LETTERS FROM INDIA;
DESCRIBING
A JOURNEY
IN
THE BRITISH DOMINIONS OF INDIA

LETTERS FROM INDIA;
DESCRIBING
A JOURNEY
IN
THE BRITISH DOMINIONS OF INDIA,

TIBET, LAHORE, AND CASHMERE,

DURING THE YEARS 1828, 1830, 1831.

UNDERTAKEN BY ORDER OF THE FRENCH GOVERNMENT,

BY

VICTOR JACQUEMONT,

TRAVELLING NATURALIST TO THE MUSEUM OF NATURAL HISTORY, PARIS.

ACOMPANIED
WITH A MAP OF INDIA AND A PORTRAIT OF THE AUTHOR.

IN TWO VOLUMES.

VOL. I.

GYAN

Published by

GYAN

Gyan Publishing House
5, Ansari Road
Daryaganj, New Delhi-110002
Phone: 011-47034999, 9811692060
E-mail: books@gyanbooks.com

Distribution Network
gyanbooks.com
India, USA, Canada, UK, Australia, France

ISBN : 978-81-212-3700-0 (Set)
ISBN : 978-81-212-4893-8 (HB)
First Published, 1834

2nd Impression 2020

Printed at: Gyan Press, Delhi.

Letters from India
Author: Victor Jacquemont

LETTERS FROM INDIA;

DESCRIBING

A Journey

IN

THE BRITISH DOMINIONS OF INDIA,

TIBET, LAHORE, AND CASHMERE,

DURING THE YEARS 1828, 1829, 1830, 1831.

UNDERTAKEN BY ORDER OF THE FRENCH GOVERNMENT,

BY

VICTOR JACQUEMONT,

TRAVELLING NATURALIST TO THE MUSEUM OF NATURAL HISTORY, PARIS.

ACCOMPANIED WITH A MAP OF INDIA AND A PORTRAIT OF THE AUTHOR.

IN TWO VOLUMES.

VOL. I.

LONDON:
EDWARD CHURTON, 26, HOLLES STREET.
(LATE BULL AND CHURTON.)

1834.

Jeffroy lith. Printed by Graf & Soret.

VICTOR JAQUEMONT.

TO THE

RIGHT HONOURABLE SIR ALEXANDER JOHNSTON,

MEMBER OF THE KING'S MOST HONOURABLE PRIVY COUNCIL,

F.R.S., F.S.A., F.L.S.,

THESE VOLUMES

ARE RESPECTFULLY INSCRIBED,

BY

THE EDITOR.

INTRODUCTION.

In giving an English translation of Victor Jacquemont's Letters to his family and friends, during his travels in India, we shall endeavour to supply a great defect in the French edition of this Work, by stating a few particulars of the life of this interesting young victim to science, prior to his departure for those shores where he was doomed to find a premature grave.

We shall also add those documents which we consider necessary to complete his correspondence.

Victor Jacquemont was born at Paris in 1801. His father, a man held in the highest estimation, is a philosopher of the Tracy school, and a writer of no ordinary power on those psychological speculations to which a long intercourse of friendship with Destutt de Tracy had probably directed his mind. He has two sons besides Victor: the elder in the army, the younger a merchant at Hayti. The three brothers received an excellent education; such a one, in short, as may be given in the public institutions of France, where instruction is not limited to a knowledge of the ancient classics, but combines with them that practical and scientific information which renders a man a useful member of society.

At a very early age, Victor Jacquemont evinced a strong attachment to natural history, which was probably strengthened by his acquaintance with the late Baron Cuvier. His intimacy with the Tracy family, and especially with Victor de Tracy, for many years past one of the most distinguished members of the French legislature, made him an ideologist, though the natural bent of his mind led him rather to investigate facts than to unravel the perplexities of metaphysics. And it is a singular contradiction, that at the very time he was pursuing his researches in natural science, doubting every thing until proved by the test of his senses, he indulged, when yielding to the confidence of friendship, in all the hypothetic ratiocination of the Tracy philosophy.

This exercise of his mind, and the opinions he imbibed from it, probably induced him, soon after he left school, to become a member of one of those societies, so numerous in France, where metaphysical politics are debated, and lead to wild and impracticable theories which mar every generous exertion for rational improvement. These societies would fain class the art of government among the exact sciences. They would establish it upon rules and principles as unchangeable as the law of the Medes and Persians, and applicable to all nations under the sun, without taking into consideration that government must necessarily be founded upon expediency,—that it is an assumption of power by a few for the benefit of all,—and that such power cannot be yoked to abstract philosophy. They appear not aware that no form of government was ever established upon abstract principles, but that all are formed and consolidated by circumstances, and the experience of events, to meet the wants of any one community, which may differ from those of another community. The only true science of government is practice; the only power to constitute it is the majority; the only test of its efficacy is a fair trial; the only way to improve it is to make its blemishes physically apparent, and then eradicate them by degrees, and not overthrow the whole fabric to build up another equally bad. But these metaphysico-philosophers have one form of constitution—I should say a thousand, but each is *the one*—adapted to all nations; one coat to fit a hundred individuals;—they have, we repeat, a thousand systems—each the best and only good one—founded upon their own Utopian notions of pure republicanism, without ever dreaming that man is by nature so imperfect—almost always swimming in so strong a current of infirmities and passions of the most fearful kind, that a republic like theirs, founded solely upon human forbearance and virtue, would be swept away 'ere its foundations were well laid. Each individual in the mass of society, loves himself best; his country, his fellow-citizens, hold but a secondary place in his regard; and, unless he can divest himself of the feelings of his species, he will naturally seek to overturn a power which has no other strength to maintain itself but the strength of opinion, whenever that power clashes with his personal interests.

Though Jacquemont imbibed freely the false theories of this visionary republicanism, though he indulged in the wildest metaphysico-political dreams, he was, nevertheless, not tainted to an irremediable extent. His unbiassed good sense led him to separate the practicable from the absurd; and in his remarks upon the rule of our Asiatic empire, he gives views of a very high order, which our statesmen would do well to examine.

Whilst very young, Victor Jacquemont undertook

a voyage to Hayti, where his brother was settled, whence he proceeded to the United States, and made a short stay there. In both these countries his talent for scientific observation was displayed in a remarkable degree; and it is this probably which, on his return to France, got him an appointment in the Museum of Natural History at Paris. Baron Cuvier now took him by the hand, and to this great naturalist Victor Jacquemont owed his selection by the Council of the Museum to fulfil the scientific mission to the East, which led to the correspondence here published.

He was instructed to investigate the natural history of India in all its branches, and collect materials wherewith to enrich the Museum, and promote the progress of science. Though the French government was not quite so liberal as could be desired in supplying him with the means of accomplishing his object, he succeeded, nevertheless, in an extraordinary manner. The light he has thrown upon parts of Asia hitherto unexplored by European travellers, must prove of the greatest benefit to science. The present letters, written to his confidential friends and relatives, and never intended for publication, give a very lively description of the manners of the natives in the different countries through which he travelled, but are almost wholly free from scientific details. The results of his scientific labours are confined to his Journal, which will soon be published, and contains a most valuable account of the natural history of those parts of Asia which he visited.

Victor Jacquemont, in pursuance of his mission, arrived in London in 1828, and was the bearer of a letter of introduction from Baron Cuvier to the Right Hon. Sir Alexander Johnston, through whose kind assistance he was enabled to overcome the various difficulties with which he found himself beset at the very commencement of his undertaking.

To Sir Alexander Johnston, who is indefatigable in the promotion of science, and ever ready to bring forward men of talent, Jacquemont was further indebted for his flattering reception from the Royal Asiatic Society, and for letters of introduction to the most influential men in India. Sir Alexander personally recommended him to the attention and kindness of Lord William Bentinck, the Governor General of India, Mr. Lushington, Governor of Madras, the late Sir John Malcolm, Governor of Bombay, and Sir Edward Owen, commanding the British naval force in India; and also obtained for him, from the President of the Board of Control, letters to all the principal personages in the East India Company's dominions. The kindness he afterwards experienced from the individuals to whom these letters were addressed is explained in his correspondence, and in a manner that does him the greatest credit.

Shortly after Jacquemont's arrival in London, he was allowed, under the auspices of Sir Alexander Johnston, to attend the meetings of the Asiatic Society, and those of its Committee of Correspondence, of which Sir Alexander is chairman. There exist two resolutions in the minutes of its Asiatic Society, which, as they refer especially to Victor Jacquemont, and to the object of his mission, are entitled to a place here.

Extract from the Minutes of the Committee of Correspondence of the Royal Asiatic Society, 19th June, 1828.

"It was resolved:—

"That this Committee, having been informed of the scientific object for which Monsieur Victor Jacquemont, Travelling Naturalist to the Royal Museum of Natural History of Paris, is sent by that institution to India, is of opinion that the attainment of that object is of the greatest importance to natural history; and therefore recommend to the Council to assist him by every means in its power in the prosecution of his scientific inquiries in India, and that C. Moreau, Esq., be requested to communicate this resolution to the Directors of the Royal Museum of Natural History at Paris."

Extract from the Minutes of the Council of the Royal Asiatic Society, June 28, 1828.

"The Committee of Correspondence having recommended to the Council assisting M. Victor Jacquemont, Travelling Naturalist to the Royal Museum of Natural History of Paris, in his scientific researches in India,

"It was resolved:—

"That the Council furnish M. Jacquemont with letters of introduction to the literary societies in India, and recommend him for election as a foreign member of this Society."

Jacquemont, on receiving information of these resolutions, wrote the following letter to the president of the Asiatic Society.

"*London, June* 26, 1828.

"MR. PRESIDENT,—Allow me to express to the Royal Asiatic Society the gratitude I feel for the resolution in my favour adopted at its last meeting of the 19th of June. I have no doubt that a recommendation by the Asiatic Society to such of its members as reside in India, will prove of the greatest use to me in the scientific voyage I am about to undertake to that country. I shall endeavour worthily to justify this favour, by arduously employing the advantages I shall derive from it, in extending and multiplying my researches in natural history. The reception I have met with from the Asiatic Society is a sufficient proof to me that science belongs to all countries; and I also know that, by labouring to make the natural history of some parts of the immense British empire in the East better known, I shall co-operate in the object to which the labours of the Society tend. I am likewise convinced that by the success of my undertaking I can give better testimony of the noble assistance afforded me by the Royal Asiatic Society. By promoting the general interests of science, which are those of every enlightened man, I shall be proud, Mr. President, to be able more particularly to pay my debt of gratitude to the institution over which you preside. I am about to pass several years in exploring the Malabar coast, and especially the mountains adjacent. Perhaps the Asiatic Society would feel more particularly interested in the verification of some obscure or contested points relating to the physical history of those regions. Among such of its members as have resided there, some perhaps may set a great value upon information which they had no opportunity of obtaining, and which would complete or confirm their general knowledge of the country. In this case, may I beg that the Asiatic Society will have the goodness to let me know its wishes, which I shall endeavour to meet by associating them with my habitual researches.

"I have the honour to be, &c.

"VICTOR JACQUEMONT."

The two resolutions were communicated to the Royal Museum of Natural History at Paris, and the Directors of that institution wrote two letters on the occasion: one to Sir Alexander Johnston, and the other to the President of the Asiatic Society. We insert both.

"TO THE RIGHT HONOURABLE SIR ALEXANDER JOHNSTON, &c. &c. &c.

"*Paris, July* 11, 1828.

"SIR,—M. Jacquemont, Travelling Naturalist to the Museum, has informed us of the interest with which you have received him, and the inappreciable advantages for which he is indebted to your kindness.

"The voyage which M. Jacquemont is about to undertake, and in which your advice and recommendations will be so useful to him, being intended for the advantage of the Museum of Natural History, we are under a real obligation to you, and we hasten to express our gratitude.

We have the honour to be, &c.

"DESFONTAINES, Director.

"L. CORDIER.

"A. DE JUNIER, Secretary."

"TO THE PRESIDENT OF THE ROYAL ASIATIC SOCIETY, LONDON.

"*Paris, August* 8, 1828.

"MR. PRESIDENT,—The secretary of the Committee of Correspondence of the Royal Asiatic Society of Great Britain and Ireland, has made known to us the resolution of the Committee, adopted at its meeting of the 19th ultimo, in favour of M. Jacquemont, Travelling Naturalist of the Museum.

"We appreciate this favour to its fullest extent, as well as the favourable effects which it cannot fail to produce in the success of M. Jacquemont's undertaking.

"We beg of you, Mr. President, to have the goodness to convey to the Royal Asiatic Society, and to its Foreign Committee, the expression of our gratitude, and to accept personally our best thanks.

"We have the honour to be, &c.

"DESFONTAINES, Director.

"A. DE JUNIER, Secretary."

About this time Sir Alexander Johnston, in his speech, after reading to the Asiatic Society the report of the Committee of Correspondence, alluded to Jacquemont in the following terms:—

"The English and French governments, equally anxious to promote scientific inquiries in India, have recently aided each other in the attainment of this great object: France, by the appointment of M. Jacquemont, an eminent naturalist, to proceed to India, and to remain there for seven years upon a public salary, for the purpose of investigating the natural history of that country; England, by affording M. Jacquemont, in every part of British India, the most ready and most efficient assistance. Both nations, by completely divesting themselves of the national jealousy which has so long prevailed between them, have set a bright example to all other nations, of the cordial and unreserved manner in which all countries ought to co-operate, according to the means which they respectively possess, in promoting those researches which are calculated to extend the limits of scientific and literary knowledge."

After encountering various delays and objections,—some of the latter fastidious enough,—Victor Jacquemont obtained his credentials from the Board of Merchant-Kings, in Leadenhall-street, who there govern a vast empire ten thousand miles off, and a hundred millions of subjects whom they have never seen. The enterprising man of science then "girded up his loins," and took his departure for the shores of British India.

In allusion to the feelings and opinions which actuated Victor Jacquemont, when he set out upon his long and wearisome travels, we cannot do better than insert the following extract, together with a letter from Jacquemont to Sir John Malcolm, from a very clever article on the correspondence of the young naturalist, which appeared in the Foreign Quarterly Review for February last.

"At the period when Jacquemont prepared to undertake his important task, there were certain opinions received as aphorisms by the liberal politicians of France, to which he had yielded implicit faith. It was held to be a self-evident truth that intense selfishness characterised the policy of England in public, and the conduct of the English in private; that insular arrogance rendered us the tyrants rather than the masters of the sea, made us reserved towards all foreigners, inspired us with a haughty jealousy always disagreeable and frequently offensive; that in India our dominion was a nuisance which ought to be abated, but that its duration depended on the will of Russia, the speedy appearance of whose forces at the passes of the Indian Caucasus was 'a consummation devoutly to be wished, and speedily to be obtained.' Full of these notions, Jacquemont arrived in England; the treatment which he received from Sir Alexander Johnston and other members of the Asiatic Society, was well calculated to remove his prejudices; but on the other hand, the difficulties and delays he experienced in obtaining his passport from the lords of Leadenhall-street, counterbalanced the impressions produced by the kindness of his scientific friends. For this, Jacquemont was probably as much to blame as the Directors; they could scarcely have imagined that a single Frenchman, even though his tall gaunt figure reminded them of the last of the knights-errant, would contest with them the empire of India; still less would they have mistaken his packing cases for parks of artillery, or his dissecting knives for a supply of military weapons; they probably doubted the object of his mission, regarding him either as a Russian emissary, or the bearer of some secret treaty to Runjeet Sing and the rulers of the Afghans; he perhaps was less explanatory than he should have been, especially with persons to whom scientific missions are by no means familiar. Jacquemont manifestly felt that his objects, if not suspected, were liable to suspicion; this appears evident in the letter he addressed from London to Sir John Malcolm, which we insert entire, as it has not yet been published.

"'TO SIR JOHN MALCOLM, &c.

"'It is in the name of science, and under the auspices of Sir A. Johnston, that I take the liberty of writing to Sir John Malcolm, without having the honour of his personal acquaintance. The accomplishment of a scientific tour through India has been intrusted to me by the Royal Museum of Natural History at Paris, and I am about to undertake it. The researches to which my attention must be directed, relate exclusively to natural history; true, that it is not the species of study and labour by which Sir J. Malcolm has so much with life, if, after several years of labour and research, he should be plundered, and lose all the results of his toils.

"'Sir J. Malcolm, whose high office in the part of the British empire bordering on these countries, must give him better information of their internal condition than any one else can possess, would perhaps favour me with his opinion respecting the hopes first entertained of the possibility of visiting them.

"'If I must renounce them, I have determined to devote all my time and all my resources to exploring the coasts of Malabar and the long chain of the Western Ghauts. This territory, naturally circumscribed, forms a kind of geographical unity, favourable under many points of view to the studies of a naturalist. The establishment to which I belong, possesses in its immense collections a very small number of natural productions belonging to this part of India. It has also been greatly neglected hitherto by the English naturalists. The geological museums in London, sufficiently rich already in collections from Nepaul and the Himalaya, are absolutely destitute of specimens from the rocks of Malabar. The zoology, with the exception of that belonging to the coast, is but little known, and the voluminous works we have on the

Flora of this country, such as the Hortus Malabaricus of Rheede, bear all the marks of the imperfect state of botany at the time they were written, and no longer satisfy the demands of this science.

" 'Finally: there is one circumstance that induces me to adopt this resolution, already nearly fixed, namely, that it will make me begin the painful and laborious part of my journey through the provinces governed by Sir J. Malcolm, and that it will permit me to enjoy the advantages of his noble protection.

" 'Giving up my visit to Cabul, should I, in my route from Calcutta to Bombay, take the road by Delhi or Agra, or should I not rather take a more direct line to the south of this great curve?

" 'These are the doubts that I respectfully submit to the consideration of Sir John Malcolm. Sir A. Johnston leads me to hope that the general will kindly solve them, and guide me by his counsel through this vast country. The kind and dear Johnston adds, that the slowness of my voyage from France to Pondicherry (slowness occasioned by a projected delay of some weeks at the isle of Bourbon) will doubtless permit me to receive Sir J. Malcolm's reply, if he would be so kind as to send it under cover to the French governor.

" 'In addressing myself to the elevated and generous

mind of the historian of India, I must not forget that Sir J. Malcolm holds an official station, and has duties to perform. I would not trespass on his kindness, had I not the honour to inform him that I have obtained an official passport from the Honourable Court of Directors, granting me free passage through all the territories of the Company. The innocent character of my pursuits would perhaps ensure me sufficient protection from the Company's officers; but I was anxious to have the special and formal assent of the Court of Directors, and it was granted me on the 25th of this month. I entreat Sir J. Malcolm to add his consent.

'VICTOR JACQUEMONT,

'Travelling Naturalist to the Royal Museum of Natural History.

'London, June 30, 1828.'

"A greater contrast can scarcely be conceived, than there is between the sober formality of this letter, and the lively sketches of life and manners addressed by the young naturalist to his family and friends. He left Europe with high hopes, unconquerable spirits, and a love of adventure almost Quixotic, but with an affectionate heart that clung fondly to his family circle,

> 'And dragged at each remove a lengthening chain.'

These feelings, combined with no ordinary graphic powers, lend an irresistible charm to his little narratives; they are dashed off with an ease and freedom such as is rarely seen; their *vis comica* frequently reminds us of Cruikshank; like that admirable artist, he extracts fun from every thing, even from subjects apparently the most hopeless; like him, too, he has a moral in every jest, not the less effective because it is incidental. In the letters now published, Jacquemont rarely alludes to his scientific pursuits; consequently they have not anticipated the interest which all the naturalists of Europe must feel in the publication of the valuable manuscripts which he sent to the Museum of Natural History of Paris; duplicates of which were forwarded by the French ministry to our government. It is on these of course, whenever they appear, that his future reputation as a naturalist must mainly depend. The chief value of the present collection rests on the account it gives of our Indian possessions, the effects of our government on the native population, the result of recent efforts to diffuse the elements of civilisation, and the future prospects of Hindústan. On behalf of England, Jacquemont is a witness above suspicion; his prejudices, which never wholly disappeared, were all against the British government; and it is sometimes amusing to see how slowly and reluctantly, in the early part of his career, he yielded to the strong evidence of facts, while in some of his more recent letters he rallies his correspondents unmercifully for repeating opinions, which he had himself entertained a few months before.

"The process of Jacquemont's conversion began at the first English settlement he visited, the Cape of Good Hope; there he discovers how honestly the British government had acted in the abolition of the slave trade, and how other powers had connived at its continuance. For this connivance, indeed, he makes rather a lame apology; but 'liberal' as he was, we shall too often see that Jacquemont was willing to sacrifice justice to expediency."

Jacquemont, during his arduous duties, never forgot the kindness shown him by Sir Alexander Johnston, to whom he wrote from Benares, but, unfortunately, the letter miscarried. He again wrote from the Ladak territory, in 1830, and this letter arrived safe. It contains an excellent, though rapid, sketch of his journey to the Himalaya, and we insert it here as necessary to complete Jacquemont's correspondence. It is rather surprising that the French editor omitted it, as we know that he must have been aware of its existence, because Sir Alexander Johnston was in communication with Jacquemont's family before these letters were published at Paris.

"*Camp, under the Fort of Dankár, in Ladak*,
3rd Sept. 1830.

"MY DEAR SIR,—I rely on your kindness to excuse my long silence, since the time I left Benares, whence I had the pleasure to acquaint you with the successful beginning of my journey. After a long interval of eight months, I avail myself of an opportunity to India, to trace shortly (as impending business obliges me) my journey since quitting the Holy City.

"I went to Delhi by the circuitous route I pointed out to you, making a very long turn to the south-west, almost to the banks of the Nerbuddah, over the table-land and across the hills of Bundlecund,—a province lately surveyed by Captain Jas. Franklin, and geologically described by him in the 'Asiatic Researches;' and I was fortunate enough to meet in several with phenomena of super-position that had escaped him in his explorations, and which will enable me to lay down another exposition of the geological structure of that country.

"From Delhi I went to the westward, through the protected Seikh country, to the banks of the Caggar, an inconsiderable stream, that vanishes in the sandy desert of Bickaneer, before it reaches the Sutledge. I was then engaged in a grand hunting-party, which I expected would have been fruitful to my geological collections, but it proved interesting to me only as showing me, in a fortnight, more of Eastern display and Asiatic manners than I had yet seen in a twelve-month. The hot winds were then threatening to invade the plains every day. I repaired to the hills, which I entered by the valley of Dheya. During about two months I travelled from the sources of the Ganges and the Jumna to the north-western limits of the British dominions on the banks of the Sutledge. Tacking, if I may be allowed that expression, between the snowy barrier of the Himalaya and its lower branches, I arrived at Simlah in the middle of June.

"It would have been impossible to experience a greater degree of hospitality than I have been welcomed with from your countrymen, during my long march from Calcutta to the latter place. The numerous letters of introduction Lord William Bentinck gave me, when my departure from Bengal left him no other way to evince his extreme kindness to me; those for which I was indebted to many of my acquaintance in the Indian metropolis; and, above all, to a gentleman with whom I became a friend,—Colonel Fagan, the adjutant-general of the army,—all these I might have lost, and still, I am sure, have been equally entitled to eulogise British hospitality. Even the last European station I reached, Simlah, is like the beginning of my journey,—like Calcutta,—amongst the most hospitable, the one I shall ever remember most gratefully. Whilst I was rapidly forgetting, at Captain Kennedy's (the political agent in that district), the privations and fatigues of my first journey through the hills, he was busily employed in preparing, and I dare say ensuring, the success of my journey over the Himalaya, by all the means his situation afforded him.

"It is now upwards of two months since I commenced travelling to the northward of the southern or Indian range of the Himalaya. I am no longer within the vast limits of British influence. I am but two days' march distant from the Ladak village, where

I shall close my reconnoitrings to the north, as it would prove very difficult, if not dangerous, to go further. Information that I got from the natives gives me reason to hope that I shall find there some strata swarming with organic remains, which will afford me the means of determining the geological age of that immensely developed limestone-formation, that constitutes the mighty Tartar ranges of the Himalaya, superior in height to the granitic peaks of the southern chain.

"Lately, whilst engaged in similar researches on the frontiers of Chinese Tartary, I had the good luck to meet with the very object of my inquiry, and also to find Chinese vigilance at fault, insomuch that no obstacle was thrown in my way. I had then to cross twice two passes, that were considerably more than eighteen thousand feet of absolute elevation, whilst the passes across the outer Himalaya scarcely average sixteen thousand feet.

"My observations on the skirts of the Himalaya, along the plains of Hindostan, are quite confirmatory of my friend M. Elie de Beaumont's views respecting the late period at which that mighty range sprung from the earth. As to the geological age of its granitic base (a question wholly distinct from the consideration of its rising up), I think that my observations in the different parts of the Himalaya, but particularly in the upper valley of the Sutledge, will prove also to a certainty, contrary to the still prevailing opinion, that it belongs to one of the latest primitive formations.

"In ten days I hope to re-enter the Tartar Hangerang-pergunnah, under British control, and before two months hence to return to Simlah. I shall then, without delay, proceed down to the plains, and resume the prosecution of my journey towards Bombay. I am in perfectly good health, and have suffered nothing from six months' exposure to the sun, during my circuitous journey from Calcutta to the hills."

The remainder of this letter relates merely to private matters. We, however, insert the postscript, giving an account of a singular Hungarian enthusiast, whom Jacquemont met in Kanawer, and to whom he more than once alludes in his correspondence.

"P. S. I will add a few lines on a subject acceptable, I presume, to your warm interest in the East. You have, no doubt, heard of M. Alexander Csoma de Kōrôs, a Hungarian, enthusiastic for Oriental philology, who has travelled through many parts of Asia during the last ten years. I saw him at Kanum, where he has resided for four years, supported by a small subsistence granted to him by the government of Bengal, to enable him to prosecute his investigation of the Tibetan language. M. Csoma has performed his task, and is about to leave Tibet, and to proceed to Calcutta. His energetic exertions and his depressed fortunes inspired me with a great interest for him; but I fear that disappointment awaits him at Calcutta, the government, in the present circumstances, being probably unable to afford him any pecuniary remuneration.

"M. Csoma will carry to Calcutta the result of his long labours, consisting of two voluminous and beautifully-neat manuscripts, quite ready for the press; one is a grammar, the other a vocabulary, of the Tibetan language, both written in English. The species of information obtainable through these new instruments of knowledge, is not, probably, of a nature to make them useful to the Indian government; and I do not believe that the circumstances of the Asiatic Society of Calcutta will enable them to undertake the publication of M. Csoma's works. I have, therefore, spoken to him of the illustrious Society in which you take so eminent a concern *, as being, in my opinion, the public body whose learned patronage is more likely to become the promoter of his labours.

"How M. Csoma de Kōrôs has performed his task, no one can decide, since he is the only person proficient in the Tibetan language. But a conjecture, and a most favourable one, may be made. M. Csoma has never been in England, and has never had an opportunity of speaking English; yet he is thoroughly acquainted with your language. Most European tongues seem to be equally familiar to him, although he has had no opportunity of a practical acquaintance with them. Moreover, for the last ten years he has been entirely deprived of European intercourse, travelling throughout Asia in the character of a poor native, without any books, &c.; whilst he has spent four years in reading, with a learned lama of Ladak, hundreds and hundreds of Tibetan books preserved in the temple of Kanuṃ. The medium of communication between him and his teacher, was the vernacular jargon of the Zeád, or Tartar tribes."

Jacquemont was most kindly received and assisted

* The Asiatic Society, to whom this letter was communicated by Sir Alexander Johnston, authorised Jacquemont to treat with his Hungarian friend for these manuscripts.

by all to whom he had letters of introduction, and by many others with whom he became acquainted in the different residencies of India. He speaks of Lord and Lady William Bentinck in the most glowing terms, as he does, indeed, of all his India friends. The following is a letter which he wrote, in English, to Mr. Lushington, Governor of Madras, a short time before his death; it belongs to this collection, as part of his correspondence from India, though never before published.

"*Tanna, Island of Salsette, September* 26, 1832.

"SIR,—I hasten to express my profound gratitude for the kindness which you have honoured me with in favouring me with such a number of valuable introductions to the officers of your Government. I have just had the honour of receiving them, enclosed in your letter of the 10th instant.

"With respect to the guard you are kindly pleased also to grant to me, if required, I beg leave to state, that the smallest,—a naick and four, was amply sufficient, in most of my travels through the Bengal provinces; and that it was only to go through the Rajpoot states, and insecure Bheel tracts, that a havildar, a naick and twelve were offered to me, and recommended by the Bengal and Bombay officers. In the well-settled provinces of your Government, I trust a naick and four, or,. at the utmost, a naick and six, will leave nothing more to desire to me for the perfect protection of my baggage.

"I shall not fail to do my best to travel the road you are so kind as to recommend to me, from Mysore to the Neilgherries; and I feel very grateful for your pointing out to me, amidst the troubles and cares of high office, such interesting particulars.

"With the expression of my fervent hopes to be able of testifying *vivâ voce* to you, in the Neilgherries, the deep sense I entertain of your kindness, I beg you will accept the assurance of my profound respect.

"I have the honour, &c.

"VICTOR JACQUEMONT."

To this we add an extract from a letter enclosing the above, written by Mr. Lushington to Sir Alexander Johnston, dated Madras, October 10th, 1832.

"MY DEAR SIR,—Your letter of introduction, given so long ago to Monsieur Jacquemont, only reached me the other day. He very prudently kept it until he was approaching our territories; and you will see, from the enclosed copy of his letter to me, that he is entirely satisfied with the arrangements made for his comfort, and for the furtherance of the important objects of his researches."

After encountering the greatest difficulties and privations in his arduous labours, the fruits of which have greatly enriched the science of Natural History, and will soon be made public, Jacquemont was attacked with that bane of Indian climes, the liver complaint. He was then at Tanna, a town and fortress in the island of Salsette, where, pursuing his researches in the pestilential atmosphere of this unhealthy island, under a burning sun, and in the most dangerous season of the year, he imbibed the seeds of the disease which terminated his life. On his arrival at Bombay, extremely unwell, his powerful constitution gave way, his complaint assumed a fatal character, and he expired on the 7th of December, 1832, after lingering more than a month in intense agony.

Victor Jacquemont was deeply and generally lamented in India. He had acquired many friends there. His amiable manners, his strength and simplicity of mind, his great power of intellect, and above all, his warmth and sincerity of heart, made him beloved by all who knew him. Though at first somewhat cold and stately in his manner, and extremely reserved, this soon wore off in the intimacy of friendship, where, as is evident from his letters, he found delight in the outpourings of his attachment, for his nature was warm and affectionate. Among his friends, he was a most entertaining companion, lively to excess, and sparkling with wit. With great depth and rapidity of discernment, he granted his friendship to those only who were able to comprehend and appreciate his mind. To strangers or casual acquaintances he was distant and uncommunicative. Not that he acted thus from reflection,—he was, perhaps, not aware of the feeling; it was mere instinct, an impulse identic with his nature, and totally free from any imagined superiority. But it was apparent to every one who saw him; and it may account for the character given of him by some who had casually met him, of being the most frigid and least communicative of men.

In person Victor Jacquemont was very tall, and had rather an awkward gait. But genius beamed from his fine countenance, and in its expression might be read the workings of a superior mind.

We shall conclude this Introduction with a letter from Sir Alexander Johnston to M. Jacquemont, the elder, Victor's father, who resides at Paris. It was written subsequently to the death of the young naturalist, and in consequence of an application to Sir Alexander Johnston for any documents he might possess, throwing light upon Victor Jacquemont's proceedings in England, prior to his departure for India.

"TO MONSIEUR JACQUEMONT, PARIS.

"DEAR SIR,—As I understand from Mr. Sharp that the letters which the late M. Jacquemont wrote from different parts of India, to his friends in France, are soon to be published, and that you are anxious, in order to prefix them to those letters, to procure from me any documents I may possess, explanatory of his proceedings while he was in England previously to his departure for India, I have the pleasure to send you copies of two reports in which I, as chairman of the Committee of Correspondence of the Royal Asiatic Society, thought it necessary to call the attention of the society to him and to his mission; and also copies of the following documents:—

"No. I. Copy of the resolution relative to M. Jacquemont, passed, on my motion, by the Committee of Correspondence, on the 18th of June, 1828.

"No. II. Copy of the resolution relative to M.

Jacquemont, passed, on my motion, by the Council of the Asiatic Society, on the 28th of June, 1828.

"No. III. Copy of a letter from M. Jacquemont to the Royal Asiatic Society of Literature, acknowledging the receipt of the resolution No. II.

"No. IV. Copy of a letter, of the 11th of July, 1828, from the Directors of the Museum at Paris to me, thanking me for the assistance which I had given M. Jacquemont.

"No. V. Copy of a letter, dated Bombay, September 26th, 1832, from M. Jacquemont to Mr. Lushington, thanking him for the preparations which had been made for his reception within the Madras territories, in consequence of the letter which I had given him for Mr. Lushington.

"No. VI. Copy of a letter from Mr. Lushington to me, inclosing the letter No. V., for the purpose of showing me that M. Jacquemont was satisfied with the preparations which had been made for his reception at Madras.

"On M. Jacquemont's arrival in England, he brought me a letter from the late Baron Cuvier, who spoke of him in the highest terms of praise. I was convinced, after a very short acquaintance with him, that he merited in every respect the character which the baron had given him, and that he was peculiarly well qualified for the important mission upon which he was about to proceed to India. I, consequently, as one of the vice-presidents of the Royal Asiatic Society of Literature, and chairman of their Committee of Correspondence, felt it to be my duty to take every measure, in public and in private, to forward his object and that of the French government. He was, on my proposal, invited to attend all the meetings of the society, and those of the Committee of Correspondence; to make use, whenever he pleased, of their library and their museum; and finally, as a mark of the highest respect which the society could show him, he was unanimously elected one of their foreign members.

"He, on his part, took every opportunity to evince to the society his readiness to adopt any suggestions which they might offer him with respect to his researches, and to assure them of his anxiety to obtain for them every information they might require from him in India. He devoted himself with the greatest assiduity to the examination of all the different works, inscriptions, and other documents, relative to India, which are preserved in the library of the Asiatic Society, and in that of the East India Company. He was indefatigable in acquiring a practical knowledge of every mechanical art, which could be of use to him in preserving such specimens in natural history as he might collect during his travels; and by the whole of his conduct while he remained in England, he gained the admiration and esteem of all those who felt any interest, or took any part in inquiries relative to the natural history, the geology, and the geography of India. On his departure from England, the President of the Asiatic Society, who was then also the President of the Board of Control of Indian affairs, at my request gave him letters of introduction to all the governors of the East India Company's possessions in India. I myself recommended him in the strongest terms to the protection and particular attentions of Lord William Bentinck, the Governor General of British India, of Sir John Malcolm, the Governor of Bombay, of Mr. Lushington, the Governor of Madras, and of Sir Edward Owen, the commander-in-chief of the British navy in the Indian seas; to the three first, that they might afford him every assistance in their power, while he was within the limits of their respective governments; to the last, that he might, by means of the different ships of war which might be, from time to time, returning to England, enabled to send such collections as he might make, with safety and without delay, to the Museum at Paris.

"The scientific object for which the French government sent M. Jacquemont to India; the liberality * with which the government was at the expense of his mission; the reputation of the men who advised the measure; the talents, the acquirements, and the zeal of the man who was chosen by them to carry it into effect; the cordiality with which Great Britain and France co-operated upon the occasion; the frankness and good sense with which M. Jacquemont himself conciliated the public functionaries in England and in India; the ardour with which he prosecuted his undertaking; the intrepidity with which he encountered and overcame every difficulty; the disinterestedness with which he sacrificed his comfort and his health to the performance of his duty; the calmness and the resignation with which he met his premature death at Bombay, and the universal regret which must be felt for his loss by every man of science in France, in England, and in India, are circumstances which must render every fact connected with the life of such a

---

* We cannot say much in favour of this liberality. The allowance made to Jacquemont was so small, that without the presents from Runjeet Sing and other native princes, and the assistance afforded him by the different governments in India, it is doubtful whether he would have been able to accomplish the object of his mission.—Ed.

man interesting to the public, and peculiarly gratifying to the friends of science throughout Europe.

"I am, dear sir, yours very faithfully,

"ALEXANDER JOHNSTON."

We have only to add that the documents, so kindly sent by Sir Alexander Johnston, were not used in the French edition of Jacquemont's letters. It was intended to insert them in a memoir of the author, to be prefixed to the correspondence; but from some mismanagement of the editor, it was not ready when it should have been. The curiosity and interest of the French public had been highly excited, and the demand for the work was so urgent, that there was not time to prepare the memoir, which was necessarily omitted. It is a question whether, in any future edition, this omission will be supplied; for the letters alone are said to excite sufficient interest without any such addition. But this is a question to be settled between the French public and the publisher.

London, September 12th, 1834.

A JOURNEY IN INDIA, &c.

BY

VICTOR JACQUEMONT.

TO M. PORPHYRE JACQUEMONT, PARIS.

Brest, 24th August, 1828, *one o'clock.*

On the fourth day after my departure from Paris I arrived here, my dear Porphyre, without accident, or more fatigue than I anticipated. I have called upon M. Poultier, commander of the Zélée; he is a lieutenant in the navy, a man about your age, and very pleasing in his appearance. He paid me every attention, and to-morrow, he is to take me on board to see the vessel which is to be my future dwelling: I say *future,* because we shall not sail for a week to come, as M. de Melay is not yet arrived.

What pleased me more with M. Poultier, was his telling me that, on our way to Rio Janeiro, we should make a short stay at Madeira. Short, however, as it may be, it will be a piece of good fortune for me, and will, moreover, considerably reduce the number of our salt beef dinners. Between each of the four stations, the Canaries, the Brazil, the Cape of Good Hope, and the Isle of Bourbon, we shall, certainly, never be longer than a month at sea; and for such short passages we can always lay in a sufficient stock of fresh provisions, live animals, fruit, and vegetables. This is a pleasant prospect for me.

The king, as they tell me here, does not provide me with a bed on board ship, but gives me fifty francs to buy a cot with three thin mattrasses and sheets. This sum is nearly sufficient, and the bedding will remain my property. I am besides, from this day, entered at the officers' mess, at which his aforesaid majesty pays for my breakfast and dinner, if I choose to take them.

I am content. To tell you that my satisfaction is not grave, and serious, would be useless. There is a conflict within me. Reflection must combat the liveliest of my instinctive emotions; and in truth, if it does not overpower, it at least keeps them silent. It was high time indeed, five days ago, that six o'clock should strike, when you saw me to the carriage, for my feelings were nigh overcoming me; yet, two years ago, when I took leave of you at Havre, it was with much more anguish and sorrow. I had then, my dear friend, reached the summit of misfortune; every day since has been more lucky to me; and now in looking forward to the future, I see an acclivity before me, more or less rugged, but which in the end will necessarily lead me to an honourable and satisfactory position in the world. It is to you, my dear Porphyre, that I am indebted for this renewed prospect of happiness. You are the cause of all I shall be, and of all that I may accomplish. I now regret nothing of what is past.

Shall I tell you the truth, my dear friend? The week which may probably elapse ere I quit France, I prefer passing alone, here, far from you and our father. I should have been much to be pitied, even during the last moments of my stay in Paris, if I had not been so overwhelmed with business relative to my departure, that I could not find leisure to ponder with you over our approaching separation. My father would have seen me pensive and sad, and I should have made him the same; instead of which, we had no time to think beforehand of the moment of our parting. Thus, notwithstanding all the delay of my departure, that moment surprised us almost unexpectedly: we scarcely said good-bye.

To-morrow, I shall write to our father. I thank him kindly for the two long lines, which he wrote on the margin of your letter. I leave him as he saw me depart, if not with pleasure, at least with security. Adieu, my friends; I embrace you with all my heart.

TO M. NARJOT, CAPTAIN OF ENGINEERS, BREST.

Brest, Saturday Evening, 23rd August, 1828.

You will see, my good friend, that I shall soon request you, who know this place, to hire me a house for six months. This morning, while I was multiplying myself by four, in order to be, at the same time, here at my inn, at the post-office, at the observatory, and on board ship, writing, countermanding, going backwards and forwards in all haste, for fear of arriving too late, it was quietly decided, that the wind had not yet sufficiently veered round to carry us out of the roads; and as to-morrow is Sunday, and of course a holiday, we shall not be impious enough to sail on that day. Thus our departure is adjourned till Monday without fail, and very early in the morning, so that to-morrow night I must sleep on board.

Then on Monday, you will see that the wind will be perhaps so much reduced, that there will be scarcely any left, so that we shall still be unable to sail. This is monstrous! and is it not also a little ridiculous? The Americans do not make so much ado; they sail invariably on the day fixed. Thus, on a certain 3rd of November, 1826, I left Havre in a ship called the Cadmus, in the very midst of a storm or squall, which retained all the other vessels in harbour, and let us off with the loss of our main-sail.

I have discovered, that, among the officers, there is one whom they term a supernumerary lieutenant: that is to say, a captain of a merchantman, pressed, for a time, into the king's service. Although still young, he has been, among other places, three times in India. He is simple and artless, and will be useful to me. Persons of his class know a great many things without being aware of it, and many interesting little facts may be gathered from them. By interrogating them with a little address, one can obtain from them information which they alone can give, because it can be acquired only by individuals in their situation.

Is it not the same thing whether a painful object meets our eyes, or an idea of sadness passes over our mind? Imagination, and memory, form a little magic lantern which makes us melancholy or cheerful, according to the things it calls to our recollection. Without rising from our chair, and without any appreciable change in the external things around us, we are by turns, passively and irresistibly, either serene or madly merry, or taciturn, gloomy, and melancholy. Others, who, with the eyes in their heads, cannot perceive these little internal tempests, see only unevenness of temper in these effects, and unhesitatingly impute it to us as a weakness inherent in our nature. You know too that M. Fortin, our skilful engineer, makes scales, which, on being changed with the weight of a kilogramme, enclosed in a glass-case, and placed in a well-closed room, will fearfully move up and down, if a poor hack but roll along the street. The happy few, my good friend, are machines equally subtle, and still more delicate and impressible. The grocer, who weighs his articles in rude scales, always tending to be in equilibrio, seeing those of Fortin trembling at the passage of a carriage, would not divine the cause of their motion, and, like *some others*, would condemn them, as bad and fantastical.

Well then! the true reason, why, yesterday evening, you found neither me, nor the hot water, to your taste, is, that I at least was in a very serious mood, and, what is worse, dreadfully *ennuyé*. In such a case, the best thing a man can do, is to go to bed; others gain by it, in not seeing him when disagreeable, and he escapes with, perhaps, dreaming sometimes of annoyances such as a pair of slippers too short, or any other bedevilment.

All my unlearned friends tell me, that I shall return very wise, doubtless, but quite worn out, and crushed by the stones and animals, with which my thoughts will have lived on very intimate terms, for many years. If such be the case, my good friend, beware of a *fiasco*, for the two or three volumes, whether learned or not, to which you have promised to subscribe, and which I wish to make amusing—a quality too much despised.

Yet, when I tell you, that *all* my friends utter this direful prediction, I say too much: some two or three pretend the contrary. But they are those who love me most, and know me best, it is true; and are the only ones who have had any specimen of my prosaic abilities. Now, it is quite natural, that their too tender friendship may blind them: but we shall see. If they are wrong, I will take to writing sermons; and, in that grave key, I hope to take my revenge. I assure you, my good friend, that, at least four times a year, I regret not being a priest or a missionary. I meet or hear none, without envying them the high and noble duties they have to perform, and without being disgusted with the stupidity of the most famous among them. I do not except from this severe judgment their defunct men of celebrity. In spite of what you will term my slander, which is nothing but my exclusive esteem of absolute honesty and sincerity, I protest that I am very devout: though it is not my habitual state, for devotion is only useful on occasions.

Good night,—adieu, my amiable friend! Retain some remembrance of the moments which chance has permitted us to pass together. Perhaps it will re-unite us! I should be glad if it were in a political assembly, for I am sure we should be near neighbours in it. We, who have no religious faith, must employ the tenderness of our souls to the advantage of humanity. That should be our religion: and unless we possess those extraordinary talents, which, by means of written language, give us great authority over our contemporaries, it is in the performance of what our peculiar talents enable us to do in public affairs, that we should place our ambition. Adieu,—Adieu!

TO M. JACQUEMONT THE ELDER, PARIS.

On board the Zélée, at sea, between Madeira and Teneriffe.
Wednesday, 10*th September*, 1828.

My dear and excellent father! Yesterday, according to the vulgar mode of reckoning, it was fifteen days since I left Brest, the Zélée having sailed on Tuesday, the 26th August. Ever since the day after our departure, we have had contrary winds, which have blown almost constantly, but without violence; so that if we have not made much way, we have not been fatigued. I need not say that my health has not been disturbed for a single instant, by the change of element; and, what is singular, another passenger quite unused to the sea, has felt scarcely anything, and the others have been but little tried. The young surgeon of the vessel, who, though familiar with the sea, paid the accustomed tribute the first week, and M. de Melay, who has paid and will pay for all, are the only two who have suffered. I knew he had not a *sea stomach:* but, in this way, he was quite beyond all my expectations. I wonder how, with a nature having such an antipathy to pitching and rolling, he can have remained a sailor. Had I been in his place, I would have changed my profession thirty years ago.

Contrary winds are not the sole cause of the slowness of our progress. A good deal is owing to the vessel: she is very good and very solid—an excellent sea boat, as they say; she has a thousand good qualities; each more valuable than the other, but—she sails badly. The captain himself is forced to allow this, and therefore, you may rely upon its truth. But, after all, what does it matter? we shall perhaps reach Pondicherry a month later than I calculated upon! Well, the first year of my travels, which ought evidently to be the most burthensome, will be a little shorter for it. This is almost an advantage. M. de

Melay lives and takes his meals with the captain, who is a young lieutenant in the navy, and but lately the comrade of two of his officers. They have had the charity to admit into their mess, and to place in a cabin at a distance from the officers' berth, the Apostolic Prefect of Pondicherry. Though this is but a trifling service done him, it is, however, a great one to us. His presence would have placed us under perpetual restraint; and with all our attempts at modesty, and to throw off the manner of the sailor, God knows to what tribulations his ears might not have exposed him among us.

There are eleven of us at the officers' mess; five of whom are officers, all younger than myself, with the exception of a poor old junior lieutenant, who seems to me to possess much professional merit, but makes no noise, and will necessarily remain in the same rank all his life. The others are a young navy surgeon, a commissary, myself, M. de Sallabery, M. Goudot, and a young man from Rochelle going to join a relation in India.

The captain's age, his comparatively low grade in the service, the circumstance of his having been the comrade of several of his officers, and his good-nature, —all contribute to our having less of tiresome etiquette, than on board any other ship of war. I could wish nothing better.

With the officers and passengers I live without any bustle; all is pleasant and agreeable. M. de Melay and myself are becoming more and more intimate every day: sometimes we walk for hours on deck, chatting *de omni re scibili.* Though I thought him a man of mind, I find him even more so than I had supposed. He has a rich fund of fact and anecdote, and is not destitute of imagination; he is a good critic, and an excellent reasoner; and his style in conversation is beautifully correct, without being heavy. I may truly say, that his being here is a piece of good fortune for me; and he certainly finds me of some advantage.

However indifferent you know me to be in matters of ordinary life, yet, as the length of the voyage renders them, for a time, less contemptible, I must tell you, that we have very good breakfasts and dinners. Bread is baked every day, and it is excellent. The wine is pretty good; and we have fresh mutton, pork, fowl, fresh and dry vegetables, so that we can hardly perceive that we are not still on shore. Sunday and Thursday are holidays, as at college; and on those days, our ordinary meal is so much improved, as to become quite luxurious.

11th September.

As the Zélée, after landing M de Melay at Pondicherry, is to make hydrographical researches on the East coast of Africa, she is provided with several chronometers, and the young officers, yet little familiar with the requisite calculations, are constantly occupied. There is not much labour on board, yet more than I should have thought. I am seldom a solitary reader or writer on the great green cloth that covers our mess table. At night, a handsome lamp, hanging from the deck above, throws its light on us, and makes our cabin look like a handsome study. I hold long sittings there, and always feel satisfied with myself at the close of each, for I work with pleasure and facility. I vary my reading, in order to rest from one subject, by applying to another. I have an excellent Persian grammar, and a tolerably good vocabulary of that language, with which therefore I have begun. The Hindostanee will come afterwards; it is already half known by a person who understands Persian. With what I shall have learned from books by the time I reach India, I flatter myself that I shall need no very long time to be able to speak it fluently, though incorrectly.

On board a man of war, there are many noises not to be heard on board a merchantman. Every manœuvre is commanded with a horribly shrill whistle; some also, which return periodically several times a day, are performed to the sound of the drum. In fine weather, the afternoon is occupied with practising the guns; now and then they have the musket exercise. At first, all this was abominable; I am so used to it now, that I scarcely perceive it. I know not whether it is from the excellence of the crew, or from the indulgence of the officers, but for the last fortnight I have not seen a man punished. All, who are not occupied in working the ship, laugh and amuse themselves. The sight of these poor ill-dressed devils, who are constantly awake, has nothing saddening in it. They are, besides, well fed, to keep them in health, and good humour: each man has a bottle of wine, and a meal with fine fresh bread. The young doctor has nothing to do. I tell you all these things, which will perhaps appear futile to you, because I attach importance to them. Care-worn countenances, and corporal punishments, would make me melancholy, and disgust me with my floating prison.

I wrote to you from Brest, that we should touch at Madeira. M. de Melay, however, has changed his mind; the uncertainty of our relations with Don Miguel, and the fear of encountering the Brazilians and Portuguese in deadly strife perhaps with each other, has made us pass that island on our right, and sail for Teneriffe. You see I do not lose by this. Teneriffe with its peak and its volcano, is one of the most beautiful places in the world. If the weather were quite clear to-day, we should already see the summit of the peak, for we are only forty-two leagues distant from it. We shall find admirable grapes, oranges, and lemons, of which we shall lay in a good store, to serve us for lemonade till we reach Rio de Janeiro.

If we are circumspect with these rabble of Brazilians and Portuguese, we are haughty enough, I promise you, with the poor merchantmen. On Sunday last, the seventh, about noon, as I was engaged with M. de Melay, the captain came and told him that a strange sail, which had kept her course very near us since the morning, was approaching still nearer; that the stranger had a suspicious appearance, and that at all events he should clear for action. In less than five minutes, each man was armed with a musket, a cutlass, a pistol, and an axe—the matches placed near the guns—every man at his post—and, instead of waiting for the stranger, we put the ship about, and stood towards him. It was blowing very fresh, and for once the Zélée distinguished herself, and sailed well. Upon this the stranger, who was in fact sailing towards us with a threatening appearance, turned tail, but we gave chase. Seeing that we gained on him, he at last had the tardy politeness to hoist English colours; we then hoisted ours, together with our pendant (the distinctive mark of a man-of-war), backing it, as they say, with a shotted gun, which raised serious reflections in the crew of the strange vessel. She brought to, and we ran close up along side her. She proved to be an English vessel, the General Wolfe, of Bristol. Our captain wished to speak her in English—a singular pretension on his part. For want of a single person among ten officers able to speak a word of that language, I was requested to take the speaking trumpet, and had the glory of telling the poor terrified devils, that the next time they presumed to bear down upon us without showing their colours, we would sink them with a broadside. I ought to tell you, that, to the great credit of my moderation, I omitted translating through the speaking trumpet certain emphatic expletives of the captain. It would have been rather a violation of etiquette

This little scene was quite a novelty for me; this real preparation for battle, without any broken limbs, interested me much. I scarcely, however, understand a sea-fight the better for it.

This, my dear father, becomes quite tittle-tattle, and I must end it. Shall I do so, however, without adding any thing more? without telling you how many times a day, in my short moments of solitude and leisure, I detect myself thinking of you and Porphyre? Yet it is without sadness. I enjoy these tender recollections, much more than I regret our separation. The time passes so quickly that I already see its termination, and I expect that you will say to me in five years, when I return, "What! already!" and this will be the best thing to say on both sides.

My barometers, and other instruments, go on excellently. You will see them again, in five years. Every thing in my trunks and chests, also arrived safe. For the last four days, on reaching the latitude of Cadiz, I have adopted linen clothes, which I shall not again leave off; for the winds bring us the heated atmosphere of the tropics. It is the climate which I love. I feel myself caressed by this genial air, and, although my long thin body can scarcely be compared to a rose-bud, I feel that I am beginning to bloom.

There is not much chance of my finding, on my arrival at Santa Cruz in Teneriffe, a vessel sailing immediately for France, or England. At all events, I should be ready, as you perceive, to avail myself of it;

but I think I shall have time to add a short postscript from thence. I have written to you, this time, without reserve; for the future, I shall have nothing to do, but to entertain you with any little changes that may happen to me.

Santa Cruz, Teneriffe, Tuesday, 16*th Sept.* 1828.
The Roads.

We put in here on Saturday morning, the thirteenth. We sail again tomorrow morning. In this short interval, I have taken care to run about sufficiently to see many things and people too. A French ship of war is quite a phenomenon here. They pay us every possible attention: yesterday, for instance, we were at a ball. I danced a French *contre-danse* with a charming Spaniard, who spoke English. The ball was given by some rich merchants, who, twenty years ago, received M. Cordier in this island. *La grande nation* has here been represented in black, from head to foot. There were many present who could speak English and French, so that I was amply indemnified for the little drudgery of the dance. I say drudgery, because these handsome Spanish women have not a word to say for themselves. To-night, we are to have it over again, and the whole city will be there. At midnight, every one retires wrapped in a large black cloak of oil-cloth. The ship's boats are ready to receive us at the quay. We jump in with address, at the risk of tumbling into the sea, for there is always a great swell here; and, by the grace of God, we reach the Zélée, which is at anchor in the roads. The return on board forms a strange contrast with the scene we have just left.

We are taking in stores of lemons, oranges, and some tropical fruits, which are found here in abundance. The fact is, we are to be forty days at sea, before we reach Rio.

Adieu, my dear father! I embrace you as well as Porphyre, to whom my first letter will be addressed. I am wonderfully well. Every thing is for the best, in this best of all possible worlds. Remembrances to all.

TO M[LLE.] ZOE NOIZET DE SAINT-PAUL, ARRAS.

At sea, on board the Zélée, lat 4° N., lon. 22° 35′, W. from Greenwich. Saturday Evening, 11*th Oct.* 1828.

It is night, every one about me is asleep except an officer and half the watch on deck. I am alone, in a tolerably capacious and elegant cabin, seated at a large table covered with a green cloth, and lighted by a lamp hanging above the middle of it. This is my hour of work, when I require silence and solitude. I came for the purpose of writing; it was to have been on natural philosophy; but instead of the MS. which I was seeking in my portfolio, chance, and a charming chance too, made me extricate from the divine disorder reigning there, your letter of July last. I began to reperuse it, my dear cousin, and I congratulated myself on having brought it from Paris, to answer it at Brest if I had time. I recollect that I did so: but I must have done it very stupidly. I was very much annoyed in that town, always uncertain whether I should sleep there the next day, and dreaded being kept there a month by contrary winds.

I believe, my dear Zoe, that although we differ much on very important questions, we have yet many feelings and affections in common. Though more of a materialist than a spiritualist, I nevertheless take but little count of matter—of positive reality. I allow an immense importance in morals—that is to say, the art of seeking happiness—to what many narrow-minded people laugh at as chimeras. The pleasures of the imagination, are not less real than those of the senses; its pains are not less cruel than theirs. It is assuredly not from our senses that we receive enjoyment, but from what you call our soul—from our faculty of feeling when excited; subject, however, in a manner which we call happy, to the physical modifications of our senses, when placed in relation with external objects. Pleasure and pain reach us continually by a route different from that; they reach us directly, without our being able to perceive the slightest modification of our organs, preceding the sense of them which we experience. There is but one thing certain in all this—sensation. It is simple in its nature, whatever may be the variety of its objects, its origin, or its causes. But let us have done with metaphysics, more particularly, as I was about indiscreetly to reveal to you those famous *real essences.* This would be disposing of my father's property, and managing it very ill, no doubt. If I marry, in India, the daughter of some nabob with a few millions, I will employ one of them, on my return, in publishing the 280 volumes of paternal eloquence, and you will there see what sensation is. Notwithstanding, I think you, my dear friend, very happy in entertaining those opinions, concerning which we differ. There is a class of enjoyments, quite independent of the material interior of our existence; and it is by them alone, that we can equalise happiness among mankind: for that which results from satisfying physical wants, will always be naturally very bad, and very unjustly divided.

Do you think that these pleasures, destitute of material reality, are unknown to those whom you call materialists? Are not the most exclusive of them subject to the laws of sympathy? Whether it be in them the mechanical result of their organisation, or a faculty of the mind, is of small importance—in all, it is a feeling which makes them share the affections of other men, not only those affections whose indications they see, but also all those of which they become conscious without the aid, without the physical impression, of their senses. There are atheists who have a worship, and a very useful one too: it is the worship of humanity. I know more than one of this description. To themselves, they are stoics, to others, angels of charity and indulgence.

You impute to physiology, pretensions which it does not entertain. It is not physiologists who have pretended to explain the most secret mysteries of the intellect; metaphysicians, only, are capable of such impertinence. It is true, that a few ill-informed physicians have believed that they could explain the functions of organic life, by the simple laws of physics, and chemistry. But even that is impossible. However admirable chemistry may have become, during the last half score of years—and mark, there are not in France six physicians, even among the juniors, who are aware of the point to which this science has risen—it is quite insufficient to account for these strange phenomena. There is a something in them, of which it is perfectly allowable for reason to form an immaterial and immortal principle. The French philosophers of the last century and of the present, who have been termed sensualists, and have been very generally supposed to be materialists, I mean Condillac, Cabanis and M. de Tracy, have seen, it is true, in the senses and intellect of man, only one of the faculties of his organisation; but they never asserted that the laws of inert matter, the laws of physics and chemistry, presided exclusively over organic life. Be that however as it may, my dear friend, the life of the shapeless lichen which grows on every thing that will afford it support and a little moisture, is physiologically quite as inexplicable as that of the most perfect of animals, man; every thing that has life, is equally incomprehensible. In this respect, nothing is either more or less so. If you grant us a soul, you must also allow something similar to other animals, which, though so inferior to us, possess, notwithstanding, many intellectual faculties, and several modes of sensation, common to all. Seneca, following Epicurus, of whose philosophical principles he partook, explains the sensibility of organised beings, by the "*anima mundi*" (the soul of the world), as the mechanical motions of the heavenly bodies have been since explained by *attraction*. This "*anima mundi*" pleases me much, precisely on account of its being so vague and indefinite a term. I see in it, something resembling a reason, but which is not clear enough not to be rejected as absurd, if it is not at once adopted as true.

I might have talked this stuff to you, at our fireside at Paris, as well as here; and yet there is nothing so out of the ordinary, as the place where I now am. We are to-day, the 13th of October, at a short distance from the equator, after having been nearly fifty days at sea, with the prospect of another month ere we reach Rio Janeiro. You, who have read Lord Byron's works, must think the sea marvellously fine. For my part, I feel none of its poetry. I see, but without admiration, the sun rise and set every day. He illuminates only a monotonous and lifeless horizon, which has nothing in it to excite the mind; any more than in the monastic sort of life we are forced to lead on board ship. I read, write, and work a good deal; but I should like some better company, for I find little entertainment in that of the young officers on board. They are excellent young men, but ill-informed, though perfectly amiable, mild, and good-natured; and in my intercourse with them, I find all I could wish, except amusement. I should be quite at a loss in this respect, were it not for the governor of Pondicherry, M. de Melay, who is a very clever man. We quite coquette with each other, though we have few infidelities to apprehend; for, except from each other, there is no one on board from whom we can expect rational conversation. You may say if you like, my dear friend, that I have concluded with a piece of vile impertinence, and you would be right, if you were any one else. But, methinks, we know each other well enough, to state without reserve or false modesty, the good and evil that we think.

On our voyage hither, we put in for four days at Teneriffe, and I wrote from that place to my father; so that he will have been but a short time without hearing from me. Teneriffe was quite a new object of interest to me, for it is a Spanish country, and I had never seen one. I made a long trip in the mountains mounted on an ass—do not suppose that these asses are like ours:—I met camels on the way; this was a stamp of locality; but at a ball in the evening at the house of a rich inhabitant of Santa Cruz, who had invited the officers of the Zélée, I had on black clothes as at Paris, and all the men were dressed, like me, in the newest fashions of London and Paris. But few of the women had any thing Andalusian in their dress; on the contrary they wore "robes à gigot," and we danced French contre-danses set to Rossini's most popular airs. Then there was écarté in the next room. Farewell to the stamp of locality! The whole world is tending to assume the same appearance, stupid, rather melancholy, and very vulgar. I shall be out of humour with it many a time, before I return to Europe.

Adieu, my dear Zoe, write to me when you think it will afford you pleasure; never mind the place where your letters will find me, only send them to my father. Tell all our friends about you, that I retain a delightful recollection of the two hours which I spent at Barly.

Rio Janeiro, just arrived, 28th October.

TO M. PORPHYRE JACQUEMONT, PARIS.

Saturday, 18th October, 1828, at sea. Lat. 6° south, Lon. 27° 35′ west from Greenwich.

I TRUST, my dear Porphyre, that before the arrival of this letter which will only be sent from Rio, our father will have received my first to him, dated from Teneriffe, where we arrived on the 13th of September, and remained till the 17th. A ship was soon to sail for Marseilles, and the consul promised to take advantage of the opportunity. Thus, you cannot have been two months without hearing from me, or having some token of my existence. Since our departure from Teneriffe, till within these few days, our voyage has been very much impeded by calms and contrary winds. The trade winds, which we had a right to depend upon to carry us into the vicinity of the equator, have, to the great surprise of the sailors, almost entirely failed us. Last year, in going to, and returning from, Saint Domingo, I saw them equally inexact at their post, so that this time, I was very little astonished at their absence; the less so, as I have always had but little faith in the theory which accounts for their constantly blowing from the same quarter. You may just as well give the same reason to explain why your daughter is dumb. Nevertheless, I make many little observations on rain and fine weather, which do not exactly confirm certain ideas on meteorology, admitted formerly on trust, and which had always appeared satisfactory to me. The calms commenced about 18° north. The sky then became constantly clouded, every day brought us some drops of rain, followed sometimes, for an hour or two, by a squall which drove us on a few miles; and thus, with much trouble, we slowly reached the fifth degree. There we were delayed several days, constantly manœuvring to no purpose, till last Monday, when the south-east wind arose, and taking us on the beam, brought us in two days to the equator which we crossed at full speed—a trim we have since kept up night and day, and which, if we can retain it so long, will take us to Rio in eleven days. With a young captain of thirty, you may guess that the crossing of the line does not take place without the customary ceremonies. A sailor

—the greatest scamp of all, and the most stupid looking—said mass—a mass after his own fashion,—with a surplice and altar got up for the occasion. He gave us a most laughable sermon, after which, the uninitiated were gravely shaved with a wooden razor four feet long; they then swore to old father Line, never to lie with a sailor's wife, and paid him ten francs for his trouble. This ceremony being over, the officers among themselves aft, and the ship's company forward, threw buckets of water into each others' faces for an hour. The fire engine also played successfully in drenching, at the mast-heads, the fugitives who had escaped from the fray. We then went below to change our clothes, and on returning upon deck we found every thing in its accustomed order, the little previous saturnalia having left no trace behind. In the evening, the captain gave us a dinner with all the research possible: we had green peas, truffled partridges, and other dainties. M. de Melay, a little excited by the noise and the pretended liqueurs of Madame Anfoux, sang drinking songs, then some of the gayest of Beranger's, and we finished with the most genuine sea songs in the world. The poor Abbé, who was next to me, was near making his escape to avoid the choruses. I confess, I never heard the like. The crew, who during this time—three hours at table—had received double rations and some liquor, were in high glee: they were allowed to come and dance on the quarter deck: and as there were no musicians among the seamen, they accompanied themselves with the voice, to tunes that would have scared the devil, and words abominable enough to bring the whole infernal host to carry off the singers. The poor Abbé went to prayers, in his little retreat, without being able to prevent these horrors from reaching him. It is impossible for a priest to exist on board ship. Accordingly, in spite of the regulation which gives a chaplain to every ship and frigate, not one will accept the office: they would have to live in the hold, if they would not be constant witnesses of the most fearful blasphemy.

Most of the provisions we brought from Brest being spoiled, we have been obliged to throw them overboard. Our fare is hence become right royal: we live on the king's salt beef and pork, dried kidney beans, and sour krout. While you doubtless are eating grapes at your breakfast and dinner, a piece of salt beef brings my meals to an abrupt close. But you have already cold and rain — I enjoy a charming temperature. I am astonished how mild it is, for it does not exceed about 26 centigrade (79 Fahrenheit). Then, in another fortnight, perhaps sooner, I shall revenge myself at Rio on the oranges, pine apples, bananas, and all the intertropical fruits, which I do not like less than our own, and which are in greater variety. At Teneriffe, we already found bananas, which, fortunately for amateurs, every one does not like. The grape of this country resembles in size that of the promised land, but it is far from being equal to ours, even the worst in the environs of Paris. Good day, for the present, my friend. Here you have enough of gossip, considering I say nothing: it seems as if we were only twenty leagues apart. I chat for the sole pleasure of chatting with you. I reserve for Rio, this bit of white paper that still remains.

P. S. From Rio, where we are casting anchor, just as a merchantman is getting under weigh for France. In good health, all well. We shall be here a week at least, and I will write before we leave.

28*th October*, 1828.

TO M. JACQUEMONT THE ELDER, PARIS.

Rio, 6*th November*, 1828, *on board the Zélée, in the Roads.*

I ARRIVED here on the 28th of October. The same evening, I despatched a letter for Porphyre, the first I have written to him since I left Brest. With regard to myself, my dear father, it is one in the morning, I am dreadfully sleepy and fatigued, although wonderfully well, and leave you to go to bed. This place is magnificent, I have never seen any thing so beautiful, but we sail the day after to-morrow, and I am plagued with cares of all kinds. Send the enclosed to J. Taschereau. I embrace you with all my heart, and Porphyre also.

Adieu! Adieu!

14*th November*.

This day week, at noon, in the finest weather in

the world, in going out of the roadstead, which is immense, we ran foul of a merchantman at anchor. I think if I had wished it, poor wretch as I am, I should not have succeeded in this difficult feat. Nobody was hurt, but plenty of masts and sides broken and driven in. The French agent will pay the damage. We have been under repairs ever since. To-morrow we go to sea again, span new, and finer than ever.

Every one has been merry at the expense of the Zélée—I as well as the rest. Besides, I am very glad to know by experience, what running foul is.

Within this week, I have discovered the three young Taunays. One of them is an artist, and professor of painting at the Imperial Academy; another, major of cavalry in the imperial army; and a third, chancellor of the consulship. This evening, I am going to see an animal extremely rare in America—an emperor. I shall take advantage of the same opportunity to see *l'Italiana in Algieri*, for it is at the opera that I am to enjoy the sight of that excellent imperial groom. I have only time to dress before dinner, and I quit you without farther ceremony, with the kindest regards.

TO M. ACHILLE CHAPER, PARIS.

On board the Zélée, at sea, between Rio Janeiro and the Cape of Good Hope, Wednesday, 10th December, 1828.

I do not wait till we arrive at the Cape to write to you, my dear friend, for I am ignorant of the time—

probably very short—that we shall be there, and I shall have leisure only for the stones, plants, things, and, if possible, the men of that country. Besides, what could I say to you from thence, which I cannot equally well say to you now? Here have we passed over half the distance from France to India; but it is more than three months and a half since we sailed. The ship sails badly, and we have frequently had contrary winds and calms. At Rio Janeiro, which we lately left, having made a previous stay at Teneriffe, we got damaged in our first attempt to leave; this obliged us to put in again to refit, and we thus remained there three weeks instead of one. I consoled myself for this delay with the opportunity it afforded me of becoming acquainted with some particulars of a country I shall not see again, for which nature had done all, but man has spoiled, irreparably ruined! I have spoken to you of Saint Domingo—undoubtedly I did not give you a very brilliant picture of it; well! in my opinion Saint Domingo has made greater progress in civilisation than Brazil. I here saw, for the first time, negro slavery, on an immense scale, forming the key-stone of society. In twenty days, I saw several vessels arrive from the coast of Africa, loaded with these miserable creatures, a prey to frightful diseases, heaped together on landing, and penned in like animals; and side by side with these horrors, the most refined luxuries of European civilisation. The Portuguese, like the Spaniards, feel not the contempt, the physical repugnance towards negroes, which few English or French can resist. They have not instituted against them, that system of refined humiliation adopted by the colonists of Jamaica and the Leeward Islands; but they are not less violent and merciless masters. Under their whip, the negroes live a few years, and die without issue. The character of this unhappy race must be very mild, innocent, and timid, for revenge and crimes not to be more common at Rio, than they are. The masters, with their polished, even elegant, European exterior, are, in many respects, as much debased by slavery as the brutalised negroes. I saw them with their golden key on their coat, with their diamonds, their ribands, their titles, their ignorance, baseness, and dishonesty, and I was disgusted. I sought a middle class—laborious, thrifty, honest, respectable—I found none. Beneath this gilt-edged rabble, I found only black slaves, or free men of colour, who are slave-owners, and the worst of all. Is that a nation? And is it not the portrait of all the new independent states, dismembered from Spanish America? The Spanish and Portuguese races are not more progressive in the New World, than in the Old. They possess liberty only in name. But what is liberty?—is it an end or a means? You will see, my friend, what inter-tropical America will become with its liberty: it will be what it was before—a country without inhabitants, and without riches, because it is without labour. Labour and economy are all that are required; and liberty is precious only when employed in working, and in laying by. An admirable use is made of it in the United States; because the English race, by whom the whole of the North of the New World was peopled, is eminently industrious and orderly. I have told you, how the North Americans crushed us French by free competition. What will their neighbours, the Mexican Spaniards, do beside them?

The colonial despotism which still exists in Canada, though much tempered, cramps the English population on whom it is imposed, in the development of its industry and tendency to improvement, and opposes an obstacle to its increase and strength. In Brazil, the oppressions and vexations, preserved by the monarchical form of government, but feebly defend the country against a contrary principle of decay and weakness.

In Brazil, all labour is performed by negro slaves. Stop the traffic, abolish slavery, and there will be no work at all. Shoot or depose the emperor Don Pedro, dismember his monarchy into several confederated republics,—and anarchy will break forth every where; it will favour the revolt of the blacks, and the whites will, in many places, be massacred. There is no escaping from this alternative, except by maintaining the present order of things. It is most melancholy!

Perhaps you will have learnt, ere you receive this letter, that Bolivar has made himself king: I wish it may be so, for the sake of his country. Our friends will exclaim "treason!"—people will cruelly repent having compared him to Washington, because he will have violated the name of a vain and useless liberty;

and they will not understand, that a despotic chief is a thousand times preferable to the frightful anarchy which now desolates the new American republics. Liberty is a superfluity for nations in want of food and laws.

The time, occupied by my long passage, goes on quietly. The most happy understanding subsists among the inhabitants of this floating prison; but my life is idle and monotonous. I have lived upon prose since I have been on board: it is the sea system and I must yield to it. If you imagine that there is any poetry in the life of a sailor, how greatly are you mistaken! Nothing is more like a convent than a ship of war. Every day resembles the one before; each hour brings periodically the same task; there is no care for any thing external, and within, a profound reliance on the return of breakfast in the morning, and dinner in the evening. One is sure, when night comes, to find one's bed made, and on awaking in the morning, a change of linen. This uniformity might suit a studious life: but beware of it. The day drags on, and is wasted on words and trifles.

I intermix, with my scientific readings, the study of Persian, which I find not very difficult. With respect to the agreeable, it is very confined in my little travelling library, being restricted to three small volumes, Catullus Tibullus and Propertius, in Latin; Moore's Lalla Rookh, and Tristram Shandy—that is all. But Tristram Shandy is a feast in itself. I like Sterne infinitely. His eccentricity pleases me. Are we not made so? Do we not pass in an instant, without knowing why, from one idea to another? Among the infinite variety of tones in his book, I can always find a page in unison with the actual state of my heart, or the caprice of my mind. No one, assuredly, has more abused the elliptical style than he has, since he has left whole chapters blank. To a fool, it is a complete mystification, and one which he would not find very piquant, because it is very easy: but is that blank page really a wordless riddle?—Why not seek to fill it up? This is to me, particularly on board ship, Sterne's greatest merit: for when I have read a score of lines, as I am walking on deck, and the ship gives a lurch, I can put the book in my pocket and continue my walk with pleasure. I have matter for thought. The pretty tales of Moore have not an equal power of pleasing me; and, as for my three ancients, I have far less taste for them than for my modern English.

Chaper, what a revolution in my existence! During the six years of our acquaintance and friendship, what vicissitudes have we not encountered—how many things have we not talked of! Sometimes, in those rare moments when I am allowed to be alone, fantastic images of happiness and misery rise before me in the dim obscurity of the past, I know not whether I am dreaming or awake: for some moments I remain dazzled, and when I again open my eyes, I perceive that I was only recollecting, while I thought I was dreaming. Yet, my friend, the memory of those piercing impressions which once thrilled my very soul, is becoming gradually effaced. The mind alone possesses memory. It recals exactly the facts of which it has had cognisance,—the ideas which it has conceived. It recals them, even when it has ceased to judge them. The heart has not this faculty: it possesses no memory—it knows only what it actually feels. If it appears to recal past feelings, it is because they are not yet extinguished, and still affect it. Do not you think so?

Do not you think so?—as if we were not a thousand leagues apart!—as if I knew whether this letter will ever reach you, and when? And your answer?—can I expect it in less than a year?—and where shall I be then! Oh, my friend, how has my youth been thwarted!—what a life of wandering is mine! Yet, do not imagine that I regret having reached the term to which the concurrence of circumstances has brought me. I would change nothing of the direction my life has taken, since my departure for the United States. Whatever sacrifice I may have made, in tearing myself for so long a period from my old father and friends, the firm hope of seeing them again, makes me endure it with cheerfulness. We shall meet again, my friend, still young, yet grown old from the agitation of our youth — we shall meet again, in the calm strength of manhood. Shall we find more happiness in that tranquil state? I hope so.

It will, doubtless, be very difficult for me to send you any news of myself. But you will henceforth always know where to find me; if not on the map, at least in life. You will, in thought, easily fill up the intervals of mine, of which I may leave you in ignorance. You see me now following a straight line; you have only to prolong it to find me.

Adieu, my friend! be happy.

Cape of Good Hope,
Tuesday, 18*th December*, 1828.

We arrived here a week ago, with splendid weather. It has lasted the whole of this week, which I have spent here, comfortably and agreeably on shore, and living in a beautiful spot. I am surrounded by so many interesting objects, that I know not how to manage to examine the whole. I have seen as many as possible, and of every possible kind.

Adieu, my good friend! for I have not time to write any more.

TO M. DE MARESTE, PARIS.

On board the Zélée at sea, December 11*th*, 1828.

It is very true, my good friend, that were I to pass another year at sea, I might experience the dreadful malady with which our friend Dr. Stendhal threatened me: for I already feel myself *bien paysan du Danube*, although I have not been at sea more than three months at a time. Though I do not require a large establishment to work, I cannot do it without some accommodation; a little quiet is moreover necessary. Béranger may reckon upon a dozen leaden bullets if, on my return to France, they should take it into their heads to make me a *rey netto**. Figure to yourself, my dear friend, some fifty officers and sailors, singing together, each in his own key, and without even sticking to it, what we liberals call the *odes* of that great poet. This abominable Dutch concert, of which Béranger has furnished the first materials, makes me have a horror of him.

The young officers, with whom I live, were, on leaving Angoulême, at the age of sixteen, taken into the service of the constitutional monarchy. They were shipped off without being allowed even to visit their families; and they have now been from eight to ten years at sea, without being able to obtain more than a few months' leave of absence. This makes them tolerably good sailors; and they do not run against people in the streets, or overturn them against the posts, or into the ditch; but you will allow, that this system is not adapted to make them amiable men. They all know perfectly well, how to take the sun's meridian altitude,

* An absolute King.

or a lunar distance, and can calculate, methodically, from these observations, and those of the chronometer, their exact situation at sea—all things of little difficulty; but they have not the most superficial notions of astronomy, mechanics, or general physics. No one here distinctly knows the difference between a thermometer and a barometer. Several have remained three years in the Mediterranean, constantly in harbour, in the Levant, the Archipelago, or Italy; others have passed a year in Chesapeake bay; yet not one knows a word of either Italian, or English. This is monstrous, and I am not yet used to it.

The most perfect understanding, however, subsists here; and that is a great deal. I play chess with them; and chat with them upon the only subject they understand—their profession. This curiosity of mine surprised them at first; they satisfy it with a good grace, and without making any remark. If you have any interest at head quarters, pray get me appointed, on my return to France, minister of marine: I warrant I should make a capital one.

The Zélée is a log, and sails very badly. You will see it by the little way we have made since the 26th of August, when we left Brest: for, since that time, we have remained only four days at Teneriffe and twenty-one at Rio Janeiro, and we are now hardly nearer the Cape, than we are to Brazil. These passages are child's play to the first voyage I made, in winter, from France to the United States. I suppose my début, at sea, must have been one of the warmest: for I have since heard people complain of little gusts of wind, which, on my first voyage, occurred every day. Hence I am more than ever *Monsieur sans tempête*, and if, at Bourbon, I do not see a hurricane blow a few ships into shivers, nothing will drive this idea from my head *.

Brazil is the abomination of desolation. Imagine some hundreds of viscounts and marquesses, with the gold key on their coat, five or six gold, silver, or diamond stars, of all sizes and colours; ignorant, cowardly, and subservient to the emperor's pleasure; and under them, no middle class of respectability, nothing but a rabble of retailers and rogues, nearly white; then a terrific number of negro slaves almost naked, who live a few years and die, commonly without issue. They are driven to labour with the whip: a small portion of their labour feeds them, and they receive a belt and a pair of trowsers: the rest goes to find the carriages, cambric shirts, and silk stockings of the 300 marquesses. Depose Don Pedro, and all the provinces will separate into federative republics. Anarchy will burst forth every where: then, soon after, will come the revolts of the negroes, and there will no longer be any European rule in Brazil. Keep the emperor, but abolish the slave trade, and there will be no more labour, no income for any body; all must decamp if

* We shall see, that Jacquemont completely changed his opinion, regarding the non-existence of storms, Bourbon having offered him one of the most splendid, but horrible spectacles of the kind.

they would not starve; and you will see all the 300 fashionables, with their stars and gold keys, arrive at the hells of Paris, Cadiz and London. The *statu quo* is the only thing possible. The emperor, though sincerely devoted to the constitutional theories of M. Constant, is convinced of this, and governs accordingly. He lives from day to day, not caring for the future. Don Miguel is much loved at Rio Janeiro, as it was he who consummated the separation of Brazil from Portugal.

What few political journals there are here, are edited by foreigners, mostly French. The emperor cannot give his subjects, his *macaucos*, as he calls them—for he often tells them, they are a set of mischievous apes—the liberty of the press. He has established it by law, but the manners of the country are opposed to it. Several journalists have been knocked on the head, in the streets, at night, for telling the truth. This disgusted the rest, and they do not say a word more. Besides, no one would be at the cost.

Scenes of violence are frequent. I was near being struck by a pistol shot, fired by a robber, who was escaping, at his pursuers. He was taken, pinioned, and conveyed to the palace guard-house in the emperor's vestibule. There he was examined quite after the Turkish fashion. The police deliberated whether they should release, beat, or kill him; the officers looked calmly on, smoking their cigars, with their hands behind their backs. He was beat with such severity, as to break one of his arms, and then imprisoned. The same evening, I saw one black beat another to such a degree, that he killed him on the spot. I was told it was a father who had killed his son, the latter having attempted to assassinate him. He was not apprehended. Besides, the law scarcely ever condemns to death, even slaves; and when by chance there is an execution, there is a general consternation throughout the city; and the devotees have mass performed for the salvation of the culprit. Almost all crimes and misdemeanours lead indifferently to the galleys: and they are frightful. Figure to yourself, that the administration of justice does not even order a regular distribution of provisions in the prisons. The prisoners live entirely on alms: when these fail, they die of starvation, unless the chancellor sends them some bananas.

The Brazilian navy is composed of two ships of the line and some fine frigates, manned with tolerably good foreign crews; but so badly commanded by native officers, that the smallest French, English, American, or Dutch squadron would not, in a few hours, leave a single plank of them floating.

Admiral Roussin, with the threat of destroying the whole, obtained from the government the promise of restoring all that had been lost by French commerce in La Plata. It was necessary to use violence, to obtain this indemnity.

The Americans have, for a long time, had only a corvette on the Rio station, notwithstanding which, no one ever attempts to show them the slightest incivility. They are not loved; but they are feared. It is because they are in earnest; and the commander of this corvette lately threatened the Brazilian admiral, that he would sink him and his whole squadron, to the last man, if he dared to overhaul any ship of his nation forcing the blockade, which he never would acknowledge.

I think, my friend, that France is rapidly returning to that state of low estimation, which it *enjoyed* at foreign stations, about the year 1760, in the time of Alfieri's youth. We are laughed at every where; it would be no worse, even if we did not expend fifty-eight millions of francs annually on our navy, and two hundred millions on our army.

At Rio, we keep up our reputation as hair dressers, and dancing masters. The Rue Vivienne of this country, called Rua d'Ouvidor, is peopled by Parisian milliners, tailors, and hair dressers. These milliners are the —— of the highest ton. The emperor amuses his fancy with almost all. The people at Rio therefore believe, according to a rule-of-three undoubtedly very deceptive, that Frenchmen are all hair dressers, and Frenchwomen all ——. For that reason I spoke English.—I put on a stiff, and almost insolent air,—and every one received me kindly.

There is a fine theatre at Rio, where a detestable Italian company, with a still more execrable orchestra, murder Rossini three times a week. I saw L' Italiana in Algieri. The higher ranks yawn there as they do at Paris, by way of ton, and, I believe, a thousand times more. The fashionables of the environs of the city come at eight o'clock in post chaises. The postillion unyokes the two mules, which feed on the grass of the square during the performance; at eleven they are again put to, and he resumes his seat, ready to take his master. The emperor is always present; for, besides the milliners of the Rua d' Ouvidor, he allows himself all the dancers and figurantes, of the theatre.—He pays them according to their merit; that is, from ten to twenty francs. The ballet at Rio is in the taste of that of Brest, or Draguignan. It is the most pleasing part of the performance.

You are well aware that I unfortunately am acquainted with Naples only by means of pictures and panoramas, and you will most likely not acknowledge me as a judge of its beauty. But the roadstead at Rio appears to me to be still more beautiful. The virgin forest of M. de Clarac is not thick enough; the sky is seen among the trees, and this is incorrect. Enormous parasitical plants, whose scientific names I spare you, but whose foliage resembles the noble leaves of the pine-apple, and their flowers those of the iris, but variegated with a thousand colours, grow on the trees like our misletoe. A thousand different species of creepers climb, and hang in festoons over the flowery masses, and interlace in a hundred different ways. If you wished to pluck one, you would bring down a whole forest.

Then, in the environs of Naples, I, as a botanist, can find only sixty species of trees, both great and small, seven or eight at most of which are common. Around Rio I reckon a thousand very common: hence a prodigious variety of foliage, form and colour. M. de Clarac's engraving does not give these interesting details.

I think, my good friend, that you will not forget me during my long absence, and that, although distant, you will give me assurance of your existence and your friendship. I shall be dreadfully alone in India! Letters from Paris have already become very valuable to me! How will it be two years hence? You know that, in spite of my rather grave profession of savant, I still have still a tolerable taste for trifles;—let me have some, for it is precisely what I shall be in want of among the English in India.

To finish with a *bonne bouche*,—I have here a prisoner on board, like myself, a very clever and amiable man, the governor of Pondicherry. I knew him at St. Domingo, at my brother's, the American. We protect each other from ennui. He has seen many men, and many things,—has not forgotten them, and talks to me of the whole with candour and elegance. He has nothing of the sailor in him, though a captain in the navy. I shall regret leaving him at Pondicherry. He lately lent me Simond's excellent "Voyage en Angleterre," which I was barbarian enough to know only by name. I say amen! to almost every page in this book—one of the most amusing with which I am acquainted. M. Simond, whose authority the baron de Stendhal assuredly respects, has, notwithstanding his taste for the arts, put storms in their proper place. This passage in his book was a little triumph for me.

Adieu, my dear friend!—kind remembrances to all about you that we used to see together. My trade of traveller will perhaps wither me some day; but, at present, I have still a feeling heart. I do not love you all less at a distance, than near at hand.

Yours, for ever.

Closed at the Cape of Good Hope, the 28th December.—I arrived here on the 20th. It is no less a vessel than the Astrolabe * which brings you this. The day after to-morrow I sail for Bourbon. All well!

TO M. JACQUEMONT THE ELDER, PARIS.

On board the Zèlée, at sea, 18th December, 1828.

I WROTE to you for the first time from Teneriffe on the 18th of September, and then on the 6th of November a few lines from Rio Janeiro. In the interval, and also from Rio, I wrote to Porphyre on the 28th of October. You will, therefore, my dear father, have

* The Astrolabe, commanded by M. d' Urville, was on her return from a voyage of discovery, and also from researches relative to the shipwreck and fate of La Peyrouse.

known of my pleasant passage from France to the Canaries, and you will thence have also concluded the happy continuation of my sea voyage.

The slow sailing of the Zélée will make it very tedious. We are to-day fifteen hundred leagues from the Cape of Good Hope, and it is the eightieth day since our departure from Brest; namely, nineteen from Brest to Teneriffe, forty-one from Teneriffe to Rio, and thirty-one from Rio to this place in the broad ocean. It will take us twenty-five days or a month to go from hence to Bourbon, and six weeks more to reach Pondicherry; for we shall have the north-east monsoon almost in our teeth.

My life on board is a little tedious, but very quiet. Dinner and breakfast are not much like those we had before we reached the Canaries. Dried vegetables, salt meat and cheese, are our usual first and second course and dessert. All is hard and tough, and bad-looking. It would be rather unwholesome if we ate too much of it; but as this cookery, though highly spiced, stimulates the appetite but little, we eat only just enough to silence hunger; and our health is better than in the Rue de l'Université, where man, in a state of society, eats too much every day. My experience, since I left Rio, confirms me in my system on this head.

For a fortnight past, we have had the cool temperature of our own September. We have resumed our cloth clothes. In the morning we enjoy the warmth of our bed; during the rest of the day, we have fine weather and a beautiful sea. Thus we proceed slowly, but without fatigue. The chess-men stand on the table without falling. I prefer this motion of the vessel to one more violent, which would shake us. It is a canter compared to a trot. M. de Melay had the folly to catch a cold on our departure from Rio, and is only now recovering. We shall remain some days longer at the Cape, in order that he may get well on shore. For my part I shall enjoy life there; for, notwithstanding the extreme salubrity of salt meat and dried vegetables, taken in small quantities, I am in want of the green. The Cape being an English town of Dutch origin, all its inhabitants, like those of New York, keep a boarding house. It will cost me a piastre and a half a day, for which sum I shall have the pleasure of stretching myself on a bed, longer and wider than myself, between nice soft sheets. There is nothing like privation for making people delicate and voluptuous. Look at Porphyre with his eider-down: if he had not been to Moscow, I am persuaded he would have remained content, like ourselves, with the triple blanket.

There is a total absence of incident on board—nay a perfect understanding among us all. It is a *rinforzando* of reciprocal good humour. M. de Melay is, however, the one who most deserves my thanks; for the good-will of the others only makes my life void of any thing unpleasant, while his makes many of its moments agreeable. The sphere of our conversation widens every day; we often make little discoveries, which suddenly bring us in contact. They come within the scope of scientific knowledge common to both; or else they are identical opinions on subjects, which we do not see in the same light as the multitude.

We talk of the future, and of Paris: his lot is to reside there on his return from India with his little fortune, and his retirement as flag officer, which cannot fail him. You may easily suppose, that we have spoken of the places we shall have to pass through, in order to return to that incomparable Paris. As for him, his way is by sea; but for me it is a much greater affair; that same way is my end, and not my means.

After running foul, on first sailing from Rio, of a ship at anchor, and ten days after, being refitted and sailing anew in earnest, we were for five or six minutes within pistol-shot of some rocks, against which the current was driving us, whilst the wind did not allow to pass them. Had it not been for the thousand crowns in my trunk, my barometers, and other unreplaceable objects, I should have looked on the matter with indifference; I could have saved myself easily by swimming. The barks filled with rowers, which were towing us out of this dangerous passage, redoubled their vigour, and we passed at last, our fear being all we had to suffer.

A fortnight ago we had a hard gale which lasted two days. Every one cried out against it; but it was nothing but what was our daily fare from Havre to New

York, on board the Cadmus, of rolling and pitching memory. It is lucky for me that my first voyage was so rough. Since then I cannot allow that it is bad weather.

I yesterday re-perused your letter written to me at Brest. It begins by rectifying the orthography of one of mine, in which I had said, "*Tout va de sire* (All goes on well)." You will have a *c* instead of an *s*. I think you are mistaken; for "*Aller de sire*" (or "*de cire*" according to you) is in Italian, "*Andare da signore*. That affair goes on well, or, "*va de sire.*" "*Questo affare va bene,*" or, "*va da signore*"; wonderfully well—"*da signore*"—because signors, without doubt, do things marvellously well. What say you to my simile? If you live long enough, you will see me become a philologist, when I am old. In fact, I shall not return from India without a fair provision of Persian and Hindostanee, or without becoming perfectly acquainted with English. It will be already knowing by half that terrible German, since I shall know more than half its vocabulary.

From time to time, I spend an hour or two in writing every thing that strikes me. I yesterday made the trial of reading a little manuscript of prose, written these two months, and forgotten. It was not always tedious, and that is a great deal; for it is not a fault of mine to be in love with my own works. In India I shall put down every thing, that I may select when I return.

Cape of Good Hope,
Sunday, 28th December, 1828.

We arrived here a week ago, with the finest weather in the world. It has lasted the whole week. I have profited greatly. I live on shore, and eat fruit—the fruits of Europe, which are beginning to grow dear to me, and those of the tropics, of which I am never tired. I have walked about a great deal, asked a number of questions, and seen a great deal. Two days after my arrival, M. d'Urville, whom you ought to recollect, my dear father, and who formerly brought me the plants of Greece, and moreover begged some others of me, has just cast anchor at the Cape, with his immense treasures. We are constantly together. I have just spent the whole day on board the Astrolabe, which he commands. He is a very clever man, and I like him exceedingly. I here saw one of the sacred anchors and cannons of La Peyrouse, which he raised from the bottom of the sea, on the reefs of Vanikoro, with immense trouble and danger. His vessel is dreadfully shattered; and many of his men have been killed, or have died. But, on these hard conditions, he has succeeded beyond all sea voyagers. He sails in two days, as we do—but for Toulon. He will bring you this letter, which, but for him, I should have sent you by M. Séguier. I am in excellent health, and am just going to bed; for at four in the morning, M. d'Urville is to knock at my door, to go and make a very close inspection of the giant *Adamastor*. Yesterday I walked twelve leagues in the mountains, in search of stones and strata. I passed near Great Constantia, where I found M. de Melay, who introduced me to the proprietor of the celebrated vineyard of that name; and after my twelve leagues on foot, I refreshed myself very magnificently with some small glasses of that rare Constantia wine, and a seat in M. de Melay's carriage, to return soberly by the high road, having nothing more to do among the mountains. It is very warm, but breezy. I am perfectly well.

Adieu, my dear father, and Porphyre also.

On my arrival I received your letter containing a page of Porphyre's; two letters from M. de Humboldt, one for myself, and the other to introduce me to Lord William Bentinck; and some ludicrous and amiable phrases of Koreff's.

In Lord Bentinck's place, I should look very cross at any one who brought me so many letters to read, as I have letters addressed to him.

TO M. VICTOR DE TRACY, PARIS.

On board the corvette Zélée, at sea, Monday, 12*th Jan.* 1829, *between the Cape of Good Hope and the Isle of Bourbon.*

One of the first letters which I wrote after I left Europe was for you, my dear friend; the other was for my father and my brother at the same time. You shared with them in my last thoughts, as I was leaving my native country. Since that time, I have lost no opportunity, from Rio Janeiro and the Cape of Good Hope, at which we successively touched, of writing to my family, through whom you have, no doubt, heard of me. One of the most valuable advantages I have derived from my voyage to America, is the more intimate acquaintance which it has caused you to make with persons who are dear to me, for so many reasons. Since that time, you have better known my father and my excellent brother Porphyre. In knowing them better, you would love them more both for their sakes and my own—I who owe them both so much, and though far from them, find such delight in the tender feelings which they have for me. I will not leave Bourbon without addressing to you, from thence, some words of remembrance, and I therefore set to work beforehand. I avail myself of a calm day to visit you in thought, but I am surrounded by strange, and indifferent people; I am interrupted with unpleasant noises; I cannot isolate myself in this tumult, and I know not what delicacy of friendship restrains my secret outpourings, and leaves me before this paper with an overflowing heart, without daring to say to you those tender things, which the presence of a third person suffices to prevent me from expressing. In your company, I have frequently experienced this embarrassment, when we were not alone; I could then only squeeze your hand as I departed; but that pressure said every thing—and now we are more than two thousand leagues asunder.

I remained twenty days at Rio Janeiro. A happy chance brought me in contact with some fellow countrymen, of a character unfortunately too rare among the greater number of Frenchmen who seek their fortunes abroad. I soon became intimate with one of them, a son of Taunay the painter, an artist, like his father, but a philosophical one. He and his brothers, whose professions are different, have been settled in Brazil these six years. They have conversed with me in a very interesting manner about what I was desirous of knowing with regard to this country, where my short stay did not allow me to study the objects of nature. All that man has done there is detestable. There is no *nation* in Brazil; the population of the empire is composed of negro slaves, who die without issue, and require constant renovation; and some hundreds of Portuguese, decorated with titles and ribands, dressed, in spite of the climate, in the Parisian fashion, but displaying meanness and ignorance which would in vain be sought in Europe, united in the same individual. The emperor, who undisguisedly despises his subjects, and is better a hundred times over than the aristocracy of birth and riches by whom he is surrounded, is nevertheless not far above his courtiers; he can drive extremely well through the narrow and crowded streets of Rio, without running against either the posts or the passengers; he is coarse in his tastes, often brutal in his manners and conversation; and yet he is one of the most distinguished men of his country.

The political bond, which forms a single monarchical state of the different provinces of this empire, is very weak. The whole policy of the emperor consists, as he himself says, in preventing it falling to pieces before his death. As he gives no external strength to the terri tories, which he unites under his rule—and this is fully proved by the issue of the war with Buenos Ayres—the remote provinces, those of the north in particular, Bahia and Pernambuco, are always ready to throw off the yoke of a power, whose central seat is four or five hundred leagues distant, doubled at least by the want of roads, and which pretends to govern them, without affording them any protection. We shall therefore infallibly witness a new shock of republics in this beautiful portion of South America. They will not go far, I think. The primitive matter of future existence is absolutely wanting in them.

They will be involved in anarchy; and insurrections of the negroes, atrocious quarrels, perhaps the extermination of the whites,—the inevitable consequence of a violent emancipation of the slaves, will soon follow as a matter of course. With slavery labour will end, and want devour the remains of the population.

The abolition of the slave trade, which, according to the treaties, is to cease in a year, but which the form of the Brazilian coast will always protect from the vigilance of the English cruisers, would be the abolition of the empire. I have had a near view of this horrible traffic at Rio, carried on on an immense scale. From the sight of this human wretchedness, I have retained a feeling of horror which will scarcely ever be effaced from my mind. Nevertheless, whoever will have the end, will also find the means. It may truly be affirmed, that slavery is the *sine quâ non* condition of the existence of Brazil, as of European domination in all parts of America situated between the tropics, without being much elevated above the level of the sea.

As regards ourselves, in particular, if Cayenne and Bourbon have for a few years experienced a little prosperity, it is solely owing to the government of those colonies, having connived at, not to say its openly protected the landing of several cargoes of slaves. Were I in your place, my friend, in the station which you occupy, I would employ my power in the suppression of such crimes. You do not fear extremes in good: say, then, that the general voice of opinion accuses the administration of these colonies of a criminal connivance at the slave trade. Say, that you are convinced that they can prosper only by this traffic; that they could not even support themselves without continual importations of negroes; and that their actual prosperity is the highest censure of their administration. If it were honest, if it prevented the introduction of slaves, the number would gradually diminish, and these colonies, instead of prospering, would fall into decay. The law, which prohibits the slave trade, has condemned the sugar islands to perish. They do not perish; far from it, they are flourishing! Then the law is not carried into execution.

Its execution would, however, be very easy. An attempt is made to enforce it with cruisers on the coast of Africa, and about the places where the slavers usually attempt to land. This method is expensive and ineffectual. Suppress all cruisers against the traffic; but appoint in each colony a civil officer, charged with settling the civil condition of the slaves. Let every slave owner be obliged to keep a book, in which they are all to be inscribed, with their name, their exact description, and their filiation. The officer thus protecting the civil condition of the negroes, shall go from one plantation to another, without previous warning. On his arrival, he shall do as our military sous-intendants do in the army; he shall pass the slaves in review, and shall make the owner account for the possession of each. Apply to delinquents, unable to explain how they came by any slave in their possession, the penalties awarded against the accomplices of the slave dealers, and the traffic would, from that moment, absolutely cease; and if a slave ship was to land negroes on the estate of any colonist, you would see the latter eager to denounce him to the authorities, for fear the civil officer should arrive at his house just at the time, render him responsible, and accuse him of being an accomplice.

Yes, the colonies must perish. The law prohibiting the traffic has decreed it: but they must fall slowly:

they must perish from exhaustion :— In the first place, to avoid the scenes of carnage which would inevitably follow the premature emancipation of the negroes; and in the next, to cause the burthen of the loss of the property, in the actual possession of the colonists, to fall on two or three generations of whites instead of one.

The colonists are certainly not a very interesting class; yet humanity should rejoice that there are means of withdrawing only gradually from them their iniquitous property. However ill-acquired their riches may be, however contemptible such wealth may appear in the eyes of humanity, the law which makes them masters of the descendants of their actual slaves, does not condemn them to sudden ruin, but to gradual decay. It will leave their families the time and means of re-entering French society.

26th January, at sea, near Bourbon.

This desolating question of slavery constantly recurs to my mind. Had you, my friend, like me, seen the sales of slaves at Rio, you would be unceasingly tormented by them.

The colossal magnitude of the English sway is a blessing. There are doubtless many iniquities, many odious falsehoods in the national and colonial administration of that government, but it every where proscribes atrocities. The war, which it carries on against the slave trade, is sincere. At the Cape of Good Hope, since the British have been masters there, not a slave has been imported. The great caution they must use with regard to the interests of the Dutch colonists, who form the great majority of the population of that colony, has not yet allowed them to establish in the colonial law provisions for the redemption of slavery, and the enfranchisement of the children of actual slaves; but they impose such charges and such conditions on slavery, that the keeping of slaves becomes too expensive to pay a profit on the price they have cost their master. Thus their labour becomes too dear to be lucrative, and it is their personal interest which leads the colonists not much to regret this horrible species of property.

A singular meeting enough at the Cape, was that of a naval officer of my acquaintance, called D'Urville, who put in there at the same time we did, on his return to Europe, after being three years occupied in physical and geographical researches in the Polynesian islands. He will obtain celebrity by his labours. He gave me news from New Holland, New Guinea, and New Zealand; I told him those from Paris: and this exchange was to our mutual liking. There is a town in Van Diemen's Land, where three journals are published; the roads in the neighbourhood Mac-Adamised; there are inns where you may dine sumptuously, if you consent to pay your guinea; learned and literary societies, such as they are; and no slaves. And we know not the name of this place! That great English nation invades the whole universe.

Adieu, my dear and excellent friend, adieu. I leave you, because on one side I am consulted about a hit at backgammon, while at the other ear, I am asked the meaning of an English word. These annoyances are odious to me. In India, no doubt, I shall have the opportunity of writing long letters to you; but in a few lines written during my solitary journeyings, you will find more of myself. Adieu—I embrace you tenderly.

Saint Denis, Isle of Bourbon, 1*st Feb.* 1829, *Sunday at night.*

I have been here six and thirty hours. I here found your letter, from Paray, dated 8th of September, which contains one from Madame Victor, and another from Madame de Percy. I am indebted to you, for many soft emotions, in a place full of immense interest, but only mental interest; and where the mind finds no place of rest.

Chance made me live, for twelve hours, with some slave dealers. It was without my knowledge. Chance, afterwards, caused me to be received with the noblest hospitality by some very rich inhabitants of this colony. I enjoy a short period of magnificence; in a few days, the privations of life on board ship will return. Such will be my life for several years: luxury to-day, want to-morrow. What matters it at my age? What food for thought in this infinite variety of scenes, presented by man and by nature!

You, my friend, who know me, know whether there is any thing in me that can lead to the enjoyment of waking dreams. Those melancholy recollections of times and places, which you recall to my mind, and where the thought of you remains attached to my memory, make me shudder. These images make me, for a few instants, lose sight of the present, of my actual life; I penetrate into the past, I seize on it again. I walk about on your lawn, on your heath, under your birches. I saunter on the margin of your pond. I have your arm linked in mine. The strangeness of the scene, in which I now am, checks and destroys the illusion; and I resume my actual life, in which my thoughts are exercised only on real and positive objects.

I measure, I count, I calculate; I estimate the value of things capable only of moral appreciation. In the morning I am in the country among the rocks, with a compass in my pocket, and a hammer in my hand; in the evening I throw off my linen clothes and straw hat, and resign myself to my black cloth dress, to see the lords of this place. They are in general clever; I learn a thousand things from them.

Adieu, my dear friend. It is very late, and I wish to be up by sun-rise. I am alone, in a pavilion in the middle of a garden, hidden by jasmine and lemon trees. The fragrance, which they exhale in these warm moist nights, passes through the Venetian blinds, and makes me feel sleepy. But as Arimanes always comes with Orosmades, the musquitoes enter along with these perfumes, and contend against their drowsy influence.

I enjoy and suffer at the same time. This is better than not feeling at all. I embrace you with all my heart.

TO M. JACQUEMONT, THE ELDER, PARIS.

On board the Corvette Zélée, at sea,
Monday 12*th Jan.* 1829.

My dear father, I wrote my No. 3, from the Cape of Good Hope; it was commenced at sea on my passage from Brazil to the Cape, and closed on the 28th of December, on the *terra firma* of Africa. That letter, which I confided to the care of M. D'Urville, commander of the expedition of the Astrolabe, to forward to you on his arrival at Toulon, where his vessel is to be paid off, will have informed you of the very agreeable, but very slow continuation of our voyage from Rio Janeiro; the pleasantness of our short stay at the Cape of Good Hope; and the fortunate chance by which I there received the first packet you have sent me since my departure. The Madagascar, which like ourselves had touched at that colony, hastened to carry it to M. de Melay, under cover to whom, it was addressed to me. I found in it your No. 1, that of Porphyre, and M. de Humboldt's letters.

We left the Cape of Good Hope on the 30th December. I spent the previous day in making, along with D'Urville, a last and magnificent excursion to the mountains overlooking the town; and I could not return on board, in the roads, but the very morning of our sailing. The kindness of the officers, who had promised me a boat to come ashore for me and my baggage, enabled me to enjoy, to the last moment, the pleasure and convenience of *terra firma*. The week which I spent there, has greatly refreshed and rested me. Not, however, that I remained idle in the shade; but I drank milk, which I had not had an opportunity of seeing since I left Brest. I ate fruit, and fed upon fresh and succulent food. The evening meal made me forget the fatigues of the day, of which some hours' slumber in an immoveable bed, longer than myself, left me no feeling in the morning when I awoke. When one can recruit in this way, a great deal may be spent without growing poor.

I again found myself, without discomfort, in my floating prison. It was peopled the day before our departure with a number of new inhabitants, whose society is infinitely agreeable. They consist of some thirty large sheep, which Porphyre would certainly charge with smelling of wool; but we do not find fault here. We thus have, that is to say, we had, two hundred fowls, and a profusion of vegetables; so that twice a day, we can literally forget that we are at sea. The whole crew partake of these niceties; hence the general health on board is excellent. For ourselves, the aristocracy of this little society, they will last till we reach the Isle of Bourbon.

Two days after our departure, we encountered off the Cape of Tempests, and as we doubled it, the gale rendered a matter of course by poetical tradition. It drowned a few of our fowls, and that was all. You know that decidedly there are no tempests. The longer I am afloat, the more I am convinced that they are only a happy fiction of poets. The word is hardly known to seamen, and they never make use of it. The maximum of the species, speaking prosaically—that is, sticking to the truth—is a very strong wind: it breaks a mast or two, and drowns nobody. It is not terrible to look at; it is only *vexigenous* (engendering vexation), disagreeable, and ugly. The picturesque in it is very rare.

Nevertheless, we had a slight specimen three days after our *soi-disant* tempest. It was in the evening; the night was clear enough, but no moon. It was nine o'clock. We had on deck only half the crew; these keep watch while the rest sleep. A ship which we saw the whole afternoon astern of us, sailing in a slightly different direction, at two leagues' distance, changed its course to bear down upon us; and the advantage of the wind permitted her to gain rapidly upon us. This suspicious manœuvre caused us to clear for action, which was done quickly and in silence. The stranger, having come within hearing, hailed us. We thought we heard English. The captain desired me to go up to listen, and answer. Behold me, then, mounted on the poop, my ear to the wind, stationed in the first tier of boxes, to receive the cannon-shot if there were to be any. The stranger, of whose strength we could not judge in the position in which he presented himself to us, but which all the officers asserted was a ship of war, asked us in English, "*What ship ours was?*" to which I answered, that he was very impudent to think of asking such a question—that he must immediately tell us who he was. He spoke again, without our being able to understand each other; but his attitude became more and more hostile. We thought that he meditated boarding. Immediately, a seasonable turn of the helm placed us so that we could fire with advantage. We then gave him a broadside of round shot and grape; and then directly, while all the guns were being reloaded, the ship was worked so as not to wait for his broadside. But the stranger seemed to be stopped. I re-mounted the poop, and thence, with a gigantic speaking trumpet, the only one of real use, I ordered him to bring-to, and an officer to come on board, or we should continue to fire. We did not at first hear their reply, but we saw them execute the submissive manœuvre which had been ordered; and we waited patiently for their boat, which, however, did not come. As, however, people are not very patient, when they have sixteen guns ready to pour forth their contents, without any more trouble than saying "Fire!" the captain and M. de Melay, who thought the stranger was a pirate, and owed him a grudge for the trouble he had given, begged me to repeat the threat of complete destruction. So I sacrificed my larynx to play the stentor, and with success. Their people soon arrived. I proceeded, with the captain, to interrogate the officer who had come in the boat, which was done in the most pacific style in the world, at least apparently. However, the captain and M. de Melay desired that his ship should be searched. I communicated, therefore, our intended visit to him. One of our boats was lowered; there was a heavy sea; and the lieutenant of the Zélée was charged with the office of boarding the vessel, to reconnoitre her in detail. But as he could not speak English, I was wanted again. I complied with a good grace—the circumstance seeming, besides, not to offer any danger, for I believed in my Englishman's sincerity. We were nevertheless on our guard. Our boat's crew were armed; we had at our feet, in the boat, a number of pistols ready loaded. The officer and the four sailors belonging to the stranger, were detained on board during our absence, and were there, besides, to answer for our safety. After struggling for ten minutes against the sea, our boat ran alongside of the stranger, which we immediately perceived to be a merchantman. We were received with the greatest politeness, by people of very good appearance, but extremely terrified.

The vessel was from Liverpool, bound to India with merchandise and three passengers. Ever since her departure from Europe she had communicated with nobody; and seeing another vessel so near, had veered round to say "Good night!" and exchange longitudes. They had taken us in the night for a merchantman, and had approached without fear. Our shot had broken a yard, and one had passed through one of her courses about five feet above the deck. Fortunately no one was killed.

The harsh part of our expedition was terminated in an instant. The innocence of the accused was evident from their weakness. I pretended to read the papers of the Nancy, and told the captain that he had been only guilty of extreme imprudence in approaching an unknown ship at night; that, however, we were very happy, as it had turned out, that none of his crew were killed; and that we should return on board our own ship, and send him his men. The poor devil confessed his error with all due humility, and made a thousand excuses for the shot we had fired at him; and then it was impossible for us to leave him without accepting something to drink. The passengers, who were of very respectable appearance, and for whom our arrival was a pledge of the termination of that horrible music, had received us with the most vehement goodwill. We were *fêted*, and caressed. They would have been hurt if we had refused to allow them to uncork a bottle for us. The steward was called, who asked me respectfully what I would like to have. I replied, with a disdainful air, "A glass of champagne." The cork flew to the ceiling, and our glasses were filled. I recommended my companion only to moisten his lips, in order to make these people believe that we had in our hold two or three feet of the same. In this respect I preached to them from example, although their champagne was excellent, and I was very thirsty from shouting so much. We then adjourned, after a little admonition which I gave the English captain, with whom his passengers seemed to be very angry on account of the danger to which his imprudence had exposed them. We were lowered into our boat with a thousand precautions, they wishing us all kinds of prosperity. We were no less polite. At midnight, we returned on board our own ship, where they were under no apprehensions about us. We dismissed the five hostages, who passed under the fire of my English eloquence, and pursued our course.

But in the tumult of the preparations for battle, one man had been seriously wounded; yesterday, he was obliged to make up his mind to lose his fore-arm. Our young doctor had never performed any operations any more than myself; it was a grand affair for him. I had the pleasure of being very useful to him, by encouraging beforehand, and assisting at the critical moment. I tied the arteries. You may tell Jules Cloquet, that instead of tying only three, the radial, cubital, and inter-osseous, I tied five, without more trouble than if I had been operating on a dead body; and if you, my dear father, or Porphyre, say again that Victor is awkward with his hands, I will send you a stamped paper, signed by twenty witnesses, as a certificate of the contrary. I agree so much with the opinion of these witnesses, that I regret, for the sake of the patient, that I did not perform the operation myself. In spite of all I did to encourage the doctor —a good sort of young man of twenty-three, tolerably well versed in ordinary anatomy, and the minor operations of surgery, but nothing more—his hand shook at the beginning of the operation, and it was only after some minutes that he recovered completely. The limb was then amputated, and I think badly enough: tell Cloquet that I should have kept more skin to cover the stump. I shall not close this letter at Bourbon, without letting you know the result of the operation, and I will then tell you, whether I should have been right or wrong in keeping more skin. I reckon confidently that when Frederick is minister of marine, which he wishes much to be, he will make me at least a knight of the Legion of Honour, for the services I am doing on board the king's vessels.

The priest, whom we have on board, of course availed himself of our man's amputated arm yesterday, to go and puzzle him with salutary thoughts on life and death. But, being informed of what was going on, by M. de Melay, who had seen his reverence going on tiptoe towards the hospital door, I went immediately, and caught him in the act of frightening the poor devil. He understood me directly, and sheered off as soon as he perceived me. I have advised the wounded man's friends not to quit his bedside, but to keep the *curé*, as they call him, at a distance: if he insists, they will receive him with a good broadside of slang. My vocabulary, as you see, my dear father, is enriched with very choice expressions.

M. de Melay is more and more amiable: he is an immense resource to me; his conversation, though extremely graceful and elegant, does not the less abound with thought and facts. Our backgammon sometimes excites a revolution between us, but never coldness. He is gay. As we are always inclined to discover merit in those who find merit in us, you will hence, no doubt, conclude that M. de Melay is sensible how amiable my lordship is.

27th January, at sea, morning.

We shall see the island of Bourbon in the afternoon, and shall very probably go on shore to-morrow. Unfortunately it will not be for more than six days. Afterwards, we shall, at last, come to the beginning of the last part of our voyage, but it will be a long and hot one.

The voyage had somewhat impaired my health, ere we reached Rio Janeiro. From the Canaries to Brazil, the salt provisions heated me extremely; and I slept badly. This indisposition has entirely passed away; I have been very well ever since we left the Cape of Good Hope. They say I am growing fat; perhaps this appearance is caused by my whiskers, which I have allowed to grow for the last two months; but I certainly feel myself full of vigour.

Every thing on board continues to go on *de sire*, or *de cire*—whichever you please. It is a great pity that

Domergue is dead, for you might have consulted him on that great question, by objecting to his *cire*, the *signore* of the Italians: "Tutte cose vanno da signore." *Signorilmente*, an adverb, is also used, though seldom in the same sense.

I reserve the small space I have left for Bourbon itself. Good-bye, my dear father. Porphyre must have received my first letter. I think of both of you without sadness, because I see your existence flowing on in tranquillity. We are all happy in being so constituted. The love we bear to each other would serve only as a reciprocal misfortune, if this feeling had with us the form which it often has. We are all well here; we are satisfied with our situation in life, be it what it may. Methinks that, at a distance, I enjoy your satisfaction, as you share in my contentment.

When I can have an hour's silence and solitude, I easily quit the ground on which I stand, and transport myself to you. I lose all thoughts of the enormous distance which separates us. Of course you also pay me similar visits: they are full of delight. Adieu.

Bourbon, 3rd February.

I have been here for three days, in the handsome and elegant mansion of a rich colonist, an acquaintance of Madame Ramond. He has a son-in-law of forty-five, an old naval officer, amiable, witty, and well informed. All is for the best in this best of all possible worlds. I sleep little but eat heartily; I work a great deal, and am extremely well pleased here. I learn twenty things every hour. Adieu, my dear father: I embrace you and Porphyre. This letter will go off this evening.

TO M. PORPHYRE JACQUEMONT, PARIS.

Quarter or Town of St. Denis, Island of Bourbon, Tuesday, 10th February, 1829.

I WRITE to you, my dear friend, in the midst of public consternation. We are, you know, in the hurricane season, the summer of this country. It is the dangerous season, that of those frightful rains and tempests which desolate the islands situated within the tropics. The weather since our arrival has been always rather threatening; a whole day has seldom passed without a squall. It has, however, become fine again. During the last four days of last week, which I employed in making a very interesting excursion in the north-east part of the island, I was caught only in one heavy shower. On my return here on Saturday evening, I regretted not having prolonged my little journey, on learning that the Zélée's departure was postponed till Tuesday, this day; but yesterday, at sunrise, the sea became tremendous, a heavy swell of unusual violence beat on shore, and destroyed the boats and light craft moored close in. Every vessel at anchor in the roads immediately weighed, on the signal being made. All cut their cables, leaving one or two anchors at the bottom, and got out to sea, taking advantage of the south-east breeze, which fortunately blew with sufficient force, and without which they would have been dashed to pieces on the coast. I went two leagues from hence to an estate belonging to my host, in front of which there is also a small roadstead, where the European vessels take their sugar on board. They had already sailed at eight o'clock in the morning.

The day was pretty fine. I spent it in galloping through the cane and other plantations on the estate of M. Martin de Flacourt, my host, whose son, a man of my own age, obligingly acted as my *cicerone*. We returned to the town at four o'clock, to dine. The sea, whose margin we followed in our carriage, from Sainte Marie to Saint Denis, had increased but little since the morning; it had, however, caused several small streams, which our cabriolet had passed easily in the morning, to rise so that they had become by no means pleasant to cross in that manner. We heard of some new accidents on our arrival. A small vessel from St. Paul had capsized and eight negroes were drowned. The Zélée, in getting under weigh, had shipped three enormous seas. There were on board, at the time the signal for sailing was made, only two officers, the lieutenant on duty and a midshipman.

The wind, which had been only fresh and steady during the day, began to blow in the evening in sudden and violent squalls, and the sea again rose. It demolished some advanced works which served to protect the landing-place. A hurricane was apprehended;

and every thing moored there, or left on account of its weight, was hauled on shore, as far as possible from the water's edge. The rain poured down in torrents.

At two in the morning the hurricane began.

As, during the previous week, I had been constantly galloping about in the day-time, up all night conversing, *mundanizing*, or writing, I had an arrear of sleep to pay—so much so, that the terrible shaking of the houses was lost upon me. I awoke as if nothing had occurred, when, at six, the negro who waits upon me came into my room with the morning's cup of coffee, and pulled me by the legs. The roaring of the sea, the whistling of the wind, and the creaking and trembling of my pavilion, stunned me a little. I was however, soon up. I went to the harbour—at least what they call the harbour. I found a crowd of inhabitants collected to contemplate the disasters of the night, and those of each fresh breaker and each fresh gust of wind. The pier had been carried away, and they were hastily emptying the warehouses which it protected. An indiscreetly curious person received a stone on his head, and was carried off bleeding, in a palanquin. He was scarcely noticed. Every one was thinking of his own sugar, his cloves, and his coffee, and cared very little for his neighbour's limbs.

The sky is charged with rain, which is falling in torrents. Nevertheless, the wind is increasing, and the sea is rising higher and higher. By not staying on board the Zélée, I have missed the opportunity of seeing, or rather experiencing, a tempest. The sea has never before risen so high here, and we must go back to the year 1806 for an equally violent hurricane. That year it was much more terrible: it was a hurricane like those whose velocity is reckoned in the "Annuaire du Bureau des Longitudes" at forty-five metres per second. As such storms are common here, the houses are built very low; they therefore offer but slight hold for the wind. None have been blown down yet; perhaps there will be some by and by. Notwithstanding that, I esteem myself in perfect safety in my pretty pavilion. Neither do my hosts, whose principal habitation is a story higher than the ground floor, fear being blown into the garden. Their house, it is true, is the handsomest in the town, and I know many in which I should not like to sleep to-night. All are built of wood—for they must also provide against earthquakes; but there are different kinds of wood: good and bad. M. de Flacourt's house, as well as the pavilion in which he has placed me, is built of large logs of a red wood as beautiful and as heavy as mahogany, but harder; so that I say to the wind, "Blow on, you rascal! Blow on: I defy you."

Good-by, my friend: for all this is no reason why I should not dine, and I am reminded that it is three o'clock. Adieu!

11th February.

Two small schooners, which had been drawn on shore for repairs, and were lying more than thirty feet above the water's edge, were carried by a sea on the roof of a warehouse, which they broke through. Guns were torn from their places. I returned to the sea shore yesterday evening. It was covered with fragments, which the waves sometimes carried off to throw back again: anchors, wood, and enormous rocks. Several houses had been demolished. One part of the town, threatened by the progress of the inundation, was deserted. It was evening: the light was disappearing, and night commenced fearfully. The wind still blew with the same fury, and the rain was dreadful.

The wind, however, has ceased. The crisis is over. The sea is less terrible than yesterday, and can add nothing to the damage already done, which is going to be estimated. The shipping will not be able to return to their anchorage for five or six days. I know not how they will be able to take in their cargoes afterwards. This is an iron-bound coast. The landing-places have been destroyed, and it will take time to repair them. The Zélée, which had taken in all her provisions, and being a King's vessel, passes before the rest, will be able to sail the first; but, like the rest, she will have to get up her anchors. We are to remain here ten days longer. Perhaps our vessel has suffered damage ; in that case we must go to the Isle of France to refit.

So far as regards me individually, I should console myself for this delay, if in the meantime I could go through the island ; but it is impossible to proceed half a league from the town without finding an impracticable torrent. The roads are masses of mud, and the deluge of rain continues without intermission.

There were twenty merchantmen at anchor abreast of Saint Denis, and at least an equal number must have been in the other roads of the island. Several stood out to sea without officers on board. There will certainly be some lost.

As men of war must have this justice done them, that, if they get more damage in roads than merchantmen, fewer serious accidents occur to them on the high seas, I rather regret that I was not on board the Zélée when the signal for sailing was made. I, who deny tempests, might perhaps have had reasons for changing my opinion.

If, which is impossible, she should not return,—if she should have perished, I must make up my mind to return to Europe, for I only brought on shore a small trunk with a coat and six shirts. My letters are on board, so is my money—all my means of travelling in India. But, in truth, I must not think of it.

Adieu ! I will write again to you in my prison.

Monday, 18*th February*.

The Zélée returned these three days since, with the loss of her top-gallant masts, an anchor, all her boats, having part of her nettings carried away, and several ports driven in, &c.; she has been almost swamped. There were three feet water between decks, which they were obliged to let run into the hold in order to pump it out. It is probable that my clothes, which I left on board, are damaged, or lost. The provisions just taken in, are spoiled.

Notwithstanding this damage, she sailed again the day after her arrival to cruise round the island, in order to assist any vessels in distress that she might fall in with. As I have no taste for horrors, I had no wish to re-embark during this short cruise, in which she will undoubtedly see some. Two crews, struggling with death on the wrecks of their ships, have already been brought in by merchantmen which had been more fortunate in weathering the gale. It is known, moreover, that there are at least ten ships in the offing entirely dismasted, perhaps without provisions, and entirely without crews. The hurricane was also felt at the Isle of France. The ships at anchor there were obliged to put out to sea; these also must be assisted. The only two officers on board the Zélée remained sixty hours on deck, without sleeping. Not a life has been lost, nor any one seriously hurt; but all on board expected to perish.

The damage suffered by the Zélée does not affect her solidity. On her return to her anchorage she will take in a new supply of provisions, purchase boats from the merchantmen who have saved theirs, get up her spare top-gallant masts, repair her bulwarks, and we shall proceed again to sea in three or four days. It will not be necessary to put into the Isle of France. M. de Melay will send her to refit at Calcutta, whither she will take me.

The hurricane of the 10th of February has caused more disasters than all those remembered by the oldest inhabitants of the island. The sea was never seen so high. M. de Melay, who has often been stationed in the classical sea of hurricanes, the Leeward Islands, never beheld any thing equal to it. My host's son-in-law, who is also an old naval officer, told me that he never before saw such a "feast of the winds." I have therefore been favoured.

As I had serious apprehensions concerning the fate of the Zélée, I am quite consoled for the possible, even probable loss of my black coat, waistcoat, and trowsers. My letters for India were carefully enclosed in parchment, and a month ago they were taken from my trunks and placed in the highest drawer of a chest of drawers which shuts well, and stands in the purser's cabin. He will have taken care of them, at the same time as his own papers. My barometers were in the captain's cabin, which the two officers inhabited during their campaign, because it was less exposed to the irruptions of the sea. Thus my mind is at rest in regard to these instruments. The books I most value, I know to be safe. My guns alone remained to be wetted, which they no doubt have been, for they must have had a foot deep of water over them, although stowed away between decks. In proportion to my fears, these probable losses are a considerable profit.

The old sky, as the sailors call it—the beautiful blue sky, has reappeared for several days; the breeze is gentle; and the sun alone, of all things in nature, commits excesses. But this great heat at Bourbon is not unwholesome; it is not even debilitating. On Saturday I went ten leagues on foot into the mountains, and four on a restive mule. I was caught in two showers. I passed ten or a dozen rivulets or streams without taking off my clothes, and I returned without fatigue. I wished to go as far as Saint-Paul: I was but half a league from it; but my progress was arrested by the torrent, which they told me had been fordable since the preceding evening, and which I found frightful.

I yield very quietly to the custom of this country, which is to take three or four cups of coffee a day. I only defend myself against the good cheer of an opulent house, that of my host. Man in a state of society eats too much: you, my dear friend, know my system on this point. I am more and more attached to it, from personal experience, as well as from the observation of others. I am fortifying myself in a devout love of abstemiousness, which, I have no doubt, will cause me to enjoy perfect health in India, amid hepatitis, fevers, dropsies, and disorders without number, which afflict the rich English, who commit excesses at table seven hundred and twenty times a year.

The slaves here, who work like horses, and have for the most part the appearance of health, with a most certain reality of strength, eat nothing but rice and coarsely ground maize boiled together in water. Some of the masters add to their ration on a Sunday a small bit of putrified cod. Now we whites, who expend no muscular strength, eat five, perhaps ten times more nourishing food than they do; consequently we digest badly what we eat: we are lean, or else loaded with an undue quantity of fat. The negroes are all in good condition. There is neither leanness nor obesity among them.

Coffee, and highly spiced rice, as it is eaten here, and as they prepare it also in India, do not heat me. This new regimen agrees with my digestive system, no less than with my head. All these parts of my person enjoy a wise, moderate, and constitutional liberty.

Good-by, my friend. This is the hour of the day (half past eight,) when the thermometer rises abruptly from 26° or 27° centigrade, up to 30° and 31°. I leave you, because the servants are about to shut my windows, which are all wide open. Then I have my little call to make on M. de Melay, at the government house, in search of news; and then to breakfast. You, no doubt, are warming yourself in this villanous month of February; you are at this moment buttoning up to get ready for your journey to your office. I pity you;—and think myself happy that I perspire, when I am dreaming of the miseries of cold weather.

24th Feb., morning.

The Zélée is returned; she will sail to-morrow; and I must go on board to-day. I have only time to take leave of you. My books and barometers have suffered no injury.

The Zélée has found nothing. Nevertheless, there are still twenty-three vessels, concerning whose fate great apprehensions are entertained.

Adieu, my friend,—I embrace my father and you.

TO MADAME VICTOR DE TRACY, PARIS*.

Saint Denis, Isle of Bourbon, 24th Feb. 1828.

My dear Madam,—I received here the kind note which you wrote to me from Paray, a month after my departure. Let me, I beg, hear frequently from you.

What diverse aspects, what varied forms of human existence, do I not see while in search of plants and

* This letter, and all bearing the same address, were written by Jacquemont in English. Madame Victor de Tracy was kind enough to translate them.

Not having the original English of our author at hand, we have been compelled to translate Madame de Tracy's French back again into English.—T.

stones? What food for thought, in the long intervals of solitary life which I shall often have to go through, and in which, from taste, I have already begun to fancy myself.

What beautiful objects you would have to paint, if your eyes saw what mine look upon! One is never tired of admiring the noble elegance and magnificence of nature in the tropics. But, in my moments of sadness, I regret the touching grace of the weeping birches of Paray, scattered about the flowery heath. I cannot recollect, without emotion, those long and narrow meadows which penetrate, and are lost in the thick foliage of the woods. Take care not to let your husband ravage, as you called it, with his agriculture, all your picturesque views, in order that my memory may know each spot on my return, and that I may find you both with the same beauties around you.

What pleases me most in my recollections of Europe, is the figures in our landscapes. Here we have only naked and brutalised negroes. I cannot get used to them.

To-morrow, I shall no longer look upon these scenes of wretchedness; to-morrow, I shall bid farewell to views of slavery. But shall I not find them again in India, though under another name? I know not. Before two months are past I shall know, and will tell you.

Adieu,—continue to be my friend. I am so far off that it seems to me almost as if I were dead. But this is no reason you should forget me. Adieu.

TO M. VICTOR DE TRACY, PARIS.

Pondicherry, Sunday, 26th April, 1829.

My dear Friend,—I arrived here a fortnight ago; to-morrow, at day-break, I shall re-embark in the Zelée, for Calcutta, which I shall reach in a week. I will write from thence at length. To-day, I have only time to tell you of the excessive astonishment and interest excited in me by every object I see in this old world of Asia. Men are not wanting to me either, and I have the pleasing satisfaction of convincing myself anew every day, that persons worthy of being loved are every where to be found*. In a few interviews, of an hour or two in all, I have become almost intimate with the *procureur-général* of this colony. I had never seen him before, nor did I even know him by name; but the day after our arrival, at the installation of M. de Melay, I heard him say, with the truest emotion, things so noble and beautiful, that I went up to him without any introduction, and without making myself known except by the expression of my sentiments, which agreed so well with his own; and it is not without regret that, on leaving this place, I shall separate from him. This man's generosity rendered the line chalked out

* Jacquemont says elsewhere, " There exists between tender and generous minds, of all countries, a kind of natural and holy free-masonry, which leads them to discover and acknowledge each other through the external differences of age, language, and nationality."

for him by ministerial prudence and reserve, incompatible with his principles; and, though bereft of fortune, I saw him sacrifice his office with an indifference I might well admire. He returns to France, where he will undoubtedly assume an eminent political station. You will probably meet him; his name is Moiroud.*

I have had another piece of good fortune: I found a college companion here, who has been useful to me. He is chief engineer of bridges and roads in this little country, of which he did me the honours.

Adieu, my dear friend. How many things we shall have to talk of four years hence. Adieu, I love you, and embrace you with my whole soul.

TO M. VICTOR DE TRACY, PARIS.

Calcutta, 1st September, 1829.

My dear friend,—I know not whether my letters have been more fortunate in their carriage than yours; but I wrote to you from Teneriffe, the Island of Bourbon, Pondicherry, and from hence a short time after my arrival; and since I left France, I have yet

* M. Moiroud, on his return to France, was attached to the council of state as *maître de requêtes*, and to the law faculty at Paris as adjunct professor. In 1832, he terminated a life which mental afflictions had rendered insupportable.

received but a single letter from you, written from Paray, shortly after my departure from Brest. It reached me at Bourbon in the month of February last, during my prolonged stay at that island. Yet my father, from whom, after a very long interval, I have just heard, tells me that he has forwarded other letters from you. I have every reason to believe that they are at the bottom of the Ganges, with many others.

In acquainting you with my arrival here, I was still struck with the disagreeable and almost horrible impression produced on me by my recent navigation in the mouths of the Ganges. This river, at different seasons of the year, is nothing but a sea of mud, raised by furious winds, and intersected by rapid currents. When the strength of the tide conspires with the efforts of the wind, no anchor can hold, no cable resist. After touching several times on banks, and being unable to steer with certainty through the narrow channels which are alone navigable in the midst of this immense surface of water, we let fall our anchors, and in less than half an hour they were lost. The hurricane at Bourbon had deprived us of all our boats, and we had no means of getting on shore, if our vessel, which had grounded on a bank and was lashed by a furious sea, went to pieces. Besides, what shore were we to reach? Saugur island: the lowest and most hideous of this vast Delta—the classic region of tigers! This critical situation lasted a whole night, during which I served as interpreter between the English pilot and the officers. But what frequently occurs, happened to us: we were only near remaining there; so that, after all, we did not remain any more than if we had never encountered this danger.

I am now reconciled to the sacred river of the Hindoos. I have been living for six weeks in a delightful spot on its banks, crossing it twice a day to visit the botanical garden, opposite to which I resided with hosts whom I left this morning.

The flattering and kind reception, which I met with on my arrival, continues. The honourable recommendations I brought, have thrown all respectable houses open to me. I chose those in which I thought I should be most at liberty to pursue my studies without interruption; and such has been the foresight of my friends, that there is not, in this country, a single man I have seen with pleasure and profit, to whom I had not letters of introduction from Europe.

People do not come here to live, and enjoy life; they come—and this is the case in all states of society here—in order to gain something to enjoy life elsewhere. There is no such a thing as a man of leisure at Calcutta. The governor-general has the most to do; next to him the chief justice; and, after these, the advocate-general, and so on. It is almost wholly among this class of men that some are to be found, whose taste for study can enable them to steal a few moments of leisure amid the duties of their station. All who are not men of highly gifted intellect soon lose their energy, and yield to disgraceful indolence. Immediately below the higher ranks, you find the most vulgar and common rabble;—yet, for a truly small number of Europeans, there are journals without number, both political and literary; there are learned societies, or societies calling themselves such, of every denomination—craniological, phrenological, horticultural, literary, medical, Wernerian, and I know not how many besides—whose members scarcely yield either in science or appetite to similar institutions in the United States. I could not hesitate between such *savans* as these and very eminent men, devoted to studies quite different from my own. Thus, as I sent you word, my first host was Mr. Pearson, advocate-general of Bengal, and the only lawyer who ever came from England with a great reputation already established. He is a man of at least your age, full of sense and good humour, and a liberal, like ourselves—which, in English, means a radical. I know not what confidence I inspire these people with, but they open their hearts to me on points about which they are afraid to speak to each other after years of acquaintance. They have the most favourable prepossessions with regard to the reason, liberality, and independence existing in the opinions of a Frenchman. In the country, where I have been living six weeks with Sir Edward Ryan, one of the judges, I was next door, or rather next garden, neighbour to the Chief Justice, a man of the highest talent in his difficult profession of English

Judge—a profession assuredly of the gravest cast, with also the gravest appearance. Well! he was the first to inform me, that Lady Ryan was very strict; and that, notwithstanding the good humour and want of strictness of the Knight himself, I might find Sunday a very dull day with them. He therefore invited me to take refuge with him on that day, at least to dine, take a walk, and play a game at chess in the evening, whilst his wife gave us some music. You may imagine, my dear friend, that I learned many things, during those charming evenings, from a man who has for the last eight years held a judicial situation in India, either at Madras or in Bengal. He wished me to see a criminal trial of natives; and I am indebted to him for the honour, here deemed very great, of having sat for two days on the *King's Bench* with the supreme court.

The office of crown-prosecutor is not considered odious in England, as it is in France. My present host, Mr. Pearson, who holds that office, is certainly, from the nature of his duties, better informed than any one else, concerning the character of the natives; and from the facts which he relates to me, and the opinions he expresses, as well as from the decisions of Sir Charles Grey, the Chief Justice, I have become acquainted with a thousand interesting matters relating to the people of this singular country, with which my own observation alone could not have supplied me. In India, the creature man is a very singular being. He, who having decided on death, throws himelf before the sacred car to be crushed by its wheels, jumps up at the moment of being touched by them, and runs away, because a European passing on horseback gallops towards him whip in hand! Here are to be seen united in the same individual, the greatest contempt for death, the greatest indifference, the greatest insensibility to physical pain, and the most excessive cowardice. Instances are frequent of the most atrocious cruelty, combined with habits of charity; nothing is so contradictory, so whimsical, so mad, as this people.

But the man who, perhaps, does most honour to Europe in Asia, is he who governs it. Lord W. Bentinck, on the throne of the Great Mogul, thinks and acts like a Pennsylvanian Quaker. You may easily imagine that there are people who talk loudly of the dissolution of the empire and of the world's end, when they behold the temporary ruler of Asia riding on horseback, plainly dressed, and without escort, or on his way into the country with his umbrella under his arm. Like you, he has mixed in scenes of tumult and bloodshed; and, like you, he has preserved pure and unsullied that flower of humanity which the habits of a military life so often wither, leaving in its stead nothing but good-nature. Having been tried also by the most corrupting of professions, that of diplomatist, he has issued from the ordeal with the upright mind, and the simple and sincere language of a Franklin, convinced that there is no cleverness in appearing worse than one is. I have been his host *en famille* for a week in the country, and shall always remember with pleasure and emotion the long conversations I had with him in the evenings. I seemed to be talking with a friend like yourself; and when I considered the immense power of this excellent man, I rejoiced for the sake of humanity.

Lady William is very amiable and very lively. I had the pleasure of conversing with her in my own language, and it was very great. I know not how it was, but she discovered that, like all Frenchmen, I was but a lukewarm Catholic, and not a very ardent Christian. As she is devout, or tries to be so, she endeavoured to convert me. For my part, I am not a whit better than before; and I fear, indeed, that she is now a little less sure of her aim than she was at first. This divergence has not been at the expense of the kindness which she was disposed to show me.

Thus then, so far as agreeable society goes, I want for nothing; and although I had already experienced English liberality towards foreigners, I met with more here than I had dared to hope for. You will even find that I have derived real and positive advantages from these trifling successes. I had postponed, till my arrival in Calcutta, several branches of study requisite for the undertaking of my journey, and for which I expected to find greater facilities here than at Paris. I have been seconded with all the assistance possible: the walls of my immense sitting-room are covered with maps of all kinds, geographical and geological, and in my migrations from town to the country and back again, every thing has followed me. I have read, with pen in hand, all that has been published at Calcutta, Madras, and Bombay, having been often obliged to have recourse to English compilations, in which interesting memoirs of this country have been published. Thus, I have acquired an exact knowledge of all that has been said about it, with respect to what interests me more especially, and have fixed the point from which I shall myself start in commencing my researches.

In the midst of this mass of business, a *pundit* of Benares came every day, in town, to pass an hour in teaching me Hindoostanee. I had, during my voyage, thoroughly studied Sir William Jones's excellent Persian Grammar; this has been an useful preparative to the Hindoostanee, which, as you know, is nothing but a sort of compromise between the language of the conquerors of India and that of the conquered—a contemptible shapeless medley of Persian and Sanskrit. I regret being obliged to devote so much time to such a study; but what should I do if I were compelled to speak to people only through the medium of an interpreter? So I do not spare myself. It is a difficult study. You, of course, when at Constantinople, learned some little Turkish. You know the detestable system of writing of the Mahometan nations of Asia—a sort of short-hand; and so difficult to read, that the natives themselves can never do it readily. Then again, the whole vocabulary is entirely new to us, with the exception of some Sanskrit words which we have obtained through the medium of the Latin, the Greek, and the Gothic idiom of the Franks; add to these difficulties, that of hearing nasal sounds which scarcely differ in anything from a balked sneeze, and of forming gutturals taken second-hand from the Arabs, which require throats of rusty iron, parched with thirst, and you will have Hindoostanee. When, by hard study, you have mastered these difficulties, you have acquired after all, only a contemptible *patois* without any literature—a language of the court and courtiers, and of the guard-house, as its name imports (*urdu zaban*, the language of camps), which will be neither useful nor agreeable out of the country in which it is spoken.

The Calcutta botanical garden is an immense and magnificent establishment, in which are cultivated a great number of the vegetables of British India, of some neighbouring territories, and particularly those of the Nepaul, a curious country, whose heights sending, into the gulfs of Bengal and Cambaya, the waters which drop from their eternal snows, nourish a vegetation very similar, in some points, to that of the Alps and the Caucasus. A Danish botanist, of mediocre talents, who passes here for the first in the world, is the director of this establishment; he has certainly the best income of any *savant* in existence. Being on a two years' leave of absence, he has left the garden under the care of a member of the council, who has amicably installed me in it, in the best possible manner for working well and quickly. I have, in six weeks, been able to scrape acquaintance with the whole vegetable host of India, collected together in a small space. A very expensive and very complete botanical library, annexed to the superb habitation of the absent director, serves me as head quarters.

In this beautiful spot, I gradually accustomed myself to the sun of this country. Undoubtedly it is powerful, and certainly raises unwholesome exhalations from a soil which is nothing but mud imperfectly dried, and filled with the remains of insects and worms without number; but I believe the danger of exposure to it is much exaggerated. Though I flatter myself I have been very prudent, I ought, according to the Indians, to have been dead ere this. It is true that, according to the physicians who have most experience of this climate, and whose great skill I willingly allow, my constitution is wonderfully adapted to its most prominent features. I arrived in the hot season; it ceased only with the deluge of rain which still lasts, and, during the intervals of which, the temperature rises exceedingly. It is the most unhealthy season, and they who are not attacked with very well marked fits of fever are for the most part languishing and debilitated. It is a universal custom to poison one's self with mercury, as Louis XIV., and, of course, his whole court, did with cassia and jalap. I have not had the slightest febrile sensation. I sleep well at night, in weather which others, who ought to be accustomed to it, condemn as immoderately hot; and at day-break, in the cool and calm morning, I glide to my table and books, or else into the country. I go out long before sun-rise, when others are just beginning to fall asleep. This happy state of health is certainly owing to some little good management. My secret is abstemiousness: I recommend it to every body, and show its success; but they think the remedy worse than the evil, and every one about me goes on taking his three meals, and religiously abstains from all mixture of water with the strongest wines of Spain and Portugal. Then, in the cool of the evening, they mount on horseback, and young and old gallop about for an hour like automatons, and for no earthly purpose; they return home bathed in perspiration; and in order to prepare for an easy and comfortable night, sit down to table, where they remain a couple of hours, and rise from it only to go to bed. There is a great deal of stupidity at the bottom of this exhibition of manliness which the English think themselves bound to make; it forms a very ridiculous contrast with the cumbrous multitude of sumptuous articles necessary for their comfort.

If I had the same wants and exigencies, I should certainly have to give up my enterprise, being sure of never combining the means of execution. Were I to follow the example of the English, and take with me, on my journey, a bed, a table, a couch, and a bottle-case, I could scarcely expect to find means for my equipment; nor can I reconcile any vigorous labour with an existence so encumbered with *soi-disant* material conveniences, and *soi-disant* enjoyments, which I find the most tiresome and disagreeable in the world. To whatever simplicity (privation, these people would call it) I reduce myself, I shall nevertheless require a retinue which would appear tolerably splendid to us in Europe. But the units of labour, intellect and strength, have not the same value here as in our own country. An ox weighs scarcely three hundred pounds, and drags two hundred weight, but not very far, in one day; each domestic performs only a few hours of the most detestably executed service. The latter have, like all their fellow-countrymen, that insurmountable strength which is the attribute of weakness: I mean indolence. One must yield before this obstacle, and, to obtain the smallest action, must consent to maintain a troop of these wretched creatures.

In my uncertainty, my dear friend, respecting the steps you are taking in my behalf, I have refrained from commencing any researches which might lead me into expenses surpassing the only resources of which I am certain—those I have in hand. This prudent reserve is unfortunately but too well founded, since up to the 1st of April, this year, nothing had been decided on in my favour. I have just written a long letter on this subject to the administration of the Jardin des Plantes, and moreover to the friends I have there, in order that they may take into consideration the means of setting me afloat in a permanent manner. If, contrary to all my hopes, nothing has been done for me when you receive this letter, may I beg, my friend, that you will look around you for every thing that might tend to the success of my application; and may I also ask of your friendship to do all that you may deem compatible with your situation. You may say that it would be a pity to lose the precious opportunity of which I may be the instrument. Acquainted as I now am with all the most influential men of this country, their kindness and support will follow me, facilitate the means of seeing and knowing, and greatly multiply my own means of action, when the latter are sufficient to allow me to begin.

What I have hitherto done through prudence and necessity, I ought to have done under any circumstances. It was the proper beginning of my enterprise if I would render it successful; and before setting forward across this vast country, it was proper for me to gain some knowledge of men and things. The slenderness of my means has hitherto done me no prejudice, but I shall most certainly miscarry if it is prolonged.

Do not fancy, my dear friend, that these vexatious difficulties—that this anxiety about the future, assails me unprepared, or affects me severely. No: when I left Europe for these distant climes, I was prepared for accidents, obstacles, and misfortunes: I knew that such things were incidental to a traveller's life; and yet I embraced it, because I knew it to be also mingled with pleasures, emotions, and enjoyments, which a sedentary life does not admit of, and because I flattered myself that, with courage and perseverance, I might acquire here what would, on my return, place me in an honourable station in the world. Now, my mind, though sometimes painfully preoccupied, preserves, nevertheless, its habitual liberty, which renders work easy and light. I feel myself in full progress, and with that feeling a man is never unhappy.

In looking after my interests, you may assert that, if from a parsimony of the most ill judged description my salary is not raised to 15,000 francs, I shall be obliged to renounce the undertaking, and that all it has already cost will be lost at the moment of reaping the fruit, but without reaping any.

I must conclude this already very long letter, for time presses, and I have not yet written to my family, who I know entertain a just sense of my situation, aware of the good and evil belonging to it, and confiding in my perseverance. For the last three days, being occupied in writing to Europe, and returning in thought to all that is dear to me, this intercourse has affected me. I must leave you, my dear and excellent friend, to repress an emotion ready to burst forth. But, believe me, never have I so strongly felt how dear you are to me—never have I enjoyed so exquisitely the pleasure of being loved. How little, when compared to ours, is that friendship which unites the men of this country, who call each other friends! I am speaking of the English; and I cannot but praise their kindness —it is extreme towards me. I sometimes tell those by whom I am best known, and whom I esteem the most, that, in banishing from their manners every lively expression of tenderness, they deprive themselves of one of the greatest pleasures within their reach; and that many of them shut their hearts entirely against it. I say this, my dear friend, to those who I know ought to say yes, after a moment of pensive silence and sad reflection.

I am often astonished how I can please men so different from myself, whose thoughts rest on objects so remote from those, which mine visit when I set them at liberty. They would scarcely expect to find aught but lead in the head of a man who goes breaking stones on his road; and saving a very small number of exceptions, the most illustrious of which they overlook, botany, with them, is only a puerile and ridiculous study, a nonsense, which only makes the people who take to it more nonsensical. The revolution, which has drawn men of science from their closets to mingle in the world like those of France, has yet to take place in England, where they are as far from it as they formerly were among us. I am in high estimation for having read some of Shakspeare's tragedies, some of Byron's poetry, and some of Scott's novels; for having seen and admired some of Reynolds' pictures, and for having heard of one Mozart and one Rossini, who wrote very beautiful music. They think it strange that I should question them concerning the commerce of this country, its internal administration, and the mechanism of the different public services which the local government performs; yet this desire of knowledge is very agreeable to them, since it enables every one to talk of what he knows best, and because I thus wage war, without premeditation, against the insipid conversation of their long dinners. They think me gay; not perceiving that I only excite their interest whilst I am gaining information. The truth is, my dear friend, that, without being melancholy, I am not a bit gayer than you have ever seen me; but this comparative seriousness is gaiety to them, whose gravity is, to us, a dull and gloomy silence.

Adieu.—What feelings, what ideas press upon each other in me to reach you; but I cannot give them utterance: I will tell you all these things on a future day.

I have written to M. de Broglie to thank him for his letter of introduction to Lord W. Bentinck; express my gratitude to him when you have an opportunity.

My father and Porphyre will tell you how my affairs stand. If you wish to have the direct testimony of one of the professors at the *Jardin*, I have a friend there, who is very amiable and very clever; you may write to him without ceremony and concert measures with him.

You will speak of me to your family, and apologise

for my not writing, on account of the number and variety of my occupations.

Madame Victor must have received a few lines from Bourbon. Adieu, my friend. I love you, and embrace you with my whole soul.

TO M. JACQUEMONT THE ELDER, PARIS*.

Calcutta, September 3, 1829.

After remaining six months without letters, I have just received some. Your No. 3, my dear father, came first; next day I received No. 1; as for No. 2, which must enclose the letters of M. Victor, Dunoyer, Mérimée, &c. &c. &c., I would wager that it is at the bottom of the Ganges, with a hundred Arab horses, which a Madras ship recently shipwrecked on the shoals was bringing hither—an accident which you know was near occurring to myself, and which is much less rare than I thought. They talked a great deal of storms two months ago in the Bay of Bengal; and I have to fear that I have suffered other losses. I hope my letters have had a more fortunate voyage

* Between the former letter to M. Jacquemont the elder and the present, there ought to be one which never came to hand, in which Jacquemont speaks of his arrival in Calcutta, and the manner of his reception. Its contents, however, are reproduced in the letter immediately following, and in that to M. Jacquemont senior, of the 26th August, 1830.

than yours. Not receiving any, I had no taste for writing; and not looking towards Europe, I absorbed myself in the things of Asia. Since I wrote to you, the kindness of the governor-general and Lady William Bentinck has been unremitting. I spent a week with them *en famille* in the country. After a few visits, I found Lady William Bentinck, as I must have told you in my first letter, a very amiable and distinguished person; but she is religious, or rather endeavours to be so. There is a great discrepancy between us, in this respect, as on some other points equally strong; but the French are allowed not to believe ——. In short, in spite of these little national failings of mine, Lady William continues to treat me in the most amiable manner, and I am always welcomed by her when I appear at her residence. She is, as I told you, the second person I saw in Calcutta, and her husband the third. I was introduced to him by her without more etiquette than if they had been here in a private station.

I have this moment come from their house, for I had left you to pay them a visit. It was a fortnight since I had called, having lived six weeks in the country. I was obliged to stay to *tiffin* (lunch), as it was on the table; and this leaves me little time to write to you.

Lord William is an old soldier, who has a holy horror of war, thinks and speaks straight forward, and, on the throne of the Great Mogul, somewhat resembles a Pennsylvanian quaker. You may easily imagine that this character has seduced me. I know not whether he is influenced by the sincere respect with which he perceives that he has inspired me—but his kindness to me is unbounded.

As at Barrackpore, when I was his guest there, whenever I dine with him during his residence in town, he voluntarily allows himself to be made prisoner by me in a corner of the drawing-room, where we converse the whole evening in a low voice. He talks to me of India, I repay him in American coin; and when half-past ten strikes, the signal of a general *good night*, we seem to part mutually satisfied with each other.

He laughed much, when I told him what dilatoriness I experienced last year, in London, from the Court of Directors, when I applied for my passport; and the mistrust with which some old drivellers in that country used to look on me. "Why," said he, "have I not two hundred and fifty thousand men to march against you?"

He is a liberal. They call that radical in English—a term which sounds worse in the ears of good English society than that of *sans-culotte* in ours. In this point I agree with him, as with the excellent M. de la Harpe, of whom he often reminds me.

Had I been without letters of introduction, the flattering marks of distinction which I have received from the governor-general would have served for an introduction every where; but my packet was so well filled, that of all the men I have seen with pleasure and advantage, there is not one to whom I did not bring one or more letters.

Socially, my situation is the most agreeable I could desire. In society, I find pleasure for my vanity, and interest for my mind. I learn many things which direct observation could not teach me, and I form acquaintance with men of influence, whose support and good offices may be materially useful to me.

Madame Lebreton will tell you of my last moves; you will know from her that I left my host, Mr. Pearson, to go and live in the country opposite the Botanic Garden, at Sir Edward Ryan's, one of the judges. He is younger than Porphyre, as good as he, and, notwithstanding his judgeship, a great lover of science. I brushed up his memory, and made him acquainted with modern improvements—and that, every evening with my elbows on the table, and without loss of time to myself. A solid and elegant boat took me every morning across the Ganges to the garden, where I remained at work all day, assisted by an admirable botanical library. At ten in the evening, when all had retired in the house, which Lady Ryan's bad health rendered quiet, silent, and quite favourable for study, I used to go *en voisin* and without ceremony to the chief justice of India, Sir Charles Grey, to chat over a game at chess, about India, where he has been a judge eight years; while his wife, the prettiest and most graceful person in the world, gave us music; and this amiable family too will help to shorten my letter, for

I am to dine with them. Sir Charles Grey is, perhaps, the cleverest man in the country. His office is very high; he holds the second in rank in India. Our hooked atoms caught together easily. He is extremely gay, and what surprises me most, is always hearing people speak of his icy gravity. The fact is, a Frenchman has much greater facility in entering into an Englishman's friendship than another Englishman—they are like bodies similarly electrified, which repel each other. We are decidedly much more amiable than they, much more affectionate; and I see that all who are worth anything are charmed with my manners. No one but myself goes on Sunday to the Chief Justice's to seek a refuge from the devotion of his countrymen. It is true that in my presence this man dares to be sincere, which he could scarcely do in that of his fellow-countrymen, or friends of his own nation.

I have often heard Frederick say, that it required stiffness to make one's self respected by the English. That is true of the ordinary English, but I am quite convinced that I please here only because my manners are perfectly natural. I show myself such as you know me to be; it is only in a numerous and consequently mixed company, that I drawl my speech and make myself heavy, after their fashion. When I am sure of my little auditory, I speak by the shortest cut, and spare both them and myself the ennui of speechifying, in which, however, I am wonderfully improved.

One with another, the people I see, and with whom

I live, have an income of from a hundred and fifty to two hundred thousand francs, and they spend it. You will ask how I manage among them! It only requires address. I am a traveller—which is an excuse for not spending anything. I seldom hire a carriage; I am in excellent quarters, and have both water and land carriage at my command. The Governor General one day lent me his yacht and his steam-boat: now, the hire of the boat alone would have cost me a thousand francs; moreover, I have no bravado—I do not boast of being rich. Those I visit are not people to esteem me the less on that account. They now know me; I have talked politics to some, metaphysics to others, and to all on subjects interesting to them. I am not to them a superficial drawing-room acquaintance; I am more and better than that. It is on esteem and consideration that is founded the liberty I enjoy among them, and which entirely overthrows all the etiquette that separates from them those of their countrymen who are not their intimate friends. My character of foreigner serves me in this.

After all, my dear father, I dare say you imagine your great boy has become a sort of dandy, quite the pet from one end of Asia to the other, and perhaps already ogling some heiress. No, indeed, far from it. I will now tell you what I have been doing in other respects.

Since my arrival, I have made the anticipated discovery that six thousand francs a year was absurd.

I wrote my conviction to the *Jardin*, begging those gentlemen to consider the means of executing what they expect of me. During my residence in town, I wished to make the best use of my stay for the furtherance of my object. The necessity of understanding the language first presented itself. That low jargon, the Hindoostanee, which will be of no use to me on my return to Europe, is difficult: besides, it is not the language of the people here. I cannot speak it to my servants; two of whom, at fifteen francs a month, are stupid Bengalese, who fan me, carry my letters, brush, clean, &c. &c.; and the third, a Tamul of Madras, speaks it but imperfectly, mixing it with his own and with Bengalee; so that it is only with my moonshee or pundit from Benares that I can study and practise. It would be dreadful to be dependent on a domestic interpreter during my journey; I already know what would be the case, as I need my Tamul—called Samy—to help me with the Bengalese. This man will nevertheless be useful to me, because he is intelligent; and as he calls himself a Christian, he can give me a glass of water occasionally to prevent me from dying, which the other true Hindoos would not do. Besides the necessity of being acquainted with Hindoostanee, I have found that of reading a good number of quartos published here or in England, on this country, in order to be well acquainted beforehand with all that has been said about it, and thereby advance as far as possible the point from which I shall start in my own researches;

and I declare I have got through more quartos than Frederick has been able to make out quadroon women, during his eight years' residence in Hayti. Duodecimos? None! Doubtless the rich have a better library in this small form; but they do not lend their books, nor even suffer their friends to see them, much less strangers. I have therefore had no intercourse except with the quartos of the Asiatic Society, and of some acquaintances. These works are very serious, and mostly in double columns, small print. I do not get on very fast, but I do not spare myself.

From a quantity of bad memoirs on geology, I have been able to make out tolerably well where to lay the blue, red, yellow, and green, on the map of India. By confronting, correcting, and rectifying these suspicious and incoherent accounts one by the other, I have frequently been able to see the objects described, which have been dragged out of the dust for me: and they have taught me more than was learnt from them by the persons who had collected and described them. I have guided the pick-axe for a dozen hours without stopping, waking my drowsy fanners twenty times. It was in the evening, or I know not when, but always, I think, without prejudice to my occupations, that I paid or received visits. I returned them by a note of a line or two, when it would have been inconvenient for me to make them in person, and said that I was only at leisure at dinner time, thus offering myself to be left or taken; and faith they took me. I have told you elsewhere how I had selected my places of study; the evenings, which were a relaxation, a pleasure to me, were at the same time a new study. Those I spent at Mr. Pearson's house were not the least agreeable, nor the least instructive—that is, in India.

I thus studied both the language and the country. I improved daily, preparing vigorously for the future, and in more than one way; for my ingenious economy (in spite of my three servants—an admirable proof of it) did not permit me to spend five hundred francs a month—far from it. So that up to this day I have not broken in upon my credit for six thousand francs, which I might have received on the first of January this year; and my banker will owe me twelve thousand francs on the 1st of January, 1830. If I had been desirous of associating the smallest practical researches in natural history with these studies (the season prevented them in Bengal), they would have made me lose an enormous quantity of time in these very studies; and, however small the scale on which I might have carried on such researches, I should have required an establishment which could not have been kept up with five hundred francs a month.

I stated all this to the Museum, with the *why* and the *how*. Thereupon Sir Edward Ryan came and told me that he should be very happy if I would become his guest; he mentioned the proximity of the Botanic Garden, the convenience of his boat to take me there at all hours, the silence and seclusion of his house, &c. &c. I remained at Mr. Pearson's until I had finished the business in which I was then occupied, and I afterwards went to the knight's, at the distance of five miles, on the river side. I there did my utmost, going to town only occasionally to dine with the Governor General, and twice to witness a criminal trial of natives, a truly memorable circumstance, as I had the honour of being seated with the three judges on the *King's Bench*,—an act of extreme politeness on the part of the Chief Justice, which has caused me to be taken for a kind of judge myself by the rabble of Calcutta, who are constant in their attendance at the court, and gains me salaams wherever I go. I brought to Sir Edward Ryan's, at Garden Reach, some other books which I had to get through; and while inuring myself, during my residence with him, to what was most pernicious in the climate of India, my literary were wonderfully combined with my botanical studies, which I carried on vigorously at the Company's garden; making in six weeks an honourable acquaintance with the *multàm sine nomine plebem* of Indian vegetation, collected together into a small space, and sparing myself a great deal of useless trouble in my future expeditions. Very frequently I did not breakfast till noon; and in the midst of a frightful luxury, whilst others drank nothing but hock at a louis a bottle, I made many meals on rice and *eau sucrée*, rendering my hours for eating subordinate to my studies.

Night approaches, my dear father, and I must leave

you. Perhaps when I rise in the morning I shall learn that a new delay of the ship which is to bring you this, leaves me still some hours to write to you: I desire it more than I hope for it. I have written, within five days, a hundred and twenty pages of letters.

There will soon be another opportunity of sending to France direct, and I shall avail myself of it. You will learn from my letters to Madam Lebreton, Victor de Tracy, and Dunoyer, many things which I have not had time to tell you. Ask them to communicate what they think will interest you. Rely on my courage and perseverance. My prudence has been known to you ever since I first left you on distant journeys. My health is excellent.

I embrace Porphyre very tenderly. He loves me well, and I return it. Adieu, my dear friends; adieu, we must part. My heart is swelling. But I return again to you to tell you to be at ease, and happy on my account; I am full of strength, vigour, and resources.

Money matters will be arranged; and when the news reaches me of the increase of my means, they will also be increased by my prudent sparings, and I shall be in every respect admirably prepared for setting them in action.

The delays which have hitherto taken place have not cramped me in the least. Under any circumstances I should have done that which prudence led me to begin. I have no uneasiness with regard to the future;

and besides, I expected that there would be some in a traveller's life. There will be misery and privations; I reckon upon all that, and when these evils come they will not take me unawares. But there are, on the other hand, lively pleasures, and deep emotions which will never be effaced, and the remembrance of which will form the charm of my life. Adieu, for it is very late. I leave you for pleasure; to dine in a palace, in the middle of a beautiful garden, with a pleasant, amiable, learned, and clever man, very kind to me, and a pretty woman, the only one who speaks French besides Lady William Bentinck: I mean Sir Charles and Lady Grey. I shall be welcomed and almost caressed *à la Française.*

But the scene of it will be two leagues from this, and I have but half an hour. Adieu!

TO M. FREDERIC JACQUEMONT, SAINT DOMINGO.

Calcutta, November 5, 1829.

If I have a good memory, my dear Frederic, I have not written to you since I left Rio Janeiro. I am mistaken, for my journal reminds me that I wrote from Bourbon. You will have heard of me through my father and Porphyre. Let me, however, continue my history in a few words. Like people who are not in a hurry, we came from Bourbon to Pondicherry in forty days without accident. At Pondichery I continued the guest of the new governor with whom I had formed a friendship on our voyage, although ten days before our arrival we engaged solemnly by oath never more to play at backgammon together: and when I was well rested and refitted inside and out by the good cheer of this "*roi d'Yvetot*," and the comforts of his fine and extensive mansion, I came here in the Zélée with the governor of Chandernagore, who had been acting provisionally at Pondichery until M. de Melay arrived. At Pondichery I found our old school-fellow Rabourdin, engineer of bridges and roads in the colony. We saw a good deal of each other, and I think with mutual pleasure. We talked a great deal of you. You know how well I was recommended here: no European, I think, ever presented himself with so respectable a mass of introductions.

After losing, at the mouth of the Ganges, all the anchors we had left, and being, during a whole night, near running aground, and perhaps perishing, we moored at last before what they call the City of Palaces, which is only the city of large houses. They kept me in the first house I entered*; it belonged to the advocate-general of this presidency, one of the three or four Europeans who make most money, and spend most in this country (four or five hundred thousand francs

* The detailed account of his arrival in Calcutta will be found in the letter of the 26th of August, 1830, in which he repeats it to his father, who had not received his first letter.

a year), and the most distinguished for his profound knowledge in his profession, and out of it by his wit and learning; he is a radical besides, and a good and pleasing man. I could not have made a better hit. The second person I saw was Lady William Bentinck. Half an hour afterwards she introduced me, without etiquette or ceremony, to her husband, and I was obliged to stay tiffin (a slight meal at half-past one) with them, and then promise to return and take a family dinner. The next day, in a hired carriage, I paid, in the town, which is immense, and in the beautiful country-houses near it, some fifteen visits at least, to judges, members of council, great people, physicians, and merchants, some of whom are very rich. The first days were thus spent in gaining a footing, getting acquainted with faces, names, and the people themselves; then, when I had discovered and settled the use of which each might be to me, or the pleasure he might afford me, I set myself to work; that is, I borrowed maps, engravings, manuscripts, books, &c. Notwithstanding the extreme heat (it was May, the hottest month in the year), I began to work vigorously at the tedious task of searching, taking notes, and learning, morning and evening, what has been done, in order if possible to go farther. Observe, I beg, that there is not a young cadet, much less a young writer, attached to the company, who does not drive his cabriolet, and that I allowed myself that expensive luxury but very seldom. A modest palanquin, which is the *ne plus ultra* of the modest in this country, was my sole equipage, when my host's carriage was engaged. Truly, I do not think I have a mind better constituted than any one else, but my vanity has not once suffered on account of my poverty, and I am poor, very poor. What more could I desire than I obtained—attentions, kindness, and flattering marks of distinction? Nothing. My manners, which I have left natural, and have not made stiff, as it is perhaps expedient to do with the English of the common class, has had the good fortune to please. I have spoken of all things to the best of my ability and without affectation. Some, perhaps, have liked me on that account; all have shown me attention; none have offended me. Very seldom, I think, has a Frenchman had such extensive and universally agreeable intercourse with the English. I forgot that I knew the language very little:—I spoke like a Frenchman. They were infinitely pleased with my want of pretension, my genuine simplicity, and my unaffected manners. My academic dignity from London has been of no use to me, any more than my official title from Paris: and no modesty can prevent me from saying, that it is on my own personal account that every one has been kind and hospitable. Wherever I went, I tried to pay in ready money, by giving some interest and a little diversity to the tiresome monotony of English wherever I went; talking, in fact, when I thought the folks fit to taste that pleasure so little known among the English.

The character of Lord William Bentinck inspires me with a profound respect; which he no doubt perceives. He is an old soldier, abhorring war; a patriot without reserve, though son of an English duke; and, although Grand Mogul for the time being, he is an honest man after my own heart, plain and open; in short, he won my regard! And as no people are so amiable as those who love us, Lord William showed me great kindness. I have passed more than one evening with him talking politics in a retired corner of his lady's drawing room, as I do with two or three friends at Paris. I was happy to see so much power in such pure hands.

Three weeks after my arrival, I was drawn from the studies in which I was already deeply engaged, by an invitation from my lord and my lady to go with them into the country. They have a palace on the banks of the Ganges, five leagues from hence. Round it, in an admirable park, are scattered, as if to add dignity to the landscape, several large cottages containing a suite of elegant apartments. I remained here a week with a friend, whom I owe to Lord William, a Spanish refugee (Colonel Hezeta), a man of probity "*quand même*," and unfortunate. He has taken refuge here under the protection of his general, whose friend he is; for he formerly served in Spain under Lord William.

His character is somewhat like that of Dunoyer, with some physical resemblance. There, for a week was I overwhelmed with attentions. There was no Lady William Bentinck for any one but myself. She would have me mount an elephant for the first time, with her; and then for a whole week she had no other companion in her walks but myself. I spent several long days with her *tête-à-tête*, talking about God—she for, I against; of Mozart, Rossini, painting, Madame de Staël; of happiness and misery; and of love, in reference to both—of all things, in short, which require, if not intimacy, at least a great deal of confidence and reciprocal esteem, especially on the part of a woman—English too, religious and strict, with a young man, a bachelor, and a Frenchman. We never conversed on insignificant matters. Lady William Bentinck, who has lived a good deal on the continent, particularly at Paris, experienced anew the pleasure of talking with a Frenchman; and as she is a very intellectual woman, she took great delight in a style of conversation in which she excels. This is truly all very strange, and it sometimes makes me think that I am tolerably original. Things of this sort used sometimes to happen to Yorick, and yet I look at myself and find no resemblance between me and that sentimental hero.

The rainy season commenced while I was at Barrackpore (at the Governor General's seat), and the temperature was a little moderated. I continued my labours in town; having returned to my host's, the attorney-general Mr. Pearson; and I soon yielded to the invitation of one of the two judges (150,000 francs a year, and a retiring pension for life of 36,000 francs after ten years' service), who lives a long league from the city, but below it, also on the river side, opposite to the most magnificent botanical garden in the world. I remained six weeks at his house, crossing the river every morning to have a little botany: being lord and master of this garden, the superintendent of which (a tolerably good Danish botanist with 72,000 francs a year, lodged in a superb house, &c.) is now in England. I was settled in the magnificent library which the Company have purchased for him; and there, assisted by the multiplied means of labour, I studied the plants of India which I gathered in the garden. I have discovered that I possess a talent of which I was not aware, that of drawing! Astonished at my success with plants, I tried the human figure, and here my surprise was still greater. You shall see all this some day. Each head cost me ten minutes or a quarter of an hour. I shall bring back with me some hundreds. The friend at whose house I resided, at Garden-reach, notwithstanding the gravity and importance of his office, is a young man of thirty-six, married at twenty; he has ten children in England. His name is Sir Edward Ryan. I wish you to become acquainted with people to whom I am indebted for so much kindness. He has some knowledge of the physical and natural sciences. I treated him as a man of thirty-six, and not as one of his grave pursuits, and we are become sufficiently intimate to live very agreeably together. Next door to him resides the chief justice of India (200,000 francs a year, and 52,000 francs for life after ten years' service) a stout man of forty-five, who is considered the gravest in all India, where he holds the second rank, and whom I found to be the pleasantest man in the world. He, like Mr. Pearson in his profession, and like him out of it, has the longest and best furnished head in the country. I caused a revolution at his house, by introducing the custom of chance visits in the evening after dinner, for the sake of conversation, or a game at chess, while his wife, a handsome, clever, and amiable lady, amused us with music. Nothing is more whimsical than my connexion with them. I was made much of and caressed by them in trio, and always distinguished in the most flattering manner on the days of having company. Sir Charles Grey, that pearl of judges, is consulted by the Governor General on the politics of the country, although his functions are purely judicial. He views India from a higher point than any other man ; I have gained a great deal by frequenting his house. He has dared to give me coffee on the chess-table, and I have dared to ask his lady to sing some Italian airs which I have heard a hundred times given by her in the finest style. It was at the hour when the whole English population of Calcutta was either asleep in bed or on a sofa, that we thus pleasantly wiled away a couple of hours. Till seven in the evening I worked like a devil, and so did he. On returning from the garden dirty and wet, I frequently found a horse bridled and saddled waiting for me, and before I washed and shaved, &c., I had half an hour's, or three quarters of an hour's gallop; every day visiting some new place, and taking a close view of the life of those singular beings, the Indians. It was a life well filled with labour, physical enjoyment, noble pleasures, and corporeal activity. It suited my health extremely well. I there learned to walk in the sun without absolutely expiring; but I dined moderately and drank only claret, whilst the most abstemious took an ample portion of Sherry, Burgundy, Claret, Port, and Champagne;—and that daily. I found Lady Grey so beautiful, although she is really not so, that it was very well done on the part of Mr. Pearson, to recal me, that I might accompany him and his family to finish the rainy season and the vacation at another seat of his near Barrackpore. I took with me a Persian and Hindoostanee master, whom I made to earn, in reality, the hundred francs a month which he cost me. He has enabled me, for two hundred francs, to speak tolerably, to understand in the same degree, and to write (and to read some little of the current writing of) that most widely disseminated language the Hindoostanee, which is a mixture of Sanscrit, Persian, and Arabic. During this last residence in the country, I paid a visit to the governor of Chandernagore, an old retired sailor, an excellent man, with whom I came from Pondicherry in the Zélée; I was but three leagues from Chandernagore.

Nothing would have been wanting to my satisfaction, which would have been complete, but for those confounded money-matters. I was in continual hopes of receiving the news that the negociation set on foot at the time of my departure, was concluded, and that I should have nine thousand francs a year more. With the slender resources actually at my disposal, I did not dare to press forward in this immense country. I have been obliged to write, to remonstrate, and to insist; but all this to Paris, and it is only after a lapse of six months that I can hope for an answer. However, my severe economy has enabled me to live hitherto on the funds I brought from France, and I am about to commence the coming year with the two years' allowance, that is, with twelve thousand, perhaps fourteen thousand. Whatever *unusual* moderation I may adopt in travelling, this is not sufficient to go very far, nor for a long period, if I have the foresight to add the expense of returning back again; and I have been compelled by this untoward circumstance to modify my original project. If I were to proceed straight to Bombay now, I should arrive there with too little money to carry on my researches in that quarter with any effect. I therefore economise my resources, and reconciling pecuniary prudence with the wants of effective exploration, as much as they can be brought to agree, am going to set out from hence across the country to Benares, thence to Agra and Delhi, making some circuits, in order to see certain rocks, and get to the highest mountains in the world. I shall ascend them in April, and spend the summer there. Thence, according to the turn which my pecuniary affairs may have taken in the interim, I shall make a start upon Bombay the following winter—or—or—truly, if no amelioration is to be expected in this matter, I shall remain in the mountains as long as they continue habitable for a poor devil like me.

In another week, I shall begin this journey of six hundred leagues to the north-west. A bamboo cart, drawn by oxen, will carry my luggage. A bullock will be laden with the smallest tent in India. Your humble servant, devoted to white horses, will ride an old steed of that colour, which will cost him only a thousand francs (a good horse costs from 3000 to 3500 francs), at the head of his six servants; one carrying a gun, another a skin of water, a third the kitchen and pantry, another with the horse's breakfast, &c., without counting the people with the oxen.

An English captain of infantry would have five and twenty instead of six; namely—in addition to those I have—one for his pipe, one for the *chaise-percée*, without which no Englishman in India travels, seven or eight to pitch his tent—which would be very large, very heavy, and very comfortable—three or four cooks, a washerman, and a sweeper, &c., then a constant relay of twelve men to carry his palanquin, in which he may stretch himself when he is tired of riding on horseback. Your poor Victor, with the miserable plainness of his ambulatory establishment, is going to do something new; but you know, my dear Frederick, that he has a pride of his own, and, if his poverty allows him, notwithstanding, to employ himself upon plants, stones, and animals, he will bear it easily. Besides, he travels with letters from the Governor-General of India; and this is some little satisfaction, occasionally very useful, in his situation, and not possessed by many colonels at 52,000 francs, and civilians at 60,000, who formed the crowd where he was, and still will be, distinguished. I say, *will be*, for precisely at the same time as I do, Lord and Lady William Bentinck, a large part of their establishment, and several of the high officers of the government, are to set out by nearly the same route, for the extreme north-western frontier, nearly eighty leagues north of Delhi, to pass the summer, in a climate similar to that of Switzerland, and producing the same fruits. They intend visiting the various parts of their empire, in their progress. Lord William has exactly a thousand times more people than I, having six thousand servants, of all kinds; he is escorted, besides, by a regiment of infantry, one of cavalry, and the company of the body-guard. I shall see him in the month of April, in a wooden house, which he has had built, six hundred feet above the level of the sea. I myself shall be a little higher still, ten thousand feet beyond any European establishment; but in very peaceful regions. You will ask, no doubt, how a man who is so favoured a friend of the Great Mogul's as I am, can be reduced to travel at the head of six beggars on an arrant jade, without palanquin, or *chaise-percée?* Well then; it is because the present Great Mogul has introduced very rigorous, and, in this country, very unpopular measures of economy; and a sinecure, which was possible under other governments, is no longer so. If, moreover, I had some temporary mission from the Indian government, while I raised my income to 30,000 francs, for a few months, I should descend prodigiously from my social position. I should enter the ranks and be stationed at the bottom; whereas, in my native poverty, I am something apart; not classed according to money, and apt to class myself according to my own personal good and amiable qualities. By the vulgar method, that of splendid carriages, grand dinners, and extravagant houses, I should require at least a hundred and fifty thousand francs per annum to maintain the position which I occupy with my 6000 francs, and should probably remain beneath it.

Let us now talk of dangers. I have obtained statistical accounts of the army, which inform me that the average deaths, one year with another, are one officer in thirty-one and a half in the Madras army, and one in twenty-eight in that of Bengal. It is no great matter, as you perceive. It is true, they do not lead the life of hardship which I am about to do, and they do not go in the sun, &c.; but, as a set-off, they drink a bottle or two of beer and one of wine every day, not to mention grog; and I shall drink nothing but water mixed with a little drop of European or native brandy. I possess one of the best syringes in India; but I conceal it, as my moral reputation would suffer. It is for want of *lavemens*, that the English for the most part die. I have, moreover, an ample provision of quinine against intermittent fevers, and all that is necessary against cholera, which is very rare where I am going. The tigers seldom say any thing to those who do not speak to them;—bears the same. The most formidable animal is the elephant, but he is excessively scarce in the countries through which I shall pass. After all, I am resolved never to speak to these animals except to whisper in their ear, and never to fire but when sure of hitting. When on horseback, I shall always have a brace of pistols at hand; and my *syce*, or groom, who follows me, running on foot for six hundred leagues, at the rate of six, seven, or eight leagues a day, and my grass cutter, are always at my heels like shadows—one with my carbine, the other with my gun. All this makes five bales, weighing together a quarter of a hundred. Some robbers or brigands have certainly appeared in that direction, but they have the stupidity to rob only their brethren, the natives, whom they kill, without mercy, for a few rupees; but I have never been able to discover a single instance of a European being killed by them.

The people here are dreadful cowards, and the English impatient. In this respect, I have been obliged to adopt their disagreeable manner. The domestic service is so divided, and each servant does so little, except the special object of his engagement, that an almost military exactness is required of him, by means of severity equally military; which is indeed natural enough. I have one man who has nothing else to do but bring me water. I shall want him on my journey, because, although there are two men attached to my cavalry, (the aforesaid jade) she would die of thirst if it were not for the water-carrier. The man who cuts the grass for her food, and he who dresses and saddles her, cannot draw water at a tank. True, I give my waterer, who also gives me drink, only ten francs a month, but when I find this man, who has almost nothing in the world to do, negligent in his office, you may imagine what a kick I am inclined to bestow upon him: and so of the rest. Would you believe that I have but two plates, yet I must have a man to wash them on my journey? So if they are not clean, woe to him! By an unusual artifice, I have accumulated on a single head the attributes of cook and waiter at table. At table! As if I were going to have a table! An English ensign, when on a march, has one in his tent, as well as chairs: for my part I shall eat kneeling or standing.

Hitherto I have received letters from our family pretty regularly. My father assures me, and the rest confirm it, that he is perfectly well in mind and body. He feels a confidence in me, which I also place in him. This is a happy feeling on both sides. Adieu, my dear Frederick, adieu; no doubt for a long period. Kind regards to all about you—if you are still in your island, the remembrance of which sometimes affects me. I do not know what I am soon to see, but it is only beyond the tropic that I expect to find scenes of grandeur in India. They will consist of inaccessible peaks, eternal snows, masses of oaks and pines—nothing equinoctial. Since I left Haiti, I have seen great things in the tropics: Rio Janeiro, which is admirable; and Bourbon, which is only an enormous mountain, crowned with a volcano. But with the verdant hills of Marquisant; with the noble rampart of palm-tree forests, which rises over them, and separates the two sides; with the cocoa-nut tree, whose summit hung over the court of your modest dwelling—are associated recollections of the heart, which will make me always consider Saint Domingo the finest part of the equatorial world. I left there the first fruits of my admiration. Since then, when I see things worthy of being admired, I seem to admire them coldly. I have not yet been touched or affected by them! Adieu, my dear friend: the whole diameter of the earth divides us, but my heart is with you.

20th. I set out instantly.

TO M. PORPHYRE JACQUEMONT, PARIS.

Calcutta, Sunday, November 8th, 1829.

My dear Porphyre. I have spent the rainy season, fifteen miles north of Calcutta, at Mr. Pearson's country house, principally occupied with the study of Hindoostanee, which I speak, understand, and write tolerably well. I availed myself of a few rainless days, to pay a visit to the microscopic governor of Chandernagore, with whom I came on board the Zélée from Pondicherry, of which he was the acting governor, until the arrival of M. de Melay. He is a very obliging man, and no one could be kinder to me.

I have accustomed myself to walking, getting wet, and going in the sun without dying on the spot, taking with me my *moonshee*, or master, from whom I have gained more information in the presence of things and people than before a writing table. The Hindoostanee, you know, is a rude medley of Persian, Arabic, and Sanscrit. In the parts of India where Sanscrit was formerly the vulgar tongue, it still prevails in the Hindoostanee now spoken there: in those, on the contrary, which are geographically in the neighbourhood of Arabia and Persia, the Hindoostanee is scarcely any thing but very corrupted Persian. I have preferred this kind of corruption, in order that I might be intelligible, both to the people of India and to those of Persia, in case of necessity.

The intelligence on money matters which I have successively received, since my arrival in Bengal, have given me much food for reflection during my studious retirement at Titaghur. I have in imagination supplied the money for different journeys, without any oriental pomp, as you may easily imagine, and I have in reality been obliged to stay where I was.

Meanwhile, the rains are becoming less frequent. The fine season, winter, is approaching; it is necessary to avail myself of it, and make up my mind to something. I have resolved on the only project which can be executed with the funds at my disposal.

In a few days, I shall set out for Benares; hence, without delay, I shall go on to Delhi, and from Delhi to the frontiers of the empire, among the highest mountains in the world.

I shall arrive there in April or May, and shall hire, in a neighbourhood which may appear good for forming collections, the house, hut, cabin, or perhaps cottage, of some mountaineer, in a spot elevated, no doubt, ten or twelve thousand feet above the level of the sea; and there I shall stay till winter.

I shall then descend with all that I may have collected during the summer; and, according to the credit I may have at Calcutta, shall proceed to Bombay, or remain in the mountains a little lower down, to ransack another valley next season, if I think I shall find sufficient there to make it worth my while.

I shall thus have come to India, crossed the line twice, to live in a smoky hut among eternal snows. If, as I hope, I find something new in this place, I shall not complain of my abode. These wilds have been travelled over by a good many English, and I have reason to believe that their Flora is sufficiently well known, although, no doubt, they have left something to be done on a close inspection. By most, the preference has been given to geology; but they had all learned geology from books and in India, and I have no faith in their decisions.

Lastly, my friend, if what I am about to do is not the best that can be done in India, the fault is not mine, and I shall enter upon my project with this feeling of satisfaction: that of all possibles, if there should happen to be another possible, this is the best.

Take your map and follow me.

Mounted on a white horse (I am predestined to have white horses), pistols in good order, &c. &c., I shall open the march, followed immediately by two poor devils, who will cost me twenty-four or thirty francs a month; one of whom, called *syce*, is properly the groom; and the other, *gassyara*, or grass-cutter, is laden with my horses' food. Each will carry one of my guns loaded with ball or shot, according to circumstances. When I gallop they will run; this is the custom.

In divers groups round a rude car made of bamboos, and drawn by two oxen, on which my baggage will slowly advance, will walk the grand-master of my wardrobe, *sirdah beerah,* a *ketmadgar,* as waiter at table, and (by an ingenious combination) at the same time cook, a *mochaltchi* or plate-washer (nota benè, I have two plates) and a *beetcheti* or water-carrier.

Besides the driver of the car, another will drive, as far as Benares, an ox of burthen, carrying the smallest tent in India.

I shall travel six, seven, or eight leagues a day; living upon rice dressed in the native fashion, fowls, and milk, and drinking water mixed with French brandy as long as I have any; never any bread. I shall sleep in my tent on a mat, or in a light cot.

In thirty-five or forty days, I shall be at Benares: it is two hundred leagues from hence, passing through Bardwan, Rogonatpore, and Sasseram.

At Benares, I shall refresh myself and my people, at some judge's or receiver-general's, and shall hire camels to go to Delhi by the right bank of the Jumna, leaving it a little to see an interesting country, the Bundlecund, passing by Murzapore, Callinger, and Agra. This will be going on excellently. The camels, they say, are admirable; they are hired at nine rupees (twenty-three francs) a month; at seven, when more than three are taken. There is no trouble about their fodder, nor that of the people who drive them. It is the same, however, with all kinds of servants, who are paid absolutely nothing more than their wages; they get on as they can afterwards. A camel will carry three or four hundred weight. As I shall then have a stronger animal to carry my tent, I will have a better one, and the whole will be cheaper than the oxen and car from hence to Benares. But, on this first part of my route, there are no camels; and besides, there are houses built and supported by government, but who support only the roof and four walls, in which I shall often sleep on my ridiculous little tent which will serve only for a mattrass: I shall be better on than *under* it. From Delhi to the foot of the mountains, passing through a part of the territory of the Sikhs, I shall go on with the camels; then in the mountains with mules and oxen; and at last, at the end of my journey, on men's shoulders.

The road which I shall follow is very safe; there is no particularly unwholesome place to pass. Tigers and bears, whose existence I cannot absolutely deny, though much inclined to do so, are not common, and they seldom say anything to people who say nothing to them. If they speak first, you know that, at all events, I have five balls ready to give them an answer; and I believe that, as I am determined not to fire except within range, meeting them will not be dangerous.

If, however, unforeseen circumstances should make me desire any other protection than that of my own resolution, I might have an escort. Here is the passport which I yesterday received for that purpose. My father will translate it to you.

" Monsieur Victor Jacquemont, a native of France, engaged in scientific pursuits, being about to travel in Hindostan, with the permission of the honourable the Court of Directors, and of the supreme government of India, it is the desire of the Governor General in council, that every necessary assistance and protection shall be afforded to him by the officers and authorities of the British nation; and farther, that he shall receive from them any attention they may have it in their power to offer."

This is better than the "*prions de laisser passer et circuler librement*," &c. &c.

But in addition to this general recommendation to people to whom I shall have no particular letters of introduction, Lady William Bentinck is procuring me a great number of the latter kind, and I shall have some from herself. My London packet, of which I did not exhaust one half at Calcutta, is nothing to what I shall carry from hence. To-morrow I shall arrange with my banker, how, while on the road, I am to draw upon him: and this will be settled satisfactorily. It will be only to-morrow that I shall break in upon my credit account for 1829, to pay for my horse. I have almost reached the end of the year without touching it.

Thank Colonel Lafosse for the introduction he gave me to his friend. Colonel Fagan and myself are like two unfortunate lovers. A singular succession of little chances has broken off twenty appointments to meet. We have seen each other but seldom—though like people who know they have no time to lose, and will soon be separated. A widower overwhelmed with business—for he is a major-general in the army—and ill, he lives by himself, goes nowhere, and receives no visits. Nevertheless at whatever hour I call, I am admitted: we converse about European affairs, and he informs me of those of this country. In spite of his being an Irishman by birth, and an Englishman by nation, I call him a Frenchman like myself, and more a Frenchman than many born in Paris.

I have the agreeable conviction, that the long use which I have made of Mr. Pearson's hospitality, has not been indiscreet. He pays me a thousand attentions. When the French ships arrived a short time ago, he had people running backwards and forwards two days in search of a Perigord pie; and this morning at breakfast he made me violate my Asiatic sobriety, by the surprise of a *pâté de cailles truffées*, which is so delicious, that we shall make it last as short a time as possible. In becoming as familiar as it is possible to be with an Englishman, I have constantly received from him the same flattering attentions with which he greeted me the first day. I am now a companion for him in life; I am, properly speaking, his only society, as he is mine, when I dine at home. In matters of idle stories, theoretical politics and literary taste, we agree admirably; and he appears to take much pleasure in our hour's chat after dinner, which is very profitable to me as he is a man of great information.

A small part of his knowledge and talents as an advocate, brings him in 400,000 francs a year; 160,000 of which he spends nobly. His office of Attorney General only brings him in 100,000.

I could not possibly have been better billeted. What would have become of me if I had not spent twenty days in London? I well remember that I did not spare myself there. Adieu for to-day, my friend, for I scarcely spare myself any more now, leaving you to try a new horse, which has just been offered to me—a young Persian horse, saddled and bridled, and for 250 rupees (650 francs)—although I had this morning a heavy fall with the white jade in question, which has made my chest very painful. Adieu.

Monday, 9th.

I make you present at my departure, writing to you in the midst of my preparations. I have cut the connexion with my white horse, to which I owe a grudge for the harm he has done me; and it is on my new acquaintance of yesterday evening, approved of by a person of knowledge in those matters, that I shall start. It is a little bay-horse in which nothing is wanting, and this gives me a guarantee, that he will take me into the upper provinces, the circumstance of his having already been there once, as he was born there. His paces are good, and he gallops well when required. I have, moreover, along with the horse, the groom, a native of the upper provinces, speaking excellent Hindoostanee, and who understands the *morale* and *physique* of the beast, having taken care of him for a year; a cheerful vigorous fellow, glad to return with me to his own country. I have formed an escort as I could wish, of people accustomed to wait on officers, and to be harshly treated by them; and I am already so much modified by the contagion of example, that I will suffer no relaxation of discipline. A man is degraded, and brutalised, by living among such debased beings. I now understand and excuse Frederick's harshness—I was going to say violence, and his great readiness in planting a kick on the hinder part of one of God's images. I already feel a similar inclination.

Your reminding me of another time and another place, has come very seasonably to repel far from me all idea of suffering in the long excursion which I am about to make. I am governed by the feeling most suitable to my situation. I consider myself entirely as a soldier in the field, taking the good where I find it, and enjoying it the more from the anticipation of the contrast, and soon lying down gaily on a mat in heat or cold—sometimes in rain, and sometimes necessarily too without dinner, although I have two servants for my *cuisine* only. After all, my caravan, the most wretched that ever traversed India, will be magnificent in comparison with your equipage on your return from Minsk. I remember, my dear Porphyre, your letters of that period, as well as if they had been read to me yesterday. It is on your particular case (which was then that of a million of

Frenchmen,) that I have formed my ideas of war and a military life; and I am, no more than yourself, appalled by the complaints which we have received from some of our warriors in Greece.

I shall recollect, in my worst days, those you formerly passed frozen, famished, and scarcely twenty years old; and I shall never think myself miserable.

The English have habits of opulence and numberless artificial wants, which would necessarily make them the same in the different situations in which I am about to be placed. I do not speak through envy; no, I despise this ignoble dependence on external things from the bottom of my heart. For my own part, I am sure that I shall, on the contrary, sometimes find a charm in the rather antiquated and biblical simplicity of my caravan.

Of course, in the states under the government or protection of the English, or merely in alliance with them, I preserve my European costume; it is sufficient to make a man, ever so little white, a Sahib or lord.

Nevertheless, in the upper provinces, it is convenient in winter to add a shawl and girdle to the European costume. The fashionables, of course, seize the opportunity of circulating the rupees, and envelope themselves in shawls. I shall think myself sufficiently magnificent, with a thick and very warm silk stuff, over a nankeen dressing gown. The whole, on the aforesaid bay horse, surmounted by a pale face, with spectacles and a large straw hat covered with black taffety, would afford Mérimée a good subject for a picture.

My banker, a correspondent of M. Delessert, is the most obliging man in the world; he has given me the best possible information on the questions of finance which I have put to him. I may draw upon him from nearly all points of my route, and thus future contingencies are provided against. On being informed of my proceedings, he will immediately let me know the increase of credit which he will be able to allow me.

I have told you nothing about my health—here is the bulletin. I have not had the slightest touch of fever. When the excessive heat here prevented every one around me from sleeping, I have slept as I used to do in winter at home. I have but little appetite, and eat little. I am very subject to colds in the head, which I shall probably avoid by wearing a turban; but here the thing is impossible; we shall see by-and-by. When I am in my hut, or under my tent, without having any hosts to respect, I may perhaps adopt it. Our father will be pleased to observe that the cold extends to the nasal fossæ and frontal sinuses, but never lower. My old disposition to sore throats, seems entirely gone.

The hygrometer is, like me, in every country—at the point of extreme dryness; but there are means, which ingenious art —— and they are used with discretion. It is, I am persuaded, from not using *lavemens* that many English die in this country. Their medical men cannot bring them to it.

Good day, my friend : I leave you to dine *tête-à-tête* at the quiet little table of my amiable invalid, Colonel Fagan.

Lord William has just lent me the French papers, which he has received from Bordeaux, up to the 17th of July, and I read them rapidly and with interest. It will be the last print I shall touch of my native land. In six days, farewell to the things of Europe. But, adieu. They make wine and brandy on the frontiers of Thibet, and I shall eat grapes next autumn ; meanwhile, I shall only have plantains and bad peaches.

Barrackpore, November 21st, Saturday.

To a ship-owner, my dear Porphyre, I may say without impropriety, that yesterday evening I weighed anchor. You know how many sources of delay there are, in collecting all the things necessary for a departure. But yesterday at three o'clock, seeing my cars loaded in the street, and surrounded by my little army, tolerably complete, I gave them the order for departure. You sailors would have objected that it was Friday ; but what could I do ? If I had waited, some of my people would have lost their fathers or brothers in the night, and been obliged to remain to-day to bury or roast them according to the Hindoo custom. In short, I should have been still detained, and how long ? God knows. At night-fall, I mounted my horse, and joined my troop on the road outside the city, and pushed them on five coss. I have ten men with me; I think there are some good ones among them. Moreover, my cook's father follows me *en amateur* to return home. This fellow will end by costing me four rupees a month, for I cannot do without a *tchaokedar* or night-guard; and I shall be forced to confer this dignity on him, with a pike, or a sabre and buckler, according to which may be the most economical. The pike will cost half a rupee, and I fear the other will exceed the other half. My attendants cost me about fifty rupees per month, and the two cars from hence to Benares, eighty.

The engineers being essentially *wigmakers**, one of them in this quarter who presides over the *materiel* of the arsenals, has given me a pike, I think at the honourable company's expense, under the pretence that it was not new, because it had been used for an instant in order to show it; and for a hundred and ten rupees (the price of the second class, *old repairable tents*) he caused to be delivered to me a handsome little mountain tent, which, in my conscience, I consider quite new.

In taking leave of me yesterday, as I was mounting my horse, Mr. Pearson told me, that he looked upon me as a member of his own family; and that if any

* In the artillery, the superior officers and managers who apply to their own personal use objects and materials belonging to the Government arsenals, are called by this name.

unforeseen event should bring me back to Calcutta, I must have no other home but his house.

I am full of strength and resignation, happy that I am *en route*, and that I owe it to my prudence. Adieu, my friend, adieu ; I love you with all my heart.

TO M. JACQUEMONT, THE ELDER, PARIS.

Calcutta, November 10th, 1829.

For the friends of local character, my dear and excellent father, there is a tolerably Asiatic appearance in this letter. Look at the edge of the Chinese and prodigiously economical paper, and tell me if that is not local character in earnest*. I have, at last, the pleasure of replying to a letter written in answer to the first of mine, which went from this side of the Cape of Good Hope. You were then afraid that my successful *début* among our countrymen of Bourbon, would not be maintained among persons of a different nation. But long ere this you probably know, without understanding it any more than I do myself, that the English in India have received me with a *crescendo* of flattering attentions and noble hospitality. To people

* This letter, like several others, is written on Chinese paper with rose-coloured edges. Jacquemont calls it economical, on account of its small size, which admits of considerable abbreviation in purely complimentary letters.

whom I find agreeable, I translate my French thoughts literally; this is something new and uncommon to them, which excites and often spurs them, to reply. In public, I deliver little sententious, well-rounded speeches; and as I am far from speaking English correctly, there are frequent gallicisms in my language, which take my truisms out of the class to which they really belong, and sometimes elevate them to the dignity of new and profound truths. The oral part of libations being suppressed in this country, I have had no opportunity of improving myself in that species of eloquence in which I made so successful a *début* last year in London.

You are going to scold me; but I must confess to you, that I have not spoken to three young ladies. They are, in every respect, the most insignificant in the world. Besides, I have always found them silly in every country.

It is long since I have had four cups of coffee, such as I had at Bourbon. Under this name, by an enormous abuse of language, the English inject into their stomachs the same number of cups of hot water and milk, dirtied a little with powdered charcoal. It is considered to be Mocha: But I accommodate myself wonderfully to these changes of regimen, not being the worse, I think, for not having real coffee.

My letter to Porphyre will inform you of the journey I am about to commence*. With my two years'

* See the preceding letter.

income to be expended in one, I think, taking all things into consideration, I may undertake that to the mountains, but no other. I shall wait there, and work hard, until the horizon, as the newspapers say, grows clearer, before I trace my further progress.

I shall write to you from Benares, Delhi, and Semla, where I expect to meet Lord William Bentinck in the mountains; but, as my letters will have to be jolted across India, they will, no doubt, reach you very irregularly; and afterwards, being secluded far from Europeans in the solitudes of the Himalaya, I shall be necessarily several months without writing to you. Put then in practice your just theories of confidence. After all, people are not glass to break, nor butter to melt in the sun: only one officer in twenty-eight dies annually in the Bengal army; and one, in thirty-one and a half, in that of Madras, and they do all they can to die. What then is the chance against me? One to sixty, perhaps? Would it not be the same at Paris?

If you hear that Runjeet-Sing has invaded the Company's frontiers, congratulate me on the opportunity I shall have of seeing an Asiatic campaign *en passant*; or if the Himalaya should sink to the level of the plains of Bengal, (which is not more probable than an invasion by Runjeet-Sing) remember the hurricane at Bourbon; and congratulate me on the sections of strata, junctions of rocks, &c. &c., which this accident would present to my view.

Friday, 10 o'clock, Evening—Calcutta, Nov. 13th, 1829.

I went out on horseback at four o'clock this morning, and did not return till eight: I rode no less than twenty miles. These are the last days of my stay here, and I must not lose an instant.

Before nine I was on my way to Garden Reach, where I was to occupy the morning in paying visits of leave-taking, and to dine in the evening with the chief justice, Sir Charles Grey. I breakfasted with Sir Charles Metcalf, one of the two members of council: it was he who so obligingly placed the Botanical Garden at my disposal, during my stay at Sir Edward Ryan's. To-morrow he will send me a letter to his brother, the collector, and a magistrate at Delhi, where he was himself resident for a considerable period; nothing could be more seasonable.

Those of his neighbours to whom I was indebted for some attentions and dinners, were soon despatched. I longed to arrived at Lady Ryan's, who had done more than show me attentions. I had not seen her for six weeks; and we met again like old friends. However, I was obliged to cross the Ganges, to take leave of the Botanical Garden, and complete some arrangements there. I found the gardener ill, and unable to assist me in this business, which I could not do without him. Another day's delay! I shall be obliged to return on Monday, accompanied by the chief of the native gardeners, a tall Brahmin with a very handsome countenance, and very intelligent. I employed the time which the unlucky illness of the Englishman left at my disposal, in going over this immense and magnificent establishment in every direction. This time I had no need of an interpreter with the Brahmin. He appeared much surprised at my recent progress in Hindoostanee.

Having crossed the river and returned to Sir E. Ryan's, to make a third change of dress, as black as possible, the remains of the wreck of La Zélée, which still does honour to Porphyre's tailor, I went to Sir Charles Grey's. We dined *à trois*, in a very un-English manner. The English of this character, and I can say the same of my host in town, never completely accustom themselves to the insipidity of their national mode of living. My departure and journey formed the sole subject of a most agreeable conversation. To such people I jested about the smallness of my tent, and the projected patriarchal simplicity of my fare during my long pilgrimage; upon which Sir Charles Grey, who spends three hundred thousand francs a year, said that I could not do better; and that were he not a judge and married, he would willingly accompany me on my unusual, and perhaps hard conditions, but picturesque and proper for study. As Englishwomen follow the fortunes of their husbands more than ours do, Lady Grey regretted that she could not be of the party.

Now, you know, my dear father, that I have always been very much disposed to consider Lady Grey handsome, graceful, and amiable. I setting the thing agoing, we began to be affected, and sought the means of depriving my departure of this melancholy solemnity. It was then settled, that if Lord William Bentinck should, as is very probable, be prevented from making his journey into the mountains in this year, Sir Charles Grey will avail himself of the preparations made for him, and proceed in his steam vessel as far, and as quickly as possible, in order to arrive at Semla before the heats, where he will inhabit the only comfortable house of the cantonment, that which has just been built on purpose for the Governor-general.

This is not unlike building castles in the air; but at table what can we do better? and why not? The chief justice is only useful, he is not necessary. He will be blamed a little for giving himself a year's holiday, without any appearance of pretext but his own good pleasure; but no one can prevent him: his high rank, which is immediately after that of the Governor-general, renders him in that situation, on the bench, much more independent than the Governor-general on his revocable throne. Besides, the immense respect in which he is held on account of his great talents and activity, allows him to do what no one else could venture upon. In that case, I shall sleep in a good bed a couple of nights at least at Semla.

I reckoned upon finishing this evening quietly and alone, as we had begun it. But Lady Grey had promised to be present at some amateur theatricals in town, and we all three went together. The performance was, as might be expected, very tedious; and we passed the time in chatting, as we should have done in her drawing-room. She was very beautiful that evening; and, thinking of the fools who formed the crowd around us, I had the weakness to rejoice at her beauty. In the morning these people gallop about on magnificent Arabs, while I trot almost in my dressing-gown, without boots or whip, on my strong but nimble Persian pony. For this they despise me a little, assuredly; but in the evening you will see them make their *entrée* with some feathered owl on their arm; and it is then I have my revenge, escorting the beautiful Lady Grey. Without the happy chance of these aristocratical friendships, the place would not have been tenable by me; and, thanks to it, no one could have been more overwhelmed with attention and distinction. Good night. My dear father! Conclude from this chapter, if you will, *that I am, perhaps, a too great admirer of the foretold lady, and that it is high time for me to depart with the occasions of meeting her often* *.

Barrackpore, 21*st November,* 1829.

The time is past, those days are gone. Had I waited till evening, I could write you fastuously from my camp of—POLTAGATE.

I left Calcutta yesterday evening with my oxen and people. There were some laggers behind, among the rest unfortunately the cook; but the case was anticipated,

* This and the following paragraph are the author's own English —T.

and I faced the appetite I had gained, in riding five coss, (five short leagues,) with two biscuits and a glass of *sub-alcoholised* water. It was useless to pitch the tent, as there was a government bungalow at hand.

What a fine thing a European inn is! I have furnished an apartment with my camp bed; my shaving apparatus, to which is annexed the medical department, the whole in an herbalising box; guns and pistols, in a corner behind my head. I gave the word—*vigilance, responsibility, prison;* and ordered our departure the next day at four o'clock.

At half past four I was on my march. Every thing goes on better than I expected. The laggers have come up. I have just enjoyed the agreeable sight of my cook; and my Persian pony, which has not made its appearance, is rather in the front than the rear. In that case, I shall find him by-and-by on the bank of the river, which I shall cross, in order to pitch my tent near Chandernagore, where I shall dine to-morrow with our governor. I shall leave this letter and several others there.

So here I am on my route. This evening my education, as an Indian traveller, will be complete when I go to bed (that is to say, when I throw myself, without taking off my clothes, on a cane cot under my little tent, and with a pilau in my stomach); added to this, it is fine, mild, cloudy weather; dressed as I am in linen, it is perfection. At night, I wrap myself up in as many blankets as an Egyptian mummy.

They have offered me at this place—a military post of the presidency—in consequence of having received particular orders from the governor general, a guard of seapoys without my requesting it. As my groom and my cook's aide-de-camp, a fellow I hope to make something of, as a stuffer of animals, &c., walk before me each with a gun, as I have always pistols in my holsters, and as all the robbers on the high roads of Bengal could be put to flight with a rush, I declined the useless honour, notwithstanding the good appearance it would impart to my entrance into Chandernagore to-morrow. I am very well. Adieu, my dear father, adieu in earnest this time. I shall write in five weeks from Benares.

I embrace you with all my heart.

TO M. JACQUEMONT, THE ELDER, PARIS.

Thursday, December 24th, 1829. *Camp of Huinguilisse, on the Banks of the Sone. Lat.* 24° 55′ *N. Lon.* 84′ 10° *E. from Greenwich;* 340 *Miles N. W. from Calcutta, and* 90 *Miles E. S. E. from Benares.*

THIS time, my dear father, it is not from a little corner of Europe, transported beyond the seas, that I write to you; it is from India. I speak no more English; I eat no bread nor do I sleep in a house. What a difference between this strange life and my existence at Calcutta among the refinements of all kinds of European opulence, grafted on Asiatic luxury! It is scarcely more than a month since I turned Arab, and it already seems that I could have been born no where but under a tent. Borrow Arrowsmith's Atlas, or a map by Major Rennel; and start with me from Calcutta on the evening of the 21st of November.

I informed you from Barrackpore, where I stopped the next morning, of the total absence of events on my first day's march. On the second day, I arrived at Chandernagore, after crossing the Hoogly. I found my knife and fork placed and my bed permanently made at our good governor's, the same who formerly made war on M. Duvancel, with his thirty-two seapoys. (N. B. they had no cartridges). He is thirty years older than I am; but at the moment of leaving Europe, I felt myself drawn towards him by the mass of opinions and feelings in which men of the same country partake, without nevertheless having any proper or individual resemblance. However, I stood firm against all his entreaties, and stayed with him only one night, to afford rest to my men and cattle from the hurry and disorder of my departure. On the 20th, I sent them only as far as Hoogly, five miles to the north of Chandernagore, on the banks of the river of the same name. All the laggers had joined, and those whom zeal had led the first day beyond my first halt, had been overtaken the day after on the banks of the river.

At Hoogly I found my baggage arranged round a pretty bungalow, my bed made, and first pilau ready in an unfurnished, but very clean room. I was about to make an assault on my first mountain of rice, when a *djemadhar*, a sort of native usher, a servant of some rank, was despatched to me from a neighbouring house—that of the collector. I found that he wished to know who I was, and I sent him Lord W. Bentinck's passport. Immediately there was a second message, an invitation to dine and sleep; I refused, on pretence of having a long beard. On this, the collector's steward was despatched to me with half a dozen cooks, tables, chairs, saucepans, spits, &c., to assist mine (as the collector supposed) in preparing my dinner. In return for this, I thought I could do no less than pay him a visit; and having only a garden to cross, I went and thanked my obliging neighbour, accepting of his kind offers only a chair and a table. In the evening he sent me a guard to watch, during the night, round my little domain, and a *tchouprassy*, a kind of armed messenger, very useful to a traveller, like the defunct janissaries in Turkey. This man, who brought me a very polite note, had orders to accompany me as far as Burdwan, forty-five miles to the north west.

This was a notable addition to my caravan, at the head of which I arrived in this city on Thursday morning without accident. It is the seat of a civil station. There are eight Englishmen here, who judge, tax, and in one word govern, a million four hundred thousand Indians, including a Rajah, who is upon paper the richest private individual in India.

I had a letter for the poorest of these eight Englishmen, the engineer officer superintending the roads. My reception here was even kinder, if possible, than at Calcutta. To tell you why, or how, is really impossible. Captain Vetch is a Scotchman, religious, &c. Moreover he is old enough to be my father; his wife, much younger than himself, is a rigid presbyterian. Are these, I ask you, a happy prelude to sympathy? Nevertheless, they have since written to me *con amore;* you would be touched if you saw their letter. Being introduced by my host to the seven other Europeans, a grand dinner was organised without delay for the next day, at the house of the colonel of the provincial regiment. I owed my people a day's rest, and I wanted some myself to adjust my paraphernalia, prior to entering the jungle. Captain Vetch having mentioned to me the propriety of a guard, in those districts unfrequented by Europeans, I demanded one from the magistrate, and sent my passport to him. It was immediately returned with five seapoys in full uniform, cartridges in their cartouches, &c., who are placed under my orders, as far as the first military station, Hazarubaug, eighty leagues from Burdwan.

Since I left Burdwan, I have travelled with a military escort, and shall have this guarantee around me as long as I am in India: Lord William did not tell me the magic effect that his firman would produce. My little guard, which I can increase according to circumstances, adds little to my personal safety here, which would be nearly perfect without it: but with it, I am certain of not being robbed. When I start in the morning with some of my men, and two of my seapoys, I am sure that my cars will arrive behind, and that my servants will not plunder them and run away. No obstacle will stop them: if they sink in a bog, or are stranded in the bed of a torrent—if the oxen stop at the foot of a mountain, without being able to get over it, my serjeant with his red dress will know how to find hands to help them along. Where should I now be without my guard? Undoubtedly, drowned in the mud of some river near Burdwan. For a month past I have tasted of the sweets of absolute power; it is certainly a very convenient thing. Of course, I make the most temperate use of it; and you know that under a Marcus Aurelius, this most simple of all forms of government is, at the same time, the best.

When my baggage arrives at the place I have marked out for my encampment, my generalissimo, with the most formidable and stiffest air in the world, comes to say that all is in good order; he then urges on the little operation of pitching the tent. At night he comes to receive his orders for the morrow, and to inform me that he has posted a sentinel at my canvas door. Pistols and guns sleep in their holsters and cases, unless the vicinity is very fertile in tigers; in which case I have always something ready at hand to make, at least, a great deal of noise. You know how Porphyre has provided for that.

But let us resume our map. From Burdwan, I proceeded for seven days to the north west on the left bank of the Dammhoudæurr, called also Dum-moodah, Doonna, &c., by geographers (it may, how-ever, be the exact pronunciation of its name in other parts of its course), passing through Manniore and Dig-nagur. It was there that I first encountered jungles, and I confess I was very much disappointed. I had ima-gined a thick impenetrable forest, offering all the richness of form and colour to be found in tropical vegetation, bristling with thorny trees, interlaced with sarmentous shrubs, and climbing plants, mounting to the tops of the highest trees, and falling grace-fully back, like cascades of flowers. At Rio Janeiro and Saint Domingo I had seen scattered features of this picture; but here I found myself amongst woods still more monotonous than those of Europe, with some stunted underwood; and instead of the roaring of tigers in the distance, the noise of the woodman's axe.

I have since viewed scenes less remote from those which my imagination had pictured. I have proceeded a hundred leagues along a road, traversed by no path, bordered, shut in, walled on either side by the forest or desert plains through which it has been opened. I have penetrated into these solitudes along the dried-up beds of torrents. As for tigers, I must believe in their existence; for I saw and touched one, which was killed at Hazarubaug six hours after my passage on the road, and the next day a leopard of the same growth; then again, my English host at the mines of Runnigunge, on the banks of the Dummoodah, has eighteen scars on his face, made by the scratch of one of them. But, incredulous by nature, I shall believe more in them, when I see but the shadow of a living one's tail. You will see, that after travelling in India like no one else, I shall return to see tigers at the Jardin des Plantes. Do not, however, be afraid that my incredulity will expose me to any danger, in this world at least: I am always on my guard, and never go on foot without a gun; nor alone on my exploring expeditions.

A recommendation from the proprietor of the mines of Runnigunge (banks of the Dummoodah, twelve leagues east of Rogonatpore) to the subaltern agent, who superintends the works, made me master of his house. After sleeping seven nights on a mat, I found the sensation of sheets on my naked skin in bed very pleasant. I remained at Runnigunge thirty-six hours; thirteen up to my knees in mud and cold water, a hundred feet under ground, with my hammer, compass, chemical tests, and measure at hand. It is the only coal mine that has been worked in India, and I spared no pains to make myself geologically and commercially acquainted with it. The thirteenth part of the hardships, or miseries of this examination, would, no doubt, have given me a desperate cold at Calcutta; but I know, and you know, by the experience of half a score of years, that my constitution is singularly modified in travelling; becoming strengthened, and easily getting over a variety of things which would be serious obstacles, were they to present themselves in the midst of a quiet and regular life. At Calcutta, I was continually taking cold, from a change of temperature of five or six degrees: now, at three o'clock, the thermometer is at 87° in my tent, which is not sheltered from the sun by any tree; to-morrow, at three or four o'clock in the morning, the cold will come, as it does every day, to pull me by the legs under three blankets, and the temperature will have fallen forty degrees: and yet I do not take cold.

From Runnegunge to Rogonatpore, where I rejoined what they call the new military road, I travelled two days and a half through the sands of the Dummoodah; a terrible business for my oxen, though assisted by fifty people more or less benevolent, who were requested to shove the wheels. Then the desolation of desolation!—beyond the river no road. You must travel in the midst of thickets, and sometimes seize the opportunity offered by a ravine. Bless the seapoys! it was arm, leg, and head-breaking work, for both beasts and people: it is a miracle that my lantern alone perished. The children of some poor villagers lost in the midst of these forests had never seen a European: they paid me back the annoyance, which I must have caused some twenty years ago, to some poor devils of Turks whom I followed in the streets and stared at, like other little blackguards of my own age.

From Rogonatpore, although the engineers have displayed but little ability, the road is nevertheless always good for a horseman; and my oxen and cars, tried as they had been, rolled on gloriously. Relays of porters are stationed along this line, to carry travellers who go post in palanquins; I have met two within the last sixteen days. There are also bungalows to receive them, as well as those who travel, like me, by marches. They are about the distance from each other that the oxen, camels, elephants, or servants on foot, can go in a day: five, six, seven, and eight leagues, according to the difficulties of the road. In these bungalows there are two very neat apartments, two bedsteads, two tables, and six chairs: in fact, two families might, at a push, find accommodation in them. Three servants attached by the administration of the post-office to each, are particularly useful to those who travel by palanquin alone. I found that at Rogonatpore, occupied by a collector, on a journey with his wife and young child. He has an elephant, eight cars like mine, two cabriolets, and a particular car for his child, two palanquins, six saddle and carriage-horses; sixty or eighty porters to carry him from one bungalow to another, independently of at least sixty household servants. He dresses, changes his dress, and dresses again, breakfasts, *tiffs*, dines, and in the evening takes tea exactly as at Calcutta, without abating an atom; glass and china are packed and unpacked from morning till night; glittering plate, clean linen four times a day, &c. &c.

I appeared in the midst of this magnificence with a ten days' beard and a foot of mud below my knee, politely requesting half of the house to which I had a right, and of which he had disposed entirely, not expecting any visit. The table which was laid, apparently for half a dozen persons, was immediately removed on my declining to sit down, and carried into the other room. I waited in my own, with a heap of stones and plants, till my pilau arrived. Having despatched a note to my unknown, offering him a bed in my room, for himself or any gentleman of his party, he came to thank me, telling me that he was alone with his wife, and remained some time conversing, extremely puzzled by the difference of my dress and my language. I amused myself by increasing his perplexity, talking about all the great people of Calcutta, like one perfectly acquainted with them, and of the most general topics of conversation, politics, and literature. Afterwards, finding him a good-natured fellow, I told him who I was; we entered into a community of arrangements. Like me, he was going to Benares each day, from one bungalow to another, and I annoyed him extremely by arriving every evening at the same quarters as himself: in the day-time he famished me, his people not leaving a glass of milk within two leagues; and in the evening I came to deprive him of half his lodgings. He offered to stop a day, and to travel after me. I preferred going a double stage, and getting on before him; thus gaining time, without causing any loss of it to him. So, after keeping company two days, which I required to know the style in which these gentlemen travel, I left him behind me; and, though he followed me very closely, I have not heard the sound of his voice since.

But finding afterwards that my tent was better lighted in the evening with a wax candle, and much more cheerful than the bungalow; and that I was much more comfortable under it with my people lying round me, and my horse at the door, than within four naked walls as cold as my canvas, I have returned to the desert fashion, and encamp, and shall continue to do so in spite of all the bungalows, serais, and caravanserais in India. Besides, on this road, the only one on which they are decent, being reserved for Europeans, their use is not gratuitous, far from it. The company ask two rupees (five francs) a day; and you cannot give less than a rupee to the servants. It is not an objection, not even the subject of remark, to the English, who are all munificently paid: but ten pounds, more or less, from Calcutta to Benares, is a matter of some consequence to me: the sum is nearly half of what the whole journey will cost me.

Evening.

In the evening, proceeding from Rogonatpore in a west north-west direction, I re-entered the forests, which are somewhat thinner about that place, and again crossed the Dummoodah, near Gomeah. For a week I travelled over a table land, at an elevation of four or five hundred metres—of several points of which I have taken the level—constantly ascending and descending, crossing several large torrents every day, and encamping at night in the vicinity of a few huts.

Hazarubaug, which is scarcely more than a village, is a little political residence. The English establishment consists of a resident—who is colonel of the provincial regiment—a subaltern and a medical officer. Having a letter for the latter I remained twenty-four hours at this house. A note, with the usual compliments, seconded by my passport, was immediately sent to the resident, and returned with a fresh escort to release that from Burdwan, and an invitation to dinner. The two houses being contiguous, I paid a visit during the day, which was repaid before dinner-time. My Amphitryon was the remains of a very elegant, clever, and amiable man, ruined, but not brutified by drink.

Starting from Hazarubaug on the 17th, after a day's rest, of which my attendants stood in great need, I am now on my way to Benares, where I shall arrive on the 31st of December, or 1st of January, after travelling a hundred leagues without stopping a single day.

I must count them: the mountains are at such a

distance! nearly four hundred leagues farther! the hot winds at their foot are so terrible! sometimes they begin to blow at the beginning of March, but usually in April. You have read Bernier's Journey into Cashmere, with the Padishah Aurung-Zeb. You recollect the recital of his sufferings in the plains of Lahore when he encountered the shifting of the spring monsoon? I must leave Delhi on the 1st of March at the latest: it is unfortunate that I could not leave Calcutta ten days earlier. But you have seen my perplexities, and the embarrassments which stopped and detained me there till 20th November.

The circuit I made, in order to inspect the coal-mines of the Burdwan district, makes the distance which I have passed over amount to two hundred leagues. I have travelled more than half on foot, the rest on horseback. I set out at four, five, or six o'clock in the morning, according to the phases of the moon and the nature of the country. At noon, two, three, and sometimes not till four in the evening, I arrive at the end of my day's journey, the whole of which, like a native, I pass in the sun. Before mounting, I eat by moonlight a plate of rice and milk well sugared and cooked over night; I put a biscuit in my pocket, and, with this ballast, I accept as a windfall, but without at all depending upon them, all the cups of milk which my cook, sent forward with a seapoy, succeeds in procuring on the road. I dine when I am ready, and when dinner is ready at the same time; if not, it waits, no matter what the hour is. The uniformity of my food fortunately compensates for the irregularity of the hours of my meals: I invariably eat a chicken cooked with a pound of rice, plenty of *ghee* or native butter, detestably rancid, but to which I have got wonderfully used; and some spices according to the fashion of the country, but very sparingly used. This is the dinner of a musselmaun with an income of twelve hundred francs. I drink two large glasses of water with a few drops of brandy, sometimes only pure water. The whole, including the illegal profits of the *khansama* (for my *maitre d'hôtel* is my only cook), costs fifty francs a month, half of which is stolen. I was forgetting very unreasonably, for I am this moment drinking a large cup of it, that in the evening I sometimes take tea. In cold weather, I find it very pleasant; or useful to keep me awake, when I have worked a great deal, and have an inclination to fall asleep.

After all, whatever may have been said of the laziness, stupidity, and mendacity of the servants of this country, their service is very convenient and very cheap. For twelve francs a month, I have a groom, who has my horse saddled and bridled at the hour of the morning ordered the previous evening for our departure. This man follows me like my shadow; when I gallop, he runs; it is the custom. If I dismount, he is at hand to lead my horse by the bridle, or to wait according to my order; now, I mount and dismount from ten to fifty times in the course of the day. The other servant attached to the horse, the *gassyara*, goes on before, and I find him at the place marked out for evening halt, with a bundle of grass, leaves, or roots, which he gathers as fodder for the animal. In carrying the wages of these two men to my cavalry estimates, its maintenance costs me forty or forty-five francs a month.

The collections of all kinds, which I go on making on the road, require care, in which I must be seconded by several servants; but this species of service is not included in any of the preceding. So when I told my water-carrier to put his water-skin into one of the cars in the day-time, and walk near me with my portfolio under his arm to dry plants, he said that it was not his business, and that too in a very impertinent tone. I did not hesitate to give him a hearty kick immediately, otherwise another would have told me that it was not his place to carry my gun, another refused to carry my hammer, and so on. I take good care not to order any thing forbidden by their religious laws; with this exception, I exact imperiously, in addition to his own special occupation, every service that each can render. I hope that the majority will have time to grow accustomed to this little revolution before we arrive at Benares, and that I shall have but few vacancies to supply in that city. I was afraid, on leaving Calcutta, that I should soon be forsaken on the road by persons paid in advance; but not one has thought of doing so. Henceforth, with my escort, they will not dare. Moreover, at this moment I am in their debt.

I harden myself against cold as well as heat. I have, it is true, covered my whole body with flannel, but over it I wear only linen or cotton as in summer at Calcutta. Tired of constantly pulling off my stockings to cross torrents, I do not put them on, except at night to sleep in. Over my day-clothes I put on also at night, when I go to bed, a second flannel waistcoat, very thick and very ample, which I keep on in the morning on the march, till the sun renders it oppressive; but the wind is sometimes so piercing, that I do not throw it off. My Pondicherry hat, made of date leaves, and covered with black silk, is more brilliant than ever. In the morning I pull it like a cap over my ears, and find it very warm. It takes every shape that I wish; it is an admirable invention of mine, light, water-proof, firm, &c.

December 25th, the other Bank of the Sone.

It is a sea of sand of not less than a league in breadth, and my cars have taken four hours to cross it. To animate this desert, Providence kept in reserve two elephants and thirty camels, which it made to defile past my caravan. I shall, by a forced march, push on this evening as far as Sasseram, an ancient Indian city.

There is not a tree to shelter me. I am writing to you under a broiling sun, and just now I found the water in the river frozen. I avail myself of the moment that my horse is at his breakfast. It is a meal which he seldom makes, having to submit to the chances which decide the hours of his master. He can, however, bear fasting very well in the day-time, and cold at night; and as he does not seem to have got out of condition during the last five weeks, there is no reason why he should not carry me to the world's end. The rogue justifies tolerably well the character of viciousness enjoyed by those of his colour, a sorrel, if there ever was one. Sometimes he throws me, when I am stupid enough to dispute with a beast without reason. In falling, I promise myself for the future to imitate Figaro, who always gave way to fools, instead of contending with them; and then, when the opportunity offers, I forget my plans of moderation and want him to pass what frightens him; hence there is a conflict, with kicking, and twenty other mischievous tricks, of which your horseman, Porphyre, will give you the nomenclature. However, we always arrange the matter amicably, as follows: one day he gives way, the next I yield to the *inclination which draws me.* In spite of these rebellions, which are, however, rare, I go on reading, sleeping, and studying my plants with a magnifying glass all the time I am on horseback, and congratulate myself on my purchase.

My Hindostanee vocabulary increases daily. Far from preventing my people from speaking near me, I invite them to do so, in order to break-in my ear to the inflexions, so different from those of the European languages to every one who has an ear. I converse with them and the soldiers of my escort; I seek to penetrate their existence, their feelings, their ideas. I am becoming impregnated with India, instead of dipping the tip of my finger in, as many of the English do, who pretend to study it. In this respect my escort will always be very useful to me; the people of my little caravan, both servants and soldiers, are not the least interesting subjects of observation which I meet with on the road. The English encourage the higher castes to the military service. Among my five men from Hazarubaug, I have two Brahmins, and the others are Rajpoots; my Burdwan serjeant was also a Brahmin.

I have given up all thoughts of comprehending any thing of the Hindoo theogony; I am persuaded that it always has been unintelligible nonsense to the Europeans who have pretended to explain it, Bernier, Sir William Jones, &c. The arranging of the castes appeared to me impossible. I tried, with my little skill in classifying as a naturalist, and I convinced myself that there is no exact coincidence between those of one part of India, and those which bear the same name in others. It is impossible to establish among them what we botanists call a critical synonymy. On my return to Europe, I shall endeavour to acquaint myself better with what will be accessible to me on this topic, without knowing Sanscrit. You have surely seen Mr. Wilson's Hindoo Theatre; it will be a novelty to me. I saw the book every day at Calcutta, and the author very frequently, and have only yet had leisure to read his excellent preface. Wilson has Mr. D'Arcet's place at the Mint, and several others, all sinecures, and very well paid. He is the best pensioned certainly of literary men; he is besides the first Sanscrit scholar in the world, and moreover a man of mind and taste. He resembles Frederic the Great of Prussia prodigiously.

My solitude is far from being irksome. I am quite certain that I shall pass my six months' seclusion in the mountains, without melancholy: I shall not see a single European. Thoughts full of sweetness and tenderness fill the moments of my life which are unoccupied by study. Certain periods of the past seem like dreams. I sometimes cannot believe that I am he that has done this, that has been there, &c. &c. For a moment I doubt my identity, and am near suspecting, in this country of the transmigration of souls, that some one else's has turned mine out of doors. The source of enthusiasm is exhausted, and when the cold keeps me awake under my bed-clothes, I contemplate the world, not as an actor, but as a critical and disinterested spectator of its different scenes. I no longer *perceive* past things, I only recal them, and so judge what was formerly in me, as well as what is without.

The admiration of the beauties of nature has its virginity; but it is soon sullied by enjoyment. Saint Domingo will always be to me the *beau idéal* of equinoctial nature. I cannot recollect without emotion the first scenes of the tropic, which chance presented to me.

Perhaps this profound impression depended on the disposition of my mind; and, if I were permitted to see them again, I might not find their beauties so touching. I have written so to Frederick. It is also for his sake that I love the corner of the world which he inhabits.

M. de Humboldt has been happy in his description of this first impression made by scenes near the equator: a natural philosopher ought to be more sensible when the study of nature's details does not close his eyes to its whole. You will conclude justly from this soliloquy that I do not blacken my paper with poetical prose. I write a great deal in all tones, and without effort, according to my humour, the state of my stomach, and the quality of my pen. No one is all sublime, all dignified, all cheerful and smiling. After a geological description, will come a confidential page, which none but myself ought to re-peruse. I should be afraid of telling falsehoods if I wrote otherwise. Adieu, my dear father, till I reach the holy city. Tell my friends that the recollection of them follows me, and charms many moments of my solitary life; but I have not time to write to them all the sentiments of tenderness which my heart contains. I do not tell you to be at ease concerning me, because I flatter myself that the eloquence of the two hundred leagues, which I have travelled so fortunately, will render a request of that kind on my part needless. Adieu! may you enjoy as good health as I do; and Porphyre also imitate me. I wish I could send you some sunshine, of which I have too much in the day-time, for a little of the warmth of European houses in the morning. Consult M. Azaïs *en passant*, on the possibility of the exchange.

December 31*st*, 1829.

This last day of the year I arrived at the holy city. I brought an introduction from Lord W. Bentinck, one from my friend at Burdwan for a very rich rajah, whom I shall see to-morrow, and two from the major-general of the army, the friend of Colonel de Lafosse, and also mine, the most amiable of men, for two of his excellent brother officers. The first who saw me kept me and put me in possession of his house, and after breakfast I found an elephant at my door to take me on my visits. Then the director of the mint, whom I first went to see on my moving mountain, a man whom I knew by correspondence to be the wittiest in India, would not let me go alone, but said he would introduce me to each. The elephant was sent home, where his back will remain exclusively at my service during my short stay here, and I went my round of visits with the *spirited mint-master* in his carriage. He was expecting me as his guest, and had provided for my reception; letters from you and Porphyre, a letter from Taschereau, one from M. Victor, introducing me to Dr. * * *, another from Madame Le Breton, a long one from Miss Pearson, one from Sir Charles Metcalfe, &c., the whole directed to me at the post-office, by the obliging governor of Chandernagore, who had picked them up, some at Pondicherry, others at Calcutta, and had forwarded them under official cover, postage free, to await me here. I have read the whole over and over again. Add to this, that I had ridden five leagues on horsèback at night, to arrive at the holy city by sunrise. I have traversed it on foot, admirably favoured with a most beautiful Provence May morning. I know not what to begin with. I smiled at reading your fears respecting my reception in this country. No: we should not do in France for any stranger what is done here for me. The London streamlet increased at Calcutta into a river, which is now growing into a sea. Half the letters which I leave on the road bring me four times the number. I shall want another camel to keep pace with this geometrical progression. The bad taste of these figures is the fault of the eastern sun.

I will return to you, my dear father, before I leave this place: I leave you for the day. Yesterday I shaved off a beard of a fortnight's growth; I resembled Robinson Crusoe, and used to dine in my tent scarcely more magnificently than he did. To-day, I put on black silk stockings, as if I were going to a ball in Paris or London. I am going to dine with a dozen Europeans, who govern a portion of the British empire. Their ladies will be dressed in the Parisian fashion of six months ago. They are not vulgar nabobs, a character which exists no longer, except on the stage of the London minor theatres. In the evening I shall enjoy an elegant and solid conversation: every means will be combined, to show me as much as possible of the wonders of the city in the short time I shall stay there. Trust to my star. There is certainly in this continuation of success, something besides good luck: it is a series of happy chances, which have by their repetition, ceased to be chances. But above all, the miracle is, my not having suffered in the estimation of others on account of my poverty!

January 1*st*, 1830.

If a thousand of my countrymen were to come into this country, with double or triple what I brought, they could not probably succeed in showing themselves any where. My host here, an infantry captain, exercising the functions of sub-intendant, has a hundred and fifty thousand francs a year; and all, you know, is on the same scale. By a peculiar favour, I have obtained a dispensation from riches; and my relative poverty has, on the contrary, been only a source of enjoyment to my self-love. Some of the most intimate of my acquaintance are not ignorant of it, and they accommodate themselves accordingly, the best way they can. I was seldom obliged to hire a carriage to go to dine at the Chief Justice's of India; when I was not next door to him, at Garden Reach, he asked my hour and came to fetch me. The fools who saw these attentions gave me credit, no doubt, for some mysterious virtues, more worthy of esteem than the vulgar possession of a cabriolet, and took it upon trust.

Portionless girls, who have not succeeded in getting married in England, arrive here in cargoes, for sale, on honourable terms, I mean, to the young civil and military officers, who, along with their commission and the assurance of a fortune sufficient for two, receive orders to go and be rich all alone in some village, a couple of hundred leagues from Calcutta, and govern a territory equal to several French departments. Those, whose places are very lucrative, select a wife from the society of Calcutta as they would a girl in the street: it is well understood, that the small number of families forming the circle in which I moved, are an exception to the rule. For a man like me it is matrimonially the worst of countries.

There are still enormous incomes in India, but immense fortunes are hardly made there now. The daughters of those who grow rich are educated in such habits of luxury, that they are only marriageable to collectors, or others of the same rank. Then the English, who are the most matrimonial people in the world, have children by dozens, and no fortune could resist a division by so Christian a divisor. Lastly, the young ladies of the most polished, and at the same time, most opulent classes that I have had occasion to meet, are still more insignificant than those of any other country. They are as afraid of the little, very little, reason of a married woman of five and twenty, as of the polar ice.

It is not, however, because they are cheerful, but the few serious ideas which marriage always forces into the most empty head, frighten the absolute insignificance of those whose wit has yet to come.

Miss Pearson is the only person I have known worthy of the consideration of a man of sense. The poor girl, whom I left very ill at my departure from Calcutta, writes me that she is dying. I must direct to England the letter which I wrote to her on my journey. The physicians are sending her there without delay: her mother accompanies her. I am afraid my letter will arrive too late. But whatever may happen, and if chance brings us again together under the same roof, we shall never be to each other different from what we are at present. Although possessed of intelligence above her twenty years, and of a very serious turn of mind, she did not seem to perceive that I was a young man; and sometimes she would talk to me of matters of feeling, as she would have done to some old friend of her father's, or her own.

It gives me pain, my dear father, to overturn your castles in the air. But, were I to suffer you to go on building, without disturbance, you would end by believing in them, as in the famous system raised on the ruins of all others (style of the *Real Essences*) and would look with displeasure at me on my return, were I not followed by the family of king Priam.

How your letters have charmed me! they have effaced the surprise and ill humour, which the news of the ministry of La Bourdonnaye, Mangin, and Co. caused me on my arrival in the holy city. I cannot answer those nine pages, which are worth fifty, for my letter would be endless. Your tenderness for me raises illusions which I cannot share, but with which I am much affected. Your reliance upon my firmness is a great happiness to me. Whatever evil may happen to me, you will know that I am provided with defensive arms, which is in me a whimsical principle of internal satisfaction, and simplicity of taste, belonging not to my age nor to my education; a sort of savage pride which will console me in bad times, should any happen. There are a thousand degrees of misfortune above the possibility of which I shall henceforth be placed.

I did not neglect writing to almost every body, during the last days of my stay in Calcutta. I must now give up that correspondence, in which all that I ought to reserve for myself would evaporate. Adieu, my dear father; my next letter will be from Delhi in two months. I embrace you, Porphyre, and the eternally absent Frederick, with all my heart: it is all that I can do now.

TO MADEMOISELLE ZOÉ NOIZET DE SAINT PAUL-ARRAS.

Camp of Moneah, Monday, December 28th, 1829.

Do not look in the map, my dear Zoé, for the place whence your cousin is now writing to you. It is nothing but a clump of trees near a miserable hamlet. I, who have a tent to lie under, can do without their shelter, which is however very necessary for my people who sleep around in the open air. Although scarcely beyond the 25th degree of latitude, the clearness of the sky, and the north wind which precipitates upon the plains of India the icy air of the summits of the Himalaya, make the nights very cold: and although under a double roof of cloth, more warmly clad than in the day time, and wrapped in a triple blanket, I often wake quite chilled. Yet at noon, the temperature often rises to 86°.

I have travelled two hundred leagues in forty days, without perceiving that I am in want of any thing. At four o'clock in the morning, I eat half a pound of rice, boiled with sugar in milk; I drink milk on my road, when my servants succeed in procuring it. I sometimes see a hundred cows put in requisition for a single glass; and my cook's zeal would set fire to the village to warm it, if I did not prefer it cold. I encamp at two, three, four, or five in the evening; I then invariably dine on a hen, pullet, or cock, some bird or other, in short, made into pilau, with a pound of rice; I drink one or two large glasses of water, often very bad, and throw myself on my rush cot when sleep closes my eyes before my paper.

Having left Bengal, the country in which the rivers can find no slope to run into the sea, and their waters stagnate and fill the atmosphere with noxious vapours, I no longer mistrust the sun, and expose myself to it like the natives. I journey more on foot than on horseback, and being turned out of my road by a thousand objects, I travel every day double the distance that my heavy baggage does. In these reconnoiterings, I am neither unarmed nor alone. I have made of four of my men, who are more active than the rest, a vanguard, which follows me like my shadow. Meanwhile, I every day feel myself full of new strength. No Englishman ever thought of living as I do, and it is for this reason that those are dead who attempted to expose themselves to the same physical influences. They laugh at my milk, my *eau sucrée*, my two meals separated by a mean interval of thirteen hours, and my abstinence from spirituous liquors: they would cross themselves (were they not heretics, and call the holy sign of the cross superstitious) if they knew that, notwithstanding all my abstinence, I am often obliged, in order to avoid gastro-enteritis to—(Well! how shall I say it.) In short, you understand, I am not, like them, afflicted with hydrophobia; and I, in my turn, laugh when they are buried, pickled in champagne, or preserved in brandy and mercury, which their doctors give them by the half pound.

At Benares, where I shall arrive in three days, I shall substitute half a dozen camels for my cars, and my caravan will be a little more picturesque for them. I nevertheless assure you, that it is so even now. What gives it rather a European, but infinitely respectable appearance, is the red coats of a little escort of seapoys, which I renew every sixty or eighty leagues, and shall keep near me as long as I am in India. It makes me absolute master of the places through which I pass, adds a great deal if not to my safety, at least to my feeling of security. My generalissimo is a serjeant of the highest distinction, who stiffens himself like a post into the position of the soldier without arms at whatever distance he catches sight of me, and leads all my people in military fashion. He is a Brahmin, if you please; as was likewise the one I had before. A sentinel, relieved every two hours, guards my little camp at night, and sometimes wakes me with a shot at some suspicious-looking rover. In the hundred leagues of forest which I have just traversed, notwithstanding this guard outside at night, I had always at hand something to make a great deal of noise in the tigers' ears, in case of a visit from them; but I saw none.

Carrying on, at the same time, several kinds of research—applying myself in the midst of the studies and mechanical cares which they exact, to perfect myself in the language of the country, the only one which I speak at present—charged with a correspondence with several of my new Bengal friends—my long solitary days run away very rapidly. My being shut out from all communication with Europeans does not bear hard upon me. You know that from Benares I shall cross Bundlecund (a mountainous province between the Nerbudda and the Jumna) to Agra,

Delhi, and thence to the Himalaya mountains, to pass five or six months of the summer in some place, almost as much above the level of the sea as the summit of Mont Blanc, where I shall remain the whole time without seeing a man of my own colour. By the short experiment I have just made since I left Calcutta, to turn myself into an Arab, I know that this long and studious seclusion, entirely separated from the men and affairs of Europe, will not be painful to me.

How different, my dear cousin, from the life I led at Calcutta, where I spent the leisure which study left me, in noble and serious pleasures—the most exquisite of European civilisation. I have talked politics, with my democratic opinions; I have talked of religion, when I have been provoked to it, with my scepticism and incredulity; I have talked of all things, in short, according to the truth of my heart, and the errors of my judgment. I had the happiness to please all that I met of those people whose distinction made me desire their esteem and good will.

Now, in the desert, I cannot recal those days without emotion. Whatever may happen to me in this country, there are men in it in whose friendship I am sure not to die; it follows and protects me powerfully in my long pilgrimage. The major-general of the army, a man from whom I parted with a swelling heart and tearful eye, and who felt for me the same sympathy which drew me towards him, has given me numerous letters of introduction (twenty-four) for such of his friends or brother officers as may be stationed on my proposed route. Every one at Calcutta contributed to increase my packet: Lord W. Bentinck made the magnificent addition to it of nine private letters. He gave me beforehand a passport in an unusual form, but so protecting, so friendly, that it undoubtedly rendered his personal recommendations useless, and I experience considerable embarrassment in showing it: for it is a formal summons made by the governor-general, to all officers in India, civil and military, to afford me the best quarters on my arrival at their residence. They would not have done as much for any Englishman. It was the same in London. There is certainly some national pride in this profusion of kindness to a foreigner, but it is of a noble kind; I enjoy it as an individual and a Frenchman.

The amiable man with whom I had the advantage to share the tedium of the sea for six months, sends me word from his Indian kingdom of Yvetot, that he shall not fail to treat to his best wine every Englishman that knocks at his door in Pondicherry; and that on my count. At the great distance at which I am from the southern extremity of India, it is agreeable to find on the map a little corner of friendly land.

Adieu, my dear Zoé! While writing to you, sleep does not come to close my eyes; but it is eleven o'clock at night, and I have given orders for our departure at four: I must therefore wind up for this day. If you expected from me a *piquant* traveller's letter, you will be disappointed; for I have not told you a word of the men, nor of the monuments, nor of the scenes of nature, in the countries through which I am passing. But I have talked to you of things nearer to me; and I flatter myself that your friendship will see a proof of mine, in the artless confessions of my self-love. It is a weakness which I do not mind confessing to you; but confide it only to those who you know love me as much as you do.

I am, besides, too much occupied by divers pursuits and too positive researches, to see in a very prominent light the picturesque interest of objects. It is not that the minute and critical examination of the productions and phœnomena of nature closes my eyes against their collective pictorial effect; but the source of the charm, and of the rapture, which I heretofore experienced on beholding their beauties, is dried up. It is henceforth with my mind, and with my taste, that I complacently contemplate a landscape or a graceful group. Yet, in the spring, I shall see the loftiest mountains in the world; I shall pass a summer, half a year, amid their scenes of eternal snow and ice. Perhaps their desolate grandeur will find my sensibility too excitable. It will be a recovery of a melancholy faculty, but still less sad than insensibility.

Adieu, Zoé! I do not know when I shall write to you, and fear I shall be able to do so but seldom; but I shall often think of you, on my Persian steed; it is the most oriental thing that I can do for you.

TO M. VICTOR DE TRACY, PARIS.

Camp at Sunniput, between Delhi and Panniput, March, 1830.

YOUR letter of the 29th June, 1829, after a journey in India, before which mine will always turn pale, reached me some days since at Delhi. You will easily imagine, my dear friend, the pleasure which it gave me, when I tell you that for two months and a half I have had no news from Europe. At Benares, a few lines of yours were brought to me from Calcutta by a young physician, to whom I was compelled to give a most negative reply as to the advantages held out to him for the practice of his profession in that city. There is but one Frenchman at Calcutta, and he is in excellent health. That is not the place for Doctor * * *. As for the English, who in general have very bad health, he will not suit them. They require a doctor of their own nation, by whom they may be sure of being understood, and who is not afraid of killing them, according to the fashion of science in this country, with calomel, opium, &c. &c.

I have not seen any European newspapers of later date than the beginning of September; so that I know quite well the change of ministry, a theme on which others would perhaps compose some tolerably gloomy variations; but which appears to me to be more ridiculous than dangerous. I recollect a time when these gentry might have risked a *coup d'état*, but now-a-days they have more interest than any one in the observation of the law, and will not dare to place themselves beyond it by raising themselves above it. The drawing-room spirit which prevails in the chamber and among the leading members, never allowed me to conceive a doubt of your success at the *tribune*, provided you were not recalled from it too soon, as happened to you the first time. The feelings to which you addressed yourself exist in the hearts of all well-born men; good sense is a thing too which nature has made common; and by speaking as you do, to principles of emotion and action, you cannot fail to exercise an influence which will be always on the increase. The liberal public did not at all like the remonstrances of its best friends; it did not at all understand being found fault with, nor even contradicted; and whoever deserved to gain its confidence and gratitude, received only an affront, after being previously imprisoned for it. Look you! Would Courier have been more fortunate? I doubt it. Nevertheless, your success makes, in the style of your *capable* and honourable friends, a *precedent*, or, in French, an antecedent, subversive of the worship of popularity, which is not one of the least ignoble forms of servility. You will open the door to others; that is what we want—new men! What good can be done with such old *able* sinners as Baron ——, and others of the same school, at present our friends? I see them from hence esteem you (I hope so for their sakes), but smile at your want of parliamentary tactics; and when you are rewarded with public favour, grow vexed, and complain that you spoil the trade, by proving that it does not require so much *finesse* to succeed. Tell me, my dear friend, is it not so? I cannot forbear laughing at this idea, without respect for Mahomet, in the mosque which serves as my lodging to-day. Tell me what the people of Moulins and the neighbourhood say of you. They who have seen you at work, making war, without metaphor, on the furze, marshes, intermittent fevers, rot in sheep, &c., in a word, on the causes of moral evil and physical evil, do they not unanimously appreciate you? If, when you answer these lines, you add to the chronicle which I ask of you, the number of your sheep at Paray, that of your ploughs, the surface, and quality of your own sown land, the misty charm of distance will cause me to think these things about you and our country delicious.

As for me, I dare not tell you any thing of this country; during the four months since I left Calcutta, with a tent and ten bullocks, I have travelled nearly fourteen hundred miles (six hundred leagues); and on this long journey so many new objects have presented themselves to my notice, my mind and imagination have been exercised on so many different subjects, that, for fear of writing you a volume, I cannot begin. It may be sufficient for you to know that I have experienced nothing but satisfaction. In the vicissitudes of a rather adventurous life, one certainly the most picturesque that can be *lived* in India, I have had good days and no bad ones. The numerous and powerful acquaintances which I formed at Calcutta, some of which ripened into friendship, make of me, in these distant provinces, a man of the country, and one of the best informed. Welcomed, though an entire stranger, because I always bring the most honourable recommendations, I am soon after caressed for my own sake, because I am furnished with articles of exchange for every one. I gain a great deal of information in my sojourning in *Europeanised* places, by making the judge talk of the moral condition of the millions of Hindoos and Mussulmauns subject to him; the collector of the taxes, of the very varied system of territorial property, and of the natural products: each, in fact, on the subject with which he is best acquainted. If I meet with a good Persian scholar, a man of critical sagacity, I seek to rectify, from his knowledge, the little I have drawn from suspicious national sources.

The variety of my studies, and also of my exercises, sometimes on horseback, oftener on foot, sometimes on an elephant, or in a litter, allows me to feel no fatigue whatever. I have never enjoyed more steady health; my Brahminic diet contends with the fatal influence of the climate.

After St. Domingo and Rio Janeiro, the magnificence of nature in Bengal possesses a fatiguing monotony. The immense mountainous forests of Behar, which I afterwards crossed between the Dummoodah and the Ganges, have more variety; but the magnificence of the tropics has already disappeared. I discern no trace of it in the mountains of Boggilcund and Bundlecund, through which I travelled with much fatigue in the month of January. The plains of this latter province, and the Doah, or immense Delta, which divides the Ganges from the Jumna, have no marked character. But repassing the Jumna before Agra, and proceeding afterwards north-north-west towards the desert which borders the left bank of the Indus, the configuration of the country, and the vegetation by which it is covered, strongly determine its aspect. It is almost Persia: salt or saltpetre in a sandy soil, dust in the atmosphere, stunted and thorny vegetation, &c. Without departing from the route marked out for me by my researches in natural history, I have seen the most celebrated cities of India: Sasseram, Benares, Mirzapore, Callinger, Kulpy, Agra, Mutra, Bindrabund, and Delhi. Benares and Delhi are the two great Hindoo and Mussulmaun capitals; and I was shown through both with the greatest politeness, by well-informed men. In order that I might see all that could be shown me at Delhi, the political resident made known to the imperial shadow, which the English Government pensions magnificently, his desire to present me to his Majesty; and the old emperor held a *durbar* last Wednesday for the ceremony. You, my dear friend, have no doubt been the victim of this honorific masquerade at Constantinople, and know what virtue it requires not to laugh at one's own face, if one has the ill luck to encounter it in a looking-glass. However, I was created *sahib Bahadur*, or lord victorious in war; which I consider equal to baron. For a hundred louis, I might have been the star of light, or the light of the age, or the abyss of science, &c.

The small retinue of Mohammed Akber Rhazi have a small share of their master's pension of four millions, and live on boiled rice and superb titles.

To-morrow I shall pitch my tent at Panniput, the field in which the fate of India has been so many times altered. Thence I shall enter the country of the independent Seikhs, and proceed to Kithul, where I shall be joined by several obliging persons, who intend getting up a grand lion hunt for me. This is what I could never see with my galloway, my eight servants, my little escort, and my bullocks; but the camp of my amiable huntsman, which I take with me, with my own establishment, which is lost in it, consists of a dozen strong Arab horses, four elephants, which are to be joined by seven others, a multitude of camels, and a hundred domestics and horsemen. From Kithul they will conduct me to the foot of the mountains at the spot where the Ganges falls into the plains. The chief of this not insignificant expedition is almost viceroy of these provinces, under the title of Assistant to the Resident of Delhi; he is therefore a most desirable companion for me. The English are so rich that no obstacle can stop them. I shall find them every where on the first and second *stories* of the mountains. They have gone as far as the other declivity of the Himalaya, and have built two houses there, one of which I count upon occupying for three or four months. On my road I shall have an opportunity of making some fine geological investigations in the thickness of the central chain of the Himalaya, opened by the river Sutledge. An abode of several months in the lofty valley of this river, on the other declivity of the mountains, on a site elevated about ten thousand feet above the sea, ought to offer for my collections of natural history objects, if not varied, at least very new. I shall push my excursions as far as the Chinese frontier. Eleven years ago, one of my Calcutta friends, an engineer officer, went thus far on a geographical expedition, and since several other inquisitive people have followed his steps. But I think I shall be the first of my profession to make this journey. Mr. Moorcroft's notes on the Natural History of the Lake Mansarower are so vague, that they are of no value to science, which will henceforth have greater pretensions. My dear friend,

I promise myself many results from this journey in the Himalaya. The cold, which I do not bear well, has, no doubt, plenty of sufferings in store for me; but I have no mercy on my body, inasmuch as the fatigues to which I expose it cannot radically alter the state of my health. I write a great deal, and yet I find that I do not write enough; but time fails me, though I do not lose any. Since leaving Benares, I have come to an admirable arrangement with my horse; he suffers me to read on his back during the whole journey, provided I do not thwart him in his whims. The *Classicists* in horsemanship would hiss me outrageously if they saw me. The magnificent English, who, in respect to horses, are extremely tenacious, consider this pace very negligent; but as they know the value of time, especially to a traveller of my description, my character as a gentleman does not suffer by it.

19th, Camp at Haberi.

In order to rest, after going fourteen leagues without stopping since the morning, and a laborious day in my tent, with a temperature of 90°, I have just allowed myself, now when I can breathe, the pleasure of re-perusing your letter. My dear friend, I have often thought what you tell me, that it is not so very difficult to speak to men, from the pulpit or the tribune. When the first awkwardness of a novel situation is dispelled,—is not the latter, on the contrary, calculated to inspire talent? There is a certain literary perfection, which is out of season in those two places; it is that which the audience cannot fail to remark and admire. Such speeches are heard and judged exactly as a composition, as a literary exercise; an enormous blunder in those who make them! The English preachers whom I have heard, good or bad, pronounce the *th* so admirably, that they have all the effect to me of teachers of English giving a lesson. The purest delivery is not the best, if it is not the most expressive. Good night: at this moment you are no doubt reading the budget at your fire-side in your little room. My friend, we shall meet there again.

Closed in the Seikh country at Kitkul, without a minute to spare to add a word.

March 22nd.

TO M. JACQUEMONT THE ELDER, PARIS.

Delhi, March 10th, 1830.

My dear father,—Leaving Benares on the 6th of January, I followed the left bank of the Ganges, till I came opposite to Mirzapore, where I crossed the river; and provided with purvannas, (firmans, or local passports) by the magistrate of Mirzapore, (to whom Lord William Bentinck had recommended me,) for the independent rajahs of Boggilcund and Bundlecund, I struck off from the direct road to the Himalaya mountains, and entered those provinces in which I knew I should find much mineralogical and geological interest. I went on to Rewah (W.S.W. from Benares), where I received a polite message from the rajah; thence to Punnah, a place celebrated for its diamond mines; and after wandering about on the lofty platform of Bundlecund for fifteen days, I again descended with considerable trouble above Adjygur, the residence of another rajah. There I was obliged to give my people and cattle some rest, as they were exhausted by their long march across the mountains. A happy chance caused me to find objects full of interest during my short compulsory stay there. Again entering the plains at Callinger, it no longer happened to me to be separated from my baggage, and to bivouac fasting among curious savages, as I was obliged to do several times in the mountains; my little tent has always followed since the 1st of February. At Bandah, a civil and military station, chief town of English Bundlecund, I refreshed my retinue, sent back my escort to Mirzapore, and, being equipped anew, resumed the road to the upper provinces, after only twenty-four hours' halt. I went to Hammerpore, at the conflux of the Betwa and the Jumna, thence to Kalpy, on the right bank of the latter river, which I here crossed to enter the Doab, a territory situated between the two rivers (Dô âb, duo aqua, in Sanscrit) Jumna and Ganges.

The winter had ended on the 1st of February at Banda; the nights had ceased to be cool, the days grew very hot. I continued, however, to travel in the day-time, confiding in my regimen, which I had gradually brought to the simplicity of that of the natives. Some violent thunder storms disconcerted me a little in the Doab. Porphyre knows what rain is, when there is no house to afford shelter. At different distances, an old mosque or a Hindoo temple served as a refuge; but more frequently I only had a tree for shelter, and sometimes stripped of its foliage.

I arrived at Agra on Saturday, the 21st of February. It was the first great Mussulmaun city I had seen; it is full of memorials of the recent grandeur of the family of Timor. I remained there three days, which were days of rest to my people, who stood in great need of it, and of extreme fatigue to me; besides the care I bestowed on my collections, I tired three horses a day. English hospitality is in general admirable. Men overwhelmed with business have been my guides round the different places I have visited; not only did they lend me their elephants, their carriages, their horses, but they always accompanied me. There are several of them to whom I am truly attached, and the recollection of whom will always be very gratifying to me. The numerous and admirable introductions with which I am provided by Lord William Bentinck for his civil proconsuls, by the quarter-master-general of the army, Colonel Fagan, for his brother officers and friends, to whom those of my letters which I have hitherto had occasion to employ have been delivered, have procured me the most flattering reception; and

I must have had very bad luck indeed, not to be convinced in the evening that it was for my own sake I was thus welcomed. I feel and think in my own way, and express myself with *naïveté* in a language which I am always told is correct, but which is sometimes unusual, strange, and often picturesque. This manner immediately forces English stiffness to unbend. I make (*bonnes gens*) Frenchmen of all the English with whom I stay twenty-four hours.

Mutra and Bendrabund are two large Hindoo cities, insulated in the midst of an entirely Mussulmaun country. I saw them both on my way from Agra.

Delhi! Delhi is the most hospitable part of India. Do you know what had well nigh happened to me this morning? I was near being made *the light of the world*, or *the wisdom of the state*, or *the ornament of the country*, &c.; but fortunately I got off with the fear only. The explanation is as follows: you will laugh. The Great Mogul, Shah Mohammed Acbar Rhize Badshah, to whom the political resident had addressed a petition to present me to his majesty, very graciously held a *durbar* (a court) in order to receive me. Being conducted to the audience by the resident, with tolerable pomp, a regiment of infantry, a strong escort of cavalry, an army of domestics and ushers, the whole completed by a troop of richly caparisoned elephants, I presented my respects to the emperor, who was pleased to confer on me a *khelat* or dress of honour, which was put on with great ceremony, under the inspection of the prime minister; and, accoutred like Taddeo in Kaimakan, (if you recollect the Italiana in Algieri,) I re-appeared at court. The emperor then (mark, if you please, that he is descended in a direct line from Timour or Tamerlane) with his imperial hands fastened a couple of jewelled ornaments to my hat (a white one), previously disguised into a turban by his vizier; I kept my countenance excellently well during this imperial farce, seeing there are no looking-glasses in the throne room, and that I could only see in my masquerade my long legs in black pantaloons appearing from under my Turkish dressing-gown. The emperor inquired if there was a king in France, and if English was spoken there. He had never seen a Frenchman, except General Perron, formerly his guard, when he was made prisoner by the Mahrattas; and he appeared to pay infinite attention to the droll figure I cut, with my five feet eight inches * of stature without much thickness, my long hair, spectacles, and my oriental costume over my black dress. In half an hour he dismissed his court, and I retired in procession with the resident. The drums beat in the fields, as I passed before the troops with my dressing-gown of worked muslin. Why were you not present to enjoy the honours conferred upon your progeny?

Of course I found Shah Mohammed Acbar Rhize Badshah, a venerable old man, and the most adorable of

* About six feet two inches, English measure.—Tr.

princes. But, jesting apart, he has a fine face, a fine white beard, and the expression of a man who has been long unhappy. The English have left him all the honours of the throne, and console him with an annual pension of four million francs for the loss of power. Do not tell this to my friends, the local character gentry, and you will see them discover at the carnival in 1833 or 34, that my oriental disguise is very badly imitated; then I will tell them what their so called badly imitated dress really is. The resident translated Victor Jacquemont, travelling naturalist, &c., &c., *Mister Jakmont, saheb bahadur;* which signifies, M. Jacquemont, lord victorious in war: it was thus the grand master of the ceremonies proclaimed me.

This lord victorious in battles is occupied here in any thing but war. He is poisoning with arsenic and mercury the collections which he has formed during the five or six hundred leagues which he has just travelled, and packing them up in order to leave them here during his journey to the Himalaya. There is no want of variety of situations in my wandering life. Here I never go out either in a carriage, a palanquin, or on an elephant, without a brilliant escort of cavalry. This is my host's politeness. I am the sole inhabitant of a sumptuous house, surrounded by magnificent gardens. If I dine out, it is with the general, or another great lord; and I do not decline. Nevertheless, it is probable that I shall spend three months of the summer in a smoky hut, horribly dirty, on the other side of the Himalaya; and God knows how I shall get there from hence, for it is very high and very far. Whatever may occur, reflect that in my past vicissitudes from Calcutta to Delhi, I have not had the slightest indisposition, and (a prosaic circumstance of the first order) I have had the admirable talent of remaining within my estimate of expenses.

Next Saturday the 13th, I shall resume my solitary and perambulatory life. I shall go and encamp fifty leagues from hence to the north-west, in the country of the Seikhs, near a city called Kitkul. The first assistant to the resident will arrive at my camp on the 20th, with an immense escort of men, horses, and elephants; and, joining our unequal fortunes, we shall march together to the place where the Ganges escapes from the mountains. The object of my future companion is to hunt wild hogs and tigers. In order to procure this pleasure, he is going to spend 10,000 francs in a month or six weeks; but he has sixty thousand a year. He is a bachelor about my own age, and destined by his talents to rise to a high station in the country. I shall have one of the best informed companions concerning the things of this country, and the opportunity of seeing and sharing in sports which will naturally turn to the advantage of my collection. Mr. Trevelyan pretends to be infinitely flattered at my allowing him to be my companion. This people will make a coxcomb of me, if you do not think that I am become one already: nevertheless, I do not fall upon them treacherously; I do not tell them that I am rich or noble; I do not put on my cravat better than at Paris; my coat is not in the fashion, and, after nearly two years of existence, eight months' navigation, and a fortnight's submersion after the hurricane at Bourbon, is tolerably rusty. In spite of that, there is no distinction which they do not lavish upon me.

Do not be afraid of the Seikhs; they are crafty thieves, but I am not suffered to go among them without a strong escort. When Mr. Trevelyan unites his little army with mine, we shall travel like conquerors. As for the danger of lion and tiger hunts, I have often put this question:—How many English gentlemen have been eaten, while hunting, since the time of Mr. Hastings? Answer:—Not one.

Panniput, March 17th.

I am writing to you to-day from the field of battle, where the fate of India has been so often decided.

You will perhaps laugh at this celebrity, which is new to you. Panniput, or Lilliput, is, perhaps, all the same to you; but you must change, my dear father, on that point, and become a little of an Indian for my sake. Is not D'Eckstein * at hand to instruct you? I

* *Le Catholique*, a monthly publication, edited at that time by the Baron d'Eckstein, often contained articles on the literature and religion of the Hindoos.

would give you a less sublime introduction to the history of this country; but I know only Mill, and his five enormous volumes would justly frighten you. Well—come—you believe *in me*, if you do not believe me.

The Delhians, with whom you ought to be in love, have conducted me two days' march from their homes. I followed their fashion with a good grace: that is to say, I showed myself as indifferent as they were, to the mishaps of my head and my limbs, while hunting wild boars with them. Fortunately, I met with no fall, which happened solely because they gave me the best Arab out of our whole cavalry. Falls from a horse come immediately after chronic hepatitis and cholera morbus, in the scale of causes of death in this country. A few broken legs, and shattered shoulders, are so much a matter of course in Indian hunting, that none is ever undertaken without a surgeon. As for hunting lions and tigers, it is (for gentlemen mean) a most harmless amusement, since the game is never sought on horseback, but only on an elephant. Each hunter is perched, like a witness in an English court of justice, in a strong and lofty box, fastened upon the animal's back. He has a little park of artillery near him: namely, a couple of carbines and a brace of pistols. It sometimes happens, but very seldom, that the tiger, when brought to bay, leaps on the elephant's head, but that does not concern us; it is the affair of the conductor (mahout), who is paid twenty-five francs a month, to run the risk of such accidents. In case of death, the latter has at least the satisfaction of a complete revenge, for the elephant does not play the clarionet unconcernedly with his trunk, when he feels he has a tiger for his head dress; he does his best, and the hunter assists him, with a ball point blank. The mahout is, you see, a sort of responsible editor. Another poor devil is behind you, whose duty it is to carry a parasol over your head. His condition is still worse than that of the mahout; when the elephant is frightened, and flies from the tiger, which charges him and springs on his back, the true employment of this man is to be eaten in the gentleman's place. India is the Utopia of social order for the aristocracy: in Europe the poor carry the rich upon their shoulders, but it is only metaphorically; here, it is without figure. Instead of workers and consumers, or governed and governors—the subtle distinction of European politics—in India there are only the carried and the carrying, which is much clearer.

In this key I should never finish. I return then to myself. On the eve of my departure from Delhi, the 12th, I received a packet, returned from Loodheeana on the banks of the Sutledge to Runjeet Sing's outposts. It contained a letter from Porphyre (29th July, 1829), a note from you too short to be counted any thing, and a letter from Victor de Tracy. The whole had come to the good governor of Chandernagore, who spares no pains to seize my property wherever he finds it. He will forward this to you through the same channel, and also another, written yesterday, to the Jardin des Plantes.

A Catholic bishop resides at Agra. Although I did not even know his name, I was so much in fashion, that I did not hesitate to send him a very polite note in Italian, to request the favour of seeing him. Confounded by the superlatively Italian politeness of his reply, I hastened to his *palace*. This episcopal palace is a small mosque in ruins, which the government has given up to him. He there lives in great poverty. I found him dining at noon with excellent appetite and a very slender dinner; ruddy, active, jovial, fat, he had the finest face and most splendid gray beard I ever saw. The English, who cannot believe that so poor a priest can be a bishop, content themselves with calling him *padri*, a mangled Portuguese word, which is applied in Hindoostanee to every kind of Christian and Mussulman priest; and the *Monsignore* by which I called him, seemed to delight him the more as I had an English companion with me. The good prelate, without pride or embarrassment, pressed us much to share his dinner; and as we refused, we were forced at least to take wine with him. He confessed that his wine was good for nothing, and told us that the wine of his native village in Tuscany cost fifty times less, and was a hundred times better. I asked him the extent of his diocese—the number of his flock. *La caldaja*, said he, *e molto grande; ma*—

la carne, molto poca. As, in speaking this, he pursued with his iron fork, the remains of a poor fricassee, lost in an immense pewter plate, I found in his reply an *à-propos*, which his Italian pantomime rendered the more expressive, and which made me burst into a fit of laughter. The Englishman, who, by the bye was, a Scotchman and a saint, asked me, *What is it?* seeing the bishop laugh as heartily as I did at the joke. I explained it to him. He did not laugh at all, but on going out, observed to me that it was especially unbecoming in a priest, to speak so of Christian souls.

I have no more chance of meeting Sir Charles Grey in the mountains this summer. He has just been travelling for two months in a palanquin, in the provinces in which I now am, and has seen that part of the mountains which the snow does cover; this will be all he can do. Lady Grey, in the meanwhile, has remained in tedious solitude at Calcutta, where she has not, like her husband, the pastime of judging people. I found I had been announced by Sir Charles Grey at Agra, Mutra, and Delhi; he thus served as my quarter-master general. The Calcutta newspapers, which Lord William Bentinck leaves as free as those in England, have libelled the chief justice terribly for this little gratification of his curiosity. I felt so disposed to become too great an admirer of Lady G——, that it was perhaps better that our fine projects of November last should be reduced to this journey of the knight's.

About the 1st of April I shall be at Hurdwar, a small town situated on the banks of the Ganges, as it issues from the mountain. It is the epoch of a celebrated fair, held every year, where I shall see Chinese, Tibetians, Tartars, Cashmerians, Usbecks, Afghans, Persians, &c. I shall buy warm clothing there, for myself and servants. I shall see three or four people I want; and, as an object of curiosity, the old Begum Sumro, who made war more than sixty years ago on the Mahrattas with the best cavalry of the period in India. It is not very well known whence she comes; however, she is generally considered to have been a slave, brought either from Persia or Georgia. I shall not have to regret not having seen her principality of Serdahna, whither I should not have gone but on her account. The resident of Delhi gave me letters to her. She was married some sixty years ago to an Italian adventurer in the service of Shah-Allum, and has since passed, I know not why, for a Christian and a Catholic. Would she not be a fine match for me, if I was to inherit her sovereignty? I will think about it on my way to Hurdwar.

I shall enter the Himalaya by the valley of Dhoon, above Hurdwar and Sharunpore. Dehra is the chief town. A Major Young *reigns* there, with the title of Assistant to the Resident of Delhi, and Commander of the Mountain Militia. Thence I shall go to Subhatoo, a similar place, the capital of a like establishment; whither I shall also carry numerous letters to its chief, two of which are letters of credit. From Subhatoo, I shall go on to Kotgur, on the second platform of the Himalaya, near the Sutledge; and thence, either by a hanging path, above the precipitous banks of that river, or by a gorge, across the eternal snows of the central chain, I shall cross this chain and enter a little country called Kanawer, politically independent of China; but which, from its geographical position to the north of the Himalaya and its climate, belongs to Tibet. Its productions must be nearly the same as those of Tibet, and for the most part unknown, if not very varied, which its hyperborean winter renders improbable. Captain Herbert, who discovered the way to this country in 1819, is the only man of information who has visited it. He travelled through it merely as a geographer, with a repeating circle and a chronometer. Since then, some inquisitive people have been there empty handed, and have built two houses, one of which I hope to occupy. If any first comers have anticipated me this year, I shall build myself a hut or a shed, or agree with a villager to hire his. Such, my dear father, I suppose will be my abode for four months. I shall live at the height of nine or ten thousand feet above the level of the sea, in a country where the summers are like those of Hungary, and the winters like those of Lapland. The nights, however, will always be cold: eternal snows will shut in every part of my horizon. The principality of Kanawer is independent of the English; but I shall enjoy the same security in these mountains as at Delhi or Calcutta. The last English authority resides at Kotgur. All my letters will be addressed to me there, and the Commandant of Kotgur will forward them to me at Kanawer by express.

Meanwhile, before I go to freeze at such a height, the spring is come to broil me in the plains. It is very fortunate for me that I take with me to Kithual the camp belonging to my Delhi friends. They have immense double, quadruple tents, which I have pitched in advance of me on the road, so as to find a shelter when I arrive at my quarters at ten or eleven in the morning. I must leave off (it is ten o'clock) to lie down under mine, that in which I am writing to you; it will be struck in an instant, taken to pieces, rolled up, packed on camels, and will take the van at midnight; and as I do not set out till four in the morning, I shall find it pitched to-morrow on my arrival. Good night; it blows hard. Oh, what fine things houses are! If you did but know how disagreeable it is to be caught in one's bed like a net, in a tent overturned by the wind! Adieu.

Closed at Kithul, in the Seikh territory.

March 22nd.

TO M. PORPHYRE JACQUEMONT, PARIS.

Camp of Cursali, at the head of the Valley of the Jumna, near its source, 2615 *metres above Calcutta—May* 15*th*, 1830.

It is a very long time since I wrote to you, my good friend; yet I cannot give credit to my journal, which, after "*Chandernagore, the* 21*st of November*, 1829, *a long letter to Porphyre, No.* 2," is silent about you. If I really have not written to you since, I have often thought of you; you have so often accompanied me in my solitude, that I am completely under the illusion of being the most faithful of correspondents. The last letter to our father, No. 10, written at Delhi, travelled with me as far as Kithul, in the country of the independent Seikhs, to the north-west of the English possessions, till the 22nd of March, the day on which it took the road to Delhi, and thence to Calcutta, commencing its long and adventurous journey in the cartouche of a Seikh cavalier, sent forward purposely *en estafette*.

The day after, I mounted my horse at sunrise, with the amiable people to whose good fortune my very slender one was allied for a fortnight, and for three days we galloped enough to kill our horses. Of course, my faithful Persian galloway, notwithstanding his modish appearance, came in fresher than my companions' superb Arabs, each of which cost five or six thousand francs. We found another set of tents; and, before our encampment, the Rajah of Patiala's seventeen elephants, and four hundred horses, drawn up in battle array. An elegant and simple breakfast served up on our arrival, without abating a single useless fork, was quickly despatched; and immediately after we each mounted our elephant. They were polite enough to give me the rajah's, with its royal seat of velvet and tinsel. We placed ourselves in the centre of the chain formed by the multitude of these animals, most of them without riders, or carrying the ministers (wakils) of the neighbouring rajahs deputed to our young friend the sub-resident of Delhi. Our cavalry deployed on the wings of this imposing line; and with the rajah's two drums placed in front beating the royal march, we entered the desert.

It consists of vast, sandy, salt plains, covered with thorny shrubs, interspersed with large trees here and there, or else grassy steppes. There are no obstacles for elephants: they laboriously tear down the trees which they cannot pass, and the branches which would strike the hunter on their back. Being stopped by the forest, our cavalry was sometimes obliged to fall back, and passed afterwards through the large gap which we had opened; where it could act freely, it formed on each side into a semi-circle, which beat the surrounding space at a great distance, and drove all the game in the plain in front of the elephants. Among us six, we killed hares and partridges by hundreds. A hyena and many wild hogs passing under our fire, were wounded *as the hunters say;* for they escaped from our horsemen, who went in pursuit of them. We saw troops of antelopes and nylghaus, but without being able to get within gun-shot of them. Lions, not the shadow of one; but we hoped for the next day, and returned at nightfall to our encampment. I was in raptures with the strangeness of this novel scene. I saw more of the East that day, than during the whole year I had been in India.

On our return, we went to the bath and toilet; the bath was a skin of cold water, which a servant spouts with force over your chest and shoulders; the toilet was the lightest cotton garments; and then dinner in an immense tent, lighted up like a ball room. The bottles fell before us, as the hares and partridges had done in the day-time. I, the only unworthy one, was present at both fêtes; nevertheless I did my best. Water was excluded, the weak-headed and timid drank claret instead—it does not reckon as wine; champagne even is considered only as an agreeable mean proportion between water and wine; this latter name is reserved for the wines of Spain and Portugal. The solid part of the dinner equalled the liquid in elegance and perfection. And in order that nothing might be wanting in the soirée, which lasted till midnight, at the dessert some Persian comedians entered, whose extravagant burlesque obliged us to quit the table and throw ourselves flat on our backs on the carpet, in order to laugh with less danger. These being dismissed, the dancing girls entered; they sing and dance alternately: nothing is more monotonous than their dance, except their singing. This latter is not without art, and they say that the loud tones, which pierce at intervals through a feeble plaintive murmur, which is scarcely heard, please, in a peculiar manner, those who have forgotten the melody and measure of European music. I am not yet Indian enough for that; but their dancing is already to me the most graceful and seducing in the world. The entrechats and the pirouettes of the Opera appear to me like the gambols of the South Sea savages and the stupid stamping of the negroes; it is in the north of Hindoostan, however, that these nautch-girls are the most celebrated.

Next morning, at five o'clock, the maître d'hôtel woke me as on the preceding day, with a large, clear, smoking cup of Mocha coffee, made on purpose *for their French friend.* Ballasted with their cup of tea, *my English friends* were already mounted. We gallopped forward ten leagues, and found, as on the day before, all things and all the people ready on our arrival. During the night, our elephants had brought the set of tents, kitchen apparatus, &c. &c. Our whole camp marched during the cool of the day; and, having rested and taken refreshment, we found after breakfast the same order of battle as the day before. We hunted the whole day in the same manner, began again on the next, and thus continued for a week. At last, after we had beaten all the covers in the country, exhausted and ruined the few villages scattered over it, and worn out the Seikh cavalry, we returned home, taking with us only a troop of cavalry and the elephants which were to serve in the tiger-hunt, at the base of the mountains. The joyous and magnificent company accompanied me as far as Sharunpore, a small town in which the Government maintains a wretched botanical garden. The director of this garden, who is also the physician of the station, was very useful to me. At his house I made my new preparations for travelling, leaving my heavy baggage and my collections, formed since my departure from Delhi, under his care; and taking only what was strictly necessary, I bade farewell to the plains on the 12th of April, two days after the shifting of the monsoon, and the commencement of the south-west winds, which have a temperature of 95° in the day-time, and 92° and 93° at night. I shall go up as far as Dehra in the Dhoon, with cars and bullocks; which I shall there dismiss. I sent back my poor poney to Sharunpore for my botanist's stable (the English have five or six excellent and polite names for our unique and ignoble *bidet*, which I cannot resolve to apply to my horse any longer). In his place, I provided myself with a long and strong bamboo, and after having carefully visited the first platform of the mountains, whilst, in my camp, basket-makers, harness-makers, and workmen of all kinds were making preparations for my journey to places accessible only to man, I ascended the second platform of the Himalaya on the 24th of April. No traveller was ever seen fitted out so plainly as I am. Thirty-six carriers are sufficient for me, at the expense of nearly 400 francs a month: it is true, that I have been able to reduce the number of my servants to five, even although I have added a gardener to them. I have besides an escort of five gorkha soldiers, commanded by a chosen havildar, who perfectly understands how to make my men get on; so that, including myself, my party amounts to twenty-six. You will consider this a royal cortège. Nevertheless I have a very bad dinner every day, deeming myself very fortunate that I have not had to go without it hitherto. It consists of boiled rice, some insipid and tough kid, and water from the next torrent. I drink brandy only at day-break to warm me; a few drops are sufficient. I sleep upon a very hard bed, without a mattrass. My tent is very light: the icy wind, which at night falls from the snowy tops of the mountain, blows through it in gusts, and freezes me in my clothes and under my blankets. Tempests, of a violence and continuance quite unknown before in the mountains at this season of the year, have assailed me since the day which followed my departure. This vein of adversity is not yet exhausted; every day brings at noon a little storm of hail and rain. At Dehra, the lightning struck a tree under which my little tent had been pitched. Two of my people were in it with me, and both were for some instants paralysed in the left side. On the heights of Mossouri, which overhang the valley of Dehra, the space around me was strewed with the splinters of a blasted rock; whilst, chilled with cold and wet, I made my careful and slender repast. It seems in truth that they are aiming at me from above. The two first shots have not touched me; but I must beware of the third.

The influence of elevation entirely effaces here that of the latitude, 31°, on the climate and its productions. I am encamped under a grove of wild apricot trees, which are only just coming into leaf. The carpet of my tent is, without metaphor, enamelled with flowers; they consist of strawberry plants, which are found everywhere here amongst the grass. The wind brings me the smoke of a large fire, around which my mountaineers are sleeping or rather dozing: its odour is agreeable; it is either a cedar or a pine that they are burning. Most of our forest trees, or species so allied to them that a botanist alone can perceive the difference, prevail in the middle zone of the Himalaya, associated with some others which are foreign to us, but which nevertheless have their representatives in the plains of North America.

My sight has certainly grown shorter within the last year: I only take off my spectacles to read and write, and even with them I do not see far enough to make use of my carbine. The range of my gun is just the same as that of my eyes: so I have left my carbine at Sharunpore. You must compliment your comrade of St. Etienne; his arms are excellent.

But in the inventory of my person, this is the only deficiency I feel: a year's residence in the plains has not affected my constitution. I have again found, in the mountains, the legs I had in the Alps. I suffer from cold, just in the same degree that I was formerly incommoded by heat; these contrary extremes only affect my temper, without touching my health. My policy of insurance against cholera, dysentery, and jungle, three great diseases of India, never leaves me; and I think, indeed, I shall not open it till I get to Paris, as I may never be obliged to open it till then:—it is a little box, containing the violent remedies proper for an attack, with an excellent instruction or little treatise on their use, which the cleverest physician in Calcutta was good enough to make for me. When I recollect his attentions, I cannot help retracing the uninterrupted series of kindnesses, and flattering distinctions, which I have not ceased to meet with, since my arrival in this country. They have often almost affected me by their true cordiality. In this respect, nothing has been wanting; old and young, great and small, overwhelm me. The oddest thing of all is, that my fortune has been the same, even among the fashionables. Although I have just travelled seven or eight hundred leagues on horseback, without whip or spur, the officers of the most dashing corps of the English army, in which the major, in order to become lieutenant-colonel, pays 240,000 francs, &c. &c., are my sworn brothers; and when I descend from the mountains, in October or November,

I shall find a relay of horses prepared by their care, to take me in one day, without stopping, from Sharunpore to Meerut, a seven days' march, without any kind of expense (fifty leagues).

It is late; I must bid you good night, my dear friend. Good night, and adieu, for a time. To-morrow I shall go up to the sources of the Jumna: they are, I believe, two thousand metres above this place, the last inhabited part of the valley; which makes six thousand feet, or twelve thousand steps of a staircase a hundred and fifty times the height of ours. Adieu! —adieu!

Camp of Rana, May 20th.

Again under apricot trees, my friend, but two days' march below my last station; and although the height of this still exceeds two thousand metres, the sun is nevertheless very hot now, and I am just arrived, exhausted with fatigue, and sick, from the change of regimen to which I have been forced by necessity in these lofty mountains. For the last six months, the foundation of my breakfast (if my slender repast merits that name), and my dinner, has been rice. Here is nothing but wheat and barley. I thought myself well stocked with my usual provender; and as I have little desire to put my nose into my cook's den of iniquities (I mean the provision basket), I took the blockhead at his word, and a deficiency of rice was soon declared. But my Gorkha havildar, who is my lieutenant-general, by violating the domiciles of the few inhabitants of this lofty valley, found some baskets of potatoes. We had a fine feast; although I ate them with salt, as Bonaparte did artichokes. But if you have your Paul Louis Courier present in your memory, you will recollect that he who was not yet called the Duke of—I know not what—exclaimed, "Great man! admirable in every thing!" Although I relatively am a very great lord, no one paid me the compliment; and the passing from dried to green vegetables had the fatal effect on me which you felt eighteen years ago, on the banks of the Niemen, when walking from precaution, and leading your horse by the bridle. Nevertheless, the weather was very fine; and at the foot of the lofty pinnacles where I was encamped, it was too precious a circumstance not to be immediately taken advantage of. I ascended them twice, at the interval of a day; being stopped on the first occasion by the superstition, and above all by the stupid cowardice of my men, much below the point which I had purposed reaching. I should in the same manner have been thwarted in the object of my second expedition, if, to the first promises encouraging them to follow, I had not added threats of chastisement, to be inflicted on those who refused to march. One only, my gardener, the most stupid and timid of the Hindoos, remained faithful to me. The rest of the band, squatting, in the sun, on a rock which pierced the mantle of snow upon which we had been marching for two hours, became perfectly mutinous, and called to my poor gardener. I did not expect that his fidelity would succumb; and though it is difficult to climb over soft snow, some hundred feet above a certain level, when the rarefaction of the air renders respiration quick and laborious, and exhausts a man at the end of thirty paces, slightly bending my knees, supporting myself with my two hands and my long and strong bamboo, which moderated my velocity as I needed it, when I made it plough up the snow deeper, I darted like a stone upon the rock of revolt, where the bamboo played another part. The traitor whose voice I had recognised calling the gardener paid for all, and very dearly too. The least weakness on my part—a half measure—would have been the most dangerous of all measures. The culprit being besides the most active, the most robust, and habitually the most evil-intentioned of all, I gave it him so heartily on his shoulders from the first that he would not have been able to reply, had he made the attempt. As these poor devils, notwithstanding their piteous and humble condition, are of high caste, and essentially military, I really did not know how the others would take this lesson. Rajpoots, and mountaineers though they are, they took it as true Hindoos; that is, joining their hands, and asking pardon. The one who had been beaten, recovering from his stunning, took the head of the file, holding the end of a long rope, which all the others took in their hands, like a rail, for fear there should be crevices under the snow. Fastened in this way, along with my botanical aide-de-camp, I marched along on the flank of the column like a true shepherd's dog—a toilsome matter in such places—exhausting all the tropes of my Hindoostanee rhetoric to stimulate their fainting spirits. Had it not been for the snow, there is not one of these people who, though loaded with a weight of a hundred pounds, would not travel along the most detestable paths of the mountains, three times as far as I could do in the same time; but they are not used to these deserts of snow. Having left their accustomed roads, and the snow concealing entirely from them the often fatal danger of a false step, their instinct of progression expires before these snowy declivities, which require neither address nor courage, for there is no danger in a fall. I fell down frequently; all I had to do was to shake my clothes. I wished to ascertain the height at which all vegetation ceases. I saw it on the point of expiring; but the delays of my march, and its extreme slowness, obliged me to think of returning before I had reached the last crests of rock which rose above the snow, and which are probably the limit of the vegetable zone. In returning from the country of Kanawer (Kannaur), this opportunity will not be wanting; but I should have liked to have fixed this point in different parts of the central chain of the Himalaya.

Do not blame too much my violence with the people of my escort. Between the hammer and the anvil, between contempt and servile respect, there is no neutral situation possible. You do not thrash people for not calling you "your lordship, your highness, your majesty:" now it is the rule in India for the natives never to address the smallest English gentleman but by these titles, the same which they give to their rajahs, their nawaubs, and the emperor of Delhi. An ill-tempered fellow on the road having called me *you* this morning instead of *your highness*, I was forced to give him a very severe lesson in politeness. I had fully as much right to do so as the Parisian philanthropist would have in boxing the ears of a rustic for *thee* and *thouing* him. I ought to be the more jealous about etiquette, as the simplicity of my equipment, the hard life I lead, the privations and fatigues I endure along with my people, my dress of common stuff proper for this kind of life, and every thing in me and around me, tempts them to depart from it. "My lord," therefore, is not sufficient for me; I must have "your majesty," or, at least, "your highness."

. You would undoubtedly laugh at his majesty, if you were to appear before him, in his dress of white bear's skin and long mustachios, an ornament which has a very imposing effect on the scarcely-bearded people of the Himalaya. Fortunately I have no looking-glass to settle the question, and I figure to myself that the reddish reflection, which I perceive on looking down, is only the effect of a false light.

In more than one disagreeable respect, my dear Porphyre, my little misfortunes follow your miseries in

Moscow at a respectful distance. The horrible dirtiness of the mountaineers, against which I cannot defend myself, is one of the evils to which I have the greatest difficulty in submitting. I hope I shall not grow used to it. The storm has just moderated the heat. A military therapeutic experiment has had full success. A burning infusion of the tea-pot, for want of tea, edulcorated with equal parts of brandy, set me on my feet again. They are bringing me a kid at last to interrupt my Brahminical diet; in the style of the *Constitutionnel*, the clouds which were covering, &c. &c. are dissipated, and I catch sight of the dawn of a curry on the fire, that is with red pepper, absolutely uneatable for a Parisian, although but little burning to me, and which will completely replace me in my saddle: without it, I should have been dismounted.

This (evil be to him that evil thinks) reminds me of a pharmaceutical episode (in this very modest country I know not what decent name to give it) of my journey among the Seikhs. One morning I was awakened by the cry of "thieves!" Day was hardly breaking, after a dark night. Servants, soldiers, horse and foot, were all aroused. A robber had slipped into my tent, which is very small, by making a large entry with his sword, and passing under my bed, which is very low, stole at random from amongst the objects lying on the ground. My pistols and watch were almost in his way; but, disturbed in his operations, no doubt, by some noise or false alarm, he had not time to choose, and escaped, carrying away with him what was under his hand, namely, my powder flask and shaving apparatus; then, disturbed in his flight, he abandoned the least precious of his booty, the razor strop, shaving box, a phial of nitric acid, &c. &c. These articles were found on the road to the neighbouring village. The shining of the pewter in the twilight made the Seikh believe that he had stolen some precious vessel; whereas he had only taken ———. The plenipotentiaries of the Seikh rajahs immediately waited upon me to request the value and description of the stolen articles, in order to cause them to be sought for everywhere, and to restore the price, in case of ill success, at the expense of the freeholders of the place. As they understood but ill my description of the one I most regretted, I illustrated it with a drawing of the natural size, and prepared to make copies of this *signalment* for distribution among the inquirers, when my English friends came up at the noise. My drawing threw them into consternation; they blushed to the white of their eyes, and were heartily vexed with me, that having the unfortunate custom of using a ———, I did not take more care to keep it secret. I told them gravely that it was a matter of life and death to me. — "Ah, death a thousand times over rather than keep one," they exclaimed altogether. "No!" I replied, "a thousand ——— rather than a single headach?" Then followed a serious eulogium of that admirable remedy, and a medical satire of calomel, jalap, &c. which the English have the folly to consider its efficacious equivalents. My speech was no doubt eloquent; for the rajah himself was immediately written to, to request him to rummage all the huts, and beat all the bushes of his paltry empire, to find the stolen article, and, if they chanced to recover it, to send it to me under a good escort, at whatever place I might happen to be. I do not despair seeing a party of Seikh cavalry bring it back to me to Paris, in a few years, on a velvet cushion. Meanwhile my English friends, reconciled to the reason of the thing, had the politeness to overcome their scruples, and to send messengers in search of a substitute to the directors of the neighbouring military hospitals. They succeeded in procuring me one, which I suppose to be of a venerable antiquity, and the first attempt of the kind. Our father and you would both laugh at it. The noise of this accident has given me the most perfect reputation, not of immorality precisely, but as a freethinker, passing into cynicism. Adieu, dear Porphyre; I was quite melancholy when I came to you, exhausted and ill: and now punch and this gossip with you have revived me, and almost made me merry. I leave you to do honour to my aforesaid English friends. In my isolated situation, and in this remote spot, I feel the inestimable value of health, and I take every care of it that circumstances will allow. Rely on my prudence, moderation, and address; rely also on my honour (for there is something else besides good management in it) to see me return some day without the loss of a hair. Adieu.

Encampment in a forest below the summit of Kedar-Kanta, May 27th, evening, at the height of 3200 metres.

You are the sole confidant of my sufferings, my poor friend; since it is you who hear all my complaints. I was well enough to continue my march, trusting that my return to my habitual regimen would completely cure me; and, having arrived yesterday at the head of the valley of the Boddiar, I left this morning its highest habitations to come and encamp in this solitude, in order to climb the neighbouring peaks to-morrow, and pass to the other side, into a valley parallel with this. I arrived, overcome with fatigue, after a march of only seven hours. Nevertheless I had collected ample material for work, and set to without delay—besides, my bed is so hard that I rest as well in my chair—but on a sudden I was seized with such excruciating pains in my bowels that I became almost delirious. The spot was ill chosen for sickness: behind me the nearest habitations are seven hours' march, before me two days', and my people have only provisions enough for this interval: so that I must either advance or go back; and for what purpose? This is the reverse of the medal:—on the side of health it is magnificent; but on the side of illness it is very bad, and there is not a woman who cannot bear acute suffering better than I can.

I scarcely know it except by very rare cramps, a fit of fever eight years ago, and my suffering of to-day; and the idea has always come to me to make an end of it, to get rid of the evil at once by strict diet. What my legs will be to-morrow I know not. But night brings counsel—and it is come. Adieu, then; it is so cold and wet in my tent, that from prudence I leave you, in order to put my bed-clothes between its atmosphere and myself. The scoundrels of Seikhs are perhaps the cause of my indisposition. Good night. Oh, how happy you are to live in a house.

June 4th, Camp of Adjalta.

Quite alive, I assure you. If I was paid at the rate of six thousand francs for that (and would to God I was so) I would explain to you in the most satisfactory manner how, by the influence of air and water, from being ill as I was, I am restored to health; but the fact is, without having a single day of perfect rest, I am now the best in condition of my whole caravan. Such is the state of the case—for there is not a day passes that I have not to ascend and descend twelve or fifteen hundred metres, without reckoning parentheses. I have substituted milk for water as my beverage, and I drink two bottles of it without scruple every evening at my dinner. It is a sort of antidote to the essence of fire, which forms the sauce of my eternal curry. It costs me three sous a day more, and a little of the arbitrary. I ascend to the mountain in search of cows, (observe, that to-day I am encamped at the height of two thousand three hundred metres—yesterday I was two thousand six hundred) and before the door of my tent a dozen are brought to obtain this small quantity of milk. I pay magnificently—three sous did I say?—it is half as much again as it is worth; but they must make haste, and the arrival of the milk coincides with the last touch of my cook. Nothing, besides, is so easy as to be arbitrary when one has only to say, like Monsieur de Foucauld, *seize him!*—I imitate him with a wonderful word of the Hindoostanee jargon, before which the *seize him* turns pale—*pacarau!* and my Gorkha seapoys would seize the devil and Monsieur de Foucauld himself. Besides the people in this country seem to think there is a degree of honour in being so treated. Those you want do not stir from home unless you despatch a soldier to them in form. What a useful thing arbitrary rule is; but what a villanous country, that which requires it! I cannot think of my own country without experiencing a feeling of admiration and affection.

Semla, June 22nd, 1833.

I have just, my dear friend, given my father such a broadside of writing, that, unless I quit the subject of my own affairs, I am at the end of my news: since the essential is told, let me amuse myself. I have been disagreeable enough with you in the preceding pages.

So you too, my dear Porphyre, are in love with the Afghans; and, not content with this, also with the

Kabulians, Kandaharians, and others, after the fashion of Messrs. of the *Courrier* & Co. Oh! oh! No one is a prophet in his own country.

Those two heroes, the two brothers, Mohammed Khan and Purdile Khan, have no more effect at Delhi than the Duke of Saxe-Schwerin, or of Anhalt-Cobalt, who may, however, be very great princes, but incognito.

Know that the Company's army consists of three hundred thousand men; thirty thousand of which are king's troops, seven or eight thousand entirely European corps in the Company's service, such as almost the whole artillery, and, lastly, the native army is commanded by numerous European officers and non-commissioned officers: it is disciplined and drilled as well as the king's army, dressed like it, fights very nearly equal to it, and is commanded by officers in whom it has the greatest and justest confidence;—that in a country like this, intersected by deserts, and in which the richest provinces, with the exception of Bengal, which is extremely distant from Erzeroum, could not support the smallest army, the smallest body of troops, in order not to die of hunger, and often of thirst, would have to drag along with it an immense number of elephants, camels, and wagons;—that the company has three thousand elephants, forty thousand camels, and *materiel* of all kinds and proportion;—that it is always ready to take the field;—and ask yourself if, from this place Semla, at a distance of seven leagues from Runjeet-Sing, I have not reason to scoff at him indefinitely, *quand même;* as well as at all the Afghans, Kandaharians, Kabulians, the brothers Mohammed and Purdile, the *heroes*, and lastly at all the varieties of vagabonds, brigands, and mendicants, both horse and foot, who flourish on the right bank of the Indus.

If you can find a discreet and inoffensive mode of insinuating this information, tell Messrs. of the *Courrier* not to believe easily in heroes, which are a sort of animal more rare in this country than elsewhere, and in general exotic everywhere.

If I had more money, I would go to Cashmere, which belongs to Runjeet-Sing. The Resident of Delhi, whom I would request to ask a passport of him, would write immediately to him for that purpose, and would receive forthwith the desired firman. Perhaps it is not to be regretted that pecuniary prudence interdicts so interesting a journey, because Runjeet-Sing may die one of these days. He is not young; and on the day of his death there will be war between his two sons; and a pacific naturalist is sure of being pillaged, if not worse—how shall I say it?—the Seikhs are such Turks in that respect.

M. Allard is quite the Soliman Bey of Runjeet-Sing. He comes from time to time to Loodeeana (on the banks of the Sutledge) to visit the English officers on that station, one established beyond the Company's territory, among the independent Seikhs, in the dominions of my friend the Rajah of Pattiala, who has not yet sent me back my syringe. He is well paid (a hundred thousand francs, like a general officer on this side the river), but he is half a prisoner. Runjeet-Sing takes great care to make him spend the whole of his income every year, in order to take away all desire of leaving him. He pursues the same policy with regard to his other European officers, upon whom he only half relies. A Mr. Mevius, a Prussian, commander of one of his regiments of cavalry, having very lately excited a revolt in his corps, by the application of the German procedure of the whip to his Seikhs, was obliged to take refuge in the tent of the king himself (Runjeet-Sing) to escape the fury of his men. Runjeet saved his life, but refused to retain him in his service; upon this, sharp words ensued upon both sides, and at last Runjeet, dismissing him, exclaimed with an oath: "Germans, Frenchmen, Englishmen, those —— are all the same!"

I ought to have left an enormous blank for the oath, which is very short in Hindoostanee, but so energetic that it would require a whole line to express it in French.

The English Government has every interest in Runjeet's preserving his sovereignty. Before the establishment of his power, parties of cavalry used constantly to pass the Sutledge, and pillage the independent Seikhs on the left bank, the friends and protégés of the Company. These it was necessary to succour; and, unless the fugitive aggressors were pursued on the other side of the river, no satisfaction or reparation was possible: the petty princes of the Punjab being too weak to be responsible for the robberies committed by their subjects. If such a thing was to happen now-a-days, the political Resident at Delhi would send Runjeet an apothecary's bill, with an immediate demand of the value of the crops and cattle plundered, and moreover a respectable number of the culprits, in order to have them hanged with all due ceremony. Runjeet would care very little for their hanging, but the payment of the rupees would concern him much; he therefore takes care that nothing of the kind shall happen. There has been no example of it since the establishment of his authority.

Although my host is the political agent who exercises his control over the only Tartar and Tibetian states to which the English power extends, we have never heard of the anonymous savant who is travelling in Tibet with an escort of twelve hundred cossacks, and other mounted *canaille* of the same kind*. The twelve hundred horses of these twelve hundred cossacks would run a great chance of starving in the part of Tibet which extends to the foot of the Himalaya on the northern side. I am not without some fear as to the means of feeding the only steed which I reckon upon the pleasure of riding in Kanawer.

* Jacquemont here contradicts an article in a French paper, concerning which his brother had questioned him.

My artilleryman, with his thousand foot Gorkhas, is so much the master of these mountains, that, during the last nine years since his arrival, he has not had occasion to resort to force. He deposes the kings in the neighbourhood when they kill too many of their subjects. He imprisons and fines them: he has only to give information to the Resident of Delhi, under whose orders he is politically placed. The Hindoo Tartar rajah of Bissahir takes great care to inform him of all that passes on the other side of the mountains where he resides, and I have reason to believe that the savant in question, with his twelve hundred cossacks, must have stopped some months' march from this frontier.

You appear to me to be pretty confident about the Afghans, and you commence with a very pleasant reflection about a pie; to which I am happy to be able to answer that I have the prospect of eating here in four months a *Strasburg pâté de foie gras*, and also a *Perigord pâté de foie gras*, which are not inferior to the *Boulogne pâté de becasses* in their finest season. The Bordeaux vessels bring them every year to Calcutta, where they arrive as fresh as at Paris; and your colleague the artilleryman, my host at present, has just written to the capital, in order that he may regale me with both at our next meeting. Since we are talking of pies, I will tell you that upon the peaks of Mossouri, in the mountains of the Himalaya, another artilleryman, a general, a grey-haired old bachelor, whom you would love to distraction if you knew him, made me taste—taste! I devoured a *pâté de lièvre truffé* and a quantity of *Perigord pâtés de perdrix-rouges truffées.* The proceeding of both is very simple; the one on account of his high rank in the army, and the other on account of his office, have an income of a hundred thousand francs, which diminishes distances in a singular manner, and exercises the action of a sucking-pump on all the good things of Europe, raising them to a height of seven or eight thousand feet above the level of the sea. Why are you not the captain of artillery *aux pâtés de foie gras?* In your absence, know, however, my friend, that the treacherous islander, your compeer, drank your health yesterday with me, and (do not tell our father or Taschereau) that it was not with *vin de Tours.*

June 25th.

I close this packet with announcing to you that I set out the day after to-morrow for Kanawer. Adieu.

TO M. JACQUEMONT, THE ELDER, PARIS.

Semlah, Semla, Simla, Simlah, ad libitum, June 21st, 1830.

My last letters were addressed to you, the one from Benares, called in my memorandum *enormous;* the latter was commenced at Delhi and closed at Kithul, in the Seikh country, on the 22d of March. Under the same cover as this, Porphyre will receive a sort of journal of my march from Kithul to the centre of the Himalaya, which almost dispenses with my mentioning it to you.

This place, like Mont-d'or or Bagnères, is the resort of the rich, the idle, and the invalid. The officer charged with the military, political, judicial, and financial service of this extremity of the British empire, which was acquired only fifteen years ago, bethought himself, nine years ago, of leaving his palace in the plain during the heats of a terrible summer, and coming and encamping under the shade of the cedars. He was alone in the desert; some friends came to visit him there. The situation, and climate, appeared admirable to them. Some hundreds of mountaineers were summoned, who felled the trees around, squared them rudely, and, assisted by workmen from the plains, in one month constructed a spacious house. Each of the guests wished also to have one; and now there are upwards of sixty scattered over the peaks of the mountains or on their declivities. Thus a considerable village has risen, as it were, by enchantment. In the centre of the space which they occupy, splendid roads have been cut through the rock; and at a distance of seven hundred leagues from Calcutta, and seven thousand feet above the level of the sea, the luxury of the Indian capital has established itself, and fashion maintains its tyrannical sway.

Porphyre has a right to be jealous of my host. He is

an artillery captain of his own age, and, like him, of long standing in his rank. He has a hundred thousand francs a year, and commands a regiment of Highland chasseurs, the best corps in the army. He performs the duties of receiver-general, and judges with the same independence as the Grand Turk, his own subjects, and moreover those of the neighbouring Rajahs, Hindoos, Tartars, Tibetans; these he imprisons, fines, and even hangs when he thinks proper.

This first of all artillery captains in the world is an amiable bachelor, whom the duties of his viceroyalty occupy for one hour after breakfast, and who passes the rest of his time in loading me with kindness. He had expected me for a month past; some mutual friends having informed him of my design of visiting Semla. He passes for the stiffest of dandies, the most formal and vainest of the princes of the earth! I find nothing of all this; it is impossible to be a better fellow. We gallop an hour or two in the morning on the magnificent roads which he has constructed, often joining some elegant cavalcade, among which I meet some of my Calcutta acquaintance. On our return we have an elegant and *recherché* breakfast; then I have the entire and free disposal of my day, and that of my host, whenever I think proper to put it in requisition, to view men and things. At sun-set fresh horses are to the door, and we take another ride, to beat up the most friendly and lively of the rich idlers and imaginary invalids whom we may chance to meet. They are people of the same kind as my host, bachelors and soldiers, but soldiers employed in all kinds of departments: the most interesting people in India to me. We sit down to a magnificent dinner at half-past seven, and rise at eleven. I drink hock, claret, and champagne only, and at dessert Malmsey; the others, alleging the coldness of the climate, stick to port, sherry, and Madeira. I do not recollect having tasted water for the last seven days; nevertheless there is no excess, but great cheerfulness every evening. I cannot tell you how delightful this appears to me, after the dryness, insipidity, hardness, and brevity of my solitary dinners, during two months in the mountains. And I have not one arrear to pay off. Having the approaching prospect of four months of misery on the other side of the Himalaya, I revenge myself by anticipation. I arrived here so much exhausted by fatigue and the consequences of an obstinate indisposition, that I thought I would avail myself of the period of my stay, to recruit my health; but my host's cook cured me in four and twenty hours.

Do you not see Semla on your map? A little to the north of the 31° of latitude, a little to the east of the 77° of longitude, some leagues from the Sutledge. Is it not curious to dine in silk stockings at such a place, and to drink a bottle of hock and another of champagne every evening—delicious Mocha coffee—and to receive the Calcutta journals every morning?

The king of Bissahir's vizier, whose master is the greatest of my host's allies, is here at present; Captain

Kennedy (that is my artilleryman's name) has introduced us to each other; and I am assured of receiving all sorts of attention at the other side of the Himalaya.

One of his officers will follow me everywhere, and I shall take with me from hence a couple of Ghorka carabiniers belonging to my host's regiment, the most active and clever of them, and one of his *tchourassis* (a sort of usher or janissary) who has already visited that country, having gone thither with his master some years ago.

The people on this side the mountains are horribly afraid of their neighbours on the other. It is rather difficult to procure porters for the baggage, and constitutionally it would be impossible to make a single domestic follow one thither; but Captain Kennedy has obligingly offered to imprison any of mine who refuse to accompany me; and although they declare that they prefer being hanged on this side the mountains to being free in Kanawer, I think that by availing myself, in one or two instances, of my host's kindness, I shall make the rest decide upon following me. What the simpletons fear I know not:—but it is no longer India on the other side; there are no more castes; instead of Brahmins there are Lamas. Besides, in my suite there will be perfect safety. The rajah of Bissahir knows very well, that if any harm happened to me he would suffer for it, and he will take great care of the *francis saheb, captânne Kindi sahebké dôste,* which means "the French lord, friend of the great General Kennedy."

June 22nd.

Yesterday was the solstice, and the periodical rains, which that period brings, invade all the southern slopes of the Himalaya, notwithstanding their distance from the tropic. It is already several days since this disagreeable change of weather took place; I can scarcely see sufficiently to write, so thick are the moist clouds in which we are inclosed. Nevertheless I shall be obliged to march a fortnight before I reach the Tibetian valleys, where it never rains. It will be the worst part of my journey.

A few lines in answer to your two letters. I cannot help smiling at your fears, arising from the news of an insurrection of the Company's troops at the time of my arrival in India. What must you not have thought, when you saw the *Half Batta* affair in the English papers! You must have believed the army to have been in full mutiny, and Lord William Bentinck compelled to embark for Europe, with his council—the natives availing themselves of the quarrel among Europeans, and arming on all sides against them.—Now to me this monstrous ignorance of Asiatic affairs in Europe is the height of the unimaginable, for an enormous mass of correspondence is constantly exchanged between the two countries; the fluctuation of travellers between them is no less so; and, lastly, though the Government of India is despotic on principle, and ought to be so, it is in fact as free as any other in Europe. There is no preventive censorship exercised against periodicals, which are numerous; first, *at Calcutta—John Bull;* second, *the Hurkuru, (which means in Hindoostan the Messenger);* third, *the East India Gazette; the Government Gazette; Literary Gazette,* &c. &c. without mentioning the journals published in Bengalee and Hindoostanee language. From the contradictory reports of these different papers, nothing would be more easy, it seems to me, than to deduce the true state of affairs: all of them go to England, and yet the mass of the English public is as ignorant of India as we are in France. Some of the little newspaper scraps which you sent me, to inform me that the Afghans had sent an embassy to the Russian general at Erzeroum, and that the king of Lahore, Runjeet-Sing, was inclined towards the Russians, have excited the mirth of my Indian friends. Here we are precisely a day's march from Runjeet-Sing, and in five days we can see a considerable part of his dominions:—now he is as supremely indifferent to us as the emperor of Japan. The forces maintained by the Company on the north-west frontier, at Delhi, Kurnal, Meerut, Agra, Mutra, and Loodeeana, would be sufficient to invade the whole of the Punjab without any movement of troops in the interior of India. Runjeet-Sing might risk a battle behind his actual line of defence, the Sutledge, and he would afford the English a precious opportunity of annihilating him in half an hour. As for the Afghans, "a warlike nation," says your estimable journal, "which has so many times invaded India, and can bring thirty thousand cavalry into the field," this is a little too much: the days of Mahmood, and Ghirni, and Timour, are past. The Afghans are very inferior to the Seikhs, and, at most, just strong enough to do battle from time to time with Runjeet-Sing.

This latter disciplines his little army in the European fashion, and almost all his officers are Frenchmen. Their chief is one M. Allard, of whom a great deal of good is said on this side the Sutledge. A month ago, three young French officers, one of whom is a younger brother of M. Allard, passed through this place on their way from Calcutta to enter Runjeet-Sing's service. Not only did the local government allow them free passage, but they also received many attentions on their long journey. Lord William Bentinck regrets that the Russians were blockheads enough not to take Constantinople; and, though they were to occupy the whole of the Turkish empire, he would not feel himself in less security at Calcutta, or even at Delhi or Semla, than he does at present.

In order to maintain his little army (from thirty to forty thousand men) on a European footing, Runjeet-Sing is obliged to grind his country with imposts, which are ruining it. Several of his provinces are calling for the English; and I do not doubt that some day or other (but not for some years) the Company will extend the limits of its empire from the Sutledge to the Indus. It is not a hundred years since the Punjab was dismembered from it, after the invasion of Nadir Shah, and it naturally forms a part of it: the religion is nearly the same, the language also scarcely differs; and the course of the seasons is the same. But the English will make this conquest only at the last extremity. All that they have added to their territory for the last fifty years beyond Bengal and Bahar, beyond the empire which Colonel Clive had formed, has only diminished their revenues. Not one of the acquired provinces pays the expenses of its government and military occupation. The Madras presidency, taken in the lump, is annually deficient; Bombay is still further from covering its expenses. It is the revenue of Bengal and Bahar, principally of the former, which, after making up the deficiency of the north-west provinces recently annexed to the presidency of Calcutta, Bundlecund, Agra, Delhi, &c., sets the finances of the two secondary states afloat. In France, we consider a hypocritical farce, the excuse of *necessity* alleged by the English for the prodigious aggrandisement of their Asiatic dominions: nothing, however, is more true; and certainly no European Government was ever more faithful to its engagements than that of the Company.

Your map, in four sheets, is not the same as mine. But I know it is a very good one; and you will be able to follow me step by step, except in the mountains. Since you love this country for my sake, and desire to become acquainted with it, summon all your courage, and ask at the Library of the Institute, or at the

Royal Library, for the five octavo volumes of Mill's History of India. It is beyond all comparison the best work on that country. Perhaps the two quarto volumes of Dr. Heber, the late Bishop of Calcutta, might amuse you more, but they would give you very little information: *it is regular milk and water!* Those parts of the Deccan left blank in the map, and marked *unexplored countries*, annoy you. You are afraid that I should have to cross them. Be of good cheer. Should it so happen, I shall take a strong escort; besides, the danger to be encountered there is that of dying of hunger and thirst, or of atonic fevers, rather than that of being attacked by parties of marauders. But there is no interest in visiting them. They are deserts without water, covered with wretched forests, through which a few hovels are scattered at great distances. I saw a good specimen between Rogonatpore and Sheergottee, in the beginning of my journey. In many parts of India every one is certain of death who passes through those terrible places between September and January; and the danger is the same to the natives as to Europeans. Rely on my prudence, and my complete submission to the exigencies of places and seasons.

The learned or literary societies of the United States are about on a par with those of India. As societies, the latter are below every thing that can be conceived in ignorance, folly, and puerility. However, there are necessarily some men of merit in each; in that of

Calcutta particularly, Horace Wilson, for instance, the first Sanscrit scholar in the world, a linguist, literary savant, and poet, at the same time. Read his Hindoo Theatre: this book cannot be wanting at the Royal Library. I wrote yesterday to my old host, Sir Edward Ryan, and my amiable neighbour, Sir Charles Grey, chief justice of India, and explained to the latter why I sent no memoir to the Asiatic Society of Calcutta. I concluded my chapter of grievances against it with the very circumstance of his being the president without having any title to be even a member, and as a proof that the society itself is absurd. The very great talents of Sir C. Grey will find employment in politics. His short hours of leisure are for European literature; and he cares as little for the history and antiquities of this country as you do. I have the same contempt for them. The Sanscrit will lead to nothing but Sanscrit. The mechanism of this language is wonderfully complicated, and nevertheless they say it is admirable. But it is like one of those machines which never issue from museums, and are more ingenious than useful. It has served only for the manufacture of theology, metaphysics, history intermixed with theology, and other stuff of the same kind: triple nonsense for the makers and the consumers; and for foreign consumers especially—nonsense = $\frac{1}{0}$. The Arabic is not exempt from these evils. The allegorical mysticism of the Orientals has penetrated even into the elementary notions which they have acquired of the physical and mathematical sciences; and the Trinity, translated into good French, is not so clear but that the interference of Brahminic fables with the planetary motions and principles of physics, complicates the understanding of it with singular difficulties.

The fashion of Sanscrit and literary Orientalism in general will last, nevertheless; for those who may have spent or lost fifteen or twenty years in learning the Arabic or the Sanscrit, will not have the candour to allow that they possess a useless piece of knowledge. D'Eckstein is, I think, very right to go on as if he understood them; and the trash which he gives, *se non e vero e ben trovato.* Try some of Schlegel, who is honest and conscientious, and see if there is much difference. Try some of Cousin. Have not the absurd at Benares and those in Germany a family likeness?

Let us go on to your second letter. Here come back your Afghans—then the probable war between England and Russia, occasioned by the latter's hostile designs upon India; the sedition of the Indian army: —all this is broad farce at Semla. Porphyre's moustaches are something new; but I flatter myself that mine owe them nothing. They are an ornament which ecclesiastics almost alone, in the north of India, dispense with, and which is particularly appropriate to the country in which I am now travelling.

I am much surprised that the *Jardin* had not

received a letter from me on the 9th November, 1829, the date of your letter, as I wrote to those gentlemen from the Cape of Good Hope, on the 27th December, 1828, by Captain D'Urville, who arrived in France in the month of March or April, 1829. I also wrote to them from Bourbon after the hurricane; and I have already received news of other letters, written at the same time and intrusted to the same ship, having reached Europe. What astonishes me no less is their silence respecting me. I wrote to them from Kithul, and I also write to them to-day, that, my credits expiring in the year 1831 inclusive, if new ones do not soon arrive for the year following, and supplementary ones for the present year, to enable me to carry on to the next, I shall be obliged to start for Europe from Bombay by the shortest and least expensive route. Whatever may happen, do not be any thing more than vexed at it; but entertain no fear that I shall allow myself imprudently to be cast on the shores of India, by the unforeseen retreat of the wave which has carried me thither. My confidence being restored in that respect, I do not suffer myself to be turned from my present studies by any uneasiness as to the future.

What need had you of the testimony of V—— to be convinced of the extravagant absurdity of a scientific journey into equinoctial America? Mexico in particular? One had need be French, to be so completely ignorant of external affairs. M. de Humboldt was very fortunate in the period which he fixed upon to make his great journey; and the social confusion of the countries which he visited is a literary god-send for him, since he drives away new observers, and restores a sort of monopoly for his works on America. Besides he had to describe the finest part of the world.

With regard to the picturesque, India is very poorly gifted. Can it be, I have sometimes asked myself, that the source of admiration in me is exhausted? I have passionately admired the scenes of nature at St. Domingo, and afterwards in Brazil. The evil is not in me; the fault is in the objects in the country.

The English papers are filled with the complaints of all Europe about the excessive cold of the winter. I am more disturbed about it on your account, than by the changes of the ministry on account of the prosperity of our native country. I think there is no Government capable of doing much harm in France henceforth. The "Association Bretonne" was invented, nearly two hundred years ago, by Hampden. The invention will remain with the English. Its adoption among us appears to me, as well as to you, a revolution, if it is adhered to.

A letter by M. Jomard, translated into the English journals, informs us that the Pacha of Egypt has availed himself of Courier's advice to the King of Spain, and given himself the productive amusement of a little puppet of a representation. But I am afraid he will scandalise our liberal friends, by shooting from time to time some of the members of the opposition, unless he associates with them some rivals of the counter-opposition, in order to prevent jealousy. However, this is the way to begin: and until Bolivar becomes a king, or, remaining president (never mind the name), shall have the power of acting in this way, every one will kill his neighbour, according to his own convenience. This right must be limited to a single person; and though he should be half mad, like Christophe, public order would still gain by the immoderate and often absurd manner in which he might exercise it.

I thank you for M. Humboldt's letter to M. Arago, and for the report of the labours of Beaumont.

I leave here, with my regal artilleryman, all the collection which I have formed since my entrance into the mountains; and I shall leave him, in a couple of days, to proceed by Kotgur, Rampore, and Seran, along the banks of the Sutledge, through one of the hottest valleys in India. I shall be carried in a sort of arm-chair. At Seran, the summer residence of the Rajah of Bissahir, I shall re-enter the mountains, where I shall dismiss my porters, and probably substitute in their place a *ghounte*, or mountain horse, of wonderful strength and activity, though of small size. My suite will then be reduced to fifty persons, at an expense of seven or eight hundred francs a month, and it is only by reducing my personal baggage to what is strictly necessary (and in truth, all that is necessary is not among it), that I can proceed with so few people. In the autumn, I shall return by the Barunda Pass, over the central chain of the Himalaya, either to this place, or directly to Subhatoo (Sabatoo, Subatoo), Captain Kennedy's winter residence, if he be already come down to it, sending my baggage on before me; and from Subhatoo to Sharunpore, without the mountains, where I shall reinstate my travelling establishment for the plains. I have left a considerable part of my baggage and collections there. The whole will be despatched to Delhi, which I have constituted my first depot; and when I see my wagons start for Sharunpore, instead of marching slowly after them, to bring up the file, across a province entirely destitute of interest, I shall gallop in a single day to Meerut, where I shall rest for several days from fatigues, privations, and miseries of all kinds, which I shall have experienced. I do not know Meerut; but I have a number of acquaintances, almost friends, there. Perhaps I shall have some leisure in Kanawer, and may find an opportunity of writing to you; however, that is not probable. Expect, therefore, a long interval of silence after this. Long as it may last, be assured I shall then be in a country as salubrious as Europe, eating apples and grapes, drinking the wine of the country, which is execrable, and lastly,

> Sachez, sachez,
> Que les Tartares,
> Ne sont barbares,
> Qu'avec leurs ennemis.

Adieu, adieu; I love you and embrace you with all my heart.

TO M. VICTOR DE TRACY, PARIS.

Semla in the Himalaya, June 23rd, 1830.

My last letter, my dear friend, was addressed to you from Kithul, in the country of the Seikhs, dated the 2nd March. For a fortnight I was running after lions there, which we went in search of nearly to the edge of the desert of Bikaneer, but we did not so much as catch sight of one. In this short space of time, deducting the lions, I saw more of the East than in the whole year which had elapsed since my arrival in India.

On the 12th April I entered the lower valleys of the Himalaya, and on the 23rd I ascended the peaks of the secondary chain. In the midst of the extreme disorder of the often very lofty mountains, which cover so large a space to the south of the line of its eternal snows, I proceeded as far as those above the sources of the Jumna. I also approached those of the Ganges. Thence, by the most tortuous paths, I came hither, near the banks of the Sutledge, but six thousand feet above its waters.

For two months, I have been living among the wildest and most desolate scenes of the north of the Upper Alps, and under their inclement sky. I have had many fatigues and privations to suffer; but I think myself sufficiently rewarded by the interesting nature of all that I have seen. It is a purely scientific interest: the landscape is poor and monotonous. In the highest mountains in the world there is necessarily grandeur; but it is grandeur without beauty.

My health has suffered a little from the want of some articles most necessary to life. The numerous suite, with which I cannot dispense in a country inaccessible to beasts of burthen, and where all my baggage must be carried on men's backs, does not permit me to remain in any village to take the rest which would recruit me. My people would soon exhaust the resources of the most considerable. Here, however, I have again found the abundance, luxury, and riches of European civilisation. After two months of misery and absolute isolation, without seeing a single European, I cannot tell you all the charm of this transition. My health is perfectly restored; it is necessary for the journey which I am going to undertake through the eternal snows of the Himalaya, a barrier but lately considered insurmountable. I shall pass the summer in Kanawer, a country at once Hindoo, Tartar, and Tibetian, where I shall escape from the solstitial rains, and which has scarcely hitherto been visited at all. Its climate is extremely severe. The English protection will accompany me, and leave me exposed to no other dangers than those which result from the country and climate. I shall not return to India for four months.

As I am hurried by different cares incidental to the preparations for this journey, I must confine myself to these lines. Perhaps I shall have leisure on the frontiers of China; and if at the same time I have an opportunity of sending a letter for you to India, you shall receive one longer than the present. The European newspapers, which I have found here after being so long deprived of them, interest me exceedingly; perhaps they would alarm others. But I have a happy confidence in the strength of the party on the side of reason. I do not believe that there could be any Government henceforth capable of doing much harm in France. Nevertheless, I should like the English journals to bring to me the *denouement* announced for the second of March: for the meeting of the Chambers must bring one.

My correspondence has become very irregular since I left Benares. For the space of five months I have been without any intelligence from Europe, and I shall have to wait the same length of time before I receive any. What a melancholy idea! Adieu, my friend, adieu! Write without delay, in order that I may find a letter from you on my arrival at Bombay, next spring. I love you with all my heart.

TO MADAME VICTOR DE TRACY, PARIS.

Semla, June 24th, 1830.

Dear Madam,—Although this place (an unknown desert nine years ago) is situated at the extreme limit of the British dominions, thirteen hundred miles from

Calcutta, at a greater height from the sea than St. Bernard and Mount Cenis; although the roads to it seem impracticable, except for mules and men devoured by curiosity; in spite of several days' march through a thousand difficulties: notwithstanding all this, your countrywomen come here and pass whole months of the summer to avoid the insupportable heat of the plains. Braving the wild and sterile solitude of the desert, they mount their horses every morning and evening in very elegant costumes, adorned with ribands, and without the omission of a single pin; they could not be better dressed in Hyde Park. Sometimes this amuses me; at other times it is detestable. It is a discord; and you know how variable is the effect which contrasts produce on our nature.

I have just been travelling for two months among mountains without meeting a single European. I have lost my small provision of English, and am afraid you will find too great a mixture of Hindoostanee in this letter to understand me easily. For want of French, English pleases my ear as well as my own language, which I have for a long time only been able to make use of in writing; it is grown like Latin to me.

I am going to pass a very cold summer. I shall cross a range of mountains adorned with snow, to arrive at those which are the highest in the world. You would laugh a good deal if you saw my disguise, and you would make a caricature of me still more amusing than that in which you represented my tall figure on one of the little Bourbon ponies, the beast and myself with hair streaming in the wind. I resemble a white bear, enveloped in thick woollen coverings; my head thrust into several silk caps, my legs concealed in thick gaiters, and my face ornamented with a pair of very long mustachios. This latter part of my costume is altogether indispensable; it is the *dustour*, a tyrant infinitely more absolute in this part of the world than fashion in England. This powerful Persian word is as much above *fashion* as this latter is above *mode*. The individuals of my escort have the ideal figures of banditti, such as one dreams of. We have no fault to find with each other.

I have latterly travelled through strange scenes of wild and savage solitude, and I flatter myself I shall find some of a character still more curious when I arrive at the frontiers of Chinese Tartary. As for danger—that proceeding from the hand of man—none exists; for man is so scarce in these deserts, that my numerous escort shields me from being carried off, and gives me the air of a conqueror.

After so many marches and counter-marches, seas, the burning sun of India, the snows of the Himalaya, what shall I still see before I return to my country?

After all that, with what delight shall I enjoy the calm prospect of Paray!—with what a sweet feeling of repose shall I walk about those peaceful domains!—Sometimes I think I am dreaming; I seem to be already a hundred years old. As for you, you will never grow old. Adieu, I embrace your husband with my whole soul. God bless you both.

TO A. M. ACHILLE CHAPER, PARIS.

Semla, in the Himalaya, June 25th, 1830.

It is more than a year since I wrote to you, my dear friend: and, if I recollect right, I then sent you only a few lines, to inform you that I had at length arrived at the end of my long voyage, and was receiving from every one most distinguished in India for rank, intellect, and learning, a reception which confounded, by the flattering excess of its kindness, all the hopes I had conceived of the noble pride of the English. Since then I have often been inclined to retrace my wandering life to you, and confide to you the emotions excited in me by the sight of so many new objects, to make you the partaker of my pleasures, and my associate in the fleeting troubles which interrupt them —but I have too much to say; and being limited by the short space of my rare moments of leisure, I have found it more convenient not to write at all, than to do it with the restraint imposed by this want of time. In your journeys to Paris, you have, I think, sometimes seen my father, and from him you must have learnt at least that I am alive, and moreover content. I have seen Benares, Agra, Delhi, and have travelled to the north-west of that city, beyond the frontiers of the English possessions, into the country of the Seikhs, and scarcely stopped till I reached the margin of the desert of Bikaneer. From thence, returning to the east, I entered the Himalaya; on the 12th April I visited the sources of the Jumna; I also approached those of the Ganges, and ascended considerably above them, on the eternal snows of the colossal chain which separates India from Tibet. This latter part of my journey kept me for two months from all European society.

Under this severe climate of the Upper Alps, among their most rugged and desolate scenes, the remembrance of you more frequently presented itself to my thoughts. I often recal to mind those mantles of snow which you were the first to teach me to climb, and the nakedness of the rocks which here and there pierce through them. How many times have I not been moved before those first pictures of our friendship, which my imagination renews with so much freshness! Alas! I am alone here; no friendly recollection will associate itself with that which I shall preserve of these strange places to render them dear to me! To live alone, to be solitary in feeling! oh! my friend, it is not because I am so far from our country, lost in the icy deserts of the highest mountains of the world—that my isolation is painful to me; I should perhaps feel this cruel void quite as much in the midst of the sweets of European society—perhaps in the midst of its tumult and its pleasures, I should not suffer less—and I am not yet thirty! Let us drop the subject.

The forms of the Himalaya, the progressive elevation from the base of the mountains heaped upon each other on the plains of Hindoostan, up to the crests of ice which cover the line of their most elevated summits, the absence of platforms, valleys, and escarpments, singularly disguise their height. I have several times encamped, at an absolute elevation of three thousand metres, habitually at 2000; however, it is always in the lowest and best sheltered places, near villages, that I must make my halts. You see, then, what subtraction must be made from the absolute height of mountains, in order to measure their relative or apparent height. The latter is still enormous; but as the eye seeks in vain to oppose horizontal to vertical lines, and as the declivities, notwithstanding their great inclination, do not shoot up all at once, but are added to each other on planes successively more distant, there is no point from which the highest peaks can be seen under a very large visual angle. Lastly, where there is grandeur—beauty and grace are wanting. Oh! how beautiful the Alps are!

The Indian acclivities of the Himalaya, which I have just visited, are pretty well known. But a very small number of travellers have crossed to the Tibet side, at least with the information requisite to study that mysterious country. In two days, my dear friend, I shall undertake this journey. The productions of nature must be little varied in so cold a country, but I may hope that a great number will be unknown to us. I reckon upon going as far as the frontiers of Chinese Tartary; the admirable protection of the English Government will defend me so far from all dangers which may proceed from men. The half-Hindoo half-Tartar rajah, who rules the lofty valleys hollowed out of the northern base of the Himalaya, has also some states on the Indian side, which make him absolutely dependent on the English power. I am besides obliged to have a very numerous suite, nearly fifty men, and it is rather in order to be absolute master in my camp than for any other object, that I take an escort of Gourkha seapoys with me, whose utility I experienced in my first excursion. You must, my dear friend, give me absolution for my little acts of arbitrary power: without them all that I have done here would be impossible. Some day or other we will philosophise and theorise on their morality. Adieu; you will easily conceive how much occupation the multiplicity of my researches gives me—I am overwhelmed with work. But my health has remained perfect, except in the snows at the sources of the Jumna, where cold, fatigue, and bad nourishment slightly deranged it. I am restored to my accustomed vigour, which is very necessary for me, in order to resist the fatigues, privations, and miseries of all kinds which I shall have to endure on the other side of the Himalaya. I embrace you with all my heart.

TO A. M. JACQUEMONT THE ELDER, PARIS.

Chini, in Kanaor (Kanawer), July 15th, 1830.

ONLY a few words, my dear father, to avail myself of an opportunity which may not very probably offer again until my return to Semla. I left that place on the 28th of June, overwhelmed, by my host Captain Kennedy, with still more attentions than I had perhaps ever yet received. He made admirable preparations for my journey into this country; and on my arrival at Seran, the summer-residence of the Rajah of Bissahir, that sovereign came in all haste to pay me a visit, and make me all kinds of offers of service. I had a draught on his treasury, the amount of which it was not convenient for me to receive immediately; and another on one of his subjects who was absent. The amount of both will be paid at sight, in the Rajah's name, whenever I may think proper to demand it; his little Chancery has written to all the chiefs in the Upper Country, and to the Lamas of Ladâk, to comply with all my desires. I hope then to be able to penetrate as far as the platform. The Rajah, besides, has given me, as Captain Kennedy had done, the highest in rank among his servants, to serve as interpreter, and to give orders everywhere in the name of his master, whom nobody here contradicts. My Semla janissary has, besides, under his orders, some Gourkha soldiers; so that, what with persuasion and coercion, I shall be but little exposed to die of starvation, or to be stopped in the middle of my journey for want of people to carry my baggage forward.

A story-teller might find something superb in the visit of the Rajah, with his fan in his hand, during a furious hurricane, which threatened to overturn the tent in which I was expecting him and his viziers, for such is the Hindoostanee and Kanaor name of his ministers. His court and people assembled to shout *God save the King*, after their own fashion. Like Louis the Fourteenth, on another occasion, I regretted the weight of my grandeur, which did not permit me to return the King of Bissahir's visit, for I was very anxious to see the interior of what is called his palace; but Kennedy had justly reproached me for having spoiled his allies by this excessive condescension. It was the Rajah's place to come with all the pomp of his royalty, and to consider himself honoured at my allowing him to take a seat before me, and at my shaking hands with him. I could neither have embraced him, nor returned any present, or his visit, without derogating from my dignity.

Nevertheless do not believe, I beg, that he is a bandit of the lowest kind, in a cavern, covered with scarlet rags, with plenty of daggers, pistols, and other melo-dramatic instruments at his girdle. The Rajah of Bissahir is a legitimate king, who reigns *de sire* or *de cire* over a degree of latitude, and two or three degrees of longitude; and although the greater part of his dominions lies buried under the eternal snows of the Himalaya, although nine-tenths of the rest are covered with forests, and the remaining tenth nothing but sterile, arid pastures or naked rocks, he has a revenue of a hundred and fifty thousand francs a year, without pressing on his subjects, who are the most wretched in the world. His *nuzzer*, or offering, consisted of a bag of musk in the animal's skin, a rarity indigenous in his mountains, which is not wanting, I hope, either in local character or in Tibetian perfume. The only thing I gave him in return was a lesson in geography, of which he stood in great need. He leaves the trouble of knowing it to his viziers, and passes his time with his Cashmerian slaves, whom he fattens in their cage, and who are probably not very handsome:—whatever may be said, they are not generally so.

On the 11th of July, I crossed the Sutledge, or, if you don't think that fine enough, the Hyphasis; and have been travelling ever since on its right bank, or, more correctly, three, four, or sometimes five thousand feet above its right bank. The climate here begins to be very different from that on the southern side of the mountain: on this side there is nothing but wind and fog, while on the other the rain falls in torrents. There are apple trees and vines in the gardens, but unfortunately without either apples or grapes in this season; that will be for my return. Budha here begins to steal the clouds of incense of which Brahma has the exclusive right on the Indian side of the Himalaya. They practise the religious precepts of Miss Frances Wright on the community of the sexes, for there is *polygamy* as in India, and *polyandry* at the same time; and this latter institution prevailing, the consequence is an excess of females, who retire into convents, situated, no doubt for mutual convenience, in the neighbourhood of little abbeys of Lamas.

At Kanum, I shall soon see that incredible Hungarian original, M. Alexander de Csomo, of whom you have no doubt heard: he has been living for four years under the very modest name of *Secundœur-Beg*, that is to say, Alexander the Great, dressed in the Oriental style. He is now about to throw off his sheep's-skin, and black làmb's-skin cap, and resume his name, in order to go to Calcutta, and no doubt annoy you, with the *galimatias* of the Tibetian Encyclòpædia, which he has just translated. You will see that M. d'Eckstein will have some fault to find with it; and yet M. Csomo is the only European in the world who understands the language. The Tibetian Encyclopædia abounds in astrology, theology, alchemy, medicine, and other stuff of the kind, no doubt translated from the Sanscrit at some distant period. If M. Csomo gives us ever so little of it in German, and M. d'Eckstein turns it from German into French, it will be nonsense, raised to the fourth power—an expression, the magnitude of which Porphyre will explain to you, if your algebra will not carry you so far.

I am very well. I shall find milk everywhere. I have rice for three months, sugar for the same period, and forty-six pounds of tobacco of the finest quality, which I bought at Rampore, to make presents to the Tartars of the Spiti (and which cost me seven francs). On my road, when the mornings are cold, I smoke the best leaves in a little roll of paper; it is better than what is sold for forty-six times the price at Paris. Since leaving Semla I have had a new cook, my steward and maitre-d'hôtel at the same time; he has the character of being a terrible rogue, but makes me fare as well as the resources of the place will admit, that is to say, very badly, but no worse—an immense amelioration in my establishment; for his predecessor was an honest man, but his works defied the rudest appetite. The mountains here produce rhubarb, *celestial happiness!* But this is not all; after three months' research, the Rajah of Pattiala, one of those whom I should embrace, and whose visits I should return—a man with a revenue of four millions—this admirable ally of the English power has written officially to my friend, the ex-sub-resident of Delhi, since promoted to the political agency of Kotah, that he has recovered my syringe. The news is in the *Akbars* (manuscript gazette) of his court: he has sent it to the Resident of Delhi with a strong escort. It is deposited in the palace of the residency, and I am officially asked for instructions, either as to the manner of sending it, or keeping it till my return. One would say that it was a barometer or pneumatic machine: however, at the top of the letters written to me on the subject is printed

"POLITICAL DEPARTMENT."

I shall thus bring back to you the most diplomatic and historical syringe that has ever existed. You shall leave it to Porphyre, and it shall pass from male to male. If Porphyre does not marry, he has brothers worthy of possessing such an object.

I fancy that Porphyre's *moustachios* might be thicker and of a more equal tint. Mine are irreproachable—an inch long, as thick as a postilion's queue, and of the most uniform red; they are extremely admired in Kanawer, but I regret their beauty every morning when I eat my porridge.

Whilst the political resident at Luknow, with an income of two hundred thousand francs a-year, is sweating and stifling in his palace, I am warming myself at the fire-side, in a wretched little house, costing one or two thousand francs, which he built two years ago, in order to spend a fortnight in it. What a luxury a house is, let it be ever so little or wretched!

I am extremely busy, and shall only stay here to get through my arrears of business. I close this letter, by adding, that it will go, with my No. 7, to the Jardin des Plantes. Twenty-three months have now elapsed since I left France, and I have not yet received a line from you.

Adieu, my dear father! Do not be afraid of the revolt of the Birmans, nor of the insurrections of the army, nor of the great approaching collision of interests in the debates of the British parliament; it is always from the English journals that we learn that we are upon a moving soil here;—I assure you that there is not a firmer. As for the only real dangers, those of the climate, let the treasure-trove of the rajah of Pattiala quiet your fears. I embrace you and Porphyre with all my heart.

A MADEMOISELLE ZOÉ NOIZET DE SAINT PAUL.

Camp of Tashigung, on the borders of Ladak and Chinese Tartary, August 24th, 1830.

My dear Zoé,—I had only just sent off one of my mountain servants to Semla when a Tartar arrived from Soongnum, a great Lama village of Kanawer, and brought me, among many others, your charming letter of the 10th of February. To answer you properly would require a volume; and it would be a delicious task to write that volume, if I had some days to remain unoccupied in a camp. But I am overwhelmed with labours of all kinds—botany, geology, &c., give me no leisure. I must go forward, and can only allow myself a few lines. If your letter had joined me yesterday with a great number of others, these lines would now be on their way to India. But, at the distance we are from each other, a few weeks sooner or later matters little.

I have this moment returned from a half military excursion into the Celestial Empire, which I conducted in the most fortunate manner; for, without being obliged to commit any other hostility than a display of murderous arguments when the Chinese made any show of opposition, I saw the object of my curiosity very quietly. I had to march five days without finding any village, and to cross two lofty chains of mountains, more than five thousand five hundred metres, or eighteen thousand English feet high (two thousand five hundred feet higher than the summit of Mont Blanc). I was obliged to have provisions carried with me, sufficient for the whole journey till my return, and my troops amounted to more than sixty men. I had, besides, a quantity of new plants, and organic remains, which I found at the enormous height of five thousand six hundred metres, so that a great number of interesting observations amply repaid me for the trouble and fatigue of my expedition. I am now exploring Ladak; and am going to visit some mountains, where, according to the reports of the mountaineers, I expect to observe several interesting geological phenomena. I this morning crossed the Sutledge, to follow the course of the Indus at no great distance. Both of them are but large torrents here, being very near their sources. The Sutledge rises in the celebrated lake Mansarower; as do the Indus, and the Barampooter, which are the two largest rivers in its immediate neighbourhood.

The Tartars of the mountains have certainly nothing of the ferocity generally attributed to them; and though there are in my numerous suite only six armed men, the *Francis saheb,* or French lord, as they call me, would drive thousands before him like a flock of sheep. They are, on the contrary, mild and peaceable people, who keep pressing round my tent to obtain a little tobacco, several parcels of which I brought from India to distribute among them. When their extreme curiosity grows troublesome, a single word disperses them. They have nothing of the servile manners of the Indians; and the progress of our corruption is so rapid among the latter, that at Bekar, the Chinese town to which I laid siege, the head man coming to me to complain of this violation of the territory of his most *Tea*-ific majesty, and advancing very near me without alighting, I felt really so indignant at this want of respect, that in a transport of rage, I seized the fellow by his long plaited queue and pulled him off his horse.

Does not the second person plural, which I am obliged to make use of when writing to you, sound strange to your ears, my dear Zoé! This language is at present as familiar to me as my own; nevertheless I am not yet reconciled to the coldness of the *you.* In my opinion this is a great defect in the English language; and it will always make it disagreeable to me to speak it with those to whom I am accustomed to address myself in our own language in a more tender way.

Here is my dinner—spring water (for I preserve carefully for bad days, snow, &c. &c., my almost exhausted supply of French brandy)—very coarse cakes made of barley meal, scarcely ground—spinach, or rather, instead of that vegetable, the leaves of buckwheat, which have nearly the same taste;—apricots, the only fruit of these lofty regions, but small as cherries, and without flavour; and, as a foundation for all this, the bones of a cold leg of mutton. This is a faithful testimonial of my cook's skill; for to obtain so wretched a dinner, I must keep a cook and his assistant, properly called scullion, whose duty it is to wash the two only dishes I possess.

As it would be a thing worthy of the bitterest censure to *embrace* you at the end of this letter, I ought, in order that I may be English to the last, sign myself, my dear Zoé, your very affectionate Cousin.

What an insipid thing an English letter is! Yorick was right: "they manage it much better in France."

TO M. PORPHYRE JACQUEMONT, PARIS.

Camp Nates, in Kangarang, August 25th, 1830
(frontiers of Zadah and Chinese Tartary).

This Delhi paper, more botanical than literary, blots with European ink; I must therefore, my dear Porphyre, give you blue and white, instead of black. The place from which I am writing to you is twenty-five days' march from the last English station; and is probably one of the most lofty inhabited places on the surface of the globe. Its height above the level of the sea is four thousand metres. As I was ascending yesterday from the banks of the Sutledge, which flows a thousand metres below, a Tartar belonging to the Vizier of Soongnum, nimbler than myself in climbing almost vertical declivities, gained on me, and delivered me a packet pretty well covered with grease and dirt, but in which I found, among many others, letters from you, our father, Madame de Paray, and Zoé. These were all from Europe; but from India and Africa there were a great many more. I read my father's immediately; yours at a thousand feet above; and it was only this morning that I finished those from Africa and India. It is curious that the day before, another courier (couriers who, although Tartars, scarcely ever run, but manage with hands and feet to clamber up the rocks, and when they have gone thirty steps puff, and take their breath to go another thirty): it is singular, I say, that the day before, a messenger also succeeded in finding me. The latter brought me only letters from India, but a well furnished packet. There are some which I thought proper to answer without delay; and yesterday morning, raising my camp at Nanija, I despatched one of my people to Semla (one-and-twenty marches) to deliver them to Kennedy, who is charged with forwarding them to their destination. One of them

—this will astonish you—is addressed to M. Allard, Chevalier of the Legion of Honour, Commander-in-Chief of Runjeet-Sing, Rajah of Lahore; a man, in fact, who appeared to frighten the Company's Directors in London so dreadfully, when I went to ask them for a passport. I sent you from Semla (perhaps they were addressed to my father) some information concerning M. Allard, who enjoys the most honourable reputation among the British officers. In my day before yesterday's packet, I found a letter from him, addressed to me, which he sent to me at Semla. Here is a copy, since it is of no great length.

" *Lahore, July 28th*, 1830.

" SIR,—I am informed by Dr. Murray, of the arrival at Semla of a French traveller, distinguished for his attainments and the mission with which he is charged. This news gives me the hope that an old officer may find it in his power to be serviceable to one of his countrymen, in regions so remote from the mother-country. I therefore have the honour of addressing to you the present letter, by one of my hurkarus—(a sort of footmen, chamberlains, janissaries, or what you please)—to offer you all that my situation at the court of the Rajah of Lahore may enable me to be useful to you in. Dispose of my services, Sir, as freely as I offer them; it will be a mark of nationality. In the meanwhile receive the assurance of the high consideration with which I have the honour to be," &c.

This cordial offer from a stranger, who thus came in search of me on the frontiers of China, affected me, and I am sure I answered it with some sentimental effusion. My answer is too long to be transcribed, although I have kept a copy. But here is the substance of the most important part:—" To visit the plains of Punjab (a country between the Sutledge and the Indus, where Runjeet-Sing is firm in his stirrups), would be no great service to me; but if M. Allard could overcome the repugnance of the Rajah, to suffer Europeans to penetrate into Cashmere, and succeed in obtaining this permission for me, guaranteeing me perfect safety, I should feel under very great obligation to him. As a motive to induce the Rajah to suffer me to see the mountainous parts of his empire (Cashmere), M. Allard may inform him that my researches will enable me, more than any other, to discover mineral masses which it might be advantageous to work."

His letter is evidently a proof that he has no doubt of getting me as far as Lahore; and in fact there is no reason to doubt it. Whatever he may gain beyond, I am nearly resolved, at least to pay him a visit; for on the spot, it is possible that I may find some means of getting something out of Runjeet-Sing.

The possible is impossible to be foreseen, on acconut

of its variety; perhaps it may amount only to zero. This is what I shall very probably ascertain at Lahore. In order to arrive at that great city, where I shall of course be the comfortable guest of the French commander, there are only fifteen days' march on a plain. Admitted by the Rajah, I cannot fail to be taken to his durbar, and to hook *en passant* a good Bukhara horse and a Cashmere shawl, instead of the shabby thing which the Grand Mogul of Delhi, like a Jew, sold me. In any case I shall not pass the Sutledge (that is to say, from India and Lahore, for here I cross it every week, yesterday for once) without writing about it to Lord William Bentinck.

I pass on to your two letters. It is indeed very extraordinary that in the month of February 1830, none of my letters from Calcutta, of May, June, and November, had reached you; but, my friend, you promised me, in your security, to take a large share, not of my personal accidents, but of those of my correspondence. A letter of mine to M. Victor de Tracy arrived seasonably after a very long time, to show you the risks which it had run. You have, besides, indirect news of me in my letter to De Mareste, in the months of July and August from Calcutta, and you persist in making yourself uncomfortable: this grieves me, when I consider that still longer intervals may elapse without your hearing of me at all. Unless you wish to condemn us mutually to a great deal of uneasiness, you must rely on my dry and stringy fibre, my prudence, and—what more shall I say?—my dexterity. I know how to fill up the blanks of our correspondence with nothing but fortunate things. I have always done so when I thought of you; however I will confess, Porphyre, that I long to know how our father got through the terrible winter of unheard-of rigour, as the English journals have informed me.

From the Jardin and its inhabitants not a word since the amiable letter which I received from Jussieu and Cambassedes at Calcutta. If the fault is theirs, the devil take them! Not a word from England. Yet Sutton Sharpe, M. Seguier, and Sir Alexander Johnson cannot fail to have answered me. Yes, if they have received my letters. It is provoking! I return to yours.—I agree with you on the name which you give to your musical fanaticism; it is truly a slight tinge of madness. You might have told me who sang to you, and what they sang to you for your subscription to the Italian opera. That would have appeared singular to me in Tibet, where they sing a great deal also (one or two inhabitants per square league), but only a single song of three words, *oum mani pani;* which means, in the learned language, which neither the villagers nor their Lamas understand, "oh! diamond water-lily!" and leads the singers direct into Buddha's paradise. Laugh colossally at —— in my name; and his accidents by flood and field. Tell him that it happens to me to be several months without hearing the sound of a European voice, also that my dinner is fundamentally detestable; and that I do not complain. A-propos of dinner: I have hit upon a mode of preserving my health; spinach made of the leaves of buckwheat produced the desirable result; coarse cakes of corn scarcely ground strengthened this amelioration, by means of which I am in every respect as well off as you. It is wonderful: on bad days, for instance, when I am encamped at the height of six thousand feet, or have been obliged to cross mountains of more than eighteen thousand three hundred feet high, I have set before me the bones of an ex-leg of mutton smoked *à l'Ecossaise*, which bones I shall finish by eating likewise; for they cannot be harder than the flesh that was on them. But Kennedy sends me word that he will treat me with truffles every day on my return to Semla. The excursion in which I have been obliged to ascend four times to so enormous an height (seven hundred metres higher than the summit of Mont Blanc), had for its object some beds of shells which I presumed were there, and in fact proved to be so: it furnished me at the same time with many new plants. But with five days' march without a habitation, and the lowest of my encampments at the height of fourteen thousand feet, I was obliged to carry twelve days' provisions; for the Chinese town or village, where at the beginning of my expedition it was very uncertain that I could arrive, would in no case furnish me with any for my return. My little army, for it was truly an act of hostility

I was committing against his *Tea*-ifying Majesty of Pekin, exceeded sixty men; six of whom, reckoning myself, were fighters. By rare good luck, I found Chinese vigilance at fault on the frontiers; and the unexpected arrival of my caravan, in close column, surprised the people of Behar so much that they fled on my approach instead of offering any opposition. I encamped peaceably in a chosen spot, and next day received in my little tent the visit of a Chinese officer, who commands a turret of sand-stone, fortified with two leather guns, at no great distance. He came to complain. I transformed him into the accused; put a multitude of questions to him without allowing him to speak, except in answer to them; then dismissed him and his staff with a nod, after I had sifted him to the bottom. I designedly put on a threatening look, and commanded my people to do the same, in order that such demonstration might suffice. The Beharites had no idea of a double-barrelled gun, still less of a percussion one.

The effect of two balls which I shot, one after the other, into a tree at hand, a moment or two before giving audience to the Chinese officer, and in the presence of several of his followers, made a wonderful impression on the subjects of the celestial empire. I gave them a little tobacco, which made them love me as much as they had before feared me. A whimsical incident immensely increased their respect for the French lord. I was exhausted with fatigue, and was, nevertheless, going to continue my march: I therefore drank the stirrup-cup, filling my spoon with brandy, in order to put a bit of sugar in it. The sugar remaining solid, I set fire to the brandy, and when it was melted, after blowing on my spoon, I swallowed this dose of punch. The Beharites, who are no artillerymen, thought that I was drinking *fire*, and almost took me for the devil. It was on that day that I encamped so high as sixteen thousand feet. I was still on the Chinese territory, where I wished next day to determine the direction of some strata. During the night, some horsemen came to lie in ambush near my camp. However, I had intimation of their arrival, and of their small numbers. Not caring at all for them, I commenced my examination at day-break, followed by six servants at most. The Tartar-Chinese cavalry immediately got into motion, following my steps, but at a respectful distance. I commanded one of them to approach; and the fellow doing so without alighting to speak to me, I laid hold of him by his pig-tail and threw him off his horse. This comes, my friend, of living a year in India: a man thinks himself very sincerely insulted by every act which is not servile. Here I was wrong, for the poor devil of a Beharite was ignorant of Indian etiquette. But I saw only one thing, the colour of his skin; and, forgetting the difference of places, I took his ignorance for deliberate insult: *inde iræ*. His comrades had gallopped away. The poor man remounted his nag with a good deal of trouble, and joined them as quickly as he could.

Afternoon.—Here I am, in spite of my thick woollen clothes, wrapped up in blankets from head to foot. I am obliged to do so every evening, and yet I suffer from the cold. This is a strange climate: it snows moderately in winter, and there is no thaw for four months; it scarcely ever rains, but blows a violent hurricane every day at three o'clock, which lasts far on in the night. I often awake long before day-light, frozen through my five blankets.

The good-natured vizier of Soongnum joined a little present to the packet of letters; this was a small basket of bad apples, such as divine Providence has made them. Great feasting on the occasion. But the grapes will be ripe when I return to Soongnum, the highest spot where the vine prospers (ten thousand feet): then there will be thorough feasting. In my Indian packet of the day before, were some newspapers: an attention of Captain Kennedy's. I saw the speech at the opening of our Chambers, attacked in an article in the Globe, entitled, *La France et les Bourbons en* 1830: an article criminally prosecuted, adds the English journalist, with many others of the same description, which appeared daily in the liberal papers. I do not know what to think of the issue of this. Is the question only to know which of the two will be most afraid and give way? I wish it were so; but in truth I know not well what to think.

Supposing, what will not take place, that the direct government of the king should succeed that of the Company in India, this change would not cause the slightest shock in Asia. Our father appears to be uneasy about the attitude of Mahrattas and Afghans, &c. &c. (and other canaille who are not worth a kick ———) in this *crisis.* Let him know, then, that the sixty millions of Indians about whom he was so much alarmed, are ignorant of the difference between the king of *Valaïte* (Europe altogether, England, America, &c. &c., for they are no geographers) and the Company. This subtle distinction is understood only, and but indifferently too, by the superior (mercantile) classes at Calcutta, Madras, and Bombay. But the peasant who ploughs, the mechanic who works, and the seapoy who mounts guard, have not the slightest idea of it. The ideas entertained in France about this country are absurd. The governing talents (St. Simon and his crew of the *Producteur* have no doubt manufactured a better word to express this idea) of the English are immense; ours, on the contrary, are very mediocre; and we believe the former to be embarrassed when we see them in circumstances in which our awkwardness would be completely at a stand still. Our father also regrets that I have not brought with me all the papers, which might assist in verifying my character as a Frenchman; as if it was by papers, truly, that it could be proved to people among whom, in his idea, it might be useful to me! as if they could read the Roman letters!

as if they understood a single word of a single European language! Let him take courage; he may live till he is a hundred before he learns that a general massacre of the English has taken place in India. The cold redoubles, my dear Porphyre, and I should never get warm in bed if I delayed any longer getting into it. I embrace you.

August 26th.

I return to you, my friend:—I have just written to our father, and have determined to despatch a courier (of the description mentioned above) to take the whole to Semla; whence Kennedy will forward it to Calcutta —thence it will be despatched to Chandernagore, to the obliging care of M. Cordier, my agent for Europe. I shall take care to write to you as soon as there is something determined upon about my Lahore affair; but—for heaven's sake—if six months elapse between the receipt of this letter and the arrival of the following, do not be uneasy, my friends. For your own information, Porphyre, do not refuse me the modest title of Esquire, which you appear to fancy sometimes, that the F.R.A.S. excuses you from giving me. It is not *ad libitum*, but indispensable. The F. R. A. S. is facultative.

When you speak of the excellent table kept on board merchant ships, I would willingly say, "Vous êtes orfèvre, Monsieur Josse." Do I not recollect the very hostile manner in which you spoke of the passengers, their appetite, &c., and the nautical artifices of a certain captain to excite tempests just at dinner-time, and other accidents, which rendered it necessary to adjourn the sitting before the attack on a certain pie, of which the messmates of his ship had only seen the outworks on their arrival at Port au Prince. It must have been a pasteboard pie, or such as they have on the stage, if there was any at all. But it is true all ship-owners are not captains of artillery; and it is said that the ,Bourdeaux gentlemen, whose ships come to Calcutta, do things liberally.

My annual credit of six thousand francs expires in 1831 inclusively. On the 1st November, on coming down from the mountains, I calculate that I shall have three thousand or two thousand five hundred francs left, in all eight thousand five hundred. This is enough for my journey to Lahore (if I must return without proceeding further), and from thence to Bombay, perhaps even to Pondicherry, where, on my arrival, I shall have something left to pay for my passage to Europe on board one of those excellent merchantmen, where there is such good cheer. That, my friend, is what I call making the best of the matter; that is to say, calculating the chance that the Museum forgets to send me a prolongation of credit.

You will have to sell two or three shares in ships to pay for the carriage of this letter, and our father a few volumes of his *Essences* to some silly bookseller, to whom Taschereau is specially charged to recommend the undertaking.

Adieu, my dear friend; envy me my mustachios, which are now five months old, a foot long, and of the brightest red. My cigar takes fire at them whenever I smoke a moment or two in the morning to warm myself on bad days. Adieu! I love you, and embrace you with all my heart.

TO M. JACQUEMONT, THE ELDER, PARIS.

Camp of Nako, August 26th, 1830. Long. 78° 40′; Lat. 32°. Frontiers of Chinese Tartary.

MY DEAR FATHER,—To write a letter every evening by stealth, either in Europe or India, in order gradually to liquidate my correspondence, would occupy my mind and distract it from the horrors of this hell of ice, upon which it would otherwise have to sleep. But I make a great sacrifice, and take a whole day of rest in order to finish all to-day, and not think of anybody till my return to Semla. I am writing to you on Indian paper, with a magnificent peacock's feather, and indigo rubbed down; a goose quill would be a great deal better, and some *petite vertù*, whether indelible or not, and some of the paper of those dogs of Christians. But what would you have? The necessities of past times have been such in this way that those of the present impose this wretched epistolary apparatus upon me.

I already *blued*, yesterday evening, ten or twelve

feet of this vile paper for Porphyre; and I send you many articles of this akbar or gazette as a reply to several chapters of your volume-letters. Until insurance companies are established for the contents of letters, I am perhaps wrong in risking such large packets; but at the distance which separates us, I cannot write short notes. So I commit this to the care of God: may he watch over it.

As it appears that he, or his favourite substitute, Providence, suffered my first from Calcutta to be lost, I return to that place, and beg to inform you that his Most Christian Majesty's log, which carried me and my fortunes, cast anchor before Fort William, on the 5th May, 1829, and after the customary salutes from the guns of the aforesaid vessel, I arranged my plans of landing for the next morning; they were put in execution as follows.

My Portuguese valet from Pondicherry having called a palanquin, I bid farewell to the Zélée, dressed in black from head to foot; and, throwing myself into the little ambulatory house, I said to the carriers, "*Pirsonn sahebka ghœur me;*" a Hindostanee sentence, which I had been meditating ever since I left Pondichery; it caused me to be set down without hesitation at the door of Mr. Pearson's magnificent house, which happened to be the one nearest to the river. A sort of Eurybates preceding me, between a double hedge of servants lining a wide staircase, introduced me into an immense drawing-room, where

I found three ladies in full toilet, and a man with grey hair in a light cotton dress, all four being fanned by a complicated machinery of hand-screens. My unknown name announced by the herald, and the simultaneous entrance of my tall black person, produced the effect of a thunder-clap; but the excessive pre-occupation of my mind, caused by the novelty, strangeness, and extraordinary appearance of every thing I had seen in the six minutes after my landing, paralysed my English eloquence mortally. Thus, at the critical moment when the spectre should have spoken, there was a pause. I would have given ten louis for a glass of port wine, which would have given my sail some little wind—unable to stir, my début was the candid avowal of my inability to proceed. "I spoke a few words of English formerly, Sir, but I perceive I have forgotten the whole; so I must entreat you to help me!" and so the grey-haired gentleman did, and so did the three ladies, the two young ones in particular, and so well, that an instant after I was swimming in English like a little fish in the river. The strangers were Mr. Pearson, Mrs. Pearson, their daughter, and her governess or companion. I delivered my letters of introduction, on the effect of which I did not rely with implicit confidence, because they were second or third hand; however, they caused me to be considered a guest at the breaking of the first seal. I was asked if they were the only ones I had brought to Calcutta; a question, which I answered, by exhibiting an enormous packet which deformed my pocket, and which, being charged beforehand, like a judicious firework, commenced on opening it with a few trifling squibs—Dr. —— Mr. * * *, merchant, or Captain —— ; then by degrees shot out the name of a judge, then that of the chief justice, then a member of council, and terminated in a grand crash with the name of Lady William Bentinck, and then the Governor-general's five times repeated. Each drew a chair near mine, and loaded me with questions and kind offers.

Eleven o'clock struck, and Mr. Pearson said to me: "This is the hour at which I must go to the Supreme Court, and I regret exceedingly that I cannot introduce you to the persons whom you are to see; but my daughter will inform you of every thing, and my carriage is at your service." He then left me, giving me a hearty shake by the hand. Miss Pearson told me that my first visit ought to be to the palace; and without informing me, she wrote and despatched a note to Lady William Bentinck. The answer, according to etiquette, was addressed to me direct, and delivered in less than a quarter of an hour, by the aide-de-camp on duty, who gave me to understand that her ladyship expected me. I got into Mr. Pearson's carriage, with footmen before and behind, and on arriving, I was received at the palace by the aide-de-camp, who conducted me into Lady William's private drawing room. She is a woman of fifty, who must have been very handsome, but is now without any of the pretensions of youth. My letter to her was from Lord Ashley, one of the members of the Indian Government in London, whom I met only once at the famous dinner of the Asiatic Society. I confessed therefore how slight was the title of recommendation which I brought; it was scarcely mentioned. Lady William had already discovered that I had seen several of her acquaintances at Paris. We chatted an hour and a half on a multitude of subjects, till her physician and also her guest entered to offer his arm to conduct her to the dining room, where the collation was served. Lady William despatched the doctor to her husband, to inform him that she had a new acquaintance to introduce to him; and a few minutes after I entered the refreshment room, giving her my arm. Lord William Bentinck came at the same time from the opposite side, with the ministers and two members of the council, which met on that day. Lady William introduced me in the most friendly way; and I sat on the right of the Governor-general, who read his five letters rapidly during the collation, and introduced me, when we rose from table, to all the persons assembled round it. I reconducted Lady William to her apartment, and did not leave her till I had promised to come and dine in the evening at eight. She taught me by heart all about the family on which my good star had fallen.

On returning to the Pearsons, who were a little surprised at the length of my absence, I found the two best rooms in the house placed at my disposal; and when I retired there to congratulate myself on my happy début, a host of servants pursued me armed with fans to cool me. I had some trouble to get rid of them. At five o'clock, Mr. Pearson, returning from the court, paid me a long visit, and acquainted me with the form of his material and domestic existence. I related my history, the last incident of which, my engagement with Lady William for the evening, rather embarrassed me; but he seemed more satisfied with his acquisition than vexed at losing it for a few minutes on the first day. I was a recherché guest. At six, he took me on a drive in his carriage along with his wife and daughter: this is the daily pastime of the inhabitants of Calcutta for an hour at sunset. They return to dinner by candle-light. After a short toilette, mine being changed, I went to the palace in Mr. Pearson's carriage.

The company was assembled in Lady William's drawing-room. I was once more her *chevalier*, and sat next to her at dinner, that being of course the place of honour. Every thing around was royal and Asiatic: the dinner completely French, and exquisite delicious wines served in moderation, as in France, but by tall servants with long beards, in white gowns with turbans of scarlet and gold. Lord William asked me to take wine, a compliment which I immediately returned, begging the honour of taking wine with my fair neighbour, who was conversing with me on a variety of agreeable topics, and offered to act as my Cicerone. To give our appetites time to revive for the second course, an excellent German orchestra, led by an Italian, performed several of the finest symphonies of Mozart and Rossini, and in a most perfect manner. The distance from which the sound proceeded, the uncertain light flickering between the columns of the neighbouring room, the brilliancy of the lights with which the table was illuminated, the beauty of the fruit which covered it in profusion, and the perfume from the flowers by which its pyramids were decorated, and perhaps also the champagne, made me find the music admirable. I experienced a sort of intoxication, but it was not a stupid intoxication. I chatted with Lady William in French on art, literature, painting, and music, while I answered, in a regular English speech, the questions put by her husband concerning the internal politics of France. I did not avoid showing, in my opinions, all that might excite disapprobation, employing, however, to express it, the most modest forms, which a lad of sixteen in England considers himself entitled to dispense with. Returning to Lady William's drawing-room to take coffee, of which I drank five or six cups without perceiving it, I found myself complimented by every one enough to turn my head. You will imagine that I did not fail to engage the physician, who is still young, in conversation, on the novelties in physiology; for I had no opportunity, in the general conversation, of speaking on subjects connected with my own profession of naturalist, and I wished to show myself in character before the hour of departure.

Next day, I tired my host's pair of horses, in going my round of visits, which however could not be finished till the day after. That day, I waited on the persons by whom I had been particularly noticed at the Governor-general's, and for whom I had brought no letters: you know the rest. A fortnight after, the Governor-general went to reside in the country, and I was of the party. Lady William would have me ride for the first time on an elephant with her; and she seemed so pleased with our gossip on the top of this moving mountain, that she never had any other companion but myself. As long as we stayed at Barrackpore, I worked during the day-time in the cottage, in which I had been settled near the palace. Sometimes after lunch, which, at two o'clock, brought together all the inmates, and where I refrained from appearing very often, for want of virtue to resist the *pâté de foie gras*, I used to go with Lady William to her drawing room, where the afternoon slipped away very pleasantly, in talking of the antipodes, rain, and fine weather. In the evening, after dinner, we had sometimes a little music, *en petit comité*. I used to monopolise Lord William at the end of a sofa in the furthest corner of the room; he talked to me of India, and I talked to him of the United States; then at half past ten, the signal for departure, I retired, taking the arm of the friend, whom, among so many kind acquaintances I had already gained: I mean Colonel Hezeta. Often before entering the bungalow which we inhabited together, we used to stroll till midnight through the immense walks in the beautiful park at Barrackpore. He related to me the two revolutions which he had witnessed in his native country; the last of which had cast him upon this without any other resource than the old friendship of Lord William. There is a strange mental resemblance between Hezeta and Dunoyer; and though he has strongly marked Spanish features, this resemblance physically struck me no less. Such, my dear father, was the way in which I spent the first days after my arrival in India. Why have I to relate them to you a year after they are gone by? The uneasiness in which the loss of my first letters has left you, concerning this period of our separation, afflicts me exceedingly. You had promised to fill up the prolonged intervals of my correspondence, which accident might leave blank, with none but pleasing conjectures: let your affection for me make you keep, in future at least, your promise of August, 1828.

What a contrast between my life at Calcutta and the isolation of my present situation, and the fatigues, privations and miseries which I now experience! But this opposition is not without its charms. I often eat my crust with extreme pleasure, when past recollections arise. Besides, the future has still lucky days in store for me.

Must I tell you that in the midst of the whirl in

which I then was, my life was less exempt from cares than now, solitary and independent as it is, in all its austerity. I contemplated with avidity this immense country which was opened before me, and I often considered, with bitterness, whether the access to it would not be closed against me by my poverty. I now look with satisfaction on the distances I have travelled; and am in nowise dispirited by the remoteness of Madras and Bombay.

What was agreeable and mild in my life then, is often recalled to my mind even in these deserts, in a manner which delights and affects me. You will yourself enjoy all the affecting testimonials of remembrance that reach me from such a distance. The English having nothing which resembles what we call society, and are almost universally destitute of that facility which we learn in it, of talking gracefully about nothings, and without dullness on serious subjects. We thus have an immense advantage over them, when we can lead them to a somewhat general conversation, the subject of which is sufficiently familiar to allow us gradually to take the greatest share in it, and to give it its tone. It is to this artifice that I owe most of my success in what they call their *society*; and it is incumbent on me to practise it, as it is on every traveller, on every man who is but a passer-by, and has only a few moments to show himself to make himself known. Although I have not succeeded in speaking their language entirely like themselves, the necessity of making use of this foreign instrument is, I know, far from being disadvantageous to me. I am quite certain of speaking properly when I think rightly.

Tell all whom it may concern, among the people in Europe, that I consider myself very much neglected by them. If those in Asia imitated them, I should not have so much to write to-day. But perhaps it is with the English post-office I ought to find fault. What letters I do receive, continue to fall upon me like manna in the desert, as to the Hebrews of old. I do not see the sons of the prophet. In general, I suppose, it is the good governor of Chandernagore, who plays the part of Moses here ; then at Delhi, there are new addresses and collections of letters, made by my baggage-master, the judge, or king of the city, under a single cover. Kennedy, at Semla, commonly tacks something of his own to this mixture ; and the whole arrives like anchovies preserved in butter and oil. It is the hydrophobia of the Kanaoris and Tartars, which, by making them carefully avoid all their life the contact of water, collects on their surface treasures of the conservative principle. It might rain in this country, but my letters, I assure you, would not be afraid of travelling in the open air in the hands of the courier.

But I shall never finish, if I do not set seriously to work to answer your letters. As to the chance of being devoured alive, by serpents which swallow an ox without winking, as we would an egg, I think it useless now to assure you of my safety. I have not yet seen a single tiger, lion, or leopard, though I went to look for them for a fortnight among the Seikhs, assisted in my search by five companions considered clever in discovering them, a score and a half of elephants broken-in to the sport, and five or six hundred horsemen. In one of the darkest of nights at the foot of the Himalaya, I discharged the two barrels of my gun in the direction in which they supposed there was a leopard, in order to account for the disappearance of a goat from a flock in a fold near my tent. My escort fired at the same time, and it is probable that there really was this time something like a tiger or leopard near, for the shepherd found the goat at the foot of the precipice, strangled and torn. It is very true, as Malte Brun tells you, that the Fakirs murder very cleverly on occasions. But I am none of their game: they seldom kill any but children, whose hands and feet they cut off, in order to steal the copper and silver bracelets which their parents attach to their arms and legs. If I were to meet several together, with a suspicious appearance, and had any doubt of their intention, I should begin by killing a couple of these horrible brutes on the spot; but from Calcutta to this place, a few kicks on the posteriors were sufficient to drive away the most importunate of their species; and I shall no where see so many of them in any part of India, as I did in the woody desert and mountainous region which I crossed in the first part of my road to Benares. They were going to Jagrena.

Mangoes and mangosteens have nothing in common but the first syllable of their name. The mango accommodates itself to every climate within the tropics; the cultivation of the mangosteen has succeeded scarcely any where except in the Moluccas, in Ava, and in Cochin China. There is a tree at Bourbon. My hosts in that island had the kindness to send a servant twelve leagues from their house, with a note to the proprietor of this rarity to obtain two specimens for me; it was just in season. I found the fruit excellent, but nothing more; whereas it often happens that mangoes surpass all epithets—it is therefore best to say nothing about them. Common mangoes are execrable. It is a fruit which is either adored or detested;—there is no medium. A mangosteen, on the other hand, in an intermediate limit, pleases universally. Mangoes are very common at Hayti, where their quality varies between delicious and bad. At Bourbon and Calcutta in particular, I ate mangoes, which must not have a word said against them. In the North of India, and at Benares, where the tree vegetates very luxuriantly, the fruit ripens badly.

I have no time at all to keep up the scientific correspondence, the occasional publication of which my friends think likely to be of advantage to me in a professional point of view. Although I do not spare myself, my time is sufficiently occupied without that. I shall therefore return with a full budget to be then wholly emptied. If some persons have thought me dead, I shall come tò life again for them. Tell Cambassèdes this, with my kind regards, if you have occasion to see him; if not, let Mérimée, to whom this message is also addressed, deliver it to him. Besides a want of the necessary ingredient, time, there is another cause, which would discourage me were I disposed to undertake such a task: I mean the uncertain fate of my letters, and the fear of these being lost like the others, or arriving only at rare intervals. Appoint an attorney to convey my friendly regards to M. de Beaumont. Tell Dunoyer and M. Taboureau that I receive and return theirs, without talking of it; and the same with regard to every other friend near you.

I have not here the register which would inform me what number I am to put upon this letter. But the last, despatched a month ago, is dated from Chini in Kanawer, and the one before it from Semla, about the 20th of June. Write to me through the Navy Board, as it is so good a channel. M. Cordier of Chandernagore will manage, with his frank, to find me in any part of India, no matter whether it be Pondichery or Calcutta. It is an age since I heard from M. de Melay. Adieu, my dear father. I am in admirable health. Continue, as you have done, to govern your coming years; patience and confidence—and we shall have much to tell each other. Adieu; I love you and embrace you with all my heart.

P. S. From horror of white, I resume my peacock's quill to *blue*, to the end of the page.

At Danum in Kanawer, I saw M. Csomo de Koros —Boûmi—or Alexander the Great (Secundœur-Beg), the Hungarian original, in short, of whom you must have heard. During the last ten years, he has been travelling in Asia, under a wretched disguise, to discover, by a comparison of language, the tribe of which his nation is a swarm.

I am now going to Ladak, a Tartar or Tibetian country tributary to China. The projected boundary of my course is seven marches hence towards the North. Thence I shall descend to Kanawer, and return to India by the Burunda Pass, through what the Indian and European public improperly term the great chain of the Himalaya. The Burunda Pass scarcely exceeds fifteen thousand feet in elevation; this will be mere child's play to me, who have reached, four times, an elevation of eighteen thousand three hundred, and eighteen thousand six hundred feet. Kennedy promises to come from Semla and meet me on the Indian declivity of the mountains, and we shall travel together some days, in order that he may make known to me the petty mountain sovereigns subject to his political control. Adieu.

TO M. ELIE DE BEAUMONT, ENGINEER OF MINES.

Lari, September 9th, 1830. *Territory of Ladah.*

DEAR M. DE BEAUMONT,—I see forming on the horizon, in Kanawer, a storm of work which only awaits my return thither to burst. I therefore take advantage of my last leisure of the desert to write you a few lines. Those fire-side geographers are fools, with their independent Tartary. The natives of this country pay tribute, on four sides; and the rajah or khan of Ladah, between the Seikhs of Cashmere and the Mantchous of China, is much less at his ease than the badshah of Persia, between the Russians and the English. However, fire-side geographers are happy fellows; I would willingly be a blockhead on such agreeable terms.

I found it very piquant, on the 21st of November last, to awake under a tent for the first time; but after having had no other dwelling for the last ten months, I have learned the value of a house; a place on the floor of the Hostelry of Courmageur would be better than my unmattressed bed, under my little mountain tent, which the frozen night-blast threatens to upset. I do not recollect, without regret, M. Durr's good dinners at the Union at Bex. Not that I, yielding to Asiatic luxury, have not my cook and sub-cook or scullion to provide good cheer; but for the five months I have spent in the Himalaya, these artists, by combining their talents, can produce me nothing daily but a pyramid of coarse cakes made of flour with all the bran in it. Now as one gets tired of all things in time, be they ever so nice, it is allowable to turn up my nose at the daily fare of my lordship, highness, or majesty, as they call me. But this is croaking too much; and as my health has suffered from neither cold, heat, rain, or the miseries of an ambulatory life, you know me well enough to believe that I care little about comforts. You will have known through Adrian dé Jussieu, Cambessèdes, or Prosper Mérimée, the admirable reception I met with at Calcutta. The season in which I arrived, and the necessity of learning the abominable jargon of the country detained me there several months; and I successively lived with people the poorest of whom had a hundred and fifty thousand francs a year. The law of drainage of rupees, nevertheless, gave me intervals of care even when I was thus magnificently treated. Nevertheless, since I find water enough to float, without running aground, from hence to Paris, I shall not complain to you of these miseries. An isolated and unknown stranger, placed in the circumstances under which I arrived at Calcutta, would inevitably have stranded. It is to the kilogramme of admirable letters of introduction with which I was provided, that I entirely owe the possibility of writing to you from Lari, six hundred leagues from Calcutta. In the great number of new personages that I have seen in India, there are none of our profession. Not that I did not, during my stay at Calcutta, become more or less acquainted with some skilful in the line; and, by means of the Asiatic Researches, with their predecessors. But abstracting localities, the Asiatic Society of Calcutta and the Lyceum of Natural History in New York, of a meeting of which I think I gave you an account, have the greatest resemblance. Geology is very much the fashion. It is a science much cultivated, in order to learn how to name scientifically the stones found in the road, and picked up and placed in the palanquin on a change of residence or garrison. So there is granite, gneiss, micaslate, clayslate, sandstone (which is always new red sandstone), and limestone (which is invariably lias.) I think I have said all. If M. Pentland has found in Peru some mountains higher than those of the Himalaya, I would not advise him to come to India; and as it is generally admitted that this mighty range, before which the Andes sink into inferiority, is the eldest-born of the creation, I beg you to abide by what I shall tell you some day concerning the phenomena of this eldest-born in the creation; for your beautiful work on the relative age of the elevation of mountains, of which I yet only know the sketch given by M. Arago in the *Annuaire du Bureau des Longitudes*, will in India be considered a personal insult by the geologists of Calcutta, their wives, their children, and their children's dolls. At Bombay I shall take care not to say I am a friend of yours. Some ten years ago, in Switzerland, a learned man of Zurich proved that the History of William Tell was a Danish legend of the eleventh century, and they could not but yield to his proofs; nevertheless he was condemned to death for having destroyed a belief which was one of the dearest heir-looms of the Swiss peasant. Being fortunately contumacious, the poor devil is now a professor in some university in Germany. To touch the antiquity of the Himalaya is no less a sacrilege in India.

A few words concerning my route. From Calcutta I went to Benares nearly in a straight line across low mountains, which form a very regular chain from the platform of Bundlecund to Rajomal, where they are terminated by a small escarpment above the Ganges; from Benares I proceeded to Mirzapore, and going from thence, I spent the whole month of January in Bundlecund, over the platform or its sides, or in the adjacent plains. In order to go from thence to Agra by an interesting route, I should have had to pass through Gewalior; but the material circumstances of waggons and escorts obliged me to reach the Jumna at Kulpy, and to go on from thence by the Doab, from Agra to Delhi, and from Delhi towards the desert of Bikanere, to the W.N.W., in the country of the Seikhs. I was then engaged in a hunting party, most admirably got up on my account.

This was at the end of March, and the hot winds threatened every day seriously to invade the plains of the north of India. Quitting my companions, therefore, I re-mounted my faithful Pegasus to reach the foot of the mountains by short marches, in the same manner that I had come from Calcutta to Delhi. I entered the Himalaya by the valley of Dehra or the Dhoon of Dehra, commonly called by the English the *Valley of the Dhoon*, which means literally the valley of the valley. It is a longitudinal valley hollowed out between the foot of the Himalaya, properly so called, and the elevated diluvial soil. I there bid adieu to the comforts of the Indian traveller in the plains; changed my horse for a stick; put my baggage on the shoulders of five-and-thirty mountaineers, and commenced the series of miseries with which I have annoyed you above. I went to the sources of the Jumna, and near those of the Ganges; thence I returned westwards to Semla, a summer station near the Sutledge; ascending along its banks, or rather on the side of the mountain overlooking them, I passed to the north of the Himalaya, in the country of Kanawer, the Rajah of which is tributary to the English. This is the commencement of Tibet, in respect of climate, productions, and the religion of the inhabitants. My researches have carried me twice from Kanawer into the Chinese territory; and in the first of these expeditions (for they were rather military, and invasive,) I had to pass four times through defiles at a height of five thousand five hundred metres, and to encamp at five thousand metres. I am now on my return from an excursion towards Ladak, without perceiving that the mountains begin to diminish in altitude. The village from which I am writing to you, seated on the banks of the Spiti, a very considerable feeder of the Sutledge, is about three thousand seven hundred metres high. Three days ago I was encamped near a village in Ladak, called Ghijourmul, at an elevation of five thousand metres. On the Indian slope I have seen none above two thousand seven hundred metres. Cultivation also is arrested on the southern side two thousand metres lower than on the Tibetian. The temperature is not the predominant circumstance of climate which determines these differences; it is particularly the state of the sky which produces them: covered with clouds and charged with rain on the Indian side, clear and void of all humidity as soon as the peak of the Himalaya is past. Having gone from that side by the natural cut of the Sutledge, I shall return into India by one of the gorges of the southern or Indian chain. Their mean elevation is from fifteen to sixteen thousand English feet; that is to say, three thousand feet below the mean level of the passages across the branches which cover Tibet and Tartary.—In the same manner as you have found that all the Alps are far from being contemporary, so it appears doubtful to me, whether the Tibetian chains of the Himalaya are of the same period of elevation as the southern chain. I will not tell you the sufficient reason of these doubts, because this letter would have no end, and my leisure has but narrow limits.

Adieu, my dear Beaumont. I shall expect your answer at Bombay. Believe in my sincere attachment.

TO M. CHARLES DUNOYER, PARIS.

Semla, in the Himalaya, October 23rd, 1830.

I REGRET much, my friend, to learn by your letter of the 1st of April, that I have lost another of an anterior date, which required a special answer. Perhaps, when it has travelled several times from Europe to Asia, it will reach me at last; and then doubt not the eagerness with which I shall endeavour to satisfy your wishes. To-day I have only to thank you kindly for your friendly remembrance of me. I have certainly explained to you why I did not take leave of you: notwithstanding the pretty things that Romeo says about the pleasure of bidding good bye, I am not of Shakspeare's opinion. In every parting, which is likely to be of some duration, there is a *perhaps*, so melancholy, that I systematically avoid the pain of the last shake by the hand. Thus I show myself worthy of my father, who, you know, is a hero of stoical insensibility—that is, on paper. He assures me, that he was as gay as possible, and quite at his ease, about me, when he had not received a letter from me for nearly a year; and his friends thought him very uneasy. I should be delighted if he had told the truth, without saying more; for at the distance at which I am not only from Europe, but also from Calcutta and Bombay, nothing is so much a matter of chance as the arrival of my letters. What ought to satisfy him as to the future, whatever the intervals of my correspondence may be, is the fortunate experiment I have made of the climate of India, the acquaintance I have contracted with men, and my general knowledge of the country. It is now nearly a year since I left Calcutta. I have travelled in the meanwhile twelve or fifteen hundred leagues on horseback, and nearly a thousand on foot. In Tibet, whence I am just now returning, I have made war on the emperor of China, encamped several times at a greater height than the summit of Mont Blanc, and am all the better for it; but this is a particular case, and proves nothing against the insalubrity of India. It is true that the English add greatly to the dangers of the climate by their want of sobriety. Excepting when I am at their establishments, I live not only like a Brahmin, but like a Carthusian friar, not having altered my opinion as to the relative merits of quartos and duodecimoes:

Hydrophobia in a whole nation is a frightful disease. On my journey into Tibet, I had a small escort of Gorkhas. It would certainly have sufficed for me to conquer the whole of central Asia, if I had taken a fancy to make myself a king. These folks had the custom of brutally driving away the Lamas and other Tartar villagers, whom the curiosity of seeing a white man had attracted round my encampment. One day, when it was less cold than usual, I undressed myself to take a bath after the Indian fashion, that is to say, to have a skin of water poured over my head and shoulders. At the splashing of this little cascade, the crowd of Tibetians pressing round me fled in a fright; and since that day I have always got rid of their importunities, by stationing my water-carrier or Mussulmaun bisti with his large black beard, who was an object of admiration to these beardless people, as sentry at the door of my little tent, with his skin well filled, which excited their terror. Instead of a score of Gorkhas, I should only take half a dozen apothecaries to make myself great khan of Tartary. You will easily think, that, when king of such a water-fearing people, I should be little tempted to use all the rights of an Asiatic prince, and would make myself a Lama, if I did not remain a Carthusian monk. A very singular trait in Tibetian manners, with which you are surely acquainted, is a plurality of husbands. All brothers born of one mother have but one wife in common. It never happens that she has any preference for either of her husbands, which might trouble the peace of her numerous family: love and jealousy in their rudest forms are therefore feelings unknown to these people. However, the great Lama of Kanawer, whose portrait I will show you some day, has the episcopal mitre and crosier. He is habited like our prelates; and a superficial observer would, at a distance, take his Tibetian or Buddhist mass for a Roman mass, and one of the most orthodox. He makes a score of genuflexions at different intervals; he turns to the altar and people alternately, rings a bell, drinks out of a cup of water which an acolyte pours out for him; he mumbles Paternosters to the same tune;—in every point there is shocking resemblance. Men of a robust faith, will see nothing in it but a corruption of Christianity. Nevertheless it is incontestable that Buddhism, now confined to the north of the Himalaya, the east of the Burampooter, and in some islands of the Indian Archipelago, preceded, in India, the worship of Brahma. It still partially existed there at the period of the invasion of the first Afghan conquerors, who proved, like the Spaniards in America, that persecution, in spite of the proverb, is no feeble engine of religious conversion. A considerable library is deposited in the temple of Kanawer. I saw there several books on theology, printed in Tibet, consisting of a Sanscrit text, with an interlineary Tibetian translation; and their date is only of the century before last. The Buddhist church at that period still kept up some friendly relations with that of Brahma; and they still preserved at Teshoolombo, at Tashigung, and in several other great monasteries in Tibet, a knowledge of the sacred language of Benares. The common herd of Lamas are ignorant of the sense of the devout ejaculation which they utter from morning to night:

"Houm! màni, pâni houm!
"Heu! gemma lotus heu!"

But, though composed of three Tibetian words, it is evidently of Indian origin, and I have proved it *botanically*. The lotus, or λωτὸς of the Greeks, is a plant peculiar to the lukewarm and temperate waters of India and Egypt: there is not one of its genus, or even of its family, in Tibet. Its extreme beauty, and its abundance in the tanks dug near the Indian temples, have rendered it celebrated in the Hindoo legends.

But enough of this. I very much doubt the existence of the table land of Tibet. I have travelled northwards 32_0 10′ of latitude. The snowy chain of the Indian Himalaya was to the south very far behind me, and yet the country was constantly rising before me. I had, in my caravan, people who had travelled three months' march to the north-east, and six months to the east, of the furthest point to which I advanced. Their accounts agree too well not to be exact. They represent all the countries which are unknown to me, as very similar to those I visited with them: that is to say, covered with mountains, heaped up without order, ramified irregularly, and prolonged into chains, which cross each other in every direction. The Himalaya, whose eternal snows are seen from the banks of the Ganges, even as far as Benares, and which forms a spectacle so full of grandeur for the plains of India, is but an humble and modest preface to the Tibetian Alps.

My being a Frenchman, is far from disadvantageous to me: an Englishman could not have undertaken the journey which the *French lord* has just terminated so fortunately. The Government forbids English subjects to approach the Chinese frontiers, in order to avoid the trouble of the complaints which violations of territory might excite. Being free from this restraint, and persuaded that my little caravan would march in these deserts like a conquering army, I fearlessly ran my chance. Several times I found, in much greater numbers than my retinue, people assembled from all the villages around, to stop my progress; sometimes on the summit of a mountain, sometimes in a narrow defile which a single man might have defended against thousands, sometimes on the banks of a torrent. I never hesitated to push forward without paying attention to their injunctions; and I had very seldom occasion to use any of these good people roughly, in order to disperse their astonished companions. Notwithstanding their bold appearance before the engagement, I never saw in them any signs of resistance by open force; but they endeavoured to famish me, in order to force me to retire. They did not dare positively to refuse to sell me provisions, but laid a very high price on them, and the farther I advanced the more they increased it.

At length I adopted the resolution which I ought to have taken in the first instance. I dictated the price myself, on a very liberal scale, and warned them that, if they did not submit to it, I would plunder the village, and carry off their cattle: a menace which was sufficient for my purpose, and which I had never any occasion afterwards to repeat.

From so cold a country I have not been able to bring a very large number of organic productions. My collections are, nevertheless, considerable, and, contain a great number of new objects. The excessive nakedness of the mountains was favourable to geological observation; and I do not think I flatter myself in putting a pretty high price on those I have made.

English hospitality, so far as I am concerned, is truly admirable: the most flattering attentions have always been paid to me. But here especially, I have had the happiness to form, in a few days, quite a familiar acquaintance with my host, the king of kings, like Agamemnon of old, for he governs absolutely a number of petty mountain princes; and my residence at Semla will always leave me most agreeable recollections. For four months I had been deprived of all European society. None of my people speak a word of English, my adopted language; and I have heard nothing during the whole duration of my solitary journeys, but the wretched Hindoostanee mountain patois.

With your letter, my dear Dunoyer, I found here a

number of others, come from the same point, but of an equally old date; nevertheless, from the English newspapers, I have learnt European news up to the 1st of June. On quitting Calcutta, I had made a very secret vow to forget the things of that part of the world, or at least not to think of them so long as I should be in this. Impossible! and lo the English newspapers are no longer sufficient to give me a satisfactory account of our political affairs. I related my distress to Lord William Bentinck, who is five hundred leagues from hence, and receives several French journals regularly. He will be so good as to send them on to me, after having read them. Sometimes I fear that the king is still more of a fool than a coward, and that the *dénouement* of all this will be a revolution. If we were forced to come to blows, I know very well who would remain master of the field; but I am frightened at the immense number of good timid people always ready to second passively a movement of reaction. I think the bastard system, imposed on the Martignac ministry by the composition of the chamber at that period, was rapid enough in its legislative ameliorations to allow us to have patience with it, at the same time that it caused the votes in parliament to be for us, and brought the great body of the nation out of it, to our side. I am waiting with great impatience for news of the 3rd of June. What becomes of Algiers?—and Greece, the crown of which Prince Leopold's declaration permits no honest man decently to accept on the conditions prescribed by Wellington? Who is to be regent in England? The answer to all that is, that it is fourteen thousand miles from Calcutta to London, and fifteen hundred from hence to Calcutta; and that the post in India goes on foot, and tigers sometimes eat the letter-carriers.

Adieu, my dear friend: here is a great deal more than I should have written to you, if I had read the book of M. Jullien (of Paris, mind!) on *the employment of time;* for I have broken in upon your leisure, and left myself but a small share to answer a little mountain of letters from all corners of the world. If you think too much is not enough, deprive posterity boldly of a page of *real essences*, and go and pass an hour with my father, who will tell you more. Explain, I beseech you, my stoicism, to Madame Dunoyer; and if you think she will allow me, add some dose of friendship to the respects which I beg her to accept. As for you, my dear Dunoyer, without any more ceremony, I embrace you with all my heart.

TO M. ELIE DE BEAUMONT, ENGINEER OF MINES, PARIS.

Semla, in the Indian Himalaya, October 24th, 1830.

So many people whom I have never seen before, call me and write to me, *my dear Sir*, that I shall henceforth suppress the *Sir* to you, my dear Beaumont, and beg you will have the kindness to make the same reduction in my favour. People of our age, with friendship for each other, ought to call each other ingenuously by their names. I have no reason to treat you more ceremoniously than Charpentier or Adrien de Jussieu, both of whom I did not know till after you. When I return to Europe, I shall perhaps find you married, and grown ten years older by that simple fact; then the ice of our past ceremony would be very hard to break. Let us break it, then, before it grows too thick, and call me Jacquemont in return for calling you Beaumont.

The acre of scrawl which will accompany this note will prove to you that my thoughts have anticipated yours. Your letter of the 22d February last has only this moment arrived. I wrote to you more than six weeks ago. I reckoned that by this time that long letter would have been at least at Calcutta; but I kept it here by mistake—it is very lucky that it was not lost*. It answers by anticipation several parts of yours, without excusing me, however, from returning to it.

Every one is talking of the fame which you have just acquired by your ingenious discoveries. I shall esteem myself happy if I bring back some proofs of the justice of your views; and in spite of wild elephants, tigers, and, what is worse, of dangerous fevers, of which the forests covering the foot of the Himalaya are the constant abode, I shall go and collect them there. As for animals, though it would be an excess of scepticism not to believe in them, I give myself little concern about them; and as for the Jungle typhus, I rely greatly on my dry and tough fibre and my alimentary regimen, to preserve me from it. I shall have finished this expedition in a fortnight, and shall perhaps have some leisure at Sharampore to tell you the result.

I have found, accumulated here, all my collections made during the space of six months in the Indian and Tibetian Himalaya, and am busied with the cares necessary for their preservation. I likewise found a little mountain of European correspondence, formed here during my absence. I must answer on all sides; and it is almost without pleasure that I scribble these lines to you, bewildered as I am with business.

I am rejoiced to learn that you see Mérimee from

* The letter addressed to the same person, of the 9th of the preceding September, was despatched only with the present one.

time to time; I have an extreme friendship for him, with which he will also inspire you, when you know him as well as I do. I suppose he is going on getting an abominable reputation by his literary hardihood, whilst at bottom he is the best fellow in the world. You are more fortunate: your brilliant success against the obscurity of the ancient revolutions of the globe, does not expose you to troublesome interpretations. It is better to show only one's reason to the public, and reserve one's imagination for friends; this is the advantage of those who cultivate the sciences.

You have obliged me according to my taste with your friendly mosaic. There is no doubt a great deal of the ridiculous in the *industrialism* of M. de Saint-Simon, because the exposition of it is exclusively dogmatical, a form without which it would appear perhaps less original, and would border upon a *truism*. But the interest which it excited, and which is also awakened by the doctrines of Mr. Owen, the *Méthode Universelle* of M. Jacotot, all those speculative and practical novelties in short, occupy too great a number of minds not to prepare considerable changes in the formation of human communities. God grant that this slow but inevitable revolution may not be checked, delayed, and turned back in its progress, by vulgar commotions of brute force. I have just run through the English papers up to the 16th of June; they are very disquieting as to the future prospects of France: the question must be decided now, but five months will elapse ere I can learn its fortunate or deplorable solution.

Adieu, my dear Beaumont. I am ashamed of this disjointed stuff, and shall cut it as short as possible. Thanks for my health, in champagne, at Edon's. This evening I shall make a little speech to my English hosts, and the whole company will rise and drink to my toast of *absent friends.* I shall think of you as I empty my glass.

TO M. DE VICTOR DE TRACY, PARIS.

Semla, in the Indian Himalaya, August 25th, 1830.

If you had ever been deprived, for four months, of all European society, you would understand, my dear friend, the joy I experienced on my return to this place. In order that nothing might be wanting, your letter of the 12th of March was waiting for me, with several others from my family, all satisfactory; and the day after my arrival I received another packet from botanical and geological friends, Elie de Beaumont, Adrien de Jussieu, &c. &c. I am not yet recovered from the very common pleasures of sleeping under a roof, not eating alone, hearing the sounds of a sister language, and receiving at the same time so much pleasant and agreeable news: I still feel a sort of nervous agitation, which scarcely allows me to remain the whole day before a writing table, and which the fatigue of my long journey across the mountains can alone calm. This must be my excuse for the confusion that must reign in this letter.

I have succeeded, in spite of the jealousy of the Chinese government, in visiting some parts of Tibet subject to its authority. An English physician, some years ago, had almost as much success in a similar undertaking; but he was destitute of the information which might have rendered it interesting in a scientific point of view. Mr. Moorcroft afterwards penetrated a good way beyond the point reached by his countryman the doctor, and that at which I was compelled to stop, since he visited Leio, where he died, no doubt by poison. Before this journey, which proved so fatal to him, Mr. Moorcroft had travelled into another part of Tibet, equally shut against strangers by the suspicious policy of the Chinese. If you have read the account of his pilgrimage to the sacred lake of Mansarower, you will doubtless have had considerable difficulty in understanding how to satisfy, a vague curiosity, he could have resolved to expose himself to the dangers of a fanciful disguise, and resign himself to the privations of all kinds which it entailed upon him. Mr. Moorcroft visited Mansarower and the eastern Kailas, in the borrowed guise of a fakhir, dumb in consequence of a vow. In his last unfortunate expedition he had adopted the Persian costume, and traffic was the ostensible object of his journey. He could ask questions, but with reserve; curiosity however led him too far: he gave the lie to his Asiatic dress, and soon perished the victim of his imprudence.

I took much higher ground with the emperor of China: for him I did not change my dress, nor voluntarily deprive myself of all means of observation, without which my journey would have taught me nothing. I directed my caravan in a manner to avoid troublesome encounters as much as possible; and when I could not prevent them, I put a good face upon the matter, and ordered the people, who were collected to stop my progress, to retire immediately. Their astonishment was extreme, and they always withdrew murmuring. You will easily imagine, my dear friend, that I should not have risked menaces, if I had not had the moral certainty that it would prove sufficient to open the road to me. Perhaps these Tartars, if provoked by verbal abuse, would have shown the determination which anger often inspires; but I was as silent as the deserts around us. It was with the most indifferent tone that my Tibetian interpreter, at their injunctions to me to retire, gave them a similar order in reply. I continued to advance slowly, at my horse's or Yak's pace, followed by my men, who marched in close order, most of them loaded with bundles, some armed. My little caravan had an appearance of cool resolution, which left the Tartars to the mildness and natural timidity of their character, and I never met with any resistance but of the passive kind. One day, accompanied only by a few servants, all unarmed, with the exception of the one who carried my gun, I fell in with a party of two hundred mountaineers, all Lamas from their dress. Though I had already experienced their *circumspection* many times, I confess that I relied, with some misgivings, upon the small number of my men. My interpreter being far behind, I had no means of communication but by signs. I made a very imperative one, and this crowd retired from the pathway; two men only remained in it, who left me no passage. I pushed the first gently; for a violent shock would have precipitated him down the sides of the mountain, which are too steep to hold on by; he caught some tufts of grass, and joined the more docile troop grumbling. The other, who was without doubt the Cid of the band, did not stir. I removed him in the same way without showing any anger. This is the simple recital of my greatest battle.

If I did not know the value of the calling of Tartar-king, I could here perform the double of Dr. Francia. I would willingly undertake the conquest of central Asia with a hundred Gorkhas. The name of these latter is a terrible bugbear, it is true; and my tall white figure, though it has nothing very terrific, appeared very formidable to the peaceful Lamas.

The Indian Himalaya has something in it like Europe. It is covered with forests, whose trees have a family resemblance to those of the Alpine forests: they consist of pines, firs, cedars, sycamores and oaks differently associated with each other, according to the height of the mountain. Above the limit of the forests, there is green pasturage intermixed with dwarf shrubs, willows, and junipers, and this zone extends to that of the eternal snow. But towards Tibet, the whole region is so elevated that the bottom of the valleys exceeds the level at which the forest stops, on the southern declivity of the chain. The vegetation, reduced to some creeping, thorny, stunted shrubs, and scanty dried grass, forms here and there blackish spots on the margin of the torrents; the sides of the mountain are covered with nothing but what the rushing waters wash down; and the immense horizon offers a uniform scene of sterility and desolation, terminating on all sides by the snowy summits of the mountains.

Such is the strange peculiarity of the climate, that these Tibetian chains, if their height does not exceed twenty thousand feet, are entirely stripped of snow towards the middle of summer. I have several times encamped higher than the summit of Mont-Blanc, and to the north of the 32° of latitude; and as it was always the vicinity of a stream that decided my halts, almost every day brought me an opportunity of examining, at leisure, the rare traces of their singular vegetation. At the same elevation in the southern chain of the Himalaya, I should have been surrounded by scenes of snow.

Though my attention was principally directed to

the study of the phenomena of nature, and the observation of its productions, I did not neglect that of our species, oddly modified, as might be expected, from such peculiar circumstances of soil and climate. One of the most singular traits in Tartar and Tibetian manners, is polyandry. However numerous a family of brothers may be, they have only one wife in common; and it is with absolute confidence in the correctness of the information which I collected, that I consider the feeling of jealousy to be entirely unknown to this strange people, for it never disturbs the peace of these populous households. I could scarcely make myself understood when I inquired, whether the preference of the wife for one of her husbands did not sometimes cause quarrels among the brothers. This is certainly a most ignoble compensation for polygamy, which prevails throughout the rest of the East.

The collections of natural history, which I made in the north of the Himalaya, could not be very considerable; nevertheless the number of objects I have brought from thence exceeds my hopes, and I think that most of them are new.

My geological observations, on the southern girdle of this great chain, so far confirm the views which M. de Beaumont has hazarded concerning the period of its elevation. But in the same way that he has proved certain parts of the Alps to have been raised at different epochs, the Tibetian Himalaya, according to my observations, appears also of a different age, (not of geognostical formation, but of elevation,) from the Indian Himalaya.

As for the age of its geognostical formation, the researches with which I have been occupied to determine it, have put me in possession of an immense number of facts, from which I hope to deduce a very simple and satisfactory theory on the primary earths.

My professional friends are urgent that I should send them from time to time a scientific paper which they might publish as a certificate of my existence. I am as convinced as they are of the advantage which would result to me from such publications, but I absolutely want leisure; and if I wished to write some pages with care, pages which I should not regret at any future time having written, I immediately feel the want of books, which are not at hand. I had rather pass for dead than for dying, which might be concluded from feeble and neglected works. I cannot flatter myself that I shall bring home from my journey materials enough to live *upon India* for a score and a half of years, as M. de Humboldt has done on his concerning America; but if I could, I should not like such a thing.

I am now ready to descend into the plains; but whether it will be to proceed to the south or to the north, I know not.

I am negociating with the rajah Runjeet-Sing and the government of Calcutta, to obtain from the latter permission to leave their states by the Sutledge, and from the rajah that of entering his. This point being gained, I shall have to run after Runjeet I know not where, for he is making war on the revolted Afghans of the Upper Indus. I shall have to make a score and half of bows, give him a few louis for a Turkish dress, and remove the suspicions which he conceives of all Europeans.

How charming it would be for us to meet again at Paray, when you will have so many nice new things to show me there, and I so many stories to tell you! How much more should I be attached to that secluded and tranquil spot, if, on returning to France, I could spend the winter with you there, free from care, reperusing the journals of my travels, and preparing some work which might draw my name from obscurity.

Thanks a thousand times for the details of your long and kind letter. I keep my reflections on these novelties to myself, for my letter would be endless.

The extracts from our journals in the English papers, selected without discernment by the journalists of Calcutta, and which reach me here after this double test, give me great uneasiness concerning the issue of the absurd quarrels at present carried on in France. With an august imbecile like ours, there are no longer any probabilities to guide one in conjectures about the future.—Every thing is possible; and the circle of possibilities encloses great misfortunes! I shall know in a fortnight the result of the first electoral operations, but I easily foresee it. What I cannot foresee is the consequence of a new liberal majority in the chamber of deputies.—Adieu, my friend. I wish to turn my thoughts from such melancholy and irritating subjects. Adieu! Write to me oftener; speak to your father of my filial attachment to him, and remember me kindly to the rest of your family. A few words more to answer what you tell me of your children. Is it not ten years ago since I began to say that Louisa would one day be very beautiful, and the same time nearly that I made the engagement for Mary, which she keeps? Adieu again; I love you and embrace you with all my heart.

TO M. JACQUEMONT THE ELDER, PARIS.

Semla, in the Indian Himalaya, October 28th, 1830.

My dear Father.—Among my European, American, Asiatic, and African correspondents, I have already written thirty-four letters (some of which will come to you), and I have not done yet, although I have limited my correspondence to what is strictly necessary. I wanted to keep you for the last, but I knew not when your turn would come; so then, without farther preamble, I shall answer your two letters, which I found here on my return from Kanawer, on the 13th of this month. It is a great affair to reply properly to six pages of your close and small writing. But fortunately several of my letters, written since my departure from Calcutta, will have satisfied you on many points which made you uneasy at the date of your No. 13. You hiss the wild elephants, tigers, lions, and serpents; and you care very little for the blanks in your map designating the *unexplored countries* which you find sometimes on my route, or for the 12mos. (with regard to which my opinions do not vary), &c. &c. If there is any other danger about which your affection alarms you on my account, tell Porphyre to show you how to make a *rule of three;* and from my success against the obstacles which your perfect security about me has drawn up in battle array, on my road, conclude that I shall be equally fortunate against future difficulties.

I am returned from afar; I have often been very cold; I have had a hundred and eighteen very bad dinners;—but I think myself amply recompensed for these Trans-Himalayan miseries, by the interesting observations and vast collections which I have been able to make in a country perfectly new. The Tartars are very good sort of people. It is true, that to please them I made myself a little heathen after their fashion, and joined without scruple in their national chorus, "Houm! mâni, pani, houm!" and liberally distributed among them fifty pounds of tobacco, to enable them to smoke the calumet of peace with me. Near Ladac, however, they endeavoured to stop my progress by the excessive price they put upon the provisions of which my caravan stood in need. Their refusing them altogether, which they should have done as faithful

Chinese subjects, would have been compelling me to plunder their villages, and take by force what I required; but their circumspection preserved them from such a measure. I however considered the excessive dearness of their consent as a refusal, and reformed the prices by authority, still leaving them very high. I added the formal threat of plunder, if my camp was not well provisioned on these conditions; and I was allowed to want nothing.

If I was not the son of so great a philosopher, hereditarily insensible to worldly greatness, I should not have returned to Semla, but have remained in Tartary, king or khan of some villages. Assisted by three servants, I literally took the fort of Dunker, in Spiti, which you will find somewhere astride on the 32° of latitude.

Sabhatoo, October 31st.

If I were not candid, as the Baron de Stendhal calls me, I should not want matter for plenty of stories; I will only tell you that I believe less than ever in adventures, precipices, &c. &c. I used to repeat to Madame Micond, when I formed the project of visiting the Alps with Hippolyte Jaubert, "people do not kill themselves." It was then only a conviction of feeling in me; it is now experience, and of long standing. The English doctor, who travelled without the slightest advantage, part of the journey which I have just brought to so fortunate a close, left half-a-dozen servants on the Sutledge, in Spiti, and in the snows of the summits of the Himalaya. Of this, he somewhat boasts. He says he experienced excess of sufferings, when they had to pass the highest gorges. I encamped, and even sojourned in places at a greater height than those over which he only passed, and felt nothing of these miseries. But I drank water, and he brandy. Not one of my people (and I always had fifty) was seriously indisposed in this more than six months' expedition; there was not a fall, nor an accident of any kind. I learned the value of discipline on board the Zélée of immoveable memory; and I introduced some of it into my caravan, to prevent mishaps, or, at all events, to remedy them immediately. My people soon understood that this regulation, which at first seemed irksome to them, was made for their safety and welfare; and on my return to Semla, there was not one who did not wish to remain with me. The English treat them like dogs and beasts of burthen, the labour of which these poor devils in truth perform. For some days I imitated cold English *hauteur*, but returned afterwards into my natural character of a good-natured fellow. I shall frequently regret my mountaineers. I shall no doubt take one or two with me into the plains. Although, since my departure from Calcutta, I have not yet been robbed by my servants, and have still two of my Bengalese, I have not more confidence in them than I had the first day I hired them. The mountaineers are like the poor Lafleur whom Yorick took at Montreuil, full of good will, but not knowing how to do anything. In this country it is no great fault in a servant to be fit for nothing. My *pahari* will have no other business than to carry my gun and guard my imperial treasure. It will be a sort of insurance which will cost me thirteen francs a month.

You ask me for some personal details about myself. What could I add to those which I have so often given you since my departure from Calcutta? My Semla friends tell me that I am returned from Tibet a little stouter, and that I have brought back with me the appearance of perfect health. I possess the reality of it. I am very brown; I have large mustachios of a distressing colour; no whiskers, long hair, a very small light and flexible palm straw hat, made at Pondichery—every two or three months it is covered with a new black silk shirt; I have not lost a single tooth. Thus I am not a bit the worse. Having returned yesterday to the hot country, I dressed myself in white cambric muslin from head to foot; in the evening, to dine tête-à-tête with my host, notwithstanding our intimacy, I was in full dress, silk stockings and black everywhere instead of the white I wore in the morning. It is my ceremonious and perhaps foppish formality of the evening which permits me to do as I like in the day-time. My Parisian tailor stands greatly in need of a successor; and I shall soon find one at Meerut. Were it not that I am ashamed of exhibiting my calves, which are not so flourishing as my shoulders, I should increase my actual etiquette so far as to adopt breeches; but I am not yet enough of a philosopher for that. I shall be content with substituting a dress coat for my black frock. The judges in Calcutta often wear trousers; so will I—the whole will be of a thick black Chinese silk stuff (economical). For the mountains, I have thick dresses of white woollen stuff. I have brought from Tibet a stuff of this kind, as soft as a Cashmere shawl, and I now wear it. I have also had a dressing-gown made, in which I do not despair of doing metaphysics in my old age. In cool weather I wrap round my neck a large white shawl without a border, and consequently of no value. In the evening, in order not to be frozen in my tent, I have twelve ells of my superb Thibetan flannel (which cost me ten francs) rolled over my body from head to foot, and I do not look much unlike a mummy. On a march, I never wear stockings; and in the evening, if I can keep my legs warm, I never suffer from cold feet. Formerly this was doubtless a morbid disposition, which is effectually effaced, as well as my tendency to sore throat. I breakfast invariably before I start. This is contrary to the English custom; but it is because their marches last three hours at most, and mine frequently do not end till night-fall. I set out, then, at four or five o'clock in the morning, ballasted for fourteen or fifteen hours, and my meal is very plain. It is a large cup of cow's or buffalo's milk—goat's where there is no better—with some cakes of coarsely ground corn. These cakes are what the natives call their bread (roti). After trying them six months, I have completely given up rice. The poor sub-lieutenant, when on a journey, drags after him a few sheep. In order to eat meat at dinner, I have only the very uncertain chance of getting an old cock or hen. But I do not sleep the worse for lying down after a repetition of my Brahminical breakfast; besides, if I find honey anywhere, I have my empty bottles filled with it; this rarity I carry everywhere with me, when there is no milk or fowl—for instance, when I encamp in a desert.

I have still four pint bottles of brandy left out of the twenty-four which I brought from Calcutta a year ago; but my majesty's maitre d'hotel has broken—that is to say drunk—about six or seven, and I have used four or five to preserve different objects of natural history. But I have just done an admirable thing at Semla. A man died there the other day. When he was buried, his house and furniture were sold by auction; such is the law. But there were no purchasers, as there then was scarcely any body left in the mountains. I bought a basket of port wine, which connoisseurs pronounce the best in India. It cost me exactly three francs and half a bottle, and it is worth fifteen or twenty. When I have to cross the unhealthy forests I shall drink a small glass to your health, and it will not injure mine.—Very middling claret costs ten francs a bottle at Calcutta. When it arrives at Delhi it is always little better than vinegar. My port is proof against such a transformation. I shall endeavour to bring you a bottle to make Porphyre tipsy with, or failing in that, Frederic, without any other witnesses. My cellar will be quite stocked for more than a year.—Good news of my cavalry which I left at Sharunpore last April. My host there, Dr. Royle, sub-Wallich by profession, sends me word that I should hardly know my poney again. Happily the soil is very sandy about Sharunpore, where the acquaintance will be renewed between him and his rider; for this extraordinary vigour of my old companion promises me many a fall.

Evening.

Although we Europeans number only seven in this place, I am just returned from a funeral. The deceased was a young officer, who had five or six good reasons for dying; the brain injected, the lungs tubercled to the last degree, the liver disorganised, the peritoneum inflamed, &c. &c. I know this, for I myself opened the body, which appeared to me to gratify the survivors, who begged me to do it. I do not avoid mentioning this event of the day to you, because my head is always cool, I never feel any pain in my liver or bowels, and I can climb and run without being out of breath, the longest and steepest acclivities;—a proof that all parts of my lungs are in good order and perform their functions properly. With the exception of some formidable places, which no one can pass in certain seasons of the year, without exposing himself to an almost certain death, I do not believe the climate of India to be so fatal as it is generally represented. You recommend me to be my own physician; this I always am. My alimentary regimen is generally so mild, that when I travel or stay in suspected places, I can, by modifying it, obtain medical effects sufficient to remove any suspicion of intermittent fevers which I might conceive. A glass of brandy in the morning before going out, some spices in the evening at dinner, and before going to bed, a little sulphur, sugar, or resin burnt in my tent. I shall henceforth add a *chillum*, or tobacco pipe, in the oriental fashion, adopted by the great majority of Europeans. The tobacco which is stuffed into this little apparatus is mixed with different kinds of dried fruits, particularly apples, and a little conserve of roses; and the smoke, traversing a vessel full of water, reaches the mouth cool and divested of all acridity. Every other mode of smoking is barbarous when compared to this.

But I am speaking too much of myself, although you desired to know all about me. The ignorance which prevails in England about India is inconceivable. The English papers, when they speak of it, are scarcely less absurd than our own. Never believe any thing you read in them. I am perfectly well informed of the commercial and political relations between the English factory at Canton and the Chinese Government, and can assure you that there will be no war in that quarter for a long time to come. The two governments are sometimes sulky with each other, and the question then is which of them shall not make the first step towards an accommodation: the factory orders all English vessels to remove, suspends its immense purchases, and consequently the receipts of the Chinese custom-houses; and, as a deficiency in this respect would cost the viceroy of Canton his head, it is always he who has to come forward and yield the point in dispute. As for political insurrections in China, nothing is more common, as in every other part of the East. A province revolts, the emperor sends forces there, his troops are very bad and seldom risk a battle; but the hostile forces pass the time in observing each other, and the Government always succeeds in corrupting some of its enemies, who deliver up their chiefs; these have their heads cut off at Pekin, and there is an end of the matter. But they immediately begin again in some other part of the empire.—In the Indian principalities, nominally or really independent, there is constantly the same sport. Look for Belaspore on your map, near Subhatos, on the banks of the Sutledge. The rajah hung his vizier a week ago, and is now here because his subjects have taken the part of the dead man. The prince in short is come to claim the assistance of Kennedy. The latter is making an inquiry, which he will submit to the resident at Delhi, who, without referring the matter to Calcutta, will, no doubt, condemn the rajah to bestow a pension on the family of the vizier unreasonably put to death, and make him give good security not to repeat such an act. If the people of Belaspore were to persist in not receiving their petty sovereign back, Kennedy would march a company or two of his gorkhas, and all would be restored to order immediately.—We are making war in Bikaneer on the western frontier, not far from hence, which means only a hundred leagues off. Some great feudatories of this wretched crown, refused tribute to their legitimate prince. The latter immediately demanded the assistance of the English; and the resident of Delhi has just ordered three regiments of infantry and one of cavalry to march into Bikaneer. Their approach is sufficient to appease the rebellion. The dukes and counts of the desert will come and arrange matters with the commander of this little expedition. They will pay the rajah something more, in the shape of a fine, and will defray the expense occasioned to the English Government by displacing its troops.

The English officers of the Indian army are exceedingly dissatisfied with Lord William and the Court of Directors, on account of the reduction recently made in their pay. It is possible that a regiment may openly revolt. Twenty years ago, a sedition of this kind, provoked by the same cause, broke out in the Madras presidency: the governor was put on board ship almost by force, and driven away. This happened at a critical period. If Runjeet-Sing had then crossed the Sutledge, the Mahrattas and Bundlecund, which were not then reduced to submission, and marched to Bengal, the British power would no doubt have re-entered into the limits conquered by Lord Clive;—but the revolted of Madras soon perceived the danger, and returned of themselves to their duty, with the exception of a regiment or two, which the others immediately reduced; and the Government had the weakness not to shoot a single officer. Lord William would have been more severe: his invincible firmness is well known. There are only a few fools who will perhaps brave it without any chance of success. All the officers, however, agreed, in their correspondence with Europe, to draw an exaggerated picture of the exasperation of the army (that is to say of the European officers of the army—for the soldiers and subalterns, that is the Indians, do not take the least part in this quarrel, in which they are peculiarly disinterested), and of the dangers to which it exposes the Government, in order to intimidate the Court of Directors, and obtain the revocation of the economical measures carried into execution by Lord William; but the latter, you may easily suppose, wrote also to the Directors that these dangers were imaginary, and that they must remain firm.

Lord William, on arriving in India, found that the expenses of the Government exceeded its receipts (six hundred millions of francs) by a twelfth, that is fifty millions. He immediately wrote a curious letter to the Court of Directors, which has just been published in England by order of Parliament :—It would, he said, be the worst of measures to continue on this footing. The imposts must be raised fifty millions of francs, or the expenses reduced by so much. Each of these remedies offers great inconveniences; the latter is the least evil, and I adopt it.—Great joy on this occasion amongst the natives, assured of having nothing more to pay; great anger among the Europeans. They wished the *Dutchman* at the devil (Lord William is of Dutch origin; his great grandfather arrived in England with William, in 1688); they hope he may be drowned in the Ganges, or break his neck in the mountains, whither he is now coming—but be assured that they will not ship him for London.

The Calcutta papers inform me that Rammohun Roy is sailing for London. He is a Brahmin of Bengal, the most learned of the orientalists. He is acquainted with Greek, Latin, Arabic, Hebrew, Sanscrit, and writes admirably in English. He is not a Christian, whatever they may say. He has converted several skilful clergymen of the English episcopal church, who had been sent to him, to Unitarianism. The honest English execrate him, because, say they, he is a *frightful deist.* The Hindoos, of the priestly order, abhor him for the same reason. If I find him in Paris on my return, I will bring him to talk metaphysics with you. I used to see him often at Calcutta.

The political hubbub in our country often disturbs me: I catch some bits of it here and there in the Calcutta papers, in extracts from the English journals, but made without skill or discernment. Notwithstanding my scepticism, not to say my habitual incredulity, I confess I consider inevitable a revolution more or less complete. I know well what will be the issue of it, and I do not dread it; but I do fear the passing evils which will perhaps lead to it. I have lately written to Lady William to beg she will send me the French journals, after every body about her has read them. I shall thus have the *Gazette de France*, the *Constitutionnel*, and the *Courrier Français*.

The arrival of the new Governor of Bombay annoys you. It is true that it will render useless the numerous recommendations which I had brought from Europe for General Malcolm. I had also some for the Judges of that presidency; but they have all died within the last two years, and their successors also. However one remains firm, the *Chief Justice*. He is an intimate friend of Sutton Sharpe's, and was only a barrister at Bombay eighteen months ago. I have so admirable a letter for him from Sharpe, that I do not doubt of being perfectly well received. He is moreover a young man of four-and-thirty, and of our own school. He will serve as my introducer to Lord Clare, whom nobody here knows.

Adieu, my dear father. I am now going to discharge my account with Porphyre. It will be long, and you will find in it all that is wanting in this. Kind regards to every one. Adieu!—Once more, I am in excellent health, and next year shall get excellently well over thirty. I embrace you with all my heart.

TO M. PORPHYRE JACQUEMONT, PARIS.

Sabaton, November 1st, 1830. *Sobatoo, Sabatoo, Subatoo, Subhatoo, ad libitum.*

My dear Porphyre,—My last letter was a very long one, and accompanied one to our father of an equal extent; both dated from Nako in Hangarang, the 26th August. It replied to two letters which had miraculously succeeded in finding me in Tibet; but it contained also a great deal more. For fear it should be lost, I return to a part of its contents, without which this would be unintelligible. Runjeet-Sing, king of Lahore, has several French officers in his service. His generalissimo is a Monsieur Allard, formerly aide-de-camp to Brune, who, I think, has shown himself at several Asiatic courts for the purpose of obtaining a military command. He has been in

Egypt, Syria, at Constantinople, at Teheran; and he came at length to Lahore in 1822. Runjeet did not engage him until he had obtained the consent of the English Government; for, according to the terms of the treaties, he ought not to admit any European into his army. But British policy having changed considerably since the time when this treaty was made, the cabinet of Calcutta answered the rajah that they did not insist upon the execution of that article. Since that period they have allowed several other French military men to travel, without molestation, from Calcutta to the frontier of the Sutledge, particularly a younger brother of M. Allard, whose avowed object was to enter Runjeet-Sing's service. The British Government beholds without jealousy these attempts at discipline and European, though French civilisation, beyond the Sutledge, and the individual English appear to entertain great good will towards our countrymen in the Punjab. Of M. Allard, in particular, I have never heard them speak but with esteem.

Jacquemont here gives M. Allard's letter, which the reader has seen before; then his own, and adds—

Here is the answer which I found at Semla, the 13th October last.

" *Umbritsir**, *September 27th*, 1830.

" Sir,—Your answer, which I expected with the greatest impatience, has reached me at Amretsir, where the rajah usually collects his troops for the festival of the *desere*. When I had the honour of addressing you, I flattered myself that you would receive my letter with pleasure; but I was far from expecting that it would draw so many obliging things from you, which I receive with gratitude, but which add nothing to the sincere desire I have of being useful to you. I shall be happy if, from my situation in this kingdom, I can facilitate the scientific discoveries which, with truly astonishing courage, you are come to make in regions so full of dangers. However, my good will, to which will be joined that of my good friend and brother in arms, M. Ventura†, who is not less impatient than I am to become acquainted with you, gives me the certainty of easily smoothing many difficulties for you, if you decide on crossing the Sutledge. It is true that our rajah is not pleased to see Europeans coming from India, visit his kingdom, particularly the province of Cashmere; but if you could obtain letters from the Governor of Delhi for Runjeet-Sing‡, or

* Umbritzir, or Amratsir, Umretsir, Amretsir, &c., is a large city, between the Sutledge and Lahore; it is the holy city, the Rome of the Seikhs. (Author's note.)

† Ventura, an Italian officer in the service of Runjeet; formerly in our army. (Author's note.)

‡ Runjeet, Runjeet-Sing, the Rajah,—Maradjah,—one and the same person, King of Lahore. (Author's note.)

even from Captain Wade*, the first difficulties would be removed; and as to what remains to be done, it will be our place to provide for your safety and necessities: all these things are necessary for a countryman of ours, such as M. Jacquemont, to travel in the Punjab. Lord William Bentinck and Sir Charles Metcalfe did not deceive you when they assured you that a journey into the country of Kabal was impracticable. To undertake it would be to expose yourself to almost certain danger. I address my letter to Dr. Murray at Loodheeana, who will have the kindness to forward it to Captain Kennedy, in order that it may be delivered to you. I hope it will reach you soon, and that it will induce you to continue a correspondence to which I attach the greatest value. I repeat, Sir, the offer of my services in whatever way they may be useful, as also the assurance of the high consideration with which I have the honour," &c. &c.

My reply to this second letter from M. Allard was, that I had determined on paying him a visit, and to put his credit with the rajah to the test. I wrote at the same time to Lord W. Bentinck to inform him of my design, and to beg of him to procure for me, in the form most favourable to the success of this negociation, a letter of introduction to Runjeet. I shall have his answer in twelve days or a fortnight.

* Political agent at Loodheeana, subordinate to the Governor or Resident of Delhi. (Author's note.)

Runjeet-Sing is not without resemblance to the Pacha of Egypt. No doubt, Europeans in his service are exposed to occasional injustice, but nothing very grievous. When M. Allard has reason to complain of Runjeet, he is not afraid to look coldly on him for a month or two; and he knows how to oblige the rajah to reconsider the measure which had justly offended or irritated him. Runjeet has a singular tact in discovering suspicious adventurers, and getting rid of such characters.

I have begged Lord William to entitle me *Lord Physician Victor Jacquemont*, and to support the title of *hakim*, I shall carry with me some pounds of cantharides. Mr. Elphinstone, in his embassy to Cabul, made himself adored for the Venetian pills which he distributed. One of the most common diseases in the East is precocious impotence. The Levantines know very well how to relieve themselves from it, from time to time, by the use of cantharides; but to the eastward of Persia such means are unknown.

Whatever Dr. Wallich may have done, or caused to be done, there will remain a sufficiency of novelties for me to afford a pretence for a book on botany, which will not merely be a *flora*, that is to say, a description of the different species of plants in the Himalaya; and, if I am not mistaken, the book of which I have an idea, not a very voluminous one, will not be devoid of interest. I shall compare the vegetation of the Himalaya with that of the Alps, the rocky mountains to the west of the Missouri, and the lofty Cordilleras of equinoctial America.

Six months of geological observations, occupying many pages of my journals, will permit me to produce something different from the vulgar work, of which many parts of the Himalaya have frequently been the subject: that is to say, a lòcal description. From the whole of my observations, I think I shall be able to conclude against the ideas generally admitted concerning their primitive formation. I cannot deny to M. de Humboldt the correctness of the observations which he has made in the Cordilleras and in Europe; but I think the statement of my own will render his very doubtful. A book of geology on the Himalaya, or on the geology of the Himalaya, will be much more sought after in England than in France; and I presume that an English version would find a sale in London. I think I shall give myself the trouble of translating myself into that language, with some variations, so that the English book may not be considered a mere translation, made by a translator at so much a sheet. Perhaps I shall find something besides trouble in writing in a foreign language? Even now I should have the boldness to undertake such an affair; and certainly it will become still easier to me in a few years. My English correspondence, of which I often complain, will have been very useful to me.

Eating creates appetite. If I pass some years in

the Punjab it will not be without acquiring a perfect knowledge of the *quantity* and *quality* of the Persian requisite for the transaction of official matters; and amid the political changes which the future reserves for our country, perhaps I shall for a time find some advantageous employment in the East! Laugh at me, my dear Porphyre, and I will join heartily in the chorus. But it is amusing to build aerial castles in a smoky hut.

I have received the *Annuaire du bureau des longitudes* for 1829; but alone, and without any letters in company.

I neither eat opium nor chew betel—no European chews betel, very few eat opium. I have just accepted a little present from Kennedy before leaving him; it is a hookha, of which I will make you a present on my return, if it is not stolen between here and Paris. You talk to me of cigars—the hookha is not portable, it is a rather complicated apparatus, weighing three or four pounds; but the smoke you draw through it is so mild, so cool, and so perfumed, that I predict you will keep one in your old age, and I hope it will be my Himalayan one. I do not see why Sir John Malcolm's departure should annoy you. No one here knows Lord Clare, his successor; but I shall arrive in Bombay no less well recommended on that account.

To-morrow Kennedy goes back to Semla. I shall at the same time go down into the plains with a new acquaintance, who pleases me much: this is Mr. Fraser, the viceroy of Delhi, a civil, judicial, and financial officer of the highest rank. Mr. Fraser was in the Punjab with Mr. Elphinstone, of whose embassy he formed a part; he is the person best informed concerning the Seikh country. My meeting with him is providential. The day after to-morrow he will continue his route to Delhi, and I shall return hither, whence I shall start again next day for Sharunpore, through Nahun. I am not yet accustomed to the singular attraction which I exercise over the English: its effects often astonish me. I have what is much better than the pleasures of self-love: the sincere attachment to me which many evince. At Semla I frequently saw an invalid officer, Kennedy's friend and predecessor. He left us some days ago for Hyderabad (the capital of central India), of which he has just been appointed viceroy. Our hearts swelled as we said good-bye. I shall be very melancholy to think that I may never see that good and amiable man again. I shall be gloriously feasted if I go to Hyderabad. The people who please me most are the military men detached from their corps, and employed for a long period in political duties, or more frequently in political, civil, judicial, financial, and military all at once. It is from them that I obtain the best information about the country. I seem like one of their comrades.

P. S. Umbala, in the country of the protected Seikhs, quite at the top of the map. 9th February, 1831.

What things have happened, my friend, since the

commencement of this letter! Do not be angry with me for not finishing and despatching it to you sooner. I was waiting from day to day, in order to have some good news to send you—but none arrives from any quarter.

TO M. JACQUEMONT THE ELDER, PARIS.

Delhi, January 10th, 1831.

How shall I begin, my dear father? My last letter, written at Semla and Subhatoo, was dated the 1st November. The most recent news from Europe for us folks in the Himalaya, came down only so far as June; and now I have just been reading the *Débats* of the 8th August, and the *Gazette de France* of the 10th, and I know the whole series of events that have filled this interval.

It was towards the latter end of November, when at Sharunpore, that I heard the first sound of the tocsin. It was at night, after a long day's study, spent far from Europe, and I was about to lie down and sleep on the thoughts of the day, when a messenger arrived in my camp at full gallop. He brought from a neighbouring European habitation a Calcutta Gazette, printed in an unusual form, bearing this title in large letters,

"THE NEW FRENCH REVOLUTION."

I accepted the chance of it at once, and bargained for freedom at the price of some thousands slain and a month of civil war. The perusal of my bulletin soon informed me that the Parisians had made better conditions. Not that the slain were wanting; but it only required three days' fighting to crush the counter-revolution at Paris. The great towns in her vicinity had done like her; and, although my undigested chronicle stopped at the 31st of July, without answering for even the events which it related under that date, I slept peaceably till morning, without fearing to be awakened by fresh gun-shots.

This news had been brought to Calcutta by an English ship, which had sailed from Southampton on the 2nd of August. Since then, another has arrived from Bourdeaux, having left that city: it entered the Ganges with the tri-coloured flag, which was immediately hoisted by all the other ships of our nation moored in the river. I was at Meerut, the largest military station of the English in India, when the flood of news which she brought, arrived there. Friends and strangers all came to congratulate me on being a Frenchman; I defy M. de Lafayette, in America, to have shaken more hands in one day than I did. My host, a cavalry colonel, who was the only one of his regiment that escaped at Waterloo—not without a ball through his body—wept for joy as he embraced me. Enthusiasm had put the rigid etiquette of English manners to the route; the *sauve qui peut* still lasts! I might throw my passports, and letters of introduction, into the fire, change my name, and, preserving only my French tionality, and set out for Cape Comorin—there is not an European in India that would not receive me with open arms. These enjoyments are new to me; I cannot describe them. All shades of political opinion among my hosts are confounded in the same feelings of admiration, love, and gratitude to the French name; and as I am the only one that bears it, I receive proofs of these feelings from all sides.

All the civil and military officers of this province joined in giving me a fête on the last day of the year just ended. Of course, a constitutional and moreover an English *fête* was a banquet, and you may guess that I did not escape from this enthusiasm without a speech; but I was wound up to the same pitch as my hosts, and words cost me nothing.

The following, among many others, is the best, I think, of my English improvisations: do not forget that it came after several toasts and furious cheers in favour of France and plenty of bottles of Champagne.

" Gentlemen, I have no words to express to you the tumultuous feelings of happiness that excite in my heart your hearty cheers for the prosperity of my country. If any thing can console me for being so far from it when I might have shared in the dangers and in the glory of my fellow-citizens, it is certainly the present circumstance of my sitting a guest at your banquet; it is the sublime spectacle of your enthusiastic sympathy for the righteous victory of my countrymen in a holy cause. I shall remember always with the deepest emotion this memorable, this most poetical occurrence of my life. These British acclamations for the liberty of France, resounding in this far distant land of Asia, at the gates of Delhi, will awake in my grateful heart as long as it breathes, a poetical echo of admiration.—— Here I resume these glorious colours which adorn alike your breasts in this patriotic meeting, and which wave over us, mixed by your friendly hands, with the noble colours of free England. Gentlemen, let us hope they may be never divided! Too long indeed they were opposed to each other!—Both then waved over victories unparalleled hitherto in the records of history.— Mournful were those victories, which proved often ruinous to the conquerors as well as to the conquered!— Gentlemen, it is not as the symbol of the military glory of my nation that the tricolour is so dear to me.—I am a man before I am a Frenchman; I do not cherish the recollection of a glory bought by the miseries, by the oppression of all the continental nations of Europe, and by the political servitude of France herself. I admire— but I lament that glory which united all the people of Europe in a feeling of hatred for the French name, and which finally made, twice, the deserted eagle and the independence of my country a prey to the storm of European popular revenge. The gallic cock which surmounts the tricolour banner of the 28th of July brings to me no such recollections: it is not a bird of prey, a symbol of conquest; but a national and spirited emblem of industry, of watchfulness, and of strength also, and of undaunted courage. Iniquitously attacked by the Prussian eagle during the domestic struggles of our first revolution, it drove it fiercely back to the Rhine.—Had it stood there—had it not undergone its imperial metamorphosis, and flying over the frontier, inflicted desolation on the people of Europe for the wrongs of their kings!——Gentlemen, believe me that those feelings which I have so feebly expressed to you through a foreign language, but which live so warm in my heart, are shared in by the immense majority of the generation to which I belong, and which now assumes the political power in my country.—Believe me, that equally proud of British friendship, equally convinced that the union of France and England, the leaders of modern civilisation, would prove a blessing to both, and countenance everywhere the generous efforts of liberty, and secure throughout Europe the steps of social improvements and promote human happiness—believe me, Gentlemen, that all my countrymen would rise with me and rapturously propose with me the toast I beg to offer: FRANCE AND ENGLAND FOR THE WORLD *!"

It, of course, costs my modesty as an author a great deal to add, that flattering murmurs several times interrupted me, and that these agreeable murmurs swelled more than once into a thunder of applause—but as an impartial historian, I am forced to confess it.

* The above speech is in Jacquemont's original English (T.)

Do not from that, my dear father, form an unfavourable opinion of the literary good taste of my friends; but recollect the place, the circumstances, the Great Mogul near us, &c. &c. All to me was like magic.

I had very seasonably disciplined myself to the fire of speeches at Meerut which I chanced to visit at the time of the grand military reviews, each of which was followed by a dinner given to the inspecting general officer. I was at all these parties without being able to help it, and they seldom terminated without a toast to the health and success of the traveller, &c. &c. "May he sometimes forget among us that he is far from his native country," &c. Every morning I made new resolutions of insensibility for the evening, in order to speak better; but they always failed me at the hour of need, and yet I did not regret them: for my thanks, receiving immediate birth from the compliment which called for them, were always favourably received.

I travelled in one day from Sharunpore to Meerut, though the distance is eighty-four miles. My Meerut friends arranged for me that which does not exist anywhere in India, relays of horses to the number of nine. I arrived at dusk, so little fatigued that finding my host, Arnold, ready to mount his horse for a ride, I asked a tenth horse of him, and accompanied him without delay. My friendship with that excellent man is really an odd thing. We both live in a very different order of ideas. The exterior of our existence has no greater resemblance. He is a brilliant, superb cavalry officer, dotingly fond of his profession and of the magnificent corps which he commands. But you know it is my fate to please the English. I suffer it to take its own course, for I really am not aware that I have any thing to do to attract it: this kindness to me seems spontaneous.

It is three days' march, about forty miles, from Meerut to Delhi, which I galloped over with my "*fidus Achates*" between breakfast and dinner on the 15th of last December.—The evening before, I had received your letters, Nos. 16 and 17 (15 is still on its way with its companions, Beaumont's book, &c. &c.) and one from Lord William Bentinck, in answer to mine from Semla, in which I expressed my wish to visit Cashmere, and requested his diplomatic good offices with Runjeet Sing to open the gates to me. From Lord William's letter, I hoped, on my arrival here, to find the resident disposed to second me vigorously. But he has received only the most limited powers for that purpose; and as he had arrived at the residence of Delhi from that of Hyderabad, only a fortnight previously, was but ill-informed concerning the relations of his court with that of Runjeet-Sing, and alarmed at his own responsibility, he seemed to be afraid to act on my behalf even in the narrow circle which had been traced for him. I consequently again wrote to the Governor-general. The answer which I received from him to my second letter is a great proof of his esteem.

He has authorised the resident to do for me what has been invariably refused to every British officer who has of late years made similar requests.

By order of the Governor-general, the resident has introduced me officially to the minister of Runjeet-Sing accredited to him. He has explained to him, which is very difficult in Persian, what I am, the nature and object of my studies, the friendship of the English Government for me, the protection with which it has surrounded me while travelling in their dominions, the personal interest which the Governor-general takes in me, and his wish to see me succeed in extending my researches into the regions subject to the absolute power of Runjeet-Sing, &c. &c. In short, this little but delicate negociation was conducted with all possible address and success. I spare you the Persian superlative with which the resident thought proper to load me, in order to give the Seikh minister a high idea of my importance: I was nothing less than the well of science, the VERUM LUCENS of the chevalier Antoine Lafont, *luisant le vrai, jaillisant la vérité* *. I think, indeed, that I may certainly rely upon being graciously received by Runjeet-Sing. M. Allard, his French commander-in-chief, has already taken upon himself to send me firmans for all the officers under him who command on the frontier. He enjoins them to obey my

* Le ver luisant, le vrai principe du mouvement des invisibles et des visibles: par le Chevalier Ant. Lafont. Paris, 1824, 4to. —triple distilled nonsense.

wishes, and escort me from Loodheeana to his head-quarters at Lahore. I shall set out in a few days.

I should have regretted all my life not having availed myself of this admirable opportunity of visiting a celebrated country, inaccessible to European travellers since Bernier, in 1663; for Forster only saw by means of a disguise which compelled him to look at nothing. After the despotic prince who, by terror, at present maintains order there, the anarchy which for a century desolated it will certainly revive, and render impracticable every undertaking similar to that which I am about to attempt with so many probabilities of success. It is to the happy chance which brought about the friendly relations I have formed and keep up with the Governor-general of India, that I am indebted for the flattering prospect now smiling upon me. No Asiatic friendship could recommend me, better than that, to the king of Lahore.

Lord W. Bentinck always finds time to write me long letters when my interest requires it, and always with his own hand, although he has secretaries, who have also their secretaries. Yet what does he owe me?—A passport once for all, and no more. It is not the same with the gentlemen at the Jardin des Plantes, whom I had reason to think attached to me by other obligations. However strange this may appear to you, it is not less true that I have not received a single line from them since my departure from Paris. You have announced to me some paltry additions to my allowance:

but what use is my knowing it, if I only know it through you? Is that an authority for me to demand more extended credit in this country? The only funds I dispose of in this country are those which I brought with me; they expire with the year just commenced. Prudence would perhaps urge me to set out for the nearest sea-port, instead of going to the distant regions of Cashmere; but I considered the opportunity offered me of visiting them, as an urgent circumstance, for a century might elapse before it could be afforded to another traveller. When this letter reaches you, I must absolutely have the means of returning sent to me. I should like to see those people, who will perhaps blame me for undertaking this journey, exposed to the fatigues and privations which await me. The pleasures of Cashmere! The delights of an enchanting climate! Oh! many fine things might be said of it for those who remain comfortably seated at their fire-sides in Paris! The tales of the west about the east are truly absurd! Ask Colonel Fabvier what Greece is; I will tell you some day what Cashmere is.

It is not impossible I may have a companion in Mr. William Fraser, the commissioner at Delhi, which means the head of the civil, judicial, and financial administration of that province. Mr. Fraser is a man of fifty, who, but for some eccentricities of character, would hold a higher office than the one he occupies: he would be resident, with two hundred and fifty thousand francs a-year, instead of one hundred and fifty thousand, the salary of his present appointment. I am only acquainted with him from having seen him for two days at Subhatoo, at Kennedy's, in the month of November last. He was on his return hither from the mountains, whither his health had forced him to emigrate during the frightful rainy season. He pleased me extremely, and I pleased him no less. In order to enjoy each other's company longer, we agreed to travel together two days, each out of his way—and when we parted we were firm friends. This man, possessed of great qualities and talents, to which every body in India does justice, but who is generally considered a misanthrope, I found the most sociable person in the world. He is a thinker, who finds nothing but isolation in the intercourse of words without ideas, miscalled conversation by the society here, which he therefore very seldom frequents. He has travelled much but always alone, because, as he told me, he never met a companion to his taste. The only singularity which I can find in him is a complete monomania for strife. When there is a war anywhere, he forsakes his tribunal and goes to it. He is always the first at a storming party, an amusement in which he got two good sabre cuts on his arms, a pike-thrust in his loins, and an arrow in his neck, which nearly killed him. At this price he has always been able to extricate himself from the actions in which he has thrust himself, without being obliged to kill a single man. This he related to me as the finest part of his history, known besides to all in this country, as is also his humanity. The emotion of danger is the most voluptuous to him: that is the theory of what is called his madness. Of course, with this form of courage, Mr. Fraser is the most pacific of all men. You would take him for a quaker, notwithstanding his large black beard.

I did not find him at Delhi on arriving there from Meerut. His duties during winter are ambulatory; he had been gone, ever since the 1st of December, to judge appeals in civil and criminal causes, as well as from the financial decisions of the magistrates and collectors of the different districts of his court. He is now transacting his business at Hansi. He wrote to me from thence, a few days ago, to confide to me a thought of his, which, since our separation, he tells me has never left him: namely, to request my permission to accompany me in my journey beyond the Sutledge. The condition on which he will acccept what he is pleased to term this great favour, is the sincere assurance on my part that such an arrangement is quite agreeable to me. I gave it to him with perfect sincerity; and with the same absence of flattery I told him that he was the only man of my acquaintance in India that I would desire as a travelling companion. The reason why he is so desirable a companion is, that being endowed with a superior mind, enriched by long experience in the different branches of Indian administration, he has a multitude of facts to tell me, doubts to remove, and enigmas to solve, concerning the mechanism of that singular government. His mode of life has familiarised him, more perhaps than any other European, with the customs and ideas of the natives. He has, I believe, a true and profound knowledge of their domestic existence, which few others could possess. What information may I not expect from his conversation? Hindoostanee and Persian are like his mother-tongue to him; I shall therefore derive the greatest advantage from his knowledge of those languages.—And if at the corner of some wood a band of ambushed rascals——I should do my best, no doubt; but a little assistance is not to be despised, and I should receive the most vigorous aid from such a companion.—Although I have very little faith in the chapter of accidents, and have rendered you sufficiently incredulous, the imperturbable coolness of my friend may, perhaps, serve as a protector to your imagination against the disagreeable chances of possibility.

Mr. Fraser has asked Lord William Bentinck for leave of absence for ten months. He will, no doubt, obtain it; but the kindness of the Governor-general to him will be confined to permitting him to absent himself from Delhi. He has reason to hope, however, that his hospitable intercourse with several Seikhs of high rank, and his name also, which is as well known on the other side of the Sutledge as on this, will ensure him a good reception from Runjeet-Sing. Besides, he will leave me as soon as his junction with my caravan appears to throw political obstacles in its way.

I forgot to tell you the conditions of our joint expenditure. In truth, I have not thought of speaking to him on the subject; it being well understood that, as I am the poorer of the two, I shall regulate them as I please. I have seven hundred francs a month to spend this year. If I think proper to stipulate that my companion shall incur no greater expense than this, he will passively submit. I might have only a hundred francs a month; and if such were the case he would cheerfully agree, if I wished it, to limit his expenditure to this trifling sum.

The aerial castles which I had amused myself with building in Cashmere, on receiving the first overture from M. Allard, when I was in Kanawer, are almost entirely vanished. All that I can expect from Runjeet Sing is a Turkish dress and a horse,—two things I little need, and which are always given in the East to persons of distinction on their first appearance at any prince's court. Perhaps,—but that is uncertain, and not less so whether I should think proper to accept it,—perhaps Runjeet, as a mark of his royal favour, may grant me a few rupees a day at the charge of the towns and villages through which I shall pass. This also is done in the East. M. Allard, who is expecting me at Lahore, will there determine upon every thing for me, and each decision of his will present more aspects than one.

My intention,—but God disposes,—is to enter Cashmere by the northern road, that which leads to Peshawar through Attock, and return through Independent Tartary, through Ladak, of which I have already seen some little, or else by an infinitely more direct route which ends at Rampore the capital of Bissahir, situated on the banks of the Sutledge, five days' march above Belaspore, the name of which pleases you so much.

Semla will be on my road from Delhi. Lord and Lady William, the Major-general of the army, Colonel Fagan, and a number of other people of my acquaintance, will be there to make me forget the miseries of my laborious pilgrimage in the enchanting valley, &c. &c.; not to speak of my former host Kennedy, who will expect me there at the end of September.

All my collections are here, and in a most satisfactory state of preservation. They are all so well poisoned that they have nothing to fear from the ravages of the insects engendered by the climate; moreover they are carefully packed, and ready to take their departure for Paris. Were it not for the expense, I should perhaps make them, with the grace of God, begin their travels to-morrow, on the Jumna and Ganges; but the cost prevents me, and it is perhaps so much the better for their safety; for after all, shipwrecks are very common on these rivers, as is proved by the high rate of insurance on their navigation. Having resolved on leaving my collections here, until I increase them with the products of my campaign in Cashmere, every one offered his house to receive them. I preferred the military store-house, where it is impossible that I shall not find them again, ten months hence, just as I place them now, unless the powder blows up—or, what is not more probable, unless the English cease to be masters of Delhi.

But a few words about my journey from Subhatoo. There are some very pretty girls there,—a remark I have very seldom had occasion to make to you since I have been traveling in this country. They form a little *corps de ballet*, which has to me all the appearance of being one of the regal acts of magnificence of my friend Kennedy, the least jealous of sultans, and a good friend besides.

I there left the king or rajah of your favourite village, Belaspore, a very hopeful young scoundrel, who used to amuse himself last summer by causing the first comers into his paltry empire to be trodden to death by one of his elephants; and who, being tired of his prime minister, hung him that he might have another. His subjects revolted and drove him away. The fugitive prince came to demand forces from Kennedy, to reduce them. He was far out of his reckoning. Kennedy without ceremony told him he deserved to be hanged himself; and, moreover, that he would take care he did not hang any body else. Lord William has only to make a stroke of his pen to efface these kingdoms.

I had seen the valley of Pinjoor, in company with Mr. Fraser. I therefore came over the crests of the two mountains from Subhatoo to Nahun; but not without accident. I was riding up a tolerably wide but very steep path. My steed, like a true mountaineer, was peaceably stepping upon the brink of the precipice, when on a sudden the ground gave way under its hind legs. The poor animal made sundry attempts with its fore feet; and after hesitating a few seconds fell backwards. A proof that I lost my senses is, that I had no idea of my danger. A miracle had placed a small, thorny, stunted tree, twenty or thirty feet below; and I found myself perched upon it, without having the slightest consciousness of the manner in which I had been carried there. In my passage, I only received a contusion on my head, no doubt given me by that of the horse as he fell upon me. As for the latter, I looked down to the valley for his remains, but the miracle was double: twelve or fifteen paces below me there was another tree, which had stopped him in his fall. He waited very peaceably, like myself, till my people went to release him. With ropes, gentleness, and patience, in less than an hour we were both fished up again. We must believe in miracles, for animal magnetism cannot explain this.

Nahun is the capital of Sirmour, a petty kingdom in the mountains, which for the last forty years has been mercilessly clipped by the Seikhs, the Gorkhas, and the English. The rajah has, nevertheless, two hundred thousand rupees a year. His little city, one of the handsomest in India, is seated on the brow of a mountain, which overlooks on all sides deep, humid valleys covered with thick forests. It was in one of these gorges that I met the rajah, who had come three miles from his residence to receive me. The moment I perceived him, I alighted from my horse; he at the same time descended from his elephant, and we advanced gravely towards each other on foot. We embraced each other on either shoulder, like uncles on the stage; and, after exchanging every other form of Indian politeness usual on such occasions, the rajah invited me to mount his elephant, and climbing up after me, we took the road to Nahun. Several other elephants followed ours, carrying the viziers and other great officers of the modest crown of Sirmour. Some fifty horse, armed and dressed in the most picturesque manner, pressed round us; the foot were much more numerous, and bore silver maces, banners, halberds, the fan, the royal parasol, &c. &c. I had never, till then, seen any thing so like the groups which a European imagination delights in placing in an Indian landscape.

The rajah was a handsome young man of two and twenty, elegant in his manners, like the Indians of high rank in the plains; open, active, and communicative, like the inhabitants of the mountains. He pleased me so much that I remained two days in his capital, spending the greatest part of that time with him. From the bungalow, which he has built for the convenience of English travellers, and which he immediately placed at my disposal, I went each morning, sometimes on horseback, sometimes on foot, to see him in his palace. He received me there with all the pomp of his court; the morning was spent in conversation, to which we admitted (and it often became matter of discussion) those courtiers whose rank gave them the right to sit on the royal carpet, near the prince's throne or arm chair, and mine. In the afternoon the rajah came, with all his cavalcade, to pay me a visit; examining all things about me, asking the use of each, and admiring the faculty of locomotion belonging to Europeans. We then remounted his elephant together, and went to take a ride about the town or its environs; at night he set me down at my own door. I liked this evening ride, because, being alone on the elephant, we were at liberty to say every thing we pleased to each other. On these occasions, I gave him a little course of lectures on morals and political economy, which would assuredly have been very little to the taste of his ministers. Every year, about five or six English travellers go to Nahun, in order to seek health in the mountains. My young protégé, notwithstanding his politeness, has not succeeded in seeing more than one or two of them, and it was only to exchange formal compliments with them. Nothing, it is true, is so rare among the natives of India as the slightest inclination to become sociable; but the English never try to discover it, nor do they cultivate it if it chance to exist. This is the reason why they remain such complete strangers to the people whom they govern. The climate of Nahun is very healthy; but at certain seasons of the year the forests in the neighbouring valleys cannot be passed through without exposure to an almost certain death. The use of tobacco and bitter and generous wines, is recommended as a preservative. My old port from Semla flowed plentifully; and Kennedy, when I left him, made me accept a hookha to smoke after the fashion of the country. These precautions succeeded perfectly, and I returned to the plains of India in all the integrity of my mountain health.

I cannot tell you, my dear father, with what feeling of melancholy I found myself once more on the sandy and desolate plains of Hindoostan. They are covered in some places with tall, yellow, withered grass; elsewhere with a poor, thorny, whitish shrub, which gives the same sad and wild aspect to the whole of India and Persia. You often pass near the ruins of a village, consisting of a mound of clay, interspersed with fragments of earthenware, and tombs scattered around. Sometimes you will pass, twice in a single day, through a considerable city, whose buildings and mosques are still standing, and which, though perhaps erected less than a century ago, no longer contains a single inhabitant. I reached Sharunpore by forced marches, in order to abridge this tedious part of my journey.

I have just been reperusing your last two letters, 16 and 17; they both relate to mine from Benares; so that one must wait a whole year between a question and its answer! Be it so!

You wish me to become somewhat of a Sanscrit scholar. You think that being in possession of a great number of the roots of that language, its study would be easy to me. You are mistaken. In the first place, in the Hindoostanee that I speak, that of the upper provinces, the proportion of Persian is much more considerable than that of Hindoostanee. I write in Persian characters; and the system of writing, which after all is but a rather illegible short-hand, is sufficiently difficult to make me dispense hitherto with using the *Nagaree* characters, which are very like the Sanscrit. The Sanscrit syntax is horribly difficult, and the system of compounding words.

But on my return to Paris, I shall say, like the fox, "they are sour," with this difference, that I shall be sincere in saying so. The Sanscrit will lead to nothing but the knowledge of itself. As for Persian, my contempt for that language is unbounded; and I am persuaded that every one who knows a little of it, and is not paid six thousand francs a year for admiring it, thinks of it as I do. I am availing myself of my stay here to perfect myself in it. A young Brahmin comes every evening to pass an hour with me; we do not read, as is usual, the eternal *Gulistan* of English students, but the *Persian Gazette of Calcutta*, written in vile prose, but such as is spoken. The English, who learn Persian, begin by buying lace, and often die without having a shirt. Hafez, Sadi, and other insipid and tiresome poems of the same kind, are only useless lace to us.

You ask me if I have gathered any of the beautiful white roses of the environs of Delhi? Be you suspicious of those flowers which embalm the whole country. I am still in search of them, without having seen any. Malte-Brun, I perceive, has allowed himself some travellers' licences. The finest roses in the world are those of Paris. Not that fine things are wanting round Delhi, but roses are very scarce.

My manuscript is of a terrifying length. I often think of the means of melting together, or skilfully separating the many different subjects which are crowded together in it. But this would be a difficult matter, and I should not be able to attempt its execution until I reached Paris. We will hereafter hold a council together on it. I imagine that we now have with the Duke of Orleans a little model of a government, quite economical, if such can exist. However, I flatter myself that my friends will obtain something from it for me. I am going to forward a little memorial to support them.

I am expecting your next letters with great anxiety. I do not know the name of one of the killed at Paris; and my newspapers agree in saying that there were several thousands. Fortunately I do not see near our house any public building which may have attracted the battle to its neighbourhood.

Adieu for to-day. I am writing to you wrapped up in shawls and blankets, and my feet in carpets. The sun is however very hot, but the air in the shade is so cold, that there is sometimes a little ice in the morning, and the wind makes the temperature appear a great deal sharper than it really is. There are no fire-places in the houses, at least in that of my host, an old general, who is otherwise without fear, but is singularly afraid of fire in his house. I owe him a dreadful cold which is just over. I forgot to tell you that they have made me a present here of an assortment of medicines which I shall philanthropically distribute among the Seikhs, Cashmerians and others, according to circumstances. I have been advised to carry with me greater quantities of those abominable cantharides pills; stimulants of that description being the most necessary to the Orientals, whom debauchery very often reduces to premature debility, of which the poor devils complain without shame. Dysentery is making great ravages here, especially among the natives. One of my people was attacked, but I succeeded in saving his life. Nine out of ten die of this disease in the hands of the English doctors. The great thing in the complaints of this country is to take them in time. For my own part I scarcely think of them, but am nevertheless always ready to give them a good reception. Make yourself easy, therefore. You talk to me about the plague: it is unknown in India. Adieu; for you to be as well as I am, is all that I wish you.

Camp at Panniput, January 29th, 1831.

Here have I begun a new campaign. Four days ago I left Delhi; to-morrow I shall be at Kurnal on the frontiers of the protected Seikhs, and about the 21st of February I shall reach Lahore. The exercise and irregularity of my travelling life, together with its frugality, have already restored me to my mountain health. Fraser returned to Delhi ten days ago; he doubts whether the leave of absence which he has requested will be granted him. Yesterday I received a very friendly message from him at Samalkha, where I was encamped. With his letter there were two elephants and two trusty and good-looking servants, whose services Fraser begged me to accept as far as Umbritsir; a useful reinforcement to the two poor starved camels which carry my tents. It moreover adds singularly to the pomp of my caravan. My host, at Delhi, who was the general of the division, has also given me a strong escort: this is necessary for the security of my slender baggage during the night. All this nearly justifies the *bahadur*, with which the Delhi engraver has gratified me on the plate I ordered from him for my herald at arms, a servant whom I have just added to my establishment, which you may easily suppose, notwithstanding this increase, to be the worst in India. Your arithmetic will enable you to discover the cause of this inferiority.

Good night. I am encamped here in one of the most celebrated fields of battle in India. It is late; I leave you for dinner—a sad affair, nothing but an old peacock, but which only cost me a shot this morning. God preserve you from such a *rôti*, and from brackish water to drink!

Camp at Kurnal, February 3rd, 1831.

The rain has kept me here two days, and I have availed myself of them to liquidate some little of the arrears of my correspondence. I yesterday despatched a packet containing a long letter to the Jardin, and another for Madame V. de Tracy. To-day I am writing the memorial which you engaged me to draw up to serve as *corpus petitionis* to the solicitations of my friends in my behalf. I will endeavour to despatch it hence to-morrow; and in the leisure of my march to Umbritsir, where I shall have a new opportunity of sending a courier, I shall finish paying the rest of my epistolary debts, informing you at the same time to whom I have written; for letters get lost here. Three days ago the courier was attacked and robbed in broad daylight near Panniput. Other districts through which he must pass on his way to Calcutta are in the same state of confusion. A poor naked man running on foot laden with a bundle of letters is quite a prize to these robbers. Although I have two sentries all night near my little tent, I think myself very happy in the morning when I find under my head the cushion on which I rest, and my shirt on my back. You would not believe the stories of robbers that I could relate to you, since it is not very long ago since I put no faith in them myself.

Six days on foot and horseback in the open air have completely restored me to my wonted state; and I have recovered the enjoyment of my mountain health. Like a true Mussulman, I have made a vow of absolute abstinence from spirituous liquors. I live pretty much like the natives, and I find after several experiments that it is the regimen which agrees with me best. I have a three months' beard, which is three inches long. With wide calico trousers, a green dressing-gown, and a large black fur cap, I shall make a very decent Afghan, if it is thought necessary that I should undergo such a metamorphosis at Loodheeana, which would moreover be very convenient. The dogs in this country bark after a Christian; the buffaloes and cows present their horns, and lower their heads before him; the horses on the road are frightened, turn their heels towards him, and kick at him if he approaches them. But the bipeds of our species make magnificent obeisances to him. It is through love of these obeisances that Europeans in British India persist in retaining their national dress, which gives them as a compensation, bites, kicks, gores, &c. &c.

Adieu, my dear father; remember me kindly to my friends. Tell Porphyre that I have already a square metre of manuscript all quite ready for him, and that I will add another centiare from hence to Umbala. Adieu, once more. I embrace you with all my heart.

TO M. VICTOR DE TRACY, PARIS.

Delhi, January 12*th*, 1831.

It was on descending from the Himalaya that I learned, in the month of November last, the glorious events of July. So it is all over with divine right and legitimacy, the granted charter and the other absurdities of our old political system! What admiration this victory excites among our former enemies, whose guest I am in these distant regions! What nation has ever awakened the concert of enthusiastic and grateful feelings which rise on all sides for the French name! What a regeneration! what glory!

It was at Delhi that I resumed the colours of liberty! What a remembrance for the rest of my days! If this great drama has a development worthy of its first scenes, it will not only produce a beneficent political revolution in the greater part of the European states, but it will also entirely change the political relations of nations with each other. Envy and hatred have been their bane hitherto: good will and good faith will henceforth preside over them.

I have just read the French papers to the 12th of August, and in the last of these journals I saw with pleasure your name in the commission charged to report on the proposals of M. Bérard. I do not understand the proceedings of the Chamber, I confess: its members seem to forget that a revolution separates them from the last session. Moderation in victory is a fine thing, but I dread the excess of a good thing.

I honour the Chamber of Deputies of November, 1827, for its address to the king. The principle of the re-elections of the voters for this address, being so faithfully executed, makes the Chamber of 1830 in some measure the same assembly as that of 1827: and perhaps after all we must not be surprised if, under the conditions of its existence, being elected under the double vote, and the minimum of age being forty years, it is not more vigorous.

Nevertheless, it appears to me to have but little understood the immensity of the power which the revolution of July 29th has placed in its hands. A revolution is never made in legal form.

Samalkha, near Panniput, January 28th, 1831.

I was unable to conclude this letter at Delhi, though detained there much longer than I expected; for I was so overwhelmed with business that I had no leisure left to write to you. I am now taking advantage of those moments of leisure which occur on my march through a monotonous and uninteresting country.

Since the day I wrote to you from Delhi, I have seen the English papers up to the 24th of August. Though all their intelligence from France is not equally agreeable to me, I cannot on the whole help feeling satisfied.

Have you not, like me, the melancholy conviction

that there are men who are unfortunately born destitute of every moral feeling? What education could supply this deficiency? Abolish capital punishment if you like, but substitute perpetual imprisonment for it. If your bill passes in France, I am persuaded that it will not be long before a similar one will be proposed in England; and the influence which we are called upon, I think, to exercise on the political destinies of Spain and Italy, might cause the same principle to be adopted there. When all the European governments have thus become quakers internally, war will appear a very strange and horrible thing. You are still young enough to see the dawn of this new age.

Keep for me what you write. Some day or other I shall again be your guest at Paray; there I shall love to follow the course of events which have taken place in our country since my absence, and to read the accomplishment of those projects of which we have so often conversed together. However elegant my little tent may be with its coloured canvass, and however comfortable it may appear to me, in the middle of a plain of arid sand, heated by a burning sun, I would willingly desert it, I assure you, to go and chat by your fireside. But I am not taking the road thither; and from the plan laid down for my journey, you may conclude I do not suffer from the *mal du pays*. I am going to Lahore, and Attock, to visit the banks of the Hindoo-Koh, and then to Cashmere; and I think of returning to India by Ladac, or some other province of western Tibet. I thought it incumbent on me to visit a celebrated region, the entrance to which is closed against British travellers, by the jealousy of Runjeet Sing. You know, on the contrary, what chances of a favourable reception await me. I have neglected no means of making them more certain: my father will tell you how. He will also tell you that in this affair I have rather consulted zeal than prudence. My credit from the Jardin des Plantes expires with the present year, and I cannot expect to return to Delhi before the 1st of November next. Thus, I have no means of returning to Europe at present. But I have the firm persuasion that the minister of the interior will grant them to me as a matter of urgency, since urgency alone makes me contract the necessity of them. I should, after my return to Europe, have regretted all my life having had an opportunity of visiting these celebrated and mysterious regions, without availing myself of it. Good night, my dear friend; I hope to write you a few lines more from Panniput, where I intend to encamp. I recollect having written to you ten months ago from that celebrated place. I look back with satisfaction at the time which has since elapsed, because I feel that it has been well employed. Adieu.

TO M[LLE.] ZOE NOIZET DE SAINT PAUL, ARRAS.

Delhi, January 18th, 1831.

MY DEAR ZOÉ,—I wish I could write you a volume; but I have scarcely time to send you a few lines. Ask my father about me; I wrote an endless letter to him.

You ask me for a flower; I send you three: one is an anemone, which I found last May among the snows at the source of the Jumna, the most sacred place on earth according to the Hindoo faith; the second is a primrose, a tolerably exact specimen of the humble stature of the Alpine plants of Tibet. I found it only once blooming at a height greater than the summit of Mont-Blanc. Until the whole of my collections have reached Europe, you will be able to boast that you possess, in that humble primrose, a plant gathered at a greater elevation than any of those actually existing in European museums. I add another rarity in the third flower, which I found in Tibet at a still greater elevation: you will recognise it to be a violet. Accept a fourth, which will be the last; it is one of the pacific trophies of my first campaign against the Emperor of China. It enamelled the ground on which I fought his most *tea-ific* majesty's forces (consisting of a few horsemen, whose commander I gave myself the inexpressible satisfaction of seizing by his long plaited tail). I doubt not that your knowledge of botany extends as far as the myosotis; but if I presume too much upon it, I must inform you that several species of the same genus exist in Europe, and that one of them, extremely pretty and very common by the water side, is called in English, the Forget-me-not.

The field of battle where I gathered it does not deserve to be remarked in a military point of view; but it is seventeen thousand feet above the level of the sea, being three times higher than the passes of the Alps, which Hannibal and Bonaparte have rendered so famous; so that my victories rank considerably above the victories of those two conquerors. You are at liberty to give these plants any specific name you please, because they are all entirely new, as well as all those I have brought from Tibet.

If we are destined not to see each other again, preserve this little flower as a remembrance, and always recollect its name—Forget-me-not.

TO M[LLE.] ZOÉ NOIZET DE SAINT PAUL, ARRAS.

Camp of Panniput, January 29th, 1831.

You are, my dear Zoé, the favourite sultana of my thoughts. I write to nobody so often as I do to you. My friendship alone would explain this; but I suspect that there exists another reason: I long for female society. When I leave the deserts to stop at a British settlement, I meet those of my own sex, sometimes full of merit and learning. But there is absolutely nothing to be said of the European ladies one meets in India: they may be accomplished wives and mothers, but they are nothing else. They read nothing but the *Mirror of Fashion*, a stupid periodical, principally devoted to the toilet, something like the *Journal des Modes*. They have, it is true, all the external qualities required in good society, but nothing more; and their husbands seem to be perfectly satisfied with the small talents they possess. You have probably heard of the domestic life of the English; well! what is said of it is not truer than a proverb. There exists scarcely any reasonable intercourse between husband and wife, in this the so much boasted English private life. They meet at meal times, and only during the active part of that operation; for when they have done eating, the ladies are politely turned out by John Bull, who feels perfectly at his ease when they are gone. Then the bottle begins to circulate round the mahogany table; and if anything is to be made of an Englishman, now is the time. Meanwhile the poor women remain in the drawing-room, amusing themselves as well as they can, till the arrival of the "lords of the creation," who sometimes keep up this circulation of the bottle so long, that when they enter the drawing-room, they find it deserted, and the lights extinguished.

People of fashion do not now remain long at table after the cloth is removed; but what can you talk about to an English lady? If she attempted to join in a serious conversation, she would be immediately set down as a blue-stocking, which is a grievous affront. You are playing a fool's part if you are not slightly acquainted with the people whom they may talk about; for things are out of the question, except those which may be collected from the Mirror of Fashion. God preserve me from ever having an English wife!

Thomas Moore is not only a perfumer, but a liar to boot. I am now pursuing the same route that Lalla Rookh formerly did; and I have scarcely seen a single tree since I left Delhi. I am encamped here on the celebrated field where the fate of India has been several times decided: it is a vast plain, covered with jungles, and full, they say, of tigers; but I have only seen a few peacocks, one of which I shot. I am sorry I did so, because it is truly a pity to destroy so graceful a creature, and because, to colour my crime with a pretence of utility, I have ordered my majesty's cook to make a mulligatawny of it for my dinner. Now the very worst of chicken would have been superior to it. I have not the heart to kill large animals which are inoffensive.

I managed so well with my horse and my two elephants yesterday, that I was obliged to walk the whole stage, lost in the jungle; but I feel all the better for it. It is incredible how greatly my constitution is strengthened after a few days of a solitary, frugal, active, and wandering life. My little band has a much better look than when I left Calcutta. I have men of the upper provinces, much taller and handsomer than the Bengalese; and lately at Delhi I added a sort of lackey or herald, called *chroprassy*, because he wears, like our old uncle *, a broad red belt from the right shoulder to the left side, and a large plate of copper, with a Persian inscription, signifying "M. V. Jacquemont, a very mighty lord." My name is engraved in Roman characters, which is the most imposing of all, as nobody can read it. This man superintends and directs the pitching of my tents, and the grazing of my camels; on the road he follows me, carrying my gun, and immediately seizes any person I may point out to him, even though it should be the magistrate of a village, of whom I want any thing. Moreover, I have infantry of the most regular kind, consisting of a serjeant, a corporal, and eight men. Robbers are so plentiful, and so strongly protected by the indulgent justice of the British, that these my forces are not too numerous.

Adieu, my dear Zoé; this letter is longer than I intended, for I have many others to write less agreeable than this. I hope to receive in Cashmere a letter from you in English, in answer to mine from Tibet. I enclose in this, one of the emerald feathers from the egret of the poor peacock, shot this morning on that historical spot the plain of Panniput. To-

* M. Noizet de St. Paul, major-general of engineers, knight commander of St. Louis.

morrow I shall reach Kurnal, on the frontiers of the British dominions, and those of the protected Seikhs; thence to Loodheeana, on the banks of the Sutledge, there are eleven or twelve days' march. I hope to be at Lahore on the 20th of February, with a beard three inches long, and quite prepared to look like an Afghan gentleman, and to play the part of one. Adieu, my dear Zoé. *Forget me not.*

TO M. JACQUEMONT, THE ELDER, PARIS.

Loodheeana, February 16th, 1831.

MY DEAR FATHER,—I arrived here the day before yesterday, and am warming and drying myself at the British political agent's, being faithful this time to my hygeinic principle of a bad breakfast and an execrable dinner. I am perfectly well. All goes on capitally for my expedition into the Punjab. The rajah will become to me, that which he often is from caprice, very amiable. M. Allard is loudly calling for me: his horsemen are here at my orders. Nevertheless I shall stay here a few days, to learn how they make the Cashmere shawls, of which country Loodheeana is the out-parish. My host, Captain Wade, is a clever, well-informed man, and his society is equally profitable and agreeable to me. He is the king of the frontier, and an excellent fellow. We visit together the workshops of the weavers and dyers, on foot, and like plain, homely people, which is seldom the case in India. To-morrow or next day, I shall be introduced to two ex-majesties, Shah-Shoudjah and his brother, each formerly, by turn, king of Cabul or Afghanistan. They live here as pensioners on English charity, which owed them nothing. One of them has had his eyes put out, a ceremony which an Ex of the East seldom escapes.

Adieu!—I leave you to make myself black from head to foot, majestically mount an elephant, and go and dine with the colonel of the garrison, who does me the honour to give a grand dinner on the occasion of my passing through this place. I shall have the courage to drink nothing but milk, whilst the champagne is going its rounds. But health before all things. Good night, I embrace you.

TO MADAME FANNY DE PERCY, PARIS.

Loodheeana, February 22nd, 1831, *on the banks of the Sutledge.*

It is a long time, my dear Fanny, since I wrote to you; but if you knew the extent of correspondence I have to get through, you would not be surprised at the scarcity of my letters.

Lord William Bentinck has just sent me the French

papers of the months of July and August 1830; they contain the latest news I have received from Europe. I have been informed by these papers of the change of situation of some of my friends, and many other things besides; but I would willingly give all this news for a few lines from Porphyre or my father.

There are two ex-majesties here, who preserve the title, and before whom I did not appear without taking off my shoes; these are Shah-Zeman and Shah-Shoudjah his brother, formerly kings of Cabul, Afghanistan, and Cashmere, and great sovereigns twenty years ago. The British Government sent them a magnificent embassy, and sought their alliance, at the period when the presence of General Cardanne at Teheran raised some suspicion in the cabinet of Calcutta with regard to the views, generally not very pacific, of your friend, the great man, as Courier used to say. Mr. Elphinstone, the British ambassador, disputed for a fortnight with the grand master of the ceremonies, and the chamberlains of Shah-Shoudjah, about the etiquette of his presentation to the king. The latter agreed at last to exact from Mr. Elphinstone only thirty-nine bows; while he himself, the king, would show his nose at the window, the ambassador remaining with his whole suite in the court-yard, at a distance of three or four hundred paces.

His ex-majesty has the most magnificent black beard I ever saw; and I found him a very gracious personage. A pensioner on British generosity, to which in truth he has no claim, Shah-Shoudjah lives here in freedom, but under the surveillance of the British political agent, my present host. By this officer I was conducted to a private audience of the shah, with whom I spent an hour conversing about Cashmere, whither I am going, and where he formerly made war, from Cabul, his country—from his mountains, of which he spoke to me with affecting eloquence. Do you recollect that the women broke open the doors of the hotel Sinet, to see the Tunis envoy's handsome secretary? I know not what they would do if Shah-Shoudjah went to Paris: the national guard would not be sufficient to preserve public order, he is so handsome! The old emperor, Shah-Zeman, has had his eyes put out; he spends his time in devotion, which however does not prevent his having a large seraglio. He related to me his pilgrimage to Mecca, which he undertook after his fall, and after he became blind. There is a numerous colony of Cashmerians here, who manufacture shawls similar to those of their own country, but generally of an inferior quality. Were I richer I would bring you a couple, or rather from Cashmere itself, where I shall be in two months; but I must not think of it.

I am well, very well. Adieu, my dear friend.

TO M. PORPHYRE JACQUEMONT, PARIS.

Loodheeana, on the banks of the Sutledge,
February 23rd, 1831.

My dear Porphyre,—If you knew how I write in the open air, often on my knee, on a tomb, or any thing else I can find, you would not be surprised at the want of coherence in my letters.

On the 16th instant, I wrote to our father a short letter from this place; and I liquidated all my correspondence before I cross the Sutledge, which alone separates me from the Punjab; but I have apprised all my correspondents, that when I have once passed it,——silence! I answer no one.

Lord William has just sent me the *Constitutionnels* for the months of July and August, up to the 26th. My head is still confused with them. I am a royalist to excess, although there are here and there things which hardly please me. In other respects, it is quite delightful: we are all honourable now. For instance, our father is an honourable metaphysician, you are an honourable captain, I am an honourable traveller, Frederic is an honourable merchant; in short, were we nothing that we are, we should be honourable married men, or at least honourable bachelors. That strange Hungarian original, whom I met in Tibet, wrote to me one day in English on an immense sheet of paper: "Sir, I have the honour to acknowledge the receipt of the letter which you did me the honour to write to me yesterday, and I have the honour to be, &c. &c." I sent him to the devil with his *honour*, and replied with *friendship*, that he was out of his senses. What should I say to *la grande nation*, which collectively is the honourable French people? What a farce!—Adieu; I shall perhaps write to you again to-morrow. William Fraser sends me word from Delhi that his affairs with the powers at Calcutta are taking a bad turn, and that he despairs of joining me in the Punjab. I am sorry for it.

An English ship is, for the first time, going up the Indus and the Ravee, to carry a present of Norman and Flemish horses to Lahore, which the king of Great Britain is sending to Runjeet Sing. On the other hand, my arrival at Loodheeana is known at Lahore and at Umbritsir; and the report prevalent in the *bazaar* (literally, in the market, which corresponds with the talk of the cafés and streets with us) is, that my arrival at the same time as the British envoy is not without design. They make me out to be a sort of secret minister from the king of France, deputed to the rajah. As a traveller, like me, does not answer the description of any these people have seen before, I am exposed to all sorts of absurd interpretations. Kennedy writes me that his petty rajahs, whom I saw last year, take it for granted that I am one of the Governor-general's aides-de-camp. Well! there is no great harm in that. Runjeet knows very well who

I am. M. Allard writes me from Lahore that this rajah (Runjeet) talks of the pleasure that he shall have in seeing me—flummery—he is a perfect old fox. Adieu, till to-morrow. I embrace you with all my heart.

TO M. ACHILLE CHAPER.

Loodheeana, on the banks of the Sutledge,
February 24th, 1830.

I OFTEN think of you, my friend, but seldom write to you, because, at the distance which divides us, the ordinary dimensions of a letter would not satisfy me, and I want leisure to converse with you at sufficient length, to make you acquainted with my internal and external existence. I recollect, however, that I wrote to you last summer from Tibet. Has my letter reached you? I entered India again on the 4th of October, through the eternal snows of the Himalaya, and resumed my researches on its southern slope. On the 15th of November, I left the mountains. A month after I returned to Delhi, where I was detained by my affairs till the end of January. Now I am journeying towards Cashmere. To-morrow, or next day, I shall cross the Sutledge; but although I shall enter a country absolutely independent of the British power, and which is even deemed hostile to it, I shall not lose all the advantages of British protection. It is a sort of court coquetry with the Governor-general, that induces Runjeet Sing to allow me to enter his dominions; a favour which the cabinet of Calcutta had hitherto invariably refused to ask of this prince, for other travellers. In the Punjab, therefore, I shall not only be encompassed by perfect safety, but meet with kindness and distinction. The rajah sends his prime minister's son to meet me. I shall let them do as they like till I get to Lahore; but there I shall beg Runjeet Sing to release me from these tiresome honours, and to allow me to pursue my journey *incog.* with only one of his household servants, who will serve me as a guide, and command respect in case of need.

My intention is to visit not only Cashmere, but the whole of the unknown part of the Himalaya, which extends from the Sutledge to the Indus, and to re-enter India through Tibet again. On my return from this expedition, I shall have completed half of a general work which will embrace the whole Himalaya from the Indus to the Burrampooter; and my most ardent desire would be to continue this work—two years will suffice to finish it. I have written to the Minister of the Interior to inform him of my project, and to request the means of executing it. I think it would do some honour to the spirit of scientific enterprise of our nation. A concourse of fortuitous circumstances offers me a crowd of advantages to favour its accomplishment, such as no other traveller could expect. Every thing helps me, even my French nationality. It is doubtful whether Runjeet Sing's jealous mistrust would have granted to an English traveller that which he allows me; and, again, the personal kindness of the Governor-general follows me everywhere in the provinces subject to his authority. Add to this, a condition which is generally wanting in this country to those who lead the laborious and active life which I do—perfect health; lastly, a correct knowledge of the two languages, Hindoostanee and English. I prefer concentrating my labours on a space so magnificently marked out by nature, to scattering or losing myself in the vastness of all Asia. If my project is well received, I will give up the thought of seeing Persia and Asia Minor. I am now well informed enough about those countries, to be convinced that the plan of the journey in the Himalaya, which I am now carrying into execution, promises more results than any other.

I do not suffer from the solitariness of my life. Whatever consolation or happiness I may have found in friendship, when I was near my friends, it is only since my lot has been cast so far from them, that I have become properly acquainted with all the delicious charm of that feeling. No, I am not alone! If your thoughts follow me they will sometimes meet me. Ah! how often I have secretly conversed with you since we parted. Since that day I have received but one letter from you; I keep it near me, with several others equally dear to me; and when I am annoyed, I reperuse these letters always with a new pleasure. I have a great deal to praise in the men of this country (I mean the English). I almost always find some sympathy in them, and sometimes a lively one. I have seen few of them who are not cordially inclined towards me, and whom the world would not call my friends; and I give this sacred name to two men, whom I did not know till I came to this country. They have won my heart, and given me theirs. I cannot tell what it is in them that has captivated me. They are both twenty years older than myself, and both unhappy; one from his situation, the other on account of his disposition.

I would speak to you of the scenes that surround me; but their interest disappears in my eyes, before the grandeur of the spectacle presented by France. It was in descending from the Himalaya into the plains of India that I received from a Calcutta newspaper the first news of those great events. Since that time, other vessels have arrived from Europe, which have brought the continuation of the particulars; and a courier of the Governor-general, who is now near Delhi, has just delivered me the series of *Constitutionnels* for July and August.

The reading of these papers has left a painful impression on my mind: the fatigue of living a month in twenty-hours; and such a month! Shall I confess to you, my friend, that the details of the reality have destroyed the brilliant vision which I had formed of a still purer and greater glory?

The ordinances of the 25th of July attacked the rights of the whole nation. But their attack was more direct on certain classes: the richer and better informed, who had the exclusive privilege of the electoral right, and whose easy circumstances and education caused them more particularly to enjoy the liberty of the press. It was therefore the part of the richer and more enlightened class to be the first in this contest! It appears to me that during the three days they kept behind the people. I have read the lists of the killed, and have found but one name that I knew.

This is not enough! a single name is not sufficient! It is the people that have achieved the revolution—the people rather than we; and yet it was rather our duty to achieve it than that of the people. It was against us rather than against the people that war was declared.

The courage and moderation of the people are admirable; but the victory would have been still more glorious, had it been won by other hands, by ours. Then it would have borne a character of political morality.

Among the victims, I see a great number of poor mechanics, inhabitants of the Faubourgs. The killed and wounded show very well to what classes the majority of the combatants belong. Among them were unhappy mechanics, destitute of all political education, and who no doubt could not even read. The liberty of the press should not have stood in need of the support of such defenders. I repeat, I honour their courage, I bless it, since it has probably saved us from a civil war at least; but, if I am not strangely mistaken as to the deplorable ignorance that still afflicts the lower ranks of society, it was only a feeling of unreflecting hatred which armed the people against the Government.

After that great victory, I dreamt of a new era in political honesty, a new species of intercourse between nations, and a new eloquence for the tribune and the press——I created an Utopia! The *Constitutionnel* has miserably overturned it. It still speaks of the *necessities* of the *times*. What means this jargon? We still continue to wallow in the mud of parliamentary phraseology; and this corrupted language is but the symbol of ideas which are not very pure.

I know not the fate of M. Victor de Tracy's motion, on the abolition of capital punishment. If it is rejected, and the ministers of the 25th of July are condemned and executed, they will inspire the small number of the sincere men of their party with the same interest which we have for the memory of those noble youths who died for liberty in 1822. God forbid that I should compare the action of the former with that of the latter! but both have fallen the victims of a defeat, after an attack upon the law. The martyrs for liberty had in their favour the internal feeling, the consciousness of the justice of their cause, of the morality of their action, and assuredly that was not the motive of ***'s rashness. But M. de Polignac's life has been uniform; it is absurdly consequent upon the principle of the absolute Government of France by a single family. It is possible that he thought he was acting for the best: he has violated the law; let him be punished. I hate him; but I have some pity for him. Let us take care not to say "Blood for blood!"

Popular insurrections have commenced in the Netherlands. Their beginning is not glorious. But this is owing to the cowardice of the middle classes, who have taken no part in the movement. The future prospects of Spain seem melancholy; the van-guard of Spanish civilisation consists of scarcely a few thousand men; and this little force is four or five centuries in advance of the rest of the nation, which remains too far behind them, to understand their manœuvres or to support them. It is the same with Italy.

It was at Delhi that I resumed the tri-coloured cockade. The ancient capital of Timour, which has been for twenty-eight years in the power of the English, is occupied by a strong European garrison. It is also the metropolis of a vast political, judicial, and civil residency. All the officers of the British Government joined, on the 30th of December last, in inviting me to a patriotic dinner in commemoration of the French revolution. The British cannon accompanied our cheers for the victory of freedom. Strange music for the descendant of Timour, who could hear it from his palace! For my part I never heard any which awoke in me such enthusiasm.

Adieu, my dear and amiable friend; I must return to Loodheeana, from which my thoughts were already very far. I have notes and collections to arrange, workshops to visit, and a thousand other things to do besides. Adieu—speak of me to my friends with the feelings which you know that I entertain for them. Adieu; I love you, and embrace you with all my heart.

TO M. JACQUEMONT THE ELDER, PARIS.

Loodheeana, on the banks of the Sutledge,
February 25th, 1831.

My dear Father,—Maharajah Runjeet Sing is an old fox, compared to whom the most skilful of our diplomatists is a simpleton. At Loodheeana I expected to find the passports which had been promised me by his minister at Delhi, but they had not yet arrived. Runjeet had written to the British political agent residing at Loodheeana (my present host); and though all the while protesting the pleasure he should have in seeing me, he was attempting to begin over again an affair already concluded, and to gain time with me. I might have cut the matter short, and gone on; but as we every day expected a new courier from him, I exercised my patience. This courier is at last arrived. The rajah, or to speak more politely, the maharajah, sends the son of his prime minister to receive me on the frontier, that is at Falour, on the further bank of the Sutledge. Runjeet himself has marked my stages to his capital, where I shall entreat him to deliver me from those importunate honours. Umbritsir, the sacred city of the Seikhs, is on my road; my travelling companion will do the honours there. As the country from this place to Lahore is nothing but a great plain, cultivated in a uniform manner, I shall not have much to see in it, and shall avail myself of this circumstance to live as much as possible with my spy. I say spy, because one of his duties is to despatch a messenger every evening to the rajah, to inform him of what I have been doing during the day; whether I have gone on foot, or on horseback, or on an elephant; whether I have hunted or drawn; whether I am satisfied or otherwise, &c. &c. I do not know what particulars he may favour the rajah with. You may fancy me on the road to Lahore, starting at day-light on horseback, with my young companion prancing away near me, and a respectable troop of horse following us, the elephants in the rear, and some servants on foot. At each halt, the chief men in the place come to pay their respects to me, being introduced by the minister's son; and their respects are not without rupees. They will be very agreeably surprised at seeing me touch their offering, without pocketing it. On the road I go on conversing with my companion, he in Persian, and I in Hindoostanee, but which will grow more and more Persian every day. I here increase my house by a chair and a carpet, as I have a thousand visits to expect from people who are of sufficient rank to sit in my company, and not to walk on the ground barefooted. M. Allard writes me frequently, that he longs to embrace me; and for my own part I feel very much disposed to like him. There is another European at Lahore, called Ventura, an Italian, who has served in our armies, and who has on this side the water a great reputation for skill and bravery. He commands Runjeet's infantry; M. Allard being at the head of the cavalry. His letters give me an idea that he possesses literary knowledge and taste.

You can ask at the library of the Institute for the "Account of Kaubul by Elphinstone:" you will find a great deal of information about the country whither I am going; for Mr. Elphinstone returned from his embassy to Peshawer through the country of the Seikhs, which Runjeet was at that time far from being in entire possession of.

The two ex-majesties of Cabul, who are here, received me with less ceremony than one of them, Shah Shoudjah, imposed on Mr. Elphinstone, twenty-two years ago. These Afghans are magnificent men. I paid Shah Shoudjah a very long visit, because he delighted me by relating the wonders of his mountains of Cabul and his ex-paradise of Cashmere.

Morning 26*th*.

I have this moment received the following lines from M. Allard.

"Maharajah has just ordered the son of the fakhir Ezis-el-Din, to start with thirty horsemen to meet you. We hope, therefore, to embrace you soon. The young fakhir, Shah-el-Din, sets out at the same time as these few words; but the horseman who will be the bearer of them will be two days before him on the road, in order that you may be in readiness to cross the Sutledge when this young nobleman arrives at Falour," &c.

I hold myself ready, therefore, to start the day after to-morrow, and these lines are the last I shall write to you from British India. M. Allard has an agent here who speaks Hindostanee and Persian equally well: I shall take him to Lahore with me, in order to perfect me in the pronunciation of the occasional diabolical Arabic consonants, which are more rare in Hindoostanee than in Persian, and of a less guttural sound. I hope to write to you from Lahore in less than a fortnight, and to give you a good account of Runjeet.

There was a little ice this morning, but it is the last cold of winter, and the sun is already very hot at ten o'clock.

I have still the same horse which has carried me

from Calcutta to the foot of the Himalaya: he continues to justify the reputation of a bad temper enjoyed by sorrels. But I am grown more cunning than he, and since I left Benares he has not thrown me once. Judges of horses make theories in which I do not at all believe. They say that an Arab of ordinary size would have some trouble to carry a man of mine. Well, my *tattoo* is much under the size of an Arab; he often does hard work, and was never behind hand; not once has his foot slipped since he has had the honour of carrying my majesty; never ill—never lame—never galled. I consider myself, moreover, a very good horseman; of a species, however, which I confess, is not very classical. I am quite used to my long beard, and I know nothing so comfortable. I really believe that we are wrong in depriving ourselves of this ornament, which, if you like, you may call natural; and that many toothachs proceed from the nakedness of our jaws.

Lord W. Bentinck, and Lord Dalhousie, the commander-in-chief, are, at present, the one at Murat, the other at Kurnal, on their way to Semla. The baggage of the former is carried by a hundred and three elephants, thirteen hundred camels, and eight hundred waggons drawn by bullocks. Two regiments, one of cavalry, and the other infantry, serve as his escort; yet I am going to Lahore with only one waggon and a couple of camels.

No French ships since the arrival of the *Gange*,

which left Bourdeaux on the 11th of August; no departures either: I presume, therefore, that the enormous quantity of letters which I have written for six weeks past, and sent to Chandernagore under cover to Sir E. Ryan, who is to forward them to M. Joseph Cordier, are arrived at that place without having yet been forwarded to Europe.

It is impossible to talk of politics, for I should never leave off. In a list of prefects, I see Dunoyer and Chaper side by side; I am writing to both.

Adieu, my dear father: speak of me kindly to those of my friends to whom I have not had time to write. Adieu; I have health, courage, and hope. Write me very long letters, and let Porphyre follow your example.

TO M. JACQUEMONT THE ELDER, PARIS.

Camp near Jullindar, in the Punjab,
March 4th, 1831.

My dear Father,—The day before yesterday I took leave of my amiable host of Loodheeana, Captain Wade, mounted my elephant, and, surrounded by a troop of Seikh cavalry, crossed the Sutledge. A squadron drawn up on the right bank of the river received me, on my landing, with military honours, and escorted me to my tent, near which it remained under arms, till the arrival of my *Mehmandar**, fakhir Shah-el-Din, who soon came, accompanied by several officers. Wade had given me a lesson in Seikh etiquette, and I repeated it without difficulty. The young fakhir took the greatest interest in the conversation: he used the most suppliant forms to put into my hands a heavy bag of money, while a number of his attendants marched past my tent, depositing at the door a large basket of fruit, and a vase of cream or preserves. This was a present from the rajah. I begged Shah-el-Din to write to him to express my thanks, giving him to understand, however, that I expected no less from his hospitality.

In the evening I had a fête of a more quiet description. I took a long excursion on the level banks of the Sutledge, without being attended by the importunate honours which I dreaded. No inquisitive face came to spoil the landscape: I felt as free as on the banks of the Niagara. On my return to the camp, my mehmandar's secretary having come to receive orders for the morrow, I appointed the hour of departure, and the place for the next encampment. I made this journey on an elephant, and alone, according to my taste. This solitude, however, is comparative; for I was not without half-a-dozen servants on foot, and as many horsemen: but in the East, such is the grandeur of *Self*, that it easily absorbs a dozen men and horses.

Fakhir Shah-el-Din, as I had not invited him to

---

* A Persian word, literally the guardian of hospitality.

travel in company with me, marched two or three miles in the rear with the squadron. On arriving at the camp, I was not long in receiving a message from him. He wished to know when it would be convenient for me to receive him. He soon arrived, with his compliments of the day before, a fresh bag of money, and provisions of all kinds. In the evening I paid him a visit; a civility which he had a right to expect from me, but perhaps not so early. He exhausted himself in the superlatives of Persian gratitude. I soon withdrew, as I had come, to the sound of trumpets. Were it not for my long beard, which continually tells me that I am a grave personage, my seriousness would not have stood the proof of this music; but I kept my countenance till my return to my camp, when I shut myself up in my tent, in order to laugh at the sublime part I am playing, and again take possession of my own identity. In India, it is the custom in speaking of one's-self to say *we*,—a form of no great modesty; but since I have passed the Sutledge, I speak of myself only in the third person, as follows: the sahib, (that is the lord) is not tired—the lord is charmed at seeing your lordship—express the lord's respects to the king—the lord invites your lordship to mount the lord's elephant, &c. There are more *lords* in a quarter of an hour in my Seikh conversation, than in all Racine's tragedies.

This morning I came to encamp near this ancient city, travelling on an elephant, which for a certain cause I find more convenient than a horse. The cause I do not know how to tell you. I will tell it to you, however, because I have promised to be candid. The confidence of noble souls is sometimes ill-requited. But with my certificate of *clarissimus et doctissimus vir*, I hope soon to have forgotten the dancing girls of Loodheeana.

Fakhir Shah-el-Din came yesterday to hear my news, and offer his compliments in the usual form; that is to say, with another bag of money, the superlatives of yesterday, and provisions *ad infinitum*. He presented to me, at the same time, the governor of the city, a long grey-beard of the old stamp, who related to me the war between Lord Lake and the Mahrattas, when they took refuge in the Punjab. The governor had an endless retinue; and in order to turn my visiters out politely, I proposed to my mehmandar to take a ride through the city on my elephant. I told the long-beard that I was in despair that I could not have him for a companion.

I am now returned. Never did any one receive so discordant a serenade as the clatter with which the Julindur musicians are now regaling me. Through my cloth walls, I do not escape a single note, and I am not yet Alcibiades enough to take pleasure in such music. I pass the time in writing to you, because I could not do better in waiting till this din ceases: for, since they play by the king's orders, the least I can do is to bear it patiently.

But, you will say, what is there in the bags that you are collecting?—a hundred and one rupees, or about two hundred and fifty francs. If Runjeet Sing thinks himself obliged to treat his friends in this fashion, I can easily understand why he is reluctant to receive visits. I ask myself where this attention on his part will end? At Lahore, perhaps; but certainly not before. Now as there are six days' journey from hence to Lahore, I shall collect, before I arrive there, six hundred and six rupees, to add to the three hundred and three which I have deigned to pocket since the day before yesterday. Till now I had always detested the slowness of travelling in India, but Runjeet Sing has arguments which would reconcile me to the speed of a tortoise. Here am I become as covetous as if I were rich: it is from a refinement of avarice that I regret not having more of those large Spanish doubloons which I brought to Calcutta; I would have offered them to him as a *nuzzer*, on the day of my presentation, whereas I shall be obliged to give him some Indian pieces of gold, to which he will pay but little attention.

I know not whether it is through an optical illusion, but the Punjab and its inhabitants please me much. Perhaps, you will say, that it is because I see them through a shower of gold; but the unsophisticated Seikhs of this country have a simplicity and open honesty of manner, which a European relishes the more, after two years' residence or travelling in India. Their fanaticism is extinguished, and such is their tolerance, that Runjeet's grand vizier (my mehmandar's father) is a Mussulmaun, and his two brothers are Mussulmauns, and all are equally in the good graces of the Seikh monarch.

Lord William will soon be at Semla. Runjeet will send my mehmandar's father to compliment him. Wade will conduct the Seikh ambassador from Loodheeana to Semla, and will afterwards come to Lahore, bearing in return the Governor-general's compliments to the rajah. I received another letter from Lord William before I left Loodheeana: he promised me the French papers for September; and I expect to receive them at Lahore with letters from you; for I know that a Bourdeaux ship which sailed in September, is just arrived in Bengal. So adieu till then, if I do not resume this gossip before, to speak to you of the holy city of the Seikhs, Umbritsir, which I shall soon pass through.

Lahore, 12th March.

I skip the holy city, to arrive the quicker at Lahore. Yesterday, at two leagues from the latter city, I met M. Allard and two other French officers, MM. Ventura and Court, who were coming to meet me in a calash and four. We all alighted, and I gave M. Allard a rude embrace. He introduced me to his brother officers, and we all got into the carriage. An hour after, having crossed a wild country, covered, like the environs of Delhi, with the ruins of Mogul grandeur, we alighted at the entrance of a delicious oasis, consisting of a large parterre of carnations, irises, and roses, with walks of orange trees and jasmine, bordered with basins, in which a multitude of little fountains were playing. In the centre of this beautiful garden was a little palace, furnished with extreme luxury and elegance. This is my abode. Breakfast served up on plate awaited us in the háll. I spent the day in wandering with my new friends through the walks of the garden, and suffering myself to be stifled with their caressses. You may imagine the excess of our curiosity on both sides. Night came, however, very quickly, and we were obliged to part; for M. Allard's residence and that of M. Court are more than two leagues from my habitation, and people scarcely ever travel at night in the environs of Lahore. I remained alone, in the enchantment of my new residence, which is quite like the fairy palaces of the Arabian Nights' Entertainments.

In the evening, my mehmandar, who had informed the king of my arrival, came to bring me his majesty's congratulations and presents; the latter consisted of exquisite grapes from Kabul, delicious pomegranates from the same country, a collection of the choicest fruits, and, lastly, a purse of five hundred rupees. A splendid dinner was served up to me by torch-light, by a host of servants richly dressed in silk. I had courage to take as usual only bread, milk, and fruit. I ought to be grateful to this regimen, for permitting me to come to Umbritsir on horseback, without the least inconvenience.

This morning I was awakened by M. Allard and M. Ventura, who were going to the king, from whom they had received, at midnight, a summons to attend him this morning. You must know that I enjoy (I know not how) such celebrity at Lahore, that every body longs to see me, and Runjeet is not the least curious among them. It is in order that he may enjoy a foretaste of this pleasure that he desires a visit from those gentlemen at so unusual an hour. He knows that they spent the day with me yesterday; and he will be fully acquainted with me by the time I am presented to him. This will, no doubt, take place to-day, or to-morrow at the furthest. Adieu! I leave you, that I may *Persianize* a little more the insolent compliments I intend paying him, and those which I shall not refuse myself in his presence. M. Allard said just now that I knew everything—that I had seen everything—that I was acquainted with the whole earth; and such being the persuasion of the respectable public of Lahore, I shall take very high ground even with the king. Too much honour cannot be done to a man like me—that is the point whence I must start.

Lahore, March 16*th.*

I have several times spent a couple of hours in conversing with Runjeet "*de omni re scribili et quibus-*

dam aliis." His conversation is like a nightmare. He is almost the first *inquisitive* Indian I have seen; and his curiosity balances the apathy of the whole of his nation. He has asked a hundred thousand questions to me, about India, the British, Europe, Bonaparte, this world in general and the next, hell, paradise, the soul, God, the devil, and a myriad of others of the same kind. He is like all people of rank in the East, an imaginary invalid; and as he has a numerous collection of the greatest beauties of Cashmere, and the means of paying for a better dinner than any one else in this country, he is generally annoyed that he cannot drink like a fish without being drunk, or eat like an elephant and escape a surfeit. Women now please him no more than the flowers of his parterre, and for a good reason—and this is the cruellest of his afflictions. He had the decency to call the function which he complains of being weak, a digestive one. But I knew what *stomach* meant at Lahore, when in the king's mouth; and we conversed minutely about his complaint, but the words were well wrapped up on either side. To prove how much reason he had to complain, the old *roué*, the day before yesterday, in full court, that is in the open field, on a fine Persian carpet on which we were seated, surrounded by some thousands of soldiers, sent for five young girls of his seraglio, whom he made to sit down before me, and concerning whom he smilingly asked my opinion. I had the candour to say that I thought them very pretty, which was not a tenth part of what I thought of them. He made them sing, *mezza voce*, a little Seikh air, which their pretty faces made me think agreeable; and told me that he had a whole regiment of them, whom sometimes he ordered to mount on horseback for his amusement; and he promised to afford me an opportunity of seeing them.

The four Frenchmen (two of them by the way are Italians,) who are at the head of his armies, which they have trained very well in the European discipline, often excite his suspicions, although he has had ten years' experience of their probity and devotion to himself. He sometimes suspects that they are Englishmen or Russians; and the poor fellows, whom, however, he pays very well, and does not use badly, are compelled to be very circumspect, in order to preserve his confidence. I spoke to him so as to keep up the semi-officiality of the British character which I had brought with me. It is of all titles the best in the estimation of a pagan like Runjeet. I eulogised the strength, honesty, and pacific policy of the Government of Calcutta; and Runjeet, when I had done, said, that the Governor-general and he were but two hearts in one body. In sum, he pleases me extremely; and when I am not at court, he lavishes the highest encomiums on me. Yesterday, in my absence, he lauded me as a demi-god, and greatly amused himself at the expense of one of his courtiers, who wanted to bring me some remedy of his own for a cold in my head, which makes me sneeze very violently and frequently.

Yesterday morning, I had a prescription written in Persian, which I sent to the rajah with some very innocent drugs, for he has had me beset day and night to obtain them. Observe, however, that he will take care not to use them himself, but will amuse himself with making his friends and servants take them. To-morrow he will tell me a hundred lies about their effects, and will ask me for more.

Nothing can be more ridiculous than the reports in the city about my interviews with the king. The latter takes care to inform me of them, and is the first to laugh at them with me, though I have no doubt he takes me for a spy. He appears, however, perfectly satisfied as to my nationality. When I left him, after my first audience, he exclaimed, that I certainly was not an Englishman. An Englishman, he said, would not have changed his posture twenty times; he would have made no gestures while talking; he would not have spoken in such a variety of tones, high and low; he would not have laughed at proper times, &c.

I shall go to Cashmere, and anywhere else, I please. The king will have an eye to my safety everywhere. I shall enjoy the same security as in the British territory.

This pattern of an Asiatic king is, however, no saint: far from it. He is bound by neither law nor honour, when his interests do not enjoin him to be just or faithful; but he is not cruel. He cuts off the nose, ears, and a hand of very great criminals; but he never puts any to death. He is passionately fond of horses, quite to madness; and he carries on a murderous and expensive war against a neigbouring province, in order to obtain a horse, which has been refused him either as a gift or a purchase. He has great bravery, a somewhat rare quality amongst the princes of the East; and although he has always succeeded in his military undertakings, it is by perfidious treaties and negociations alone, that from a simple country gentleman he has become absolute king of the Punjab, Cashmere, &c., and is better obeyed by his subjects than the Mogul emperors in the zenith of their power. A Seikh by profession, a sceptic in reality, he every year pays his devotions at Umbritsir; and, what is very singular, these devotions are paid at the tombs of several Mohammedan saints; yet these pilgrimages offend none of the puritans of his own sect.

He is a shameless scoundrel, and cares not a bit more about it than Henri III. formerly among us. It is true that between the Indus and the Sutledge, it is not even a peccadillo to be a scoundrel. But what horribly offends the morality of these good people is, that the king, not content with the women in his own seraglio, often fancies those of others; and what is worse, those which belong to everybody. In spite of the mystery which the orientals, even of the lowest class, throw over their intrigues, whether purchased or not, Runjeet has often exhibited himself to the good people of Lahore, mounted on an elephant, with a Mussulmaun courtesan, amusing himself with her in the least innocent manner. Although he is only fifty-one, he is now reduced to the scandalous resource of old debauchees, and complains of it without shame.

He is about to quit Lahore; and has directed M. Ventura to proceed to Moultaun with ten thousand men and thirty pieces of cannon, for the purpose of collecting the tribute from the distant provinces of his empire. M. Allard will no doubt soon have a destination of the same kind. Runjeet will find some analogous occupation for himself; for he is a Bonaparte in miniature, and cannot remain in one place. In a few days we shall decamp from Lahore. At my audience of leave, I shall receive some new presents, and a dress of honour, which will be a very handsome dressing-gown, made of Cashmere shawls. I intend this for you, my dear father, in your great days of *real essences*. My military chest is grown very weighty with his highness's rupees. I have wherewith to go to Cashmere and remain there four months, without further curtailment of my wretched credit at Calcutta. At all events, M. Allard opens an unlimited one for me in Cashmere. Then, in order to return to Semla, I shall have to cross some districts of Kanawer, the king of which, as you know, is one of my friends, and will willingly lend me some hundreds of rupees, if unforeseen accident should cause me to arrive in his dominions without money. Like a man of foresight, I wrote to Kennedy, and Murray (the political agent at Umbala), to let all the mountain rajahs under their controul know that, in six months, I shall come and knock at some of their doors. It is probable that he of Belaspore will be the first whom I shall honour with my company.

Yesterday, our countrymen, my hosts, gave me a splendid fête at my palace—for palace it is—with accompaniment of dancing and singing Cashmerian girls, &c., one of whom would have passed for very pretty, if not even for very beautiful, in any country. I do not know how it happened, but in the dusk of the evening, when the servants lighted up the saloon, I found myself *tête-à-tête* with this opera-princess; my hosts had maliciously retired with the rest of the band into the garden;—maliciously and charitably. They understand hospitality like Kennedy, at Subhatoo. At the dessert, I had for a moment forgotten my frugal regimen, and had drunk a glass of champagne to the health of M. de Lafayette, which is a very curious thing at Lahore.

The general's flag has been lucky in this country. M. Allard, eight years ago, caused it to be adopted in the armies under his command. The Seikhs are a good sort of people, but no conjurors: Runjeet only knows that it was Bonaparte's flag, whom he is fond of persuading himself that he resembles.

I have just received a letter from the Jardin des Plantes, and it is the first! It is dated the 19th of May, 1830; acknowledges the receipt of my No. 1, 2, 4, and 5; approves of what I have done, and what I propose to do; and informs me that from the 1st of January, 1830, my salary has been increased two thousand francs. It is, moreover, written in very kind and obliging terms; signed Cuvier, Cordier, Jussieu. It was forwarded to me by Messrs. Eyriès, brothers, merchants at Havre, who remind me that they are the agents of the Jardin, and offer me their services if they can be useful to me. They would have done much better if they had sent me a letter of credit for two thousand francs a year on some good Calcutta house, since the Jardin appears to have made no arrangement with M. Delessert for him to send me supplementary credits. However, I know that the money is at my disposal somewhere, and that it will belong to me wherever it is; and I shall find some means of getting at it in case of need. I have to-day answered these gentlemen, and Messrs. Eyriès also.

For four months, at least, from the present time, it will be difficult for me to write to you; so do not be uneasy if, after the present letter, you have to wait half a year. Be assured that I am going into the terrestrial paradise with a good stock of health: in less than a month I shall breathe the salubrious air of the mountains, whence I shall not descend into the plains of Hindostan till the beginning of winter. Adieu, then, my dear father, adieu! The only thing that vexes me is to be deprived of news from you for so long a period. I embrace you and Porphyre, with all my heart.

Lahore, March 18th, Evening.

To-day I had my audience of leave of Runjeet Sing, to which I was conducted by M. Allard. I spent, for the last time, a couple of hours in conversing with that extraordinary man. He gave me the khelat or dress of honour, and that too of the most distinguished kind: it costs five thousand rupees, or twelve thousand francs. It consists of a pair of magnificent Cashmere shawls, *lie de vin;* two other less beautiful Cashmere shawls, and seven pieces of silk stuff or muslin, the latter of extraordinary beauty: eleven articles in all, which number is the most honourable. Add to this, an ornament, according to the fashion of the country, of badly-cut precious stones.

And, in addition to the value of this present, a purse of eleven hundred rupees; which, together with the sums before received, make two thousand four hundred, which is more than a year's salary from the Jardin.

Nor is this all. The king is going to give me some people to take care of me; horse and foot soldiers to watch over my safety; one of his secretaries, in order that I may send letters to him occasionally; camels to carry my tents and all my baggage to the foot of the mountains; and, lastly, carriers to do it, when the beasts of burthen can advance no further. Lastly—for there will be *lastlys* till to-morrow,—at the salt-mines, where I shall arrive in ten days, I shall receive a purse of five hundred rupees, and at Cashmere, one of two thousand.

Lastly, to conclude; if any thing takes my fancy at Cashmere, the king has recommended me to inform him of it, in order that he may satisfy my desire.

Of course we parted very good friends. What I was afraid of, was being detained longer at Lahore, or in the Punjab; and in fact, the minister came to ask me if it would be agreeable to me to accompany the king in a hunting excursion, on which he is going in a few days, and that too in a manner which solicited an affirmative answer. But, from the very first, I took very high ground with Runjeet: I answered unceremoniously in the negative; so that my diplomatist insisted no farther. M. Allard, who was several times condemned to the honour which the king destined for me, congratulates me extremely on having escaped it.

Runjeet asked me if I should continue to wear the European dress. I told him that I should, since he honoured it so much. I shall only leave it off to return from Cashmere to Semla, if I effect my return through Independent Tartary.

It is now M. Allard's turn. He is taking the inventory of my *menage* and stable; and he has, without my being able to decline it, been making such additions as he judged necessary for my convenience. I shall carry away with me a charming recollection of Lahore.

I wish you could assist me in returning M. Allard's kindness. He has a younger brother, about my own age, who has served in France. He sent for him, fifteen months ago, to enter into the maharajah's service, and at some future period to take his own place; but the climate has been so adverse to him from the first year, that M. Allard has sent him home this winter. This young man is now at Calcutta, on the eve of sailing for France. What will become of him there? As a claim to the favour of Government, I think he might put forward the honourable distinction of his brother's services at the extremity of Asia; and of the celebrity he has gained for our nation among a people who were almost entirely ignorant of us. I shall write to our friends to recommend him, and Porphyre must help him as much as he can.

Adieu, my dear father! It is midnight; I am falling asleep. The first letter will be from Cashmere.

Put Runjeet's Cashmere shawls forward, in order to help in winning those charitable (female) souls, who would wish their name to fill up the blank in a certain notarial act, which you gave me at parting. Adieu! I embrace you.

TO M. PORPHYRE JACQUEMONT, PARIS.

Lahore, March 21st, 1831.

My dear Porphyre,—There is such a principle of inaction in a caravan, that if it stops ten days anywhere, it becomes very difficult for it to resume its march. Thus you see I am still at Lahore, though on the 18th I received my audience of leave from the king. But, on the day of departure, a crowd of little affairs always come, and to necessitate an adjournment, there is baggage to arrange, divide, and load differently, if new means of transport are employed—workmen who promise, and keep their word no better than ours, &c. &c. However, I shall review my little army to-morrow, and the day after I shall cross the river.

If you have read my letter to my father, I hope you are satisfied with Runjeet-Sing. I have just turned his purses of rupees into a bill at sight for two thousand five hundred rupees on Cashmere, whither I likewise carry a royal mandate for two thousand rupees; and I unfurnish my chest for fear of accident, since, in ten days, and while on my journey, I shall receive another five hundred rupees from the king.

If you reckon properly, you will see that all this amounts to five thousand rupees, or about twelve thousand five hundred francs, which I intend to reserve and send to Calcutta, where it will accumulate at the rate of eight per cent. per annum.

I cannot tell you, my friend, with what pleasure I receive this money, because it is the first of which the free disposal belongs to me. I consider myself as but the steward of my allowance from the Jardin; but these twelve thousand five hundred francs are a windfall, and I consider quite charming this *terne* in the lottery without having purchased a ticket. I sadly curtailed your fortune, my dear Porphyre, by my voyage to America, and I must repair the breach with his highness's rupees; or, if you prefer it, in case you marry, you must let me make your wife's *corbeille*. I shall put my khelat into it, and it will gain you a fine reputation of conjugal munificence. But in six weeks, you will attain the terrible age of forty, which is rather late to take the leap. So let me restore you your shares in the ship General Foy, and keep my superb shawls, to tempt the infinitely beautiful, good, amiable, and rich young ladies who may not have any aversion for me.

Have I not seen in the English papers, that our late Spanish funds had resuscitated from the nominal 7 or nothing, to 25? It would be singular if you were to sell them at 40! After all, it would still be a bad speculation, for, since the 24th of March, 1824, of mystifying memory, we have received no interest for that money; but as, at that very time, I thought it lost, I think that, in finding it again, we have a gratuitous gain.

My new mehmandar is a most desirable man. He is

the man of business of the king's favourite; which favourite is a very great Seikh lord, who possesses the sovereignty of the greater part of the Himalaya mountains, of which Runjeet has the political possession. It is exactly as if I had the king's favourite with me. He will let me want for nothing, and will not leave me till I quit Runjeet's dominions; and I think of remaining two or three months in the valley of Cashmere.

I have a sufficient escort of cavalry to have nothing to fear from the *Akhalis*, or immortals, a species of fanatics or armed beggars—the more dangerous, as their sacred character renders them very respectable, at the same time that their indolent life forces them to rob for subsistence.

On the road from Peishawer to Cashmere, another fanatic, a Syed, that is to say, a pretended descendant from the Prophet, is playing the devil at the head of ten or twelve thousand bandits of the same species as himself; and it is probable that Runjeet, whom he has provoked for several years, will, at no distant period, decide upon vigorously giving him chase. But I shall always stay in the rear of the line of military operations. If the Syed caught me, he would cut my throat on the spot, for the glory of God.

I am rather losing sight of our politics. It is no great harm, for they seem to me to be going all wrong.

I yesterday received a farewell letter from Calcutta, from that distinguished and amiable man, whom I chanced to meet in the Himalaya, Mr. Inglis, a very rich Canton merchant, who is on his return thither to play at losing or winning millions. He promises to write to me frequently from that country, with which he is admirably acquainted. He is almost a friend. If, in a couple of years, Marlot receives a chest of Chinese plants, addressed to me, he must not be surprised; for I have given Mr. Robert Inglis his address, and he has promised me a present of that kind.

Adieu, my dear friend. I embrace you with all my heart.

END OF VOL. I.

LETTERS FROM INDIA;
DESCRIBING
A JOURNEY
IN
THE BRITISH DOMINIONS OF INDIA

LETTERS FROM INDIA;
DESCRIBING
A JOURNEY
IN
THE BRITISH DOMINIONS OF INDIA

TIBET, LAHORE, AND CASHMERE,

DURING THE YEARS 1828, 1830, 1831.

UNDERTAKEN BY ORDER OF THE FRENCH
GOVERNMENT,

BY

VICTOR JACQUEMONT,

TRAVELLING NATURALIST TO THE MUSEUM OF
NATURAL HISTORY, PARIS.

ACOMPANIED
WITH A MAP OF INDIA AND A PORTRAIT OF THE AUTHOR.

IN TWO VOLUMES.

VOL. II.

GYAN

Published by

Gyan Publishing House
5, Ansari Road
Daryaganj, New Delhi-110002
Phone: 011-47034999, 9811692060
E-mail: books@gyanbooks.com

Distribution Network
gyanbooks.com
India, USA, Canada, UK, Australia, France

ISBN : 978-81-212-3700-0 (Set)
ISBN : 978-81-212-4894-5 (HB)
First Published, 1834

2nd Impression 2020

Printed at: Gyan Press, Delhi.

Letters from India
Author: Victor Jacquemont

LETTERS FROM INDIA;

DESCRIBING

A Journey

IN

THE BRITISH DOMINIONS OF INDIA,

TIBET, LAHORE, AND CASHMERE,

DURING THE YEARS 1828, 1829, 1830, 1831.

UNDERTAKEN BY ORDER OF THE FRENCH GOVERNMENT,

BY

VICTOR JACQUEMONT,

TRAVELLING NATURALIST TO THE MUSEUM OF
NATURAL HISTORY, PARIS.

ACCOMPANIED
WITH A MAP OF INDIA AND A PORTRAIT OF THE AUTHOR.

IN TWO VOLUMES.

VOL. II.

LONDON:
EDWARD CHURTON, 26, HOLLES STREET.
(LATE BULL AND CHURTON.)

1834.

TO THE

RIGHT HONOURABLE SIR ALEXANDER JOHNSTON,

MEMBER OF THE KING'S MOST HONOURABLE PRIVY COUNCIL,

F.R.S., F.S.A., F.L.S.,

THESE VOLUMES

ARE RESPECTFULLY INSCRIBED,

BY

THE EDITOR.

A JOURNEY IN INDIA, &c.

BY

VICTOR JACQUEMONT.

TO M. JACQUEMONT, THE ELDER, PARIS.

Camp of Pindee-Dade-Khan, among groves of pomegranate and orange trees in blossom, under large mulberry trees.

April 6th, 1831.

I OUGHT not to be writing to you, my dear father, this evening: for business, of which I have enough, ought to come before pleasure; but I am so bruised, from a late terrible fall from my horse, that I grant myself this pleasure as a whim to a sick person. I left Lahore on the 25th of March, and on the 30th I arrived on the banks of the Chenaub or Acesines, at Ramnaghur. On the 1st of April I crossed this river, opposite to Khadabad, fifteen miles west of Ramnaghur. Rajah Gulab Sing, whom the king had commanded to receive me at Pindeedaden Khan, had come three days' march to meet me; after Runjeet Sing he is the greatest lord in the Punjab. As I suppose you are tired of the honours with which I am received, I will spare you all the details of Seikh politeness which Gulab Sing observed in the morning. In the evening I paid him a visit of ceremony in his camp, where he was expecting me, in the midst of all the pomp of his little court. We embraced each other for about a quarter of an hour, enough literally to stifle each other, till we raised each other from the ground, by turns; and as I found him a good fellow, understanding from the first my Hindoostanee, which I have strangely *Persianized* and *Punjabized*, during last month, I remained conversing with him till night.

Next day, at the following halt, the Rajah returned my visit, and added to the presents which he had made me the evening before, in the king's name, a double-barrelled gun, made in the mountains, after an English pattern. I should have preferred one of their long matchlocks, as a curiosity; but he considered his double-barrelled gun a master-piece of Himalayan industry,—but you will see that it is not a very brilliant specimen. Yesterday morning we crossed the Jelum, or Hydaspes, and came to encamp here. I spent the evening with my friend the *Rose-water Lion*, (for such is the signification of Gul-ab Sing: Gul, rose; ab, water, Sing, lion.) He is a soldier of fortune, a sort of usurper. I am persuaded that the legitimate Rajah of Jummoo Kangia, and other mountain principalities, which Runjeet has transferred to Gulab Sing, would please me less. The latter is a lion in war, but by no means a rose-water *petit maitre;* he is a man of forty, very handsome, and with the plainest, mildest, and most elegant manners. He took me this morning to see some salt mines, situated, at a distance of three leagues, in the mountains. We set out at break of day: the temperature was delightful. As I had barometers with me, I regulated our pace according to my horse's slowest rate, and did not excuse Gulab Sing a single new plant. Every stone which appeared at all suspicious was also examined; and my Punjabian eloquence was such, on botany and geology, that my companion, delighted with knowing the Sanscrit-feringee name of so many plants, (their Latin names it was that I was telling him,) set to work herborising along with me, and I owe him more than one plant which escaped me. A European must be a very absurd person who cannot attach an Oriental by his conversation, unless he has to do with a stupid one. Europe, in the most common details of its civilisation, is a mine of wonder to these people. They will listen to you all day with pleasure, if you are disposed to exhibit those treasures without rounded periods or a figurative style. Two arm-chairs went on before us; and when we passed near a tree, or I had bundles of plants to tie up, the Rajah and I sat down; and if we halted ever so short a time, Gulab Sing made a couple of secretaries dismount, who, seating themselves behind us, wrote down hastily what I said. Thus am I taken down in short-hand, like Cousin's metaphysics! but I am more positive. What these people love more than anything is the political statistics of Europe, of which they have no idea: the population, strength of armies, taxes, product of each branch of public revenue, the axioms of our civil and criminal law, and, lastly, the great results of the application of sciences to manufactures. I have no need to employ any quackery to do justice to the character which the Governor-general directed should be given of me to Runjeet Sing's envoy at Delhi. I have only to state the commonest truths.

When we arrived at the mines, Gulab Sing appeared very uneasy, and began to tell me long stories about the catastrophes which sometimes bury the miners by the falling in of the mine,—about the heat, bad smell, dirtiness, winding paths, &c.,—reserving for the *bouquet*, that no gentleman had ever descended into such a common sewer. However, he asked me what my pleasure was. "To leave you here and go down alone," I replied.—"But if the stones should fall in upon you, and I not be with you, what could I say to the king?" exclaimed the good man. It appears that he is answerable for me with his head, all the time I am intrusted to his care. He accompanied me, therefore, not into one mine, but into several, and forgot that it was derogatory. I taught him, while there on the spot, a little geology; and to continue the lecture, he will accompany me to-morrow into another part of the mountains. He has this moment sent me word, to my great satisfaction, that a road has been discovered by which I may go the whole way on horseback. This is good luck for me, for I am too much bruised to walk. A week ago I had a fall, which might have been more serious, for I fell under my horse, which fell backwards in rearing; but this time I escaped with only being buried in the mud. To-day I saw the same catastrophe about to happen, but on sharp stones; I however disengaged myself, and fell backward alone.

Do you recollect, my dear father, that you often used kindly to find fault with the disagreeable asperity of my manners, and their repulsive stiffness? and I admitted these unhappy defects in my character. Well, these last few years since I left France, my humour must have been a good deal modified to my advantage; for I have received too many proofs of interest from too many different people, not to attribute a part of them at least to those very qualities of which you were formerly so much vexed at my being completely destitute. Chance would not be so constant in my favour: there must be some good management on my part, which is nothing but the desire to please, produced, unknown to me, by a more kindly disposition, become habitual to me. Yesterday, one of my servants, who acts as my treasurer, because he can read and write, and because I thought him honester than the others, robbed me; he pocketed a few rupees which I had ordered him to give to some boatmen. By accident I obtained proof of his roguery. Instead of falling into a passion, and perhaps giving him a lashing with my whip, as I should probably have done not more than a year ago, I spoke very mildly to him; and though I punished him with a fine to the advantage of the people whom he intended to rob, and the refusal of leave of absence, which he requested of me, I made him do what I verily believe no Indian had ever done before, confess his fault and his repentance.

Good night; for if I go on, I know not where this scandalous trumpeting one's self will stop, and you would properly take a dislike to me for it. Moreover, I have great need to stretch myself in bed.

Jellapore, on the right bank of the Hydaspes.
April 11*th*, 1831.

God be praised! my dear father, not forgetting the blessings due to M. Augustin Taboureau, M. Cordier of Chandernagore, Captain Wade of Loodheeana, and M. Allard, who, each adding his good offices to the others, have just caused me to receive, on the banks of the Hydaspes, your No. 15, with the other letters which accompanied it, and under the same cover Beaumont's book. Lord William Bentinck had contributed a small contingent of Constitutionnels, and several other Indian friends the expression of their kind remembrances. This is quite a festival; so I have just ordered a whole day's halt, in order to celebrate it. Half of it I shall occupy in writing, and the remainder in rummaging anew the low mountains, at the foot of which I am encamped.

I began to despair about the fate of this packet, No. 15, which had allowed itself to be overtaken by the two following ones, 16 and 17; and I am entirely ignorant of the cause of its delay. The chain of our correspondence has so many links that some frequently escape me; it is always a little mystery to me how it gets over them in succession. It falls to me from heaven like the manna of the Israelites; and were I pious, I should give many thanks as I picked it up.

Though late, your letter is not less welcome. I owe to its perusal a nervous emotion of pleasure, which sleep, in the stillness of the night, will alone calm. I should have to write twenty pages to answer it; for it calls up a crowd of thoughts which I should like to communicate to you, and which would not be less pleasant for you to receive; only day-light lasts but sixteen hours.

You remind me of the beginning of my journey; my first marches from Calcutta to Benares. I survey myself from head to foot, in search of what is in me that is admirable, but cannot find it. I recal to mind the silence and monotony of those first marches, and do not perceive the wonders that you see in them! Nothing appears so simple and natural to me as to botanise and geologise on the banks of the Hydaspes, and gallop in the desert with my long-bearded escort. The sequel of my journey will have a *crescendo* for your charming surprise; and if your enchantment begins with *forte*, what will remain for it to celebrate my arrival at Lahore? You should begin with *piano*.

You guessed me at Benares. I spent last summer with the Lamahs, and now I am very near Cashmere, where I shall spend this. There are four roads to it from the Punjab side,—that of Jummoo, that of Bembur, that of Murpour and Prounch; and lastly, to the north, that of Mozufferabad. It would have suited my geological convenience to take the latter, whence I might have made an excursion into Hindoo Cosh; but a chief of Afghan fanatics, Sayd Ahmed by name, has occupied it for some months, and Runjeet Sing, who might crush him by a decided measure, is contented with acting timidly, and confining him to a poor mountainous district. Ahmed plunders and burns the few villages in it, and would do worse than a Musulmaun with me if I were to fall into his hands. It is with regret that I am obliged to forego this route; which, moreover, the king, in his care for my safety, for which he considers himself answerable to the English Government, would not have allowed me to take.

I parted the day before yesterday from the Rajah Gulab Sing, delighted with him, as he was with me. A courier will leave my camp every day, to carry him news of me; and I have promised to write to him sometimes, with my own hand, in Persian, which appeared to give him extreme pleasure. We are friends enough, and he is sufficiently good-natured, to excuse some omissions of etiquette, to which I shall be exposed in not borrowing the hand of a secretary. My safety, the attentions lavished upon me in this country, and the facilities afforded to my travelling, all depend on the idea of consideration attached to my name; and I must neglect no means of maintaining and increasing it. Gulab Sing can neither read nor write; and he has little esteem for that vulgar talent in a man of the middle class, whose trade and livelihood it is: but in a lord, and what is more, in a feringhee lord, it is an admirable talent in his eyes.

I shall go with my ten camels, that is to say, with the king's camels, as far as Mirapore. There, mules will be substituted for them to carry my baggage, which I shall lighten a little: and at Prounch, carriers will replace the mules. I have none of the trouble of these arrangements. My Mehmandar Sheik Bodder Bochs, being provided with the king's firmans, takes care of and provides for every thing. Fowls, kids, butter, milk, eggs, and flour are brought to my camp from every village. Since I left Loodheeana, my cook has never brought me any bill; and after feasting myself, there is enough left for my people to enjoy themselves like princes. Wade sends me word from Loodheeana, that Runjeet has written to him about me, and that of all the European lords he had seen, no one pleased him so much as I have done. He proves it by his attentions to me.

Mr. Ventura is marching towards Moultaun, with ten thousand men, to receive the tribute of the southern provinces of the Punjab. Mr. Allard thought for a moment that the Maharajab would send him into the mountains against Sayd Ahmed; he is encamped on the Acesines, and flattered himself at first that we should perhaps meet in Cashmere; but his courier of this evening overthrows that hope. He has behaved admirably towards me; every day I discover some new attention on his part, which he has performed unknown to me. As the people of my escort belong to a body of cavalry under his command, in which the promotions depend entirely upon him, you will easily imagine that I am well guarded. The lieutenant of my troop has a good chance of being made captain (resseldar), if he brings to his general a satisfactory certificate of his conduct from me; and he certainly shall have it.

I have the rajah's firmans for the protection of the collections which I shall send from Cashmere to Loodheeana as soon as I shall make them, when Wade will direct them with the same protection to Delhi.

I do not know by what road I shall return from Cashmere; but I will write to you more than once before I think of returning, and will constantly apprise you of my intended marches, as soon as I have determined upon them.

My purse, a very ignoble object no doubt, but, as they would say in Haiti, very necessary *metal* for travelling, is excellently well lined. I take a thousand rupees with me (one hundred louis), and I shall receive four thousand more in Cashmere. It is Bunjab Sing's present to me, being just two years of my ridiculous salary from the *Jardin*, before the addition of the two thousand francs, made since 1830. At Calcutta there remains about six thousand francs in my banker's hands, to which I ought to add the aforesaid supplement for the years 1830 and 1831, which makes ten thousand francs.

I am not afraid of being robbed: besides my having six sentinels in my camp during the night, every district through which I pass is responsible for all that may happen to me. Every thing, even the course of the seasons, is favourable to me. In common years, already at this period, the south-west monsoon dries up the Punjab with its burning heat. Bernier, in the beginning of March 1663, wrote, every morning, that he should no doubt perish during the day; and this year storms, more frequent than usual at this season, often clear the atmosphere. It is yet only very warm; and in five days I shall enter the mountains at Mirpoor, when I shall not care for the summer monsoon.

You speak contemptuously of European thunder and storms, compared to those of India. It is true, that in the Himalaya, they are terrific; and, for a sample, I received one this morning, which was felt gigantically in the vicinity of that great chain. It is nevertheless in Europe, and in the Alps, at the foot of Mont Blanc, that I have witnessed the finest of this kind of spectacle. Elie de Beaumont was of the party, and assuredly has not forgotten it.

To prove my filial piety, I have just changed my clothes, and am drinking your health in a glass of punch, which will not injure mine; it is to obviate the bad effects of the wet, of which I got plenty this morning, galloping three hours in the deluge to get over this stage. On these occasions, the vigour of my horse, a pretended Persian, reconciles me to the defects of his temper. I have several times thought of cashiering him on account of his vices; but, since I left Benares, in spite of all his malice, he has not succeeded in throwing me; he himself has never tripped, nor fallen lame, and it is likely that he will carry me as long as I travel on land, except in Cashmere, where his sudden starts, shying, and obstinacy, might throw him and me over some precipice. In Cashmere, I shall buy, without regard to the price, the best *ghounte* in Tibet (ghounte is the name of the wonderful race of mountain horses). He will not only serve me for this campaign, but also for that which I shall make in the Himalaya east of the Ganges, if the Minister of the Interior approves of the project which I have explained to him in my memorial. If not, I shall make a present of the animal to Kennedy, or to Lord and Lady Bentinck; and it will not be a vulgar present.

There are few people I have known in India, with whom I do not keep up some correspondence. It is on my side less frequent than I could desire, for want of leisure; but the number is so great! I am the only one of our nation enjoying the attentions of this little English society, transplanted into India to govern it. My passing through any place necessarily forms a little event, of which each preserves a remembrance, whilst these changes of scene, being constantly renewed, do not leave a durable impression of faces on my memory; but there are, nevertheless, many that I shall never forget. My preceding will have sufficiently informed you of them.

You speak very modestly of your *Real Essences!* What can be more real than what you owe them?—the innocent amusement of these twenty years! The working part of the community would no doubt deny their utility, because they are stupid enough not to comprehend how the possession of an idea or a feeling can be the source of our enjoyments, quite as well and much better than a coat of M. Ternaux' finest cloth, and that the greatest utility in life is pleasure. So, continue to distil those precious *essences*.

Lord William's *Constitutionnels* have informed me of the new composition of the Council of State, by M. de Broglie, whom I am disposed to quarrel with because he has not made M. Amédie Taboureau one. Taschereau and he will always have a few lines from me, with which they must be satisfied; for, once more, the day is only sixteen or eighteen hours long. Adieu, my dear father: the share of others would be too small were I to make yours larger. Take care of yourself: do not make an octogenarian of yourself before your time, which will come of itself soon enough. Write to Frederic for my sake; and tell him all this, for I think he will hardly come to Paris to read my letters.

Adieu! I embrace you with all my heart.

TO M. DE MARESTE, PARIS.

On the banks of the Hydaspes, at Jellalpore, April 11th, 1831.

How many things I have to tell you, my dear friend: first, about myself—*primo mihi,*—then about your own people, whose heroism, patriotism, and immortal glory the English papers and the *Constitutionnel* have related to me. The month of July, 1830, has completely relieved us from the contemptible character which our nation—*la grande nation*—was rapidly assuming in the eyes of others. It is very fortunate for me that I am among the Sheiks and the Afghans, for if I had remained longer on the other side of the Sutledge, where they reign, the English would have surfeited me with dinners. I was, to tell you the truth, prodigiously in fashion amongst them, before the great *amende honorable* of the 28th of July, but since then I have been quite the rage; and I was the only animal of my species,—that is to say, the only French gentleman, whom they could get hold of; I was bound to pay for the whole nation, of which I was the sole representative. I was obliged to eat like an ogre, drink like a fish, talk like an advocate, and make speeches, in season, out of season, and in all seasons:—*Gentlemen, the deep emotion which I feel, &c. &c.*: then comes, the *inadequacy* of your very humble servant *to do justice to such an eloquent, &c. &c.*—But, thank God, as I have not an alderman's stomach, I am released, till my return to Semla, in six months, where I shall begin again, with renewed vigour. In the meantime, I am picking up plants and stones in the Pentrapotamis,—which appears to me infinitely more classical than the Punjab—and am going to Cashmere, where I shall spend the whole summer in these innocent occupations. Runjeet Sing, the king of Lahore, has had the good sense to fall in love with me, on honourable terms, however,—a circumstance to be remarked; for when these Seikh gentlemen are in love, it is in general not in a very virtuous manner. He proclaims me the wisest of feringhee lords—a demi-god: he overwhelms me with the most flattering attentions,—surrounds me during my journey with the most complete protection,—provides for all my wants, camels, mules, carriers, breakfasts, dinners,—and, not satisfied with this, he sometimes sends me monstrous bags of money, which is considered in this country as the greatest politeness.

There is no want of local character here. The English, who have no political influence in this country, and are totally excluded from it, have not been able to efface it, as they have in India. If I had leisure, I would tell you what this singular court of Runjeet Sing is, and the in-door and out-door mode of life of these Seikhs, in their different conditions. But, my dear friend, I have other fish to fry, with a paper on geology begun, which I must finish upon the spot. The time will come, I hope, when we shall be able to spend a couple of evenings in the week together, and you will lose nothing for having waited till my return. You will say that I imitate Baron Stendhal, and his tender remembrance of Timothéus, *the most fiery of his charioteers;* but I shall have to pass in review before you a multitude of camels, saddle-horses, elephants, and brilliant escorts of cavalry, forming my lordship's cortege. However, I promised you not to tell any lies: if you accuse me of them, I shall say it is envy.

At Lahore, I lived in a little palace of the Arabian Nights' Entertainments; a battalion of infantry was on duty near me; the drums beat in the fields when I put my head out of doors; and when I walked in the cool of the evening, in the alleys of my garden, fountains played around me by thousands! A most splendid fête was given to me, with an accompaniment of Cashmerian girls, as a matter of course; and, although they had their eyes daubed round with black and white, my taste is depraved enough to have thought them only the more beautiful for it.

I have a long beard,—a red one, I must allow; but in other respects I have retained my European dress. The dogs, nevertheless, bark vigorously at so unusual a figure; the children pay me back, with interest, the vexation which I inflicted, some twenty years ago, with other blackguards of my own age, on the poor devils of Turks whom I met in the streets: they are never tired of looking at me; but I move about with my atmosphere of servants and horsemen, who are perfectly accustomed to my proceedings, and keep at a distance in the back-ground, all who exhibit an indiscreet astonishment. Some days ago, I gave a lesson in botany and geology to the Rajah Gulab Sing, successor to the late Taxiles; and as it is allowed that I am an admirable man, the pearl of sages, every one feels the greatest veneration for plants and stones. Adieu. I have talked so much about myself, that there is nothing left for you. What became of you in the uproar? Write to me, my dear friend. You owe it to my sincere friendship. I embrace you.

TO M. VICTOR TRACY, PARIS.

Camp near Jelialpore, on the banks of the Hydaspes, April 10th, 1831.

I WROTE to you, my dear friend, from the English frontier of the Sutledge, at the end of February. On the 2nd of March I entered on the Seikh territory, where I was received in the most distinguished manner. My father, to whom I wrote from Lahore, will no doubt have told you the flattering reception I have met with from Runjeet Sing, the high protection with which he surrounds me, and the solid proofs of kindness which he lavishes upon me. The hospitality of the king of the Punjab is as careful of my personal health as it is magnificent. He provides for all my expenses, and I enjoy the utmost liberty in all my motions.

I regret much, my friend, that I have not leisure to converse with you, to relieve my mind, as you do with me. But I have a great number of letters to write,—such an arrear of business already, and the day is so short, that I must for this once refuse myself the pleasure of writing at greater length.

The *Constitutionnel*, which I have just read on the banks of the Hydaspes, has interested me greatly. Newspapers are excellent things. I have the pleasure of reading your own speeches here without your knowing it. You do not say a word in the tribune which I do not pick up. Is it not the same thing as if I heard you? How often do I not feel myself, by these means, brought near to you?

My English papers go much further than my *Constitutionnels*, and from them I think I can make out that your motion for the abolition of the punishment of death has passed both Chambers, and that the king has joyfully given his assent. I long to see the confirmation and details of it in our papers, and to read the proclamation of this glorious triumph which you have just obtained.

A thousand thanks to you for not forgetting our dear Paray. How well I feel all the charms which that beautiful spot must have for you. I tell myself that, in your place, I should no doubt have done as you did; that while I made war on the furzes, I should have sought, at the same time, to preserve that peculiarly mild and melancholy character which pleases us both.

We shall meet each other there again some day, I hope, and shall again walk together along its grassy avenues, in the cool of the morning. We will retrace together the years of our separation. Then will the scenes of Asia be vividly pourtrayed in my memory, opposed to the mild soft tints of the peaceful Paray.

Is not your friendship mistaken as to the true interest which my letters may possess? My father seems charmed with the first two I wrote him after my departure from Calcutta, on my road to Chandernagore and Benares, and which he sent to you to read the very day you finished writing to me; but if the sincerity of his testimony is not doubtful, its value is at least very suspicious; and I confess, my dear friend, that it is the same with yours, and for the same reason. I know not what difference there may be between my journals and my correspondence; but I have sometimes tried the experiment of reperusing the former after a long interval, and I did not judge of myself as you do. Nevertheless, I cannot write them with greater negligence or precipitation than I do letters; for of the latter, for instance, I have written to-day fifty-four pages of this small size, after galloping three hours this morning, to get through my stage, and the evening is still long. The compliment you pay me would be in truth the most agreeable of all, if I were to receive it from others not prejudiced in my favour as you are. Where plants and stones only are to be talked about, there is no occasion to be amusing: it is out of place; but beyond the technical details of science, it is, I agree, the first requisite in black or white. What object can a

Parisian have but his pleasure, in seeking, in a book on India, to become acquainted with its social and political organisation, and the description of features under which nature presents itself there? If the book which teaches him all this is a bad one, he is wrong to shut it; for after all he is seeking only for amusement.

Science has philosophical eminences which it is not impossible to render accessible, or at least visible, to minds unfamiliar with them. My ambition would be to intermix general physics and the higher branches of natural history, with pictures of political history and sketches of Indian manners. But could I do it without imparting to the latter a disagreeable dryness and heaviness, and without forgetting the simple severity of language in which matters of science ought to be expressed; could I master this concord, nothing more would remain for me than a series of special, and absolutely technical, memoirs.

This will form one of the objects of our first conversations when I have the happiness of seeing you again. But think of it; and do not wait till my return before you give me advice. Adieu! my dear and excellent friend.

TO M. PORPHYRE JACQUEMONT, PARIS.

Camp at Jellalpore, on the banks of the Hydaspes,— April 11th, 1831.

My dear Porphyre,—Packet No. 15, which I thought lost, as I had already received Nos. 16 and 17 four months ago, came to hand this morning, along with Beaumont's book. I have read the few acres of manuscript which were so carefully inclosed in it, and the additions made by several Indian friends. I have written the ten letters which you will find in company with this, and you may suppose I have done enough for one day; nevertheless, I must finish, in order to devote to-morrow entirely to my minerals,—and it will be the worse for you, as, coming last, you will have the smallest share.

You were perfectly right to object to the publication of any portion of my letters. It is impossible for them not to be written with too much negligence to please any but my friends. I think my father has completely surrendered to your objections against his premature if not indiscreet publication.

Writing to-day to each, I have endeavoured to forget what you tell me about your exchanging letters with each other. This thought would have stopped my pen, or at least would not have allowed it to run carelessly over the paper and blacken fifty-eight pages a day, as I have done. Nevertheless, chance has sometimes helped me. From Lahore, for instance, I recollect letting out, in my letter to my father, some incongruous confession which would hinder him from showing it to many people. I like very well to chat *tête-à-tête*, but when there is a third party it is a very different thing; it is the same with writing. To speak as I think, and without humbug, I must persuade myself that I shall be read only by the person to whom I write.

But you, my friend, poor Porphyre, ask me, modestly enough, for a word or two of friendship and gossip. It is not a tune always at command, and I cannot play it to-day; but when I feel myself in the vein, I will think of you, and as I always have pen, ink, and paper at hand, you shall have it to your heart's content.

Cambessèdes is a capital fellow, to whom you would do well to say a hundred kind things from me, when you meet him. I shall write to him from Cashmere in less than a month.

I am dreadfully sleepy. Adieu, then, my dear friend; I love and embrace you, with all my heart.

TO M. PORPHYRE JACQUEMONT, PARIS.

Camp at Nur, near a village in the woods, among the mountains, on the road to Cashmere,—April 20th, 1831.

It is almost as much as I can help, my dear friend, not to swear on paper; but I shall take a hearty revenge in the open air. The fact is, peripateticism exposes its admirers to such a complication of vexations, that they have often a good mind to seat themselves on the first stone, cross their arms, and d——n heaven and earth. For the last five days, I have been continually and very legitimately (if our liberal friends have not scratched the word out of the dictionary) in a deuse of a temper, or rather in a positive fury. It is since my entrance into the mountains. I was to have found a number of mules and carriers there, which the King had ordered for me long since; but the power of a sovereign in Asia decreases at least as the cube of the distance from the place where he may be. Hence at Soukshainpore, my last halt in the plains on the banks of the Jelum, the people said they cared very little for the king's orders, and received only those of his eldest son, their dauphin. The Thanadar (mayor or commandant) took refuge in his mud fort, with a few wretches armed with matchlocks, and threatened to fire at my caravan, if I persisted in demanding that to which I was entitled. The surrounding villages paid for the rebellion of the chief town. My people visited them as marauders; and, after seizing my share, helped themselves pretty plentifully.

At Mirpore, where I ought to have found the mules and carriers, nothing was ready. I wanted forty of the latter; they were to come every day; and after waiting three days, not one came. I rated my mehmandar and the lieutenant of my escort: I accused them of laxity and indolence; but they defended themselves by imputing the blame of these delays to the total insubordination of the petty mountain chiefs to the king, and the habitual rebellion of their wretched subjects against them. When my people talked too loud, the Mirporeans, who had also their mud citadel, threatened to retire within it and shut the gates. If my friend Gulab Sing had not been six days' march off, I would immediately have written to him, and requested him to send three or four hundred regular infantry, in order to make an example, and give a hundred lashes to the gentlemen of the staff at Mirpore; but I should have been obliged to stay there twelve days, and the place was entirely destitute of interest. The thermometer, besides, rose every day to 94°; and yesterday morning, seeing a score and a half of carriers, I had them loaded with the most indispensable part of my baggage, and leaving my two officers in the rear, to get out of the business as they might, and see to the forwarding of the remainder, I started forward. I arrived before all my people, near the banks of a river where I meant to encamp; and I found nothing to receive me but a burning sun. The poor devils arrived at last, one after the other, a quarter of an hour between each; and at four o'clock in the afternoon I breakfasted. I had entered the estates of Gulab Sing. Wonders of all sorts were promised me. The chiefs of a neighbouring fort came to make their salaam. According to them, it rained mules and carriers in their mountains. However, nothing fell in the night, but the oxide of hydrogen in immeasurable quantities; and my yesterday's collection of carriers, far from increasing by the rain, melted in it like salt. This morning, when I asked if fresh ones had arrived, I was told that those of yesterday had decamped. I ordered my twenty mountaineer soldiers, ten only of whom had arrived the evening before, to set out in search of them; but if the carriers were not made of salt, the soldiers were made of sugar: not a vestige of them remained after the rain. The remainder of my caravan, dragged on with asses taken by force, were dreadfully fatigued. I took your spy-glass, and swept the horizon in search of some village whither to wend our way, or rather to make a treaty, for it was porters that I wanted; but not the slightest trace of smoke could I discern, except on the other side of the torrent, which the storm of the night had rendered impassable. However, a score of my Cashmerians were at last unearthed: they had hid themselves in the high grass; and leaving my fat mehmandar behind me to play Prometheus, and create men in the desert, in order to provide for the transport of half of my baggage, which was lying on the bank of the torrent like the remains of shipwreck, I pushed forward, followed by a small column, carrying with me what was most necessary. So I am writing at breakfast, although it is not yet noon; the reason is, I have made so many circuits, and climbed so much, right and left, in the mountains, that I have arrived after this first division. Here I may wait. My cook has forty eggs, flour and rice in proportion; and around the village there are some fields of green corn for horses. I have a tent, a chair, table, ink, pens, and paper, as you perceive. The situation is high enough not to be very warm; and I leave my rear-guard to the grace of God. As for the mountain soldiers, with their matchlocks, and their swords, and bucklers, some came here, as a sample, to tell me that they had eaten nothing since the day before yesterday; that is, since they have been what they call on duty, in my neighbourhood. I drove them away like dogs; and the spokesman does not know how near he was getting a few kicks on the nether end of his person. To every symmetrical mind, but to a naturalist in particular, who recognises himself only by means of method, and by logical and ingenious classifications, the general *sauve qui peut*, and the *va comme je te pousse*, in this country, with both men and things, are truly confounding. Last year, when I left Semla, on my way to Tibet, I asked Kennedy for only two of his gorkhas; these two men being broken into European discipline, had drilled my carriers like a ship's crew; and the latter often amounted to sixty. A single one would have sufficed. Why have I not a detachment of them now? They would do more business, and spare me more trouble, than all the rabble of horse and foot with which I am encumbered. Kennedy, indeed, offered me some; but it would have been contrary to rule, and, as it appeared to me, at the risk of committing himself with the Government. Besides, the king might have taken offence at my invading his territory with soldiers in the

English service. I therefore refused my good friend's offer. I repent having done so now.

To fill up the measure this morning,—and mark I know not what may have happened to my rear-guard, which is perhaps where it was yesterday, waiting, like the emigrants at the camp of Villejuif, in March, 1815, for men to advance,—well, to fill up the measure, I was obliged to prove my insolubility in water, in order to arrive entire in my person; for I was caught in a couple of deluges on the way. The tickets on a bag full of minerals were reduced to a sop, and I shall have to find out their former order. This is the devil,—then, two of my horsemen's horses fell down a precipice, whence they were got out very lame; mine has lost his shoes. This is not to be borne. Water for drinking is nothing but mud; a kind of chocolate, very disagreeable even to an Indian traveller, who, after two years' running about like me, ought not to be very nice as to his potations. Adieu, my dear friend; I am going to take a little walk near my tent, and to give myself the satisfaction of swearing like a roll of drums. When you escorted parks of artillery, with bullocks, through the mud of Poland, you perhaps experienced a slight tinge of the vexation which excruciates me. Nevertheless, one must have a good head, if not a good heart, against temptation; use patience; untie, but break not; lay down, and do not throw. Heavens! how rank the butter was in my omelette! such a smack of stinking cheese! how hot the sun is shining between the two acts of the deluge, under a thin cloth, where the air is stifling! Damnation! This is one, at least, which my father, if you give it him to read, will not be tempted to communicate to all our friends. For a diversion, I will add, in Indian, a *bhanne tchoute!* which is an oath compared to which all ours are but very little boys. Adieu!

20th, Evening, at dinner.

MY vexation had not attained its zenith this morning, when I blotted a long sheet of hieroglyphics for you. But the sun is brighter after the storm; the reprimand which I gave my mehmandar has had its effect: here he comes with all the rest of my baggage, and twelve Cashmerians besides, whom he made prisoners in this village, which thought itself safe from my people's attacks because the torrent was impassable; but my man crossed it, he told me, on skins filled with air, and has taken by storm with four soldiers the twelve poor devils whom he brings with him. Meanwhile, the vizier of a neighbouring petty mountain chief brought me ten of his own growth, so that I am swimming in abundance; and as I pay them, which they by no means expected, being apprehended in the king's name, and said to be paid by him, the band about me are in excellent spirits.

It is the abomination of desolation to want the necessary hands; since, when some are wanting, the rest that have been seized become useless: so I keep a number to the amount of four or five hundred francs a month, in order to have a good reputation, and find every where volunteers who are the best carriers, as well as the best soldiers. If I were to make use of the royal privilege which is granted me, the peasants would forsake their villages at my approach, and my people find nothing to eat. This morning, as I was rambling at some distance from the road, among some very rough hills, covered with thick wood, I discovered three men hid. I was in search of something quite different; nevertheless, I thought them a good prize, and I said to one of my men, "Seize them!" They were peasants of the neighbouring village, who had run away to escape domiciliary visits. They looked very foolish at being thus dislodged by chance. I promised them that they should be paid, instead of being ill-used, and they went gloomily enough to join the main body of my troop, because they had never seen a European, and put but little faith in my gilded words.

The horizon, without metaphor,—that is to say, the sky above the mountains and plains,—has also cleared up. I feel myself quite alive, and in a humour to finish the perusal of Beaumont's book this evening. Since I have been twice only just missed by the lightning, I prefer every kind of cracker to Father Jupiter's, in the Himalaya at least, where they are loaded with ball, and not badly pointed. It lightened enough to singe my moustachios, and the fluid seemed every instant to strike some tree of the group under which I was encamped. Then I was under the same tent in which last year, in the Dhoon, two of my people, who were changing my linen, were struck to the ground, and for a moment paralysed, by the fall of the lightning on a neighbouring tree. I recollect that at sea I had no greater liking for thunder. When you are alone in a storm, with an accompaniment of this music, whether in ship or encamped in a desert, your chances of being struck seem much greater, because you are the only one that Jupiter can aim at; and, although he is not very skilful, the most awkward have their lucky hits.

Curse my infamous writing if you like; I will allow you to do so. However, you must excuse it, as well as this Cashmere paper, because in writing so badly on this slippery paper the pen follows the thought, and never remains behind; and the *metal* (in the style of St. Domingo) which is precious to me is time. You will at least see, my friend, in the disorder of these long letters, that although I am some thousand miles from you, the thought of you is not the less vividly present to my mind, and that one of the most agreeable illusions of my solitude is to recal you to my recollection, and to converse with you exactly as if you were present.

Adieu! On account of the rain, with which I have been so completely soaked this morning, I shall allow myself a cigar after dinner; but it will be while I am reading Elie de Beaumont's memoir.

TO M. JACQUEMONT THE ELDER, PARIS.

Camp at Berali, in a small plain in the middle of the mountains, on the road to Cashmere,—April 22nd, 1831.

MY dear Father,—I promised myself never to believe in adventures; but I have been compelled to give way to evidence, and you will be converted too.

The Indians and Persians call Cashmere the terrestrial paradise. They tell us that the road leading to the other is very strait and difficult: it is the same with that to Cashmere in every possible sense.

It was at Soukshainpore, on the banks of the Hydaspes, at the foot of the mountains, that the first shadows appeared in the picture of my ambulatory prosperity.

The chief of this little town, which is a fief of one of the king's sons, refused to obey Runjeet Sing's firmans for furnishing my camp with all the necessary provisions. He shut himself up in his mud fort, with a few wretches armed with matchlocks, and threatened to fire at my horsemen, if they insisted any further on obedience.

I wrote immediately to the king at Umbritsir, to complain of this contempt for his authority, so prejudicial to the hospitality which he meant to show me. My cavalry dispersed themselves in the surrounding villages; and I saw them return from their foraging excursion pretty heavily laden. This is according to rule.

Next day, 16th of the present month, I entered the Himalaya with my camels, and encamped at Mirpore, where a numerous troop of mules was to be assembled, ready to supply the place of my camels, which were incapable of proceeding farther into the mountains.

Instead of mules, I found at Mirpore a hundred rascals, with their matchlocks and little mud fort, indifferent enough to the Rajah's commands, for which they would have cared still less had not my friend Gulab Sing been encamped at the distance of a few days' march, with three thousand regular troops. Ten times a day did messages and promises of mules and porters pass between my mehmandar and the chief; but for two days without effect. On the evening of the third day, a score of Cashmerian porters arrived. This was half the requisite number; but I was so enraged at being kept in a horribly hot place, entirely devoid of interest, that on the 19th I loaded these twenty men with the most necessary part of my baggage. I pushed forwards, leaving my mehmandar behind with the rest, reprimanding him a little for his pusillanimity.

Towards the middle of the day, I arrived on the banks of a torrent, near which I meant to encamp; but my little rear-guard did not arrive till long after; and I breakfasted at sunset. It was night before the rear-guard appeared, in the most pitiable condition. Sheikh Bodu Bochs, my mehmandar, and Mirza, the lieutenant of my escort, had, as M. de Foucauld would say, seized half a dozen poor devils and a troop of asses; these brought the remainder of my baggage.

A terrible storm lasted the whole night; and, as a half-drowned cat dreads cold water, and warm water still more, I recollected that last year, in the Dhoon of Dehyra, on the pinnacles of Mossouri, the thundering god did not aim badly, supposing that he was firing at me; and hearing the crackling of the trees around, and seeing my tent almost constantly illuminated by the flashes, I confess I should have preferred a calm serene night,—moonlight, of course.

It seems, however, that Jupiter only fired blank cartridges that night; for his terrible racket neither killed nor paralysed any one.

But the torrents of rain, which served as fuel to this conflagration of the skies, melted my asses, horses, soldiers, and carriers, as if they had been sugar.

At sunrise, I found only my escort, among whom there is a kind of discipline. But the rain had made them as benumbed as serpents buried in the snow; and their poor horses looked as if they were made of wood, they were so stiff. This little chosen band, however, by degrees got into motion, literally disinterred some of my foot soldiers; and, assisted by the latter, succeeded in picking up, right and left, the twenty Cashmerians of the day before. All the rest had entirely disappeared.

I administered a fresh reprimand, and this time a

severe one, to Boddu Bochs; and, wishing him the art of Prometheus, to improvise twenty carriers in a desert, I pushed forward, followed, as on the preceding evening, by only the most necessary part of my baggage.

The road was extremely difficult; we were obliged to alight incessantly; and, in spite of their care, the horses belonging to two of my escort tumbled over a kind of precipice, whence they were rescued very much bruised, and very lame. For my own part, I was constantly on foot, hammer in hand, and continually quitting the path, which was only a low and narrow gap in a wood very thick with thorny shrubs, to gain some neighbouring eminence, and determine the direction of the strata with the compass. Some armed servants followed me in the smallest of these circuits; prudence demanded it. In one of these excursions, I discovered three men hidden; and, cocking my piece and bringing it to my shoulder, the three suspected figures proved by their terror the excess of my circumspection. They were poor peasants belonging to a neighbouring village, who had taken refuge in the fastnesses of the wood to avoid the passage of the avalanche which chance had brought near them. They gained nothing by it; I had them seized and carried along the road, promising them that they should be paid for their trouble. They were, so far, an addition to my means of transport.

Nur is the name of a wretched hamlet at some height

in the mountains; it was my second halting place. I arrived late, wet through to the skin. Boddu Bochs was not long in coming up; he arrived with the rear guard and some prisoners. He had crossed the torrent in the morning on skins filled with air. On the other side, the inhabitants of a considerable village were sleeping in tranquillity; and in the first moment of surprise he carried off some score and a half of men.

I therefore thought myself at the end of my troubles; but in the evening famine appeared in my camp. All my people came to tell me that they were hungry, and that there was nothing to eat in the neighbouring wood. This was the fault of the mehmandar, who had not told them to take provisions with them. I recommended them to wait till the next day, and commanded the soldiers to watch them well during the night.

But there was another deluge that night: and the soldiers, who did not consider themselves insoluble in water, deserted their guard in quest of shelter; and yesterday morning a new deficiency was found in the number of my carriers. I acted as the day before, and started the first with a small troop. The distance was greater than usual, and the road very bad even for a Tibet walker. Nevertheless, I arrived, without accident to myself or my escort, at Nekhi, a still more miserable village than that of the evening before. My horse had lost his shoes, and was very lame: I did not fret much about this, because the nature of the road only allowed me to go on foot.

Night approached, and I was a little astonished at not seeing my mehmandar; the more so, as the rest of my baggage, sent on by him, had joined the camp. At length one of his servants arrived, breathless, to tell me that his master had had a fall, and broken his arm.

Contrary to the Asiatic rule of not advancing a step towards an inferior, I seized one of my Cashmerian's sticks, and followed by several of my people and horsemen, descended from my mountain to help my wounded man. They said he was lying in a valley three leagues from the camp; but I ran about three hours, at the risk of breaking my neck pretty often, before I found him. I confess his excessive cowardice disgusted me, and made me almost regret coming so quickly, if not so far. This pusillanimity in an herculean body appeared only the more prominent. It was impossible for me to examine his wound properly: this visit only served to prevent him making himself ill with drinking bad arrack, to keep up his sinking spirits he said. I had the bottle broken. The night promised to be fine; and I left the wounded man stretched on a bed, in the midst of a pine forest, surrounded by a score of servants and soldiers, to take care of him and watch him. He was to be brought here to-day, on his couch. I returned very late to the camp, by the very doubtful light of an exceedingly new moon, and through frightful roads. However, I made all my people take the same precautions as myself: we dragged ourselves along without accident, for half an hour, close to immense walls, along vertical escarpments.

I was worn out with fatigue, exhausted by an abundant perspiration during a fifteen hours' march, and without appetite for supper. I had a little bad punch made; and as I had entirely abandoned the use of fermented liquors for the last four months, it sent me to sleep immediately, if it did not intoxicate me during my slumber without my knowledge.

At last, this morning, nobody failed when summoned—I mean those of my band. They passed the ridge of the mountain at sunrise in good humour, to breakfast at the first halt; for we were to reach this place, Berali, the first village after Mirpore.

I went on foot, following my lame horse, in bad humour with the rocks, on account of their nature and the direction of their strata, thinking about my sick mehmandar, and the difficulty of carrying him to this village, along the frightful roads, and about the impossibility of his accompanying me on my journey, and the annoyance of applying to the king for a substitute, &c.; when I found myself this time, with my rear-guard, at the foot of a lofty mountain, with nearly vertical sides, and a flat summit, on the edge of which I observed a fortress. I was told that it belonged to the king, and was garrisoned with three or four hundred soldiers, under the command of a royal governor. In fact, I soon saw some people of very suspicious appearance, with their matchlocks, swords, and bucklers, coming down by the only path leading to the summit, and the only one by which it was possible to pass.

They made their salaams, and told me they came on the part of their master to show me the road, and to look to the safety of my baggage. Their master, they added, was waiting for me in the plain by which the mountain is crowned, to offer me his salutations, and a *nuzzer* (a present offered by an inferior to a superior). In this account there was nothing but what was very probable; and, after an hour's painful climbing, I reached the top, following my escort. It was a very pretty, smooth plot. The fort rose in the middle, on a mound, and greatly contributed to the picturesque effect of the landscape. Numerous groups of soldiers, in their oriental accoutrements, were not wanting, and gave this picture all the local character which the gentlemen of the *Globe* could desire. I found my caravan reposing under an immense sacred fig-tree, the only tree in this strange place. I ordered them to continue their march. My servants then came to tell me that they were not allowed to do so, and that it was the people of the fort who detained them.

A great number of the latter had approached me: they crowded round my horse, which I had again mounted; but curiosity seemed their only motive, and the crowd opened at my bidding. However, it had so increased, that the men belonging to my escort were lost in it. Impatient at this delay, I commanded them to bring the governor as quickly as possible. He soon came, in the midst of a new troop of soldiers, much worse-looking than the preceding ones, and so wretchedly clad himself, that I was obliged to ask Mirza which of these vagabonds was the chief. From respect to the king, whose officer he is, I dismounted to receive his compliments, as he was himself on foot. He offered me a kid, which my *maitre-d'hôtel* carried off. I could hardly wait till the end of his speech, to express my indignation at the refusal to allow my caravan to proceed. I addressed him vehemently, demanding if it was true that he had dared to give such an order. Neal Sing (for that was the name of this bandit) appeared a little disconcerted at my violence; and, without answering my interrogatories, offered me as many soldiers as I wished, to guard my baggage. I told him that he and I being the only inhabitants of this desert, I had no need of his soldiers; and the only thing I required of him was to draw them off. He then gave me to understand that such an order on his part would not be obeyed, and again requested me to take a guard of his troop. I then thought it prudent to accept his offer.

My situation, however, visibly became that of a prisoner. My djemadhar Mirza spoke only with joined hands to Neal Sing, whose tone rose in proportion. At last, the latter, after a long statement of all the injuries the king had done him, and which Thean Sing his minister (the brother of my friend Gulab

Sing) had provoked, declared to me with joined hands, —mark this—and the humblest and most submissive language, that having in the possession of my person the means of forcing the king to redress the wrongs he had done him, he should keep me prisoner until justice was done him; and that myself, my escort, and my baggage, should serve him as hostages and securities.

The man grew warm with the recital of his misfortunes. They were, he said, the reward of his fidelity. Gulab Sing wished to make him surrender his fortress, which had been intrusted to him by the king. It was on account of his having constantly defended it against that lord, that his brother Thean Sing, being near the king, had rendered the latter's orders for his pay of no effect. He had for three years received nothing; he had no better dress than the rags which he showed me; his soldiers lived upon the grass of the fields and the leaves of the trees.

I saw, with a secret—oh! a very secret—displeasure, the effect of his eloquence upon the famished and armed multitude in whose power I had fallen. A general clamour rose, frequently above the voice of the chief; and the conclusion of his oration was not the passage the least applauded in this menacing manner. Each, as he listened, examined the lighted match of his gun, and knocked off the ashes. Several of the soldiers wished to speak in their turn; but I imperiously commanded this frightful rabble to be silent; and I no longer heard any more than slight murmurs, which the chief himself was not afraid to suppress. The calm indifference which I affected, and the unstudied loftiness of my language, imposed on these wretches. My contempt overpowered them. They certainly had never heard any of their rajahs talk of himself, as I did, in the third person. Runjeet Sing is the only one who does so in the Punjab; and while I paid myself these compliments, I spoke to them only as to servants. By this manœuvre I succeeded in detaching the greater number from their chief, whom I treated with the same familiarity, but with a tone of kindness and protection. I led him under the shade of the great fig-tree I have mentioned, to converse less publicly with him. I made him sit humbly on the ground; whereas I had one of my chairs prepared for myself. He seemed eager to enter upon business; but I called to my mehmandar to bring me a glass of *eau sucré*, which was a long time preparing. I complained of the heat, and commanded another of my servants to hold a parasol over me, and a third to fan me with a plume of peacock's feathers. I took all my little comforts, not only without abating any thing of them, but, I assure you, adding largely to them; leaving Neal Sing on the ground, in all his humility, to reflect in silence on the enormity of the crime he meditated committing, and its terrible consequences. I then explained to him under what auspices I had come into this country, and the terrible vengeance which the king would not fail to exact for any affront which I might receive in his states, in order to convince the English government that he was not the instigator.

Neal Sing protested that he had entertained no criminal design against me; he doubted not that the king, knowing me to be in his hands, would pay him what he had so long owed him, in order to extricate me. I represented to him, that, after offering such an outrage to Runjeet's power, he could never flatter himself that he would be sincerely pardoned; and that sooner or later he would pay the penalty by some cruel chastisement. I affected to say these things, not in a menacing tone, but as if I was speaking for his own interest; and this artifice was not without success. Neal Sing then proposed to set me at liberty, and to retain only my baggage. I rejected this idea, with reasons which would make him still more conscious of the distance between us. To travel without my tents! my furniture! my books! my clothes! I who change twice a day! The proposal was absurd and impossible! I looked at my watch, and told my *maitre-d'hôtel* it was breakfast-time, and ordered him to get it ready without delay. I knew very well that there neither was nor could be any thing ready; since all my caravan were prisoners under the custody of Neal Sing's people, before whom my servants took care not to open a single package. I ordered some milk to be brought. The *maitre-d'hôtel*, at his wits'-end, asked me where he was to get it. "Don't you hear," said I to Neal Sing, "that the saheb desires to have some milk? Send directly into the neighbouring villages, that some may be brought without delay.". The brigand was a little confounded by this policy; and in his uncertainty, he despatched some of his band in quest of the required beverage. I saw them go; and when they had gone a hundred paces, I called them back, and told my *maitre-d'hôtel* to explain to them that it was cow's milk, and not buffalo's or goat's, that I wanted, and that they must see the animal milked before them.

I designedly accustomed these bandits to obey me in trifling things, in order to facilitate the arrangement of the great affair I had yet to treat with them, the moment of which I delayed by a number of artifices, as I saw that this species of truce favoured my interests, by the ascendancy which Neal Sing allowed me to assume over him. When I thought the moment favourable, I proposed him a present, and the support of my recommendation to the king.—He had shown me so many good royal bills, that a slip of paper more, written by my hand, would not appear a great addition to his riches; and I therefore offered to add something more solid. He immediately demanded two thousand rupees. Some of his band, who were collected around us, cried "No! no! ten thousand!" which only gained them a contemptuous exclamation from me, which none dared to resent, and which seemed so much to confound them, in the eyes of the rest, that none of them afterwards ventured to interrupt my conversation with their chief. "Neither ten thousand, nor two, nor even one;" for the very good reason that I had not got them; "but, in consideration of your wretched position, I will give you five hundred rupees." "Five hundred rupees!" he exclaimed: "what is the good of that? We number four hundred men, who have been dying of hunger these three years. Two thousand rupees; or you must remain a prisoner." Without appearing to attend to his alternative, I shrugged my shoulders at the absurdity of his demand, and offered to allow my treasurer to convince him of it. He easily accepted the proposition of seeing my treasure counted. I reproved him with haughtiness, severity, and contempt, for this movement; as if what I had said could be otherwise than true. "The Asiatics," I told him, "are wretches who will perjure themselves for a crown; but have not you heard what the word of a Christian lord is?" He made excuses with joined hands, protesting that he believed me; but repeated, that five hundred rupees would not be sufficient for his people.

I changed the place of our conference. Perceiving a little shady valley, I told Neal Sing to go there with me to continue it; and I took great care to be constantly wanting something out of my trunks, in order that all my baggage might follow me, and to prove, in the eyes of the wretches who surrounded me, that there was a limit to the rebellion of their chief, and that I did not consider myself at all their prisoner. I stopped twenty times to look at some plant, to examine it with a magnifying glass, have it gathered, and put into a book, by one of my servants whose business it is. Neal Sing had to answer my questions about their names and uses. These delays and this haughtiness put the mob of mountain soldiers out of humour; but they kept silence.

I had, however, much bettered my situation. This man, who held me prisoner, who was the master of my life, allowed me to offer him my protection. He complained that he had never been able to let the king know his grievances, because Thean Sing intercepted his correspondence. He begged me to write to Mr. Allard, to request him to be the channel of it; and immediately I wrote to this kind friend, relating my adventure, and regretting that I could not acquaint him with its termination. This letter was received with every demonstration of respect. Politeness is always something in a robber. The idea of keeping me prisoner had been gradually abandoned, although I firmly repeated that I had not a thousand rupees. I collected information concerning the roads, distances, that of the next village (where I am now), the resources it offered my hungry caravan. I succeeded in getting my tents and my pantry sent forward to it. I manœuvred so as to save even the five hundred rupees which I had first offered, while the knife was at my throat; but I saw the unpopularity of the chief increase so much, that to prevent the explosion of it, which would have been the general pillage of my baggage, and perhaps a good many shots, I anticipated the tempest, and, with the greatest air, told my treasurer to count out five hundred rupees to Neal Sing.

The rest of my adventure is simply comic. The robber in chief assured me that he would not take this money, and that he would not even receive it, unless I declared it was my good pleasure to give it him. He almost made me laugh at the humility of his protestations. "He would henceforth be my servant, because *he would have tasted of my salt* (a popular figure in all the Indian languages); were it not for his excessive misery, he would have made me a very different *nuzzer* (offering) from a kid; but I well knew, by that, his submission to all my desires, and how poor he was, I who treated him so generously." My servant only had to take a few rupees from a bag, and put them into a larger one, in order to make up five hundred rupees. He gave this bag to Neal Sing, who, with an humble and suppliant air, begged me to condescend to touch the money and his hand when he received it, in order to prove to him that this present was the pure effect of my kindness, and my satisfaction for his services. I consented, but with my left hand; and when my robber felt the finger with which I had touched the bag that was given him, pressed lightly on his hand, he prostrated himself, and said that he was the most faithful, the most grateful, and the most devoted of my followers, and, if I permitted him to take that name, the most attached of his friends. He then said a few words to Mirza, to extract a few rupees from him; and my poor devil of a lieutenant, with his hands joined, and a very piteous look, excused himself on the score of his poverty; when I restored his confidence, by telling the robber imperiously that he had eaten my salt, and that Mirza had also eaten my salt. I made them shake hands to cement this theatrical friendship, and then commanded my caravan to resume their march to Berali.! Neal Sing offered me fifty of his bandits, which I prudently refused; I asked only for five, and ordered him (for in words I was the master, and had scarcely ever ceased being so) to make all the rest go back into the fortress. In taking leave of me, which may be translated restoring me my liberty, he asked me, in a low voice, for a bottle of wine, which I had the good faith to send him, after promising it. I thought, however, that it would be too ridiculous to have a bottle of my old port emptied to my health by such a scoundrel. I sent him one of Delhi arrack, which serves me instead of spirits of wine.

The five bandits he had given me appeared very uneasy at finding themselves in the minority. They escaped at the turning of a mountain, and, joining some others who had secretly left the fort, stole the lean kid which one of my attendants was driving before him, and which would most assuredly have been the dearest meat I ever tasted.

This village is exposed to Neal Sing's attacks, when famine drives him from his forest fastnesses; and it might be possible that the scent of my rupees, though they know that I have not three hundred left, attracted some of his band to-night. But my men are on their guard, and capable of giving a repulse, if they have courage enough, which I doubt, to any attack not made by Neal Sing's whole troop. I am writing to you with my pistols on the table, and others under my bolster, and my gun leaning against my bed. I have no doubt that bringing down two men at the first shot would make an impression on the minds of the rest, unless they form, as they did this morning, an overwhelming majority.

To-morrow I shall encamp near a small town; my safety will then be complete till I reach Cashmere. My caravan will be re-victualled there, and I shall despatch carriers by another road to inform the king of my adventure, and demand reparation; likewise to acquaint Mr. Allard with its amicable issue. Woe to the most devoted of my servants, the most attached of my friends, if Runjeet Sing commissions Mr. Allard to chastise his insolence! He has a good chance of being hanged on the sacred fig-tree, which witnessed his treason, and it would be the greatest service Mr. Allard could do him; for if he delivers him up to the king, Runjeet will only preserve his life, if it resists horrible mutilations; and I trust Mr. Allard will do Neal this kindness. It is true I solemnly declared that I was charmed at giving him five hundred rupees, and it is true that I was charmed at getting off for that. My satisfaction, you will easily imagine, is only relative.

I suppose this evening (ten o'clock) that Bodder Bochs, having got wind of my adventure, will not thrust himself into the wasp's nest. But there is no other road forward, and the want of provisions will make it impossible for him to return to Mirpore. Neal Sing will make him pay dearly for his welcome, if he catches him, for Bodder is the confidant of Thean Sing, the author of Neal's misfortunes. He appears, besides, a very bad character, and not worth regretting as a mehmandar.

I hope, my dear father, that I shall not have to increase this letter, already long enough, by other stories of the same kind; however, if you are henceforth obliged to acknowledge that there are really adventures, you will see to how little, after all, things can be reduced. This has cost me fifty louis, but the rajah has given me five hundred. I therefore play upon velvet.

I have nothing to find fault with myself in this matter: no human prudence could have avoided it. Violence would have cost the lives of some of the brigands, without giving one of my people the least chance of escaping massacre. I could only play the diplomatist, and I esteem myself very fortunate in getting out of it, saving, at the same time, a bill at sight on Cashmere for two hundred louis and the king's khelat,—and observing forms so completely, that I believe that the Marquis de ——, the Duke of ——, the Prince ——, my old schoolfellows, but now very clever, high and mighty lords, and of the stuff they make ambassadors of, (which appears comical enough,) could not have done better. But some day, when I am near you, and have returned to the monotonous circle of sedentary European life, I shall have more pleasure in recalling these diplomatic recollections of my youth, than their aforesaid lordships in recalling their embassies. I envy them nothing. The strolling life, whose vicissitudes I have had to relate to you to-day, has also, and in the present instance, its pleasures, which are unknown in Paris. I let my imagination give way to the charm, whilst my mind is continually employed with real objects of study. Add to this, some philosophy for which I do not think myself much obliged to our friend Seneca, good health, and a pair of excellent legs;—and believe me that I am in a more enviable condition than they. Adieu!

April 23rd. Camp at Koteli.

Well, I am rid of Neal Sing, and have nothing more to fear from his nocturnal attacks! Why was it not written above that I should arrive a day later on his territory? He would have robbed me this morning; but now I should have made him refund, and have given him a hundred lashes, as a token of my gratitude for his good and loyal services. This morning, at a short distance from Berali, I met on the road the army on its return from Cashmere, and as it was impossible for two horses, and often even for two men on foot, to go abreast on these paths, along precipices, I sat myself down in the shade by the side of the road, and reviewed two or three thousand men, who defiled before me. Their commander, Sheik Nur-Mohammed, alighted from his horse, and advanced respectfully towards me, offering me some rupees as a nuzzer. I made him sit down by my side on the grass, without ceremony, and remained more than an hour in conversation with him. I related to him my discomfiture of yesterday; and before I got up, I wrote all the essential particulars to M. Allard, in order that he might as soon as possible lay them before the king. Sheik Nur-Mohammed promised to deliver this letter himself to M. Allard, whose camp he will reach in six days. On his march he will ascertain whether Neal Sing has laid hands on my mehmandar, in which case he will besiege him in his fortress. He offered me at all events to do so, to punish the bandit as quickly as possible; but I dissuaded him from it, because I wish the king to have the precedence in the satisfaction I expect. In order to have the pleasure of sharing in it, I should no doubt have accepted Nur-Mohammed's polite offer, had I met his army yesterday.

This army is returning to Lahore very discontented. The last Soubah of Cashmere, who had raised it, treated it generously, and the troops know that they shall be badly paid by the king. They are, moreover, irritated against him on account of the revolting injustice which he committed against their former chief. Were it not for a few companies formerly disciplined, who marched along intermingled with the irregular Seikhs, my baggage would probably have been plundered; but no sooner had I met the Sheik than this terrible rabble was silent, and presented arms as they passed me.

On the road side, I saw the body of a man hanging to a tree, apparently executed that morning. I asked who he was, and why he had been hanged, but all the passengers seemed so indifferent to the spectacle that no one knew more about it than myself. A poor man's life is considered of but trifling importance in the East!

One must have travelled in the Punjab to know what an immense benefit to humanity the English dominion in India is, and what miseries it spares eighty millions of souls! In the Punjab there is an enormous portion of the population who subsist only by their guns. It is perhaps the most wretched of all; however, in all justice, they would only have a right to be hanged. I cannot witness the frightful evils of such a system without ardently desiring to see the English extend their frontiers from the Sutledge to the Indus, and the Russians occupy the other bank of the river. It is generally believed that it would be the period of a dreadful shock between those two great powers, which would decide the fate of Asia to the west of the Irady; but I think, on the contrary, that then alone would peace reign throughout those vast regions. European civilisation *deserves* to invade the universe. For want of the civilisation of the west, its dominion alone is still an immense benefit for the people of the other parts of the globe, and it is probably the only one which the religious institutions of Asia will permit us to confer on the East.

May 1st. Camp at Kohoutah, valley of the Betar.

I have made but little way for the last week; but man and beast had great need of rest at Koteli, where there was nothing that would have refreshed them readily. On the 27th, I arrived at Prounch, in a pitiable state, spitting blood. I cut the disorder short by a bold manœuvre. I made some of my men catch leeches in the neighbouring rivers, and applied sixty-five to my chest and epigastrium; and to repair this great loss of blood, I had two sheep a day killed, of which I ate as much as I could; and now I am perfectly recovered. It was no doubt a cold, in consequence of my forced march, which had struck on my chest. There is no helping it: there are marches in which one has to cross four torrents of icy water, higher than the girdle, and you may think yourself lucky if you escape drowuing.

The threatening horizon with which I was surrounded on all sides at Koteli, has very much cleared up. The day after to-morrow I shall cross the chain which separates the basin of Cashmere from this sea of mountains!

There is indeed, at a short distance, a fortress belonging to the king, at Oeiri; but it is too near the great centre of authority, Cashmere, for the killadar (governor) to allow himself the liberties which Neal Sing took with me. Besides, I am pennyless.

I wrote to the king from Koteli, relating my adventure, and demanding satisfaction. In a fortnight I shall have his answer.

I also wrote to Wade, whom Lord William Bentinck is sending on a mission to Lahore, to return the rajah the compliments of which he had sent him a whole cargo to Leula. It is important to my safety in my future excursions that the brigand should receive an exemplary chastisement.

Cashmere, May 13th, 1831.

Here I am at last, and have been several days. The pass of Prounch, though still encumbered with snow, was but play to me. Last year, in Tibet, I several times ascended to nearly double the height.

I found, to be sure, people on the road who cared very little for the king's orders; but their insubordination caused no considerable obstacle. I arrived here on the 8th. The governor, being informed of my approach, sent his boat and officers to receive me, two leagues from the city, and conduct me to the garden prepared for my residence. It is planted with lilacs and rose-trees, not yet in flower, and immense planes. On one of the angles stands a little pavilion, looking over the lake: I am settled in it. My attendants are at hand, in my tents, pitched under the large trees. They are building barracks in haste for my cavalry and horses.

If the governor of Cashmere had been a great lord, I should not have hesitated to pay him the first visit.

But he is a man of low extraction, who only holds the office temporarily; and I refused to pay him this deference. For a *parvenu* he was very tractable. It was agreed, at once, that our interview should take place the next day, at Shalibag, the Trianon of the ancient Mogul emperors. It is a little palace, now abandoned, but still charming by its situation and magnificent groves. It is two leagues from my house, on the other side of the lake. The governor sent his barge, with a numerous guard, which made quite a flotilla, and I went to Shalibag on board my flag ship. The governor had ordered a fête to receive me. The fountains were playing in the gardens, which were crowded; the Seikh troops, in their magnificent and picturesque costume, occupied every avenue. Dancing and music only waited for my presence to commence. The governor rubbed his long beard on my left shoulder, whilst I rubbed mine on his right. We sat close to each other on chairs; the vice-regal court sat round us, on the carpet; and, after exchanging the common-place compliments, the fête commenced.

This insipid interlude of songs and dancing, which the Orientals can witness with pleasure from morning till night. is called *nautch*. It is graceful nowhere but at Delhi. The Cashmerian beauties had nothing in their eyes to compensate for the monotony of their dancing and singing. They were browner, that is to say blacker, than the chorusses and corps de ballet of Lahore, Umbritsir, Loodheeana, and Delhi. I remained as long as I was pleased with looking at the fantastic architecture of the palace, the variety and splendour of the groups of warlike figures crowding around, the colossal size of the trees, the greensward, the water-falls, and in the distance the bluish mountains, and their white summits. After half an hour's stay, I took leave of the viceroy, and returned home in the same order in which I had set out.

My pavilion has but very flimsy walls: it was closed only by Venetian blinds, elegantly carved, with infinite art. It was open to every wind, and to the inquiring looks of the Cashmerian idlers, who came by thousands, in their little boats, to look at me, as they would at a wild beast through the bars of his cage. I have had it hung inside with curtains, which shelter me tolerably from the wind, and completely inclose me from public curiosity. The governor has sent me a numerous guard of a half regular corps, under his more especial command. There are sentinels all round the garden, and the indiscreet persons who approach it come in for their share of blows. I was obliged to give orders to this effect: I should not be respected without it. This pretty spot will serve as my residence, or rather head-quarters, for the next five months to come. Its situation is very central, in the middle of this country. I shall leave the heaviest part of my baggage there, and make a series of excursions round it, by boat, on horseback, or on foot, according to the nature of the places I have to visit. The king's munificence allows me to go into the expenses necessary for forming large zoological collections. I think in five months I shall double the baggage I have already.

I was not without some fears, on coming here. For several years past, an Afghan fanatic, Sayed Ahmed, has been threatening Cashmere ; but the day before yesterday the fort fired a royal salute, and the governor sent me word that Sheer Sing, one of the king's sons, had just given him battle, near Mozufferabad, in which he and his whole army had perished. Public report adds that Sheer Sing is coming here as viceroy. Although I have good reason to boast of the attentions of the present governor, I wish for the prince's arrival : he is a great friend of Mr. Allard's, and cannot fail to treat me well. His authority will be much more powerful in this country than that of the present chief, and will protect me much more effectually in my excursions. However, every one knows at present that I will not be trifled with. A royal firman arrived the day before yesterday, announcing that, the king being informed of my adventure, Toloochee has driven Neal Sing away, ruined him, and ordered his nose and ears to be cut off if he shows himself at Lahore. The same firman enjoins the governor immediately to send me five hundred rupees, which is evidently intended on the king's part as a restitution of the sum which Neal Sing extorted from me. The manner in which the king speaks of me in this firman expresses great esteem and real kindness, and has produced a wonderful effect here. In a few days I shall write to Runjeet to thank him.

As I dreaded the cruelty with which Neal Sing is threatened by the king's vengeance, I took the liberty, in the letter in which I informed him of my adventure, to point out the punishment which I desired to be inflicted on the culprit. I related to the king how he had mystified me so far as to oblige me to declare that it was my good pleasure to give him five hundred rupees; and I requested that he would make him disgorge them for the benefit of the poor; and that he should have, moreover, five hundred lashes; obliging him, moreover, to declare that it was his good pleasure to be flogged. If Runjeet was in good humour the day he received my letter, he no doubt laughed at the pleasantry; and Neal Sing will receive the punishment in question, of his own free will, and for his own pleasure.

I mentioned to you a man hanged at Koteli. There were a dozen suspended on trees near my camp, on the banks of the river. When the governor visited me, he told me, with a very careless air, that in the first year of his government he had hanged two hundred, but that now, one here and there was sufficient to keep the country in order. Now mark that *the country* is a miserable and almost desert province. For my part, if I had to govern it, I should begin by putting in irons the governor and his three hundred soldiers, who are robbers *par excellence*, and I would make them work in the formation of a good road. They now live lazily on the labour of the poor peasants: they would continue to subsist on the same rice, but then they would earn it.

The cleverness and roguery of the Cashmerians are proverbial in the East. Crowds of pretended people of quality come and offer their services as *ciceroni;* they know every thing, they have been everywhere; and when I question them closely, I discover that their knowledge is only a witty imposture. Some, however, have been recommended by Mr. Allard, and I frequently receive them. I have an hour's lesson in Persian every morning from one who is of Mogul extraction. As for the pundits, who are all of the Brahmin caste, their ignorance is extreme; there is not one of my Hindoo servants who does not think himself of a superior caste to them. They eat every thing but beef, and drink arrack. In India, none but the most infamous castes do so.

It is not possible for me to return by Ladak, as was my intention; that journey would be too dangerous. My scientific baggage will, on my leaving Cashmere, be too precious for me to risk it in the desert. From Prounch to this place I have had an escort of fifty men; but this is not enough; in case of an untoward encounter, I should require five hundred—an army. I shall no doubt return to Semla, by way of Kishtewar, Chumba, and the Koolloo country, or else by Rajoor, Jummoo, and Belaspore. I shall manage so that every petty prince through whose territory I may have to pass shall receive a firman from Runjeet Sing, to inform him beforehand of my arrival. But half of this road traverses the states of the Rajah Gulab Sing, whose regal residence is Jummoo; and there I shall have nothing to fear. Nevertheless, whatever weather it may be, it will be a fine day when I recross the Sutledge.

My health is now perfectly good; it cannot be otherwise in so salubrious a climate. In a month, I shall eat cherries out of my own garden, then apricots, peaches, and almonds, then apples, pears, and lastly, grapes. I walk every evening under a superb vine arbour, the vines of which, though still young, are two feet in circumference: I never saw any thing like it. I am also promised delicious melons, and even water-melons. This latter promise is the threat of a very warm summer; but it resembles ours in the south of France. The productions are the same. We have now the same weather as at Paris, but finer, and less inconstant.

I saw at Sharunpore a hundred Cashmerian plants, brought into India by native merchants. Half of them grow in the Himalaya, also to the east of the Sutledge; and, having determined the mean altitude at which each grows, I made a conjecture, of remarkable accuracy, on the absolute elevation of Cashmere. I supposed it to be five or six thousand English feet. Now, some barometrical observations, made since my arrival, which I have yet been able to calculate only approximately, by the comparison of the meridian means for the month of May, at Calcutta, Bombay, and Sharunpore, give me an elevation of five thousand three hundred and fifty feet.

I have discovered that my cook had been a long time in the service of an English physician, a great epicure, and I have given him *carte-blanche* for the exercise of his talents. As the raw material is not scarce here, I almost feast since this discovery. These good dinners that I boast of are, however, without bread or wine. The aqueous regimen, to which necessity dooms me, often makes me long, like a pregnant woman, for a bottle of light wine. I have much better servants than I had last year; particularly the head one, who acts as my treasurer. I could not touch a piece of money in this country without forfeiting all respect; and it was very fortunate for me to find among my attendants a trustworthy servant, to keep, open, and shut my purse, keeping an account of every thing received and disbursed. I have also a greater number than during my first campaign in the Himalaya—double—it is a heavy expense; but it is unavoidable. After all, the number does not exceed fourteen; and Mr. Allard has a hundred and fifty,—and they are not enough for him.

I yesterday heard from Mr. Allard, who sent me letters from India, Loodheeana, and Delhi, all of very ancient dates, his courier having been lost a week in the snow. They inform me from Delhi of the fall of the Wellington cabinet; and they have sent me a Bombay Gazette, from which I learn the insurrection of

Warsaw. But not a word about the affairs of France. In my ignorance of the way in which they are going on, I rejoice at the elevation of Mr. Brougham and Earl Grey to the ministry. It seems to me a pledge of friendship between France and England, whose good understanding appears the necessary condition of the peace of Europe. It remains to be seen whether the Duke of Wellington will not be able to secure a majority in the House of Lords against the Whig ministry, which may oblige it to quit the field, or at least to contend for liberty without effect or advantage.

I shall write to the *Jardin* shortly, and a letter which will be agreeable to M. Cuvier, for it will promise him all the fishes of the waters of Cashmere. This will make a hundred jumps ere it reaches you; I know not whether it will still find M. Cordier's kindness at Chandernagore to forward it. For these three months I have known nothing of what is going on in *French India*, as we have the comical impertinence to call it. I cannot conclude without adding a melancholy reflection—it is, that your last letters were dated the 22nd July, 1830:—ten months without news! It is a very long time! Adieu! my dear father, adieu! I would place the same confidence in you that you justly do in me:—but I am thirty; and you—are more than double. Is it not thirteen days since Porphyre has reached forty?—And Frederic speaks of his grey hairs! Well, be it so! Let us all grow old together, and try who can do it the fastest.

I have not the *maladie du pays*:—No: but when my thoughts turn towards it and you, it is not without strong emotion. The solitude of my situation would be nothing but common-place to a man made like the multitude, who love without passion. But you, my dear father, and those who know me as you do, can alone imagine all the sadness in my soul sometimes, when it is uneasy about the objects of its affection.

I shall not write to Porphyre to-day: this letter is for him, as well as for you; but I find in my portfolio a few pages addressed to Frederic, from I do not know where. Send them to him. Adieu once more.

TO M. PORPHYRE JACQUEMONT, PARIS.

Cashmere, May 14th, 1831.

If I did not think, my dear Porphyre, that a despatch weighing a kilogramme * would be heavy enough for the Honourable Company, I would have added a few sheets to the monstrous packet of manuscript which I despatched yesterday, under cover to Sir Edward Ryan, at Calcutta, to be forwarded to Chandernagore, and thence to our father; but the post-office people would have cried out about the abuse of the privilege. I therefore divide my works into two

* About two pounds and a quarter English.—Tr.

volumes; this one for you will, I hope, join the other one at Chandernagore, and proceed with it. I have detailed at great length to our father all the accidents of my perambulations. After all, there is no danger: quite the reverse. This country is a land of beggars, scoundrels, and bandits; but I am prudent. Nothing is so common as for them to kill a man in order to rob him of an old pair of breeches, worth twenty or four-and-twenty sous, half a rupee. The whole population are armed with swords, in the use of which they are said to be very dexterous; and the figures met on the roads, all carry a long matchlock on their shoulder—not very formidable, in my opinion.

It is possible I may see Mr. Allard again in the mountains. The mother of a brood of little mountain rajahs has just died, leaving nine lacs of rupees (two million two hundred and fifty thousand francs). Her children are fighting about the inheritance; and Runjeet has just sent Mr. Allard to the spot to remove all cause of quarrel—that is, the nine lacs.

The day I arrived here, the 8th, the governor sent me as a nuzzer, ten sheep, forty fowls, two hundred eggs, several sacks of barley, rice, flour, sugar, some native brandy distilled from the wine which they make, and which resembles a mixture of bad *anisette* and bad *kirschen-wasser*, &c. All this I distributed to my suite; but the king has just sent a new order, that my table is to be constantly provided at his expense, a favour which I only act upon for form's sake, but which is essential for form's sake. I should almost fare well had I but bread and wine; but my old Semla port, so much admired by the English, is stronger than brandy, and I keep it for cold and rainy days, in the mountains. I am very well; the colour of my hands disagrees with that of my arms, but I look well. At Delhi, I allowed myself the luxury of a looking-glass, and I look at myself every month. Nevertheless I am frightfully thin.

Know that I have never seen any where such hideous witches as in Cashmere. The female race is remarkably ugly. I speak of women of the common ranks,—those one sees in the streets and fields,—since those of a more elevated station pass all their lives shut up, and are never seen. It is true that all little girls who promise to turn out pretty, are sold at eight years of age, and carried off into the Punjab and India. Their parents sell them at from twenty to three hundred francs—most commonly fifty or sixty. All female servants in the Punjab are slaves; and, in spite of the exertions of the English to abolish the custom, it nevertheless prevails also in the north of India. They are treated tolerably well, and their condition is hardly worse than that of their mistresses in the harem. The wives of the old king of Cabul, whom I saw at Loodheana, Shah Shoudjah el Molauk, are driven with great kicks by their guardian eunuchs: their servants are certainly less ill-used.

Every day, innumerable bands of girls present themselves at my garden gate. An Asiatic nobleman in my place would always have forty of them singing and dancing around him; but I preserve my European character entire in my manners as in my costume: it inspires respect.

The Cashmerian politicians whisper that I am come here to reconnoitre the state of the country, and its resources,—and to treat with Runjeet Sing concerning its cession to the English government. Others assert that I am come with the design of farming it from Runjeet, as viceroy, for so much a year which I shall engage to give the Maharajah. You may guess that I weigh all my words in order to furnish no cause for all these silly reports: I stick to my *ilom*—my science. With the Mussulmauns, who visit me, I talk about the Koran, which I call the holy Koran, and about Mohammed (his name be praised!) and their religious matters; with the soi-disant Pundits, or Hindoo doctors, who at first came by hundreds, I made them ashamed of their ignorance of the *shastras*, and their relaxed discipline. Here, every man who is a little less ignorant, and openly less of a rogue than the rest, is looked upon as a saint, and the respectable public of Cashmere take me for a very saintly Christian. When I am reading, it is always a prayer-book; this is good policy.

The season for the arrival of the Bordeaux ships at Calcutta is approaching. If they bring me any letters, I can receive them here in a month. I shall work with new ardour when I have received them. It is also very long since I have seen an English newspaper: it makes me feel the more keenly the privation of a comparatively sedentary situation. Adieu, for to-day.

Cashmere, May 20th.

ONLY a few words, to tell you that Runjeet Sing is an admirable man—which I hope you think already, and have long thought. An officer of his household has just arrived this morning, in a fortnight, from Umbritsir, where the king is at present encamped. He brings me a very gracious royal firman. Runjeet writes to me that he has received my letter from Koteli—that is to say, my complaint against Neal Sing—and that the Rajah Gulab Sing, who had been much earlier informed of the affair, had not hesitated to have that chief arrested;—that having him thus at his disposal, on the day my complaint arrived, he immediately pronounced judgment (and in a manner to prove his tact): he ordered none of the cruelties or barbarous mutilations which are customary, but had the culprit put in chains and imprisoned in a fortress, where he will remain until I solicit his pardon. This, my friend, is what none but Runjeet would have done. He knows that his penal code is repugnant to us, and he punishes this man as he would have been punished in a European country. The five hundred rupees which were sent to me by the governor, on the day of my arrival here, without prejudice to the two thousand which Runjeet had long ago decreed me, were an additional act of kindness of the rajah; and not, as I thought, the restitution of the money of which I had been plundered by Neal Sing. Runjeet, in his letter of to-day, informs me that he has ordered his vizier to make that restitution in his name. Every thing, therefore, is for the best, in the best of all possible worlds. The king, besides, enjoins me to make myself at home in Cashmere. "That country is yours," he writes: "establish yourself in whichever of my gardens pleases you best; order, and you shall be obeyed." I leave you, in order to take a boating excursion on the lake and the river. I have the state boat of the late magnificent governor, and thirty rowers, in my monthly pay. Guess the monthly pay of a rower—two francs forty-six centimes; so I shall have to give thirty rupees a month to these thirty men; but as my situation compels me to be grand, I give them forty, and presents likewise whenever I get out of the boat. What charms me is, that I am drilling two men who promise a good deal for my zoological preparations: the one is a hunter by profession, the other is an embroiderer, with slim fingers. I will make them a bridge of gold, to decide them to follow me into India, where I have yet found no one, even of the lowest class, who would do this business, even for gold. Good-by, my friend: I regret much that you cannot be of the party; but gun, nets, and books of plants will; nor shall I return empty-handed. The worst is, that I must show a little state and pomp.

My little court follows me in these excursions, seated in two rows, like onions, on each side of my arm-chair. At first they started when I fired over their heads. Now they can stand fire; but they continue to be astonished when I pull off my coat, and turn up my shirt sleeves to my shoulders, to lay hold of the plants floating in the water. Adieu!

Cashmere, May 29th.

At last, this will go this evening, with several others, one of which is for the *Jardin des Plantes*. I have received courier after courier from M. Allard, which is very friendly on his part, considering the great distance which separates us,—about a hundred and fifty leagues. They only brought me Indian letters, and ditto newspapers. M. Cordier writes to me that he is expecting a vessel from France immediately. May it bring me letters from Paris. Adieu, my dear friend: I embrace you with all my heart.

TO MLLE. ZOÉ NOIZET DE SAINT PAUL, ARRAS.

Cashmere, May 16th, 1831.

My dear Zoé,—Living, as I have done for the last three months, among Orientals, who, each after their own fashion, treat me with some horrible jargon or other, it seems as if I had lost some part of the treasure of my English eloquence; and that is the reason why I write to you to-day in French. I dread the severity of your criticism; but I do not well know what I should gain from it by writing to you in our own language; for I seem also, from want of practice, to have grown awkward in its use.

A few days ago, I sent my father a sort of volume, journal, or bulletin (call it what you like), which he will forward to you; in which case, you will know, before you receive this note, a small part of the vexations against which I have had to struggle, with prudence if not courage, since my entrance into the mountains dividing Cashmere from the Punjab. I was purified from all my past sins, for three weeks in that purgatory, before I was admitted into the terrestrial paradise. But God and his prophet Mohammed be praised! (as I often have the politeness to say to the Mussulmauns who surround me) the days of trial are past. I now enjoy the fruits of my perseverance, a virtue which carries one a great way; since, in spite of the repugnance of the English Government to favour this pretty episode of my journey, and the originally still greater repugnance of Runjeet Sing to allow it—in spite of the more or less decided rebellion of the mountain chiefs against the Rajah's commands respecting me, here have I been, for the last week, settled in a handsome bungalow, on the banks of this agreeable lake (which Moore, however, has by far too much embellished, according to the lying custom of the gentlemen of Parnassus), in the midst of a garden planted with trees of our own country, where I gather roses in my morning's walk. At the gates of a very large city, I seem to be encamped in a solitary plain; and it is not the only advantage of the situation of my garden that it is raised ten feet above the surrounding plain, a circumstance of importance in the terrestrial paradise, where robbers are not wanting. Besides, a strict guard is kept up around me. The governor sent me, on the day of my arrival, a company of Seikh infantry, which is on duty near my excellency. Two of the horsemen of my escort superintend all the details; and a gentleman of my chamber, at six rupees a month, stands all day at my door, and shows six rupees' worth of discernment in his selection of the applicants of all kinds whom he admits. The rogue has been strutting about, since yesterday, in a dress which is worth more than all the money he has legitimately received (I say legitimately, in the supposition that the French Academy, always animated with an inviolable devotion to his Majesty's person, has not yet erased the word from their dictionary) since he has been in my service. It is the custom in the East, that no one can approach a man of higher rank than himself, without paying both master and men. The English in India discourage this practice as much as possible; but in Cashmere, where the European conventions which we term honour and probity, have not yet penetrated, if I were to punish my chamberlain for receiving a revenue from his key (this is figurative, for I have not so much as a door to my house), Cashmerian public opinion would stigmatise me as an unjust and capricious lord. The rogue will thus keep his fine dress and silk turban, but with a strict injunction to stop there, on pain of punishment, as his worship the mayor would say.

Extraordinary culinary talents have suddenly manifested themselves in my *maitre-d'hotel;* but unless I have been fifteen or twenty leagues on foot or on horseback, I have no appetite in the evening for a good dinner, if I have not Locke, or Sterne, or some other illustrious dead, to bear me company at table.

Lalla Rookh, whose Persian name you will never be able to pronounce unless you choke yourself on purpose with a fish-bone, in order to utter the Persian *kh* properly, forms a part of my library; but I am tired of it. A page of this style would perhaps please; but thirty (and all his tales are longer) make one sick. So the finest music pleases for two hours and a half, but fatigues and annoys, if prolonged beyond; so one of Lamartine's harmonious reveries may charm in an hour of idleness, but it is impossible to read in succession ten or twelve of his best poems; and so Chateaubriand amuses by his picturesque style, as far as the second column of a newspaper: but he is tiresome even in a pamphlet, and intolerable in a romance. However, without knowing much of the matter, you intended, when you learnt English, to read Lalla Rookh. Know, then, that it was in the very gardens and palace in which she was received by the king of Bucharia, that my first interview with the governor of Cashmere took place, who after this first meeting on neutral ground, came yesterday to pay me a visit at my own house. He has all the look of a fool; but he possesses the very rare virtue in this country, of obedience to his sovereign, and executes punctually all the kind orders of the king in my favour. I have every reason to be satisfied with him.

It was very lucky for me that I met a scoundrel bold enough to stop me and extort money from me. The prompt example which Runjeet has made of this bandit, who was no less than governor of a royal fortress, has produced the most useful moral effect for my safety in this country. Every one now perceives the danger of an unbridled passion for my rupees. There were three hundred in my box when I left Loodheeana; and now I have five thousand. I boast of this as I should of playing a game at chess well and winning it, on account of the difficulty overcome. There was a great, an immense one, I assure you, in my not being nailed, as it were, to the shores of India, where the vessel in which I came landed me. I sometimes reflect with real pleasure, on the wisdom and prudence of my commencement. I began modestly with having only one servant; then two; then a palanquin; then six other valets, and a horse. I set out from Calcutta with a single bad tent; no chair nor table;—and by degrees I have increased my household up to forty servants, (without mentioning my thirty rowers,) three tents, two horses, and all the rest in proportion. And yet there is as much prudence in my actual establishment, and the same proportion between what I have and what I ought to have, as there was in my wretched outfit between Calcutta and Benares. When I return to India, whether I enter it by Loodheeana or descend the mountains from Semla, what a difference between the reception which awaits me there and the profound solitude of my situation at the commencement of my journey! There is now on the other side of the Sutledge an enormous mass of kindness, which even in my absence exhibits itself in a thousand ingenious ways. This flatters me much, I will confess; for, being neither a duke nor a *millionnaire*, and falling as it were from the clouds among the people who at present show this extreme consideration and truly friendly kindness towards me, I owe it all to myself—I am the real architect of my fortunes; I do not allude to the five thousand rupees in my strong box, but to the honourable reputation I enjoy with every one.

But, you will say, where is the local character in all this?—and is there none in Cashmere? To which I reply, that the shades are little varied in the East. I know no country on earth where so many witches could be enlisted for Macbeth, if, instead of three, Shakspeare had collected a hundred thousand, on the heath of—I know not the name. However, the men are a remarkably handsome race, and the ugliness of the women is explained by continual exportation of every pretty Cashmerian face to the Punjab and India, to stock the harems of the Mussulmauns, Seikhs, and Hindoos. The king of the Sanscritists, Mr. Wilson of Calcutta, has been at the trouble of translating some old chronicles of the Cashmerian monarchy, before the invasion of the Moguls, in the reign of Akbar. They reckon seven or eight hundred kings, which is little for the country, where, in every thing relating to times past, ciphers cost the liberal humour of their historians nothing. Whatever these old histories may say, there can be no doubt that the population of Cashmere, originally Buddhist, like that of the Punjab, and afterwards Brahmin, like it,—that is to say Hindoo,—have had, for a long period, chiefs of their own religious faith, and under their sway enjoyed absolute political independence—the defence of which nature had rendered very easy, by means of the enormous mountains with which she has on every side surrounded the country. Of this long period, only some vague recollections survive among those who are now called the literati, and here and there a few ruins. In their massive structure, and the style of their ornaments, they possess a Hindoo character. There are still some traces of ancient works of public utility, which date from the same epoch. Mohammedanism has done nothing but destroy. The emperors of Delhi have built nothing but kiosks and cascades. The Mogul government was the masterpiece of absolute monarchy: all the revenues of the state went to the civil list, which never either erected bridges or dug canals, but raised palaces, tombs, and mosques for itself. The Afghans, last century, having deprived the Moguls of that conquest, and the Seikhs having driven the Afghans from it, a general plunder followed each new conquest; and the intervals of peace, anarchy, and oppression, doing their best against labour and industry, the country is now so completely ruined that the poor Cashmerians seem to be in despair, and are become the most indolent of men. If one must starve, it is better to do it at one's ease, than bent under the weight of labour. In Cashmere, there is scarcely more chance of getting a supper for him who tills, spins, or rows all day, than for him who, being rendered desperate, sleeps all day under the shade of a plane-tree. A few thousand stupid and brutal Seikhs, with swords at their sides, or pistols in their belts, drive this ingenious and numerous, but timid people, like a flock of sheep.

The southern slope of the Himalaya always preserves something of an Indian character at every altitude. The section of the seasons, to the limit of perpetual snow, is the same as in the plains of India; the summer solstice brings rain every year, which falls uninterruptedly till the autumnal equinox. Hence there is a peculiar character in the vegetation, which is different from that of the Alps and Pyrenees, not being exposed to the same influence. But Cashmere being on the northern side of a lofty snowy chain, is separated by this high barrier from the climate of India, and has one of its own, very similar to that of Lombardy. The wild and cultivated vegetable productions, taking into account the law according to which the temperature decreases from the equator to the pole, speak so precise a language to one who can interpret it, concerning the height of places, that, in the complete ignorance which existed before my journey of the level of this celebrated valley, I had fixed it at between five and six thousand English feet, from a small number of plants which I had seen brought by merchants. Now, my own observations make it about five thousand one hundred and fifty feet. It was with the most lively satisfaction, that I saw the final logarithm of my calculation transform itself into this number. The Italian poplar, and the plane-tree, are predominant in the cultivated tracts. The plane-tree is colossal, the vine in the gardens gigantic; the forests are composed of cedars, and different varieties of firs and pines, absolutely similar, in general, to those of Europe, and, in a more elevated zone, of birches, which seem to me not different from ours. The lotus appears on the surface of still water; the flowering rush and water trefoil, with which you are no doubt acquainted, and the elegance of which you must have admired in the humble ditches of Arras and the environs, rise above it, associated with the same kind of rushes and osiers. All this is strangely European; but if I took it into my head to write an epistle to Liberty, I should not begin like Voltaire:—

" Mon lac est le premier," &c.

Voltaire had no taste for objects of nature or the fine

arts. For any one who has a grain of it, his Lake Leman was one of the last to cite in *The Alps.* That of Cashmere would make but a poor figure by the side of the Lago Maggiore in Lombardy, or those of Thun and Brientz in Bernese Oberland. There is one in the north of the United States, which, without the sublimity of the latter, possesses all their grace, and quite a peculiar character of loveliness,—I mean Lake George, on which I spent a delightful day, on my return from Canada to Albany. If I could tell what I feel,—if I could copy on paper the perfect images which I see in my mind,—what charming pictures I should make of those places whither chance has by turns directed me. I have felt their charm so vividly—so profoundly! sometimes they awakened emotions of pleasure so tumultuous that I could preserve but a recollection as confused as themselves;—for instance, such as I felt when I galloped for the first time through a tropical forest in Haiti. But there is so perfect a calm in the cold landscape of North America, that the impressions it excites, when it possesses any attraction or beauty, are peaceful and serious. I regret having suffered the time to pass when I could perhaps have reproduced with fidelity the images of the different forms of happiness of which I dreamt in the valleys of New Jersey, on the banks of Lake George, and in the desert forests of Tonnawanta. I am no longer under the spell of the illusions which gave life to those day dreams; the vivid lustre of those flowers is faded, and their fragrance evaporated. After all, the world, as it really is, is a miserable affair. There is a feeling which makes one see it other than it is, however cruel in their consequences may be the optical errors which it causes us to make: I nevertheless often doubt whether we are not always indebted to it for more pleasure than pain.

Enough, however.—You will say that Sterne's sentimental traveller does not make more turnings in his journeys than I do, and you will be right. But it is thus I love to write,—leaving to my pen the apparent free will of its turnings and windings on my paper. I shall stay several months, not *at* but *in* Cashmere, and will write to you again before I leave that country. I may even now tell you that I shall not return to India by Tibet; a part of that journey would expose me to so many dangers, that a very strong escort would not be sufficient to ensure my safety. I should require a little army. Adieu, my dear Zoé; my table is covered with minerals, which I must look over, and give an account of. I leave you, to resume a paper on geology, which is nearly completed. Adieu. Think of me, and write to me.

TO M. JACQUEMONT, THE ELDER, PARIS.

Cashmere, May 26th, 1831.

TO-DAY, my dear father, you will have only my smallest size. Porphyre, as a compensation, will receive some yards of bad Cashmere paper, blotted with my worst writing of a month past, together with a little addition of a more recent date. I received yesterday a courier from M. Allard, who brought me several letters from India, and one from his master. I shall not let him return without loading him well. M. Cordier writes me from Chandernagore, under date of the 22nd April, that he has just put on board the Jean-Henri, bound to Havre, all that I had addressed to him for you from Lahore, up to the 11th March, the day on which the king granted me my audience to take leave. I am happy to think that the good intelligence which I sent you on that day is perhaps by this time near the Cape of Good Hope. Kennedy writes to me from Semla that M. de Polignac and his colleagues have been condemned to imprisonment for life. Another from Kotta, in Rajpootana, of which he is *de facto* king, under the modest title of political agent, writes me in haste to announce that Lord Grey has taken the Duke of Wellington's place, as if my Delhi friends had not informed me of it a week ago. But Wade, the political agent of Loodheeana, and the principal channel of my correspondence with India and Europe, being at Semla for the purpose of introducing Runjeet Sing's embassy to the governor-general, I get no papers—that is the devil! Moreover, he is no doubt to-day at Adenanaghur, between the Ravey and the Beyah, in the Punjab, complimenting Runjeet Sing, in his turn, in the name of the governor-general; and I think he has brought me some papers from Semla, which I may receive in a fortnight, through M. Allard. At any other time I would wait very patiently; but it seems to me that in the actual circumstances of Europe, every day may bring such great events that the prolonged ignorance of them is truly painful.

Kennedy also sends me word that in the autumn, Mr. Thoby Prinsep, one of my Calcutta acquaintances, (the secretary of state,) will be sent on a political mission to Runjeet. I am puzzling my brains to no purpose in guessing the object of it, which must be very important, to be confided to the minister himself.

I am in no small degree curious to know the questions which Lord William will put to me about this country, when he sees me again at Semla. My prudence here is extreme. I measure my words; for every thing that I say or do goes to the king, and, beyond him, through his *ukkbars*, to all the political officers in India. I ought also to tell you that I have received the letter which I expected from Runjeet, touching my affair at Tolootchee: it is very gracious, and has turned my adventure into quite a piece of good luck. M. Allard, at a distance, continues to act in the most admirable manner towards me. How friendly it was in this good man to have hunted me out and sent me his first communication on the frontiers of China, ten months ago! Nothing is so uncertain as his future prospects: perhaps he may never return to France; perhaps he may do so before me,—in which case, receive him cordially, and without ceremony; let him drink your oldest wine; and Porphyre must pilot him about! How happy I have been since my departure! What excellent people I have met at Rio Janeiro, Bourbon—and India, every where in short. A misanthrope travelling with me would be cured of his malady. I am writing to the *Jardin*, to promise M. Cuvier the fishes of the lakes of Cashmere, and a very respectable number of the animals of this country. It is to Runjeet Sing that they will be under obligation, for if I had only had their wings to enable me to fly, I should not have taken so high a flight. I have huntsmen whom I send out on all sides, and among them I have one clever enough to learn very quickly how to prepare zoological specimens. I pay this man eight times more than he earns, and I hope, by increasing his salary still farther, to prevail upon him, in the hope of making a little fortune in a year, to follow me to India. When I want fish, I shall have only to choose among my most intelligent boatmen, and being sent on extraordinary service, they will lose nothing. The governor has given up to me the boat belonging to the late viceroy. Thirty men are requisite to work it; add to this, twenty porters to carry the most necessary part of my baggage, in my excursions on dry land, across the mountains; fifteen servants besides, amounting to not much less than eighty in all, making a heavy expense, obliged, as I am, to pay magnificently, that is to say, double or treble the value of things. I now almost fancy that British India is Europe; a man is able there, to a certain extent, to regulate his expenses by his means; but here, in this virgin Asia, you must leave the country if you cannot be magnificent when there is need. Runjeet Sing, in fact, will have paid the expenses of my campaign; but there will scarcely be any surplus, unless he exhibits some new coquetry towards me, when I am on my return.

A Seikh lord, returning from the battle of Mozufferabad, in which the Sayed fell, has interrupted me by a visit. His animated recitals having interested me much. I kept him a long time. He was an old greybeard, reddened by the fire of many battles. "I never had so much pleasure in a battle," he told me: "the Sayed's people fought like tigers; they killed us three hundred men, and wounded four hundred; but we did not leave one of them free or alive. Such sport!"

Adieu! I have written at greater length than I at first supposed I should. I love and embrace you with all my heart.

Apropos, M. Cordier, of Chandernagore, has sent me word that he had forwarded to you a Calcutta journal in which he had found my Delhi speech. At Loodheeana

I saw in the same paper this piece of eloquence of mine; but it was so badly printed, and the punctuation so bad, that it had no common sense, nor indeed any other sense. It is true, that, being rather indisposed, I was not able to drink a bottle of Port or Madeira, in order to gain inspiration; and water, reddened with bad claret, seldom fills the sails of English eloquence, either my own or other people's; but I think, that, notwithstanding the *intensity of his feelings*, the *gentleman* was not so incoherent in his speech—since speech there was.

TO MADAME VICTOR DE TRACY, PARIS *.

Cashmere, May 26th, 1831.

My dear Madam,—It is so long since I received any letters from Europe, that I begin to lose patience, and feel myself much more melancholy than I have hitherto been, on account of the frightful distance which divides us, and the profound solitude of my situation.

This dearth of news happens at the very moment when I am devoured by impatience to receive some; for up to the present time, when I have thought of my friends, I could fancy what you were doing, and where you were, according to the different seasons of the year. But this revolution, all the details and results of which I do not

---

* See Note, p. 79, Vol. I.

yet know, has cut the thread of my conjectures. My thoughts are lost in space while seeking you, and the recollection of you escapes me in the circle of a new political world. My wishes will perhaps hasten the arrival of those letters which I so much desire.

In order to withdraw my attention from you, I will speak about myself. I will tell you that my journey across the Punjab has been very fortunate and interesting. But when I penetrated into the passes which separate that country from the kingdom of Cashmere, I encountered a multitude of obstacles on which I had not reckoned. The state of disorder reigning in those mountains was something new to me, and procured me a sort of adventure which has proved useful to me. I have experienced the emotions of a little melo-drama, of which I was the hero; and virtue triumphed over crime, which is something moral, and does not always happen.

This valley of Cashmere, the fame of which has extended far and wide, perhaps deserves it only on account of the frequent visits paid to it by the court of the Grand Mogul, usually shut up within the burning walls of Delhi or Agra, in a most naked country, parched up by a cloudless sun. The lakes are poor things in comparison with those of the Alps; and of all the palaces built by the Mogul emperors on their banks, that of Shalimar, the most famous of all, is the only one left standing. I was received there by the governor, who did his best to welcome and dazzle me. The place pleased me much, on account of its limpid water and magnificent groves. But how many towns on the banks of Lago Maggiore surpass Shalimar in beauty! The appearance of these mountains is rather grand than beautiful,—like that of the Himalaya: magnificent outlines, and no more. Nature has done nothing to adorn the interior—it is an immense border, inclosing nothing. There are none of those picturesque details which make the Alps so attractive, so constantly new to you.

I have pitched my tent in a royal garden, on the banks of a pellucid lake. This garden is filled with roses in bloom; but they are small, and have but little perfume. What beautiful plants I have found, and how often have I thought of your Flora of the Bourbonnais! I hope you are not relaxing in your labours, and that you really surpass those artists who make the flowers larger than nature, in order to render them more beautiful. You were right in saying that it is reflection much more than practice that ensures perfection in the arts. I think I have become a painter, since I have viewed nature so much with its effects of light and shade. Were I manager of a theatre, or of a strolling company performing Macbeth, I should have but little trouble in finding witches: for I meet plenty every day. This may assist your imagination in forming an idea of the women in this part of the world. It is true, I have no taste for brown or gloomy beauties; I do not like stormy faces, like Lord Byron; and I have never felt any pleasure in looking at a female face, if it was not white, gentle, delicate, and noble. Yet I have met in India and the Punjab, from time to time, very handsome women in their style of beauty; but Cashmere has not yet presented me with one of these exceptions. I am sorry to find my experience so contradictory to the accounts of the small number of European travellers who have visited these regions before me. If things are not dreadfully altered since Mr. Forster was here, in disguise, fifty years ago, he must have embellished the truth furiously, which ought to be allowed to poets only. I strongly believe that every thing, then under the arbitrary government of the Afghans, was similar to what is to be seen to-day, under the despotic and capricious dominion of my friend Runjeet Sing, king of Lahore. India is no longer the poorest country in the world to me: Cashmere surpasses all imaginable poverty.

On arriving here I was not without some apprehension of being a good deal disturbed in my peaceful studies, by the not very agreeable visit of a celebrated fanatical Mussulmaun, who for these two years past has carried on a desperate and continued war against the forces of Runjeet Sing, in the neighbouring provinces, constantly threatening to invade Cashmere. But he has just been killed in battle, and is gone to continue his mode of life in Mohammed's paradise. I shall probably spend the whole summer in this country, in peaceful occupations, and making excursions in all directions. When the periodical rains have ceased in the Himalaya I shall return to Semla, where I shall comparatively find the luxury and comforts of Europe, with the exception of Rossini's operas! I wish I could hear you sing *O patria!* I think I should find you immoveable in our opinion that Madame Pasta has carried taste and expression in singing to the highest possible perfection. Try and make your daughters fond of music—a taste for music is a happiness.

Adieu! I take leave of you with these melodious recollections; and to-morrow I shall write to your husband, in order again to turn my attention from the desire of having news of you.

TO M. DE TRACY, PEER OF FRANCE, PARIS.

Cashmere, May 28th, 1831.

DEAR SIR,—If I did not know that the greater part of my letters to my father were communicated by him to his friends, I should not have allowed more than two years to elapse without writing to you. But in the wandering and laborious life which I have led since my departure from Europe, so many material cares absorb the precious time devoted to study, and so many interesting objects every day dispute the short hours of repose which remain after a frequently very long march, that I have always deferred till the present moment telling you how delightful it is to me to think in present solitude of the affection of which you have given me so many proofs. The recollection of the early years of my life is often retraced in my mind; and it is never without emotion that I recal the truly paternal attention which I then had the happiness of receiving from you. I shall show my gratitude all my life by feeling towards you as a son.

I am no doubt indebted, for many enjoyments, to the three years which have so soon elapsed since my departure. Study has been a constant source of serious pleasure to me. The variety of natural scenery, from the south of India to the mountains of Tibet beyond the Himalaya, could not fail to make other and more lively impressions upon me. In short, in this long journey, through such strange regions, and among such strange nations, I have sometimes found oäses of European civilisation. At such a distance from Europe there are neither English nor French: we are all of the same country; we are all Europeans. My fellow-countrymen could not have offered me a kinder reception than I met with during the short stay I made at a great number of the English stations. My quality of foreigner was the title under which this hospitality was exercised towards me,—at first with ceremonious eagerness; but, from the second day, a friendly cordiality almost always controlled its formality. I have thus met in the course of my travels with a number of good people, to whom I am sincerely attached, and who, I think, will always recollect, with the same pleasure as I do, the chance which made us mutually acquainted.

Finally, till within the last six months, I always had the happiness to receive news from my family and yours pretty regularly; and more than once I owe to this correspondence the agreeable illusion of being for a moment transported to Europe. So much for pleasure; but I have also had many cares and annoyances.

At first, the excessive slowness and continued crosses of my everlasting voyage made it appear still more tedious, although I ought rather to have congratulated myself on those prolonged sojournings in countries which I shall never have another opportunity of seeing. I was thus able, in fact, at Rio Janeiro, to form some notion of the state of equinoctial America. I was enabled to admire the wisdom and humanity of the British colonial institutions at the Cape of Good Hope; and to become acquainted, in our paltry island of Bourbon, with the infamy and absurdity of our own. There remained for me to see, at Pondichery, the ridicule and folly of our system. I was detained there a fortnight; this was longer than sufficed for that purpose, but not long enough seriously to commence my labours;—I was therefore in haste to reach Bengal.

How deplorable is the condition of the human species in this vast East! The British Government in India, though it calls for some reforms, merits nevertheless many eulogiums. Its administration is an immense blessing to the provinces subjected to it; and I have only fully appreciated it since I have been travelling in this country, which has remained independent: that is to say, it has remained the theatre of atrocious violence, and continual robbery and murder. Society in the East is fundamentally defective. The first of its elements, a family, scarcely exists. In the upper classes, which afford an example to those below them, polygamy impedes the affection of a father for his children, on account of their large number, and awakens jealousy and fierce hatred among brothers. The wife is an impure creature, whom her husband scarcely considers as being of the same species with himself. Children, as they grow up, soon imbibe this abominable contempt for their mother; and it drives them from her, as soon as they can dispense with her services. Can sympathy, when banished from the domestic hearth, exercise itself more ardently abroad? The men are acquainted with friendship only after the ancient fashion.

Domestic manners in India, which are the greatest source of its misery, seem to me to be susceptible of no amelioration so long as this country preserves its present religious institutions; and perhaps it is generally believed that these are unassailable. All the direct attempts at religious conversion made by the English, in Bengal especially, have entirely failed. The Indians, upon whom the experiment has been made, would in no case change Mohammed or Brahma for Jesus Christ and the Trinity; but, within the last few years, the Government has wisely (and courageously too, for it requires courage in the Company to provoke the stupid and hypocritical wrath of Parliament), withdrawn its support from the missionaries, and opened gratuitous schools at Calcutta, Benares, and Delhi, whither it attracts, by every influential means in its power, children of the middle ranks, to instruct them in the languages and sciences of Europe, without telling them of any of our follies.

I have visited these schools, at Calcutta in particular, where they reckon the greatest number of scholars; and I have conversed with many young people in the higher classes, Brahmins and Mussulmauns, whose European education had naturally converted them from Mohammed and Brahma to reason. Several of them, indeed, complained that this treasure made them but the more miserable, in cutting them off from the rest of the nation, and making them conceive and desire happiness under forms interdicted by their caste; and none of them have yet had the courage to surmount this barrier.

Nevertheless, if there be any hope of ever civilising the East, it must be by these means alone. The English Government would accelerate its action immensely, by substituting, in the courts of justice and all public transactions, the use of the English language instead of the Persian, introduced by the Mogul conquerors, but the knowledge of which has remained quite foreign to the mass of the people, and has only continued in certain hereditary professions. Ten years would suffice to effect this change: for the Indians require English much more than Persian; and the latter is only of use to those acquainted with it, in the routine of their employments; whereas English would be a key for them to the whole circle of European knowledge.

There are not wanting narrow-minded individuals, foes to this generous project; but I doubt not that, in a few years, it will be adopted by the Government. It will spread the light of Europe throughout the country, and qualify it some day to govern itself.

I could have wished, my dear sir, to have forgotten ours, on leaving it. The uncertainty of its destinies, since the revolution, and amid the threatening symptoms of European politics, is a too frequent cause of anxiety to me; which is the more painful, because, since that period, I have received no news either from your family or my own. I take refuge in study; but melancholy thoughts often distract my attention.

Adieu, sir. Permit me to repeat that neither time nor distance will ever weaken my feelings of tender and respectful attachment.

TO M. VICTOR DE TRACY, PARIS.

Cashmere, May 28th, 1831.

My dear Friend—I was about to despatch a courier to India, with several letters for that country and Europe, when one arrived from Lahore, bringing me, from M. Allard, several recent Calcutta and Bombay papers, with letters from Delhi. I stopped my messenger, in order to devour my prey; and though I have already written to almost all of you, I will not allow my hurkaru to start without burthening him with a few more lines for you. My letter to Madame Victor renders it unnecessary to speak of myself; and if you are at Paris, my father will no doubt give you a still longer piece of egotism to read. If he does, it will be a great act of humility on his part; for my correspondence with him ought to please no one but himself. As, in my separation, I am the *hobby-horse* of his affections, all paper blackened by my pen is welcome to him, whatever figures may be on it; I am therefore quite at my ease, and write to him by the yard. My Indian gazettes are a confused and ill-joined mosaic of extracts from a multitude of English papers: dates must be revised, blanks filled up by induction, proper names guessed at; all of which is a very difficult job. I have had the patience to retouch this work, in order to repair the primitive sketch; but it is still very imperfect. I know only that Lord Grey and Mr. Brougham have succeeded the Wellington administration, and that they take office under circumstances the most disquieting for the internal peace of Great Britain; that the plague is ravaging Russia; that Poland is in full insurrection; that Belgians and Dutch are carrying on a war of extermination; that Germany is in a ferment; that despotism and liberty are almost equally powerless in Spain; and that, in short, war is in preparation on all sides. My papers have told me almost nothing about our own country. They report the insignificant interrogatories of the ex-ministers, an uninteresting session of the Chamber of Peers, and the Chamber of Deputies, by which I only know that the former was still in existence in the month of December, and that the latter had not been dissolved. They also tell me of an order of the day of M. Lafayette, which proves that the population of the *faubourgs* gives the national guard plenty of work; and lastly, of two lists of new ministers, who agree only in the dismissal of their predecessors. I confess that I can make nothing of the association of names which I find together in these lists.

Do you remember the autumn of 1822 at Paray? It was at that period our friendship was formed. Being then a man, I became acquainted with you. You were ill; during the last fortnight of my stay with you, I spent part of the day in your room. What a recollection I shall always preserve of those long and pleasant conversations! You were elected deputy a month after; and I remember that my father, at that time, expressed some doubts of your success in your legislative career. He thought that the inflexible uprightness of your principles would induce you to take a direction in which no one would follow you, and which many would not even understand. It was, I have no doubt, the feeling of most of your friends; my father was not the only one to express it to me—your family had the same fears. Well! among so many incredulous people, I had the most perfect confidence in you. I told my father, when I heard you declared deputy, that sooner or later you would reach the point whither parliamentary influence leads; and this is perhaps at no great distance. I do not wish it for your sake; but I desire it for the sake of morality.

Your motion for the abolition of the punishment of death produced the immediate effect which I expected. It has not contributed to make you popular, in the low acceptation of the word (and there is a very low one); but this impure wave of popular wrath will pass, and popularity will come afterwards, to surround the glory of your triumph. You recollect the explosion with which your speech on the Bisson affair was received. You never feared assaulting those vulgar idols; and at first the vulgar did not understand you: they could not. At the commencement, your opinions must have appeared *isolated*. A stranger to all coteries, and intrigues, you suffered the continuous chain of your public conduct to escape notice; but it is evident that during the last two years many people have perceived that all your parliamentary acts are to be found on the prolongation of the same straight line. Tell me, my dear friend, is it not exactly so?—just as we long ago predicted together with certainty.

In spite of the considerable armaments apparently preparing in all countries, I have a confident hope that the peace of Europe will not be disturbed. I do not think the Governor of India shares my confidence on this point; for he is about to send a magnificent embassy to

Runjeet Sing, which certainly is not an affair of common courtesy. Its object can only be to strengthen the bonds of amity between the two governments, and enlighten Runjeet as to his true interests, which are confounded with those of the Company, in the event of an aggression by Russia. Nothing, in fact, is so practicable as the march of a large European army, with all its *matériel*, from Toplis to Delhi; and it would even have the choice of three different roads, by which it might debouch in three columns upon India. And such is the stupidity of the Indian princes, that they would either forsake the British Government, or act against it, the moment a Russian army crossed the Sutledge. Yet what other nation in Europe would have left the vanquished in India so fair a portion? But the Asiatic nations will always remain in their nonage: they are never to be taught by experience. Turkey and Persia will force Russia to occupy their last village, as the Indian princes have obliged the Company to absorb them all into its power, one after the other. They have all succumbed, in the rashest the most stupid enterprises against the Colossus, which would have left them in peace, had they not madly provoked it. Thirty years ago, the English drove the Mahrattas out of Delhi, where they found, imprisoned in the fort, a blind old man, whose long life had been but an uninterrupted series of misfortunes. This was Shah Allum, the descendant of Timour. He had never reigned but by name. The English leave him his vain title, and pay him all the honours formerly enjoyed by the Mogul emperors. They give him a magnificent pension (four millions of francs): guaranteeing this title, these honours, and these advantages, to his family. What use do you think he once made of the guns which have been given him for form sake to fire a salute whenever he leaves his palace? He fired them at the English troops. In less than five minutes the imperial palace was attacked, and the guns retaken. Well! such are the Indian princes. They are all like children, who cannot be trusted with a razor in their hands; not the princes only, but the whole population, which is utterly destitute of reason and moral sense. I make no difference in this respect between the Mussulmauns and the Hindoos: both are equally uncivilisable—at least so long as they maintain their religion.

A-propos of uncivilisable people: my papers of yesterday have informed me again that from Mexico to Buenos Ayres, in the whole of equatorial America, in short, the people are fighting with fury. Without knowing it positively, I already supposed this to be the case. The liberation of South America from Spain is, I think, a misfortune : it was premature. Had it been delayed half a century or a century, the social progress which the mother country would have made during that period, the benefits of which progress it might have shared with its colonies, would have qualified the inhabitants for an independent and free government. Hayti, however rude its political institutions may be, still appears to me the pattern republic, or rather government, among all these new states. It is the only one in which the citizens are not continually cutting each other's throats.

Adieu, my dear and excellent friend, Adieu! How I long to hear directly from you. The last letters which I received from Europe were dated the 22nd July, ten months ago! Adieu: I love and embrace you with my whole heart.

TO M. JACQUEMONT THE ELDER, PARIS.

Cashmere, June 11th, 1831.

MY DEAR FATHER,—M. Allard, writing to me a few days ago by the royal daak (which, running night and day, goes in four days from this place to Lahore), has had the awkwardness to tell me that he had the evening before despatched one of his couriers with a number of newspapers and letters from India, one of which is from Chandernagore. I think his man may arrive to-day. How can I help thinking of him twenty times an hour? In my reply to the General, I forbade him ever to announce letters from Chandernagore beforehand; for the disappointment would be too cruel if they turned out to be only a few insignificant lines from that place. Having been without news from you for eleven months, I confess that unfortunately I have not your stoicism to put a good face on the matter. If, among my brothers in Adam, in Cashmere, I could find any like me, they would see me hanging my head when I think of you, my friends, and our country.

Instead of M. Allard's courier, one arrived this morning from—guess from whom?—from Ahmed Shah, king of Little Tibet, a very polite gentleman truly. He writes me, that being informed of my arrival at Cashmere, he is eager to assure me of his friendship and devotion. He places his country at my disposal; and his messenger, who is a confidential servant, like Eurybates formerly with Agamemnon, confirms his master's respect and attachment to the English. The good man adds, that the Seikhs are a pack of scoundrels, and tells me that with one or two English regiments I might proceed a great way. In order to receive his confidential communications, I did not fail to send, under pretence of requiring his services as an interpreter, for the man whom I know to be Runjeet Sing's spy here. I made him read Shah Ahmed's firman literally, and charged him to prepare the answer which I dictated summarily to him. I send him back a page of compliments; I tell him that I am delighted at being so near him (fourteen days' march), since my presence in Cashmere overwhelms him with happiness; I add, that I am not an Englishman, but only an intimate friend of the Company. As for the presents which he offers me—gold, musk, and rock crystal from his mountains, I thank him infinitely for them; but state that he will oblige me much more if he will despatch all his subjects in pursuit of the wild beasts in his dominions, and send them to me alive. I think, too, I shall put him some questions on the geography of the countries which surround his own.

This singular communication is, I have no doubt, an answer to the overtures indiscreetly made six or seven years ago to this prince, by Mr. Moorcroft. This gentleman was an English physician in the Company's service. He was superintendant of the stud in India: a very lucrative employment. The Government allowed him several times leave of absence, of which he took advantage to travel to the north of the Himalaya. Central Asia was to him what the Real Essences are to somebody else. But the jug goes to the well so often that it gets broken at last. Mr. Moorcroft died there of a putrid fever, or a dose of poison, or even a gun-shot wound: it has never been properly explained which. He went to Ludak, thence to Cashmere, where he inhabited the same garden which I occupy. He thought that by jesuitically giving himself a political character, which he no more possessed than I do, he should smooth many difficulties in the object of his journey; and he wrote a very ambiguous letter to Ahmed Shah, which did not fail to fall into Runjeet Sing's hands, who, in his turn, did not fail to forward it to the British Government without complaint or comment. But a duplicate having reached Ahmed Shah, he thought the English at his gates; and although for six years he might have convinced himself that they at least knew how to wait very patiently until he opened it to them, he takes me for Mr. Moorcroft's successor, and makes overtures to me. If Runjeet Sing still entertains any suspicions of me, I trust that my frankness on this occasion will completely dissipate them. I have acted without artifice, or rather without cunning; and this is evidently the most cunning way of acting. Shah Ahmed is quite sheltered by his poverty and his desert territories from a Seikh invasion; so I do not commit him at all, in making this parade of my honesty of purpose.

If my Tibetan ambassador were a spy and Shah Ahmed's letter a counterfeit, Runjeet would be delightfully mystified in seeing me take his known spy for my secretary to undeceive the pretended Ahmed. But the cunning Sing would not dare to play me such a trick.

Not but I sometimes perceive the little snares that he lays for me. Not long ago, the Governor sent me his secretary to say that he had just received a most mortifying letter from the king. Runjeet stated in this letter that I had written to him that he (the Governor) was a fool,—that nothing went on right in Cashmere,—that he surrounded himself with a set of asses, and left clever people unemployed. He commanded him to ask me who the clever people were, and to employ all those whom I might indicate. I told the Governor the truth: that I had never written any thing of the kind to the Maharajah; and that the latter no doubt wanted to laugh at him, and stimulate his zeal by giving him the alarm. The poor devil of a Governor insisted on my immediately becoming grand elector of Cashmere. He humbly allowed that he was no better than a fool,—a very true confession. He offered to make a clear house of it—he particularly insisted on obtaining a certificate of my satisfaction; for he seemed persuaded that I had complained of him to the Maharajah; and the fate of my brigand Neal Sing has inspired the long beards with a salutary dread of my influence over Runjeet Sing. I refused the desired certificate; but promised to continue informing the king that I was satisfied with the Governor, so long as the latter should continue to afford me the same motives for satisfaction. As for the office of grand elector, I sent it to the devil, and showed him the absurdity of his request.

Now, I believe that Runjeet played off this piece of mischief on the Governor, only to discover whether I felt the lightest inclination to interfere in his affairs. But on whatever point he presents himself, he will be repulsed with the same loss.

There is nothing upright and honest in the natives of this country: they are perfidious in every thing. It is ridiculous for a European to play at the same game with them: we must always be their dupes. The sublimest scoundrel of the kind with us, is, I am persuaded, but a child compared to Runjeet Sing. We have only to be honest people, as is natural to us, in order to disconcert them—never to understand half words, and to speak always in a loud voice.

I am getting ready for an excursion to the frontiers. The king's spy, who is at the head of the chancery, has begged the favour of being allowed to follow me. He shall certainly have it; and he shall have enough of it at once to repay his zeal, for I think of leaving the rogue frozen on some mountain peak.

The summer here is very hot. But the Governor sends me ice every morning; and I have taught my khansama how to make very light iced punch. I finish my dessert with it; and you will allow that in a barbarous country it is no slight luxury. But I have more lace than shirts. I shall have sixty-eight servants in my pay, which will procure the rajah's rupees a very rapid expenditure. They bring me every morning a sheep, a dozen fowls, a basket of eggs, a sack of rice and flour, and all other things in proportion; and—I have not a bit of bread to eat!

Adieu! for I feel myself in a humour to complain; and that would be too bad. I must reserve the right of remonstrance for bad days; and perhaps I shall have more than one before our meeting.

TO M. NOIZET DE SAINT PAUL, CAPTAIN OF ARTILLERY IN THE ARMY OF THE MOREA.

Cashmere, June 12th, 1831.

Do not measure, my dear George, the pleasure I have in writing to you by the smallness of the paper. I have not the good fortune to be a warrior, like you: far from it, especially in point of leisure. Business comes upon me on all sides; and I am forced to be concise in my supplication, prayer, or request—call it what you will.

The object of the present letter is to move your bowels of compassion as my cousin-germain—german and a half—and to stimulate your artilleryman's laziness so far as to make you take pen, ink, and paper—the largest possible sheet of the latter—and, that without preamble or circumlocution, entering at once into the matter, you tell me about the world, and how it goes on where you are—Athens or Paris, Arras or Berlin,—no matter;—though I should prefer, for your own sake, that your chronicle was dated from Paris. Gossip above all:—it is the only true thing. Truth suffers cruelly in a wig, *à l'oiseau royal;* enveloped in this way, it is no longer like itself. Gossip, then—tell me all about Greece. You are there become in a certain degree my colleague in the East. Well! tell me—Is not the credulity of the good souls of the west a blessing for us?—

for in fact, if we wish to seem to have seen wonders, our imagination has only to invent them. But between us, no inventions if you please—honesty among thieves! Tell me, then, without embellishment, all about Canaris, Mavrocordato, Odysseus, Mavromichaelis, and other famous Turk-eaters. If you are in France, politics of course; but above all, forget the papers you read in the morning. And if you are doing the hero of artillery *en tilbury*, and of liberty at Berlin or Vienna, well! sing of your glory, but in vile prose. I am the only animal of my species in this corner of the world, so far separated from all others; and, to divert me from the animals, minerals, and plants of Cashmere, I have from time to time the Persian Chronicle of the Court of Lahore — very poor nourishment for the political genius of our family. Put yourself to a little inconvenience, then, my good friend, and with a good grace. Your letter may reach me in a year. It will perhaps find me in one of those situations through which I have already so often passed.—of solitude so profound, that I shall be indebted to it for a pleasure incommensurable with the vexation which it may have caused your laziness. Tell or write to Zoé, that for her punishment she would deserve to learn Latin as we did, in order to know how to understand *pauca multis*.

Adieu, my dear friend. Take care of muskets, if any are fired near you, and get out of the way of bullets when you see them coming—at least if such is the custom. I am very well, and preparing to complete my thirtieth year, which brings us singularly near to to each other. Farewell.

P. S. For local character—which you have a right to expect from a correspondent in Cashmere—know that I am writing this to you with a reed from Kathay, and would give a thousand of them for one goose-quill.

TO M. PORPHYRE JACQUEMONT, PARIS.

Cashmere, June 14th, 1831.

MY DEAR PORPHYRE,—For several days I have been on thorns. A short time ago M. Allard wrote to me by the royal daak, that he had sent a courier to me the day before, with a monstrous packet from beyond the Sutledge, and what is more, from Chandernagore. His messenger could and ought to have arrived yesterday—the day before yesterday—or even the day before that; and he is not come yet! To-day I was to have set out on a ten day's excursion towards the frontiers; but it is impossible to start: anxiety keeps me here. If you give way to the blue devils as I do, during the long interruptions of our correspondence, I trust, my friend, that you may not happen to be deprived of letters from the 22nd of July to the 14th of June; and in order that the fault may not be mine, if this misfortune must happen, I will write either to you or to my father more frequently than I have hitherto done. I will do so on account of the distance, which will make my letters more valuable, and at the same time increase their chance of being lost on the way.

You may have perceived that since I crossed the Sutledge I have had an attack of quite a new passion,—I mean avarice. The numerous mortifications to which it has exposed me have cured me of it. The people of Cashmere have an admirable knack of borrowing money, which they do not repay. In a fortnight eight hundred rupees have thus melted away, independently of a number of presents which I am obliged to make. It is high time that I was again running about the mountains. I have at last taken the resolution to resign myself to, or I have resigned myself to taking the resolution to, recross the Sutledge, as much a beggar as when I crossed it on the 2nd of March, and to consider the rajah's liberalities only as a sort of loan, which I ought to repay by doing as much honour to it as possible in his dominions. I am, however, refitting, and shall re-enter India with a new wardrobe. My *fumée Navarin*, which has seen so many countries within the last three years,—the four quarters of the globe,—is arrived at a truly ominous state of maturity. It is serving as a pattern for its successor, which is to be made of black shawl, waistcoat and trowsers of the same, together with a duplicate of each, and wonderfully adapted to the climate of India, where our clothes of French cloth heat one red hot.

Add to this, an immense Persian dressing gown, all of the same stuff, which will come into use in five months at Semla, and elsewhere in the winter,—not to mention the service which I hope it will some day do me at Paris. Those devils of Englishmen have the wonderful art (the secret of which lies either in their riches or their debts) of procuring all the commodities of Europe at the end of the world. For our single *Journal des Modes*, ten journals of the same kind are published in London. The English in India and Van Diemen's Land subscribe to them. Their wives seek eagerly to peruse them; and every family, though living whole years in a remote district, without any European witness of their existence, ruins itself in millinery and other finery, in order to be in the fashion. This is the height of folly. I found a society at Semla, almost every member of which would be deemed ridiculous among us for the importance they attach to the shape of their boots, coat, or hat; and I have thought it prudent not to appear again among them except with a coat the material of which will compensate for its old-fashioned cut.

Where the deuce are you, my good friend? Returned, perhaps, to Wilna? For I confess I now believe in the possibility of a war, if there be a revolution in Prussia, which appears to me inevitable. But I trust it will not last long; and that we shall for the last time execute justice on the kings and aristocracies of Europe. What blunders the Chamber of Deputies committed in the first week of last August! I see by the English papers that M. de Lafayette has resigned the command of the national guard, which proves that there is discord in the camp of our friends. But now that we have returned to the famous legal order, how can we sweep off the peers by an ordinance? Peyronnet would cry out from his prison, "Set me at liberty, since you have infringed the new charter, as I did the old!" My greatest anxiety, however, is concerning my father's fate, deprived as he perhaps is of your society. It is dreadful. I should have felt more when I left him, could I have foreseen the course of political probabilities since the revolution. Adieu for to-day! I am tormented with anxiety, and not fit for any thing. Adieu!

Cashmere, August 5th, 1831.

Here, my dear Porphyre, have I begun the bundle which I lately announced from Vernague. I find it again in this city, with some other epistolary scraps; and, comforting myself with the idea that every thing of that sort is good from a distance of some thousands of leagues, I despatch this remnant to Chandernagore. I am adding an ell of this large hand for the obliging M. Augustin Taboureau. Yesterday I received a courier from M. Allard, who, for twenty-four hours, was considered dead. He has only written me a few lines to prove his resurrection; but without any particulars. I know not what his complaint has been. At this moment there is no contagious disease in the Punjab. Public health here is perfect. I have not seen a single case of cholera morbus, in spite of my curiosity to do so,—no more than lions and tigers,—no more than of yellow fevers in Haiti. It would seem as if the devil placed himself in my way, to prevent me from seeing.

The Calcutta Gazettes of the 4th July apprise me of another change of ministry at home. The famous legal order seems always to be tottering. This both vexes and grieves me. The most contradictory accounts of the fate of Poland arrive from Persia and Bombay; my Delhi friends forward them to me. Then I see that there is an indigenous regent in Belgium, without any talk of a king; revolutions in Italy; and still no general war.

I am very well, and work hard. In my weeks of sedentary labour, all day in my chair, I used to be unwell, and without appetite in the evening. I have provided against this evil, by taking a good swim at sunset. It is literally a warm bath that I take. The proof of my strength is, that I swim an hour,—to be sure without exertion, in still water. By pursuing this plan I sleep at night, which I could not do previously, without some equivalent fatigue. Bustle yourself in delivering the inclosed letters.

It is not merely a magnificent embassy that the British Government now talk of sending to Runjeet Sing: the Governor-general desires to have a personal interview with the Maharajah. My friend Wade is returned to Lahore, to negociate the etiquette at the meeting of the two stars of the East. They are counting steps and half steps, and regulating beforehand the insignificant sentences which they are to exchange, &c. This is a very grave affair; and I do not think Wade will manage it well. The high contracting parties, as they say, have irreconcilable or incompatible pretensions, which form the subject of parley at the present time. What Lord William wants with Runjeet Sing, I am unable to guess,—to frighten him, perhaps, and show him how easy it would be to annihilate him. The Colonel of one of the two regiments of English cavalry in the Calcutta presidency writes to me from Semla that he has been appointed to command, not the escort, but the army, which is to accompany the Governor-general to his interview with Runjeet, if it take place; or the embassy to Lahore, in the reverse case. He will take his regiment of lancers, a regiment of native cavalry, one of English infantry, two of seapoys, and a battery of light artillery,—all picked for the occasion. I do not know how far the Maharajah will relish so many honours.

I laughed heartily at Cashmere, nor did they laugh less at Semla, at the grand oriental sentences of General Lamarque, about Russia, the Balkan, the Caucasus, Persia, China, and the cruel oppression with which the perfidious islanders keep down a hundred millions of Indians, ripe for revolt. I could wish that legal order went on as well at Paris, as it does from Cape Comorin to the peaks of the Himalaya. It is enough to make one burst with laughter. I abandon, without mercy, to the ridicule of my English friends, all my countrymen who give way to such folly. I do not know whether it is that I read these things coolly at a year's interval; but the bulletins of the army in Africa appeared to me quite as ludicrous. Our soldiers on the Atlas were *as great as Atlas himself*!!! This is Victor Hugo all over. I believe now-a-days people laugh heartily at the Emperor's bulletins,—even their happiest claptraps. Honour to common sense!

You recommend me, in one of your last letters, not to venture to return through any country at war with France. Thanks for the advice: it is very well to be prudent among the Russians. It appears that these scoundrels have intercepted some English travellers in Persia, and sent them to cool themselves in Siberia. Be easy: I shall be prudent. Adieu, my friend! My boat is ready, and the sun sinking. Do not be afraid of my drowning myself. I embrace you, and my father too, with all my heart.

TO M. JACQUEMONT, THE ELDER, PARIS.

Vernague, at the Source of the Hydaspes, in Cashmere,—July 19*th*, 1831.

AT length, my dear father, I am happy! I yesterday received your letter of the 1st and 3rd November. It was just a year since I had heard from you. The events of the revolution, with their divers and unforeseen chances, filled up this long interval, and opened my mind to a thousand cruel anxieties. God be praised!—and thanks to you, and the chain of friendly hordes by means of whom your letter found me in the depth of these solitudes! M. Allard's courier travelled a hundred and fifty leagues in nine days to bring it to me from Lahore. But I have rewarded him well for his diligence. I keep him a day, in the midst of the forests in which I am encamped, and where I shall make a halt of twenty-four hours, to reperuse your letter and Porphyre's, after having read them many times, run through the French papers of February which came with them from Semla, and reply. But where am I to begin? The emotion of pleasure which I feel is a complete fit of nervous fever; my hand shakes, and my ideas are in confusion. This letter of the 1st of November is numbered 20; and I have not received your Nos. 17, 18, and 19. But M. Cordier of Chandernagore, writes to me that, at an interval of a few days, he has despatched to me three packets from France before this one; and M. Allard's courier informs me that another messenger, less active than himself, is on his way to Cashmere, having left Lahore thirteen days ago. I have decided that he is the bearer of these three packets from France, mentioned by M. Cordier; and you may judge whether this expectation is calculated to calm my anxiety.

Age engenders mistrust, if not timidity. What I most dreaded was, to learn that the political agitations of our country had deprived you of your habitual security of mind, to which you owe the happy quietude of your old age. I was afraid Porphyre might be absent from Paris, and you left alone in the midst of your uneasiness. But you have dissipated all my fears: and henceforth I shall always think of you with additional happiness. My nature has not a tendency to hope. It is perhaps on account of this disposition of mind that I enjoy present good more exquisitely. When it comes, it is in all its intensity: I have not anticipated its enjoyment in my dreams of the future.

I shall still be badly off with twelve thousand francs. It is less than the pay of an infantry captain in India; and I am forced into a number of expenses which do not come within the wants of an officer. My journeys, and the formation of my collections, render this necessity evident,—especially in the mountains, where my caravan can only move with the help of a great number of porters. Here, for instance, in excursions of a fortnight at a time from Cashmere, leaving the bulky part of my baggage in that city, and reducing the number of my followers as much as possible, I require twenty-nine men; and yet I have not to trouble myself, as in the Company's territory, about providing for the subsistence of these people, nor of my domestics. The rajah does it all! How could I do it myself? I have more than a hundred men in my camp. There are some acts of service excessively repugnant to the habits of the Asiatics, whether Hindoos or Mussulmauns, and which they cannot be brought to perform, except by the temptation of very considerable gain; and even this motive often fails to induce them to remain. Thus, on my arrival in Cashmere, I taught two Cashmerian servants to help me in my zoological preparations. They gained more at it in a month than they would otherwise have done in a year; and yet they have left me. One of them was a hunter; when the people saw him killing all sorts of animals, they rose upon him, beat him, and broke his gun. I had thirty of the mutineers bastinadoed, and threatened with a more severe punishment in case of a relapse. My man was not beaten again, but he became the object of general contempt and hatred, and he told me one day that he could no longer follow a craft which made him so odious. The other also resigned. I can find none to take their places. In these barbarous countries, religion meddles with every thing, aud raises a crowd of obstacles in the way of the curiosity and ardour of a European traveller, such as you have no conception of.

If M. Cordier is still at Chandernagore, which I think probable, I will send all my collections to him from Delhi, requesting him to repack them himself, with all the care required for their voyage by sea, and also to ship them. If he is no longer there, there is no one at Calcutta from whom I can request such a service. All the men I became acquainted with there are overwhelmed with business. I wrote to that effect long ago to the Jardin des Plantes, and I hope the gentlemen there will yield with a good grace to the necessity of waiting.

You ask me what I think of our Indian possessions. I have heard that there was a talk of purchasing from our Government, Pondichery and our other factories in India. The price put upon them was even fixed: it was said to be a million sterling. I do not, however, know what steps may have been taken to realise this desire of the Company. Were I to be asked as to the propriety of accepting such an offer, I should say Yes, a thousand times. Our microscopical establishments in India are always ridiculous, and a humiliating anomaly in the event of war. Young M. Desbassyns wishes to attach a degree of importance to Pondichery of which it is not susceptible. As for the consent of the inhabitants to the change of sovereignty, the British, if they desired the transfer, would buy it with money. Our trade with India, generally ruinous to the speculators who embark in it, is not capable of much extension. The productions we send thither are consumed only by the scanty population of inhabitants of European origin. They consist of Bordeaux wines, some silk goods, and Bourbon coffee; and to the latter island most vessels carry back rice bought in Bengal. M. Desbassyns' establishments at Pondichery must perish, because the British provinces have natural advantages which that locality does not possess for the same branch of industry: they have a more fertile soil, a more favourable climate, cheaper labour, and lastly capital, which we want.

What absurd tale is it of which you speak, my dear father, about Afghans descending from Cashmere to conquer Bengal? In the first place, there is not a single Afghan left in Cashmere: Runjeet Sing drove them out twelve years ago, and it was no difficult task for him. The last king of Kabul, whom I saw at Loodheeana, Shah Shoodjah el Molok, who is well acquainted with his old subjects, told me that with a regiment of English seapoys, it would be easy for him to repossess himself of his crown,—and he spoke the truth. All these people fight little, and fire, from a great distance, their shot which kills nobody, and immediately run away. If there be only a little cavalry to overtake them, or a sufficient number to surround them, they are exterminated. Should Runjeet-Sing think he could prudently absent himself for some time from the Punjab, nothing would be easier for him than to re-conquer the whole of Afghanistan. Runjeet-Sing's is the only power which has stood with that of the British. But the respective revenues of the two states will give you their relative resources. That of the Company amounts to twenty-six millions sterling; that of Runjeet to three; and he can only come up to this amount by excessive taxes, which tempt his subjects to throw themselves into the hands of the British. The latter have nothing to fear from war, unless it be with the Russians. They might crush Runjeet in a couple of months, if they wished it. The only internal danger possible for the English power would be a partial revolt of its native army.

I have but little curiosity to cross a few provinces of Persia as I return to Europe. I think I can do more and better by prolonging my stay in India, and applying myself more especially to the great chain of the Himalaya. I wish exceedingly that the minister of the interior would approve the project I have sent him to that effect, and upon which he may by this time have decided. In a work on the Himalaya, there would be a great unity, which would be wanting in my labours, were they to embrace, at the same time, and in a numerous series of scientific views, a very great extent of territory, of which I should have only crossed a few lines at long intervals. To fill up this void I should be compelled to borrow from others, and my work would therefore want originality in several parts.

I told you long ago of my contempt for what is very gratuitously termed *Indian history*. Assuredly my opinion on this subject could not be changed by the traditions preserved in Cashmere. Nevertheless, I am having a copy made of a somewhat rare book—a very modern Persian translation of a Sanscrit text, the date of which I do not know, but which I suppose to be the same from which Mr. Wilson of Calcutta has extracted for the Asiatic Researches a list of Indian kings of Cashmere. The Persian translator, who lived a hundred years ago, has added to the work. I shall have an almost perfect translation when I leave the country, for I read it with my Mogul secretary as the copyist brings the sheets. He explains in Hindoostanee the passages too elaborate for my comprehension, and lies in his beard when he meets with an Arabic quotation, for he does not understand Arabic any more than I do. However, it is a wretched rhapsody: D'Eckstein all over, and worse still.

My letters from Tibet will long ago have undeceived you with regard to the state of the population among whom I spent last summer. The natives are very different beyond the Sutledge, where the influence of order, exercised by the vicinity of the English, has not yet reached them. There is, as I sometimes perceive, a ferocious disposition in the Seikhs. Whilst I was going about the highest mountains in this country, a month ago, the two sects of Mussulmauns, confounded in a very unequal proportion in Cashmere, were quarrelling about their religion. The Seikh guard sent to restore order, set fire to the city, and disturbed the water in order to fish in it. The two parties fought, killed, and burnt each other for twenty-four hours. It was fortunate that I had left a strong guard at home, for the plunderers came, but were received sword in hand and repulsed. I found every thing at my dwelling as I had left it. On my arrival here yesterday, the chief of a neighbouring fortress, who on my passing through his territory had paid me an humble visit, sent some soldiers to me with a most insolent message. He said he would prevent me from going further. I immediately wrote him a threatening letter. He replied that he was obeying Runjeet-Sing's orders. For an instant I suspected the rajah of treachery. Nevertheless I wrote again, telling the chief that he was an impudent liar, and that I should demand a signal revenge from Runjeet-Sing. To-day, the wretch came to beg pardon!—yet he perhaps spoke the truth in designating the rajah as the author of the prohibition which he wished to impose upon me; but he knew that it would be disavowed by the prince, and that he should be punished for his indiscreet zeal. Baseness, perfidy, cruelty, and arrogance, are the prevailing features in the national character. Notwithstanding the reparation that has been made, I have just written to the king to have the fellow punished. I must not pardon the least want of attention: the impunity of one would be the signal of a general attack. Runjeet continues to be my friend, at least ostensibly. The courier of yesterday brought me another letter from him as friendly as usual. It is the third time he has written to me since my arrival in Cashmere. I was going to demand my passports in spite of all this friendship, when the excuses of the governor of Islamadad arrived.

General Cartwright, my host at Delhi last winter, has written to me that he shall be summoned to Calcutta next winter, to give evidence in a criminal prosecution. He is a kind and excellent man, who has loaded me with kindness; his absence, however, will not be disadvantageous to me: it will allow me to live with Mr. William Fraser during my third stay in the ancient Mogul capital. My intimacy with Mr. Fraser is quite of a different nature; there is a good deal of resemblance between us. He is a true friend to me. We wished to live in common; but as long as the good General Cartwright was there, there was no thinking about it: the general would never have pardoned my deserting him. He also states in his letter that the Commander-in-chief and the Governor-general think of leaving Semla very soon; I may possibly therefore miss the latter. I should regret it much; for I am not arrived at the end of the obligations which I would wish to owe him. If my Himalaya project is approved of at Paris, Lord William will have to take the same steps in my favour with the rajah of Catmandoo that he did with Runjeet, in order that the prince of Nepaul may remove the interdict which he has laid on the travelling of Europeans in his dominions. Before that period arrives, it would be proper the Governor-general should have been already thanked by our minister of the interior for what he has hitherto done towards the success of my journey. His kind intentions would be thus strongly supported, and I shall have need of all his favour to gain an entrance into Nepaul; for at the other extremity of India the rajah of Catmandoo is the pendant to Runjeet-Sing: he is powerful, and suspicious of the British. The quickness of my visit to the one after leaving the dominions of the other, may, I have no doubt, appear singular to the Calcutta diplomatists, who are not very bright, though they fancy themselves so clever. They will remark that such was not at all my purpose when I left Bengal, since I then announced my intention of proceeding nearly in a direct line to Bombay. I foresaw their objections, when I wrote my memorial to the ministers, and took care to inform Sir C. Grey of it; he has therefore been long aware of the alteration in my plans, and will, when necessary, make it known to Sir Charles Metcalfe.

The Mogul Emperors were quite stage kings. The monuments of their grandeur were scarcely more than theatrical decorations. Akbar, Jehanguire, Shah Jehan, and Aurung-Zeb, reigned in the seventeenth century. They expended immense treasures on Cashmere, their new conquest. Nothing remains of their extravagant magnificence, but gigantic trees. Their palaces have fallen into ruins, almost every where effaced. Yet the ancient buildings dedicated to the Indian worship are still standing. Their number, and the immense labour bestowed on them, bear witness to a very long period of indigenous rajahs before the introduction of Islamism in the eleventh century.

I have hitherto seen no reason to surrender to the oriental proverb about the beauty of the Cashmerian women; and I despair of ever doing so. The number of sick who come to me is without end. A crowd of poor and diseased people gather round my tent, like a gayer one round our theatres. Unfortunately nearly all are incurable: there is blindness of all descriptions, and a host of wretches worn down with most dreadful diseases, which they owe to us. I give alms to those whom I cannot relieve with medicine; and I think with pleasure that some do not leave me without carrying away a feeling of gratitude.

I am sorry that M. Cordier of the museum, who has so strongly supported my interests, has not found time to tell me himself of the new obligations which he has conferred upon me. I shall write to him shortly to thank him, and shall, at the same time, make up for the silence which, since my departure, I blame myself for having preserved towards Madame Cordier.

My Calcutta banker has written to me lately about the annual settlement of our accounts. The result is, that on the 30th of April, 1831, he had a balance in my favour of two thousand six hundred rupees. I shall not want any of this money before I return to British India, having still about as much in Cashmere, from the rajah's presents. I have moreover a right to depend upon the supplement of two thousand francs from the Jardin for the years 1830 and 1831, and also the four thousand francs from the interior for those two years, which would amount in all to twelve thousand francs more than my banker thinks I have. With that, and the two thousand six hundred rupees at Calcutta, I can proceed next year in any direction whatever. My ambition would be to bring back with me to Europe the sum which I owe to the rajah alone: that is to say, about fourteen thousand francs. This I consider my own property, whilst I look upon the funds from the Jardin and the Minister of the Interior, to have been placed in my hands as a steward, to employ them in the furtherance of my undertaking. I owe the rajah much more than these fourteen thousand francs; for since my departure from Lahore, the heavy expense of all my means of carriage is almost wholly at his charge; I ought also to add that of my subsistence, to which he does not allow me to contribute. I shall have eaten four or five hundred sheep, thousands of fowls, &c., at his expense, ere I get among the English again. Do not suppose that I am the fatter for it. People do not grow fat at my trade: there are too many fatigues, and besides, my health is not very good; it often experiences little derangements, which I should not perceive if they came at longer intervals, but the repetition of them is sometimes annoying. I suspect that in this European climate, the absolute and lengthened privation of spirituous liquors is prejudicial to my stomach; and if my approaching campaign is to be carried on in the mountains, I will try and have, every day, a glass of wine to drink with my evening meal. I shall refresh myself at Kennedy's, at Semla, in the month of October or November.

The cholera which you mention is not unknown in Cashmere. It has appeared twice since the Seikh conquest, and the Cashmerians do not fail to attribute its importation to their new masters. But if this disease is attacked at first, and combated immediately with the violent remedies discovered by experience, it is not very dangerous in India. You know that the good and learned physician, whose friendly advice I received at Calcutta, did not let me depart without supplying me with those remedies prepared by himself; the box follows me like my shadow. Be easy therefore on this head. In general do not believe in any disagreeable newspaper reports, such as sedition among the troops, revolts, wars, contagious disorders, &c. &c.: these things are but little in use in the world which I inhabit. I think a man must be rather foolish to allow himself to die at thirty; and I have the vanity to believe that I shall not commit such a piece of folly for a long time to come. I take a close view of it, and do not act rashly—I am not so careless as all that. Porphyre confirms what you tell me, and what I very sincerely believed without the corroboration of his testimony—that your health is excellent. Is not this a time to live, when there is so much to see? Although you may have carried a little too far the consequences of the principle of immortality which you find in your experience of life, that is to say, in the very fact of a great age, I think with you that this experience may serve to redeem a part of its original cost. Cerebral activity is certainly a principle of longevity. See to what an age most men, celebrated for intellectual labours, have attained.

Adieu! my dear and excellent father! Your letter has restored me the tranquillity I had lost. I am about to work with an ardour which has never slackened, and with a freedom of thought of which I have for some time been in want: I shall do every thing better and quicker. Kind regards to all friends: they will understand that in a short halt in the midst of woods I can only repeat my remembrances to them collectively. Adieu! I embrace you with all my heart.

19th, Evening.

General Allard's second messenger is just arrived with all that I was expecting from you. I have fifty letters to read; for there are a score from India, and all very long ones:—a charming one from Lady William Bentinck, and one from my friend Colonel Fagan, whom Porphyre cannot know without liking him.

TO M[LLE.] ZOE NOIZET DE SAINT PAUL, ARRAS.

Mountains of Cashmere, July 20th, 1831.

YESTERDAY after writing to you, my dear Zoé, I received with fifty others at the same time, your long letter written immediately after the revolution, and resumed at different intervals. It is quite a volume. You must feel that it is impossible for me to answer every part of it. Your letter shall remain a couple of months in my portfolio; I will read it over more than once, and my thoughts will answer it, doubt it not, in my solitary marches, or sleepless nights, when the mountain storm keeps me awake in my tent. Permit me to tell you only, my good friend, that you have not sufficient confidence in me. Open the "Annuaire du Bureau des Longitudes," where you will see, in the tables of mortality, that the fatal chances are almost null at our age; I firmly believe that though I roam about the world, I increase them only by an absolutely insignificant quantity. I was formerly near being crushed to death on the Alps, by an avalanche of stones; I was also near being drowned in the Niagara, and swam during a quarter of an hour without any hope of reaching the bank; in fine, I have had many other narrow escapes;—but life is made up of such things, and we often very closely miss losing it, before we lose it in reality. I am beginning to compare myself to an old china vase, brittle in its nature, and easily broken, but hardened by accidents, and accustomed to fall without breaking. Never, therefore, couple gloomy apprehensions with the thought of me. You would do much better, if you continue to grant me the favour of thinking about me, to try to imagine the beautiful scenery with which I am surrounded in this pretended Paradise of India.

You tell me that my friends have regretted my absence on my own account; I have received the same information from several of them, but without understanding what they would have been desirous of doing with me. I think that if I had been at Paris, I should not have remained a passive spectator of the three great days. Supposing I had escaped with my life, what new claim in my profession should I have acquired by the share I might have taken in those military events? None. My friends know very well that I have no fortune, and that I want a professional income above all things. Now I ask myself and you, what use is a man like me out of his especial sphere? The answer, I confess, embarrasses me. They tell me I should have been made a prefect. But, conscious of my incapacity, I should have declined this distinction. It is true that one of my friends, a scientific man like myself, holds such an appointment. Formerly he worked in iron; but his trade of smith had brought him into contact with a multitude of affairs into which he could not fail of acquiring an insight. He had also been mayor of a small commune, and was quite a Minos compared to me: and in fact I am told, that, placed as he is in one of the most delicate of that kind of situations, he gives entire satisfaction to persons of the most opposite opinions. But does not diplomacy require some preparatory studies?—is there not a routine to be learnt, except indeed in the more elevated stations? However, I do not think my friends would have thought of getting me appointed minister to the United States: a deputyship then alone remains; all talk to me about it. But it does not provide one's bread and butter; so I go on working hard and steadily, doing my best, let what will come afterwards. I do not deny that if unforeseen chances should some day call me to the legislature, I should rejoice at it. I will even confess that I have long wished it. I think I know how to play a part in a public assembly, which, without requiring great talents, would elicit general assent and esteem, and would perhaps even give the actor some influence. In friendly tête-a-tête, or in very limited circles, I have had the good fortune, more than once, to exercise the art of persuasion upon men who would not have been supposed to take advice from me. Although perhaps peremptory, dry, and disagreeable in the eyes of the world, during the last years of my stay with my father, I was quite different in the out-pourings of friendship. It seems that since my voyage to the United States, that is to say, since the fatal period which I have mentioned, my individuality is remarkably modified and ameliorated: there is a greater stock of benevolence. It appears to me that I often exercise, towards the indifferent, some of that art of indulgence, good-nature, and persuasion, which they formerly could not discern in me. Art of good-nature and indulgence! will you not laugh at the contradiction? But, my dear Zoé, I know many men in whose hearts these feelings live, and who, notwithstanding, have never known how to express them. Timidity, false shame, and sometimes vanity, are what stops their expression. Now I am not timid, and perhaps in the eyes of some I am not over-modest, though in the sincerity of my heart I feel that I am modest, and destitute only of false modesty. The uninterrupted chain of benevolence which I have found to guide and support me these last four years, has perhaps often been unwittingly formed by myself. What I have everywhere found in my very numerous personal friendships, I might perhaps also find in public intercourse with a greater number of men at a time. Shall I tell you that I often hope so?

Meantime, I am endeavouring to unravel the confusion in the rocks of the Himalaya, and to separate the truth from their ambiguous testimony concerning the revolutions of this part of the globe. I am likewise describing new plants, and seeking to penetrate the internal form of existence of this singular race of men, each at its proper time.

I am not writing to you in English, from horror of the *you*, which I should nevertheless be obliged to employ on pain of not writing to you in English. The *thou* is printed and sung, but never either spoken or written. No relationship nor degree of attachment admits it: the most tender father, the most impassioned lover or husband, have no other form of address than *you*. A mother says it to the child in the cradle.

The studies you are pursuing will, in many respects, give you a much more extensive knowledge of the English language than I possess. When we meet I hope I shall be able to serve as a master, to teach you what alone you could not guess at: I mean the capricious pronunciation of that language; and perhaps to show you how to distinguish its double vocabulary, the one German or Saxon, and the other Latin. Shakspeare uses the former, and Milton also. Pope is exclusively Roman. It is the modern tendency; all languages are gradually approximating, by becoming every day more and more Latinised.

Your choice of the book which you are translating surprises me. Sterne's thought is almost always an equivocal reticence. It is true that in the Sentimental Journey this equivoque is always decent. Tristram Shandy, which I however confess to be one of my favourite books, is to my great regret often very coarse. The only excuse for these indecencies is perhaps their enormity, which renders the idea which they convey scarcely comprehensible. We men are little affected by these things; social conventions allow us manners so different from those imposed on women! We are almost without modesty.

I regret the more, now that I know its subject, the loss of your letter written during the winter of 1829. You must begin it over again. In respect of thought, I do not know you. Let me become fully acquainted with you, and be assured that I shall respect all your opinions, however different they may be from my own. In great subjects mine are only scepticism and indifference, but without adopting either side of the question. Adieu, my dear friend, adieu!

TO M. JACQUEMONT THE ELDER, PARIS.

Isle of Planes in the Lake of Cashmere,
August 8th, 1831.

My dear Father,—If you could see me to-day, you would scarcely recognise me, and would perhaps take me for an indolent Asiatic. Within the last few days, the excessive heat has broken down my European energy. I have deserted my garden, which is like a hot-house, and am come upon the lake in search of a breath of air. But even here, at the foot of the mountains, the same calm prevails in the atmosphere. I envy India its hot winds. I had brought materials for working with me; but I must first try to exist, which has been a very laborious task these last few days. These overpowering heats are rare in Cashmere: they only come when the periodical summer rains entirely fail, which has happened this year. The rivers, from which the country derives its subsistence, have been dry for a month past. This is a public calamity. The people wanted the Mollahs to pray in the mosques for rain, but the sky was so unpromising that the Mollahs, expecting but little success from these supplications, caused the Seikh governor, for a long time to forbid that the prayers should be offered up. Yesterday, seeing some stormy clouds about the peak of the mountains, they got the interdict removed which they had themselves called for, and the inhabitants of the country hastened from all parts, to a village which I can see from this place, and where they preserve a hair of Mohammed's beard. If there really be such a thing as faith, or true piety, in the world, it is amongst the Mussulmauns; but the poor wretches will not reap an ear of rice the more for it. The dervishes, who are the least devout of the faithful, should have come to me and consulted my barometer as to the probability of change of weather, before they asked it of heaven. The threatening clouds of yesterday dispersed during the night, as I had foreseen, and with a sort of Christian folly foretold. The hot weather has returned to the set fair of the infernal regions.

The water of the lake is so warm that I seem to derive no advantage from the change of element when I plunge into it. One must remain a considerable time in it before any coolness is felt; but the only place fit for bathing is very deep, and requires the faculty of swimming. I am grown very skilful in that exercise, and can keep it up a long time; nevertheless it is laborious in still water, and when I get into the boat again, my strength is scarcely recruited.

The sun has not spared me: with the exception of my hands and face, which have long been hardened and blackened, my whole body is become of the brightest crimson. The friction of the lightest clothing is a torment to me; I have left off the European dress, and avail myself of the conventions of Oriental fashions, which are but little troublesome. A servant stands near me with a large fan, and, from time to time, administers an artificial tempest, which alone makes me feel that life is an agreeable thing.

Bernier, whose travels I think you have read, speaks of this little island, which is a toy of the Mogul emperors. It is completely overshadowed by two enormous plane trees, the only ones remaining out of four planted by Shah-Jehan: this will show how small it is. The palace is nothing but a large hall, open to all the winds of heaven when it is their pleasure to blow; the arches are supported by columns, in a fantastic style, the spoil of some ancient pagoda. Shahlemar, with its fine avenue of poplars, stands opposite. Nichat-Bagh, with its fine shady groves, appears like a large black spot at the foot of the yellow-coloured mountains. Opposite to it is Saifkan-Bagh, which is nothing now but a forest of gigantic planes. The little mosque, to which the devout Mussulmauns of India and Persia flock to adore *azrette boll*, literally *his excellence the hair* of their prophet's beard, shows the gilded pinnacle of its minaret above a group of the same kind of trees. In the back-ground is the throne of Solomon, who was a great traveller according to the Cashmerian chronicle. This panorama which surrounds me, calls forth a crowd of recollections; the inhabitants of Cashmere look upon it all their lives and it alleviates their misery. I confess that I am still too much of a European to find any charm in it. The figures in an oriental landscape are picturesque on account of their costume, but the entire system of manners is very prosaic. The external form of material existence varies as much as among us in the different classes of society, if not more so; but internal life is the same everywhere. There are seldom any passions here to give it relief. With the system of the constant seclusion of the women, their degradation, their impurity, and their plurality, love is rare, as you may easily suppose. Friendship among brothers is scarcely less so: the respect due from the younger to the elder, checks so familiar a feeling. Violent hatred seldom produces any thing but degrading crimes; and since the introduction of Islamism, I do not believe that the manners of the people have ever differed much from what they are at present. With us it is the manners that create institutions; but the koran is a very different thing from the gospel: it is the book of general law. What variations could manners undergo when modelled upon this immutable law?

I have just made a very extraordinary discovery: I am thirty years of age to-day! The *Annuaire du Bureau des Longitudes* informs us that it is probably half the journey of life; yet it seems as if I was born but yesterday, and these thirty years which have slipped away, appear to me as a dream! After all, as nothing is certain but consciousness, all the rest may perhaps be nothing but a dream. I do not suppose that the *Real Essences* will prove the contrary: I keep to this idea in the hope that the future will be reality and evolve with less speed.

Were it only to afford you pleasure, I would not always remain a bachelor. I subscribe to the perfect wisdom of what you wrote to me on this subject in one of your last letters. Lucilius did not receive more philosophical advice. But philosophy has little to do with the matter: it is not the sufficient reason of the affair; matrimony is a lottery which does not admit of moderate stakes. I have at least this conviction, that the happiness or misery of the rest of my life will depend upon it,—and I am not naturally a gamester! Shall I, when I return to France, still retain the faculty of losing my senses?—and my losing my own senses is not all; it is not even half the miracle to be performed: I shall have to inspire another with the same madness;—and what talisman shall I bring back with me from Asia to work this charm? I shall return to you tolerably worn out for my thirty odd years, without personal attractions, or youth in manners or mind;—I ask you who would notice me? Certainly, a man at my age has left behind him more than half his chances of attracting. Our manners do not admit that degree of familiarity among young people with which I ought to be known to inspire a deep attachment; and in the world as seen by young ladies, what can they perceive either in the men who pass by or even in those who are pointed out to them? Again, here am I thirty years of age, without ever having found out that a girl was not a child. I am fraternally even paternally, disposed towards them—in short every thing which I should not be. They have always returned this feeling! The young English lady, whose fate has interested you for a moment, has written to me since she left India. All her letters are quite filial. At Calcutta she saw me forming exclusively her father's society, while a number of young men, some however not so young as myself, occasionally partook of the hospitality of her family. She has taken me at my word. Have I grown younger since?

The surest way to give a real existence to your castles in the air, would be to carry off, from Cashmere, one of those beauties said to be so common among the Mussulmaun families of rank: it would not be a difficult matter to negociate. But you would find your daughter-in-law so singular a kind of animal in every respect, that you would hasten to make a present of her to the Jardin des Plantes, where I admit that she would be much more in her place than with you. The binding of the *duodecimos* is in general of a deeper colour than that of the Saint Domingo *quartos*. You might say that beyond a certain limit there could be no coquetry in being brown: such is not the opinion in Cashmere, for the darkest blacken one half of their faces and bedaub the other with white, red, and yellow. I beg pardon of the fine ladies of the west, but this daubing is very becoming: it gives the eyes an expression which justifies all the good and bad verses of Arab and Persian poets on their mistresses' eyes.

A gentle breeze is rising, and the sun is just setting behind the mountains. Adieu then, my dear father, for this is the hour of my deliverance. I shall throw myself into the water, which will certainly be very picturesque in the enchanted lake of Cashmere. But when will the time come when I can bathe in prose in the river at Paris?—My escort suffer from the heat a great deal more than I do. As they lie on the turf at the edge of the lake, they look like fish out of water. They curse with all their heart the little strength I have left. As they are no flatterers, my Seikh officer will tell me that I am no less a Secundæur-Beg than an Aflatoune; and the intelligent Mogul who acts as my secretary and cicerone will exclaim, "God is great," and that I am Rustum.

Closed on the 16th of August, as I am mounting my horse for my last excursion into Cashmere. It will occupy five and twenty days. I have only time to embrace you and Porphyre.

TO M. PORPHYRE JACQUEMONT, PARIS.

Camp in the desert mountains which divide Cashmere from Tibet, August 26th, 1831.

THE wind blows furiously, my dear Porphyre; and it will blow much harder to-morrow on the heights which I am going to visit. The cold seizes me here by the feet, at night, as it did last year in Kanawer, and keeps me awake in bed to philosophise on the atmospheric tides of lofty mountain chains. To-night I was indulging in other reflections: I was thinking about the possibility of a visit of Little Tibetans; for they sometimes come a distance of a hundred leagues to plunder a caravan or a paltry village, carrying off men, women, and children as slaves. However, I am well guarded. The chief of this valley, which is about twenty leagues long, has left his castle to follow me, and his cavalcade increases mine considerably. He is a poor devil, nearly starved to death by the extortions of the viceroys of Cashmere. When he is hard pressed he sometimes rebels, and wages war against Runjeet Sing, holding out for six months together, with his two hundred matchlocks, against the Seikh army. I did him the honour of paying him a visit, during which I condescended to drink a cup of tea while he dined with my cicerone and Mogul factotum, and the Mussulmaun commander of my escort of lancers. In honour of me, he is turning his country topsy turvy. He has sent his army on a campaign in the forests, and I hope they will bring me some game for the museum. All this courtesy is interested: it is not from pure love of my Platonic and Socratic wisdom; for my friend Rossoul Mallick hopes through my influence with Runjeet to get released from some heavy arrears due to the treasury of Lahore—*nous verrons*. All the people in this country are not Neal Sings. For instance, my friend the saint at Cashmere, Mohammed Shah Saheb, being informed of the plan of my excursion, sent one of his deputy saints to Rossoul Mallick to act as my quarter-master; and the good-natured man, who does not know how cold it is here, sends me water-melons to refresh me. A good bottle of wine would be more seasonable. After all, the liquid crystal of the fountain is but a stupid drink. I shall need a great deal of virtue not to get tipsy, like the English, when I am Kennedy's guest again. Tea comes to Cashmere by caravans across Chinese Tartary and Tibet. I know not why the caravan tea has any reputation with us; this is absolutely destitute of fragrance, and is prepared for drinking, with milk, butter, salt, and an alkaline salt of a bitter taste. All this produces a turbid, reddish liquid of extraordinary flavour, execrable according to some, and decidedly agreeable according to others: I am of the latter opinion. In Kanawer it is made in another way: after the tea has been boiled for an hour or two, the water is thrown away, and the leaves are dressed with rancid butter, flour, and minced goats' flesh. This makes a detestable ragout; they call it tea. I make mine according to the paternal custom: that is to say, hot water and sugar without any milk; and after taking it, I stretch myself on my bed. It throws me into a perspiration, during which I quickly fall asleep. My Cashmerian *courta*, which is a very bad conductor of caloric, preserves till two or three in the morning that with which I thus charge myself in the evening. This *courta* would be a riddle to you, if I did not tell you that it is a very thick Cashmere robe, a present from Mohammed Shah Saheb. I have likewise discovered that a soft shawl, wrapped round my head and neck, is more comfortable than my round English felt hat and black silk cravat; and I give myself this comfort, which costs nothing, for I have a great number of shawls.

If our friends could get M. Allard's silver cross changed into a gold one, I believe this distinction would make me perfectly happy. I think a recompense is due to those who, at a distance from Europe, have borne the name of Frenchman with honour. I shall write soon, to that effect, to the proper quarter. His name is mentioned with respect throughout the whole of British India, and in this country he gets what is better than respect: there is but one voice with regard to his justice and humanity, as well as his wisdom. If we could be the instrument of the reward of his services in the Punjab, we should thus acquit the debt which he has imposed on me. Do you think it is so difficult to make a knight of the legion of honour, an officer of that order, for the reasons that might be adduced*? Adieu, for to-day; I embrace you. It is night, and dinner-time. The people at Semla are perhaps at this moment drinking my health, for the English take care of their absent friends in that way, or rather take care of themselves under the pretence of absent friends. Woe to those who, like myself, have nothing but spring water to return the compliment! Adieu again, my dear friend; I embrace you with all my heart.

In the valley of Cashmere, at Safapore, September 1*st.*

Here I am returned from the mountains, in every respect delighted with my excursion:—no, I must except the stones. It is a devil of a job sometimes to distinguish between primary and secondary limestones; I have here and there some doubts about them. But I have brought some new plants, and, what is of more consequence, two new animals, or at least one; and this latter is a very respectable quadruped, a species of marmot. My friend Rossoul Mallick's sub-brigands, brought me a bear and a species of chamois, the latter perhaps new; but the rogues, in spite of my strongest injunctions, had so mutilated these animals that I could make nothing of them. As

* M. Allard was nominated an officer of the legion of honour, 5th November, 1832.

I was in a discovering vein, I found out a lake here which nobody has spoken of, and which is the lake of lakes in Cashmere, being the only deep one. I am encamped on its strand. I had splendid weather when I wanted it; that is, when I was in the midst of my excursion at the highest point of the rivers Hydaspes and Indus, between Cashmere and Tibet. Rossoul Mallick has loaded me with kindness throughout; and I have repaid him in good advice with regard to his eating opium like bread, as he does. This morning a letter came from the excellent M. Allard; he announces that the interview between Runjeet Sing and Lord William Bentinck will take place on the left bank of the Sutledge, in a little Seikh district under the rajah's domination. He tells me likewise that the rajah has expressed a wish to see me, to converse about the atmosphere, water, and soil of Cashmere, and more besides, in a manner which does not allow me to decline a second visit to Lahore or Umbritsir. He adds that if this circuit thwarts my mountain projects, it is also necessary for their accomplishment. The country of Koolloo, through which I wish to enter the British Himalaya, is difficult of access, and it will be useful for me to go to court and get a new stock of credit, so that I may travel with facility: "Moreover," says he, "the rajah no doubt intends to fill your pockets as he has your strong box;" so I have just written to the king to tell him that I am now carrying on my last campaign in the mountains, that it will be terminated in about twelve days, and in ten or twelve more I shall leave this country to appear in his sublime presence, according to his wish. I shall give him a map, which I have constructed from numerous bearings taken with the compass, and laid down on a large scale, with the names of the places in Persian characters, and the mountains in horizontal projection, so that he may understand them; and I trust that my second visit to this singular personage will not be less agreeable than the first, without speaking of purse or pocket.

After all, every thing is for the best in the best of possible worlds. With my minerals, plants, beasts and fishes, I should not be able to zig-zag along the Himalaya to the Sutledge. I shall leave these things at Jummoo, the capital of my friend Gulab Sing, who has just written to me. The road from hence across the mountains is tolerably good, that is for pedestrians and horses. At Jummoo I shall find my tent, which, thanks to Providence, M. Allard, and the rajah's camels, I have had sent from Loodheeana. At this period the rajah will probably be at Umbritsir. I shall leave Jummoo in six or seven days, and shall doubtless not quit Umbritsir until the rajah sets out on his journey to the Sutledge. I shall escort my precious baggage so far, and then leave the care of its transport as far as Loodheeana, to M. Allard and the rajah's camels. Equipping myself lightly, I shall again penetrate into the mountains near Mundis (Mundeenagur) where there are some salt-mines which I am very désirous of seeing. I shall take care to avoid a district situated between Jummoo and that province, in which vast forests of bamboo cause dreadful fevers after the autumn. The lower region of the mountains which I wish to visit on leaving Umbritsir, will not be too cold in the month of November. On the first of December I shall certainly cross the Sutledge. I have no time to write to my father. I am writing to you between a basket of grapes as large as those of the Land of Promise, and some excellent pears; I am, moreover, in perfect health. Adieu, my dear friend; I embrace and love you with all my heart. My next will no doubt be either from Lahore or Umbritsir.

TO M. JACQUEMONT THE ELDER, PARIS.

Pergunnah in Cammeradge, in the mountains of Cashmere, on the banks of the Pohour, Sept. 6th, 1831. (*despatched from Sapoor* (*Sampore,*) *Sept.* 11*th,* 1831.

MY DEAR FATHER,—A few days since, I wrote to Porphyre, on my return from the mountains through which it is necessary to pass in going from this country to Ladak; and if my letter proceeds safely through the hands of * * * * (but the list would be too long, so I will omit it,) and if on reaching Chandernagore it finds a ship ready to sail for France, you will already know when you receive this that I have had every reason to be satisfied with the commencement of my last excursion to Cashmere. Since then, I have had additional zoological good fortune, followed it is true by reverses of the same species. Rossoul Mallick, faithful to his promise, turned his mountains and glaciers upside down to find animals for me, and his Afghan greybeards have several times pursued me into the plain to bring me in their game, consisting of monstrous bears, and latterly a species of panther apparently new. A journey of twenty leagues under the sun of the 34th degree of latitude, unfortunately rendered this game so high that, after infinite trouble to make something of it, I have been obliged, not without great regret, to abandon it all. I have thus misspent much time and money; the fault lies, first in the distance between the different places; next in the sun; and lastly in the rain, which is revenging itself for the unusual dryness of the summer at the expense of the beauty of the autumn.

From Safapore, where I was encamped when I closed my letter to Porphyre, I went to the extremity of lake Vooller or Ooller, at Bondehpore. While I was there, dissecting large birds, beasts, and fishes, I was informed of the arrival in my camp of a vakeel or messenger from the king of Little Tibet, and of a neighbouring mountain chief, at open war with the governor of Cashmere. The former I was told brought my lordship presents from the king his master. The other came only to pay his respects; he had two hundred of his mountaineers with him, which much displeased me. Nevertheless, I put a good face upon the matter, and commanded them to wait at a distance, until I was ready to grant an audience to the vizier of Tibet, and the Cashmerian chief. Having resumed my European dress, and majestically seated myself in my chair, under a sort of canopy hastily set up, mats were stretched on the ground, and near me a privileged carpet. My people formed a line on each side, most of them so ragged that you never saw the like in the streets of Paris; and when I was satisfied with the arrangement of my court, the Mussulmann officer of my court went in quest of the vizier. This plenipotentiary was a common-place melo-dramatic brigand as to figure and costume. He repaid me all the salaams which I formerly made to the Grand Mogul, and presented on his knees the king's letter, written in Persian, and filled with roses, narcissuses, and basil, in perpetual bloom in the garden of his friendship for me, which occupied the whole of his majesty's heart. Ahmed Shah had received my answer to his first communication; this time he wrote to me that, in order to please me, he had ordered a general battue throughout his mountains; and that, notwithstanding the season being so unfavourable to hunting, forty-two animals had been taken alive, but most of them wounded; and that all had died a few days after their capture, with the exception of the two which he sent me. His letter enumerated the articles which he offered me under the title of a *khelat* or *dress of honour*, this dress, consisting of three large lumps of rock crystal, eight immense sacks of dried fruit, two young live antelopes, and a piece of the stuff in which his Tibetan majesty dresses himself, made of the tender hair of this species of antelope. He described his envoy as having been his vizier for thirty years, his confidant, and a second himself. Aga Sheragh Ali Shah* (for I would not refuse this singular diplomatic personage any of his titles) was not long in informing me that a confidential mission had been intrusted to him; and as he saw that I was surrounded by spies, he told me that he wished to consult me about a complaint of the rajah's. I invited him to relate it to me there and then, but he told me that it was a disease that could be mentioned only in private. This invention, to remove all the witnesses of a secret interview, was not bad. But when he came to acquit himself of his mission, he had eaten so large a quantity of opium, that he could tell me nothing but that his master was passionately in love with the British (whom he has never seen, and who are at a distance of three hundred leagues from his paltry dominions), and that he was their most obedient servant, and his country theirs, &c. &c. I replied that I felt a strong inclination for Ahmed-Shah, and that with all the tulips, narcissuses, and bunches of roses in the world, I was his unalterable friend.

Two men of my ambassador's suite had been frozen

* Aga, chief; Sheragh, torch; Ali, sublime; Shah, king, in Persian.

to death on the journey; another had his arm broken; a horse had fallen down a precipice. But Sheragh Ali Shah felt so much revivified by the sunshine of my presence as to have no doubt that had he but brought his dead with him, I should have resuscitated them. In fact he gave me my heart's content of local character.

After him, the mountaineer was introduced. He was a man of my own age, perfectly handsome, with a very mild and haughty countenance. I should have loved him with all my heart, but for the two hundred vagabonds he had brought with him; however, in spite of this appendage, he pleased me much. From motives of prudence, I hastened to let him know my kind intentions towards him. I told him that I was a friend of the oppressed and a promoter of peace, that I deplored the state of war and perpetual uneasiness in which he lived, and that if he would promise henceforth to remain in peace, I would ask Runjeet Sing for the liberation of one of his wives and of his daughters, who were captives at Cashmere. He related to me his history, which affected me much, and I certainly will keep my word when I see Runjeet Sing again. But I am convinced that the best way for him to have got his wife and child back, would have been to have carried me as his prisoner into the mountains; and I take it very kindly of him to have left me to be the uncertain instrument of their freedom, instead of making me the assured pledge of it, as he might have done. My design at first was to have visited his mountains, but

I judged it imprudent to prolong the trial of his justice; and I yesterday determined upon continuing my journey round the lake, without penetrating into the valleys which come down to it. Dellaveur-Mallick (that is my new friend's name) accompanied me to the bank of a wide torrent which forms the boundary of his contested domain. In my interest for his safety, I should not have allowed him to have come farther, and was about to prohibit his doing so, when he dismounted to take leave of me. He told me, smiling, that there were no guns truer, nor of a longer range, than those of two mountaineers who always marched by his side; nor was there a sharper sabre or swifter horse than his own. I shall never forget his countenance: it was so handsome, good, and picturesque. Walter Scott could not imagine any thing better.

As for Aga Sheragh Ali Shah, he is nothing at all like a hero of romance; but he is an adventurer, whose stories would be amusing, if the fumes of opium did not obscure them so much. He is a native of Bombay, no doubt of Persian descent; for he is a Sheeah in religion, with a white skin and of low extraction. My Indian servants have found out that he was formerly of their condition. After having changed many times, and travelled from Persia to China, he was retained in Little Tibet by the present rajah, who has actually made him his favourite and minister. He is well known at Cashmere as the principal personage in that country, and moreover as a very good man, but too much of a busy-body. The man first sent by Ahmed Shah, returned this time with Sheragh Ali, whose head servant he is. This man is infinitely better adapted for diplomatic craft than his master, and I think that the rajah has only sent his incomparable Aga Sheragh Ali Shah, to do me honour and add more lustre to his mission; and that Nassim Khan, the servant, will come and make his report when he perceives me alone; for this morning, as he was walking near my house, he showed me in the scabbard of his sabre a small corner of a letter, folded after the fashion of Ahmed Shah's diplomatic messages.

It is impossible for me to comprehend what these people want with the British, whose agent they evidently persist in considering me. Ahmed Shah is unique in his way—a pattern king, though he is not a citizen king. He is very much beloved by his subjects, and dreaded by his neighbours. He freed himself some years ago from a kind of tribute (almost nominal it is true) which Little Tibet used to pay to China. His poverty, and the frightful mountains which divide his country from Cashmere, secure him completely from the ambition of Runjeet Sing. After all, in spite of my diplomatic genius, I cannot make out what he wants! Meanwhile, the individuals composing his embassy gallop or run among my suite, and have already learnt to gather plants and collect insects; and whether the secret mission of the embassy is fulfilled or not, when the horseman arrives from Cashmere, whither I have sent him for three hundred rupees, the *sublime torch* of the Little Tibetan empire will receive his present and dismissal at the same time. I have already replied to Ahmed Shah, repaying him all the flowers of his garden of friendship with interest. I am now going to write to Runjeet Sing to inform him of all: because, if he gets into an ill-humour with Ahmed Shah, he has absolutely no means of injuring him; and I will conceal nothing from Lord William Bentinck, because I am convinced that the political character ridiculously assumed by Mr. Moorcroft in these regions, where he secretly gave out that he was the precursor of British conquest, has been loudly and sincerely disavowed by the British Government. Ahmed Shah, who reigns after the devil's fashion, knows nothing of this denial. There can be no doubt that Mr. Moorcroft made overtures directly to him, and now he persists in taking me for an Englishman, and believing that, like Mr. Moorcroft, I have other objects of curiosity besides the minerals and animals of his country. Mr. Moorcroft's conduct was highly reprehensible: he brought a slur upon British honour among the Asiatics.

For my own part, as I am perfectly innocent of Ahmed Shah's mistake, and as I at first did all that depended upon me to destroy it, I am easily consoled for his not wishing to be undeceived, since without it he would never have acted as my zoological auxiliary. His lumps of crystal have no scientific value; but in

Cashmere, they make vases of it very much esteemed in the East, and I hope to take coffee with you out of his Little Tibetan majesty's cups. I am having an immense dressing-gown made of his royal stuff, which possesses a softness very superior to that of Cashmere shawl; in this I shall do honour to Ahmed Shah's munificence, and in it you will talk excellent metaphysics in winter, for I intend it for you on my return. I shall have one left, less admirably beautiful, but such as no natural or moral philosopher ever wore: it is a present from my friend Mohammed Shah, the saint of Cashmere. I regret that I cannot keep for you one of the sacks of dried apricots out of Ahmed Shah's garden. It is a pity to see them devoured by my people, whose jaws are little used to being exercised on such articles. They are exquisite. All this will cost me twenty-five louis for an *obligato* present to the ambassador; but I shall not regret them if my two animals, which are very young, live long enough to show the character of their species clearly. After all, I have hitherto been playing upon velvet, for I have more than a hundred louis out of Runjeet Sing's rupees.

It would be absolutely impossible for a European of my pursuits to travel in this country under any other conditions than those with which I entered it. I remember certain advice kindly given to me by people who had seen a little corner of the East. Nothing was easier, according to them, than to cross the whole of Asia with heavy baggage: they talk of caravans of merchants,

&c.; it is all pure romance. Merchants, it is true, go almost every where: from Cashmere to Teheran, and even to Mashed, they go through Lahore, Delhi, Bombay, Bushire, Shiraz, &c. &c., without passing through Cabulistan, and for a very good reason. The petty eastern princes use discretion in robbing them, because they will see them again: and if some of the profits of their trading are left them, they are to the chiefs through whose territories they pass, like the miser's goose that laid golden eggs: few are fools enough to kill it. But he who passes without intending to return, is stripped to his last rag; and European travellers of course can claim no exclusive privileges. They have but two alternatives: to travel as beggars, like M. Alexander Csomo de Koros, in the national costume of the country they are crossing, or else to surround themselves with a respectable substantial force, or get credit for having what they cannot in reality procure. Thus, I started on horseback from Calcutta in the evening of the 20th of November 1829, without the slightest immediate protection; at Hoogly, two stages from thence, I acquired a sort of janissary, whose place was supplied at Bardwan by a corporal and four men; I was quite a snow-ball till I arrived on the banks of the Sutledge with a serjeant and twelve men, where I found fifty in readiness to receive me; and although, since that time, I have always had nearly the same number, it was too little sometimes, and would have been so everywhere were it not for the long arms of the powers whose friend I am believed to be. There has been, however, more good luck than address in my ambulating fortunes: for instance, had not chance brought to my camp at the same time, a few days ago, both the king of Little Tibet's envoy and the mountain chief of whom I have spoken, the latter would probably have either plundered me or carried me off prisoner. But in throwing off the yoke of Cashmere, he has become the vassal of Ahmed Shah: he could not therefore venture to harm me in the face of that prince's minister; and, to go farther back, the excellent M. Allard, hearing of me, sent his offers of service all the way from Lahore to the frontiers of China: without him I should never have come here, although without Lord William it would have been equally impossible. My success required a union of acts of kindness, one of which was the effect of mere chance.

Justice in one who has power to be unjust, is a miracle in these regions; at first it is a riddle to the inhabitants, but they are not long in solving it and appreciating it. Throughout the whole viceroyalty of Cashmere, there is no tribunal to settle private disputes upon a basis of equity. But for a month past, people have several times come, and from a distance too, who wished to have me for an arbitrator. They talk of my *adawlut* (justice), which pleases me infinitely. With respect to wisdom, you must know that I have had promotion; Runjeet now calls me

Aristotiles, in addition to my old titles of Aflatoon and Bocrate, (Socrates).

My health has been perfect for the last two months; I am still as thin as ever, but am more hardy and tough. As a proof of strength, I can tell you that I have several times swam an hour and half in still water, without resting, and without any fatigue; I think I could keep up this exercise for four or five hours. This is a great deal more than Leander did. I do not yet well know how to set about breaking five hundred heads with a single blow of an ass's jaw-bone, but my secret is the same as Samson's. What hands would here cut the fatal lock? I should like to see a chorus of Cashmerian country-women make their entrance on the stage of one of our theatres, before the lovers of the Exotic. Night is coming on and my servant is disputing for half my table (which is very small) to place my frugal dinner on. Adieu, then—while writing so familiarly to you about such trifles, I seem only to be separated from you by the bridges; and it is a charming illusion which recals all the serenity of my mind for serious occupation. Adieu, once more, adieu!

8th morning at Baramoola.

Autumn is come with its chilly nights and cold mornings; it is the same as ours in favourable seasons, except the sun, which, in the middle of the day, is much hotter, and still nearly vertical. Yesterday evening, I dismissed the vizier, who is gone back to Little

Tibet with all his suite. Immediately after his departure, I wrote a long letter to king Runjeet Sing. (You no doubt curse the irregularity of my orthography of Asiatic names; it is because they are very difficult, if not impossible, to write in our European languages,—at least those that I can use. The English write *Runjeet.* We ought to write *Rounedgite*, or *Raunedgite*, or *Reunidgite*; but neither *o*, nor *a*, nor *e*, does the business, although *o* is the nearest approximation to the Persian sound. As for the word which the English write *Sing*, if they pronounced according to the analogies of their idiom, it would be *Singe*. What comes nearest in French is *cygne, cygnus*. The name of this country for us, is exactly *Câchemir*, or in English *Cashmere*. *Delhi* is written a thousand different ways by the English, none of which is the correct one. The best in English would be *Dellee*, and in French *Delli*. The English mode at present is, to write *Bunarus* for the *Bénarès* of the French; in French we ought to write *Bênârèsse*. As for the final *an*, in Teheran, Ispahan, Burdwan, &c., this sound, very easy of imitation to all Europeans, neither exists nor can be written either in French English, or Italian. The Indian and Persian *am*, like *an*, is unpronouncable by one who has not heard it from the mouth of a native. The final *ghur* of many names of places in the English maps, is a stupidly literal translation of the Persian: it is nearly *queur* in French, as in the word *liqueur:*

gueur, *abad*, *poor*, *nagur*, all signify habitation; here I close my parenthesis). I have written then at some length to Runjeet Sing, relating my little adventure to him. I think my letter will amuse him; part of its contents at least will, I am sure, be very much to his taste: this part consists of some pills of the extract of cantharides.

I had forgotten to acknowledge the receipt of young Robinet's note before. I received it at the source of the Hydaspes seven weeks ago. It has given me a very high opinion of that young man; but what is to be done with him here? It would doubtless not be easier for me to be useful to him at Calcutta. I know few belonging to the commercial circles of that great city: I am, properly speaking, acquainted only with Mr. James Calder, a rich Scotch merchant of great zeal for the sciences: the houses of the rest are formed like his. The clerks destined to rise are nephews or cousins who are sent for from Europe very young, at sixteen or eighteen. The others are native Hindoos or Portuguese, a mixed breed between the ancient Portuguese conquerors and the Indians. All children born in India of Europeans in easy circumstances are sent, at six or seven years of age, to England for education. There is only one French house at Calcutta, that of M. Bonaffé; which the English do not count, it being of very small extent. I know no example of a Frenchman having made a fortune in India by the means to be used by M. Robinet. There are a certain number who came to Calcutta with a small venture in goods, and perhaps with some honesty. After being ruined by bankruptcy, robbery, or a law-suit, they are detained in India by the impossibility of paying for their return to Europe. They live upon the profits of a small clandestine and fraudulent brokerage. I know of their existence only from the police reports, inserted in the newspapers, and in which their names appear. I should therefore advise the young gentleman not to think any more of this country. Having been consulted from Calcutta, concerning the chance of a favourable establishment in that city, by a young physician who was recommended to me by M. Victor de Tracy, I hastened to answer him from Benares, where I then was, that the best thing he could do would be to leave it as soon as possible. Tell M. Robinet, moreover, that what I have seen in other foreign countries of the existence of our countrymen, who go there to make their fortunes, has sufficed to convince me that the great majority of them are very unfortunate at New York; and it is the same at Rio Janeiro and Bourbon. I entreat him to prefer the mediocrity of his present station to the very improbable chances of a better fortune at a distance from our country.

Sampore in Cashmere, Sept. 10th.

Yesterday evening, I received a courier from the king, with a direct invitation for me to repair to him. I might have required pressing, but that would have looked ill; and, although annoyed at leaving Cashmere a fortnight sooner than I had at first determined upon, I have answered his Seikh majesty that in ten days I shall resume my route towards the Punjab. I shall have to travel rapidly to join Runjeet Sing at Umbritsir, before he leaves it for Rooper (Ropur). Look for this village on the left bank of the Sutledge, at the foot of the mountains near Belaspore. It is the place appointed for the interview between the rajah and the governor-general, which will take place, with the greatest possible pomp, on the 25th of October. Wade and Kennedy ask if I shall be present there. Certainly not. A poor devil of an *Aflatoane*, a *Bocrate*, an *Aristotelis*, like me, would be stifled by the clouds of dust raised by the contact of two such great powers. Then this eastern magnificence is, after all, nothing but a display of rich dresses, where the person is reckoned good for nothing but to fold drapery upon, or button splendid costumes on. I shall therefore leave the rajah's court only to re-enter the mountains near Koolloo, in order to visit the iron and salt mines at Mondi; and shall thus, on my return to Semla, have an opportunity of becoming acquainted with your favourite, Belaspore. Lord William renews, through Kennedy, all kinds of offers of services to facilitate my progress, whatever it may be, in my next campaign. I shall go from hence to Umbritsir by the pass of Pyr, Punjal, Radjouri, and Jummoo, where I shall again see the rajah Gulab Sing, who received me so well at Pindaden Khan in the month of April last. I am perfectly well, but over head and ears in business and can write to nobody to-day. Adieu, my dear father; I embrace you and Porphyre with all my heart.

TO M. JACQUEMONT THE ELDER, PARIS.

Djamon (Jummoo in the English maps,) October 3rd, 1831.

My dear Father,—I have at length quitted the mountains. I left Cashmere on the 19th of September. The stupid Seikh who is at present in possession of the privilege of plundering that unhappy country (at the expense no doubt of disgorging into Runjeet Sing's treasury at the end of his government) came the day before, to pay his visit of leave; he brought me, on the part of the king, a khelat, or dress of honour, of the value of fifteen hundred rupees (four thousand francs). After his visit, I went to pay one to my neighbour Mohammed Shah Sahib, whose birth, reputation for wisdom, and sanctity, allowed me to pay him that honour without derogating. There is no sort of attention which I did not receive from this excellent man. I was almost obliged to be angry with him when I left him, in order to make him keep a horse and some porcelain vases, which he wished to make me accept. I would take nothing but a very plain though handsome cup, out of which I shall have great pleasure in drinking coffee some day at Paris. There are good people everywhere, and it is my good fortune to meet with them at all the places where I make any stay: it will be delightful to me to recollect them.

Although I had fixed the day of my departure a week before hand, Sheikh Bodher Bochs, my mehmandar, was not ready. This man is no worse than the other Seikh officers, but I hate him more, because, from the time he has been with me, I am better acquainted with him. He bought six women at Cashmere, two of whom he married before the mollah, and it was the difficulty of transporting them beyond the mountains which detained him in the city. He asked me for a day's respite. I was inexorable; and on the 19th, as I had at first fixed, I mounted my horse at day-break, and took the road to the south. My caravan was much more numerous than on my arrival. Sixty soldiers formed my escort; fifty mountaineer porters carried my baggage, a few captive animals were led in the rear. A confidential officer of my friend Mohammed Shah rode behind me; the Mogul, who had served as my secretary and cicerone during my stay, followed me also. The day before, I made him a present of five and twenty louis, the well-merited reward of his good services; the poor fellow, to whom justice was quite a novelty, and who, I think, was sincerely attached to me, would have followed me anywhere. He hopes, with some chance of success, that by presenting and recommending him to Runjeet Sing, I shall make his fortune. As Bodher Bochs assured me that he would rejoin my camp at the second stage, I left, through forgetfulness, all Runjeet Sing's firmans with him; but he neither appeared at the second nor the third night's bivouac, and I doubt whether he will rejoin me before I reach Umbritsir. There was perhaps some rashness on my part in throwing myself headlong into the mountains without any mehmandar; but I thought that, in case of obstacles arising, I might show Runjeet-Sing's last letter, in which he presses me to go to him. This ensurer of respect remained useless in my secretary's pocket. It has turned out that some pervanahs or firmans, addressed in my name by myself to the chiefs through whose territories I was to pass, have caused me to meet with the desired reception from them. The rajah of Radjouri, who is bed-ridden with a painful disorder, sent his eldest son to meet me; this young man brought me apologies for his father, unable to come himself. The rajah lodged me in the most picturesque turret of his castle. As a unique exception, this rajah enjoys the reputation of being just and learned. I went to see him without ceremony, and remained more than an hour sitting on his bed near him, talking to and comforting him. I could do no better, for I had no remedies either to give or to prescribe for him.

I had at first resolved to descend from Radjouri to Jummoo straight across the mountains; but the rajah drew me such a picture of the difficulties of this route and its insecurity, that I changed my mind and came to Bimbur. There, I entered the plains of the Punjab. But I had already found its climate again at Radjouri, and even at Tunna, whither I descended in a day and a half's march from the summit of Pyr Pendjal. This rapid and immense change of climate has not even affected my skin; but several of my people have experienced fatal effects from it. One of my horsemen caught, at Radjouri, the terrible fever of the lower mountains, which almost always kills its victim after exhausting for a year or two by continued suffering. My antelopes from Little Tibet died of the heat at Bimbur. In order not to do as they did, I left off my flannel, and I find that it is comparatively very agreeable to perspire in cotton clothes. It is very odd that this Indian heat (for the Punjab is India,) which every one calls so enervating, does not oppress me in the least. It fires my skin a little as it would the skin of any one else; but I feel myself as cool within, and as vigorous as on the mountains of Cashmere, if not more so. In order to reach this place from Bimbur in three stages, I was obliged to be on horseback fourteen or fifteen hours a day; and besides, I watched during the night, for it would not have been safe to sleep. The tribes at the foot of the mountains in these districts could never be reduced by Runjeet Sing. They frequently descend into the plains, often in very numerous bands, imitating the exploits of Walter Scott's Scotch Highlanders, and Fauriel's klephts, sparing only their more immediate neighbours, who, I think, go halves with them. I was afraid of being betrayed by the latter. Had I known beforehand the risks of this route, I should certainly have taken another; for I think nothing is more silly for a man of my profession, than to get a gun-shot in a night skirmish, and thus end his days like a dog, without the smallest flower being thrown upon his tomb. Yesterday I left those dangers behind me by crossing the Chinab. I expected to find the rajah Gulab Sing here, to whom I had written to announce my approaching arrival. I was therefore a little disappointed to learn, on going up to Jummoo, that the rajah had left his capital two days previously, and was encamped at a distance of ten coss on the Umbritsir road. However, as he was to lend me a large tent, and camels to go to Runjeet Sing, I persisted in coming here. Gulab Sing is better obeyed at a distance than Runjeet Sing. His vizier received me as his master's friend. All that I can desire comes as it were by enchantment. Plenty is in my camp; soldiers, servants, highland porters, are all lodged at the rajah's expense. The poor fellows had great need to pass through this land of plenty after the privations and fatigues they have endured since we left Cashmere. The rajah's eldest son, who has remained here to receive me in his father's absence, wished to come and see me last night on my arrival. He is a boy of fifteen, a favourite of Runjeet Sing's. I received him only to-day. He interested me with his charming countenance and his modesty; at this age when children are opening into manhood, and the chance of what they will become is on the point of being decided, they interest me extremely. I therefore promised little Gulab Sing to remain here over to-morrow, in order to spend the morning with him on an elephant's back, in seeing the environs of Jummoo, and preaching morality to him without his perceiving it. The day after to-morrow, on the road to Umbritsir, I shall repay to the father the visit I received from the son. Gulab Sing, who expected me by the direct road from Radjouri, sent one of his viziers with a palanquin and bearers, and a small army to meet me. The young rajah presented me with a purse of three hundred and fifty rupees. Eight months ago I should have thought this proceeding very brutal. Being now well acquainted with the manners of the country, I should on the contrary have been offended if he had come empty-handed, as also if he had not left his shoes at the door of my tent. I am become quite insensible to the pleasure of winning in the lottery of Punjab politeness, because money on this side of the Sutledge goes as it comes, and perhaps still faster.

Yesterday I made a duplicate of my map of Cashmere, on which I write all the names in Persian; it is the present which I intend for Runjeet Sing.

As I was descending the Pyr Pendjal, I received a courier from Runjeet, who brought me, along with a letter from the king, a packet from Semla, containing one from Lord William Bentinck, in answer to the thanks I had expressed to the Governor-general for the reception which his powerful recommendation caused me to meet with from Runjeet. Lord William wishes to leave me all the merit of my success.

Here follows what he writes to me: I copy this letter instead of sending it you, because his writing is rather illegible, and, being in English, I think it not familiar enough to you for you to be able to make it out.

"*Semla, Sept. 5th*, 1831.

"My dear Sir,—I have not acknowledged the receipt of your last letter, for which I beg to apologise. It gives me great pleasure to find that your accueil by Runjeet-Sing has been satisfactory. It must be mainly due to your own address. You have the *singular* merit of having *at once* (veni, vidi, vici) conquered the distrust of that most wary politician. You must have suffered great fatigue and privation in the course of your present expedition. The thanks and applause of the scientific world will be your best reward. I was in hopes Captain Kennedy had sent you our last intelligence from Europe, but I find that he made you but a partial report. I send you therefore a copy of what has been received from Bombay. I have also seen a letter from a friend of mine, but not addressed to me, who left Paris the second week in April; he gives a favourable account of the stability of things in France, of which my correspondent remarks a less favourable opinion generally prevailed in England. We expect daily a ship which was to leave England on the eleventh of May.

"We have also still to come the *Circassian*, that left England in the beginning of April, and which contains the missing French papers, which shall be forwarded to you as soon as received. Lady William desires me to present her kind remembrances to you. I shall always be happy to afford you every assistance in my power.

"I remain with much respect and esteem,

"Dear sir, your faithful servant,

"W. C. BENTINCK."

Lord William joined to this letter a manuscript copy of a Russian newspaper, which came by way of Persia, and informs us of the great news of the dissolution of the British Parliament, and the *statu quo* of the armed peace of Europe. Is it not strange that I should be better informed about European affairs, though alone in the midst of the mountains of Cashmere, than the inhabitants of Calcutta on the same day? However, the politics of Europe have for some time interested me less—they hang fire too long.

This evening I delivered a decision, which has gained me the reputation of a Suliman, (Solomon,) at Jummoo. My secretary came to complain that one of the soldiers of the escort had stolen his shawl. I did what the meanest scribe in India or the Punjab never deigns to do in such a case. I went to the spot, thirty steps from my tent; there I interrogated the witnesses and the defendant, and was easily convinced of the latter's guilt. The commander immediately inquired if it was my pleasure that he should be hanged, or have his nose and ears cut off. I ordered that to-morrow, during my absence, before the assembled troop, a man of the lowest caste should break the prisoner's sabre and gun into pieces, and give him a hundred blows with a stick; after which my servant will give him a month's pay, in order that he may leave the country, from which he will be ignominiously driven. I am afraid the rascal will immediately buy a sabre with the five rupees he will receive after his punishment, and turn highway-robber; but if he does so, Gulab Sing's police has a good chance of catching him before long, and my responsibility ends there. There are no prisons in this country; I shall suggest to Gulab Sing the idea of establishing some in his dominions, and to substitute forced labour for the cruel mutilations so frequently inflicted by Eastern justice Good night, my dear father. The rest at Umbritsir.

Jummoo, 4th evening.

This is to thank you, my dear father, for your excellent and charming letter of last February, No. 24, which a courier from M. Allard has just brought me, together with one from Porphyre, a packet of very recent Calcutta papers, and a letter from my banker, who has received authority from MM. Delessert and

Delaroche, to increase my annual credit six thousand francs for this year, and three thousand for the year 1830; thus making an increase of nine thousand francs for this year, and extending it to twelve thousand for the years 1832 and 1833. So this year I have the fifteen thousand francs which I wished.

Your No. 23 is still wanting, which makes some passages of your No. 24 obscure. I hope my letters from Upper Kanawer, and from Spiti or Tibet, will have reached you a short time after those from Semla and Tchini; and that the continuation of my correspondence up to this day has confirmed your faith in my luck. Seeing me so near Leh or Ladak—for it is all one on the map—you expressed a wish that I should extend my expedition thither. Your ambition then will have been a little disappointed in seeing me return to the high valley of the Spiti without having been there; but you would have pitied me for the cold and hunger which I should have had to suffer, if I had persisted in going to Ladak—not to speak of obstacles of a different description. Pinkerton, whom you were going to read under the heads "Chinese Tartary and Tibet," will no doubt have given you an idea of the lamas (pronounce the word *lommmmmma*) and terrible Tartars, very different from the reality. You seemed to regret much that I could not see Cashmere. I hope I have acted like a dutiful son! have I not? If you had known all the difficulties of that expedition, you would never have thought of my making it, and would have believed it absolutely impracticable. Many of my English friends, well able to estimate these difficulties, Kennedy for instance, when he knew that I was at Lahore, still did not believe that I should succeed in getting to Cashmere. I do not know who the modern traveller is you speak of, who has given the Cashmerians so bad a character. Forster is the only one who has visited it since Bernier; he was there fifty years before me, but in disguise; and no one before me wore the dress or bore the character of a European. Cashmere is nevertheless very near British India, two hundred leagues distant at most, and its celebrity has constantly excited the ambition of British travellers. I am forgetting Mr. Moorcroft, who perished miserably a short time after he left it.

I laughed a great deal at your conjectures as to the means I should be obliged to employ to raise the money necessary for my last year's campaign. The Great Mogul is not so great as you imagine. He does not tie a trinket worth a thousand crowns to any one's hat. Being reduced to a sort of stage king, he takes care to dress in mere stage trumpery those whom he honours with a khelat. But Runjeet Sing does things in a different manner. I am truly ashamed of the enormous bale of Cashmere shawls with which my baggage has been increased during the last seven months; though if my money should happen to run short during the remainder of my journey, they would prove an important resource. I really do not yet know what I shall do with them. I should like to be able to take them with me to Europe, with my animals, plants and minerals; they would serve as presents which I should like to make to the wives of my friends. But how could I get them passed through the custom-house?

My letters last winter expressed the enthusiasm with which the revolution inspired me, and the bitter regret I have sometimes felt at being so far from France at that memorable period. Since then my opinion concerning those great events has much changed. It has been modified, like your own, in proportion as I saw so many base, absurd, and ignoble consequences proceed from so noble a principle. I see many people speak in the tribune of the events of the great week, as being their handy-work, as if they had fired a gun in the streets with the working mechanics, and as if it was not solely by the muskets of these mechanics that the revolution was achieved. The hostile tone of all parties in the chamber is a deplorable error. Shall I tell you, my dear father, that I sometimes regret not being a deputy? I know not whether I am strangely deceiving myself; but it appears to me that an honest man, who would play the part of mediator, without art or craft, and simply by showing the acute pain he suffers from these bitter dissensions between men so long united, and the misfortunes with which they threaten the country, would not speak in vain. The artifices of logic in what is termed the eloquence of the tribune, are too far-fetched: they almost always wound the self-love of those against whom they are exercised. Too great pains are taken to convince, and not enough to persuade. Some aim at oratorical display; I wish they would aim at touching the feelings: this is what I should try to do, if I were in the chamber under present circumstances. Can what is easy in a *tête-à-tête*, or in a small company, be so very difficult in a numerous assembly? Mistakes and differences may arise between honourable men; but they must be very blind, and their advisers very bad, if these quarrels are not soon terminated by a sincere reconciliation, and the mutual friendship and esteem of the parties rendered more firm than ever. All parties have wrongs to complain of from one another, and these wrongs are daily aggravated by the deplorable obstinacy with which each shuts himself up within the circle of his own peculiar views. Rather than be the impotent witness of these fatal dissensions in our own country, I prefer being at the extremity of Asia, removed from them by space and thought.

On my return into British India, it shall be my first care to write a long letter to the Jardin des Plantes, on the results of my expedition to Cashmere. I never had less leisure than since I crossed the Sutledge. I have necessarily had a multitude of relations with the people of the country through which I was passing, such as no other European traveller could, even if he wished it, have any opportunity of forming with those of British India: hence many hours stolen from my work. Sometimes I had measures of safety to take; sometimes visits to receive and politeness to show. I cannot pass in silence and *incognito*. Yesterday, for instance, I could not excuse myself from losing a couple of hours with the little rajah in visiting the neighbourhood of his capital. Had I been on horseback alone, I could have made the survey in less than an hour. To-day I am encamped near his father, Gulab Sing. While I was peaceably jogging along the plain, on my way hither from Jummoo (nine coss), looking through my spectacles at all the plants, which I held close to my nose in order to discover the new ones, one of Gulab Sing's officers came to meet me and compliment me in his master's name. I am resting a little, waiting for my breakfast; it is past noon, and I have been six hours on horseback. Then comes the ceremony of the moulakat or visit of the rajah, who will condescend to come first. I shall have to return his politeness. If he leaves me late, it will be almost impossible to-day, &c. &c. In India it is quite different. Many an English officer has served fifteen years in India, and travelled all over the Peninsula, without having any intercourse with the people of the country except such of them as are his attendants. Such a line of conduct, which is exceedingly common in the European community inhabiting and governing India, would be highly improper for doing what I am on the point of terminating: I mean making my way in a country where all is not open before me. My caravan having now re-entered India, and marching silently along the roads, will have all the appearance of a funeral, in which I shall act the corpse; and I shall certainly find the change very agreeable.

Apropos of death and funerals—the plague is making terrible ravages in Persia, especially in the southern and coast provinces of the gulf; very severe sanatory measures have been adopted at Bombay, Madras, and Calcutta, against Arab vessels coming from Busheer, Muscat, and Jedda. This terrible disease has never yet appeared in India. The cholera morbus reigns with fury at Benares, and the towns on the banks of the Ganges, below Patna, Dynassour, &c.

In one of your former letters you regretted that I had not taken a doctor's degree, that I might add the weight of that dignity to any report on the frightful malady of which India is the classic seat. But—but truly I should be very much embarrassed, quite as much as Pariset was to discourse pertinently on the plague in Egypt, and for the same reason,—for hitherto I have neither seen, nor had an opportunity of seeing, a single case of cholera morbus. At St. Domingo, and in the United States, I met with the same disappointment with respect to the yellow fever. I strongly suspect that this will be my lot with the plague.

I have just learned from the Calcutta papers, the death of a Piedmontese traveller, called Count di Vidua, who, for two years, travelled through India in a palanquin, proceeded thence to China, and afterwards to the Moluccas, on his way to New Holland. He was, I imagine, a mere tourist, with a more decided taste for heaps of stones, and old bits of brick, than for any other kind of observation. He had the awkwardness, I was going to say folly, to tumble into a boiling bog, whence the hot mineral springs of Java arise, and he died from the effects of his scalding. From his manner of acting in all things, according as I have been told, I could have wagered that M. Vidua would never see Turin again. Pliny is excusable for the fatal curiosity which cost him his life; he certainly died in a most picturesque manner for a natural philosopher. But for a poor devil of an Italian antiquary to go and get boiled in Java—what business had he there?

I am going to make arrangements with M. Cordier of Chandernagore about the forwarding of my collections to France. During the winter, they will go down the Jumna and the Ganges from Delhi to Chandernagore. I think it better to trust to the improbable chance of shipwreck than to the certainty of the accidents incidental to land carriage.

Porphyre makes you forget all your philosophy: you would have him lose his identity; well, "*trahit sua quemque voluptas*," and his *voluptas* is to be unsociable. There are few as innocent as he; and if, as times go, every one like him would remain secluded, either from humour, taste, or modesty, public affairs would go on all the better for it. The mild and gay nature of his thoughts, is a proof that he would gain nothing in changing his ways; besides, people seldom change much at forty, and however extraordinary it may seem, Porphyre has leaped this terrible ditch. When, after dinner, we all take a walk together to the Tuileries, our group will no longer be that of father Horace, as it was ten years ago at the Luxemburg.

Djessur, or Jusser, on the banks of the Ravee, or Hydroates, October 8th.

This time, my dear father, I am writing you a journal, and not a letter. The rajah paid his visit three days ago; and, as I expected, rather late. We talked about his mountains, Cashmere, the immortality of the soul, steam-engines, then the soul again, the universe, &c. &c. Gulab Sing was so pleased with these physics and metaphysics, that we kept it up pretty late in the night by the light of my excellency's torches and candles, which furnished my Rajpoot philosopher with more than one comparison and idea. I decidedly like that man ; and my reason for it is that he seems to like me. The rajah earnestly besought me to remain a whole day with him ; and I consented, on condition that I should march during the night in order to make up for the loss of a day. The day before yesterday, in the morning, I went to him just as he was getting out of bed, and we remained conversing until they came to tell us that the preparations for the chace were complete—for it was a settled point that we should hunt. Two towers had been built, in a neighbouring forest, with the branches and foliage of trees. We each took our station in one of them, while the rajah's cavalry, entering the wood on all sides, drove the game towards us. I killed a wild hog. I must have been born with very little taste for the chase, for this did not give me the slightest pleasure, although it was my first piece of good luck with wild hogs. The rajah's Brahminee cooks, who were on horseback, *improvised* a Rajpoot breakfast out of the produce of our sport, which was truly excellent, and was served up in large baskets, filled with little dishes made of leaves. Runjeet Sing himself has no other table service.

Our Mussulmaun people and horsemen, and some of the Hindoo castes, took to their heels when they saw the roasted hog, which they hold in as great abomination as the domestic pig: a horror shared by the Rajpoots of Hindoostan. I spent the day at a short distance from our hunting ground, in the rajah's camp, where tents had been prepared for me. Gulab Sing sent me his presents there: an excellent and beautiful white horse, caparisoned in the most splendid manner after the Seikh fashion, and a khelat, with Cashmere shawls, &c. I went to take leave of him; and found, as he had done the day before, so much pleasure in my visit, that I should be there now, had he not himself, at the approach of night, made me start. I reached Zafferval in the middle of the night; I was there agreeably surprised by meeting a European, the first I had seen for seven months. An old Italian artillery officer, a friend of M. Allard's, and who, like him, has been several years in Runjeet's service, received me at Zafferval, where he was himself encamped. He is governor of this province, and he loaded me with friendly and flattering attentions. He told me a multitude of things which a traveller would never discover in this country. I was obliged to spend the whole of yesterday with him. To-night, he accompanied me on horseback seven coss from our camp, and I afterwards went on alone as far as the banks of the Ravee, which my caravan has just crossed. I shall cross it to-morrow at day-break, with my light troops, and the day after to-morrow I shall be at Umbritsir with the good M. Allard.

The Italian told me too much. Had he known me beforehand, and been desirous of some friendship on my part, he would have left me in ignorance of the necessary means to enforce command in this frightful country. Gulab Sing no doubt does still worse; but his father did the same. I shall feel real pleasure in continuing my tour in India, on Gulab Sing's horse; because he did not give it to me merely from etiquette, but evidently as a token of remembrance. Is not this familiar friendship with a demi-savage of the Himalaya, very curious? I should scarcely have dreamt of it when I landed at Calcutta two years ago. I believe that this luck in travelling proceeds, on both sides of the Sutledge, from the same principle. I have preserved entire the nationality and individuality of my thoughts. With the English I did not become stiff like themselves: with the Asiatics I avoid the cold complimentary style habitual to them. I translate my French ideas and personal feelings into the language of both: in short, I retain my identity, as much as I can, in the fetters of a foreign idiom.

You ask if the Indian chief-justice Sir Charles Grey, is any relation to Earl Grey, the British prime minister. He is, but opposed to him in politics. Sir C. Grey is about to retire, after his ten years' judicial services, which give him a right to a pension for life of 50,000 francs (2000*l.*) It is said that Mr. Pearson will succeed him. It is natural that Lord Brougham should dispose of the vacancy in his favour, for Mr. Pearson is his intimate friend: his age, reputation, and knowledge of Indian judicial affairs, acquired since he has filled the office of advoçate-general, give him also great right to this high dignity.—Good night.

Between the Beas and the Sutledge, at Captain Wade's Camp, October 19th.

I stayed a week at Umbritsir, with the excellent M. Allard. The second day after my arrival, I had an audience of Runjeet Sing, without witnesses. Guess what he offered me?—the vice-royalty of Cashmere! I ridiculed both him and his proposal, which was, no doubt, only a stratagem to know my mind. He pleased me still more than when I passed through Lahore—of course on account of his caresses. I found that I had changed my title at the Seikh court, and that instead of *Jakman Sahib Bahadur*, I was now known by every one as the *Aflatoon el Zeman.* Captain Wade, with two other officers of my acquaintance, arrived at Umbritsir three days after me. He came, on the part of the Governor-general, to accompany Runjeet Sing through his dominions to Rooper, on the left bank of the Sutledge, the place appointed for the interview of the two potentates. I met him again with great pleasure. It was the festival of the Unlocked, and I saw Asia in all its picturesque pomp. Wade invited me to join him, and since that day I partake of all the privileges of the British commission. On the eve of the festival, the king had the kindness to have me shown the famous tank of Umbritsir, in the centre of which is the golden temple, in which they preserve the *Grant*, or sacred book of the Seikhs. The fanaticism and madness of the Akhalis or religious warriors, who always crowd into this sacred place, would threaten any European visitant with almost certain danger, if he had not a strong guard. It was not wanting on this occasion. I went to the temple on an elephant, with a strong escort of Seikh cavalry, the animal on which I was mounted, pushing the formidable Akhalis to the right and left, without hurting any of them; and the temple was occupied by a regiment of Seikh infantry. In its precinct I paid a visit to an old man, celebrated for his sanctity; he was waiting for me, as was likewise the governor of the town, an equally respectable old man, who was there by the king's order, to conduct me through the temple. He took me by the hand, and led me all over it. If he had let me go, the Akhalis would no doubt have done me some ill turn; but I was sacred while under the arms of the old Dessa Sing. At night-fall, the temple, being already lighted with lamps, presented the image of Pandemonium. I humbly offered the *Grant* a nuzzer of three hundred rupees, being part of what the king had made me a present of the day before; and I received a small khelat in return. The Unlocked is a Hindoo festival, and the greatest of all. The Seikhs celebrate it with still greater noise and splendour than their ancestors and Hindoo brethren. On that day Runjeet reviewed his army. I seated myself with Wade, by the king's side, in a magnificent tent, pitched on a platform, in the middle of the plain of Umbritsir. All the chiefs of the Seikh court came to do homage to the king, and then the army marched past us: it resembled a good deal the armies described by the historians and poets of antiquity; and for this once the reality far surpassed my expectations.

The next day (the day before yesterday), the king struck his camp at day-break, and departed with Captain Wade. I could not leave M. Allard soon enough to join the royal cavalry on the road, and did not reach Wade's tents till the evening. Henceforth I shall not leave them, in order that I may not be lost in the frightful melée before which the king appears to flee, and which is in reality following him contrary to his wish. The Aflatoon el Zeman, yesterday morning, on an elephant, walking side by side with that of Runjeet

Sing, discoursed to him like an oracle. As there was no longer the smallest plant to pick up in the sandy and arid plains which we were crossing, I did not regret not being able to stop according to my fancy. However, thinking I saw one to-day, I made my elephant kneel down without ceremony, and descended from it to have a nearer sight of a plant which I recognised, and neglected on being better acquainted with it. Every body stopped with me; you see what privileges Aflatoons enjoy.

I ought not to forget to tell you that I received at Umbritsir two equally long and friendly letters from Mr. Pearson and M. de Melay. The former sends me word that he is shortly expecting his daughter, whose health is completely re-established, and who is returning, without Mrs. Pearson, to bear him company at Calcutta for the rest of the time he has to remain there.

Hatteli, in the mountains between the Beas and the Sutledge, October 28th.

In the evening of the twenty-first, I took my last leave of Runjeet Sing at Ooshearpore. During the morning's march, while on horseback near him, we chatted about my projected journey to Mondi, which I am at present performing; and he had the candour (a rare virtue with him) to confess that the wretched rajah of Mondi was the most refractory of his mountain Rajpoot vassals. He is always obliged to send an army of eight or ten thousand men every year, in spring, to receive the slender tribute of a hundred thousand rupees. Nevertheless he gave me hopes that, with a little address, his firmans to the rajah, and the assistance of an old Seikh officer, a trusty man, whom he added to my escort, I might succeed in my undertaking. Our last interview was long and very friendly: Runjeet lavished a thousand caresses on me; he took my hand and shook it several times at my well-aimed broadsides of flattery, in which, without seeking it, I infused a degree of feeling. I was embarrassed with his exclusive attentions, on account of his neglect of the British officer commanding Wade's escort, who was visiting him with me. But, with the Asiatics, the English are so awkward, and so unsociable, that I am not surprised at it. They have only *yes and no* to say for themselves, and Runjeet likes to be amused. It was quite dark when I left the king, giving him all sorts of wishes for his glory and prosperity in this world and the next, and taking away with me a magnificent khelat in exchange for those gilded words. On returning to my hut, I found that, in addition, the king had sent me a present of five hundred rupees. Wade, with whom I afterwards supped for the last time, gave me a firman in his own fashion for the rajah of Mondi, who being near the English frontier, will, I trust, act up to its tenour.

It required, I assure you, all my love of minerals to make me leave the pleasures and security which

I found in his society, and again throw myself alone into the mountains. I expected to encounter some difficulties, and have not been mistaken. From the third day of my journey, I had to traverse the pontifical states of the Punjab, a small mountainous district, inhabited and governed by a centenarian, the spiritual head of the Seikhs, who not a long time ago, in a transport of rage against his eldest son—an ambitious youth of eighty—got upon his feet, and without a word's warning, cut off this son's head with a single blow of his sabre. From motives of policy, Runjeet pays this terrible old fellow every mark of respect. I thought that I should appease the Cerberus by throwing him a cake of a hundred rupees. But I was obliged to pass his fortress without being allowed to enter it, lest it should be defiled; and while I was encamped a few leagues further on, near the last village on his frontier, an order came for me to evacuate his holiness's territory forthwith. As his heralds were terrible akhalis, carrying long guns and matches ready lighted, I did not require to be told twice. I therefore pitched my tent in a valley separated from his dominions by a small chain of mountains. I here thought myself in a friendly country, because I was in the vicinity of one of the fortresses belonging to Sheer Sing, Runjeet's son; but the next morning, as I was about to mount my horse in order to continue my route, my old Seikh officer Kadja Sing, showed me, with an embarrassed air, a score of vagabonds posted in front of my camp with their guns shouldered barring my passage. My horsemen proposed breaking through them by charging with their lances; a silly proposal, which I rejected, with a shrug of my shoulders. Instead of doing this, I wrapped myself up in my splendid dressing gown of white flowered Cashmere shawl, established myself comfortably in my arm-chair, and set about smoking my cigar and drinking a drop of brandy, as a preservative against the mountain fever. In this commodious attitude I played off a little diplomacy with the enemy. Eight months ago this adventure would have puzzled me very much; but being now well acquainted with these customs, I perceived that it was only one of the most vulgar common-places of Punjabee manners. Some day or other by the fireside I will give the details of this negociation; suffice it for you at present to know, that, after a good deal of parley with my two officers, the hostile chief consented to approach me, and I complimented him on his vigilance, ordering him to call his people, upon whom I bestowed the same eulogiums; and that to their great amazement, I, with a majestic and patronising air, bestrode my white horse, bidding them adieu with a slight wave of my hand. They answered with a most respectful salaam, stammering forth some excuses (I do not yet know what for) and witnessed my departure, as confounded as so many geese, while my baggage passed forward. I came hither in three days, marching like a conqueror.

Here, however, I was obliged to stop, in order to treat with the rajah of Mondi, who, I think, will this evening answer my despatches. His capital is fifteen leagues distant, and thither I have had to send Runjeet and Wade's firmans, together with one which I had the impudence to write to him myself. Belaspore is only fourteen leagues off. The rajah of that place being informed, I know not how, of my approach, has sent me an officer of his miserable court and twenty soldiers. His vizier will receive me six leagues from his capital on this side of the Sutledge, so that if I fail with respect to Mondi, which would be a matter of much regret, in a geological sense, I have at least secured a good line of retreat direct upon Belaspore. I confess that I shall cross the Sutledge again with pleasure. It is not that knowing, as I now do, the certain difficulties and possible dangers of a journey beyond that river, I would not, if necessary, recommence this year's campaign; but if a friend of mine wished to repeat it, I confess that, till his return into the heart of the British possessions, I should sometimes think of him with anxiety. Is this courage or presumption on my part? I know not; but I think I can trace a little superstition in my feeling of security. I trust to my address in getting out of a scrape, and to my fortunate star for not getting into any very bad one: and I should not have the same confidence in the good luck and presence of mind of any one dear to me. After all, what I have just done (for henceforth all danger is past) has been attempted by only one, by Mr. Moorcroft, and there he remained, some say from the effect of fever, others, from poison : but at Cashmere I ascertained for a fact, that he and one of his companions, were miserably killed with sabre and matchlock.

I have certainly exhausted, in the Punjab and the mountains, all my chances of Indian adventures, and I am glad of it. For one travelling "en porte-manteau" an adventure might afford a very interesting diversion; but for a poor devil of my calling, who is not in want of work, it is a very inconvenient addition.

I experience an agreeable feeling of satisfaction, in looking back upon the road over which I have already passed with so much success and good luck. I have executed half my task, and that portion too which, so far as relates to human obstacles, offered the greatest difficulties. With the exception of the first summer, when I was broiled at Calcutta, I can scarcely do otherwise than admire the climate of the places in which I have lived; for during the winter I travelled in the plains, and among the mountains, in summer. Henceforward it will be very different. I must prepare myself for a terrible sweating next summer at Bombay, and then as I journey towards Cape Comorin, winter will be quite imperceptible. But I think that my fibre which has been hardened in the Himalaya, will be but slowly affected by the enervating influence of the humid heat of the Malabar coast. I shall be careful. I shall purchase shade, at the rate of twenty francs a month, by means of a very large parasol, which I intend to have made at Delhi, and which a servant, walking or running by my horse's side, will constantly hold over my head. I shall buy another large double tent, in order that when I dismount every day I may always find one ready for me. If, notwithstanding all this, the heat oppresses me, I will, in order to cool myself in imagination at least, think of the scenes of ice and snow on the lofty summits of the Himalaya, Adieu!

Subhatoo, November 22nd, 1831.

I had not yet come to the end of my adventures when, nearly a month ago, I wrote the foregoing lines at Hatteli. In order to get to Mondi I had sentinels to force. Their opposition was inexplicable; for the rajah had sent me a pressing and submissive invitation to his capital; he literally gave me *carte blanche* over his subjects, placing at my disposal, his vizier, &c. &c. The latter personage I suspected of treachery; and, as he was not in great force in my cavalcade, I had more than once a great inclination to arrest him and make sure of his person. Every new post that I forced, deputations arrived from the city entreating me to proceed no further. These people assured me that they were sent by the rajah: they promised that their master would visit me the next morning, at whatever distance from the city I might encamp. Thinking them all mad, I paid no attention either to their entreaties or to their remonstrances, and in the evening, reached

Mondi. The whole city was in an uproar: nevertheless I was received not only as a friend, but as a master. The enigma grew more and more inexplicable. At last, while I was encamped in the tents prepared for me by order of the rajah, his uncle, an old man, visited me, and looking very piteously, told me that it was an unlucky day, and that the astrologers had discovered in the morning that if my interview with the rajah took place that day, frightful calamities would fall upon the monarchy of Mondi.

This was on the first of November. I stayed several days in Mondi and its vicinity, embarrassed with the hospitality and humility of the rajah, and was forced to accept several nuzzers. The money I refused: but he passed the bags which he had brought over my head, and distributed their contents amongst the throng, which crowded round my encampment when he paid me a visit. I saw his mines, which are full of geognostic interest; and, after confounding great and small for several days with the profundity and marvels of my knowledge, I left Mondi on the 7th, mounted on a most wretched-looking little horse, one however of the noblest race of Kooloo, a present forced upon me by the rajah.

As I was internally blaming the expensive magnificence of my stud, now amounting to four horses, I arrived at Sooket, where my camp was established. The first man that met me was my groom, carrying a finger of his left hand in his right; the poor fellow was covered with blood. It was Gulab Sing's stallion which had used him thus cruelly. Without hesitating longer than Candide did when Issacar and the grand inquisitor interrupted his conversation with the fair Cunegunde, I presented my gun, which I had on my shoulder, and killed the terrible animal on the spot. The evening before I had a serious quarrel with him, and dreaded some mishap for the man who tended him. I dressed the unfortunate man's wound, after executing justice on his enemy. He will be well in a few days, and will receive his dismissal for having lied, by declaring when he entered my service that he had been a groom before. Nevertheless, to console him for his mutilation as much as I can, he will receive with his dismissal, two years' wages, amounting to a hundred rupees.

On the 9th I crossed the Sutledge—with what joy! —I cannot express it. It seemed on my landing at Belaspore, from my inflated skin, that it was but a step to the Rue de l'Université. The young rajah, who on account of some new knavery had excited an inquiry on the part of the political agent of Umbala—my friend Mr. Clerk—hastened to pay his respects. He was in hopes of obtaining my intercession with Mr. Clerk; but he only received a severe admonition, and retired in confusion.

All my trans-Sutledgic equipage having become useless, I dismissed the men, giving to each a reward proportioned to his services. This cost me a thousand rupees. I obtained, moreover, for my escort, the promotions which at my request M. Allard, their general, made among them: Ismael Beg received his captain's commission, &c. &c. &c. My Cashmerian secretary, who had been so useful to me, was in justice the best rewarded. All expressed their gratitude, and their reget at leaving me, in a manner which affected me exceedingly. You know, my dear father, that I am not brave on such occasions: I was choked with emotion. Without waiting for each of them to say his adieu, and invoke Allah and Mohammed for my happiness, I mounted my horse, and rode off with a rapidity which allowed no one to follow me.

I was galloping along the Subhatoo road towards Kennedy's residence, when one of his couriers brought me a letter, which informed me that he was expecting me at Semla. I hastened forward, and on the third day found myself under his hospitable roof.

He was not alone. I found with him some old acquaintances, and a new one, Mr. Maddock, one of the most distinguished men in the country. He has just left the residency of Lucknow for that of Catmandoo, and by this time he must have set out for that place. Must I tell you that it was in order to become acquainted with me that, in defiance of his instructions, he remained at Kennedy's, who, he knew, was expecting me daily? The cold drove us from Semla four days ago; but Mr. Maddock will remain with us at Subhatoo as long as I stay there myself. For my part, it would require a great effort of courage and unsociability not to remain as long as he prolongs his stay; for I am as much pleased with him as he is with me.

Nevertheless I have given the necessary orders for camels; and when they arrive at Bar, at the foot of the mountains, I shall take the road to Delhi. Lord William Bentinck, who has been detained at Kurnal by serious illness, will no doubt be still in the imperial city when I arrive there.

The excellent M. Allard has written to me since the interview at Ropur between the Governor-general and Runjeet-Sing. In the British camp, he found several of my friends, who received him in the most distinguished manner. He is delighted with the honours paid him on this side of the Sutledge, especially those which he received from Lord William. Nothing can be better calculated to increase the great consideration which he so justly enjoys at the Seikh court. As his countryman and friend, I learn all this with true happiness; and it is not without an increase of pleasure that I think I have aided him powerfully in this affair, notwithstanding my distance from the scene.

Good old general Cartwright has just been summoned to Calcutta, as a witness on a criminal trial. So this time, at Delhi, I shall be at Mr. William Fraser's service, and shall be able, without offence to any one, to spend the time with him that I must stay at Delhi, in order to ship my collections on the Jumna for Paris.

On the 30th or 31st of December I shall leave the imperial city, and proceed towards Bombay. Adieu, my dear father. I wish I could send you health, for I have some to spare; but I hope you have no occasion for that of other people. I am overwhelmed with business, and write this time to no one but M. Victor. A Bourdeaux ship, which sailed on the 4th of August, has been signaled in the bay of Bengal. I hope it brings me letters from you. I have none of later date than February, and they appear quite old. I embrace you with all my heart.

TO Mlle. ZOE NOIZET DE SAINT PAUL, ARRAS.

Subhatoo in the English Himalaya,
November 23rd, 1831.

My dear Zoe,—If none of my former letters have been lost on their way from Cashmere to Arras, you must have thought me almost a gossip last summer; but for the last few months you will have had no occasion to find fault with me on that account. Since my departure from the so-called terrestrial Paradise, I have had so much to do that I have entirely neglected my European correspondence. Nevertheless, during this interval, I have, as far as my journeyings and short moments of leisure would allow me, and on my father's account, blotted down a respectable chronicle of my sayings and doings; and this I yesterday concluded abruptly enough, in order to despatch it to Calcutta. I cannot speak to you of myself without repeating some of that long epistle ; and as my father will most probably send you at least some few sheets of it, this present will be very brief. I am as gay as a lark at having done what I have, and at having nothing more to do. This winter I am going to Bombay, and shall make a considerable circuit by way of Poonah, the capital of the old Mahratta monarchy. I shall remain at Bombay as long as the rainy season lasts, during which travelling is impossible ; and shall afterwards proceed to Cape Comorin, which is twenty degrees of latitude from this place : but this I think nothing—it seems only hop, step, and jump. I have no more human obstacles to fear ; no more rascals ambuscaded in a mountain defile, with their long matchlocks and their " you cannot pass;" no more fears, no more nightly attacks. *Things* will perhaps incommode me still more than the people did in my expedition beyond the Sutledge. The remainder of my Indian pilgrimage will be in a furnace and an oven by turns. Meanwhile, I stake what I have left, and still enjoy the pleasure of being cold here.

I have ceased to be the Plato of the world, the Socrates, the Aristotle of the age, the high and mighty lord Victor Jacquemont. I have no longer any right to cut off noses and ears, or to levy tribute. I shall never again be treated as I was by the rajah of Mondi, who received me as if I had been Runjeet himself, or the band of the old lady his neighbour, as the ignorant

Indians ludicrously term the British Company. On crossing the Sutledge, I lost all my lordly privileges, and am once more plain M. Victor Jacquemont, walking about alone, when I am pleased to have no other escort than my walking-stick. This change keeps me in perpetual good-humour. Notwithstanding the distance from the Himalaya to the good city of Paris, I feel that, by entering the territories subjected to British rule, I am brought some hundred miles nearer to it.

After all, my journey through the Punjab to Cashmere, and the manner in which I was allowed to make it, are singular enough. What congratulations, questions, and envy it calls forth !

A single day's march will bring me into the plains. I despaired of joining Lord W. Bentinck; but he has just been taken ill, which will delay his journey to Jaypore, and I expect to see him at Delhi.

Adieu, my dear friend: I cannot accuse *you* of gossiping; but excess is a fault in everything, especially in the pen. Make the *amende honorable* for the past and write to me in your smallest hand, on the largest sheet of paper. Adieu once more.

TO M. PROSPER MÉRIMÉE, PARIS.

Subhatoo in the British Himalaya, near the Sutledge,
November 28th, 1831.

It is a very long time since I wrote to you, my dear Prosper; but you have been still more negligent.

I am certainly at the end of my adventures. They are so rare on this side the Sutledge, that I have scarcely any chance of meeting with more. They have not been wanting beyond the British possessions; but as none of them had an untoward termination, notwithstanding the suspicious preamble of some, I do not regret having become acquainted with the oriental disagreeables of the ambulatory species.

On my return from Cashmere, I saw at Umbritsir the festival of the Unlocked. It is certainly the most magnificent in the East. I was prudent enough to refuse the most picturesque of vice-royalties, that of Cashmere, with an annual revenue of two lacs (500,000 francs),—a piece of folly according to some, and an act of extraordinary wisdom according to others; one, in short, becoming the Aflatoon el Zeman, Bocrate, Aristoon el Feringhistan, &c.

My prudent refusal has still farther exalted my reputation for wisdom. Runjeet has ever since considered me an animal quite *sui generis*, which could not be too highly honoured. If ever you fancy that, in order to write pretty exotic tales, it is necessary to cross the Rhine and the Indus, you may rely, my dear fellow, on all my protection.

Notwithstanding the *crescendo* of Runjeet's attentions, I find it still very pleasant to be once more among *the perfidious islanders*. My host for the present is an amiable fellow, the best paid of all the captains of artillery in this sublunary world; he is more of a king of kings than Agamemnon himself, without any Achilles to oppose him among the petty mountain-rajahs his vassals. A regiment of Gorkha sepoys insures his absolute sovereignty from the Jumna to the Sutledge. This morning, he paid me the compliment of having a grand review, with firing, &c. &c. to prove to me that he knew something of his incidental profession of colonel of infantry, which I had been disputing; but he insisted upon my being on horseback in full dress of Aflatoon (a black European coat), as he had in store for me all the honours due to a general officer inspecting his corps. The whole time the review lasted, I was near falling off my horse; and when my artilleryman had made his scoundrels perform all their antics, he concluded with a general advance towards the piquet where I was posted, his men presenting arms, and he himself saluting with his sword, and crying out: "Now Jacquemont, take off your hat and make a speech!" He was quizzing me, but I repaid him with interest in his own coin. With the utmost coolness, and in the tone appropriate to inspection speeches, I commenced a long rigmarole in English, without head or tail, which so upset his gravity, that he ordered the drums to beat, and dismissed the men without waiting for the end. After six months of absolute solitude, every frolic does me good, even an English one. I certainly see the English, for the most part, in a more advantageous light than they exhibited themselves to you. I am particularly fortunate with them. However, I have no very great reason to be vain of this success. They become so heartily tired of themselves in their distant solitary stations, that every new face is a God-send to them.

Those among them who are still bachelors, especially in India, have a style of behaviour which is not our *bonhommie:* but they have much more of the *good fellow* than we have, from thirty to fifty. Two other friends besides myself share Captain Kennedy's hospitality: one is a brother officer of his in the artillery, the other the ex-resident of Lucknow, the largest city in India. I know not how we manage it, but we are carried off every evening bursting with laughter.

TO M. VICTOR DE TRACY, PARIS.

Subhatoo in the British Himalaya,
December 1st, 1831.

My dear Madam,—I answer your letter of the 29th of March last, which I have received only to-day. You remind me of the date of mine, which had only then reached you, a year after. This mode of corresponding is indeed melancholy, recollection having ample time to be lost. But with so great a distance between us, and the impossibility of writing by question and answer, the only way to meet is to advance towards each other and repeat this kind of journey frequently. We must not wait till we receive a visit before we return it.

When you read these lines, time will have alleviated the bitterness of regret, left by the great and lamentable bereavement you had just suffered when you wrote. I was very young when a similar misfortune happened to me: you must remember it; but I think it was, for that very reason, the more cruel. The affections of childhood divide themselves but little. The chances of an innocent adolescence on the very threshold of youth, had not made me acquainted with the happiness of any but filial love. This faculty of loving still existed in all its integrity, and I thought that I had lost all at a blow!

I do not know, but I should think that when misfortune surprises us in the midst of our career, when our sensibility is completely developed in all its forms and is successively exercised in each of them, it must be less terrible. There are criminals whom a barbarous chastisement rouses to indignation, hardens, and causes to struggle against their punishment. Well, why do those excruciating torments of moral evil exist in the world? Is not the wounded soul sometimes hardened by a misfortune, the justice of which is incomprehensible to our intellect? Pardon me for talking to you thus, you who have wept so young: forgive me, it is better never to think of such things.

In the world with which we are acquainted, there is no life beyond hope, and the happiest that I can conceive, is that which hope does not abandon for a single instant. Happy, thrice happy, those who can believe and hope. Happy too is the child who has been able to gild the declining years of those who watched his youth! How greatly ought this idea to soothe and mitigate your sorrow.

Perhaps I should have done better by not writing, if I have only increased your affliction. But believe me, I shall always sympathise with you. In my mind I share the happiness you enjoy, in your husband, your daughters, and the qualities with which you are endowed.

Adieu, dear Madam, adieu.

TO M. PORPHYRE JACQUEMONT, PARIS.

Bussee, in the Country of the protected Seikhs, twenty four miles north of Umbala, December 5th, 1831.

In the first place, my good friend, excuse the thickness of the paper. Let me prose ever so little, this letter will weigh two pounds; but as it is John Bull who pays the postage from hence to Calcutta, and our highly esteemed public from thence to Paris, never mind. Besides, I have not the embarrassment of choice.

The excessive slowness of our correspondence is the very devil. The only compensation is its safety, since we have sent it through the ministry of the marine.—Let us begin with business.

I regret much that the ministerial decision of October 1830, granting me an annual increase to my salary of four thousand francs, has not been rigorously carried into execution, and that its effect has been confined to the last quarter of the said year, which makes the total only nine thousand francs. For, sending off my collections will cost me a great deal of money, and the campaign of 1832 will be a very dear one. I have just discovered that I owe three months' wages to some of my people, and eight months' to others. I shall smart for it at Delhi, where I must moreover buy another horse. I have three at present. One is my *soi-disant* Persian, which brought me here from Calcutta; a rascal that threw me a score and half of times before I even reached Benares, and which in 1831 ate me more than double his value, during the six or seven months of indolence which he enjoyed in the plains, while I was in the mountains. The second is the rajah of Mondi's famous ghounte, excellent in his way; but in truth he is of no use to me on my journey to Bombay, and I therefore dismiss him too. The third is my charger, which I have ridden since I left Lahore, and has lost his agreeable pace; he continues to rear and is grown hard in the mouth. Moreover, like all the horses of the Punjabee chiefs, he is accustomed to eat nothing but sugar; his keep therefore costs me double that of another, so I shall send him back to M. Allard.

Now the least it can cost me for a general renewal, will be twelve or fifteen hundred francs, and that without being extravagant; for were I to select a horse from one of the company's cavalry regiments, I should have to pay eight hundred rupees, or two thousand one hundred francs for it, that being the price at which the officers are allowed to make a choice of this kind. Near Delhi there are two studs, which my friend Mr. William Fraser knows thoroughly, and I have therefore asked him to make the purchase for me.

I have occasioned M. Allard very numerous expenses, and as, notwithstanding his hundred or hundred and fifty thousand francs pay, he is no richer than myself since the bankruptcy of Mr. Palmer (the most celebrated banker in Asia; he failed at Calcutta twenty months ago for the moderate sum of seventy five millions of francs); in devising some means of making him a present, I have thought of sending him a lottery ticket which will cost me a hundred and twenty-eight rupees, and may win him 160,000. I should tell you that every six months, there is a lottery at Calcutta, consisting of six thousand tickets, at a hundred and twenty rupees each, regulated in such a manner that only a twelfth of the capital deposited remains in the bank. This sum serves to cover the expense of several charitable institutions, which is only a pretence to sanctify this sort of gambling, and allow the saints to risk their cash, which all of them do as well as those who are not saints. The number of civil and military officers throughout India is about six thousand, being as many as the tickets. There are but few of them who do not from the day of their arrival in India, till that of their departure from it, impose upon themselves this voluntary half-yearly tax of a hundred and twenty eight rupees. Between ourselves, when I have had the ticket bought for M. Allard, I have a mind to do like the rest, and have one bought for myself out of my good friend Runjeet Sing's rupees.

But I am dreadfully puzzled, and you will certainly laugh at my embarrassment. I think myself sure of winning the great prize, 160,000 rupees, or at least the second 80,000, that is to say 500,000 or 250,000 francs. What the deuce shall I do with the money? If I send it to you, I shall be asked on my return, where I stole all that money—what rajah I have plundered, &c. &c. So that I pray my number may be drawn a blank.

The only consideration which might publicly justify me, and cause me unhesitatingly to confess the origin of my income of five and twenty thousand francs a year, would be the origin of the one hundred and twenty-eight rupees with which the hook is baited; which, of course, are part of the contents of the monstrous bags sent me from time to time by Runjeet Sing. Nothing is more of a lottery than the caprice or favour of an Asiatic prince. I have won some score thousands of francs without staking a farthing, and surely I may risk one bribe to catch another. To hoard money gained in that manner would be miserly. Enough of such folly.

Mr. Maddock fell ill at Kennedy's while I was sharing with him the Himalayan artilleryman's hospitality, and I took possession of the patient. I purged him, gave him an emetic, and made him take quinine and lavements, (a horrible thing to an Englishman,) used sinapisms, camphor frictions, &c. &c., and soon set him on his legs again. There was no time to lose: he was seized with the mountain fever, which is almost endemic in the low, hot, and moist valley all round Subhatoo. It is a pleasure to put one's self out of the way for grateful people. If I were to go to Nepaul instead of Bombay, I assure you I should meet with a splendid reception, for my ex-patient, Mr. Maddock, is the resident at the court of Khatmandoo.

I taught Kennedy, too, to cure himself, without medicine, of a complaint to which he is subject. The fact is, I think myself a better Indian physician than most of the company's doctors. Whenever I have met with any clever ones, I talked to them of nothing but their profession, thus profiting by their experience; whilst, for my own part, my camp, especially this year when it was so numerous, has furnished me every day with some patient or other. Be easy therefore about me, and be persuaded that if I should happen to be taken ill, I shall not drug myself with less success than others. Cholera is fabulous: I have never seen it, and am prepared to surprise the people of Paris a good deal, when they ask me about it. When I crossed the Sutledge, I also left behind me all chance of seeing a woman burned. But as cholera is no joke in Europe, a serious word or two about that disease. It sometimes attacks the large Indian cities, and makes very great ravages among the native population. Europeans are seldom its victims, especially *gentlemen;* but the soldiers of the European corps, all Irish, addicted to intoxication, are swept away by it in great numbers. You see that it is no concern of mine. However, be it understood, that if it pleases to reign in Bombay next May, I shall not dispute its stay in that city, and shall repair elsewhere at a respectful distance.

I will endeavour, when the time comes, to profit by your advice as to the propriety of returning to Europe during the summer. In truth, the thought of a Parisian winter makes me feel rather uncomfortable. Here, on the level plains of India, in the 30th degree of latitude, with orange and date trees, sugar canes, plantains, mangoes, and other tropical productions on all sides, I am writing to you by the fire-side in a wretched hut, built for the accommodation of the invalids who go to Semla in search of coolness. Meanwhile, I am dressed in my disguise of a white bear of Tibet, with flannel underneath, and a long, broad girdle of shawl over it; and though it be cloudless noon and I am in a house, or rather a kind of house, I shiver at the fire-side though dressed in this manner. I walked this morning more than half the way, my feet being too cold when on horseback. This chilly constitution is admirable in a poor devil who is going as far as Cape Comorin; but if it continues longer, I shall be forced at Paris to mount a puce-colour wadded *douillette*, at the risk of being taken for a priest.

I left Subhatoo yesterday afternoon; and if you look at the map, you will see that I made haste through the valley of Pinjore, which I crossed, without perceiving it, in the very teeth of the quartan ague, which prevails there nearly the whole year. To make up for the time lost at Subhatoo (Mr. Maddock does not call it lost), I shall go to morrow to Umbala; four-and-twenty English miles, or ten post leagues is a good long day's journey in India. You would be of my opinion, and that of the generality of men on this subject, were you to see the excoriated backs of the half starved camels that carry a portion of the baggage, the wagons and bullocks drawing the rest; and if you knew the necessity there is of opening, unpacking and displacing every thing in the evening, and of closing up, re-cording in the morning, &c. &c. At this season such things are pleasant, as we have constantly the finest weather in the world; but when the rain comes it falls in torrents. You have had some taste of it in your profession, so I shall spare you all account of it.

It is the jobbing in indigo that is ruining all the commercial houses in Calcutta. If they were to confine themselves to the profits of their commission, they would all make fortunes. I am glad to hear that Messrs. Cruttenden, Mackillop, and Co., do not gamble in that way.

The only thing that makes me object to them is my knowledge of a number of debts due to them which they will never recover. Nothing is more common in India than to owe 50,000, 100,000, or even more than double that sum of rupees: and the debtors are frequently captains at 600 rupees a month, or surgeons at 1000 or 1200; all proceeding from the mania of expending more than their income. The public idea is, that the bankers of Calcutta are a pack of thieves and that it is delightful to over-reach them. The English, so proud, so tenacious of their honour, suffer themselves to be dragged before the king's bench at Calcutta, for debts truly shameful, and for which there can be no excuse, except in the insanity of the debtors.

This is how they argue:—

"I am an English gentleman: that is to say, one of the most brilliant animals in the creation.

"I have forsaken the joys of Europe, and the charms of the domestic circle: I have bid farewell to my friends, in order to come and live in this beast of a country.

"Ergo, in compensation for this, I have a right to eat, drink, dress, live, and ride, &c. &c., in the most magnificent style. And if my income is not sufficient, I will run in debt to meet this necessity."

To most of them, it would seem that an English gentleman who should drink water, would lose caste and become a Pariah, like a Hindoo who drinks a glass of wine, or a Mussulmaun who eats a slice of ham. I should think it must be the same in England. The gentlemen on the other side of the Channel, have need of a strong lesson of politeness from the people, in order to learn that a gentleman may eat a bad dinner without dying after it, and wear an old coat without catching the itch. However, the thing is brewing in that quarter. You and I are destined to see the shell burst. The abolition of the rotten boroughs will do no more good there than did Catholic emancipation in Ireland. That which the Irish most wanted before all,—especially before the equality of political rights,—was potatoes to eat: emancipation has not put a single one more into their mouths. What the English people now want is bread. They have the simplicity to believe, that a reformed parliament will give it them: an error which they will soon rectify when they come to put their new electoral laws to the test. I would not exchange the lot of France for the next thirty years for that of England.

Lest our papers may make you magnify a fly buzzing about Calcutta into a monster, let me tell you that a band of rogues, fakirs, and beggars, vagabonds out of employ, and all Mussulmauns, have lately been plundering some villages on the left bank of the Hooghly. They have thrashed the "beurkondars and chokidars" (patrol and militia) of the district, and have increased to the number of two thousand men at least, armed with swords, pikes, bludgeons, and matchlocks. A regiment of Indian infantry was despatched against the moolabies (a religious appellation, which the robbers have assumed), with a hundred horse, and two pieces of light artillery. They killed and took a great number in the first engagement; a second will settle the matter. All this was going on ten or twelve leagues from Calcutta.

Farewell, my dear Porphyre. What a capital thing my bad dinners are—a chicken as hard as wood, coarse cakes, and water my beverage! Here am I, after two days of this frugal regimen, the same man again as before I spent a fortnight with Kennedy, who would most infallibly have made me ill if I had stayed longer with him. The English have no conversation: they remain at table for hours after dinner in company with numerous bottles, which are kept in constant circulation. How can one help drinking? Having nothing to do can of itself make one drink. I smoked like a steam-engine, in order to let the bottles pass without making them deviate from their elliptic orbit round our oval table. But I was obliged to do like others. Hence, disturbed sleep, indistinct ideas next morning, and the necessity of galloping about a couple of hours like the English, in order to digest the dinner of the preceding day. I have determined, therefore, to keep my savage manners whenever I chance to moor in any port of British civilisation, and to drink my milk, water, and eat my cakes among guests who will laugh at my meagre fare. With what pleasure I shall bid adieu to this system, when we are all collected round our old father's little round table with the intention of doing justice to a good soup, a leg of mutton, and a few bottles that may have patience enough to wait in the cellar till my return!

Delhi, December 21*st* 1831.

My DEAR PORPHYRE,—At this place, where I arrived on the evening of the 16th, I found four immense packets of letters waiting for me. None of the preceding ones are wanting for the last two years; I am going to answer them as fast as I can. I send you what I have ready for you: I shall only say one word now as it is growing dark. Know then that I am wonderfully well; that I arrived in time to spend six and thirty hours with Lord and Lady William; that I am delighted with them; that in ten days I shall start for Bombay, when I have shipped on the Jumna my collection, now being enclosed in tin and hard dry wood, an inch thick. I love you and embrace you with all my heart.

TO M. JACQUEMONT THE ELDER, PARIS.

Bussee, between Subhatoo and Umbala, Dec. 5th, 1831.
Despatched from Delhi, Jan. 10.

A FEW days ago, my dear father, I sent you a long letter from Subhatoo, which I began at my departure from Cashmere, and continued at different times during the remainder of my journey beyond the Sutledge, and terminated at Semla, at Captain Kennedy's. Porphyre will tell you why I availed myself of the captain's hospitality longer than I had intended, or than was convenient for the continuation of my journey.

Your No. 25, of the 13th of March last, reached me on the 1st of December, at Subhatoo, and there is not one line in its three long pages which has not afforded me pleasure. It is delightful thus to pass the period of our separation to our mutual satisfaction.

You ask me at the beginning of your letter what I was doing on that day? It was the 13th of March. I was just arrived at Lahore, and was walking alone in an Arabian Night's garden, thinking of my good fortune, or giving my arm to the excellent man who invited me thither from the centre of Tibet. I made my first appearance at the court of Runjeet-Sing, and came from this first interview much pleased with the Seikh monarch. In the elegant hall of the little palace in which I resided, I found, on my return from the rajah, a table laid out luxuriously and tastefully, after the French fashion; and by a friendly fiction I did the honours to the very persons who had provided it. A select troop of the king's Cashmerian amazons came by his order to amuse me with a concert and ball. The concert was execrable, Oriental music being one of the most disagreeable noises I know; but the slow-cadenced and voluptuous dance of Delhi and Cashmere is one of the most agreeable that can be executed. I will also admit that my Cashmerian *danseuses* had an inch of colour on their faces, vermillion on their lips, red and white on their cheeks, and black round their eyes. But this daubery was very pretty: it gives an extraordinary lustre to the already beautiful and extraordinarily large eyes of the Eastern women.

And as the *danseuses* of Lahore are quite as virtuous as those of Paris, it is useless to tell you more of the 13th of March.

A year before, and on the same day, if I have a good memory, I was paying my devoirs to the shade of the Great Mogul at Delhi. What shall I be doing on the next 13th of March?

In casting a paternally complaisant glance at the commencement of my ambulatory grandeur at Serau, you ask me what I did with the rajah of Bissahir's present, his bag of musk. Why, I played the republican, according to Montesquieu's notion, and exercised self-denial. The rajah's musk stinks at the bottom of a bale of shawls, treated with as little ceremony as itself. When it is cold enough for me to put on a girdle, I take it from another uninfected bale of shawls.

M. de Melay read M. Marle's* book, of which you speak, at sea; but he used to speak so ill of it, every day, that I drew back in affright from his six volumes. They have confirmed you, you tell me, in your contempt of the ancient literature of India. But you inquire whether Sanscrit is sufficiently well known for all the beauties of the mythological poetry of the Indians to be appreciated; to this I will reply, that, errors excepted, Mr. Horace Wilson is the only European in India perfectly acquainted with Sanscrit. There is but one of the Brahmins at Benares who knows it better than he; and whatever may be our new pretensions to the knowledge of that language, and those of the Germans, not excepting even the Baron d'Eckstein, I believe that not one of the adepts in Europe knows one quarter as much as Mr. Wilson does. The latter gentleman, of course, says that the language is splendid, that its grammatical structure is admirably logical, ingenious,

* Histoire générale de l'Inde ancienne et moderne depuis l'An 2000 avant Jésus Christ jusquà nos Jours. 6 vols. 8vo. Paris, 1828.

and perfect; and that its literature, which is exclusively poetical both in form and matter, is equally worthy of admiration.

I conceive the eulogiums lavished on the instrument to be deserved and sincere; but I suspected the honesty of those awarded to the works.

I have no doubt in my own mind that the Brahmins possessed much information to which they are now strangers. In this respect, India resembles Egypt; and the similarity between the two countries is not confined to this circumstance.

You are curious to know the degree of information at present possessed by the upper classes in Central India. I might, without wronging them, anticipate the continuation of my journey, and tell you, beforehand, that in general they are as ignorant as the lower classes. But next year I shall have, no doubt, an opportunity of seeing a good many Rajpoot and Mahratta chieftains; I will then tell you what I have seen. From Delhi to Seringapatam, the Hindoostanee is the colloquial language of the courts, as Persian is the written language of their chanceries. I now speak the former with great ease, and understand the latter tolerably well. Thus, my curiosity will be neither deaf nor dumb, when I find an opportunity, in the sequel of my journey, of exercising it on this object.

The *Journal des Debats*, which you sent me, told me nothing that I had not previously read in the *Constitutionnel*, in the month of September, at Cashmere.

I know neither when nor how the British sway in India will terminate; but of this I am certain, the poor Tartars will have no effect in accelerating its downfall. India, in a military point of view, is too civilised to have any thing to dread from the mounted hordes of Turkistan, even if she had not European officers to command her armies. Look at Runjeet Sing; he has only twenty-five thousand well-disciplined troops, and with so small a force he makes his northern neighbours tremble.

The British power in India will never perish, I think, by foreign aggression. Of physical strength, the English will always have more than could be brought against them, on the Sutledge or the Indus; but their material force possesses no other basis than moral force at present—very powerful, it is true, but which caprice might overturn. Then all would sink at once! What event can produce this shock?—undoubtedly the re-awakening of religious feeling. This may occur to-morrow, or it may not happen for a century to come. But although much may be said on this subject, I am going, my dear father, to wish you good night (for it is very late), and fall asleep with the same certainty you have at Paris, of finding every thing in the same situation to-morrow that it occupies to-day. Indeed, I even believe my chances of finding the morrow the same as the previous day, much greater than yours.

Adieu! I embrace and love you with all my heart.

TO M. PROSPER MERIMÉE, PARIS.

Soneeput, thirty miles North of Delhi,
December 15th, 1831.

My dear Prosper,—Excuse this large sheet of foolscap, which is any thing but select. May you never have to write on such paper with a peacock's feather. In India, such pens have all desirable local character, but apart from that, they are not worth a rush.

Great is my joy at finding myself once more among the British. On the other side of the Sutledge, especially in the mountains, there is always a chance of encountering a band of vagabonds, armed with match-locks, who say to you, "you pass not here;" and this unlucky chance has often been realised in the course of my journey. Upon that, my secretary would pull out of his pocket a terrible firman of Runjeet Sing's, in which he enjoins his friends and lieges of the plain and the mountain, not only to give free passage to the Plato of the age, alias the Lord Victor Jacquemont, but also commands them to provide hay, straw, &c., for the aforesaid lord, and to do all that he requires. This sublime passport having been read, the rascals with match-locks, said, very quietly, that it was all Hebrew to them; that not one of them understood a word of Persian; that, besides, they were not Runjeet Sing's servants, but those of such and such a petty jaguirdar or zemindar (vassal chief), and that they recognised no orders but those of their master; and with these words, knocking the ashes from their matches, and repeating "you pass not here." I assure you, my dear friend, that it required no mean diplomatic abilities to get on in spite of all this, and that more than one secretary of embassy would have been very much puzzled; for, however numerous my escort, its adversaries were usually in so large a majority, that it was only by negociation that I could succeed in obtaining a passage. Once only (and that was during the expedition with which I terminated my campaign beyond the Sutledge) I judged that the strength lay on my side, and I laconically showed the matchlock men the long and sharp lances of my horsemen. They saluted me down to the ground, and presented arms, after their fashion, as I passed. I almost regretted their civility: it deprived me of a pretence for having a tussle with this odious body of match-lock-men, in which they would have been losers.

On this side the Sutledge the people are very much tamed. No one ever thinks of saying to the bearer of a tolerably white face, that eternal "you pass not here!" so much used in the Punjab. The British have destroyed in their possessions the originality of Asiatic manners, beyond the domestic circle of each individual. They have no longer any picturesque feature, but are very convenient for use.

I gave the stones of the Himalaya a great proof of attachment, in leaving Runjeet Sing on their account three days before his interview with the Governor-general. We Indians, who do not think less of this interview than of that between Napoleon and Alexander on the Niemen, fancy that your papers will be greedy of the details with which those of Calcutta will supply them, as if people at Paris cared about the Sutledge, Rooper, Runjeet Sing, or Lord W. Bentinck.

In order that, when you are minister for foreign affairs, you may be tolerably acquainted with these matters, take a map of India and look quite at the top of it for the Sutledge, where it leaves the mountains. If the map is at all minute in its details, you will find on the left bank of that river, Rooper, Roopur, Rupar, Ropour, or Ropur.

In general, you may consider as belonging to the British, all the country on the left bank of the Sutledge, and lower down the Indus, after its conflux with the former river.

This is a bad line of military defence.

The Indus, on the contrary, especially in the middle part of its course, between Attock and Deyra-Ghazi-Khan, would be an excellent one.

The Russians might present themselves before it in force, almost without meeting any obstacle on their route. They would march at their ease through Persia; whilst Afghanistan, which for the last twenty years has been divided into a multitude of little independent and extremely weak principalities, would be unable to arrest their progress for a single day. It is, moreover, beyond doubt, that the Afghans would spontaneously swell the numbers of any army marching to the conquest of India. To plunder India, was the former trade of the Afghans, the road to which they would joyfully resume.

Orders have therefore come hither from the honourable Court of Directors to gain by treaty with the ameers of Sind and Runjeet Sing, the navigation of the Indus, in order to bring British troops by steam from Bombay, in case of any hostile demonstrations in Persia on the part of Russians.

The ameers of Sind are the chiefs of Tatto, Hyderabad, and other places in the vicinity of the mouth of the Indus. They have been independent ever since the dissolution of the Afghan empire. For these twenty years past, Runjeet Sing has been coveting their country, and would long ago have seized it, had he not dreaded the displeasure of the British.

The ameers have just been informed that if they do not afford every facility and protection to the commercial and military navigation of the British on the Indus, they will be left to Runjeet Sing's tender mercy. They have hastened to reply that they are the submissive slaves of the old lady of London, and that it will be their pleasure as well as duty to establish dock yards on the banks of their river for the British steam-vessels.

In the event of a threat from Russia, the British would go up the river and take up a position on its left bank, consequently in Runjeet Sing's dominions.

The interview at Rooper was no doubt intended

to cement more strongly the union of the two powers, flatter Runjeet's vanity with the attentions shown him by the old lady's pro-tempore husband, and induce him to form a defensive alliance with her against any indiscreet adversary coming from the North or from the West.

This time, many good hard lacs of rupees were expended without advancing the business one jot.

Runjeet will promise, sign, swear, all that is asked; and when the Russians come, if they ever do, which I do not think will happen very soon, he will consider himself quite as free to act according to his fancy, as we approved of his Catholic Majesty's doing so, after the taking of Cadiz by the hero of the Trocadero.

If he thinks that by his aiding the Russians they will succeed in dislodging the British from India, he will most certainly assist them, being well persuaded that these new comers will not be able to maintain their conquest, and that then his own turn will come to attempt gaining possession of India. He is already rather old, and rather too infirm to accomplish such a project, and if but half a score of years elapse before he commences it, he will fail in the undertaking.

If Runjeet were sincerely allied to the British, he would deprive the Russians of every chance of success. The folly of the cabinet at Calcutta consists in their imagining that there are diplomatic means of assuring themselves of the Seikh Monarch's fidelity.

The Governor-general gave him grand fêtes, which

Runjeet returned with no less magnificence. The Bombay and Calcutta newspapers for the last month speak of nothing else. This wretched trifling is transcendant policy with them. No style is noble enough for the recital of these things. The journalists thus find it impossible to depict the Seikh prince with his most characteristic features. Not one of these papers, for instance, has dared to say that, on his second visit to Lord William Bentinck, Runjeet gravely *committed a nuisance* in a corner of the superb tent, in which he happened to be with Lord William and his whole court.

The backs of my camels are one complete wound, my bullocks are lame: and I shall be clever if with such an equipage I can breakfast the day after to-morrow at Delhi. I long to arrive there; for I have every reason to hope that I shall there find two packets of letters from France: and the last I received are dated in March.

Write and tell me all that has happened to every one of our friends since the month of July 1830. Some news of the literary world, if it has not been entirely swallowed up by politics. Is M. Gerard still first painter to the king? Who is that M. Cavagnac whom I never heard of, and who without giving warning made such a splendid speech in the Cour Royale? What is become of the Scheffers, the Thierrys, the Globites, and the Globulars, the Baron de Saint Lazare, and the Baron de Stendhal, and of a fair lady whom you told me I frightened very much one very rainy morning?

Write, my dear friend, with your largest pen, on the strongest paper, for John Bull pays the postage, and you see I do not stint myself in quantity.

I should like to increase this packet with a couple of pages for Madame Mérimée: but I have been gossiping too much with you. I must therefore return to my work. Tell her however that from the substantive *mahogany* we have in India derived the verb *mahoganise*, which not only expresses the alteration of complexion, but also the radical mummification of the person; and assure her that in spite of my three years' service under the rays of a tropical sun, I am not too much mahoganised. If I were to go to London I should stand no chance of being admitted into the Oriental club, my complexion is so fresh-coloured.

P. S. Notwithstanding this fresh colour of which I here boast, I think the following a very decent proof of mahoganisation. Four days ago, I was at Kurnal, a great British military station on the Seikh frontier. I alighted at the house of a young officer of my acquaintance, whose regiment was to give a ball, next day, to the whole station. I was pressed to stay four-and-twenty hours. I was promised that I should see some very pretty girls at the ball. Now it is nearly two months since I saw a European female, and yet I continued my course, and refused to heave to. I should say at once of the prettiest English face at the ball, "what does it prove?"

Adieu my dear friend, I embrace you heartily.

TO M. NARJOT, CAPTAIN OF ENGINEERS, BREST.

Delhi, December 22*nd*, 1831.

PRELIMINARY NOTICE.

WHEN you become commander-in-chief, with a poor devil of a secretary, and a few aides-de-camp, whom, by way of pastime, you may amuse yourself with driving mad during wet weather, when it occurs, then, my good friend, you will be at liberty to write as illegibly as you please. But so long as you remain a simple captain of engineers, with the mere appendages of that rank—and, what is still worse, so long as you remain, what, alas, you appear insensibly to have become, a downright plebeian—cross your t's and dot your i's in a plain citizen-like manner: your hieroglyphics put me in a perfect fever during a whole hour. In future, write in well-formed Roman characters.

With regard to matter, you say so much, my good friend, in your two yards of pot hooks of last June, and I have so little time to devote to you to-day, that I must content myself with acknowledging the receipt of your charming letter. Why do you not give me the same treat every three months? Your letters now run no chance of miscarrying, except indeed by shipwreck, which, however, is scarcely heard of since the revolution, except in novels. Sea voyages are performed with so much safety, that out of eight-

and-twenty packets which my family have forwarded to me, only one has been lost; and I have ascertained how that happened. It was in the depths of the Ganges that the misfortune occurred, along with thirty Arab horses, and a due proportion of Christians and faithful (I mean Mussulmauns). This occurred two years ago. Besides which, you see that it is but a six months' trip from Brest to Delhi.

On my return to Delhi, a few days ago, I found, with your letter, about fifty others, the greater part of which require answers, and some so urgently that I must obey. I shall therefore be brief, if indeed it is possible for me to be so. If, therefore, I spin out my letter, do not thank me, for I solemnly assure you that it will be contrary to my intentions. As Lord W. Bentinck, whom I have been fortunate enough to meet again here, had sent me the French papers of June and July, previously to my receiving my letters from the post office, and as I had also read the English papers up to the 8th of August, your political intelligence came rather late. Nevertheless, for Brest politics, that is to say, coming from the world's end (finisterre, or *finis terræ*), it is so good, that I have derived both entertainment and instruction from it. I experienced a great deal of difficulty in making out your abridged formula for *henriquinquists*, which, during two days, I read *quinquinists*, without feeling much wonder at it, considering the age of folly in which we live. I took these quinquinists for some political society or club, or association composed of young doctors or apothecaries, who had succeeded in becoming an authority. Quinquinist is not bad, but henriquinquist is excellent. Whenever my stupid Indian attendants make a more than usually gross blunder, I will call them henriquinquists. It will have a prodigiously good effect. I do not recollect at what time I wrote to you last, but it must be long ago.

I will bring with me a cargo of Cashmere shawls, enough to make every husband tremble. During eight months I have been a man of great consequence, very rich, very magnificent, very benevolent, and consequently as poor now as I was before this singular journey. I have sometimes been a prisoner, frequently a diplomatist, and a warrior as seldom as possible; for in spite of the strong escort with which my friend Runjeet supplied me from his own body guard, I have seldom found myself the strongest either on suspicious occasions or in hostile encounters. But it is in politics that I shine the most. You will see that they will make a diplomatist of me one of these days. Our men of talent would have been sometimes embarrassed in my situation. These extensive regions are closed against the curiosity of Europeans by the not injudicious jealousy of their rulers. Hitherto, every thing has gone on well for me: here I am, returned safe and sound, and, I assure you, quite alive, from Cashmere, where the mountain range is not so high, the valley not so picturesque, nor the women so beautiful and the men such knaves as it is asserted. My portfolio is filled with letters from kings. The successor of Porus wrote to me every week. I sent him from the mountains very sorry dissertations upon natural philosophy, in order to satisfy him; it was such science as Seneca displayed in his *quæstiones naturales*. But the king of Lahore is a better judge of horses, swords, and matchlocks than of the sciences of Europe, and my Persian dissertations upon the four elements were fortunate enough to please him.

A six months' residence among the Mohammedans and Hindoos, has rendered me very tolerant. Religion is the favourite topic of conversation among the inhabitants of the East. It was our usual theme in the stern-cabin, or rather under the awning of my gondola, when I used to invite some fashionable long-beards to accompany me in my excursions on the lake of Cashmere, during the hot summer evenings, in order to breathe the cool air. I have learnt to speak only in terms of respect of My Lord Mohammed, because the prophet received the same distinction from Mussulmaun guests, who invariably gave him the title of Excellency. Christianity is monstrous, revolting, extravagant when compared with Mohammedanism. If ever I become a devotee, I shall certainly commence by turning Turk! There is only one thing that can be made a subject of reproach to the religion of Mohammed: it is, that principle which condemns the female sex to a state of abjection. A respectable woman cannot, without incurring shame, have learnt to read and write, to dance or to sing. These talents and accomplishments are considered disreputable, and are the exclusive attributes of courtesans, who, according to the usage of this sect, are alone allowed the privilege of pleasing.

The consequence of this custom (which indeed extends over the whole of the east, from China to Constantinople) is the dissipation of married men, the coldness of domestic affection, and the kind of love prevalent among the ancient Greeks and Romans.

I am occupied here in getting all the collections which I have made since my arrival in India, shipped and sent down the Jumna. I hope to see them, in a week, properly enclosed in tin, and in a double casing of the driest and hardest wood, ready to proceed on their journey. I shall then bid an eternal adieu to the imperial city, and take the road to Bombay. I have now done with the scenes of snow, ice, and desolation of the Himalaya. I experienced a heaviness of heart on losing sight of those mountains where I had spent two years of my life, and which I shall never see again.

New scenes await me during the remainder of my journey—scenes of tropical climes. I shall travel by land as far as I can. From Cape Comorin I shall return to the north by the plains of Mysore in the blue mountains, the highest of the Ghauts. I shall spend there the summer of 1833, and shall then think of returning to Europe, though not through Persia: the politics of Europe preclude the possibility of my adopting that route; besides it would destroy the character of my journey. I prefer remaining entirely Indian.

Adieu, my good friend. I embrace you.

TO M. VICTOR DE TRACY, PARIS.*

Delhi, December 22nd, 1831.

COLONEL FAGAN, who has been a protecting divinity to me in India, is about quitting this country for ever, to return to Europe, and will probably take up his residence in France. He has requested me to introduce him to some of my friends. It is with you that I intend commencing the circle of epistolary visits which I make for him and with him. Colonel Fagan, who is of Irish origin, was brought up in France. At an early age he entered the India company's service, and was in the expedition which the British sent against us from Bombay to Egypt, and which arrived after our capitulation. He there became acquainted with M. de

---

* Others might yield to the apprehension that this letter might prove uninteresting. For our part, we believe that it would be doing an injustice to the intentions of Jacquemont, did we not allow him to express publicly the gratitude and friendship which he professed for Colonel Fagan. The sentiments contained in this letter are as honourable to the writer as they are to the person who is the object of them.

la Fosse, with whom he returned to France, where he remained a couple of years, during which, he contracted the intimate friendship which now connects him with M. de la Fosse. Since that period Colonel Fagan has twice revisited France. This gentleman is an officer of the highest distinction. He has for many years been *adjutant-general*, that is to say, major-general of the Indian army, which, is in fact the chief command, for the nominal commander-in-chief is an English lord, who remains here four years only, and then returns to Europe, without understanding a word of the language, or having the slightest knowledge of the very peculiar manners of the army which he commands. Colonel Fagan is the object of universal regret, esteem, respect, and affection in the army. I made his acquaintance through the introduction of M. de la Fosse, and it has proved of the greatest service to me; there is not a military station in India, where he does not possess some friend, and at those places I am always sure of meeting the most generous hospitality.

I had the pleasure of seeing Colonel Fagan only for a short time at Calcutta; but our friendship was quickly formed, and since that period our correspondence has rendered us still more intimate. His manners and habits are noble, grave, and elegant. His opinions upon the great questions of the moral world are the same as ours.

I have given him a letter for your father: pray introduce him. Colonel Fagan cannot but be proud to know

M. de Tracy, and your father will, I am convinced, reap great pleasure from the acquaintance of so distinguished a character. Pray, my good friend, introduce him to your sisters and brothers in law. Is it necessary to beg of you to present him first to Madame Victor?

Adieu. It is a friend I recommend to you; I trust that on my return to France I shall find him as much yours as he is mine.

TO M. PORPHYRE JACQUEMONT, PARIS.

Delhi, December 23rd, 1831.

YOUR letter, marked Y, is extremely brief; the Annual for 1831 arrived at the same time, after a lapse of eleven months. I do not know whither it has been travelling all this while; certainly not in India, for I have become one of the most easy of individuals to find, though at the same time the least sedentary of its inhabitants. You recommend me, on my return home, to beware of the foreign powers. Every thing is settled on that score, as I have decided upon returning by sea. There are indeed examples of Englishmen having been intercepted in Persia by the Russians, and sent to Siberia, there to spend the remainder of their lives in skating. These atrocities have lately transpired, and I presume have led to energetic remonstrances from the British government.

Whenever you see my father secretly preoccupied with some thought which disturbs his quiet, try, my good friend, to reason with him on the subject. At twenty we see things under the most glowing colours; at your age, we see them as they are; but at our father's time of life they represent themselves even more gloomily than they are in reality. Thoughts of the future sometimes absorb his mind; in that case reason quietly with him about the chances of the future. If you must quit him to enter the army, show him the probability of a speedy termination of the war, and the certainty of your reaching high rank. As he advances in years, he concentrates all his affections in us, and I am convinced that the thought of seeing us again happy, would make him support his solitude with resignation. During the months of May and June he thought I was at Lahore, and he received with lively satisfaction every communication that tended to prove that I was out of the British possessions. The supposition that after having visited the Punjab and Cashmere, I should return to India, and continue my travels as I had commenced them, caused him considerable pleasure. All my letters since that period must have proved very satisfactory to him. The happiness I have experienced in my journey has been greatly heightened by the thought that he shared in it. I hope that, on my return, my future fate will be settled in such a manner that I shall no longer be a cause of anxiety to him.

Although the subject has much occupied my mind,

I have not yet decided upon the form I shall adopt in the different publications I intend to produce. I trust nevertheless to be able to extract from the very considerable mass of manuscripts which I shall bring with me, an instructive work, and at the same time of general interest.

Apropos of the new organisation of the artillery you speak of: I must inform you that in the Indian army the foot artillery is drawn by bullocks; but they are of a peculiar race, very large and very active, at least for bullocks. The horse artillery, in speaking of the other, never call them foot artillery, but bullock artillery, which appellation is horror and abomination to the latter.

What do you mean by your fears that any indiscreet communication of the letters which I write could excite the suspicions of the British, whose guest I am, upon the real nature of my travels, and my intention of visiting India with the most minute research? This absurdity is most monstrous: it surpasses all belief. I entirely belong to the country. I am upon terms of familiarity with the greatest portion of the civil officers. It is they in general who receive me, because they rank the highest, and are of the greatest importance to me. There is never any *Monsieur* or *Sir* between us. It is my dear Maddock, my dear Wade, my dear Kennedy, &c., on one side, and my dear Jacquemont on the other. At the Governor-general's I am considered one of the family, and consequently relieved from the restraint of etiquette, to which others are subjected. A secret agent! It is perfectly well understood by all my English friends that I shall gather other information from my travels than what may relate to natural history, when I have emptied my collection of stones, and analysed my trusses of plants! Why, here, at the president's table, between whom and myself the difference of age precludes very familiar intercourse, do you think that I fear to speak about the policy, the financial and judicial administration of Northern India, of which he is vice-regent? It is almost always the theme of conversation, and I am myself the promoter of it. Whenever I cannot perfectly understand some point of statistics, and feel vexed at my ignorance, I instantly write to the minister of state, and beg of him to make the necessary inquiries and calculations in his department, to ascertain what I want to know. A secret agent, indeed! Could that appellation, think you, be applied to me! In truth, the supposition is the height of absurdity. Every body in India knows who I am. I have concealed nothing, and I have found people almost everywhere who inspired me with sufficient confidence to make them acquainted with my situation in the most precise manner. It is perfectly well known that I arrived here with a salary of six thousand francs a year: I at once boldly owned it, and that it was afterwards raised to eight thousand, and ultimately to twelve thousand. I make no secret of what I have received from Runjeet. In short, my good friend, as I play an honest part, I do it in a straightforward open manner. I have adopted an open and candid line of conduct with the most suspicious, false, and deceitful of Asiatic princes, Runjeet, and I believe that Runjeet himself would laugh at any one who would insinuate to him that the stones and plants of his mountains were only a pretence of mine to investigate the rest. If ever, my dear Porphyre, they speak to you of a secret agent, you may boldly assert that there never was a stranger in India who enjoyed such testimonies of respect as those which I every where and continually receive. It will not be a very modest assertion, but it is proper that the truth should be known in that respect.

Though much further from Great Britain than you are, I am in reality much more favourably situated for judging of the future prospects of that country, by the occasional opportunity I have of reading its public journals, and my acquaintance with many of its natives. I consider the prospects of Great Britain to be truly alarming. I am persuaded that if the peers are mad enough to throw out the reform bill proposed by the commons, the present ministry will either make a *coup-d'état* with the liberal party, or else resign, and then a sanguinary revolution must be the consequence. The crisis will be a fearful one, because there does not exist a country in Europe where the inequalities of the social order offer more frightful contrasts. The mother country does not extend that solicitude to her Indian possessions which they deserve.

Farewell. I am dying with fatigue. Yesterday the engineers of the garrison of Delhi gave a ball to the still remaining red coats and black coats. I was obliged to show my long dark face, and anything but dancing physiognomy: and the mistakes which occurred among the carriages, palanquins, and horses, kept me upon a sharp trot the greatest part of the night. I did not get to bed till three o'clock in the morning, and such late hours do not at all suit me. Adieu, my dear and excellent friend. I love and embrace you from the bottom of my heart.

January 10th, 1832.

My boxes are not yet ready, which is the very devil. As there are a number of vessels always sailing from Calcutta for Havre and Bordeaux, I will write again. Nothing new. I work very hard, and my health is very good.

Your's most affectionately.

TO M. JACQUEMONT, SENIOR, PARIS.

Delhi, December 26th, 1831.

My dear Father.—Shall I tell you, that your notions on the politics of India amuse me greatly? Your quotations, made from memory, and borrowed from M. de Marlès, on the subject of the history of Runjeet Sing, are truly delightful. But is it decorous for a son to speak thus to his father? You will, I am sure, forgive me this liberty, now that by my letters from the Punjab and Cashmere, you ought to be better informed respecting the state of the Ultra-Sutledge and the fallibility of your oracle M. de Marlès. I possess all the materials requisite for a history of the Punjab for the last fifty years, but it would not interest any body. The biography of Runjeet Sing, would perhaps be amusing, but it is replete with events which could not be written in the vulgar tongue, and which it would be necessary to insert in Latin notes. In spite of every thing that is blameable in Runjeet, pray love him a little, were it only for my sake. You were alarmed lest he should make me marry, and force me, *nolens-volens*, to remain with him. I feel pleasure in thinking that you must have received, a long time ago, my first letters from Lahore, which will have destroyed any apprehensions on that score.

But what was that war of Runjeet's which made you tremble for my safety? The rajah of Belaspore would be highly flattered if he knew that the troubles of his empire had caused you such alarm. If I were to visit the Himalaya again, I trust you would do me the honour of believing me to be absolute lord and master at Belaspore.

I have entirely lost the thread of European politics, and can no longer prophecy as formerly. Did I tell you that I predicted the events of July 1830, six months before I knew them, to a friend at Calcutta, and that my letter, which he showed to others, gave me an extraordinary reputation? Every one now asks me what will happen in the Punjab and Cashmere at the death of Runjeet. To this I reply, that for the present, Runjeet, notwithstanding his grey beard and attenuated frame, has not the slightest idea of dying; and if they insist on having my opinion, I shall write my *siege*, like Vertot, and mention the chiefs who will wage war in the plains, and those who will do battle on the mountains, showing the chances of each. Wade, with whom you now are acquainted, will inform me of all these things in Paris, whenever they come to pass.

I arrived on the evening of the 16th, and found here Fraser, who I thought was on a judicial circuit. He informed me that the Governor-general's camp was still under the walls of Delhi, and that during the night it would be transported to Cuttob, on the ruins of ancient Delhi, from which it is four leagues distant. I consequently got into his palanquin, and was conveyed to Cuttob, where I remained two days with Lord and Lady

William, with whom I was still more delighted than even during my stay in Calcutta. It is impossible to describe the flattering attentions they have shown me, and the real friendly feelings they have evinced towards me. I conversed at great length with Lord William upon the countries I had visited, and with Lady William about Paris and their own journey. So many things had occurred since I had parted from them at Calcutta! I drank water with great intrepidity, to the health of all those who, according to the custom of their nation, saluted me with their glasses; and this feat was not a little admired. There were several persons of my acquaintance in the Governor-general's camp: Mr. Toby Prinsep, secretary of state; General Wittingham, who commands this division; and Mr. Metcalfe, my first host at Delhi. Lord William marches towards Rajpootana. Lord Clare, the new Governor of Bombay, comes to meet him: they are intimate acquaintances. Lord and Lady William, independently of their verbal recommendation, will both give me a letter for that nobleman; I expect it every day. I am alone in Mr. Fraser's immense house, which is a kind of Gothic fortress, built by himself, at an immense expense, upon the very place where Timour Lenggue pitched his tent when he laid siege to Delhi. My host is at the camp with the Governor-general, whom he accompanies to the limits of his jurisdiction. I am busied the whole day, undisturbed by any noise, except that of the workmen who are packing up my collections, and am perfectly free from any restraint of society. In the evening, when the weather is fine, I mount my horse; and if rainy, I take my palanquin and repair to the town, where I always dine with the resident. This gentleman has a cultivated mind and an acute understanding; his habits are retiring, but his conversation is more varied and pleasing than that of most of his countrymen. Mr. Maddock lived with him; and, to make up four persons, a young diplomatist, full of wit and spirits, never fails to dine with his patron.

The resident at Delhi receives five thousand rupees per month (or thirteen thousand francs), for table money. As he seldom has more than five or six persons at dinner, and feels himself conscientiously bound to expend this extra allowance in the object for which it is given, you may easily imagine that the dinners I have at his house do not much resemble my ambulatory meals. I, however, completely edify our little society by my stoical sobriety. At ten o'clock we wish Mr. Martin (the resident) good night, and with Maddock and Bell (the lively and witty assistant diplomatist I have just mentioned), I retire to the apartments of the latter, where, round a good fire, we talk till midnight. There is no inducement to go to bed, so cheerfully do we three spend the time together. Besides, they will not let me quit them easily. When however, the time comes, I light an excellent Havannah cigar, and folding my Cashmere morning gown round my limbs, mount my horse, and, preceded by two men, who run before me with torches in their hands, a short gallop soon brings me to Fraser's fortress. This last evening, I returned to my lodgings with a heavy heart: I had shaken hands for the last time with Mr. Maddock. He departed this morning for his new kingdom of Catmandou, and before setting out from Delhi, he wrote me a farewell letter which has affected me much. If, instead of proceeding to Bombay and to the Ghauts, I took it into my head to go to the further end of the Himalaya in Nepaul, what support should I not find in Catmandou?

You say in one of your letters that since the British are so amiable towards me, they must be very different in India to what they are at home. There may be something in that, especially among those who inhabit the superior provinces, to the north of Benares; but I take upon myself the greatest part of the merit of this kind of miracle.

You also state, that you are greatly satisfied with Frederic's opinion of my English, which he says is perfect, and the language of good society. I have at present too great a knowledge of that language to accept of his fraternal compliments. I have remained during my stay among this foreign nation too completely French—I have retained too much the individuality of my own character in the turn of my thoughts, not to betray instantly, by my language, my foreign nationality. It sometimes vexes me, but I more frequently rejoice at it. My English is English apart, which from not being perfect is not the less good. You must forgive my impertinence. I have left off writing in English to Frederic as well as to Zoë, who has also forbidden me to write in that language, on account of the *you*, which alone can be used in English. Zoë, however, in her reprimand, has hazarded a few words in the language she condemns. Tell her I did not find one single word wrong; she appears to me to understand it already perfectly well.

You will observe, that I write by fits and starts.

I cannot conceive how the London papers could assert that Lord William Bentinck had, as you state, arrested the commander-in-chief. The general in command was Lord Combermere when I arrived in India; at present the army is under Lord Dalhousie, who, after two years of service and ill-health, is going to resign the command to Sir Edward Barnes (ex-governor of Ceylon). The governors of Madras and Bombay are not, by right, so absolute as you imagine. The governor of Calcutta possesses the power of arresting both these governors just like any other European; but for these last thirty years there have been only two or three instances of arrest of Europeans. The one which created the greatest sensation was that of a Mr. Buckingham, the editor of a Calcutta paper, who was politely requested by an *acting* functionary at Calcutta, to leave the country, the tranquillity of which he endangered by his violent incendiary declarations. This Buckingham, who is a man of talent, is now in London preaching a crusade against the Company's government; but he does not enjoy great respect. Lord William has hitherto arrested nobody, for which I decidedly blame him. The number of civil and military British officers in the whole of India amount to six thousand. The European army consists only of twenty thousand men—that is all. It is evident therefore that it is not by physical force that we keep under the immense population of those vast regions. The principle of our power is elsewhere: it is in the respect with which our character inspires these nations.

A European of degraded morals ought immediately to be arrested and sent to Europe. Such a man does more injury to the European character, and to the future prospects of the British power in India, than a formidable insurrection could do. At Calcutta, where there are so many Europeans of every class, the lowest Bengalee burgher keeps his shoes on at the Governor-general's!! At Delhi, the greatest Mogul lord takes off his in the presence of a British ensign.

Runjeet Sing, a monarch absolutely independent, and possessing the greatest power in Asia after the British, always received me barefooted. If, in the Punjab, any native lord whatever had presented himself at my residence without leaving his shoes at the door, I would not have received him, but have written instantly to Runjeet to demand satisfaction for the insult. The idea, however, of so enormous an offence could have entered no one's head.

At Calcutta, the Indians every day see European sailors led away drunk by Indian police soldiers. They likewise see Europeans stand as culprits at the bar of the criminal court. There the powerful illusion attached to the name of European is dispelled. In the whole of the Delta of the Ganges, which for the most part is cultivated by indigo planters, either British or half-caste—an opulent class of men, but violent and gross in their habits—the spell is also broken. In no other part is the European population so numerous in proportion to the natives; no where are the latter so timid as here; and yet there is no province where Europeans are less respected.

My excellent friend M. Allard writes to me from time to time, since my departure from the Punjab. Runjeet Sing has presented Mirza Hede, my Persian secretary of Cashmere, with twelve hundred francs, and a pension of one thousand francs. I did not dismiss him at Belaspore without charging him with a farewell letter to the Maharajah. Poor Mirza writes me this in the overflowing of his heart, and promises me that himself, his mother, his brothers, and all his family will offer up their prayers for my happiness during the rest of their lives. This really has affected me. Allard has received a very kind letter from Lord William: he despatched it to me in order to translate it; I sent him back with the translation a lottery ticket, which I sent for on purpose to Calcutta, and which may make him gain a hundred and sixty thousand rupees, if it so please the blind goddess. This is a present of three hundred francs. I regret much that my want of means prevents me from testifying my gratitude in any better manner for the innumerable obligations I am under towards this excellent man.

Jaypoor, Ajmeer, Nusserabad, Indore, Aurungabad, and Poonah, are the most remarkable places on the road which I shall take from hence to Bombay.

I shall proceed first to the country of the Rajpoots, then to that of the Nizam, then to that of the Mahrattas. Jaypoor was not quiet last year; but order has been restored. I know the resident at Ajmeer; further, his diplomatic aide-de-camp is the son of Colonel Fagan. A son-in-law of the latter commands a considerable body of troops near Ajmeer, and so on as far as Bombay. As, however, these English posts are at a great distance from each other, in the west of India, you must not be uneasy if my letters succeed each other only at long intervals.

It appears that I forgot last year to relate to you my visit to the Begum (the Persian for princess) Sumro, at Serdhana, near Meerut. You must know, then, that Colonel Arnold introduced me to her one Sunday morning in the month of December last, whilst I was at Meerut with him. I breakfasted and dined with this old witch, and was even gallant enough to kiss her hand. Like a true John Bull, I had the honour of drinking wine with her at dinner. On my return to Meerut, on the following day, I received an invitation to dine with her on Christmas day. She must be a hundred years old, she is bent in two, and her face is shrivelled like dried raisins; she is, in fine, a sort of walking mummy, who still looks after all her affairs herself, listens to two or three secretaries at once, and at the same time dictates to as many others. Only four years ago, she caused some of her ministers and disgraced courtiers to be tied to the cannon's mouth, and fired off like shot. It is related of her, and the story is true, that about sixty or eighty years ago, she had a young female slave of whom she was jealous, buried alive, and that she gave her husband a nautch (a ball) upon this horrible tomb. Her two European husbands met with violent deaths. She was, however, as courageous as she was cruel. Some Italian monks have gained possession of her mind, and inspired her with a tremendous fear of the devil. She has built a beautiful Catholic church at Serdhana, and a few days ago, she wrote to the Government to request that, at her death, a portion of her domains may remain attached to the church to meet the expense of its service. She has addressed the Pope, asking to have a bishop at Serdhana: nevertheless she is not yet in her dotage.

Of the sixteen lacs of rupees which compose her revenue, she every year buries four in her gardens. These she might now give to whom she pleased, but at her death they will belong to the British Government. Runjeet has also, within a few years, been seized with the mania of burying his money, and since this fit came upon him, there are no bounds to his avarice.

My friends, the diplomatists of Delhi, wished to procure for me, from the Emperor, some splendid title: for instance, the pillar of science, the light of posterity, the sword of the state, high and mighty lord, &c. &c. But the imperial chancery is worse than the commission under the great seal. It spins out a dreadfully long account against those whom the Great Mogul honours with his titles; so that I have abandoned the yoke, and continue to live upon my Punjabee titles. which are not indeed standard ones, as you are no doubt aware that Runjeet is a soldier of fortune—in other words, a usurper.

Poor Jussieu, in his last letter, informed me that his wife was in the family way, and that he hoped to have a boy. I had begun a letter of congratulation to him at Subhatoo, which fortunately is still in my portfolio, so that I can destroy it. With his quiet and retiring habits, and the domestic tastes of his family, Jussieu must have severely felt the loss of his wife.

As I am determined to be amiable for once, I will address a few lines to Madlle. Duvancel. There is more gallantry in this than is usual with me; for, living, as I do, secluded from female society, I become daily more bearish than even I used to be, and I always had a terrible inclination to be so. With increasing years, I have corrected myself of a few of my defects, but I am sadly afraid I shall carry this to the grave.

We have a very extraordinary winter for this country. The weather is rainy and windy, and yet not cold. It is fortunate that this fit of bad weather takes place while I am stationary; for when rain falls during a march, it is most distressing whilst it lasts. The tents become enormously heavy; the camels which carry them, slip upon the wet ground at almost every step; for their thighs, very badly articulated in their sockets, are easily put out of joint, and frequently cannot be reset. The bullock-wagons, which carry the heavy baggage, sink into the mud. All the attendants, bullock-drivers, camel-drivers, and soldiers, look downcast and dispirited; they become deaf and dumb, and half paralysed. Thus, all is not pleasure in a wandering life.

In spite of all these drawbacks, the traveller ultimately ends his journey, it is true, but always late, wet to the skin, and not exactly certain of finding a shelter, or much to eat. At all events, he arrives, resumes his toilsome labour next day, and by dint of persevering in this way, you will see me, my dear father, in the course of about thirty months, arrive in your fourth story, or third story, above the *entresol*, as landlords usually express themselves.

January 10*th.*

One more word of adieu! My dear father, I am still detained here by my workmen, and by a variety of trifling domestic details tedious to settle. I shall be as poor at Bombay with my twelve thousand francs, as I was at the residence of Calcutta with my primitive ration of six thousand; for every thing there is exactly twice as dear as at Bengal.

There are in the Ganges half a dozen French vessels about to sail. Each of them will bring you a packet from me.

I embrace you with all my heart.

February 13*th.*

My dear Father,—I intended setting out to-day after breakfast, but luckily discovered that the casks which I have had made at a very great expense, and filled with essence of turpentine to preserve the fish, leaked considerably. My caravan was already on the move. It was a kind of rehearsal of departure; but I trust it will be the last, and that this subtle fluid, which is almost on a par with your *essences,* will be duly imprisoned in copper vessels. This is the devil! In the dreadful confusion of my table, it is impossible to write you a word more.

I shall certainly see Lord William again at Jaypoor, or between Jaypoor and Alvar. Adieu! I embrace you with all my heart, also Porphyre and Frederic, if the latter is still with you.

TO M. VICTOR DE TRACY, PARIS.

Delhi, January 11th, 1832.

MY DEAR FRIEND,—On my arrival in this town, I found what I looked forward to, a long letter from you. In recalling its date to your memory, I shall perhaps remind you also of the subjects which it contained. Its date is the 25th of last May, a short time before the elections.

As your friendship has got into the habit of paying me a thousand compliments which I do not deserve, I shall, in return, adopt the practice of commencing by a little act of humility. Many a man who is amiable and witty in *tete-à-tete,* is perfectly at a loss when a third person happens to come in. With regard to myself, I only feel at my ease, and confident in myself—I have facility in expressing my ideas with those alone whose kindness and good-will I know I enjoy. I am too expansive, especially with my pen, to be a general favourite. When the time comes to make an author's bow to the public, instead of epistolary visits to my friends, it will be a most trying moment to me: so much so, that if I could manage not to give my name with my prose I should consider myself very fortunate. The ground of that feeling usually termed modesty, is nothing in the world but suffering vanity, with which is mingled a sort of moral delicacy. Can you, without its costing an effort, expose how you think and feel, to men whose thoughts and feelings you know to be entirely opposed to yours, which they cannot even comprehend. I have never tried to pourtray scenes of nature and human life. I write much as I go along; but my notes are disorderly. It is not sufficient that I should make a choice among them ; and before I undertake the arrangement and labour they will require, I must describe a number of plants and stones, and perhaps by that time I shall acquire a facility of writing which I have hitherto been unable to attain. But what shall I ever be able to make of the immense cultivated plains of India, slowly travelling, as I do, with bullocks and camels?

It is indeed kind of you to talk to me of science and literature. Two friends, *savans* by profession, and who have nothing else to do, forward me from time to time their bulletins. These are Adrien de Jussieu, and Elie Beaumont ; but they have I believe little taste for the art, at least the latter, and they never speak upon that subject. It is natural that the house should be covered with *barricades* at the annual exhibition of pictures. In speaking of Scheffer, whose talents, like yourself, I esteem more than those of any other artist, I could have wished you had mentioned whether he still wholly confines himself to painting.

The announcement of the plays at the bottom of the Paris papers had already informed me, a long time since, that the stage was entirely invaded by Robespierre, Murat, Napoleon, and even their very contemporaries, though yet living. All this is in very bad taste. In placing on the shelf, the Greeks, the Romans, and the marquisses of our ancient stage, we have not been fortunate in the choice of their successors. Are then Delavigne and Lamartine entirely dimissed by these lovers of the horrible?

But this is carrying questions and answers too far. At the distance which now separates us, it is better to speak only of ourselves. Well then! I arrived here on the 16th of last month, just in time to join the Governor-general's camp a few leagues distant, as he had just left the imperial city. I spent two delightful days with Lord and Lady William Bentinck; and returned here to ship on the Jumna all my different collections. It is a most tedious affair, and takes up much more time than I expected: it will detain me at Delhi a great deal longer than I had imagined. The dreadful spring of India will overtake me before I can pass the Nerbudda. Others would perhaps not dare to undertake so late in the season the very long journey to Bombay; but my excellent constitution, and great abstemiousness, allow me to support with ease the excessive heat of India.

I feel exceedingly happy in the small circle of acquaintance, or, to speak more properly, of friends which I have formed here. My host, the superintendant of the province, enjoys a celebrity which extends a hundred leagues around. He is man who, delighting in the emotions of danger, goes to war as an amateur, whenever there is fighting going on, and never returns without a few gun-shot wounds; but his humanity is such, that in the midst of the many scenes of carnage to which his monomania has hurried him, he has never struck a blow with his sword; his heart fails when his arm has been raised to cut his enemy down. He is half Asiatic in his habits, but in other respects a Scotch highlander, and an excellent man, with great originality of thought, a metaphysician to boot, and enjoying the best possible reputation of being a country bear. I have succeeded in taming him, which does not prevent my being looked upon by certain persons as something of a bear myself; but with others I pass, and I believe with more justice, for a perfectly sociable being. The resident is a man of very retiring habits, and perfectly cultivated mind. In spite of the dissimilarity of our tastes and tempers, we agree admirably together, and are fond of each other's society; in short, my dear friend, I receive on all sides in this country the most unceasing marks of kindness.

I meet a great many Indians here. They are almost all Mussulmauns of Mogul extraction, the wreck of the nobility of that court. My host is the only officer of government, who, to my knowledge, keeps up any social relations with the natives. Last Sunday I paid a few visits with him to some of these long-beards. This politeness and condescension is, I fancy, blamed by the other British officers. A few days previously it was the anniversary of the nominal accession of the emperor; and the resident, who on that day owes an annual tribute of congratulation to this shadow of royal power, had the kindness to take me with him to the durbar.

Every thing is in preparation for my journey to Rajpootana. At the fifth station from hence I shall quit the British territories, but shall not want for their protection with the Rajpoot princes. The resident, whom they look upon as the successor of the Great Mogul, their former sovereign lord, has written to all of them, and I rely entirely upon their hospitality. With these still independent nations there is other protection than the friendship of the prince. A traveller who cannot claim it as his safeguard, is exposed to a thousand vexations, without mentioning the pretty certain chance he runs of being plundered. In spite of myself, therefore, I am obliged to add a Persian secretary to my little caravan, in order to decipher the abominable *chekestea* of the Rajpoot chanceries, and to carry on my correspondence when necessary. The department of foreign affairs thus makes a dreadful hole in my budget.

This secretary is a descendant from the Prophet, which is not always a recommendation; but he appears clever, and my intention is to make him earn his five louis a month, so that on my arrival at Bombay there will be no such thing as Persian hieroglyphics for me.

There is a coolness between Runjeet Sing and us—I mean the Government. The British wish to occupy the Lower Indus, and push their trade in that direction. They will unquestionably be obliged to establish military posts on the banks, in order to protect it. Hence the ill temper of Runjeet, who cannot resist and is forced to suffer what he cannot prevent.

That which he allowed me last year out of compliment to the Governor-general, he would no doubt refuse me now. In spite, however, of his dissatisfaction against the British, he still thinks kindly of me. I have lately received a letter from him, informing me that he had just granted a pension to the native of Cashmere who was my secretary in that country and in the Punjab. There is, however, no war; indeed there is nobody for the British to wage war against. The last quarrel with the Chinese was terminated amicably, though much more serious than the preceding ones. The day will however come, and no doubt we shall see it, when the British will be compelled to take by force the tea which the Chinese will refuse to sell them. It would be very easy to invade China, but I question if it would not be difficult to retain possession of it.

Good night, my dear friend. I have spent the whole day among plants, stones, and animals; this is the reason why I do not speak of anything that relates to them. The winter here is as cold as in the south of Spain, and I leave you to go, according to the expression of the country, and *eat the air*, the fresh air which I shall inhale no more during the remainder of my stay in India. I wish that you and yours may enjoy health equal to mine. Adieu, &c.

TO M. DE MARESTE, PARIS.

Delhi, February 6th, 1832.

If this be not a specimen of local character, seek it elsewhere, my dear De Mareste. Learn that it is even of the finest kind, and that royal and serene highnesses alone are treated with this paper *. But the writing only commences at the middle of the page, or even lower, if one desires to be still more stylish. During six or eight lines, a regular file firing is kept up, directed against the vanity of the correspondent. The high, the exalted, the sublime, the just, the merciful, the charitable, the generous, the mighty, the victorious, the invincible, the sage of high renown, the ornament of the universe, the pillar of the world, the great prince, the prince of princes, the king of kings, the master of the world, the arbiter of one's destinies, hail!—after this preamble, the business of their epistle is begun with protestations breathing unalterable friendship. The jasmine and the narcissus are the principal ingredients of these rose-water metaphors, nicely perfumed with this sweet essence. It is a wish as violent as the longing of a lady in the family-way, to see the king of kings, and a cruel privation to be unable to do more than pay half a visit by means of a letter. At

---

* This letter was written upon a large roll of paper, called by us *Chinese paper*, bespangled with particles of gold.

length, when the eloquence of the writer has become like a garden dried up by the parching winds of the desert, and in which not a single flower remains to be culled or added to the epistolary nosegay, then he thinks of saying what he has to say. However simple the business may be, it is always couched in ambigious terms, and accompanied with innumerable reservations. He then finishes in a laconic manner, like the Indians of Cooper, with "That is all," or "I have said,"—or, if he prides himself upon the highest refinement, he ends with "after that, what could there remain for me to say?"

When a virtuous woman wishes to write to her absent husband, she sends for an old priest, an intimate acquaintance of the family, and explains to him from behind a curtain what she has to communicate. The scribe, if he be sagacious, writes the despatch in the name of another person, and not of the wife—it being considered the height of vulgarity for a wife to write directly to her husband. Thus, if she has to inform him that she has lately been brought to bed, a little boy of six years of age is often stated to be the person in the straw. Notwithstanding this excessive delicacy of the ladies of the East, their husbands are by no means better off than their brothers of the Western world, especially in the middle and lower classes. Among the Rajpoots, whose country I am about to visit, bad spelling is as common in palaces as in cottages. Their manners resemble, to an astonishing degree, the chivalrous manners of France in the feudal times.

Read Colonel Tod's huge book.

Adieu, my dear friend. As we never write upon the back of this paper, I must abruptly offer you my farewell wishes. May Mohammed vouchsafe you his aid, and may the all-powerful Allah preserve you! When free from the burthen of my plants, animals, and other objects of curiosity, which I am going to ship on the Jumna, for the bridge of Austerlitz, I shall set out.

TO Mlle ZOÉ NOIZET DE SAINT PAUL, ARRAS.

Alwur, between Jaypore and Delhi,
Tuesday, February 21st, 1832.

I DID little more, my dear Zoé, than acknowledge the receipt of your long letter and little note, the date of which I do not recollect. I intended to answer you on my journey, after having quitted Delhi; but here have I been on the road for this last week, and have so much business behind hand, that, for fear of giving you more time than I can really spare, I will not re-peruse your two letters. This candour may appear something like rudeness; but, my dear friend, what can I do? Without a little bluntness of proceeding now and then, I should never get through my labours.

Do you know what occupied my thoughts this morning when returning from Ramgur on horseback?—our walk to Saint Cloud, which you recalled to my memory in so delightful a manner in your last note. You said that you had often returned alone to walk in that charming place. Indeed I have also frequently visited it in imagination since the day we were there together. I have since that period been in places of far superior beauty: the forests of North America in autumn, Hayti, Rio Janeiro, the Himalaya, and Cashmere: but since I have left them I return to them less often than to Saint Cloud. The temper of a traveller varies and follows the changes of the weather. This was a grey morning. The bullocks and camels, exposed all night to a dreadful storm, dragged themselves painfully along the wet roads. My horse, which had not escaped a single drop of this nocturnal deluge, drooped his ears, and did not obey the bridle. I was myself in a serious mood. I thought it would be melancholy to die without visiting once more together those places where we first knew each other. What happiness to meet there again! How much we should have to say to each other! I have seen and felt so much since that period! You know that I am not prodigal of friendship; but I have bestowed it upon a man whom I think I have mentioned to you in one of my preceding letters: his name is William Fraser. I have just spent six weeks with him, and, thanks to his kindness, Delhi will remain one of my happiest recollections of India.

How singular is my fortune with the English! These men, who appear so unmoved, who, among themselves, always remain so cold, unbend with me, in consequence of my openness. They even assume towards me an expression of kindness, in spite of themselves as it were, and probably for the first time in their lives. Your friendship for me, my dear Zoé, would enjoy the miracles I thus operate and without effort. Shall I be able to bring back the secret with me to Europe?—I doubt it. It appears that when there I did not possess it: I was little inclined to society, and left but few friends. You were able to judge of my disposition during the short visit you paid us in Paris in 1826. It is true I was extremely unhappy at that time; but I had never been happy for twenty-four hours in succession, and after my return from the Alps in 1824, my temper was always uneven. It was my voyage to America which changed me and made me better. I feel happy in being indebted to Porphyre for this.

My herbarium is a store of recollections. I commenced it at Lagrange in the month of May 1818. Every succeeding year I have added to it, not only by my own gleanings, but likewise through the presents of my friends. How many lively associations of thoughts and feelings does it not present! Paray at different periods of my life—before I rose into manhood, during the innocent enjoyments of youth fortunately prolonged beyond the usual term, in 1818 and 1819; Paray in 1821, in the first dawn of youthful emotions;

Paray in 1822, on my return from the Alps, after I had reached man's estate, initiated into the great ideas of life, alive to the feeling of arts and poetry; Paray in 1824, during the tumult of the passions. Hervy* at different periods. When you came to Paris my connection with Jaubert had ceased. From the bottom of my heart I accused him of weakness and almost of ingratitude towards me. But since that period I have forgiven him for separating himself from me, and the recollections of our friendship have assumed their wonted charm. So much for Hervy. I will one day explain to you how I came to lose a friend to whom I was once attached. When I knew him, he had a greater knowledge of botany than I had, and he gave a more philosophical direction to my studies in that branch of science. I still love to remember it. A kind-hearted German, with whom I became intimate in Switzerland, and who showed me the friendship of a brother, has enriched my herbarium with the plants of the North and East of Europe. His name is Charpentier; and he is a first-rate geologist. Mr. Ramond, an old man, who has left some good works upon science, and was the first who explored the Pyrenees, gave me the plants of those mountains, which were unknown before his travels in those regions. Contrary to his usual demeanour towards others in general, he was very kind

---

* The seat of M. Jaubert, Member of the Chamber of Deputies.

and amiable towards me. My herbarium will often recall him to my mind, for I shall constantly find in it the plants of the Pyrenees ticketed in his own handwriting. I pass over the others, my dear Zoé, to tell you that you ought to furnish your share to this depôt of recollections. I sent you some plants from Cashmere and Tibet. For professional persons, each of these plants is worth a hundred of the plants of Barly. Your friendship, I am persuaded, does not prize them less than the dry passion of the learned. Well Zoé, you must pay your debt, if you have an opportunity. Do not fear to send me only common plants. It is to think of you rather than to study, that I ask you for them. Besides, it was only on my return from America that I decided upon poisoning my herbarium with corrosive sublimate, for the worms had made great havoc among the old specimens, those of the common plants which I had collected the first. Your gifts will then come very a-propos.

Good night, my sweet friend. I answer you playfully, as you write—what can be more agreeable? I do not speak to you at present of myself, because my father will forward to you the letters which I shall write to him from Ajmeer, and the subject of *me* will be treated as fathers will have it from their sons, that is to say, in great detail. After the atmosphere of society I breathed at Delhi and Subhatoo, my solitary and wandering life pleases me much. To teach you to laugh at what you call my so-styled Hindostanee characters (it is you who thus call them), and which were true and good Persian, I will converse with Fraser in that language only, if ever chance brings us three together at the same table. I cannot be too modest: I can read with tolerable ease a letter not very well written, which is very difficult, and which many Englishmen cannot accomplish after a residence in India of ten or twenty years. But I have given myself much trouble, without speaking of the money I have spent to attain this. My Persian secretary costs me fifty rupees a month, and a camel, which is more than a hundred and fifty francs. The fellow has three servants. It was impossible to get one for less, and equally impossible to do without, obliged, as I am, to correspond with the princes whose dominions I traverse. Who would believe this at Paris? Who would doubt it in London? Adieu, my dear Zoé. Write to me often. Remember me to George, if he is with you; let him also write to me.

TO M. JACQUEMONT, SENIOR, PARIS.

Ferozpore, S. W. of Delhi, between that city and Jaypore, February 19th, 1832. Sunday.

My dear Father,—I treat you like a crowned head, for it is only to such that this paper, strewed with gold and silver, is made use of. It is the finest manufactured at Delhi, which by the way, does little credit to Indian industry. But bad as it is, the pen runs over it more glibly than over ours. You have only to sit before the table, and if you have but a pen in your hand, in the course of half an hour you will, without any exertion, find the long sheet filled on either side.

Ferozpore is not less agreeable to the ear than your favorite Belaspore: I find it much pleasanter on account of its Persian origin. Feroze, in Persian, means sublime, excellent. It is the name of the pretty stone which we call turquoise—and that is not all. Two leagues from this very Ferozpore, as I was coming this morning on foot from Naguinah, with weather as delicious as our lovely April mornings, I saw a troop of horsemen advancing, headed by a fine young man whom I recognised as the nawaub. He alighted from his horse to approach me. We embraced each other as on the stage, upon each other's shoulders, and after exchanging some other expressions of Asiatic politeness, we re-mounted our horses, and he conducted me to the elegant villa whence I am now writing to you. The guns of the adjoining fort were fired as I alighted at the garden gate. Breakfast was served up when we entered the hall, and in the European fashion, with all the elegance and style imaginable. As it is the Ramazan, my host, who is a Mussulmaun, could not with propriety set me the example at table, but he did the honours in the most graceful manner. He did not insist upon my taking tea, nor partaking of the good things which covered the table. He allowed me to drink my constitutional bowl of milk and eat a few oranges only. But his politeness knew how to avail itself of my frugality. He said to me that the most brilliant creatures of the Divinity lived only upon the honey of flowers, and that he was not surprised to see so great an *aflatoune* and *aristoune* as I, imitate their delicate frugality.

After breakfast I dismissed Shaim-Shouddin (the name of this young man); at noon I shall pay him a visit in the fort, where his little palace is situated, and where I suppose he is now breakfasting in secret on account of the Ramazan. We will then take a turn on an elephant for a couple of hours, to see the environs of his capital, and I shall return to work for the remainder of the day.

This young man is the eldest of a grand Mogul family, the chief of which, thirty years ago, had the good sense to join the army of Lord Lake against the Mahrattas. The British government recognised his services by confirming him in the possession of his principality which he had formed in those troubled times. He is like a German duke. In the event of war, he is obliged to furnish his contingent of cavalry to the British government if required, and this contingent is in proportion to his revenues. The Grand Duke of Ferozpore is richer than many members of the German diet: he has four lacs, or a million of francs, a year.

My well-known intimacy with Mr. William Fraser was quite sufficient to insure from the young nawaub the polite reception he gave me; but Mr. Martin, the resident, who is to all these nawaubs and rajahs what Prince Metternich is to the German dukes, had himself written, a long time previously, to announce my arrival. It will be the same so far as Bombay. I was much affected at leaving Fraser. In order to spare each other the pain of leave-taking, we had tacitly agreed that I should depart, and that he should let me go like a thief, without crying "stop him". But when my servant came to tell me that the camels were already gone, and my horse ready, I forgot my stoical determination of the preceding day. Fraser's heart was as full as mine, and we quitted each other after a silent shake of the hand.

Tuesday last, the 14th instant, I encamped at Cuttob, upon the ruins of ancient Delhi. I could not succeed in banishing the melancholy impressions of my departure. In the night, one of Fraser's attendants came galloping to me with a note from his master, saying that he experienced the same grief, and had resolved to defer his business and run after me to spend a few more days with me. I wished it more than I dared hope for it, because I knew that Fraser ought to have left Delhi five weeks previously, to preside at the assizes of his district; and that, to accompany me, he neglected the duties of his office, and exposed himself to the censure of Government. I therefore went the following day, in very low spirits, and pitched my camp at Goorgaon; however, on my way, I met two singular characters, who came very a-propos to divert my sorrow. The first was a young officer who recollected having seen me at Calcutta at Mr. Pearson's; he accosted me by name. He was coming from Agra, to get change of air for his young wife who was unwell. I do not know how he came to discover that I was not a fanatically zealous Christian; but discover it he did, and in order to make a proselyte of me he related his history, which in no wise resembled that of the Savoyard curate. Quarrelsome, and a duellist, he had killed one of his brother officers at Calcutta, during the time I was there: all the circumstances of the duel tended to render the result of it deplorable. My young friend told me he was near losing his senses on the occasion: he ought to have said that he became entirely bereft of them. He fell into the hands of priests, and a young and rather pretty girl who was of a religious turn; they have succeeded between them in making him the most determined Christian I ever met. He had a good stock of bibles with him, and begged me so hard to accept of one, that I conferred that favour upon him. He promised me that his wife and he would pray with all their might for my conversion; and, wishing him every success in his prayers, I took my leave of him until we meet again in Paradise.

As, however, I was travelling on foot, the very compact bible of this friendly zealot felt very heavy in my pocket. I soon gave it in charge to my secretary; this descendant of the Prophet, caring very little for the divine work, put it into the geological bag, along with the stones and hammer.

On my arrival at Goorgaon, I received the visit of the nazer, or Hindoo judge. Forming a most extraordinary exception to the inhabitants of Northern India, he spoke English as well as I did. He also related his history to me, in which there were no men killed; but the termination of which was deserving of perdition. He was a Brahmin of high caste, but very poor, and by his handsome countenance and precocious intelligence had interested in his favour an old British officer of the highest rank, who had brought him to Calcutta, and bestowed upon him a European education. His masters, who were English missionaries, had endeavoured to make him a christian; but he found that the bible was not superior to his *shasters*, maintained that, although his *vedas* did not reach excellence, still they were better than the bible, and that even they were not good enough for him.

In this manner he had become what I have heard called in Philadelphia a *frightful Deist*. This Brahmin was a man of sense; I kept him with me until the evening, in order to make him explain the particulars of his judicial duties.

Towards the close of the day, I was walking alone, in a sorrowful mood, in the great desert plain, where I had pitched my tent, when I saw a tall white figure advancing towards me. It was Fraser. I was going to dine, and he partook of my bowl of milk and cakes.

We made a princely dinner upon this simple fare, under the shelter of my little night tent, which I have carried with me to Tibet and Cashmere, and under which I have so often awakened among the most lovely and extraordinary scenes in the Himalaya, recalling to my memory that which I shall never more behold. It is impossible for me to finish this simple story: the nawaub has sent his elephants to fetch me; and, as the greatest test of politeness is punctuality, I go that I may not be waited for.

Sunday Evening.

The favourite pastime of the nawaub is to have his elephants beaten; the consequence is, that they are as vicious as devils. In order to have no altercation with them this morning, I paid my visit in a calash, for Shaim-Shouddin had sent me one. I returned much later than I expected, and it was only to mount my horse and set out for the neighbouring mines. Neighbouring, did I say?—not so much in the neighbourhood either; but I did not begrudge the distance, which was filled up in the most agreeable manner; for I travelled through a forest of date trees, extending over a wild glen between dark and bleak mountains. The mine was, as I expected, of the same formation as the surrounding soil.

On my way back, I saw four poor little quails, sporting innocently in the beams of the setting sun. I approached softly and treacherously, and killed them all four at one shot; they formed a great addition to my next day's dinner. Would you believe that my host has treated me with ices in the desert? I have just given him, at his own request, a certificate of hospitality, drawn up, in due form, for Mr. Martin. He deserves it.

To return to Fraser. From Goorgaon, we walked together to Sonah, on the 16th; on the 17th we arrived at Noh, on the frontier of his district, and of the British territory. He is as plain as myself in his habits, and we did not acquire the certainty how well we agreed in travelling without regretting not having visited Cashmere together. Yesterday morning, he bolted from Noh, before day-light; and although I am a very early riser, when I left my tent, I could perceive not the slightest trace of his, at the place where the previous evening we had dined and spent the evening together. He will come some day and see me at Paris. How many good and amiable men you find among the British of Northern India; I do not know why, but at Bengal it is not exactly the same thing. There is less cordiality and less intellect. This difference is proverbial in India, and not the less true because it is proverbial. Good night, my dear father: it is getting late, and I should be telling an untruth were I to state that I am not tired. I am going to bed. Good night!

Oojein in Malwa, April 3rd, 1832.

I continue, my dear father, my long history of Ferozpore. Fraser, as I mentioned, accompanied me to the British frontiers at Noh. I reckoned without my host, for I expected to have received some civilities from the rajah of Alweer, and he was, on the contrary, most singularly uncivil. I paid him off for it, which I could allow myself, and indeed was in a manner obliged to do. I encountered him as he was going to meet the Governor-general, at that time returning from Ajmeer, where there had been a kind of, I believe very useless, congress of Rajpoot princes. I received from Lord William the kindest invitation to proceed to his camp, and at the same time the means of doing so without loss of time; namely, relays of saddle horses, and horsemen stationed upon the road to serve me as guides. Leaving, therefore, my caravan to proceed at a bullock's pace on their route to Jaypore, I gallopped off to the left, and from Rajghur, reached at Kalakoh the Governor-general's camp. This was on the Saturday morning. Lord William always halts on the Sunday, because God Almighty, they say, rested on that day. I remained two days with him, and received greater kindness than ever from him. I have written all that to M. Victor, but by mistake in English, and my writing is so bad, that I doubt if he will be able to make it out. As I find that water agrees with me, since my departure from Delhi I have resisted the temptation of Champagne and Sauterne, which wines circulate freely at Lord William's table. An excellent orchestra played the "Parisienne" during the meal; in the middle of a desert in Rajpootana! What say you to that? In order to give me an idea of a Rajpootana court, Lord William took me with him to receive the visit of the rajah of Alwur, and the following day Lady William lent me her elephant to accompany Lord William, who returned his visit. But the poor devil of a rajah was much disappointed, as he did not receive the khelat. A great number of complaints had been made against him, and, in order to punish him for his want of civility, he was refused this distinction, granted to the other Rajpoot princes. Lord William spent the best part of Sunday in talking politics with me, and of course India was the theme of our conversation. He asked me also a number of questions relative to the Punjab. We left each other perfect friends. Lady William took up all the time which the Governor-general left me, and when I quitted her she gave me a letter of introduction to the Earl of Clare, the new governor of Bombay, who is an intimate acquaintance of hers. A few hours' gallop brought me up to my caravan, which I found in the sand; but this had given me no uneasiness, as the baggage had been guarded since our departure from Delhi by a serjeant and fourteen men. I arrived at Jaypore on the 1st of March, and remained there three days to see this town and its environs. It is, without comparison, the finest city in India, and the surrounding country is extremely interesting. Thence

I proceeded to Ajmeer, the prettiest place I have seen; I mean of those on the plains, for I prefer Nahun and Mundeenaghur in the Himalaya. From Ajmeer I made an excursion to Beawr, the capital of Mhairwarra, a mountainous country, inhabited by a race of men indigenous in India, and following no other industry, for centuries past, than that of freeebooters, exercising their depredations in the adjacent plains of Marwar and Mewar. They have been, within the last ten years, miraculously converted to order and liberty; the latter however being only for the men. The husband buys his wife, the father sells his daughter, the son sells his mother. Among the women, dishonour consists not in being sold, but in being ill sold. I will show you in my portfolio a few of those tender fathers, and delicate husbands, and respectful sons. Beg of M. Victor to read or translate to you my history of Mhairwarra. It cost me eighty miles, or thirty-four leagues, in thirty-six hours, on horseback and on an elephant. I was fairly worn out on my arrival at Ajmeer. Between Delhi and Rajghur, I had been fortunate enough to discover some very interesting geological phenomena. I had the same good luck at another Rajghur, situated in the mountains which separate the valley of Ajmeer from the plain of Nusserabad, where I remained only one day to change my bullocks, my camels, and my escort. These Rajghurs must perplex you dreadfully, by their constant repetition on the map. *Ghur* signifies a fort or castle; and every lord of a village has a great propensity to give himself the title of rajah. Thus every village has its rajghur, and often has no other name, unless it be *rajpoor*, or *rajepoora*, or *rajekote* or *kajekoti; poor, poorât; kote, koti;* and *naghur*, which I was nearly forgetting have nearly the same signification as *ghur*.

I pitched my tent at the foot of Fort Chittore, celebrated in the history of India. I should have liked to have been able to have visited it, not on account of its antiquities, for which I care little, but for the sakes of the stones of the mountains which it serves to defend. I found the grapes sour: for having no express order from the court of Odeypoor to be admitted, I could not enter it.

I wrote to Porphyre from Khachrode, which you will find close to this place, although I made a considerable circuit to get there. I went to Rutlaum, from curiosity to examine in their places some singular stones, which I had seen used at Joura, and where I had no other trouble than to get myself carried in Captain Borthwick's palanquin. This gentleman is a political agent of the British government in these provinces, allied or tributaries to Malwa. You must add this name to the list, already rather long, of Indian saints; for Captain Borthwick was excessively kind to me. I visited the quarries, which I was so justly anxious to see. I returned to Khachrode this morning, and left it again for Oudgene with the minister of the young nawaub of Joura, whom Mr. Borthwick begged to accompany me here, and who will be my cicerone. He is one of the most intelligent Indians I have met with; he is a Mussulmaun, as are almost all the people here of whom any good can be said.

We are very apprehensive of a revolution in England. Not that such an event would shake the British power in this country, but on account of the numerous failures which it would occasion. For my own part, I entertain fears of something worse; indeed I fear every thing. Our revolution appears to me much less decisive than it was a year ago, when it had allies. Wade has, with a great deal of difficulty, made Runjeet-Sing consent to open to the British the navigation of the Indus. There is something of fear of the Russians at the bottom of this negociation. Towards Hazarubang and Ramghur, on the road from Calcutta to Benares, there are some regiments employed in making a terrible example of the revolted Coles. Adieu.

Mundlesir, on the borders of the Nerbudda, April 25th.

My dear father,—I passed through Indore without finding any letters from Europe, neither were there any at Mow. Thence I proceeded to Maundoo, immense and almost unknown ruins, on the border of the plain which supports the mountains of Vyndhia. The heat had become intolerable. I there found much to enrich my herbarium. The table, on the corner of which I am now writing to you, is covered with stones which I have brought from thence. I next went to

Mheysur, on the banks of this river, and three days ago I arrived at Mundlesir. It is the residence of Captain Sandys, a British political agent, who had the extreme kindness to send me, on the mountains of Maundoo, some horsemen and guides to show me those beautiful and extraordinary places. I had no other recommendation to him than a letter from Mr. Martin, the ex-resident of Delhi, and at present resident of Indore, one of whose lieutenants is the political agent of Mundlesir; and besides that, my name is now known to everybody in India. How I know not; for I avoid appearing before the public in whatever manner it may be, though others, no doubt, in my situation, would do so in order to enjoy more consideration. I here draw back from every species of publicity, and only present myself to individuals. There are some very ignorant scribblers who have not the same reserve, and are continually thrusting themselves into notice. I should be little flattered to have any thing in common with them, and I remain as quiet as possible. But my wandering life brings me into connexion with so many men, in a country where men (I mean men from our country) are not very numerous, that I find myself known to the greatest part of this community of Europeans. In short, Mr. Sandys overwhelms me with kindness and civility; and, although Mundlesir is one of the hottest places in India, I recruit myself perfectly here. My attendants were more in want of rest than I was. They had suffered more than I from the excessive heats of my last marches. My bullock chariots had broken down in the mountains. I left half my army, and the most intelligent of my attendants, to take care of them, and get them repaired, and I came on here with the camels. The rear guard has now rejoined the camp. There is no want of sick. I physic them as well as I am able, and with success. As for myself, I enjoy the immense luxury of a house. There are in a town life in Europe many admirable advantages which we enjoy without appreciating them, and, whatever my future fate may be, I think I shall always find in my European destiny enough to be thankful for and attach to me to life. There are a thousand things of which we only know the value when we are deprived of them—the luxury of eating bread every day, of sitting upon a chair, of sleeping upon a mattress, of drinking wine, whether good or bad. After my travels in Asia, little will, I hope, suffice for my physical comforts.

I am here in the country of the Bheels, a nation indigenous in India, and robbers by profession. Their Mahratta sovereigns were incapable of governing them, and within the last ten years the British have undertaken to govern the country, handing over the revenues to the Mahratta prince. They have already operated an immense salutary change in the manners of these savages.

I shall probably pass to-morrow on the Nerbudda, which flows at a hundred paces from hence, and enters the Bombay territory; and at Ajuntah, I shall enter that of the Nizam. This country, the geological structure of which is quite peculiar, has also a singular configuration: it differs entirely from every other country I have seen before in India. The Nerbudda possesses an original character of beauty which no other river has ever presented to me; it is of a most extraordinary nature.

This morning I received a parcel from Chandernagore, the sight of which filled me with joy; its thickness made me hope that I should find some letters from Europe. There was only one from the Jardin, announcing to me the supplement of indemnity which the minister of commerce and public works has granted me, of three thousand francs for the year 1831, and three thousand francs for the current year, in all, and once paid, six thousand francs, which I have requested my banker to add to my credit. These gentlemen inform me that they have not yet verified upon whose proposal it is that M. D'Argout granted me this indemnity. I suppose it is a reply to the demand of funds which I addressed from Kurnaul to the minister, in February, 1831. They acknowledge the receipt of two of my letters, the last dated from Lahore in March, 1831; I hope, therefore, that at the time they wrote to me (November 21st, 1831) you had also received your share of my packet from the Punjab. The last letter which I received from you is dated June, 1831, and is already very old! Adieu, my dear father, remember me to all around you. One word more: M. de Melay, whom

I had consulted upon the means of converting a simple knight of the legion of honour into an officer of that order, begs me to address him a short memorial on the subject of M. Allard; he writes that he will support it with all his bureaucratic eloquence in transmitting it to the minister, and that he does not doubt of the success of our united prose. I am, therefore, going to write the best prose in my power; and shall feel happy if I can contribute in procuring for a worthy countryman a recompense for the manner in which he upholds the honour of the French name in the distant regions of the Punjab.

Adieu, once more, and for the last time; and now guard against cold, heat, and damp. Farewell my dear father; take care of yourself for your own sake and for mine. Think of the pleasure of talking at our fireside of that burning furnace Mundlesir, and of so many other things of which I shall be full when we see each other again. I love and embrace you with all my heart.

TO M. VICTOR DE TRACY, PARIS*.

Camp, in Malwa, between Chitton and Indorre,
29th March, 1832.

My dear Friend,—About the middle of February I have left the beautiful Delhi to see it no more; and

---

* This letter was written by Jacquemont in English, and is given *verbatim*.—Tr.

since that time I march in a southerly direction. I border already on the tropic: the sun in mid-day appears to be almost vertical, not a cloud in the sky, and the breeze rises gently on the morning, which when it is not yet wanted, becomes a gale of hot wind about nine o'clock; yet this is only the beginning of the monsoon. It will be fairly set in, and rage in all its fury when I shall have to cross the valleys of the Nerbuddah and of the Taptee. I should not think so much of it, since I am doomed to it for the remainder of my travels in India, and I hope I shall get by and by accustomed to it; but it is a hard trial for one lately from the Himalaya.

I wish I were again on my way to Cashmere, flying from the sun every day, instead of facing it as I do; how gladly would I take again the chances of the adventurous journey! But, alas! the drama of human life is performed once only, and my imagination, which pictures to me such beautiful scenes of the Himalaya, makes me feel bitterly that I am dead already to the reality of their actual enjoyment. You remember Dante's lines:

——Nessun maggior dolore,
Che ricordarsi del felice,
Nella miseria.

Well, there is no great difference between hell itself and a tent exposed to this Indian sun, so far, at least, as temperature goes; and this is true misery, and is felt the more so when one thinks of the cool shades of Cashmere, of its streams, and of its forests.

You know already how I was detained at Delhi so much beyond my expectations. And now, suffering as I do from the excessive heat, I cannot yet say that I regret to have made so long a stay in the imperial city. There I lived with a friend; and the sweet remembrances of friendship are blended with those of the place where that friendship originated. Delhi shall ever be one of my dearest recollections of the East. My route to Jaypore led me first through a country exceedingly interesting in a geological point of view—Ferospoor and Alwur. I spent a pleasant day at the former place with the young nawaub Shemkoodden-Khan, whom I had met with already as a visitor at my friend Fraser's; he entertained me with the greatest hospitality. By way of compensation, the Alwur rajah proved very industriously uncivil towards me. Had I been an obscure traveller, I would not have taken the least notice of his want of courtesy; but, introduced as I was to his notice by the very highest British authorities, I could not but resent it for them; and, acquainted as I am, since my journey across the Sutledge, with Eastern manners, I found it little difficult to make the foolish prince apologise for his backwardness. The Governor-general was then marching from Adjmeer to Agrah; his route was almost parallel with mine, in an opposite direction. I received from his camp an exceedingly flattering invitation to join it; horses were sent to me, and stationed in the way, with horsemen to guide and escort me: and, leaving my caravan, on the 25th of February, long before day-light, I arrived before noon at the tents of the Governor-general, after many an hour of hard riding. Lord W. Bentinck was to stay two days in the place where I met him; however attentive he and Lady William had been always to me since the day of my arrival in Calcutta, never did I receive from them such a kind reception. I spent with them two days, which I shall never forget. The camp was pitched in a weary desert of Rajpootanah. It appeared like a moving city. Though exceedingly averse to any thing like state, Lord W. Bentinck cannot dispense altogether with the pomp by which the former Governors-general of India surrounded themselves in their journeys. Many of the chief officers of the state must accompany him to despatch the business of the various branches of the service. Every one of the heads of departments has a number of deputies and assistants. Then comes the personal state of the Governor-General, then his escort, consisting of a regiment of infantry, one of cavalry, his body guards, a light battery, and comes after all an immense number of camp followers. The sight was quite new to me, and very interesting, as you may fancy. To welcome my arrival at head-quarters, my friend the Alwur rajah arrived there also on the same day. He had been summoned, that, after paying a visit to his lordship, he might receive one in return; an attention which had been paid by the Governor-General to all the other Rajpoot princes, except to him, in a first occasion. The rajah expected also to receive a khelat, or honorary dress, a distinction bestowed on many other chieftains of his rank. The reception afforded me an opportunity of seeing a Rajpoot court in all its gaiety and glittering. After the Asiatic exhibitions of the day, I sat in the evening by the right of Lady William Bentinck, at a large table, to a superb dinner. The party was numerous; an excellent band was in attendance in a contiguous tent; Lady William told me she had lately received from the Palais Royal *la Parisienne*, and desired it to be performed for me. What a strange concourse of circumstances! I felt inwardly grateful for it: I enjoyed it thoroughly. The evening before, at that time, alone in my little tent, pitched in a solitary spot at the foot of a hill, sitting to my usual meal, a plain pillau; a single candle burning on my small table, often blasted away by the wind; no noise but the loud shrieks of the jackalls about my cattle, bullocks, and camels; every thing about me of the country where I was. And but for twenty-four hours what a complete change around! All the luxuries and refinements of Europe! Lord William, the next day, was able to command some hours of leisure, which we spent together in his tent, talking of his country, of its probable destinies, glancing, too, at Europe, and concluding by exclaiming, how strange was our meeting *there*, and talking *there* of such things. He, a man from England, one of the crowd there; here the absolute ruler of Asia: I, quietly engaged in my philosophical researches amidst barbarous tribes! We smiled at the idea of deeply-laid combinations to bring in such extraordinary circumstances, which have arisen chiefly from chance and necessity. How little understood is this political phenomenon in Europe.

On the 27th, long before day-light, the tents were struck down. I found a horse and a couple of horsemen in waiting at the door of mine. I mounted, and trusting to the good eyes of my guides, and to the sure footing of my chargers, I rushed forward at a sharp canter, on a rough path intersected by ravines; and, changing horses and guides on my way, in a few hours I joined again my poor little wretched camp, where I could not but fancy that the whole of the two days past was a dream.

I have since seen the superb Jaypore, and the delightful Adjmeer: and, during my very short stay in the latter, I have contrived to visit Mhairwarrah, the former Abruzzi of Rajpootanah. It was well worth eighty miles riding in little more than twenty-four hours. I saw a country, whose inhabitants since an immemorial time had never had any other means of existence but plunder in the adjacent plains of Marhwar and Meywar, a people of murderers; now changed into a quiet, industrious, and happy people of shepherds and cultivators. No Rajpoot chiefs, no Mogul emperors, had ever been able to subdue them; fourteen years ago every thing was to be done with them; and since six or seven years, every thing is done already. A single man has worked that wonderful miracle of civilisation; Major Henry Hall, the son-in-law of Colonel Fagan, of whom I have written to you at Delhi. As I know it will be gratifying to your feelings and to your opinions on the subject, I shall add, my dear friend, that Major Hall has accomplished this admirable social experiment without taking a single life.

The very worst characters of Mhairwarrah, he secured them, confined them, or put them in irons at work on the roads. Those who had lived long by the sword without becoming notorious for wanton cruelty, he made them soldiers; they became in that capacity the keepers of their former associates, and often of their chiefs; and the rest of the population was gained to the plough. Female infanticide was a prevalent practice with the Mhairs, and generally throughout Rajpootanah; and now female casualties amongst infants exceed not male casualties; a proof that the bloody practice has been abandoned, and scarcely has a man been punished for it. Major Hall did not punish the offenders, he removed the cause of the crime, and made the crime useless, even injurious to the offender; and it is never more committed.

Major Hall has shown to me, on the field, the corps which he has raised from amongst those former savages, and I have seen none in the Indian army in a higher state of discipline. He was justly proud of his good work, and spared no trouble to himself that I might see it thoroughly in the few hours I had to spend with him. Upwards of a hundred villagers were summoned from the neighbouring villages and hamlets; I conversed with them of their former mode of life, and of their present avocations. Most of these men had shed blood. He told me they knew not any other mode of life: it was a most miserable one by their account; they were naked and starving. Now, poor as is the soil of their small valleys and barren their hills, every hand being set at work, there is plenty of clothes, of food; and so sensible are they of the immense benefit conferred upon them by the British government, that willingly they pay to it already 500,000 francs, which they increase every year, as their national wealth admits of it.

Often I had thought that gentle means would prove inadequate to the task of breaking-in populations addicted for ages to a most unruly savage life; such as the Greeks for instance. Yet the Klephtes were but lambs compared to the Mhairs; and the Mhairs in a few years have become an industrious, laborious, and well-behaved people. I see by the Bombay papers that M. Capo d'Istrias has been murdered: I wish Major Hall were his successor; for, now, I have the greatest confidence in the efficiency of *gentle means*. But a peculiar talent, too, which is a gift of nature, is required in the ruler, without which the most benevolent intentions would prove useless. We know, by a Persian express, the fall of Warsaw, and the rejection of the reform bill by the Lords, with the outrages which have taken place immediately after it. Unsatisfactory as may be the state of our country, England is much worse. Things might be settled in France without collision, whilst in England it appears to me that it cannot be done without hurting many private interests. Inequality in every thing there has grown to a monstrous degree. It must be somewhat lessened: will the gentle measures of the laws of inheritance, &c. &c. be quietly waited for? The working classes in the large towns of England are horribly degraded by usual drunkenness. I believe that in the course of our first revolution, atrocious as it was, there was scarcely a scene more shameful for the human species than the late riot at Bristol. Thanks to that revolution of ours, there is now in France such a gradual transition between the higher and lower classes, and such an absence of lines of social demarcation, that we have nothing to fear of the calamities with which England is threatened. In England there are two classes perfectly distinct. The gentry (which includes the nobility), and the people. The natives of India have long since smartly enough made the distinction. They have two expressions only to mention a European: a *saheb logue*, a lord, a gentleman, or rather of the caste of lords or gentlemen; and a *gora logue*, or one of the caste of the whites, a white man. The former character is much respected by them; the latter may be dreaded, as it is indeed very often quite dreadful, but respected never.

There are disturbances in a district of Central India, which I have visited two years ago, just after leaving Calcutta. They are of a more serious nature than it was at first anticipated, yet I believe the insurrection completely put down already. It was not political at all, but called for, it appears, by the mismanagement of the local authorities. The more I know of this fabric, the more extraordinary it appears to me. No guess can be made at its durability, it may last centuries, and may be swept away in a few months. However, this I will foretell: the British power in India will not perish by foreign aggression. Foreign aggression indeed may do much towards its destruction, but more by the spirit of rebellion it will raise every where throughout the provinces of the empire, than by the actual collision of the invaders with the British armies. *Si vis pacem, para bellum*, has been of late a maxim too little acted upon. For the sake of economy, several corps, which, it is true, were but very little useful, have been disbanded; and India is the country of the world where men are the less prone to change their profession. There are few *Major Halls*, to work the miracles he has done. Disbanded soldiers turn out robbers. There are many well organised gangs of highwaymen in these independent states, and without a strong escort I should be plundered to a certainty. Lord William will leave to his successor a more satisfactory budget, but I apprehend he will leave to him also ample occasion for many new expenses. I hear from Lahore sometimes by M. Allard. Some uneasiness is felt there regarding a claim from the English Government, supported by its diplomatic agent, to have the navigation of the Indus freely open. Runjeet-Sing is very reluctant to it; but he is too wise not to submit, though reluctantly. His son, Cheyr-Sing, is now viceroy of Cashmere. 'Tis a great pity he did not fill that situation a year ago, when I was there, for he is a great friend with the French officers in his father's service, and very friendly to the Europeans; besides, for a seikh, let it be well understood, a high-feeling, noble, young man. The low villain who pressed so hard upon the poor helpless Cashmeerians during my stay in Cashmere is likely now brought to his accounts, and severely retaliated upon. Runjeet-Sing's treasury and Cheyr-Sing's favour with his father will benefit by it, but not the poor Cashmerians certainly.

But what do you care about Runjeet and Cheyr-Sing and Cashmere? I will speak of me to atone for so much lunary matter. My health has been lately a little tried by the immense changes of temperature I was subject to. In the sandy deserts of Rajpootanah, such is the dryness of the air, the transparency of the sky, that, in the starry calm nights of the winter, the thermometer reaches the freezing point, owing to the principle of radiation. I marched two or three hours in that cold atmosphere every morning, and the sun early was so powerful as to raise the temperature of my tent, where I spend the afternoon, to 35 and 36 degrees, by and by it will be 43 and 44°, if not more, but then the nights will be almost equally hot. I caught a very bad cold, for which I was obliged to put up three days at Nemutet, the last English station which I have passed through, and where I was most kindly taken care of by a good old gentleman whom I had seen at Simlah and at Delhi, now the superintending surgeon of the army in these quarters; I made there a new acquaintance with a Swiss family, the gentleman having got a commission in the company's service some twenty years ago, is now in command of a regiment, with the reputation of an excellent officer; ten years ago he went on leave to Europe and married in his country at Berne, just at the time when I travelled in Switzerland. They knew some of my acquaintances in their country, and most of the places which I had visited, we spoke of them, helping each others' memory, and forgot entirely the Jura which makes France and Switzerland two distinct countries; we felt like countrymen, the simplicity of their manners was a thing which I had not witnessed since I left France; I was quite delighted with them, we spoke of the English as if foreigners to us, although we were adopted members of their society. Both husband and wife proved very accomplished persons, I have spent some happy hours with them, and not parted with them without a sincere promise to inquire after them whenever I may visit their country again, as they intend to retire there in a short time.

Adieu, my dear friend, through the bamboo screen of the door of my tent I see the sun setting behind a grove of date trees; no such things in your Paray, but your temperate countries have their poetry also, variety makes up abundantly for magnificence. It is time for my hot spiced pillau, after which I write a couple of hours more, before sending my caravan ahead by the cool of the night. This would-be English of mine is quite French: ten times more so than when I write to an Englishman, why the difference? I assure you without vanity that I speak and write it quite differently with the English, much more like them: perhaps because with them I think more like them and for English feelings find more readily at hand English expressions; whatever may be the incorrectness of my speech in their tongue, I have seldom to be ashamed of it with the English in this country, as Lady M. Bentinck is the only person that ever offered to speak French with me. Adieu again, the blank beneath I shall fill it up at Indore, whence I shall forward this to Calcutta.

* I must leave off writing to you in English, since it would be impossible for me to tell you in that language that I love you and embrace you with all my heart.

---

* The remainder of this letter was written in French.—Tr.

Vojein, 5th April.

A few words more, my dear friend, to fill up the page, it is not that I am in want of occupation, but I cannot work, liable as I am to receive numerous visiters. This city is the largest and most celebrated in the dominions of Scindia, at present under the British protectorate; my arrival was announced in such a manner that I found a pretty little palace prepared to receive me, and the constituted and other authorities came to make me their salaam; I answered them in my best Hindostanee; I received from Neemuch the last gazettes of Calcutta, and this morning, on horseback on the road, read the sixteen immense columns of Lord Brougham's speech in the house of lords, on the 7th of October last. What talents! but what a perverted use of talent! What a disagreeable kind of talent is that which disgusts the hearer instead of conciliating him. If I were a public man I would study Lord Brougham in order not to resemble him; what is the use of that cutting irony, that bitter sarcasm, that supercilious pride? What is the use of these quotations of Greek and Latin verses? The English entertain a sovereign contempt for our parliamentary debates, with regard both to the form and to the matter. For my part, I have the same feeling, and from the bottom of my heart for the forms of theirs, what think you of them? Adieu once more, I shall rest here two days, this letter will go from Indore, remember me to your family.

TO M. PORPHYRE JACQUEMONT, PARIS.

Khacherode, in Malwa, 31 *March,* 1832.

I WRITE you a few words, my dear friend, before the arrival of my basin of milk and its accompaniment of chepatties; and on the conclusion of my breakfast, I shall sit down to my occupations for the day. In the afternoon I shall certainly not be in so good humour, because then there will be ninety or a hundred degrees of heat in my tent, and a poor devil condemned to be baked can scarcely feel any disposition to be merry. The summer has set in these six or seven days; its arrival has been something like that of a cannon-ball, which gives no notice of its approach, and I am caught. You must recollect reading in the papers of the day, that Dr. Oudney was reported to have died of cold in the deserts of Africa: well, only a week ago, at sunrise, in the desert and sandy plains of Rajpootana, the thermometer fell almost to freezing point; in the course of the day it rose to ninety, and, under a tent exposed to the sun, to a hundred and five. The cold and hot air-baths which I was thus obliged to take, whether I would or not, produced a bad cold on my chest; I completely lost my voice for several days. I wanted to cover my throat and chest with leeches on my arrival at Neemuch, where I stopped and remained three days at the house of an old gentleman of my acquaintance, chief physician to the army in these provinces; but the good man had his prejudices against leeches, and although I had not the slightest confidence in his medical talents, I allowed him, through politeness, to do as he pleased, and contented myself with fasting, and drinking expectorating ptisans. Five days since I resumed my journey, and am almost cured; the notes of my voice, however, are still singularly hollow and sepulchral. It is evident that my throat is always my weakest part. This little accident appears to me almost a periodical return of the one which made me spend last year at Prountch, between the Punjab and Cashmere, a month later than this year, but under similar circumstances of temperature. Last year the disorder was much more severe; I experienced great pain in the chest, from which I am free this spring. It is true I had then suffered considerable fatigue since my arrival in the mountains of Mirpore; instead of which, ever since my departure from Delhi, I have, comparatively speaking, travelled very comfortably. I have nevertheless made much longer marches than in any of my preceding campaigns. But I have two horses, and even three since I dismissed the moonshee (Persian secretary) whom I had engaged at Delhi, and mounted upon the Ghounte of Koulton, which the Rajah of Mondi gave me last November; in spite of the bad state of this cavalry, there is always one of them capable of carrying me. One of the horses is lame through the stupidity of the farrier who shod him; the ghounte has a sore back from the saddle of my moonshee, and were it not for my faithful sorrel of Calcutta, I should be obliged to walk the remainder of my journey. This creature is more vicious than ever, and, about a fortnight ago, he threw me, without my being able to know how it happened, upon a heap of stones, from which I got up much bruised. This was near Ajmeer; he had not taken that liberty with me for two years past. I have been taken in by my friend Fatteh-Oulla-Beg-Khan; the horse which he sold me for four hundred and twenty five rupees (nearly eleven hundred francs) is nothing but a sorry jade. When the back of the ghounte is cured, and can again bear a saddle, I shall get rid of this pest at any price. The wags of Bombay may joke as they please about my long legs, and the smallness of my horses.

It is most fortunate for me that I met the governor-general at Rajpootana. He, as well as Lady William Bentinck, assured me that I might rely upon the hospitality of the Earl of Clare, Governor of Bombay, whom they knew personally before they met him at the species of Indian congress which Lord William had lately held at Ajmeer, and where the Governor of Bombay was present, as well as a dozen Rajpoot princes. I suppose that the fine work of Colonel Tod has put these latter in vogue in London and even at Paris, and that you have heard a great deal respecting them. Were it not for the protection of the British government, there is not one of these proud kinglings who would not long since have become a pensioner and prisoner of Runjeet-Sing. This is all fudge. I should only like to see two or three hundred of Runjeet's grey beards in the midst of as many thousands of these bullies of Rajpootana.

In India, my dear friend, every one has the pretension to smoke the tobacco of Bhilsa. The real amateurs have some doubts about it, founded upon the very limited extent of the territory of Bhilsa, which you will find somewhere in the principality of Bhopal, in Central India. But what is still better, I am assured that there never was a plant of tobacco at Bhilsa, and that the far-famed tobacco of that name is nothing more than the Khacherode sent there for sale. I am going to try it, and if I find it good I will bring you a small packet of it. I have not accustomed myself to smoking, but merely indulge in it now and then, and sometimes at intervals of months. Since my departure from Delhi, I drink nothing but pure water and milk, which is a regimen of my own choosing, entirely *ad libitum;* I find it agree with me very well. I do not eat meat every day, and find that also agree with me still better. Thanks to this regimen, I suffer much less from the heat than any other European. At this season of the year, no Europeans travel; all the movements of troops have ceased since the 10th of March; every one remains quietly at home behind mats of vetiver, kept continually wetted, which produces an agreeable freshness by evaporation of the water; or else under the draft occasioned by screens attached to the ceiling, or fanned by attendants, and pass their time in cursing the country, in drinking brandy and water, and smoking the houkha. At break of day they take a short gallop, which is continued only until sun-rise; and in the evening, at sun-set, an airing in a carriage, and that is all their exercise. This is very different from the life I lead. I have stood it now for three years, and trust I shall hold out until the end. I anticipate one thing with pleasure on my return: it is that of bringing back myself, not the least difficult thing to do, for how very few return! At Delhi I found several persons who confessed to me, that when I set out for Lahore fifteen months ago, they little expected to see me again.

A great number of robberies take place in these provinces; but beyond the Sutledge a European has seldom or never been attacked. Besides, I have a strong escort for my baggage, which without this protection would infallibly be plundered; I march on alone with few attendants, but well armed. Your arms are excellent. I lately shot an antelope at two hundred and ninety-four of my long paces, with your double barrelled gun, and you will see by the extreme smallness of the two holes made in the skin that the ball had lost nothing of its strength; sportsmen are not aware how far a good gun carries a ball, and in a straight line too.

Did I tell you that I sent from Delhi a Cashmere shawl as a present to Madame Cordier? I was apprehensive it might have been stolen at the post office, which sometimes happens; but I found at Ajmeer a letter from her husband, thanking me for the present, which had arrived safe at Chandernagore. But it seems that there was a deliberation at Chandernagore, to know what use was to be made of my present, for they had never seen a shawl of that kind. M. Cordier wrote to me that they hesitated between a shawl and a gown, and asked my opinion. It will surprise him, for I voted for breeches, according to the Cashmere and Persian fashion; in those places these shawls, called jamevars, are made use of for the immense trousers of the ladies.

The news of the Reform Bill being thrown out by the British peers, has caused considerable anxiety among the merchants at Calcutta. Several very large houses are already shaken.

I quitted Delhi, in possession of a pound of green tea, a thing quite unprecedented in my store. I make use of it now and then as fancy guides me, and I find it do me much good during this frightful heat. I drink it cold, with very little sugar, and very strong. My father would be quite alarmed if he were to see the colour, and would expect to see my nerves get completely shattered; for although I take it about half as strong as the English, I still use more tea in one day than would suffice him for a month. This beverage prevents also that excessive thirst which I could otherwise only quench by an enormous quantity of sugar and water. I wear neither stockings nor cravat, but wrap up my face and head with linen when I go into the sun. Talking of tea, as I laughed at the Tibetans who throw away the water in which it has boiled, and eat only the boiled leaves, I must not spare the Parisians, who throw away the first water poured in the tea-pot, which is exactly the best. Forget forty years of prejudices, and try.

I shall not bring you any tobacco of Bhilsa; it may perhaps be very good, still, as I have smoked scarcely anything in India but the usual mixture of moist sugar, dried raisins, conserve of roses, and tobacco, tobacco alone, even after its fumes have passed through a bottle of water, seems so powerful and so acrid, that I am incapable of smoking it.

I told you that I had dismissed my moorsha. I ought to have added the reason. He was very mild, very submissive, and even very punctual: but he appeared so very unhappy at the obligation he was under of walking, sometimes trotting, and even gallopping on horseback, that the sight of him made me melancholy. He was a Sayed, or descendant from the prophet. Before my arrival at Jaypore I had been under the necessity of sending away another attendant of high caste,—according to his own account a brahmin. I am pretty well satisfied with my other servants, but their wages ruin me. In four days I shall be at Indore, where I have some hopes of receiving letters from Europe. My last are nine months old, but through the English papers I have a little French news of the month of November; and the Hugh Lindsay steamer, which goes between Bombay and Suez, and is shortly expected at the former place, will bring us later news. I do not know how things will end in England. The line of demarcation between the rich and the poor is still more defined in that country than it was in France forty years ago. The people, who are so wretched and so ill-used, have become brutalised by the use of ardent spirits, and have sunk low in moral degradation. If there is a revolution, it will be a frightful one.

Mr. Le, President of the War Committee, becomes more and more insolent towards the British at Canton. Lord W. Bentinck has lately written him a letter perfectly to the purpose. It was necessary to make this Chinese screen understand that he may be insolent once too often. He took no notice of the warning, and even peremptorily refused to receive the captain in the navy commissioned by Lord William to deliver his letter; he would only receive it from the hands of another, and gave an evasive answer through the medium of another person of inferior rank. This will end in a war, and it will not require much to crush Mr. Le's power. The insolence of these rascals is really inconceivable. Their means of resistance amount to nothing, and they never speak of us but as of the barbarians of *Europe*. This president talks of his infinite commiseration for us, poor little creatures that we are! nothing but atoms! mere dust!

With the exception of the newspapers of Calcutta, scarcely anybody in this country thinks of the renewal of the company's charter; and it is probable that in England, amid so many great domestic interests which are now the subjects of parliamentary debate, it is not much more thought of than here.

Adieu. I have written at greater length than I intended when I began, but it was a long time since I had chatted with you. I am going to resume my occupations, or rather to begin them. Adieu, &c.

Mundlesir, on the borders of the Nerbuddah, April 24th.

I rested at Ougein, and I do the same here. This is the hottest place in India, but I am perfectly recovered. I shall be fortunate if I reach Bombay before the rains. Overwhelmed as I am with business, I have only time to forward some letters which I find in my portfolio, commenced on the road. Adieu, my dear Porphyre.

TO M. DE TRACY, PEER OF FRANCE.

Mundlesir, on the banks of the Nerbuddah,
in Central India, April 25th, 1832.

DEAR SIR,—Here I am returned within the tropic, among far different scenes than those of the Himalaya; scenes less varied and less beautiful. The provinces which I have traversed since my departure from Delhi are either occupied by the British, or have been visited by them; and notwithstanding any moral observations I may make upon their physical and natural history, they no longer possess for a European traveller that inexpressible charm of a new country, which attracted me so powerfully to my researches in the valley of Cashmere and the desert mountains of Tibet; and my occupations in natural history left me no time or leisure to pursue other studies. I have often regretted that I possessed neither sufficient time nor knowledge to make researches into the origin of the different nations inhabiting India. They are most probably all of them descended from the same branch of the human species; having been for centuries subjected to the same circumstances of climate and regimen, the slight differences of organisation, which perhaps at first distinguished their original varieties, have disappeared, so that it is impossible at present to discover among these nations characteristic features peculiar to any of them. It is by comparison between their domestic habits, their religious rites, and, above all, their languages, that we must endeavour to trace and unravel the mystery of their original migrations and filiations. This task ought to be accomplished by the British, who are permanently established in India. Colonel Tod has lately attempted it with regard to the Rajpoots; he was most favourably situated for these researches. But if you have read some parts of his work upon Rajpootana,

I presume you will scarcely have found any other basis for anthropological comparison than some strained etymologies from the Latin and the Sanscrit. But, as I have already owned to you, I am perfectly ignorant of the latter language, and only know as much of it as an Englishman does of Latin who has not learnt it: that is to say, a few isolated words, because the vulgar Indian tongue which I speak has borrowed its vocabulary partly from the Sanscrit, partly from the Persian, the Arabic, and the Turkish, just in the same manner that the Latin has given to the English language for the last eight centuries more than half of its existing vocabulary, which at first was exclusively Saxon and Gaelic.

Notwithstanding my ignorance of the Sanscrit, I maintain that it possesses scarcely any other than a philological interest. There have been already too many translations from this language without advantage either to science or to history, for us to expect any benefit from future translations.

It is the same thing with the Tibetan, of which a learned Hungarian, M. Csomo de Koros, was preparing a dictionary and grammar in conjunction with the Lamas of Kænam, when I visited that part of the Himalaya. I then had the honour, notwithstanding my unworthiness, to inhabit a temple celebrated in Tibet for the literary treasures it contained. M. de Koros often came thither with the Lama bishop, (I say bishop, because the Tibetan priest had adopted the mitre and crozier like our prelates.) He showed me several hundred volumes, rudely printed with wooden characters, in the grand monasteries of Chinese Tartary. One of these works, which passed for the most admirable of all, and which at Calcutta has received the pompous appellation of "Tibetan Encyclopedia," was composed of no less than a hundred and twenty volumes. At my request, M. Csomo translated me the title of several, and the nineteen first volumes only treat of the attributes of the Divinity, of which the first is the *incomprehensibility*, which, in my opinion, may dispense with endeavouring to discover the others. The remainder is a medley of theology, bad physic, astrology, fabulous legends, and metaphysics. This abominable trash has not even the merit of originality. It appears, like most of the Tibetan books, to be nothing but a translation or compilation from the Sanscrit, made a hundred and fifty years ago, when the religious persecutions, by Aurung Zebe, caused a great number of Brahmins from Benares to fly to Tibet.

M. Csomo de Koros, who, when I passed through Kanom, had almost completed his philological labours, was preparing to proceed to India, to carry thither the result of them; that is to say, his Tibetan Dictionary and Grammar. I asked him, if, in offering to the Orientalists the key to a new language, he had not thought it proper to present them with some choice translations from Tibetan books, in order to give them a foretaste of the literary pleasures, or of the sound knowledge which they might derive from a perusal of them. He replied in the negative; and I thought he was right, for I fancy the titles of the principal works of the sacred library of Kanom, would be quite sufficient to effect the radical cure of even the most dreaming German enthusiasts with regard to Tibetan researches. The poor man has been at Calcutta for the last year, where he cannot, to his great mortification, find a single person who has the curiosity to learn the language of the Lamas. The Lord preserve us from the Tibetan language! I feel quite indignant at seeing this theological, cosmogonical and so-styled historical trash fill up the greatest part of the works which treat on India. We adopt in Europe a completely false notion of the real intellectual habits of the Indian nations. We generally suppose them inclined to an ascetic and contemplative life; and, upon the faith of Pythagoras, we continue to look upon them as extremely occupied with the metamorphosis of their souls after death. I assure you, sir, that the metempsychosis is the last of their cares: they plough, sow, and water their fields, reap, and recommence the same round of labours; they work, eat, smoke and sleep without having either the wish or the leisure to attend to such idle nonsense, which would only make them more wretched, and the very name of which is unknown to the greater number of them.

It is only on my return to France that I shall be able to discourse leisurely with you about this singular country. If the same good fortune which has accompanied me since the commencement of my travels does not fail me before the end, I shall enjoy this pleasure in a couple of years. My father will, perhaps, be somewhat displeased with my not bringing him back some very profound system of Indian metaphysics, but I have at present upon the Ganges a boat which descends from Delhi to Calcutta, laden with things much more real than the *real essences:* they are the archives of the physical and natural history of the countries I have hitherto visited; and if these collections, which have cost me so much labour, arrive without accident at Paris, as I have every reason to hope, I shall find on my return wherewith to congratulate myself on having limited my researches to the objects of my undertaking.

Farewell, my dear sir; my last letters from Europe are very old, and I shortly expect fresh news. If my letter from Cashmere is not lost, if it has reached you, and if, on arriving at Bombay, I find a few lines from you in reply, need I say how great my delight will be? Once more, adieu, my dear sir; believe that I shall ever acknowledge by the feelings of a son, the paternal affection of which I have had the happiness of receiving so many proofs from you during my youth.

TO M. PORPHYRE JACQUEMONT, PARIS.

42—, 43—, 44—, sometimes only 40 degrees, I mean centigrades; such, my dear Porphyre, is the average state of the atmosphere in which I exist during the day, that is to say, the temperature of my tent. At a much lower temperature than that I was quite exhausted only a few months since. I then trusted I should get accustomed to it, and I was right, for I now find myself perfectly comfortable at 43 and 44 centigrades. What say you to that? I should not like to see you here; I should prefer hearing that you had recommenced a promenade to Moscow. A stout and strong man like yourself would melt here like butter; in the course of a week nothing would remain of you but skin and bones. Here is the triumph of the mathematical axis; the straight line like myself, without any other dimensions but length! This dreadful heat is in every respect inconceivable; when writing, I have no other covering than a thick white muslin turban to keep my head cool; and breeches, which, although the name is not very compatible with delicacy, (in English, at least, it is frightfully indecent,) I look upon as one of the most decent inventions which human wisdom ever thought of; jacket, waistcoat, shirt, flannel waistcoat, shoes and stockings, the devil take them all; I make a bundle of the whole, upon which I seat myself, and in the course of an hour they are wringing wet, as becomes the reservoir, the cistern of all the animal pores below the waist. It is, nevertheless, most incredible that I feel myself as fresh in mind and as light (I was again going to say fresh) in body as if, instead of having 43 centigrades, we had only 14 or 15.

It is fortunate for me that the equilibrium of my fluids is perfect, for if I were obliged to take a lavement at this hour of the day in my tent, the water, by the grace of God—(I am the only one in India who in this case says by the grace; every one else would say by the malediction of God)—the water, I say, is almost at the boiling point. Now you know that animal heat is considerably less; the lavement therefore would be too hot. *Quod erat demonstrandum.*

I breakfast upon milk and plantains, that fruit of all hot countries, of which you have heard talk, and which resembles stale jasmine pomatum, very sweet. I dine upon onions fried in ghee, which is the representative of butter in India; melted butter as rancid as a Turk. I drink lukewarm water with that, and in the course of the day lemonade warm or hot, because everything is warm or hot. I have become sufficiently Indian to like rancid butter, and on the first day of my arrival at Haity, the 18th February, 1827, I found the plantain a delicious fruit, contrary to the opinion of many Europeans, who get quite angry with any person offering them the first taste; and after having tasted it, say that a plantain is a very unseemly jest against an honest man.

I have been these four days past in the Bombay territory, the first post of which is the celebrated fortress of Asseerghur. I was admirably received by the commandant, and moreover I found there a letter from the Governor of Bombay, informing me that he had sent to all the civil and military officers stationed upon the route I intend to take towards his capital, the necessary orders that I should want nothing.

Whilst I am writing to you, a man, one of my attendants, is in my tent, looking after something I want out of my trunks, and to my utter confusion has drawn out things I had not cast eyes on for several months past; I mean my dresses of honour (khelats) of the Punjab and Cashmere. How the devil shall I make the people at the custom-house comprehend that these are my clothes, and that consequently I have a right to wear them.

This is pretty nearly the list of them :—

Five pair of large Cashmere shawls; eight odd Cashmeer shawls, large and small; five pieces of China silk and Multana silk shawls, with large gold borders; seven muslin turbans—(*Nota bene.* A turban has by no means the look of a turban, when not in use; it is a piece of magnificent muslin, very narrow, from forty to sixty feet long); two scarfs of black Cashmere shawl, embroidered in silk and gold; seven or eight pieces of muslin; two pieces of gold brocade, &c., &c. All these things are prohibited in France. I should find it very hard to sell them in this country for a very small part of their value, and I am particularly desirous to bring them to France, to give myself the pleasure of making presents during the remainder of my life. I should like to encase you, my dear fellow, in a beautiful and immense morning gown of Cashmere shawl, well wadded, and I am persuaded you would feel an inexpressible luxury in indulging yourself in such a comfortable covering.

As I am sentimentally inclined, I must tell you that I should like uncommonly to see you smoke the houkha which my kind friend, Mr. Fraser, has given me, because I am convinced you will find that this elegant little gift, which was manufactured at Delhi and given me by the best friend I have acquired in India, will recal to my remembrance Delhi, my friend, and the Himalaya, where I met him for the first time, and excite a host of agreeable recollections.

I will then return to you your beautiful and excellent pocket pistols, upon which I shall have slept in very strange places, and where sometimes their presence under my pillow—my pillow! I wish you could see what I call by that name—has made me sleep with more security. You will find them nearly the same as when you gave them to me, but if the stocks are a little scratched, you will not like them the less; is it not so, my good friend? Oh! how delightful will it be to find ourselves together again after so many years of absence, and to me of solitude. What a delight to dine all three, or rather all four of us, at our small round table, with lights; to eat soup and drink French red wine, and to rise from table only to go into your room or my father's, leaving the others to seek their pleasure out of the house, and we remaining in ours to relate our mutual adventures during our separation! I shall have dined alone and drunk water for such a length of time! What a pleasure to live in a house after so many years spent in the open air, or under a light canvass tent, admitting the rain, the wind, and the burning sun-beams! What a happiness to sleep upon a mattress! A tear starts into my eye as I think of all those joys. If I recollect right, my dear friend, the last time we embraced each other we shed no tears, and it was all the better that we did not; but the next time we have that happiness, we will allow nature to resume her sway: she can procure us nothing but enjoyment. And my father, how happy he will be! especially if we are all three with him. What a tour I shall have made! London, Philadelphia, Hayti. I have seen more of America than Frederic, who scarcely quitted New York during the two years he spent in the United States. The Niagara, a forest at the Brazil, the boreal winter of the United States, the peak of Teneriffe, Mont Blanc, all the lakes of the Alps, the Mediterranean, the table mountain of the Cape of Africa, a hurricane at Bourbon, the Ganges at Benares, Delhi and the Great Mogul, the source of the Jumna, one of the sources of the Indus, the Lamas, the Chinese; in short, Cashmere and the highest mountains in the world! During so many years, a life so essentially different, both in feeling and existence, to that which I thought myself born to, and to which I shall return after immense travels by sea and land;—the constant habit and complete knowledge of foreign languages!—Heavens! Porphyre, when we are re-united in your little apartment, how extraordinary will all that appear to me! I shall almost doubt my own identity.

Listen to me, my dear friend; you are getting old, and, besides, you have remained too poor to think of matrimony, which, without some fortune, is but a sorry thing. I, too, shall be none of the youngest when I return, and shall most probably be one of the poorest; the probabilities, therefore, are that we shall remain bachelors. Well! we must do our best to live together. In our old age we will take our walks together, play our game of backgammon together, and together we will now and then indulge ourselves in going to hear some good music. It would be much better if one of us could find a rich and good wife, who would become the sister of the other. We shall see! After all, why should it not be so? Adieu, my good brother. It is a matter of course that this foolish effusion is only for yourself and my father.

TO M. JACQUEMONT, SENIOR, PARIS.

Ellora, May 22nd, 1832.

MY DEAR FATHER,—I am here encamped this morning in a place of so much celebrity, that I cannot pass it without, at least, addressing you a few lines. Between the mountains of Nindhia, and those of Adjuntah, in the valleys of the Nerbudda, and of the Tapti, I had perfectly accustomed myself to 105 and 110 degrees of heat; nay, I had almost begun to find that it was not too much. The country is wild and mountainous: my bullock wagons broke down several times during the night marches; but there is an especial providence for broken wagons, provided you have with you a corporal and four men, who proceed to the nearest hamlet and return with a workman, and an axle-tree to replace the broken ones, and who officially put in requisition the assistance of the passers by, in order to get up the overturned wagon; for providence quite alone, without the corporal and the four men, would prove awkward in repairing the disaster. The tigers, also, twice spread terror through my caravan, and ate a poor devil of a peasant. He was not one of my attendants, who have not my permission to be imprudent. I do not allow them to scatter themselves on the road, when there is the slightest danger. Both man and beast march in a compact troop: as for me, I always belong to another small band, lightly armed, without soldiers, trotting and galloping right and left, and looking at every thing that appears. I need not tell you no tiger has crossed my path. It is certainly ordained by fate that I shall not see a tiger in India. Indeed, unless you are seated upon a good elephant, the meeting, they say, is a dangerous one, as is proved in the instance of the poor devil of a peasant, carried off the other day behind my caravan. Firing at these devils has scarcely any effect; a tiger receives sometimes twenty balls before he dies, and when he is wounded he becomes furious.

The famous fortress of Asseerghur was in my route: it was there I entered the Bombay territory. Boorhampore, which you may discover a few leagues from thence on the banks of the Tapti, belongs to Scindia, the Mahratta prince of Gwalior. At length, at Adjuntah, I entered the dominions of the Nizam, and at the same time the immense bed of the Godavery. On the 17th, I arrived at Aurungabad, the miserable remains of a great city, founded by Aurung Zebe. I was expected by the commanding officer, a colonel in the Bengal army, who commands a division of the Nizam's troops. The nawab of Hyderabad, has also sixteen thousand British troops, and commanded by British officers, in his pay. This accounts for his existence as sovereign of a great state. If he were thrown on his own resources, dependent upon the incapacity and treason of his Mussulmaun and Hindoo officers, he would lose his throne in a few years, and his monarchy would be divided into several hundred independent lordships, continually exposed to the depredations of the Maratta hordes.

My host, Colonel Seyer, is a man of great merit, in his private, as in his professional character. He literally crammed me with information; and when I left him, he filled my bags with books of the most valuable description. They will remain there a long time, as I have no leisure for reading. Coming from Bengal, where I had known so many people, I was almost a brother officer to Colonel Seyer. I was much less a stranger to him than an English officer of the Bombay or Madras army would have been, who might have come to him at the same time I did; for there is but little friendship between the officers of the three presidencies: they are jealous of each other, seldom meet, and even when they do, almost always avoid each other.

At Aurungabad I hoped to have received some letters from you, but it appears that, for several months, no French ship has arrived in India. Very few even come from England at this season of the year; but very shortly the arrivals will take place.

Lord Clare, Governor of Bombay, to whom I had written from Indore a few lines officially to inform him of my arrival within his presidency, forwarding him at the same time a copy of my passports from Calcutta, wrote to all the officers of his government, stationed on the route I intend to take, to apprise them of this great event, in order that they might make the necessary preparations on the occasion. I thus found at Aurungabad letters from these gentlemen, offering me their houses, their porters, their palanquins, &c. &c. I immediately returned an answer to the Governor and to them, assuring them that I felt both overwhelmed and flattered by their kind hospitality. Colonel Seyer told me, when I took leave of him, that he had also received instructions from the government of Bombay equally kind towards me, and that no doubt Lord Clare would invite me to remain with him during my stay at Bombay. If I am to remain but a short time in that city, the governor's politeness may prove very desirable to me; but if I prolong my stay, I shall look out for some kind of house, which does not admit too much rain, and take possession of it like an absolute monarch; for a traveller of my consequence ought to be at home. But I have heard so much of the insalubrity of Bombay during the season I intend to spend there, that if I can derive equal advantage by remaining at Poonah, I shall probably take up my abode at this latter place, for three months, and become housekeeper for the first time since my arrival in India; for my pretty bungalow at Cashmere scarcely deserved the pompous appellation of a house. I think, moreover, that Poonah will offer great attractions as the head quarters of a naturalist. If it turns out so, all will be for the best; because Bombay is very unhealthy during the rainy season, and Poonah, on the contrary, enjoys a great reputation for salubrity at that period of the year.

When I have filled my cases at Poonah, and the rains have ceased, I shall go down to Bombay, to ship them off, before I proceed to the south. I should like to be able then to send you my Cashmere wardrobe, with the animals, plants, and stones for the Jardin des Plantes; for besides that these various matters fill two trunks, which in travelling is excessively inconvenient, I am sometimes apprehensive of being robbed of them. I own I should feel the loss most acutely, as it would deprive me of the only opportunity I could have on my return of making pretty presents replete with *local character*. Aurungabad has fallen with its founder, according to the oriental custom. There is a Mogul mausoleum, much admired by those who have only seen the south of India; but after Lahore, Agra, Delhi, and their superb mosques of Shâh-Jehan, Akbar, and Jehangire, the ruins of Aurungabad are scarcely worth notice.

The most remarkable things that surround the town are the magnificent subterranean passages dug in the mountains, which extend from thence to this place, where the most celebrated are. The conclusions to which all the writers on this subject have come, is that no one can tell, when, by whom, or for what purpose, these excavations were made. The Hindoos claim these works as theirs, asserting they were executed by one of their numerous divinities. There are no longer any Buddhists to dispute their claim; but Christians, perfectly disinterested in the discussion, decide the question in favour of the Buddhists. We believe in India, that Buddha formerly reigned in the north, his power extending even beyond the Indian Caucasus. Near Cabul there are caves and idols, supposed to bear some resemblance to those of Ceylon and of Ellora; but although for the last fifty years several Europeans who have attained a perfect knowledge of the Sanscrit, have read many volumes on the subject, it has not yet been ascertained at what period Bramah played Buddha, in the east, the same scurvy trick that Jesus Christ played Jupiter and Co. in the western world 1800 years ago.

The other day I read, at Aurungabad, an analysis, made by the learned and ingenious Mr. Wilson, of the translations from the Tibetan of my friend of Kanum, M. Csomo de Kôros. They have a wonderfully soporific effect: there are about twenty chapters upon the kind of shoes that the Lamas ought to wear. Among other nonsensical absurdities, of which these books are full, priests are forbidden to help themselves to pass the ford of a rapid river, by laying hold of the tail of a cow. There is no lack of profound dissertations upon the properties of the flesh of griffins, dragons, and unicorns, and upon the admirable virtues of the horn of winged horses. To judge of this nation by what I have seen of them, and by what the translations of M.

Csomo disclose of them, one would take them to be a nation of madmen or idiots.

Yesterday I visited the famous fortress of Dowlatabâd. Both Hindoos and Mussulmauns attribute the building of it to some unknown divinity. For my own part I know not what to think of it.

This morning I encamped here by moonlight. I passed near the tomb of Aurung Zebe, who was a very wicked man, but a tolerably good king. He made roads and canals instead of building palaces. There is the same difference between him and his father Shâh-Jehan, as between Louis XI. and Francis I. or Louis XIV. Baber is the Henry IV. of this family of Tamerlane.

As I was carelessly riding on, without much regarding the essential conditions of my equilibrium, I was twice on the point of being thrown, by my horse starting at the sight of two hyenas which passed very quietly under his nose. I fired at the second, which did not induce it to accelerate its pace in the least, but made my frightened horse start worse than ever. I am too bad a horseman, I ride with too great disregard to the classical rules of horsemanship to experience many falls. I sometimes totter, but that is all. This reminds me of the little quarrels which I used to have with that excellent Madame Micour, because, in reply to her fears at the danger of travelling, I used coolly to reply, "No one kills himself."

When I was in Provence, and sometimes also in the

mountains of Auvergne, which were very hot in the month of July, Jaubert used to be angry with me, because I sometimes said "It is pleasant to be in the sun." If he were with me here, I should not be able, in spite of the 105 degrees of heat, to say otherwise, for I have at last found out, that 105 or 107 degrees of heat are very agreeable. I should drive him mad by this involuntary discovery.

This reminds me of the letters you used to write to me when I was at Grenoble or at Geneva, and the curious details of the precautions which your affection led you then to recommend me to take. You have since that period been converted to my belief, or rather to my incredulity. Although we are badly enough constituted, since our machine is so often out of order, and ultimately stops altogether without remedy, still we are not made of glass, thank God! let us then take care, great care of this outward case of ours, which resembles a violin without which our soul would be but a useless bow. Do you avoid cold and damp, whilst I battle here against the contrary elements. I meant to have written to you only half a page, and I have covered two pages with my hieroglyphics!

Adieu, then, until my arrival at Poonah, unless I take a fancy to pay you another visit. There are few fancies I can indulge in in these deserts, and I seldom fail to gratify them when they do occur.

TO MADEMOISELLE ZOÉ NOIZET DE SAINT PAUL, ARRAS.

Camp near Ellora, in the Deccan, May 24th, 1832.

As you have no opportunity at Arras of gaining any information about Asia, perhaps, my sweet friend, you are even ignorant of the name of this place of wonders. Formerly in Europe we had, from time to time, the plague; now we have the cholera morbus. In like manner in India, where Brahminism has been for several hundreds or several thousands of years the endemic malady of the mind, Buddhism formerly exercised the same ravages on the common sense of the poor Indians. Ellora, now a wretched village, was undoubtedly at that period a flourishing city, and the head-quarters of the madmen, fools, and scoundrels, who lived upon the stupid credulity of the nations of southern Asia. All the mountains towards the east are hollowed out into spacious halls, galleries, and subterraneous palaces of colossal structure, and sometimes of exquisite workmanship. I have a large volume in 4to, several in 8vo, and a great number of manuscript notices, to inform me by whom these immense works were executed, and how long ago, and for what object they were intended, &c., &c.; but after perusing all, I know no more about these wonders than the poor Brahmins who do the honours of them, and do not fail to attribute the merit of their construction to some of the fifty thousand divinities whom they worship.

This morning I discovered one of these subterraneous temples, of a form entirely different from that of all the others, being that of a Gothic church in miniature. Nothing is wanting: the nave, the choir, and that kind of gallery which contains the organ in our churches—all is there. Building the pyramids of Egypt is but a trifle compared to the labour which must have been required for excavating these palaces and temples out of the hard rock. The effect is most extraordinary; but the idols always put me a little out of temper; they give the idea of bad reasoning, and the caves of Ellora are peopled with them. An English artist, more than twenty years ago, made some beautiful drawings of these astonishing ruins*, which were engraved in London. I hope one day to explain them to you in Paris.

Curiosities here are most abundant. The day before yesterday I was encamped under the celebrated fort of Dowlatabad, which plays so conspicuous a part in the history of modern India. I am well persuaded that the engineer who built it knew less than our uncle Saint Paul in his little finger; but Dowlatabad has a finer aspect than Lisle, and even Mons, where all the discoveries of Carnot have been put in practice. George and Porphyre, and all their brethren, wholesale killers, would here waste their powder and shot. One of our countrymen however, M. de Bussy, who, about fifty

* The artist to whom Jacquemont alludes is Mr. W. Daniell, R.A.

years ago, was a personage of importance in India, took this impregnable fortress; not with artillery, however, which would have made no impression, but with the aid of that irresistible argument which made Bazile yield to the not very proper whims of Count Almaviva.

To-morrow I am going to visit the tomb of Aurung Zebe, a most abominable man, and yet a tolerably good king for this country; he was besides the last of his race who deserved the name of man. Since passing the river Nerbudda, the heat is very intense; 105, 107, and 110 degrees from ten o'clock to half-past three or four in the afternoon. In the valley of the Nerbudda, the night was almost as hot as the day. The heat of the soil stings the face and eyes in the same manner the flame from burning straw would do, if placed close to one. I have accustomed myself to it, because the French resemble dogs in that respect, and can accustom themselves to heat better than any other animal; and now that upon the elevated plain of the Deccan, there are only from 100 to 105 degrees, I almost find the nights cold. Every body else at Aurungabad, where I spent these last days, were under process of suffocation, and cursing their existence; but these were British, who drank one or two bottles of wine every day, and ate one or two pounds of animal food.

But the rains will shortly appear, and as much will fall in six weeks as usually falls in three years and a half at Arras; it will put the sun's rays to rights.

I hope to arrive at Poonah before the wet season sets in.

Since this hour yesterday, I have written the trifling number of sixty-seven pages, in which I have extracted several manuscript memoirs in English of great interest, and my hand is quite stiff; indeed it would require less to make it so; I shall therefore leave off for the day. Besides, without being unwell, I have not been quite right for these last two days; I sleep little, and have no appetite, and it is anything but enlivening to have a soul pent up in a suffering body. I take leave of you, therefore, requesting you will forgive me for not having done so before, for nothing is so tiresome as a man suffering under weariness of mind. And what am I now going to do?—throw myself upon my bed and endeavour to sleep. A man is behind me, fanning me: I hear you exclaim, "what luxury, what magnificence!" to which I reply that the thermometer is at 105, and I should like to see those who tax me with luxury exposed to it. Good night, then, although it is but noon-day.

TO M. JACQUEMONT, SEN., PARIS.

Poonah, June 6th, 1832.

My dear Father,—I arrived yesterday in this town, which was the capital of the Mahrattas, when Mahrattas existed otherwise than merely in name and in form. Lord Hastings, in 1808, exercised an act of justice upon this nation, whose last chief, the Peishwa, repaid by frightful treachery the benefits conferred by the British government, whose alliance he had himself voluntarily sought. It is now one of the strongest military stations of the British in the Peninsula.

You see me on the oriental side of the Ghauts, and from the distance to the sea of Coromandel and the proximity of the sources of the Kestnah and the Godavery, you will be able to judge of the elevation of the country above the level of the sea. It is not less than six hundred metres; this is sufficient to produce a very sensible difference in the temperature, which is much milder here than at Bombay. The rains, which will very shortly take place, are neither so violent nor of so long a duration as at Bombay, and on the rest of the coast. They tell me that these rains will keep me a prisoner at home during whole months. I shall therefore very probably pitch my tent here during the rainy season, and shall perhaps hire a house, in which I shall establish my head quarters for three months, and avail myself of the intervals of fine weather to make my researches in the neighbourhood. The situation of Poonah appears to me favourable for researches in natural history. Every thing, therefore, turns out for the best.

I found here, on my arrival yesterday, a great number of letters from all parts of India, and even from the

Punjab. A few days ago I received one from China, which I send you, because it will inform you better than the Chinese politicians who write in our newspapers, concerning the present quarrel between the company and the viceroy of Canton. Mr. Inglis, from whom it comes, is the kind and amiable man whose acquaintance I made two years ago in Kanawer, and of whom I certainly have spoken to you in my letters. He is a very rich merchant of Canton, destined to take a share in the government or controul of Indian affairs in London, either as a member of the court of directors of the company, or in parliament. Let Zoé translate this letter for you, if you cannot make out English written in so bad a hand.

The most delightful part of the treat which awaited me here, was your letter of October, 1831, No. 31, written at different times, together with those of Porphyre, Frederic, the contribution by Zoé and Adelaide, and a very long and friendly epistle from M. Mirbel. I have as usual kept you for the dessert, and read your letter over again in my bed, upon which I fell asleep in the best of tempers, and in the happiest manner possible.

Your numbers 29 and 30 are still behind hand, but the essential is this 31. When you wrote it you knew of my arrival at Lahore, and you conclude, as you are justified in doing from these fortunate beginnings, that I shall terminate in a manner no less satisfactory than I did my expedition beyond the Sutledge. This is good logic, and I shall not belie your expectations. Your letter delighted me by its gaiety, which I take for the surest sign of good health. My letters from Lahore will not have diminished your friendship for the king of that country. You ask me, what his sons do! He has only one of his own, named Curruk-Sing, a man of thirty (Runjeet is about fifty-two), without talents, without being in any wise distinguished, and, in my opinion, without any chance of succeeding to the entire power of his father. But this man so distrustful, this Machiavelian sovereign, is a good, forbearing kind of husband, and whenever he absented himself a few months from his capital and harem, unceasingly engaged as he was in distant expeditions, his family multiplied in a most extraordinary manner. All his wives (he has about a dozen) were brought to bed one after the other, each giving him a boy, and fine ones too, and seldom less than two at a time. Runjeet-Sing either thought himself, or pretended to think himself, the father of some of these children, and has brought up one of them to enjoy great honours. This is prince Cheyr-Sing. Notwithstanding his high-sounding name (literally *Lion-tiger*), Cheyr-Sing is a very good young man. He very naturally execrates Curruk-Sing, and will wage war against him as soon as Runjeet dies. I wish him good success. He is extremely brave, and, for a Seikh, not without humanity, but he possesses no talent. I met him at the palace, at the festival of the Unlocked, and conversed an hour with him. He knew me perfectly as the friend of Allard, and as the *Plato of the age;* he therefore overwhelmed me with civilities. Runjeet cares no more for his legitimate eldest son than for the equivocal younger one. His principles in politics are, "After me comes the deluge." You can form no idea of family ties in the East, especially among the higher classes. I will explain them to you some evening by your fire side. How different this world is to ours.

You ask me if Runjeet has allowed me to continue my journey upon the humble and modest tattoo, as tattoo there is, which had brought me from Calcutta to Lahore? Yes, until the festival of the Unlocked took place. On the evening of the festival, his minister, Fakhir-Ezis-el-Din, came to the camp of the British envoy, whom I had joined, with the Maharajah's compliments, and a horse a-piece, which he sent us as presents. They were superbly caparisoned, but were vicious beasts. Wade, by the rules of the service, could accept no present from the king; he therefore had his horse registered to the *credit* of the honourable company, to whom I also abandoned mine. Each horse might be worth thirty francs, and the saddle three thousand. They were both sold at Loodeeana or at Delhi, for the benefit of the said company. I thought that this liberality of a poor devil like me, would come with a good grace, and it was considered to do so. The extreme economy which I exercise towards myself, allowed me, when an opportunity occurred, to throw my money away upon Runjeet's attendants. In short, I maintained, in the best manner I was able, my character of *Aflatoune-el-Zemân.*

You reproach me with not having admitted you sufficiently into the intimacy of my palace at Lahore. The French officers were desirous of providing their breakfast, and often dinner, at my house; I had therefore in my kitchen a congress of Indian, Georgian, Persian, Armenian, Cashmerian, and Punjabee cooks, belonging to these gentlemen; those of Allard brought up the rear. Their masters arrived at eight o'clock in the morning, went a few moments to the king, and then returned. When they were all assembled, I gave orders for serving up, and did the honours of the table in French, English, Italian, Hindostanee, and bad Persian. In the afternoon I frequently went to the royal residence, and paid the king a very long visit; thence I went to Allard's, at a couple of leagues from the royal tents. The good fellow was hungering after France, and could never have enough of my society. In the evening we went, mounted upon his elephant, to see the city and the curiosities of its environs; or sometimes his friend, M. Ventura, was my cicerone. When I remained to dine with them, they would not allow me to return to my garden by night, for fear of the Akhalis, who even in the day time are very troublesome, and much worse at night. At day break I gallopped home well escorted, and was sometimes insulted notwithstanding. The Akhalis do not even spare Runjeet himself. Sensible people treat them like dogs, to whom it is wisest to say nothing so long as they content themselves with barking.

I trust that the manner I served you from Cashmere was according to your desires. The beginning was rather sorry, but schoolboys who begin with Tacitus and Horace find all other books easy afterwards; the same thing happened to me; after the difficult and rather ticklish Tolonchi affair, I got through some other difficult passages with tolerable ease. You guessed right in supposing that M. Allard would remain one of my regular correspondents during the remainder of my stay in India, but you did not anticipate that Runjeet would also be on the list. I am however about to address an invocation to the Muses, and to compose for this king, who is a very good fellow, very eccentric and a little cracked, a mixture *secundum artem;* a flattering elixir of roses, jasmine, hyacinths, tulips, musk, ambergris, eternal life, glory, fortune, renown, &c., &c., which will please him exceedingly, and I shall conclude pathetically with *Waugh Gourou Kê fotteh!* (Glory to the grand Gourou, Govind Sing!) which will complete the satisfaction of my eccentric friend. The British have so exclusive a respect for the Christian Olympus, that they become almost rude towards every other Olympus; they "my lord" the British bishops, and do not pay the same compliment to ours, nor to the saints of Mahomet's calendar. To Mussulmauns I never say *Mahomet, Ali, Omar,*

Houssaine, but *my lord Mahomet, his excellency Ali, his highness Houssaine*, the *holy Mecca* instead of simply *Mecca*. This attention, which costs me but little, wins people's hearts. As to the Hindoos, one does not know how to take them; the scoundrels have no more religion than dogs. The Seikhs, who, like the latter, care very little about the Eternal Father, entertain at least a great affection for the memory of their gourou or priest, Govind Sing. If you fire at a dog barking at and threatening a cow, you get high in their favour. I shot at several of these poor animals in the Punjab, to the great satisfaction of the long beards of my escort. This little piece of cruelty (it was only small shot) obtained for me a great reputation of humanity.

But I have already said so much about the Punjab, that I here conclude the subject.

Your indiscretion, my dear father, prevents me from relating to you in future any free stories, for you would instantly betray me. This time, at least, either fortunately or unfortunately, I am not called upon through any prudential motives to show reserve. The duodecimos of the Deccan are not inferior in colouring and binding to the quartos of St. Domingo; and coming from Cashmere, I find the jet black very serious.

The cholera commits frightful ravages at Mow, Indore, and in the territory of Meewar, through which I have lately passed. It raged with violence at Ahmednugghur when I was there a few days ago, but it scarcely attacked any but Indians. They say that water drinkers are more liable to catch it than others; I shall therefore mix a little wine with my water. Besides, I am supplied with remedies ready prepared, which, when administered at the beginning of the attack, are so efficacious that I apprehend very little from this disease.

What M. Mirbel writes to me relatively to the devoted, zealous interest which Jaubert takes in my concerns, affected me extremely. Although it is quite natural to him to do so, I felt a desire to write to him upon the subject, and my letter is inclosed.

Several French vessels are expected at Pondichery and Calcutta; some of them must have left France ages go. I trust that these stragglers will bring me your numbers 29 and 30. Part of M. Mirbel's memoirs must be in these packets.

The government of India is at present occupied in sending into Transoxiana a young officer of the Bombay army, named Burnes, by whom last year they had the lower Indus sounded, in order to ascertain how far it is navigable. Mr. Burnes arrived at Lahore last summer by the Indus and the Ravee whilst I was at Cashmere, and having an official political capacity, carried to the Maharajah presents from the "Padishah of London," as the King of England is styled here. His English horses and carriage, destined for Runjeet, were in my opinion the pretence only of his journey, undertaken to make these soundings. He has just, with Runjeet's permission, crossed the Punjab from

Loodheeana to Attock. We know that he is now on the right bank of the forbidden river, and is continuing his journey to Peshawer or Cabul, whence he intends to cross the Hindoo-Coosh and visit the basin of the Sea of Aral, and the eastern shores of the Caspian. I do not know the precise object of his journey, and even doubt if he have any. He has chosen for his travelling companion the physician of the corps commanded by Kennedy at Subhatoo. Now, the people of Subhatoo know me perfectly well, and I found here a long epistle from the above named Doctor Gerard, dated from the borders of the Indus. The poor devil already talks of the martyrdom which awaits him. The fact is, unless they travel as beggars, which is not a very commodious manner to make observations, they run great risk of being robbed, and, if they resist, of being murdered.

TO MADEMOISELLE ZOÉ NOIZET DE SAINT PAUL, ARRAS.

Poonah, in the Deccan, June 7th, 1832.

My Sweet Friend,—On my arrival here yesterday, I found your note, of I know not what date, and your letter of the 10th of October, which were waiting for me. Your note was written in a very low-spirited mood, as if there were no possibility of remaining alive in Nepaul. How can you, the daughter and sister of a soldier, give way to such childish fears? What is there so dreadful in Nepaul? I abandoned the idea of visiting it for other reasons than those which made you fear that the journey was unsafe for me; it was because I should have been almost constantly a prisoner, which, for a traveller of my sort, is dying by inches. You have however made amends in your letter of the 10th of October, by laughing a little at the fears you expressed a few months before. When you wrote me the last time, you had seen my first letter from Lahore. You call me a *lucky fellow*, your mother calls me an impudent rogue. Amen! There is some truth in both your compliments, although, after all, my impudence is nothing but ingenuousness. I still miss one of your letters, and two of my father's; they will arrive together one of these days, a year old. I shall then expect your criticism upon my famous *speech* at Delhi. It is really very stupid and very stupidly printed. One of the toasts in fashion at that time in India was, "France and England against the world!" and when the dinner guests were half seas over, they added, for their neighbours, "And by God we will give them a good licking," or, what is still more energetic, "a d—d good licking!" For a kind of quaker like myself, this hostility against the human species appeared in bad taste, and put me out of temper; and when at Delhi I said, "France and England for the world," I was in a minority in my opposition to that great ninny the public. If I had to do this over again, I would not write an *extempore speech* before hand, but, like the others, indulge myself in bumpers of Madeira or port.

It is evident to me, from the few lines of English you have found means of inserting in your letter, without introducing your enemy *you*, that you are as well versed in that language as I am; there is not a single expression of yours with which I have any fault to find.

It is really a most extraordinary thing, that six or seven years are necessary in order to acquire an indifferent knowledge of the old language which has supplied ours with almost all its roots. Latin is a mere trifle to a Frenchman; it is still easier to an Italian or a Spaniard, and especially so to a Portuguese. The oriental languages are quite different. I know but a dozen words which are the same in Sanscrit, Persian or Arabic, Greek and Latin, and the modern European languages derived from them. *Nao*, in Sanscrit, means boat; so it does in ancient Persian: *navis*, in Latin, in Greek nearly the same, *naus*; *naval*, *nautical*, with us, and very few et-cæteras.

The whole vocabulary of these eastern languages is to be learnt. This is really the very devil. I wish I had leisure sufficient to learn Persian, in order some day to vindicate the truth, and show the Parisians how puerile the literature of Persia is. But I know just enough of it to have the right of entertaining an opinion of my own, but not of imposing it upon others.

Poonah is a large city, on the eastern side of the Ghauts of Bombay in 18° 30′ of latitude, which is very hot, but being two thousand feet above the level of the sea, which makes it cooler, the people of Bombay come thither to spend the rainy season (the summer.) For that reason I shall remain here three months. It costs me the trifle of two hundred and sixty francs per month for an ugly large thatched house, the only one vacant. I am thus sheltered from the rain, and go on working very hard.

The Governor of Bombay is a great English lord. He is most attentively polite to me, and shows me every kind of favour. I went yesterday to his country house to pay him my first visit. I have refused the economical but inconvenient honour, of being the guest of Lord Clare, who wished much to keep me with him.

My little climbing horse of the Himalaya is a great curiosity here. My state charger, with his Mogul saddle of brocade and bridle of black velvet embossed with gold and silver, is not less so. In short, in every thing about me, and in myself, I have a certain air and look of strangeness, which is a source of great attraction to these people. Their ignorance relative to the things of Bengal and Hindostan is extreme. I relate many particulars to those who are deserving of it; but do not think that I make myself cheap—I am not such a fool as that. Red partridges are esteemed in our country in proportion to their scarcity, and I make myself rather scarce also. Your mother would call me not only an impudent fellow, but a precious braggadocio. What can I say?—it must be so. You taxed me with being insipid in English. With you I may have been so, but as I am an "impudent rogue," I will add, that with me it is an exception. To all my English friends, or to the English with whom I have to treat only of matters of business, I prefer writing in English, because with the former I am *humorous* in the extreme, (box the impudent fellow's ears!) and with the latter I have the stately politeness necessary, and which it would not be proper to lose sight of. I must also tell you, that my friends are men, all bachelors, and that with them I care not, sometimes, about being a little uncivil, in order to be more *humorous*. English women are most extraordinary beings. The most impassioned amongst them, she who would desert husband, children, and character, to run after another man, would, even with that very man, show a reserve perfectly incompatible with our French ideas of intimacy, which in my mind are the sweetest forms of friendship. There is a barrier of ice betwixt an Englishwoman and myself, which the most ardent passion on my part could never succeed in entirely melting. It might make some little holes, but I should never have entire possession. Let it be well understood, that when I say *me*, I mean any man from France and even from England, and not Victor Jacquemont.

The life of an Englishwoman is like a part in a play—she has been instructed in it from her cradle by her mother or her nurse. The *esprit de corp* of caste is thus perpetuated with her, and in America, separates her entirely from the other sex, sensibly, intellectually, and sociably. Read an English book in two volumes, entitled, "Domestic Manners of the Americans," by Mrs. Trollope. But I will tell you all about this some day.

TO M. JACQUEMONT, SENIOR, PARIS.

Poonah, July 7th, 1832.

MY DEAR FATHER,—All your letters have at length arrived. I have now, after your number 31, which reached me on the 6th of June last, received your number 32, which came the day before yesterday, and yesterday I got number 29, which has been twelve months on its way, on board a ship called the *Diligent*. It is disagreeable not to receive them in the same order in which they leave France; number 30 is still wandering over the world.

I have also received the Baron Humboldt's memoirs; M. Cordier had the kindness, at Chandernagore, to divide it into packets, which the post-office will take charge of. Your number 29, closed the 11th August, was in reply to my letters from Kurnal of February, 1831. It is so old, and I have written to you so often since then, that it scarcely requires any answer. You, however, ask me whether the dysentery, which I told you was making such ravages at Delhi, was not the cholera. By no means; it was the dysentery, as I stated; if it had been the cholera, I should have said so. But it is only six and thirty hours ago, that I first saw a specimen of that disease; it rages here at present, and one of my servants was attacked last night. I am acquainted with this horrible complaint, as well as a man can be who has not observed it himself, but has obtained a great deal of information about it. From the very first moment, I recognised it with unerring certainty; the symptoms are such that it cannot be mistaken for any other disease. They are moreover very numerous; the state of the pulse would indicate it, or the skin of the hands or soles of the feet, the temperature of the body, the languid circulation, the appearance of the eyes and face, or, in short, the character and nature of the evacuations.

I have attended my poor servant in the best manner I could, and after six and thirty hours of illness he still lives, which is a great deal, but I doubt if he gets over the day or even the morning. He is a Hindoo, and the best of my attendants; almost the longest in my service. The others, Hindoos or Mohammedans, constantly watch him, and keep up an appearance of confidence when near him, endeavouring to cheer him by telling him stories which he cannot understand. They afterwards retire to the garden, when they roll themselves upon the ground, and weep bitterly. My *sirdar*, or steward, who belongs to the same caste as the sick man, and besides was his comrade by the nature of the service in which they were both employed, and who is by far the most active, sensible, and most manly, among this band of full-grown children, has this instant in my chamber given himself up to a most violent paroxysm of despair.

I hope you are not a contagionist; for I continually go into the sick man's room, and even touch him, and then return to my writing. This frightful disease is not contagious, at least in India. There is no difference of opinion in this respect among either European or Indian physicians; and as the numerous accounts of cholera in Russia and England which I have lately read describe it as being of exactly the same character as in India, I look upon it as almost certain that the present European cholera is not contagious by the touch. I know of no satisfactory analysis of the circumstances of climate, in which it appears that the cholera assumes greater development. The British medical men in India, at least the majority of them, are far from being sufficiently learned or scientific to make this analysis. The cholera rages all over the Deccan this summer; a great number of natives fall victims to it even here, but of two thousand European soldiers, and more than one hundred and fifty officers, not one has been attacked with it this season at Poonah. We are always less subject to it than the Indians, but this year, and in this place, the difference in our favour is absolute; and that is the reason why I do not hesitate to tell you, and as a matter of perfect indifference, that at a few steps from where I am, in the next room, there is a poor man dying of that disease.

I take good care of myself; I drink a drop of brandy in the morning, wine at breakfast, when it happens that I eat meat at that meal, which however occurs but seldom. I also take wine at dinner, and when I write till late in the evening, I take a bowl of tea mixed with rum, after which I go to bed. I cover myself very warmly at night, and wear during the day a very long Cashmere shawl, rolled like a waistband not round my waist but upon my hips, so as to keep my stomach warm and at an equal temperature. I believe that a great number of the complaints of this country proceed from refrigeration, mostly imperceptible, of that part.

I have already answered, at least in part, your letter number 31. I proceed to number 32, a small sheet, extremely short, and about the third of my accustomed portion. It is dated October 29th, 1831; you thought me then returned among the British, and indeed I was very near them, at only two days' march from the Sutledge, but more annoyed by the long matchlocks of the people of the Himalaya than ever I had been before. Many thanks for Dunoyer's very long letter; it is a charming epistle, full of friendship, and perfect in every respect. I received it with peculiar satisfaction. His address to the people (a thousand pardons, I meant citizens) of Moulins proved to me that he had not yet, in his new official capacity of prefect, learnt the jargon of office.

Adieu. I have acres of writing for you, but there is no ship sailing from Calcutta. I shall keep the whole and make a single packet of it. Adieu.

Evening.

My poor fellow died this morning, as I anticipated, whilst I was at breakfast, which I had not the heart to finish. He had been to Cashmere with me; he was the most active and useful of my attendants, and the mildest, and had never served any body but me. This morning he still knew me, and answered *Khroudavond*, my lord, when I addressed him by name. By twelve o'clock his body was already burned. I was obliged to go and beg a dinner of a neighbour, all my servants having gone to the funeral. I should regret the poor fellow more if I had not always treated him well; but during two years he has had but few harsh words from me, and I engaged him at first at five rupees a month, but doubled his wages a long time before his death.

TO M. PROSPER MÉRIMÉE, PARIS.

Poonah, July 16*th*, 1832.

To my great confusion, my dear Prosper, this evening, in making a general inspection of all my writings, I found at the bottom of a box, among some catalogues of stones of the Himalaya, these two Himalayan scraps, which I decide upon forwarding to you notwithstanding their scandalous dates. They will prove to you that I am least deficient in one of the theological virtues, I believe order, unless it be a sacrament. (*I will be damned if I have not forgotten my catechism**.) But I shall be acquitted of the more than venial sin of suffering years to elapse without writing to a friend.—Personality! I really thought I had forwarded you my letter from Subhatoo six months ago. It is indeed a shame of you, De Mereste, and the Baron de Stendhal (if indeed the ladies allow the latter a moment's repose) not to write to me, and to allow me to remain in India as ignorant of the things of your Parisian world, as if I were an inhabitant of the moon.

The English have letters from home up to the 1st April; my last are dated October.

Our estimable captains of Havre and Nantes remain six and seven months on their voyage; they say that their ships are so fond of the sea, that when once they

* The words in Italics are Jacquemont's own English.—Tr.

are on it there is no getting them to move. This is too bad.

Our governors of Pondicherry and Chandernagore have just informed me that I have been appointed a knight of the legion of honour. However I intend to remain plain Mr. Jacquemont, were it only for the singularity of the thing, as I have not yet met with a Frenchman out of France, who was not either a count, a marquis, a baron, a viscount, or a chevalier.

I have seen, I know not where, an epistle from Beranger the great poet, to Chateaubriand the great prose writer, and the answer of the latter to the poet. Notwithstanding "liberty, which needed no ancestors," it made me think that we Frenchmen are very forgetful.

Poonah contains only from forty to fifty thousand inhabitants, mostly Mahrattas; fifty or sixty die every day of the cholera. I lost one of my servants about a week ago, and the European soldiers begin to experience the effect of the disease. Hitherto, the natives alone had been attacked; but such is the force of habit that no one entertains any uneasiness about it. It is probable that one of the causes of this malady is a sudden cooling, either internally or externally. In proportion to their respective numbers, there are fewer gentlemen who fall victims to it than soldiers. Adieu, my dear friend; write to me when the cares of your empire allow you leisure. Pray take notice that this last sentence is prose, in spite of its resemblance to Hugo's verses.

TO M. DE MARESTE, PARIS.

Poonah, July 11th, 1832.

KNOW, my dear De Mareste, that my only motive for writing to you is to give the sheet which I have just scribbled over, time to dry, an operation which requires several minutes at this season, compared to which the deluge of Moses was only a shower, for it lasted only forty days, and in this country, when once the rain begins, it lasts three months and a half without intermission. The consequence is that the animals and plants of the traveller become mouldy or rotten, and that even upon the labels of the stones grow the *mucor*, the *byssus*, and other mushrooms, which the *profanum vulgus* condemn *en masse* under the erroneous collective name of mould, but which are, I assure you, pretty little mushrooms (better described than eaten), but excessively *untoward* in the luggage of a naturalist. The hygrometer, which, for a month past, has been at the maximum of humidity, does not stir; it will only move from that point in September. This rain is the devil, or an incarnation of the devil. Success to the mild climate of France, although I have more than once been wet through in it. You are, my dear friend, a miserable fellow, and if that does not please you, an infamous one! I could say the same to many others, who, like yourself, no more write to me than if, since my arrival in India, I had gone to join the great soul of the universe. You left off with me about M. de Martignac, and the municipal and departmental law, and I know not what besides. Since that period, there have been plenty of new pieces, theatrical effects, and changes of scenery, &c., &c. Of yourself I have not heard one word. The brilliant Baron De Stendhal has also completely neglected me; but from him this is perfectly excusable: he is a thoughtless and fashionable young man, in great request among the ladies of Leghorn, I suppose, or some other city in Italy, where he represents, like an exquisite, his most Christian Majesty. But you, an honest citizen of Paris, and a good sort of husband, who have nothing to do with the vanities of this world —you are absolutely inexcusable. Politics have absorbed all my friends for the last two years, and since then I will not say they neglect me, quite the reverse, but they scarcely ever write to me, which is provokingly tiresome. The English at Poonah are not amusing; in the north of Hindostan, where every one of them is a kind of pacha, they grow great with their dignity, and, *mirabile dictu!* they even become amiable. Here I find them again natural, which is no compliment to them. However, as I am overwhelmed with business, it is perhaps better that it should be so; I am not tempted to seek any pleasure at their houses, and desert my own papers and memorandums. They remind me of my lord *What-Then*, in the "Princess of Babylon," by their prodigious indifference for every thing that is beyond the confined circle of their own monotonous existence. I prefer the Cashmerians, who alone formed my society last year; I think they had more vivacity of mind than the black and red automatons which people these head-quarters of the British power in India. Poonah is a large city, at least for India, where the towns are in general small. The population of Calcutta has not been ascertained; it contains no doubt 400,000 inhabitants, Benares, 181,000 instead of from 500,000 to 600,000; Daux, 50,000 instead of 150,000; Allahabad, 38,000 instead of 150,000, according to the general account; Delhi, about 120,000. Poonah no doubt contains from 40,000 to 50,000, and the cholera does not leave the place; for this last month it carries off from fifty to sixty persons a day: let that console you! I am however alive, and perfectly alive; enough so to be still in existence, I hope, eighteen or twenty months hence, when I trust I shall have the pleasure of seeing you again. Tell me some story in the intermediate time, and give it to Mérimée, or to my father, properly folded up and sealed. Write to me, then, and cease to be sulky, as you have been for these last three years.

TO M. CORDIER AT CHANDERNAGORE.

Poonah, July 27th, 1832.

MY DEAR M. CORDIER,—I am once more on my legs, or rather in my arm chair, after having been five days in bed in a precarious state, with a violent and sudden attack of dysentery, which came upon me like a pistol-shot, and quitted me yesterday in the same manner, in consequence of a terrible quantity of *blue pills*, calomel, rhubarb, opium, magnesia, cream of tartar, castor oil, ipecacuanha, and a mild lavement of gum arabic, which appears to me to have cut the matter short.

A traveller in my line has several ways of making, what the Italians term a *fiasco;* but the most complete *fiasco* is to die on the road. Some poor devils have been less fortunate than I, and in obedience to the dysentery that reigns here, have gone to see what there is behind the great wall. Much good may it do them!

Farewell, my dear M. Cordier. The papers will have informed you that the people of Bombay do not act with a light hand in driving away the plague from their shores. They are right. The cholera here carries off now but few people. It rains less hard than at Calcutta, but more continually. It is enough to make one die of *ennui.*

Adieu. I leave you to take by my sick man's broth, composed of arrow-root. Guard yourself from evil.

Yours sincerely.

TO MADEMOISELLE ZOÉ NOIZET DE SAINT PAUL, ARRAS.

Poonah, August 21, 1832.

My dear Zoé,—I received this morning a tolerably large packet from Paris, and before I go to bed I will write a few lines in answer to your eight little pages of the 12th of November, and 3rd of January, 1832. I have written so much to-day that my hand is quite stiff, besides which it is very late, and to-morrow at day-break I must gallop six leagues from hence, where I shall find my ghunter, or little Tartar horse, saddled and bridled, ready to climb the mountains with me, and two botanico-mineralogical attendants, completely equipped, and at their post. I shall herbarise, geologise, or zoologise at their head if the opportunity occurs, and, with my bags filled, I will return upon the same horse as if the devil was at my heels; for it will then be twelve o'clock, and I shall have eaten nothing, after having been nearly fifteen hours on horseback, on foot, and in the mud and rain. Thus I must away to bed, for it is already very late.

You laugh at my *in*, and *at* Cashmere; but you are wrong. I do not know how I can otherwise designate the province of which the city we call Cashmere, and the inhabitants Chaêr, or most excellent city, is the capital.

Although you pretend not to do so, you have carped in a most treacherous manner at the spelling of a certain word in my letter; *episode*, I believe: now certainly, on referring to its Greek derivation ὠδὴ, it must be feminine; but know that there are at least ten faults of orthography in your eight pages, and in future be less proud. In the Persian language there is no gender for inanimate things, but in the miserable Hindostanee patois, especially derived from the Sanscrit, this folly exists.

I have been on the point of dying of an attack of dysentery, the first illness I have had in India. During three days I was dreadfully shaken, my sufferings were acute, but my head was entirely free, and singularly fresh and clear. I chewed the air. My physician was an honest Scotchman; like all the world, he was incapable of rebutting my arguments. The activity of my thoughts consumed me. I imagined that the beautiful airs of Mozart, played on the violin by a clever musician, would charm me, and thus gild the pill; and and as there is here a musician above mediocrity, I was going to send for him, in order to die at least with music, when the remedies caused a reaction, and decided my recovery. The poor Scotch doctor was little edified with this musical fugue; but he dared not, nevertheless, propose to me his presbyterian brahmin. It was an endemic disease. The cholera has carried off a great number of persons here, but people are accustomed to this infliction—nobody thinks about it, any more than at sea people think of the chances of being upset.

Good night, my dear Zoé. Write to me. Good night.

TO M. JACQUEMONT, SEN., AT PARIS.

Poonah, Dec. 14, 1832.

MY DEAR FATHER,—I have a packet ready for you, but I should not wish to forward it without adding to it several others which are not ready, and that is the reason why I keep it back. It is however of little consequence, as I do not believe that there are any ships about to sail from Calcutta; this is not the season. I have received all your letters up to last March.

It is still impossible for me to fix exactly where and when I shall embark on my return. I am going to write to M. de Melay, to ask him the ordinary departures from his little port, or rather from his roadstead, and also from Madras (for although there is a port captain at Pondichery, there is no more a port there than at Montmorency or Versailles); but the general period of departures for Europe is December and January. It is therefore probable that I shall not return until the spring of 1834; but long before my departure you shall be informed of it with certainty. I should also prefer this plan on account of my health. I fear the cold. Here, in this place, looked upon as cold in this season, and whither people flock from the hot-house of Bombay to regain life, the thermometer varies slightly, for the last two months, from 70° to 75°, in my room, and I sleep with two blankets. My health is good. To-morrow I set out for Bombay, and shall visit the island of Salsette on my way thither. The fish drive me mad. I am obliged to stow them myself in a number of glass jugs filled with spirits of wine, else every thing would be broken in the hands of the stupid Indian servants. Were it not for that I would write more, but I have no time. For the honour of the principle of our correspondence, I put a number on this note. Adieu, &c.

TO M. PORPHYRE JACQUEMONT, PARIS.

Tanna, Island of Salsette, October 14, 1832.

My dear Porphyre,—I here enclose for the minister D'Argout, a few lines of thanks, and an acknowledgment of the receipt of my nomination as a legionary. Pray forward them to him.

One of the *Annuaires du Bureau des Longitudes* which you have sent me, in which Mr. Arago has inserted an article upon the beautiful labours of Elie de Beaumont, will have completely informed you, if not of the particulars, at least of the spirit of the thing. The discovery of tertiary and alluvial strata, and the different circumstances attending their stratification at the foot of the Ghauts and on the declivities of these mountains would serve to solve the problem of their geological age (age of their rising), a much more valuable element than any other kind of observation. I have therefore been forced to labour, in seeking after some particles of this soil, and not without exposing myself a great deal to the sun, and in this unhealthy waste, in the most unhealthy season of the year. I am consequently rather in a suffering state, or rather have been a little poorly for the last few days. And as, were I in the town (Bombay), I should not be able to keep myself quiet, and take the necessary repose, I prolong my stay at Tanna a little longer than I intended.

I am still without any other letter from you since that of the 10th of last March, which I received at Poonah on the 8th of September. You may feel how anxious I am to receive some news, after the dreadful visit which the cholera has paid to Paris.

Our intelligence from Europe is up to the middle of July, brought by some estafettes who have come from Constantinople through Persia. I have therefore confused accounts of the scenes of carnage to which the funeral of Lamarque gave rise, or of which it served as a pretence. It is a very melancholy thing. I saw with much sorrow, that a great number of societies, each of them of course vying with each other in patriotism, and composed of several thousand members, had followed the procession, with banners flying. Whither are we going? I dare not think of it. The fear of what I may find on my return to France, prevents me from anticipating that event with joy. Adieu, for to-day. What a perfidious climate this is! but the winter is coming on, and in a month I shall be again in the plains of the Deccan, where the cool weather is very perceptible; and when the great heats return I shall be in the Nilgherries.

TO M. PORPHYRE JACQUEMONT AT PARIS.

Sick-officers' Quarters, Bombay, December 1, 1832.

DEAR PORPHYRE,—I arrived here two and thirty days ago, very ill, and have now been thirty-one days confined to my bed. In the pestilential forests of the island of Salsette, exposed to the burning sun, during the most unhealthy season of the year, I caught the germ of my present illness, of which, indeed, I have several times, since I passed through Ajmeer in March, felt some slight attacks, but about the nature of which I deceived myself. It was inflammation of the liver. The pestilential miasms of Salsette have completed the thing. From the beginning of the disorder I made my will and put my affairs in order. The care of my interests remain in most honourable and friendly hands: those of Mr. James Nicol, an English merchant of this place, and of M. Cordier of Calcutta.

Mr. Nicol was my host on my arrival at Bombay. No old friend could have lavished more affectionate attentions upon me. At the expiration, however, of a few days, whilst I was still in a state to be moved, I quitted his house, which is situated in the fort, and came to occupy a convenient and spacious apartment at the quarter of the sick officers, which is in the most airy and salubrious situation, on the sea-shore, and a hundred paces distant from my physician, Doctor Mac Lennan, the most able at Bombay, and the admirable care he has bestowed upon me, has long since attached me to him as a dear friend.

The cruellest pang, my dear Porphyre, for those we love, is, that when dying in a far distant land, they imagine that in the last hours of our existence we are deserted and unnoticed. My dear friend, you will no doubt reap some consolation from the assurance I give you that I have never ceased being the object of the kindest and most affectionate solicitude of a number of good and amiable men. They continually come to see me, anticipating even my sick-bed caprices and whims. Mr. Nicol especially, Mr. John Bar, one of the members of the government, Mr. Goodfellow, an old colonel of engineers, and Major Mountain, a very amiable young officer, and many others whose names I do not mention.

The excellent Doctor Mac Lennan, nearly endangered his own health for me, by coming twice a night, during a crisis which seemed to leave no chance of my recovery. I place the most unlimited confidence in his abilities.

My sufferings were at first very great, but for some

time past I have been reduced to a state of weakness that scarcely allows of any. The worst of it is, that for thirty-one days I have not slept a single hour. These sleepless nights are however very calm, and do not appear so desperately long.

Fortunately the illness is drawing to a close, which may not be fatal, although it will probably be so.

The abscess, or abscesses, formed from the beginning of the attack in my liver, and which recently appeared likely to dissolve by absorption, appear now to rise upwards, and will soon open outwardly. It is all I wish for, to get quickly out of the miserable state in which I have been languishing for the last month, between life and death. You see that my ideas are perfectly clear; they have been but very rarely, and very transiently confused, during some violent paroxysms of pain at the commencement of my illness. I have generally reckoned upon the worst, and that has never rendered my thoughts gloomy. My end, if it is now approaching, is mild and tranquil. If you were here, seated at my bed-side with my father and Frederic, my heart would burst with grief, and I should not be able to contemplate my approaching death with the same fortitude and serenity—console yourself,—console my father—console yourselves mutually my dear friends.

I feel quite exhausted by this effort to write, and must bid you adieu! Farewell! oh how much you are all beloved by your poor Victor! Farewell for the last time!

Stretched out upon my back, I can only write with a pencil. For fear that these lines may be effaced, the excellent Mr. Nicol will copy this letter in writing, in order that I may be sure you will read my last thoughts.

VICTOR JACQUEMONT.

I have been able to sign what the admirable Mr. Nicol has had the kindness to copy. Once more, farewell, my friends!

December 2nd.

LETTER FROM MR. JAMES NICOL, ENGLISH MERCHANT AT BOMBAY, TO M. PORPHYRE JACQUEMONT AT PARIS*.

Bombay, December 14th, 1832.

My dear Sir,—Although unknown to you, fate has selected me to communicate to you an event which you do not anticipate. It is with feelings of the most profound regret that I am obliged to transmit to you the last letter of your brother Victor, and to give the only consolation that can still remain to you, which is to inform you of the tranquillity and absence of pain with which he received the fatal blow on the 7th of December.

* This letter was originally written in French.

Your brother came to my house on the 9th of October, on his arrival from Tanna, in a very weak state of health, ever since an illness with which he had been recently afflicted, and from which he hoped he should speedily recover, and thinking the sea breeze of this island would effectually strengthen him. On the evening of his arrival, he took a walk with me of half a league, and the following day he paid a few visits, but returned home early quite exhausted. I advised him to take instant medical advice, and the same evening Doctor Mac Lennan visited him. For your satisfaction I will inclose, in this letter, an account of the disorder, drawn up by this medical gentleman.

As your brother states, he suffered severely at the commencement of his illness; and from the beginning was informed of its dangerous nature. On the 4th of November he made his will, of which I inclose a copy. Towards the 8th of November the disorder appeared to take a favourable turn, and he cherished the hope of recovering his health, when the formation of abscess was manifest. He then became daily weaker and weaker, but during the whole time of his illness he preserved a tranquillity and contentment of which I have never before seen an instance.

I left him on the 6th of December, nearly in the same state as on the preceding days, but without any appearance of approaching dissolution. On the 7th however, towards three o'clock in the morning, he was seized with violent pains, which lasted nearly two hours. Doctor Mac Lennan was with him during that time. At five o'clock in the morning your brother sent for me. On my arrival his sufferings had ceased, but such a change had taken place in his features since the preceding evening, that I could not refrain from tears. Taking my hand, he said to me, "Do not grieve; the moment is near at hand, and it is the accomplishment of my wishes. It is the prayer which I have for the last fortnight addressed to heaven. It is a happy event. Were I even to live, illness would probably render the remainder of my life wretched. Write to my brother, and tell him what happiness and what tranquillity accompany me to the grave."

He repeated to me that he wished me to forward to France his manuscripts and collections, and entered into the most minute details respecting his funeral, which he desired might be the same as for a protestant. He begged of me to let his grave be marked by a simple grave-stone, with this inscription:—"Victor Jacquemont, born at Paris on the 8th August, 1801, died at Bombay on the 7th December, 1832, after having travelled during three years and a half in India."

In the course of the day he had several fits of vomiting, and his breathing was considerably affected, but he retained his faculties as perfectly as when in health. He was anxious only for death, saying, "I am well here, but I shall be better in my grave." Towards five in the evening, he said to me, "I will now take my last draught from your hands, and then die." A violent fit of vomiting followed, and he was laid upon his bed entirely exhausted; from time to time he opened his eyes, and appeared, about twenty minutes before his death, to recognise me. At sixteen minutes past six o'clock he yielded up the ghost, falling asleep, as it were, in the arms of death.

His funeral took place on the following evening, with military honours as member of the legion of honour, and several members of the government, and many other persons, followed the procession.

I feel sincere and deep commiseration in the irreparable loss which your father and yourself sustain by his death. I only knew your brother during his illness, and I have only had the melancholy satisfaction of offering him every care and attention which his illness required. In conformity with his wishes, I have had all the articles of natural history which have remained in my possession carefully packed up; they are contained in eleven cases and one cask, of which I inclose you the invoice and bill of lading, signed by the captain of the French ship the Nymphe, of Bordeaux. I have written to the commissary-general of the navy at Bordeaux, begging him to remove any difficulty that might arise; you will have the goodness to write to him on that subject. I have also forwarded the bill of lading of a box addressed to your father, containing all the manuscripts which your brother left in my charge.

In the case containing his papers, I have placed his order of the legion of honour, which your brother particularly begged me to forward to you. I also send you his watch and pistols.

Have the kindness to separate from the other papers the catalogues relating to the collections, and forward them to the Royal Museum.

I have the honour to be, dear sir, &c.,

JAMES NICOL.

APPENDIX.

REPORT* BY DR. MAC LENNAN,

ON THE DISEASE AND DEATH OF VICTOR JACQUEMONT, AND THE POST-MORTEM EXAMINATION OF HIS BODY.

I saw M. Jacquemont for the first time on the 30th of October, 1832, in the afternoon, the day after his arrival from Tanna. He told me that in March, 1832, he had been seriously unwell in Rajpootana; and that since that period he had experienced no marked disease, with the exception of an attack of dysentery which took place at Poonah during the rainy season. A fortnight or three weeks before his arrival at Bombay, and while he was at Tanna, he had experienced irregular attacks of fever, with disordered bowels. The day after his arrival, he was obliged to abstain from paying visits in the town, in consequence of an attack of fever more violent than the preceding. It began about noon with shivering, and was just over when I saw him.

He said that he felt an uneasiness *as feeble as possible* in the præcordia; but it was not increased by pressure

* We have been unable to obtain the original of this Report, and have therefore been obliged to re-translate it from the French.—Tr.

on the abdomen, or by an effort to draw a long breath. A sensation of heat and weight about the sacrum was the most remarkable symptom; but it did not yet appear that it ought to be considered a serious one. M. Jacquemont had no head-ach, little thirst, and less pain in the loins than he had already felt, and certainly less than is usually felt under similar circumstances. The skin was of a good colour, cool and moist (the paroxysm of fever was just over when I saw him); the pulse was at 84, and there was not the least appearance of gastric irritation. He told me that his evacuations were frequent, very offensive, and attended with tenesmus. His tongue was swollen and very foul, his mouth disagreeable, and his breath fetid.

Sixty leeches were applied to the sacrum. M. Jacquemont took a warm bath, and at bed-time a strong dose of calomel with a few grains of palo, ipecacuanha, and opium.

Saturday, 31st. M. Jacquemont had passed a tolerably good night, and though much affected with the fever, had slept from time to time. A strong pressure above the navel now produced slight pain, which was, however, not increased by fetching a deep inspiration, and seemed quite unconnected with the position assumed by M. Jacquemont in bed. The sensation of heat and weight at the sacrum had disappeared, and upon the whole the patient was better. As the abdominal pain was principally connected with the right hypochondrium, sixty leeches were applied to this part. The warm bath was repeated on the return of the fever, and three doses of the mercurial preparation of the preceding day were given at intervals of eight hours; but extract of henbane was substituted for the opium. The application of the leeches having considerably relieved the patient, and the fever having come on later and in a less degree than on the preceding day, thirty leeches were again applied to the right hypochondrium at night; and a dose of castor oil ordered, to be taken at four in the afternoon of November 1st. This purgative operated speedily and energetically. The stools were copious, liquid, of a brownish colour, and had a very disagreeable putrid smell, such as I had never yet found, except in evacuations containing a great deal of blood, and when this blood had long remained in the intestines. M. Jacquemont himself very justly compared this smell to that exhaling from a bucket used by anatomists for macerations; and he told me that he had perceived it for several days, though in a less intense degree. There was no blood in the evacuations, and no appearance of fibrinous deposit or any animal matter whatsoever. The relief he felt after these evacuations was very considerable, and from that time all pain about the sacrum disappeared.

As M. Jacquemont had greatly neglected his health at Tanna, had exposed himself to the sun without proper precautions, had encountered great fatigue, and had paid no attention to his complaint, or at most taken a few small doses of laxative medicine;—further, as it was evident, from the symptoms, that the liver in particular was affected, I thought it right to act upon the entire organism by means of mercury, and bring, if possible the whole system under the influence of that mineral. Accordingly, M. Jacquemont took strong doses of calomel mixed with ipecacuanha and henbane, three times a day, and as often a mercurial preparation was rubbed in upon the inferior extremities. He also took, at first once a day, then every other day, a mild laxative draught, generally composed of jalap or cream of tartar. During this period, great care was taken to keep up the patient's strength, and he took regularly, every four hours, a small quantity of animal soup, and now and then some wine and water.

By persevering in this mode of treatment up to the 5th, the alvine secretions assumed a more favourable appearance; the putrid smell of which I have just spoken, no longer existed, and the patient evacuated without tenesmus or uneasiness. The fever had not returned since the 4th.

Some slight indications of the approach of ptyalism appeared on the 6th, and in consequence the mercurial medicines were continued on that day and the following; but as these symptoms did not increase, and it did not appear necessary to persevere in this mode of treatment any longer, I determined to discontinue it, and do nothing more than keep the bowels open, pay great attention to diet, and palliate any symptoms that might appear. Before I made this change, I explained to M. Jacquemont the nature of my fears. I apprehended that an organic disease, probably an abscess in the liver, had been forming for some time. I begged M. Jacquemont to allow me to consult with another physician. I called in Dr. Kemhall, who entirely approved of the system hitherto pursued, and the proposed change in the mode of treatment. He also feared the existence of abscess in the liver; but as there was no direct symptom to indicate it, (and the existence of such abscess could be inferred only from an absence of morbid symptoms in every other part of the body, joined to the length of the patient's convalescence,) we both hoped that the failure of mercury in its effect proceeded from some idiosyncrasy, and not from the existence of organic disease in the liver. The mode of treatment we fixed upon was the one I had before imagined, that is to say, to give the patient meat broth, jellies, &c., and wine and water at intervals of three hours, day and night. The bowels were to be kept open with laxatives given from time to time; lastly, an opiate was to be taken every night. Further, as it has been remarked that gestation in the open air often produces a happy effect in accelerating convalescence and hastening the action of mercury upon the organism, M. Jacquemont was carried a few miles in a palanquin during several successive days; but the fatigue which it cost him being compensated by no improvement in his health, these airings were discontinued, and the above-mentioned treatment alone persevered in.

Meanwhile, M. Jacquemont was wholly free from pain in every part of the body. The pulse and skin were in their natural state, and the tongue clean. The alvine evacuations were bilious, but not more so than might be expected from the use of the mercurial medicines.

Hitherto, no change had taken place, further than a slight gradual increase in the strength of the patient, and he began to look upon his condition with less gloomy apprehensions, that is to say, he did not think his end so near as he had at first imagined. It must here be observed, that the utmost candour was always shown towards him: the nature of his disease was explained to him, and the probability of a fatal termination was not concealed from him. He was informed, however, that no present symptoms indicated that the abscess was considerable, or that it might not be carried off through some of the channels of the body, and that therefore he might reasonably hope for this favourable termination of his complaint. I felt bound to adopt this line of conduct, because it was evident to me that reserve or dissimulation would have done M. Jacquemont harm, whilst the medical particulars stated to him, and which he seemed perfectly to understand, appeared to give him hope, to quiet him, and to inspire him with resignation.

On the 15th of November, a small swelling was apparent on the right hypochondrium, but without any other symptoms. It was not till the 17th that a slight sensation of pain resulted from pressure on this region. A large blister was applied, and the same mode of treatment continued. Complete relief succeeded the application of the blister, which acted very powerfully; and the swelling on the right side diminished. M. Jacquemont also appeared to gain strength, and he had certainly gained flesh; but nothing indicated the return of health, if I except the evacuations, which had become perfectly regular.

November 26th. The uneasiness returned, and also the swelling in the side. Another blister was put on. It drew well, but the relief it afforded lasted only a few hours.

November 27th. This was a bad day. M. Jacquemont experienced violent excitement in consequence of the ill conduct of his servants, and relapses followed his knowledge of their behaviour. From this time every change in the patient's state was of an unfavourable character. The disease made rapid progress, at first manifested only by a great depression of spirits, and an aversion to all food. This aversion became so strong that the nourishment he took within the twenty four hours was not equal to half, nay, to a third, of what he took at the beginning of his illness. To these symptoms were soon added prostration of strength, emaciation, and now and then slight febrile exacerbations. The pain in the side and in the region corresponding with the edge of the liver, increased, and the swelling became considerable.

December 2nd. The swelling assumed the appearance of a pointed tumour towards the edge of the ninth rib, at the place where it is joined to the eighth. A careful examination was made by Dr. Henderson (whom I had called in because Dr. Kemhall was absent) and by myself. We could discover no fluctuation, and it did not appear that there was any adherence, even at the base of the tumour, to the subjacent parts.

To aversion for food was now added increasing difficulty of keeping it upon the stomach. Nausea and vomiting became frequent. The febrile exacerbations increased, and lasted a long time. Thirst also came, with great dryness of the mouth, and accompanied with a feeling of constriction towards the stomach and the upper parts of the abdomen.

December 4th. The patient had frequent and violent pains in the abdomen, especially when he attempted to go to stool, or to draw his breath deeply. All these symptoms increased, and were sometimes very alarming, although at the beginning of the night the patient found great relief from hot fomentations and anodyne drops.

December 7th. At three o'clock in the morning I was called to M. Jacquemont. I found him in a very different state from that in which I had left him the night before (at midnight). In changing his position in bed he had suddenly found acute pain round the pubis, and was unable to void his urine. His countenance was expressive of agony, his skin bathed in perspiration, and his appearance that of a dying man. Hot fomentations on the pubis, and repeated doses of nitric ether, and laudanum, diminished these alarming symptoms, and the pain ceased. But the vomiting soon after returned. The patient voided a considerable quantity of black and glareous matter, resembling coffee grounds. These attacks lasted during a part of the day, and were accompanied with frequent syncope.

The prostration of strength was such that he appeared several times on the point of expiring from the efforts he made to vomit. But he rallied a little after each fit. Towards sunset the vomiting diminished; but it appeared that this arose merely from the weakness of the patient, who was unable to throw up the matter contained in the stomach. He expired quietly and without convulsions, at six o'clock in the evening. He had spoken to me very rationally an hour before. During the whole progress of his disease, his faculty of observation and reflection was never affected, and this was the case up to the moment of his death.

In compliance with the wish he had expressed, a post mortem examination took place next day, December 8th, at six o'clock in the evening. I examined the cavity of the thorax and that of the abdomen, jointly with Dr. Henderson.

In the former cavity, all the viscera were in their natural state; in the second, an enormous abscess in the liver had burst, and its contents had partly flowed into the abdomen. The abscess was situated in the posterior part of the liver, and at a short distance from the backbone. It contained the quantity (measured) of a hundred ounces of clear fluid, and sanious pus. All the other abdominal viscera were perfectly healthy.

MAC LENNAN.

REPORT OF CAPTAIN BRIOLLE,

COMMANDING THE SHIP NYMPHE, OF BORDEAUX, ON THE DEATH AND OBSEQUIES OF VICTOR JACQUEMONT.

TO M. DE PRIGNY,, COMMISSARY-GENERAL OF THE NAVY AT BORDEAUX.

MONSIEUR LE COMMISSAIRE GENERAL,

Being at Bombay in the month of December last, when M. Victor Jacquemont had just ended his scientific journey, I hastened to visit a countryman whom all the papers of India concurred in placing in the foremost rank of distinguished naturalists, but who, in consequence of the fatigues and privations with which he had to contend in his laborious researches, was unfortunately attacked with liver complaint of a very alarming nature. I found him in bed, scientifically discoursing with the most eminent physician of the country, under whose care the Governor had placed him, and explaining with the utmost calmness how, in two or three days, he should be freed from his cruel sufferings, but at the expense of his life, as an effusion would take place internally, and he should not have the slightest chance of recovery.

His physician having absented himself for a few hours, he expatiated much upon this gentleman's abilities, and upon the interest and attention which the Government of Bombay unceasingly showed him; but he added again, that he had only three or four days more to live, that all the assistance of art was useless, and that having terminated his manuscripts, with the exception of some trifling parts relative to Tibet, he should die with the consolation of having contributed as much as lay in his power to the progress of a science which still left much to be done. The unfortunate gentleman died the fourth day after this conversation, preserving nevertheless to the last a tranquillity, a mildness, and a presence of mind, worthy of his noble character.

The Government of Bombay, desirous to honour the memory of a man so distinguished for his talents and private virtues, ordered a magnificent funeral, at which all the civil and military authorities were present; and the remains of the unfortunate Jacquemont were deposited in their last asylum with all the pomp of military honours.

Deeply affected by the attentions of the Bombay Government towards this illustrious victim of scientific research, I addressed them a letter, of which I enclose a copy, and received in reply the two letters also enclosed, the last of which informs me, that in consequence of a deliberation of the Council, my letter is to be preserved in the archives of the Government. I have therefore thought it my duty to send you all these particulars, to be laid before the Minister of Marine, in order that he may determine whether he will approve of my application to the Bombay Government.

I remain, &c.

BRIOLLE.

LETTER FROM THE PROFESSORS, ADMINISTRATORS OF THE MUSEUM OF NATURAL HISTORY, TO M. JACQUEMONT, SENIOR.

Paris, 21st May, 1833.

Sir,

We sympathise too deeply in the misfortune you have experienced, not to feel the want of associating ourselves to your grief. The Administration of the Museum, who had confided to your son the mission which he has so honourably fulfilled, feels his cruel loss in a twofold point of view: it is thereby deprived of a traveller who enjoyed its utmost confidence, and science is deprived of a naturalist on whom it founded the most brilliant hopes. Every thing authorises us to hope, that from the judicious precautions he took even in his last moments, all the fruits of this unfortunate struggle will not be lost; that the labours of M. Victor Jacquemont will yield their fruits, and their results be developed, less brilliantly perhaps than if they had remained in his own hands, but still sufficiently to cause what he has done to be appreciated, as well as what he would have done, had he lived. Be assured, Sir, that nothing shall be wanting on our part to attain this object, and to afford you this legitimate consolation, the only one you have now left.

We are, &c.

CORDIER, DIRECTOR,
GEOFFROY SAINT HILAIRE,
A. DE JUSSIEU,

Professors, Administrators of the Museum.

CHOLERA MORBUS.

Poonah, July, 1832.

One of the most recent publications of the English physicians in India, on Cholera Morbus, is a letter addressed to the Court of Directors, by Dr. Whitelaw Ainslie, of Madras.

Dr. Ainslie distinguishes two sorts of Cholera, the sporadic and the endemic, differing only from each other in their developement, their progress, and their termination. There is greater violence in the endemic Cholera, a more rapid progress, and a termination more generally fatal. It is the same disease as the other, but more intense.

He attributes, but without any proof, the origin of this complaint to very obscure modifications of the electric state of the air. It is principally in the south of India that he has observed it. Having found that the thick and liquid glareous matter vomited and evacuated by the patient were always acid, he endeavoured to check the disease by neutralising this acid in the stomach; and having employed magnesia in strong doses for that purpose, his practice has frequently been attended with success. Dr. Ainslie was aware of the advantages that, for a length of time, had been obtained by the use of ammonia in large doses, and attributes them, I think with reason, to the property this alkali possesses of saturising acids.

The only cases, rather numerous, of natural cure, are those in which the bile, by the convulsive efforts made in vomiting, passes from the duodenum to the stomach. It appears that this fluid possesses the property of neutralising, like an alkali, the acid so abundantly generated in that organ. A blister, produced instantaneously by the application of boiling water to the abdomen, has often been attended with happy results. Mr. Ainslie recommends the application of one, in the very first stage of the disorder, to the bottom of the leg, on the inside, in order to retain, by an artificial inflammation of the teguments, the heat of the flesh, which naturally withdraws from them.

Bleeding has long since been tried. It almost always produces immediate relief, but it appears often to have hastened death.

As the blood never flows but with extreme difficulty, on account of its thickness, and of its almost coagulated state in the veins, attempts have been made to aid the operation of bleeding by placing the patient in a very warm bath, which has had the desired effect; but it seems to exercise no influence upon the progress of the disease.

In very violent cases, calomel has been administered in

doses of from twenty to thirty grains, mixed with eighty drops of laudanum, whilst the same quantity of laudanum was injected into the rectum. These enormous doses of calomel, repeated a number of times, often appear not to have exercised the slightest influence upon the progress of the disease, even in cases where a *post-mortem* examination has shown the calomel retained by a viscous liquid to the coating of the stomach, which it had already violently inflamed.

What surprises me the most in Dr. Ainslie's work, is a fact in medical statistics, which is undeniable, and which shows that of several thousands of British and Indian soldiers who in the course of a few years have entered the hospital of the Presidency of Madras, as Cholera patients, the British and Indians have fallen victims to the disorder in equal proportions, and the proportion of deaths has been as one to four of the total number of patients.

Hence it follows, that Cholera appears to be generally of a less deadly nature in the south of India than in the Deccan and Hindostan, where the proportion of deaths is said to be much greater.

ILLNESS OF SOUDINE.

Poonah, July, 1832.

Soudine, my Hindoo servant, five and twenty years of age, in my service for the last eighteen months, always enjoying perfect health, leading an extremely regular life, abstaining from all kinds of spirituous liquors, and almost entirely from animal food, was seized on Friday evening, July 5th, with an attack of colic. The alvine evacuations were very numerous, but not copious, and were followed by vomiting in the course of an hour. It was then only that his illness was reported to me, and that I witnessed it. At seven in the evening his attitude announced a great prostration of strength. He complained of tenesmus; the pulse was very weak, and the feet were a little cold. The evacuations, both from the stomach and from the rectum, succeeded each other rapidly, more than ten times in an hour. They were composed of a fluid, a little viscid, though thick, of a greyish white, and without smell. The patient was put to bed and warmly covered; bottles of hot water were applied to the feet, hot napkins upon the abdomen, and twenty drops of ammonia were administered in a tablespoonful of water. The patient swallowed this burning draught without complaining, but two minutes after he brought it up. From seven o'clock to eleven at night, other similar doses were given, in the intervals when the natural vomiting was quieted; but the patient did not retain one of them more than three minutes. In one of these doses I mixed twenty drops of laudanum; he threw it up the instant he had swallowed it.

The natural heat rapidly left the extremities; the feet were colder than the hands; the legs became cold, and also the arms; the breathing became hard, the body gradually cold; but the patient often complained of an insupportable heat that burned him all over, and made him throw off with violence the clothing that covered him. He tore off his own clothes, and asked to be left naked. These sudden and transient invasions of heat were perceptible only by a momentary increase of natural heat in the body. On the forehead alone there was a cold and clammy prespiration, but the coldness of the legs remained unchanged.

There were cramps in the legs, and spasms in the muscles of the abdomen, during the attacks of internal heat.

The skin of the palms of the hands and of the soles of the feet, became hard and rough. The nails lost their colour and turned white. The eyes became gradually hollow, and were surrounded by an internal circle, smaller, deeper, and blacker, and by a larger circle on a level with the superior border of the maxillary bone, on the bony summit of the lower part of the orbit. Their motion was slackened, and their brilliancy faded

At midnight I administered to the patient eight grains of calomel, diluted in a spoonful of sugar and water aromatised.

But the efforts produced by the vomiting, which constantly came on after an interval of a few minutes, without being accelerated by the remedy, expelled the draught, at least in great part, whenever they began.

At one o'clock in the morning of Saturday, I administered the same dose of calomel, mixed with twenty drops of laudanum; it was thrown up again in the course of two minutes.

I passed the remainder of the night without giving the patient any thing to drink except a little sugar and water, when he complained of thirst, which only happened during the sudden attacks of internal heat.

On Saturday morning there was no pulse, except at intervals, after the convulsive efforts produced by the vomiting, but aggravation of all the symptoms of the preceding day. The legs were colder, the eyes more sunken; the features were altered and cadaverous. The purging and vomiting continued without ceasing during the night. Between the intervals of the vomitings the patient dozed; he was conscious, but faintly so.

At eight in the morning, in an interval of comparative calmness, I administered a draught of laudanum and sub-carbonate of ammonia, edulcorated and aromatised with essence of mint.

The evacuations, which were already less frequent before this remedy, continued to decrease, and were less copious, but they did not vary in their nature. The general prostration continued. Towards noon, the patient had some violent cramps. During these nervous paroxysms, he complained of dreadful internal heat. It did not affect his extremities, but momentarily warmed his arms and thighs, and covered his forehead and body with a clammy prespiration, which instantly grew cold. The pulse then reappeared for a moment, but weak and irregular. The feeling of universal burning of which the patient complained during the spasmodic fits, continued for some time after the spasms in the abdomen and stomach were past.

During the day I directed a spoonful of sugar and water to be given to the patient, whenever he asked for drink, which he did but seldom. The vomitings now took place only five or six times an hour, and the alvine evacuations two or three times.

At four o'clock in the evening, another dose of the morning draught was given; this was also rejected, in the course of ten minutes, at the first effort produced by the vomiting.

The breathing became more difficult, and all the other symptoms more aggravated. The strength decreased gradually, the coldness continued, the sensibility diminished. During the night the patient was purged less often, and was comatose in the intervals of repose. Two doses, of eight grains of calomel each, were administered as on Friday, on the Saturday evening towards night, and each remained in the stomach at least a quarter of an hour.

On Saturday morning, the patient could scarcely hear or see any thing; he however knew my voice, when I called him by his name. His eyes were fixed and dull, as if they were dead; he however told me he could still see me, but confusedly. At eight o'clock I made him take a pill of three grains of calomel and one grain of gummy extract of opium, which he swallowed with great difficulty. The attendants rubbed his abdomen with hot napkins imbibed with laudanum, to assuage the violent pains of which he complained in that part. The bottles of hot water held under his feet from the very beginning of the attack, never warmed them, not even the surface which remained cold when placed upon boiling water.

He now vomited no longer, nor had he any alvine evacuations. His head became heavy, his breathing embarrassed and difficult. His whole body was covered with prespiration, and after this last effort of nature, and a few moments of rattling in the throat, he expired without convulsion, at half-past nine in the morning.

Not one of the remedies administered to the patient had the slightest effect upon the progress of the disease. The absorbent powers of the stomach were no doubt entirely suspended, and that organ, instead of absorbing, only secreted the matter of the evacuations.

The secretion of the urine was suppressed from the very beginning.

The disease lasted about forty hours, without a moment's abatement, until the death of the patient. The prostration of strength alone appears to have moderated the violence of the evacuations, fifteen or twenty hours after the attack. The patient, overcome by the fatigue and the prostration occasioned by his exertions, when these exertions did not produce excruciating pain, appeared, from the first moment I saw him, absorbed in himself, and deprived of all power of reflection. There was no disturbance in the intellectual faculties, no delirium, but a heaviness which unceasingly increased. For nearly an hour before his death, he was in a state of stupor In no stage of the disorder did the patient appear alarmed, or even anxious, respecting its termination.